Ecology of African mammals

TROPICAL ECOLOGY SERIES

ALREADY PUBLISHED
Tropical forest and its environment
K. A. Longman and J. Jenik
Animal ecology in tropical Africa
D. F. Owen

Ecology of
African mammals

M. J. Delany and D. C. D. Happold

Longman
London and New York

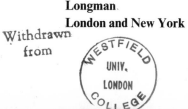

Longman Group Limited London

Associated companies, branches and representatives
throughout the world

Published in the United States of America
by Longman Inc., New York

First published 1979

QL731

Library of Congress Cataloging in Publication Data

Delany, M. J.
Ecology of African mammals.

   (Tropical ecology series)
   Bibliography: p.
   Includes index.
1. Mammals – Africa – Ecology. I. Happold, D. C. D., joint author. II. Title. III.
   Series. QL731.A1D44 599'.05'096 77 – 5611
   ISBN 0–582–44176–5

Printed and bound at William Clowes & Sons Limited, Beccles and London

Contents

Acknowledgements

In the preparation of this book we have received considerable assistance from numerous colleagues and organisations. This help has taken the form of constructive comment on the drafts of our manuscript, provision of information that has not been published and advice on sources of data. Those assisting us in this way are Dr N. R. Chalmers, Dr R. F. Chapman, Professor J. L. Cloudsley-Thompson, Dr S. K. Eltringham, Dr R. D. Estes, Dr G. de Graaf, Dr M. Happold, Dr P. J. Jarman, Dr J. M. Kenworthy, Dr K. Koopman, Professor E. Kulzer, Dr G. L. Maclean, Professor J. Meester, Dr P. Miller, Dr J. Phillipson, Dr J. Sircoulon, Dr H. N. Southern, Dr C. R. Taylor, Central Statistical Office Government of Kenya, Kenya National Parks and Uganda National Parks. We are extremely grateful for their contributions which have added greatly to the content of the book. While acknowledging this help, we do not absolve ourselves from any inaccuracies or ommisions and accept full responsibility for the account as a whole.

The authors are particularly grateful to Dr Meredith Happold for the preparation of the Index in the course of which many of our nomenclatural inconsistencies were corrected.

Our task has been made much easier through the sympathetic support and assistance we have constantly received from Dr H. Moore and Miss B. Gouge of Longman.

Preface

When we first started to teach mammal ecology to undergraduates in tropical Africa in the early 1960s, we soon found that there was no suitable reference book for our purpose. Prior to about 1960, most studies on wild indigenous African mammals were on taxonomy and zoogeography, and ecological studies were limited to natural history observations. However, from this basis there has been a very rapid increase in ecological studies in the last fifteen to twenty years. This has been partially motivated by the rate of environmental change in Africa which is making the continent increasingly less suitable for the survival of wild mammals. Many of these studies, in several languages, are published in books and journals which are sometimes difficult to obtain and therefore are inaccessible to the average student of African mammals. A book which brings together much of this scattered information to give an overall picture of mammalian ecology in tropical Africa is now possible and timely.

We have attempted to give a balanced presentation even though recent research is very unbalanced in scope and emphasis. East Africa has been the focus of ecological research compared with the rest of the continent. Large mammals, especially the ungulates, have been well studied whereas bats, shrews and pangolins, for example, have been largely neglected. Studies on savanna are appreciably more numerous than those on arid zones, forests and mountains. Similarly, most ecologists have tended to be specialists in, for example, primates, or ungulates, or rodents so that synecological studies dealing with the whole ecosystem are rare. As far as possible, fair representation has been given in this book to each order, biome, and subject without undue emphasis on those species and subjects which have been particularly well studied. This has necessitated careful selection of the available information and, regretfully, the ommision of many excellent studies.

The book is divided into four parts, each differing in its approach to the subject. Part One describes the families of living wild mammals in tropical Africa, discusses the historical events which have been responsible for the present fauna, and compares the mammals of Africa with those of certain other parts of the world. Part Two describes the environments of the four major biomes of tropical Africa (rain forest, savanna, arid, and mountain) and how the mammalian fauna is adapted to the particular conditions of each biome. Part Three takes four general ecological subjects (life histories, behaviour, ecophysiology, and populations) and discusses these in relation to the ecology of African mammals. The patterns, variations and strategies within each of these subjects are described and exemplified in relation to the requirements and environments of selected species. Finally, Part Four examines some of the beneficial and detrimental interactions between man and wild African mammals. There is inevitable overlap of some subject matter in different parts of the book. However, we hope this emphasises that the same facts can be understood and explained from different points of view.

General ecological concepts are discussed where appropriate. In this way, the reader obtains an introductory knowledge of ecology illustrated by specific African examples. Although designed principally for undergraduates, we hope this book will be of interest and benefit to all others interested in the ecology of African mammals.

Tropical Africa is defined as mainland Africa between the latitudes of $23\frac{1}{2}°$N (Tropic of Cancer) and $23\frac{1}{2}°$S (Tropic of Capricorn) and excludes the offshore islands within these latitudes. Most of the details on the ecology of particular species or communities are taken from studies within this tropical belt, but when this was not possible we extended our limits to include all continental Africa.

Nomenclature follows that of Meester and Setzer (1971–77) unless otherwise stated.

PART I The mammal fauna

Chapter 1

Living mammals of tropical Africa

One of the most fascinating features of tropical Africa is the wealth and diversity of its mammalian fauna. This fauna embraces species as varied as gigantic elephants, tiny pygmy mice, scaly pangolins, amphibious hippopotamuses, flying squirrels, naked burrowing rodents, and termite-eating aardvarks. Mammals occur in all the equally varied habitats of tropical Africa: the hot arid deserts, humid rainforests, rolling savannas, rocky inselbergs, cold mountains, the rivers and the lakes. Each species has its own unique set of characteristics enabling it to survive in a particular ecological niche, and the consequent spectrum of colour, size, shape, physiology, behaviour and ecology exemplified by these species is aesthetically and biologically quite wonderful.

It is estimated that there are about 750 living species. The characteristics of most species and the niches where they live are quite distinct, but for others it is difficult to be certain if individuals with very similar characteristics should be separated into different species or considered as a single species. For this reason, an exact number of species cannot be given. African mammals belong to 50 families and 13 orders (see Table 1.2); as a whole this fauna is more diverse than that of any other continent except South America. Despite this diversity, they are all classified as eutherian or placental mammals because the unborn young are nourished by a complicated placenta and they are well developed at birth. There is no evidence that the other two subclasses of mammals – the pouched marsupials and the egg-laying monotremes – have ever been represented on the African continent.

1.1 The relationships of African mammals

'Tropical Africa' is part of the Aethiopian* zoogeographical region. This region consists of the continent of Africa except the northern part along the Mediterranean from Morocco to Egypt, and the southern part of Arabia. The area between the Sahara desert and the Mediterranean coastline is included in the Palaearctic Region as its flora and fauna show more affinities with Europe than with Africa. The living mammals of Africa show many relationships with the Oriental Region (south-east Asia, India) and a lesser relationship with the Palaearctic Region (Europe, northern Asia). For example, old-world monkeys, porcupines, pangolins, rhinos, elephants, bamboo rats

*This spelling is preferred to Ethiopian to prevent confusion with the present country of Ethiopia in eastern Africa.

and several families of bats are found only in the Oriental and Aethiopian regions, and dormice, jerboas, hedgehogs and horses occur only in the Palaearctic and Aethiopian regions. By comparison, some African mammals, such as rodents, dogs, cats and bovids, are almost world-wide in their distribution (Darlington 1957). Historical aspects of the relationships of African mammals are discussed further in Chapter 2 and the present mammal fauna is compared with that of other regions of the world in Chapter 3.

Besides the mammals which, at the present time, are also found in the Palaearctic and Oriental regions, some families, genera and species are found only in the Aethiopian region. These are known as endemic or exclusive mammals as there is no living representative of an endemic family, genus or species in any other zoogeographical region. The existence of a large number of endemic genera in Africa suggests that there has been isolation from other regions for a long geological time so that the endemic groups have had time to evolve.

Endemism occurs at the family, genus and species level, with endemic families being much rarer than endemic species. In the Aethiopian region, there are 11 endemic families: the Chrysochloridae, Galagidae, Anomaluridae, Pedetidae, Thryonomyidae, Petromyidae, Bathyergidae, Protelidae, Orycteropodidae, Hippopotamidae and Giraffidae. The number of endemic genera is about 180 (Bigalke 1972. Table 1.1), with the Rodentia, Carnivora, Artiodactyla, Insectivora and Chiroptera having the greatest

Table 1.1 *Endemism in the living mammals of Africa. (From Bigalke 1972.)*

Order	Families			Genera		
	Total No.	Endemic No.	%	Total No.	Endemic No.	%
Insectivora	5	3	60	24	19	79
Chiroptera	9	0	0	44	18	41
Primates	4	1	25	11	11	100
Pholidota	1	0	0	1	0	0
Lagomorpha	1	0	0	4	3	75
Rodentia	14	6*	43	84	68	81
Carnivora	6	1	17	36	24	66
Tubulidentata	1	1	100	1	1	100
Proboscidea	1	0	0	1	1	100
Hyracoidea	1	0	0	3	2	66
Sirenia	2	0	0	2	0	0
Perissodactyla	2	0	0	3	2	66
Artiodactyla	5	2	40	36	32	88

*Ctenodactylidae included as endemic.

number of endemic genera. All the 11 genera of African primates, the single genus of Tubulidentata, and the single genus of Proboscidea are endemic to Africa. Compared with other regions, Africa has a large number of endemic families and genera. This high degree of endemism is one of the reasons why the African mammal fauna is so interesting and spectacular.

1.2 Taxonomy of African mammals

A mammal ecologist in Africa has to be certain that he can identify and give the correct scientific name to the species he is studying. This is not always as easy as it sounds for several reasons. Firstly, there are many examples where a single valid species has been given different names by different authors in the past. For example, the lion has been called *Leo leo*, *Felis leo* and *Panthera leo* at different times and by various authorities. At the present time, the species *leo* is included in the older genus *Felis* by some authors, while others still prefer to place it in the genus *Panthera*. This difference of opinion depends on whether the lion is considered to be more closely related to *Panthera* or to *Felis*.

Secondly, many African mammals have been named more than once in the past so that the newest of the names becomes a synonym, and many former species are now regarded as subspecies. For example, a bushbuck in the southern Sudan was originally called *Tragelaphus bor* by Heuglin in 1877; subsequently it was realised that this bushbuck was simply one of many subspecies, or geographical varieties, of the previously named common bushbuck *Tragelaphus scriptus*. Hence the name *bor* becomes a subspecific name, and the correct scientific name is now *Tragelaphus scriptus bor*.

Thirdly, the ecologist may be studying a species which has many closely related species and/or subspecies, and neither the taxonomist nor the ecologist can say exactly what the correct name should be. The African buffalo *Syncerus* shows a lot of variation in the shape and size of its horns throughout its geographical range. This has given rise to much confusion about the specific and subspecific names. A recent review (Grubb 1972) has placed all the African buffalos in a single species *Syncerus caffer* which has three subspecies groups – *nanus*, *brachyceros* and *caffer* – which show discontinuous variation in the sizes and shapes of the horns. In some parts of Africa there is interbreeding between the subspecies groups which makes it especially difficult to know how to name such individuals.

Fourthly, the taxonomist is trying to put static names in a system which is dynamic and evolving. Species and subspecies are evolving all the time, and a subspecies at the present time may have evolved into a new species in 5000 years time. It is very difficult to decide when, along this course of evolution, a name should change from that of a subspecies of one species to that of an entirely new species.

These examples show that the ecologist must be careful when naming his study animals. It is essential that he records their most important taxonomic characteristics, and the localities at which they were obtained, so that if a subsequent revision shows the name to be incorrect, the recorded information will not be wasted, particularly if one cannot be certain of the correct identity of the study animals.

There are many books, guides and papers on the identification and taxonomy of African mammals. Some works deal with nearly all the mammals over a large area, while others describe the mammals of a particular country. A different approach deals with particular orders or families throughout their geographical range, or within a specified area. Also there are many papers on 'difficult' genera and species which are of great interest to the specialist. Some examples of all these works are listed in the Bibliography (pp. 413–5).

A particularly useful work is *The mammals of Africa – an identification manual* by Meester and Setzer (1971–77) which gives keys, taxonomic data and geographical distribution for all species and subspecies in continental Africa. Their nomenclature is used throughout this book.

Table 1.2 lists the 13 orders and 48 families of mammals in 'tropical Africa'. The genera and number of species in each genus are also listed, so when a particular name is mentioned in the text, the reader will be able to classify the animal and ascertain its relationships. African mammals which occur only in Africa south of the tropic of Capricorn ($23\frac{1}{2}°$S) or in Palaearctic Africa are not included in the Table.

Table 1.2   *The orders, families and genera of wild mammals of tropical mainland Africa. The number of species in each genus is indicated by the figure after the genus name. Species and genera which are found only in northern Palaearctic Africa or in South Africa south of latitude 23°S are omitted. (Data mostly from Meester and Setzer 1971–77.)*

Order and suborder	Family and subfamily	Genera and species
Insectivora	Tenrecidae	*Potamogale* 1, *Micropotamogale* 2
	Soricidae	*Crocidura* 74, *Suncus* 6, *Myosorex* 8, *Sylvisorex* 7, *Paracrocidura* 1, *Scutisorex* 1
	Erinaceidae	*Erinaceus* 3, *Hemiechinus* 1, *Paraechinus* 1
	Macroscelididae	*Rhynchocyon* 3, *Petrodromus* 1, *Macroscelides* 1, *Elephantulus* 10
	Chrysochloridae	*Amblysomus* 2, *Calcochloris* 1, *Chlorotalpa* 3, *Chrysochloris* 1, *Chrysospalax* 1, *Eremitalpa* 1
Chiroptera	Pteropodidae	*Scotonycteris* 2, *Casinycteris* 1, *Hypsignathus* 1, *Plerotes* 1, *Epomophorus* 8, *Epomops* 3, *Micropteropus* 3, *Nanonycteris* 1, *Eidolon* 1, *Rousettus* 3, *Myonycteris* 1, *Megaloglossus* 1
	Rhinopomatidae	*Rhinopoma* 2
	Emballonuridae	*Taphozous* 6, *Coleura* 1
	Nycteridae	*Nycteris* 11
	Megadermatidae	*Cardioderma* 1, *Lavia* 1
	Rhinolophidae	*Rhinolophus* 15
	Hipposideridae	*Hipposideros* 12, *Asellia* 2, *Triaenops* 1, *Cloeotis* 1
	Vespertilionidae	*Myotis* 5, *Plecotus* 1, *Nycticeius* 3, *Pipistrellus* 13, *Eptesicus* 13, *Barbastella* 1, *Mimitellus* 1, *Glauconycteris* 9, *Laephotis* 1, *Scotophilus* 3, *Kerivoula* 7, *Miniopterus* 4
	Molossidae	*Otomops* 1, *Platymops* 1, *Sauromys* 1, *Myopterus* 3, *Xiphonycteris* 1, *Tadarida* 23
Primates	Lorisidae	*Arctocebus* 1, *Perodicticus* 1
	Galagidae	*Euoticus* 2, *Galago* 3, *Galagoides* 1
	Cercopithecidae	*Cercopithecus* 23, *Cercocebus* 4, *Papio* 7, *Theropithecus* 1, *Colobus* 10
	Pongidae	*Pan* 2, *Gorilla* 1
Pholidota	Manidae	*Manis* 4
Lagomorpha	Leporidae	*Lepus* 5, *Poelagus* 1, *Pronolagus* 3
Rodentia Sciuromorpha	Anomaluridae	*Idiurus* 2, *Zenkerella* 1, *Anomalurus* 6
	Sciuridae	*Xerus* 4, *Myosciurus* 1, *Heliosciurus* 3, *Protoxerus* 2, *Epixerus* 1, *Funisciurus* 9, *Paraxerus* 11
Myomorpha	Cricetidae Cricetomyinae	*Beamys* 2, *Cricetomys* 2, *Saccostomus* 1
	Dendromurinae	*Delanymys* 1, *Dendromus* 5, *Deomys* 1, *Leimacomys* 1, *Dendroprionomys* 1, *Malacothrix* 1, *Steatomys* 3, *Prionomys* 1, *Petromyscus* 2

Order and suborder	Family and subfamily	Genera and species
	Gerbillinae	*Ammodillus* 1, *Desmodillus* 1, *Gerbillus* 15, *Meriones* 2, *Microdillus* 1, *Psammomys* 1, *Tatera* 7, *Taterillus* 10, *Gerbillurus* 3, *Desmodilliscus* 1, *Pachyuromys* 1
	Cricetinae	*Mystromys* 1
	Lophiomyinae	*Lophiomys* 1
	Otomyinae	*Otomys* 9, *Parotomys* 2
	Muridae	
	Murinae	*Arvicanthis* 2, *Colomys* 1, *Dasymys* 1, *Hybomys* 2, *Lemniscomys* 4, *Lophuromys* 7, *Malacomys* 2, *Muriculus* 1, *Mus* (including *Leggada*) 15, *Mylomys* 1, *Oenomys* 1, *Pelomys* 8, *Praomys* (including subgenera *Praomys, Mastomys, Hylomyscus* and *Myomyscus* = *Myomys*) 22, *Rattus* 2, *Rhabdomys* 1, *Stenocephalemys* 1, *Stochomys* 2, *Thallomys* 1, *Thamnomys* 4, *Uranomys* 1, *Zelotomys* 2, *Aethomys* 9, *Acomys* 4
	Dipodidae	*Jaculus* 1
	Muscardinidae	*Graphiurus* 5
Hystricomorpha	Thryonomyidae	*Thryonomys* 2
	Ctenodactylidae	*Pectinator* 1, *Massoutiera, Felovia* 1
	Rhizomyidae	*Tachyoryctes* 2
	Hystricidae	*Hystrix* 2, *Atherurus* 1
	Pedetidae	*Pedetes* 1
	Petromyidae	*Petromus* 1
	Bathyergidae	*Heterocephalus* 1, *Bathyergus* 1, *Cryptomys* 3, *Heliophobius* 2
Carnivora	Canidae	*Canis* 4, *Vulpes* 4, *Fennecus* 1, *Lycaon* 1, *Otocyon* 1
	Mustelidae	*Ictonyx* 1, *Poecilictis* 1, *Poecilogale* 1, *Lutra* 1, *Aonyx* 2, *Mellivora* 1
	Viverridae	*Poiana* 1, *Genetta* 9, *Osbornictis* 1, *Viverra* 1, *Nandinia* 1, *Suricata* 1, *Herpestes* 4, *Helogale* 2, *Dologale* 1, *Atilax* 1, *Mungos* 2, *Crossarchus* 3, *Liberiictis* 1, *Ichneumia* 1, *Bdeogale* 3, *Rhynchogale* 1, *Cynictis* 1, *Paracynictis* 1
	Hyaenidae	*Proteles* 1, *Crocuta* 1, *Hyaena* 2
	Felidae	*Panthera* 2, *Felis* (including *Profelis, Leptailurus* and *Caracal*) 6, *Acinonyx* 1
Tubulidentata	Orycteropodidae	*Orycteropus* 1
Hyracoidea	Procaviidae	*Procavia* 5, *Heterohyrax* 2, *Dendrohyrax* 3
Sirenia	Dugongidae	*Dugong* 1
	Trichechidae	*Trichechus* 1
Proboscidea	Elephantidae	*Loxodonta* 1
Perissodactyla	Rhinocerotidae	*Ceratotherium* 1, *Diceros* 1
	Equidae	*Equus* 4

(continued on p. 6)

Table 1.2 – continued

Order and suborder	Family and subfamily	Genera and species
Artiodactyla	Suidae	*Potamochoerus* 1, *Phacochoerus* 1, *Hylochoerus* 1
	Hippopotamidae	*Hippopotamus* 1, *Choeropsis* 1
	Tragulidae	*Hyemoschus* 1
	Giraffidae	*Giraffa* 1, *Okapia* 1
	Bovidae Bovinae	*Syncerus* 1
	Tragelaphinae	*Tragelaphus* 7, *Taurotragus* 2
	Cephalophinae	*Cephalophus* 15, *Sylvicapra* 1
	Reduncinae	*Redunca* 3, *Kobus* 5
	Hippotraginae	*Hippotragus* 2, *Oryx* 2, *Addax* 1
	Alcelaphinae	*Connochaetes* 2, *Alcelaphus* 2, *Damaliscus* 2
	Antilopinae	*Aepyceros* 1, *Antidorcas* 1, *Litocranius* 1, *Ammodorcas* 1, *Gazella* 8
	Neotraginae	*Oreotragus* 1, *Madoqua* 5, *Dorcatragus* 1, *Ourebia* 1, *Raphicerus* 2, *Neotragus* 3, *Pelea* 1
	Caprinae	*Capra* 3

1.3 Insectivora

The order Insectivora are small mammals which feed on insects, molluscs, worms, and other animal foods. They have elongated snouts and numerous small pointed teeth. The typical dental formula is $\frac{3023}{1023} = 28$, a feature which easily distinguishes them from the rodents. Insectivores are mainly nocturnal and are seldom seen. There are five families in tropical Africa; two of these, the Chrysochloridae and Macroscelididae, are endemic and a third family, the Tenrecidae, occurs only in Africa and Madagascar.

The family Tenrecidae is represented by three species of otter shrews. The largest of these, *Potamogale velox*, inhabits streams and rivers in the lowland forest and swampy regions along large rivers. This species shows a striking resemblance to the true otters (Order Carnivora) which also live in riparian habitats. The convergent morphological features of these animals include a streamlined body, a thick powerful tail, long vibrissae, and dense soft fur. Otter shrews are the largest of the African insectivores with a body and tail length of up to 47 cm.

The family Chrysochloridae comprises the golden moles. They are one of the three families of African mammals adapted for burrowing, and have a cylindrical form, small eyes, very short ears and tails, and short powerful forelimbs with large claws (Fig. 1.2). They obtain their common name from the beautiful golden tinge of their hair. Although rare, these animals are widely distributed and they occur in the northern and southern savannas, in montane and lowland forests, and four species are found in the south-west arid zone.

The family Erinaceidae includes the hedgehogs which have many small spines on their backs and sides, large ears and eyes, and no tail (Fig. 1.3). In self-defence these hedgehogs curl into a prickly ball. The hedgehogs of Africa occur widely in the northern and southern savannas, and in the Somali and south-west arid zones. *Erinaceus* is the most widespread genus.

The only diurnal insectivores in Africa are the elephant shrews of the family

Fig. 1.1 Tenrecidae: Otter shrew (*Micropotamogale ruwenzorii*). (*Photo: U. Rahm, from Rahm and Christiaensen, 1963.*)

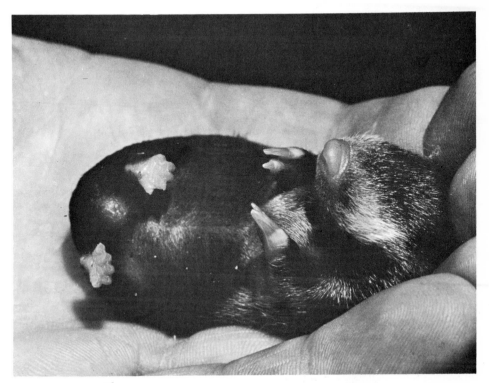

Fig. 1.2 Chrysochloridae: Golden mole (*Chrysochloris asiatica*). (Photo: J. Visser.)

Fig. 1.3   Erinaceidae: Hedgehog (*Erinaceus* sp.). (Photo: C. A. Spinage.)

Macroscelididae. These are the largest of the shrew-like insectivores; one species (*Rhynchocyon cirnei*) has a head and body length of 25 cm and a tail of 20 cm. Elephant shrews have long hindlimbs, short forelimbs, large eyes and elongated snouts, and are adapted for rapid bipedal locomotion (Fig. 1.4). They feed on insects which they hunt during the day. Elephant shrews are fairly common in the south-west arid zone, the southern savanna and the eastern part of the northern savanna. Two genera, *Rhynchocyon* and *Petrodromus*, occur in the lowland and medium-altitude forests of Central Africa. Elephant shrews do not occur in West Africa.

The most numerous and widespread insectivores are the shrews of the family Soricidae. Well over 100 species have been recorded from Africa but many of these are of uncertain taxonomic status. Shrews are small active animals with an elongated snout, small eyes, and a tail which is thick at the base and covered with long sparse hairs (Fig. 1.5). Some species have scent glands which give a very characteristic odour (e.g. *Crocidura manni*). Shrews are especially common in the lowland forest where the majority of the species have been described, but they also occur in the northern and southern savanna and in montane habitats. *Crocidura* is the most widespread genus with the largest number of species. This family contains two very small African species (*Suncus etruscus* and *S. infinitesimus*) which weigh only 1.5 to 2 g.

1.4   Chiroptera

The bats (order Chiroptera) are the only order of flying mammals. The second, third, fourth and fifth digits of the forelimbs are greatly elongated and support a membrane of naked skin called a patagium. This is attached to the sides of the body and extends on to the short hindlimbs. An additional membrane, the interfemoral membrane, may

Fig. 1.4   Macroscelididae: Elephant shrew (*Petrodromus tetradactylus*). (Photo: Zoological Society of London.)

Fig. 1.5   Soricidae: Shrew (*Crocidura poensis*). (Photo: D. C. D. Happold.)

Fig. 1.6 Pteropodidae: (*a*) Fruit bat (*Myonycteris torquata*). (Photo: A. R. Devez.) (*b*) Fruit bat (*Epomophorus gambianus*) feeding on the flowers of *Parkia clappertonia*. (Photo: H. G. Baker)

a

b

occur between the hindlimbs and enclose the tail. Bats are divided into two suborders: the Megachiroptera and the Microchiroptera.

The Megachiroptera comprises the single family Pteropodidae. These are fruit-eating bats which are usually large in size although some microchiroptera are higher than the smallest of the fruit bats. Fruit bats have a simple more or less elongated snout, a 'dog-like' face, large eyes, a very small or non-existent tail, and in all African species there is a claw on the tip of the second digit (Fig. 1.6*a*). One genus, *Megaloglossus*, has small papillae on the tongue and feeds exclusively on nectar. The other species, with the possible exception of *Plerotes*, feed chiefly on fruits and their geographical range is limited to regions where fruits are available all the year. Some species show regular daily and seasonal movements in response to food availability. The areas covered are not vast, and do not correspond to the migratory movements of birds. When a particular tree is in fruit, bats of different species may congregate to feed, and some species of trees, e.g. *Parkia*, *Bombax*, are pollinated solely by fruit bats during their feeding activities (see Fig. 1.6*b*). Fruit bats are mostly nocturnal, but their large eyes enable them to see in very dim light. Some species of *Rousettus* which live in caves have, in addition, a simple echolocation mechanism. Some fruit bats roost in very large numbers as does *Eidolon helvum*, which may live in colonies of tens of thousands of individuals, but most other genera are found singly or in small groups. Fruit bats are found throughout tropical Africa except in parts of the northern Sudanese arid zone.

In contrast the Microchiroptera contain many families of insect-eating bats, which show extensive morphological variation. Insect-eating bats are nocturnal; they navigate and catch their prey while flying by means of their ultrasonic echolocation in which hearing replaces vision. The strange 'nose-leaves' on the snout of some families, and large ears, are related to this special sense. These bats can easily be distinguished from fruit bats by the absence of the claw on the second digit, and usually by their small eyes. There are eight families of Microchiroptera in Africa; these are the Rhinopomatidae, Emballonuridae, Nycteridae, Megadermatidae, Rhinolophidae, Hipposideridae, Vespertilionidae and Molossidae (Table 1.3).

Table 1.3 *Distinguishing features of African microchiroptera.*

Family	Nose leaf	Interfemoral membrane	Type of tail	Position of tail in relation to the interfemoral membrane (IFM)
Rhinopomatidae	Small	No	Long	Tail not enclosed in IFM
Emballonuridae	None	Yes	Medium	Terminal half of tail projects through IFM
Nycteridae	Yes	Yes	Medium	Tail enclosed in IFM
Megadermatidae	Yes	No	None	Tail not enclosed in IFM
Rhinolophidae*	Large	Yes	Medium	Tail enclosed in IFM
Hipposideridae*	Large	Yes	Medium	Tail enclosed in IFM
Vespertilionidae	No	Yes	Medium	Tail enclosed in IFM
Molossidae	No	Yes	Medium	Proximal half of tail enclosed in IFM, terminal half not enclosed

*These two families may be distinguished on the shape of the nose-leaves.

The mouse-tailed bats, family Rhinopomatidae, have a long 'mouse-like' tail which is ensheathed in the interfemoral membrane only near its base, and small nose-leaves (Fig. 1.7). This family contains a single genus *Rhinopoma* with two species which occur in the Sudanese arid zone and in the desert along the Nile valley southwards to north-central Kenya. They are gregarious and roost in caves and human habitations.

The family Emballonuridae are the sheath-tailed bats. In this family the interfemoral membrane is well developed and the tail projects through the membrane

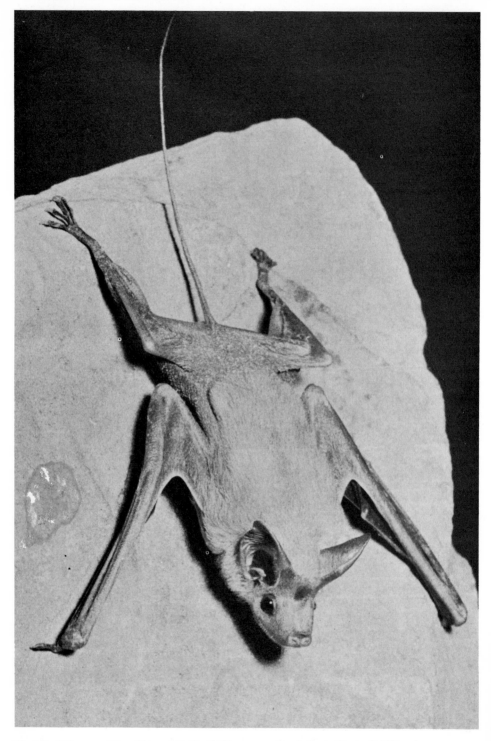

Fig. 1.7   Rhinopomatidae: Mouse-tailed bat (*Rhinopoma microphyllum*). (Photo: E. Külzer.)

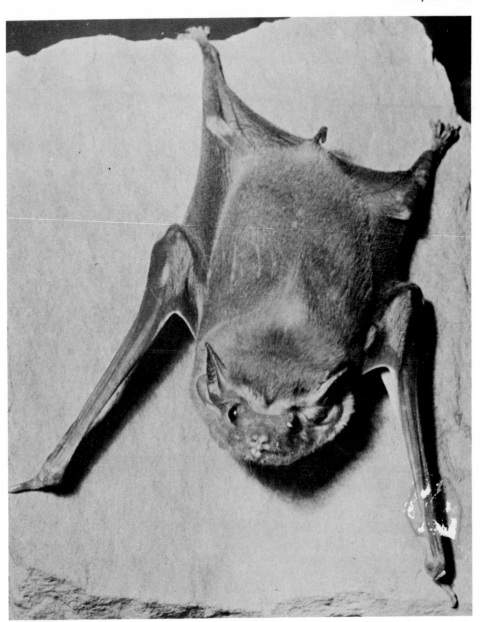

Fig. 1.8 Emballonuridae: Sheath-tailed bat (*Taphozous hildegardeae*). (Photo: E. Külzer.)

on its dorsal side so that thé terminal end is free. The ears are rather pointed and the snout lacks any nose-leaves (Fig. 1.8). The family contains only seven African species, but these are widespread throughout Africa south of the Sahara. Most species are gregarious and roost in caves and human habitations.

The slit-faced bats, family Nycteridae, are all included in the genus *Nycteris*. A deep cleft, bordered by nose-leaves, runs from the nostrils to the top of the head and gives rise to the common name of the family. The ears are large and elongated and the tail is

Fig. 1.9   Nycteridae: Slit-faced bat (*Nycteris thebaica*) eating a mealworm. (Photo: E. Külzer.)

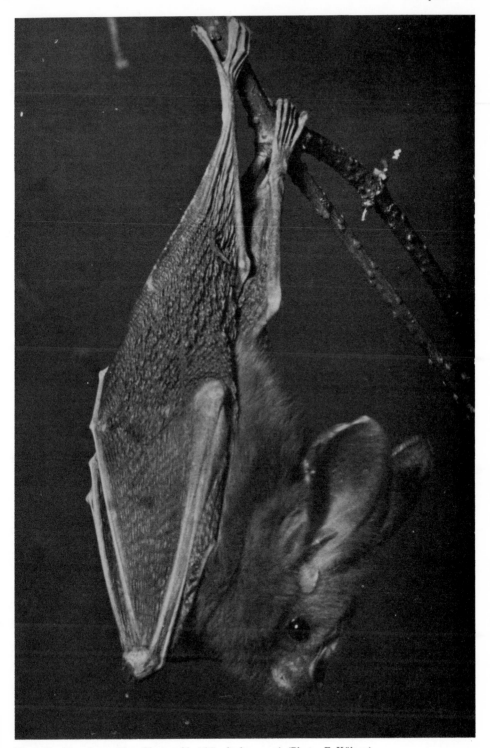

Fig. 1.10   Megadermatidae: Big-eared bat (*Cardioderma cor*). (Photo: E. Külzer.)

Fig. 1.11   Rhinolophidae: Horse-shoe bat (*Rhinolophus hildebrandtii*). (Photo: E. Külzer.)

Fig. 1.12 Hipposideridae: Leaf-nosed bat (*Asellia tridens*). (Photo: E. Külzer.)

Fig. 1.13   Vespertilionidae: Simple-nosed bat (*Scotophilus nigrita*). (Photo: E. Külzer.)

Fig. 1.14   Molossidae: Free-tailed bat or Mastiff bat (*Tadarida condylura*). Adult with young. (Photo: E. Külzer.

entirely enclosed in the interfemoral membrane (Fig. 1.9). The family is widespread though not particularly common throughout the arid and savanna zones and along the Nile valley, and several species are confined to the forest zone. Bats of this family tend to be solitary or to live in small groups. During the day they roost in trees, crevices and abandoned burrows.

The false vampires or big-eared bats, family Megadermatidae, are easily distinguished by their enormous ears which are up to twice as long as the head (Fig. 1.10). There are prominent nose-leaves on the snout, and the eyes are larger than in other microchiroptera. The tail is absent, but the interfemoral membrane is well developed. There are only two African species in the family; they occur in the savanna and arid zones from about 15 °N to 15 °S, and also penetrate the lowland forest to some extent.

The horse-shoe bats, family Rhinolophidae, have well developed nose-leaves. There is a front nose-leaf in the shape of a horseshoe, and a back nose-leaf which is usually pointed (Fig. 1.11). The tail is enclosed in an interfemoral membrane. The single genus, *Rhinolophus*, has 18 species in Africa. Members of this family are found in all habitats. Most species roost in groups in caves during the day.

The leaf-nosed bats, family Hipposideridae, are included in the Rhinolophidae by some authorities. However, an elliptical posterior nose-leaf (Fig. 1.12) and the different types of echolocation sounds made by leaf-nose bats probably merit their separation into another family. Species in this family are found throughout Africa south of the Sahara and along the Nile valley. *Hipposideros* is widely distributed but the other genera have limited distributions. Most species are gregarious and roost in caves and human habitations.

The family of insect-eating bats with the largest number of species and the widest distribution is the Vespertilionidae or simple-nosed bats. The snout does not have any nose-leaf in African species and the long tail is entirely enclosed in the interfemoral membrane (Fig. 1.13). Bats of this family occur throughout most forest, savanna and arid habitats throughout Africa. They are rapid flyers and are frequently seen on the wing at dusk. They range in size from the smallest *Pipistrellus* (forearm 26 mm) to the largest *Scotophilus* (forearm 75 mm). These bats roost singly or in small groups in holes, caves, buildings and on branches. The family is a difficult one for the taxonomist and many species are of uncertain status. Because of the number and diversity of species, the family is divided into three subfamilies: the numerous Vespertilioninae, and the less numerous Miniopterinae and Kerivoulinae.

The last family of insect-eating bats is the Molossidae, comprising the free-tailed or mastiff bats. As their name implies, they have long tails which are only partially enclosed in the interfemoral membrane, and the terminal half of the tail is free. A simple nose, thick lips, and wide rounded ears are very characteristic of the family (Fig. 1.14). An unusual feature is the presence of a fleshy pad at the base of the first finger, so that when the wings are folded the bat can run rapidly on all fours using the first fingers and the hindlimbs to support the weight of the body. Bats of this family are gregarious and make a variety of noisy sounds which are audible to the human ear. The family is distributed in all habitats in Africa including the desert along the Nile valley.

1.5   Primates

The monkeys and apes (order Primates) are primarily adapted for arboreal life. Their limbs are usually long with well developed digits ending in nails, and the thumb is opposable. The tail, if present, is not prehensile but may be used for balancing. Most species of primates are vegetarians although some are omnivorous. They are most numerous in the lowland forest zone where they have undergone extensive speciation: relatively few species have become adapted for life in the savanna. The order ranges throughout Africa south of the Sahara; some species like the vervet (*Cercopithecus pygerythrus*) are widespread and common, and others like the golden potto (*Arctocebus calabarensis*) are very restricted in distribution and quite rare. There are two suborders of primates: the Prosimii and the Anthropoidea. The Prosimii are the 'primitive' forest primates and are represented in tropical Africa by the families Lorisidae and Galagidae. The Anthropoidea includes the true monkeys of the family Cercopithecidae found in forest, savanna and montane regions, and the highly evolved forest apes of the family Pongidae.

The galagos (family Galagidae) are small arboreal primates with extraordinary abilities to leap at high speed from branch to branch and from tree to tree. They have elongated hindlimbs, long fingers, slender bodies, and a tail which is usually longer than the head and body. Galagos are mostly nocturnal although some species are active during the day. They have enormous eyes, and appear to have good vision in very dim light. Galagos sleep in tree holes during the day, and at night they forage singly or in pairs using their hands to catch insects and to grasp leaves, flowers and eggs which make up their varied diet. Several species of galagos occur in the lowland forests, and one species, *Galago senegalensis*, occurs throughout the northern and southern savannas.

The pottos (family Lorisidae) differ markedly from the galagos. They are slow-moving and nocturnal, with comparatively small eyes, short tails and limbs of equal length (Fig. 1.15). They feed on insects, snails and fruits. There are only two species: the potto (*Perodicticus potto*) which occurs throughout the lowland forests of West and central Africa, and the golden potto (*Arctocebus calabarensis*) which is restricted to the forests of eastern Nigeria, Cameroun and Gabon.

The true monkeys of Africa are all included in the family Cercopithecidae. This family contains the largest number of species and the widest distribution of all the African primates. Monkeys are usually vegetarian, but some species will also eat insects and small vertebrates. Most of the forest species are arboreal and occasionally terrestrial but the savanna species tend to more terrestrial in habit. All the species in the family are similar in structure, and therefore characteristics such as the shape of the head and the colouration of the fur are important diagnostic characters. There are five African genera: *Papio*, *Theropithecus*, *Cercopithecus*, *Cercocebus* and *Colobus*.

The genus *Papio* comprises the baboons, drill and mandrill. These are heavily built with pointed dog-like muzzles, and they have callosities on the buttocks which are highly coloured in some species (e.g. the mandrill). These primates are predominantly ground-dwellers and although they can climb in trees, they are not agile. Baboons are gregarious and are seen in large groups comprising males, females, and young. There are six species of baboons; they occur in savanna and rocky habitats, but their ranges do not overlap. The drill and the mandrill occur only in the lowland forest of Cameroun and Gabon.

The *Cercopithecus* monkeys have flattened faces, long tails, and are slightly built (Fig. 1.16). They are the most arboreal of the African monkeys, and they can move quickly and with great agility in the trees. Most species are gregarious and live in troops. The greatest number of species are found in the lowland forest, but others occur in the fringing forests in the northern and southern savannas. Some species, e.g. *Cercopithecus pygerythrus*, *C. mitis*, and *C. mona*, show considerable variation in colour within their ranges, and these varieties are considered either as subspecies or superspecies. Some of the lowland forest species have very constricted ranges, and in some localities several species of *Cercopithecus* live sympatrically, e.g. *C. mona*, *C.*

Fig. 1.15 Lorisidae: Potto (*Perodicticus potto*). (Photo: C. A. Spinage.)

nictitans and *C. cephus* in the forests of Rio Muni. In contrast, the savanna species of the *Cercopithecus aethiops* group are found throughout the northern and southern savanna wherever there are suitable riverine forests.

The mangabeys, *Cercocebus*, are similar to the *Cercopithecus* monkeys except that they have longer muzzles. They are more terrestrial than *Cercopithecus* but less so than *Papio*. These monkeys occur in parts of the lowland forest zone.

The most terrestrial of the monkeys is the widespread *Cercopithecus* (*Erythrocebus*), or patas monkey, which occurs in the northern savanna zone. Patas monkeys forage on the ground looking for seeds, fruits, and insects, and at dusk they climb into trees for the night. They often live in small groups.

Fig. 1.16   Cercopithecidae: Talapoin monkey (*Cercopithecus talapoin*). (Photo: Zoological Society of London.)

Fig. 1.17 Pongidae: Chimpanzee (*Pan troglodytes*). (Photo: Zoological Society of London.)

The colobus monkeys (*Colobus* spp.) are almost entirely arboreal. They have only four fingers on their hands. The fur is soft and long, and in some species it forms a 'mane' on the back and rump. Because of these and other characteristics which clearly distinguish colobus monkeys from the other Cercopithecidae, some authors place them in a separate family Colobidae. Colobus monkeys live in family groups or in larger troops. They are diurnal and feed mainly on shoots and leaves. They occur only in forest regions, and in some areas several species are sympatric but each species occupies a different stratum in the forest; for example, in certain lowland forests of West Africa *Colobus badius* lives in the forest canopy while *C. polykomos* lives in the middle layers. Each of the ten species of *Colobus* has a fairly restricted distribution within the forested regions of tropical Africa.

The family Pongidae includes the gorilla and the chimpanzee. Next to man (family Hominidae), these are the most highly evolved of the primates. They are large and heavily built, with the forelimbs longer than the hindlimbs, and no tail. Although they are usually quadripedal, they can also walk bipedally. They are mainly ground dwellers, but usually sleep at night in nests in trees. Gorillas and chimpanzees normally move about in family groups or in troops of up to 40 individuals. The gorilla occurs in restricted forest areas in Kivu and in parts of Cameroun and Gabon; the chimpanzee (Fig. 1.17) lives in scattered localities in lowland forest from Sierra Leone to Uganda and Tanzania.

1.6   Pholidota

The pangolins (order Pholidota) show adaptations for feeding on ants and termites. These adaptations include forelimbs with long claws for breaking into ant and termite nests, a pointed snout, a long sticky tongue for licking up the prey and the absence of teeth. The body, except for the ventral surface, is covered with scales similar in general appearance to the scales of reptiles (Fig. 1.18). When alarmed, pangolins curl into a ball. The four African species are included in the family Manidae. The rare *Manis*

a   b

Fig. 1.18 Manidae: Pangolin (*Manis tricuspis*) (*a*) Two individuals climbing. (*b*) Head and body to show details of scales, claws, ear and unscaled ventral surface. (Photos: (*a*) E. Pages and A. R. Devez; (*b*) G. Pariente and E. Pages.)

gigantea is terrestrial and occurs in the lowland forest and savanna of West and central Africa. The other three species are arboreal, and between them are distributed over most of Africa south of the Sahara.

1.7 Lagomorpha

The hares and rabbits (order Lagomorpha) are small to medium-sized mammals with long ears, large eyes, soft thick fur and a small fluffy tail (Fig. 1.19). They have long hindlegs, and hares in particular are strong runners which bound along with the body close to the ground. Lagomorphs graze on tender grasses and herbs, and their long incisors continue to grow throughout life. Both hares and rabbits are crepuscular and nocturnal, and because of their small size, speed and secretive habits are seldom seen. Rabbits shelter and rear their young in burrows, but hares use surface nests or 'forms' in dense grass.

The African lagomorphs are members of the hare family, Leporidae. There are five species of *Lepus* which occur throughout the northern and southern savannas and the arid zones. Rock hares (*Pronolagus*) are found in rocky areas in parts of southern and eastern Africa. The scrub hare or African rabbit (*Poelagus marjorita*) lives in woodlands in Uganda and southern Sudan. This species usually rests in vegetation but builds a burrow in which to rear its young. Unlike those of the other genera, the young are born naked.

Fig. 1.19 Leporidae: Hare (*Lepus* sp.). (Photo: C. A. Spinage.)

1.8   Rodentia

The rodents (order Rodentia) are a very large and successful order represented by 12 families and about 240 species in Africa. The dental formula is $\frac{1003}{1003} = 16$ or $\frac{1004}{1004} = 20$, which easily distinguishes them from Insectivora. They occur in most habitats, and show great diversity in their morphology, ecology, physiology and behaviour. The majority are terrestrial, but some species are arboreal (utilising different strata in forests), and some are entirely subterranean. The African rodents range in size from the small pygmy mouse (*Mus minutoides*, wt. 7 g) to the crested porcupine (*Hystrix*, wt. 20 kg). The majority feed on grasses, roots, leaves, seeds and fruits, but some include insects and worms in their diet. Most rodents are nocturnal, but squirrels, cane-rats and some mice are partly diurnal or crepuscular.

Because the rodents are so diverse, they are divided into three suborders. These are the Sciuromorpha for the squirrels and 'flying' squirrels, the Myomorpha for the mice, rats, jerboas and dormice, and the Hystricomorpha for the porcupines, cane-rats and their allies.

Squirrels (family Sciuridae) are the most abundant arboreal rodents. They are diurnal, active animals which are seen frequently running along branches and jumping from tree to tree. They have a long bushy tail which is used as a balancing rudder (Fig. 1.20). Squirrels have a varied diet which includes insects, eggs and grubs as well as seeds, nuts, fruits and shoots. Squirrels range in size from the pygmy squirrel (*Myosciurus*, total length 15 cm) to the giant squirrel (*Protoxerus*, 60 cm). Many species occur only in the lowland forest zone, and some have very restricted ranges. In contrast, the Gambian sun squirrel (*Heliosciurus gambianus*) is found in all savanna regions in tropical Africa. One genus of squirrels (*Xerus*) lives on the ground. These

Fig. 1.20   Sciuridae: Tree squirrel (*Funisciurus pyrrhopus*). (Photo: Zoological Society of London.)

ground squirrels spend the night in burrows. They occur in many savanna and arid regions of Africa, with the four species being similar in their habits.

The 'flying' squirrels (family Anomaluridae) are the most arboreally adapted rodents. Unlike bats, these animals do not fly, but they have a large flap of fur-covered skin between the limbs on each side of the body, which functions as a gliding membrane

Fig. 1.21   Anomaluridae: Flying squirrel (*Idiurus* sp.). (Photo: U. Rahm.)

(patagium), enabling the animals to glide away from the tops of tall trees (Fig. 1.21). Flying squirrels can glide up to 100 metres without losing much height. They land on the trunks of trees, and climb upwards using their claws and scaly plates under the base of the tail. By climbing, gliding, climbing and gliding again over established routes, flying squirrels are able to move comparatively easily and swiftly through their forest habitat. They are, however, limited in distribution to lowland forest regions where there are numerous tall trees. In suitable areas within the lowland forest zone, and some outlier forests, the three genera of flying squirrels are widely distributed but they are nocturnal and seldom seen.

The family Muridae contains the rats and mice; it has the largest number of species of any rodent family and probably the most individuals. The murids can be found in most terrestrial habitats of Africa, and some species are truly arboreal. The African murids are typically mouse- or rat-like, and are superficially similar. They differ in coat colour and pattern, size, length of extremities, tooth and skull morphology, ecology, physiology and behaviour, but in spite of these differences, the taxonomic status of many species is uncertain. This is a very large diverse group of about 23 genera and 90 species and is of considerable ecological importance. These rodents are found in forest, savanna, swamp and arboreal habitats. Several species are commensal, living in human houses and stores (*Rattus rattus, Mus musculus, Praomys* (*Mastomys*) *natalensis*), and others may be important pests of crops and stored products.

a

b

Fig. 1.22   (*a*) Muridae: Murinae: Long footed swamp mouse (*Malacomys edwardsi*).   (*b*) Cricetidae: Gerbillinae: Egyptian gerbil (*Gerbillus pyramidum*). (Photos: D. C. D. Happold.)

The family Cricetidae contains six subfamilies in tropical Africa. The subfamily Cricetomyinae contains the pouched rats which obtain their common name from large storage pouches inside their cheeks. These animals collect seeds, fruits, roots and other foods on the ground, pack them into the pouches and carry them to special food stores in their burrows. The giant pouched rats (*Cricetomys* spp.) are found in forest and savanna throughout most of tropical Africa, and may often live in human habitations. Other genera are *Beamys* and *Saccostomus* which range from east to southern Africa.

The Dendromurinae are mostly small specialised tree mice, although the terrestrial fat mouse (*Steatomys*), the burrowing *Malacothrix* and rock-living *Petromyscus* are exceptions. Many species in this subfamily have prehensile tails. The fat mice lay down considerable reserves of fat and can live for relatively long periods without water. The group is diagnosed on the basis of structural characters of the molar teeth.

The Cricetinae contains a single species (*Mystromys albicaudatus*) which occurs only in southern Africa. It is large (head and body 160 mm) compared with most murid rodents although the tail is comparatively short (50–80 mm). The subfamily is characterised by the zig-zag enamel patterning of the cheek teeth and the hairiness of the soles of the hindfeet.

The Lophiomyinae contains one species (*Lophiomys imhausi*) which occurs in the forests of eastern Africa. This 'maned rat' has long coarse black and white fur, and it can erect some of the hairs along the length of the back to form the 'mane'. It is endemic to Africa and is placed in a separate subfamily because of a strange formation of the bones of its skull. This large rat (head and body 32 cm) is a slow mover and poor climber.

The Otomyinae contains the laminate-toothed rats and vlei rats. They have blunt faces, small eyes and small tails. They are separated from other rodents by the unusual hypsodont and lophodont pattern of the cheek teeth with their numerous transverse grooves. They also show the unusual feature of the first molar being substantially smaller than the third.

The Gerbillinae, or gerbils, occur mostly in the arid zone and to a lesser extent in the savannas. They have large eyes, sandy-coloured fur and long tails which usually have a tuft at the end (Fig. 1.22*b*). They avoid exposure to hostile arid conditions by spending the day in their deep, extensive burrows. Several species which live in arid zones are known to have special physiological and behavioural adaptations for conserving water.

The jerboas (family Dipodidae) are a family of desert rodents, and in Africa they occur only in the Sudanese arid zone and the Sahara. Jerboas have large eyes, very long hind-limbs with extensive hairs on the underside of the three toes and a long tufted tail (Fig. 1.23). They live in burrows in the sand, and at night they emerge to feed on seeds and dried grasses. Jerboas are saltatorial, and their fast gaits are bipedal.

The dormice (family Muscardinidae) are myomorph rodents, which, like the Sciuromorpha, are specialised for arboreal life. Dormice sleep during the day in holes in trees. At night they climb through the trees feeding on seeds, nuts, fruits and shoots. They are small animals with dense soft fur, long bushy tails and hand-like forepaws (Fig. 1.24). Dormice are widely distributed in the northern and southern savannas and some forest regions.

The third suborder of rodents is the Hystricomorpha, which includes seven African families. The cane rats (family Thryonomyidae) are large solidly built rodents with coarse fur, short limbs and a short tail (Fig. 1.25). They live in savannas where the grass is tall, and they feed solely on grass stems which they manipulate with their forepaws. They are partly diurnal, and rest in grassy nests or in the abandoned burrows of other

Fig. 1.23   Dipodidae: Jerboa (*Jaculus jaculus*). (Photo: D. C. D. Happold.)

Fig. 1.24   Muscardinidae: Dormouse (*Graphiurus* sp.). (Photo: C. A. Spinage.)

animals. A single genus, *Thryonomys*, occurs throughout the savanna regions of tropical Africa.

The largest African rodents are the porcupines (family Hystricidae), which are

Fig. 1.25 Thryonomyidae: Cane rat or Cutting-grass (*Thryonomys swinderianus*). (Photo: Zoological Society of London.)

characterised by long spines or quills on their backs and sides (Fig. 1.26). These can be relaxed or erected at will, and are used for defence against enemies. The quills rattle as they move. Porcupines are nocturnal and during the day they live in caves or burrows. Large crested porcupines (*Hystrix*) occur throughout the northern and southern savannas, and smaller brushtailed porcupines (*Atherurus*) which have shorter quills and a brush of special bristles at the end of the tail occur in lowland and medium altitude forests.

The orange-toothed mole rats or bamboo rats (family Rhizomyidae) are almost permanently fossorial. They are cylindrical in shape, with small eyes and dense fur (Fig. 1.27) and are similar in appearance, and show many convergent features, with European moles (Talpidae) and African golden moles (Chrysochloridae). However, the forelimbs of these animals are small because they use their teeth for burrowing. The family contains one African genus, *Tachyoryctes*, with two species, which extends from the highlands of eastern Africa to southern Africa.

The mole rats (family Bathyergidae) are an endemic family which are similar in many ways to the bamboo rats. They have fairly large forelimbs and their incisor teeth protrude forwards beyond the lips. This family shows varying amounts of reduction of the fur, and in the naked mole rat (*Heterocephalus*) the skin has only a few scattered hairs (Fig. 1.28). Mole rats possess specialised physiological characteristics which are probably related to the stable nature of the temperature and humidity in their burrows. In the common-toothed mole-rat (*Cryptomys*) the vibrissae, together with the cornea of the otherwise functionless eye, detect air movements. There are four genera of tropical African bathyergids. They all occur in the drier savanna parts of eastern and southern Africa and in the Somali arid zone where the soils are sandy and well drained.

Finally, there are three Hystricomorph families, the Petromyidae, Ctenodactylidae and Pedetidae, each of which has a small number of species and a limited distribution.

Fig. 1.26   Hystricidae: Crested porcupine (*Hystrix cristata*). (Photo: C. A. Spinage.)

Fig. 1.27 Rhizomyidae: Mole rat or Bamboo rat (*Tachyoryctes* sp.). (Photo: Zoological Society of London.)

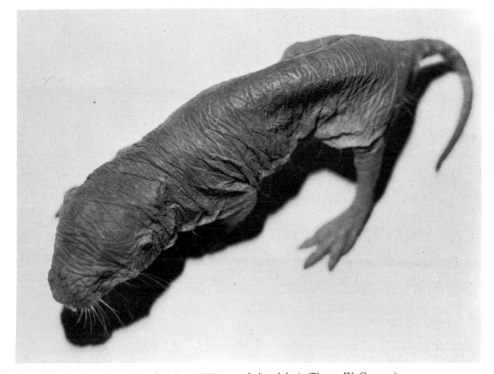

Fig. 1.28 Bathyergidae: Naked mole rat (*Heterocephalus glaber*). (Photo: W. George.)

Fig. 1.29   Petromyidae: Dassie rat (*Petromus typicus*). (Photo: C. G. Coetzee.)

Fig. 1.30   Ctenodactylidae: Gundi (*Ctenodactylus gundi*). This species only occurs in Africa north of the tropics. (Photo: W. George.)

The dassie rats (Petromyidae) are squirrel-like rodents that inhabit rocky areas in the south-west arid zone (Fig. 1.29). The gundis (Ctenodactylidae) also live in rocky areas (Fig. 1.30). One genus, *Pectinator*, occurs in the Somali arid zone, and the other two genera occur in rocky areas of the Sahara. The springhare (Pedetidae) is a large rodent with very elongated hindlimbs, a long bushy tail, large eyes and long pointed ears (Fig. 1.31). The proportions of the body are similar to those of jerboas and kangaroos. Springhares are nocturnal (and occasionally diurnal) and live in burrows. They are saltatorial, and cover long distances in search of shoots, roots and water. Springhares occur in the southern and northern savannas, and in the south-west arid zone.

Fig. 1.31   Pedetidae: Springhare (*Pedetes capensis*). (Photo: M. J. Coe.)

1.9 Carnivora

The order Carnivora contains the largest and ecologically most important meat-eating mammals. Their adaptations include good vision and hearing, sharp teeth for stabbing and cutting, sharp claws and considerable strength and agility for catching their prey. Carnivores range in size from dwarf mongooses to the large powerful leopards and lions, and they display many different morphological, ecological and behavioural adaptations. Carnivores feed on a wide range of prey animals – from worms, snails and lizards to zebras and waterbuck. Consequently the characteristic adaptations of each genus are related to the prey which is caught, killed and eaten. Carnivores are found in all habitats in tropical Africa, but even in ideal habitats they are never extremely numerous. This is simply because large numbers of the prey species are required to sustain each individual. Five families of carnivores occur in Africa.

The dogs, jackals and foxes (family Canidae) are long-legged running carnivores which have blunt non-retractile claws (Fig. 1.32). Most species live singly or in small groups, but the hunting dog (*Lycaon pictus*) may live in packs of up to 20 individuals. The canids hunt their prey by running, and then catching it with their teeth. They feed mostly on amphibians, birds and small mammals, although packs of hunting dogs can kill large antelopes which they chase until the prey is exhausted. The jackals and hunting dogs occur throughout the savanna and arid zones, but the foxes are more confined in their distribution. Four species of fox live in the Sudanese arid zone and in the Sahara desert, and one species, the Simien fox (*Canis simensis*), is found only in parts of the Ethiopian highlands.

Fig. 1.32   Canidae: Side-striped jackal (*Canis adustus*). (Photo: C. A. Spinage.)

The family Mustelidae are small to medium-sized carnivores. This family has many species in the Palaearctic and Nearctic Regions, but is poorly represented in Africa. There are three subfamilies – the Mustelinae, Mellivorinae and Lutrinae – each of which is morphologically distinct and adapted to a different ecological niche. In Africa, the Mustelinae are represented by the zorilla (*Ictonyx striatus*) and African weasels (*Poecilogale* and *Poecilictis*). These are small, long-bodied agile carnivores with short legs and a long tail, and they have well-developed scent glands which produce a characteristic pungent odour. Zorillas are mostly nocturnal, and feed on rodents and eggs. They are seen infrequently, although they may be quite common in some areas. *Poecilogale* occurs in forest and savanna habitats of central and southern Africa, *Ictonyx* is widespread in the savanna and arid zones and *Poecilictis* is found north of *Ictonyx* in a narrow belt of savanna south of the Sahara. The Mellivorinae contains only one species, the ratel (*Mellivora capensis*), which occurs widely throughout most of tropical Africa (Fig. 1.33). This medium-sized, solidly built mustelid lives in burrows during the day, and at night it searches for small vertebrates, bulbs and shoots. The otters (subfamily Lutrinae) are semi-aquatic animals which feed on fish and aquatic vertebrates caught in the water. They have an elongated body, long thick tail, short legs

Fig. 1.33 Mustelidae: Ratel or Honey badger (*Mellivora capensis*). (Photo: Zoological Society of London.)

and sleek, dense, water-repellent fur. There are three species of African otters, all of which are found in tropical Africa wherever there is permanent or semi-permanent water. In some areas, the ranges of two or more species overlap. The distribution of the African otters is not well known as they are seldom seen and probably uncommon.

The family Viverridae is a large diverse family in which there has been extensive radiation in Africa. The family is comprised of the mongooses, civets and genets. These are small to medium-sized carnivores, mostly terrestrial, which feed predominantly on insects and small vertebrates. Some species also include fruit in their diet. None of the viverrids except the genets contract their claws. The viverrids are separated into three subfamilies: Viverrinae for the genets, civet and water civet, Nandiniinae for the palm civet and Herpestinae for the mongooses. The genets are small, agile, cat-like carnivores which hunt their prey by night, and are partly arboreal. There are several species of genets which occur in forest regions, and one species, the common genet (*Genetta genetta*), is found in both northern and southern savannas. In contrast, the civet (*Viverra civetta*) is a larger dog-like carnivore which is entirely terrestrial (Fig. 1.34). This species occurs in forest and savanna habitats throughout tropical Africa. There is also a rare semi-aquatic water civet (*Osbornictis*) which feeds on fish, and lives in the lowland forests of eastern Zaire. The palm civet (*Nandinia binotata*) is placed alone in the subfamily Nandiniinae. It is a medium-sized, lithe, cat-like animal which is the most arboreal representative of the family Viverridae. Palm civets occur in the lowland forest zone and some outlier forests. They are nocturnal and feed partly on fruits. The mongooses (subfamily Herpestinae) are a distinct group of viverrids ranging in size from the dwarf mongoose (*Helogale parvula*, head and body 25 cm, wt. 500 gm) to the white-tailed mongoose (*Ichneumia albicauda*, head and body 60 cm, wt.

Fig. 1.34   Viverridae: Civet (*Viverra civetta*). (Photo: C. A. Spinage.)

3·5 kg). Mongooses have a very varied carnivorous diet, and some also eat fruits. They are terrestrial, although some species can climb to a limited extent. Some genera (*Mungos, Helogale, Crossarchus* and *Suricata*) are gregarious and hunt in packs of up to 20 individuals. Many species, if kept in captivity, transfer some of their social behaviour to humans, and become delightful, affectionate pets. In this, their behaviour differs from that of most other carnivores. There are 22 species of tropical African mongooses. They occupy many ecological niches, although some appear to overlap in their habitat and feeding requirements. Some species, such as the white-tailed mongoose, are widespread in the savanna and arid zones. Others have very restricted ranges: for example, the Gambian mongoose (*Mungos gambianus*) is found only in the lowland forests of West Africa.

The hyaenas and aardwolf (family Hyaenidae) are medium to large dog-like carnivores whose hindlimbs are considerably shorter than their forelimbs (Fig. 1.35). Hyaenas kill some of their own food, although they are also scavengers of prey killed by other carnivores. Their jaws and teeth are extremely powerful which allows them to feed on bones and tough carcasses deserted by other predators. The spotted hyaena (*Crocuta crocuta*) hunts and feeds in packs, whereas the striped hyaena (*Hyaena hyaena*) and the brown hyaena (*Hyaena brunnea*) tend to be solitary. *Crocuta* occurs throughout the northern and southern savannas where there is suitable prey, *Hyaena hyaena* lives in the Sudanese arid zone and the southern savanna, and *Hyaena brunnea* is confined to the south-west arid zone. The aardwolf (*Proteles cristatus*) differs from the other hyaenas by having reduced dentition, weak jaws and well-developed anal glands; because of these differences some authorities place this species in a separate family Protelidae. Aardwolves feed solely on insects. They occur in parts of southern Africa, and in the drier regions of East Africa and Somalia. Despite the dog-like

Fig. 1.35 Hyaenidae: Spotted hyaena (*Crocuta crocuta*). (Photo: C. A. Spinage.)

appearance of all the Hyaenidae, these animals are closely related to the cat family Felidae.

The cats (family Felidae) are the most specialised of the carnivores. They are efficient predators being strong and agile, and possessing powerful jaws and sharp retractile claws. The smaller felids, such as the caracal (*Felis caracal*), serval (*F. serval*), golden cat (*F. aurata*) and sand cat (*F. margarita*), stalk and pounce on their prey which includes rodents, birds and lizards. The larger species – lions, leopards and cheetahs – prey mostly on antelopes and display diverse means of hunting and killing their quarry. Lions (*Panthera leo*) hunt by night or day either singly or in small groups. They stalk their prey, chase it a small distance and kill it by biting the throat, breaking the neck or by suffocation. Leopards (*Panthera pardus*) also stalk their prey. They are solitary, mainly nocturnal, excellent climbers and often haul their prey into trees out of reach of scavengers. In contrast, cheetahs (*Acinonyx jubatus*) run down their prey often attaining speeds of up to 100 km/h (60 miles/h). Cheetahs differ from the other felids in having very slender limbs and non-retractile claws (Fig. 1.36).

Although felids are such efficient predators, they play an important role in the conservation of African wildlife. They weed out the old and unhealthy prey animals, and prevent overcrowding in habitats which could be degraded if the herbivorous animals became too numerous. Felids occur in most habitats of tropical Africa although each species varies greatly in its distribution and abundance. Lions and leopards are common throughout most of the northern and southern savannas provided there is sufficient prey. In contrast the sand cat is a rare species confined to the Sahara desert and the Sudanese arid zone. Similarly the golden cat is also rare and found in parts of the lowland forest zone and adjoining savanna.

Fig. 1.36   Felidae: Cheetah (*Acinonyx jubatus*). (Photo: Kenya Information Services.)

Fig. 1.37   Orycteropodidae: Aardvark (*Orycteropus afer*). (Photo: Zoological Society of London.)

1.10　Tubulidentata

The aardvark or 'earth pig' (*Orycteropus afer*) is the only species in the order Tubulidentata. It is endemic to Africa and is specialised for eating ants and termites. Aardvarks have an almost hairless skin, long snout and ears, powerful short legs, and the tail is thick at the base tapering towards the tip (Fig. 1.37). The senses of hearing and smell are good, but sight is poor. Aardvarks break open the nests of termites using the long claws on their strong forelegs, and then the long sticky tongue is inserted into the nest and the prey is drawn into the mouth. The number of teeth are reduced since only crushing teeth at the back of the mouth are required for chewing. Aardvarks are solitary and nocturnal, and during the day they rest in burrows which they dig themselves. They are distributed throughout the savannas of Africa, and also in some parts of the rain forest, but they are generally uncommon due to the scarcity and scattered distribution of suitable ant and termite mounds.

1.11　Hyracoidea

The hyraxes (order Hyracoidea) are compact little animals with small ears, short legs and no tail (Fig. 1.38). They look like rodents but in fact they are closely related to elephants and Sirenia. Like the elephants, they have strong ridged cheek teeth, and their third upper incisors form small tusks. They are also vegetarians. The soles of the feet are moist, and although hyraxes do not have claws they are able to climb surprisingly steep smooth surfaces. *Dendrohyrax* is entirely arboreal and occurs in the lowland forest zone. *Procavia* and *Heterohyrax* are found in rocky areas in the savanna and arid zones.

Fig. 1.38　Procaviidae: Rock hyrax (*Procavia* sp.). (Photo: C. A. Spinage.)

a

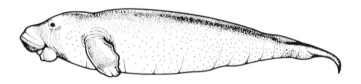

b

Fig. 1.39   (*a*) Dugongidae: Dugong (*Dugong dugon*) The whole animal to show cylindrical shape, modified forelimbs and horizontally flattened tail.   (*b*) Trichechidae: Manatee (*Trichechus senegalensis*) A manatee feeding on submerged vegetation; only the snout, nostrils and upper lip are above the water. The small eye is almost invisible. (Photo: D. C. D. Happold.)

1.12   Sirenia

The order Sirenia includes the manatees and dugongs. These are large aquatic mammals which browse on submerged waterweeds in permanent rivers and lakes, in estuaries and brackish lagoons, and in the sea. They have elongated bodies with reduced paddle-shaped forelimbs, no hindlimbs and a horizontally flattened tail called a fluke (Fig. 1.39). There are two families of Sirenia (Trichechidae and Dugongidae) each with a single species. The manatee (*Trichechus senegalensis*) occurs in the large permanent rivers and lakes of West Africa. The dugong (*Dugong dugong*) is found off the eastern coast from the Red Sea to Mozambique; it typically inhabits estuaries and coastal lagoons.

1.13   Proboscidea

The order Proboscidea includes the largest of the African mammals. The African elephant (*Loxodonta africana*) is characterised by the elongation of the nose and upper lip to form a trunk, the development of the third upper incisor to form tusks, large flap-like ears, a grey skin with sparse bristles and a small tufted tail (Fig. 1.40). Elephants

Fig. 1.40   Elephantidae: Elephant (*Loxodonta africana*). (Photo: C. A. Spinage.)

are entirely vegetarian. They use the trunk to obtain leaves from trees and tussocks of grass from the ground. The tusks are used for breaking branches, pushing down trees and scraping off the bark. Because of their size and feeding habits, large numbers of elephants can modify the vegetation of a region within a few years. Wooded savanna is transformed into grassland and scrub, and this extends the preferred habitat of grazing mammals and their associates.

Elephants usually live in small groups but occasionally they form large herds. The groups tend to be of two kinds; female groups, often with their young up to 15 years of age, and all-male groups comprising adult bulls and young bachelors. Adult males are often solitary. Elephants reach sexual maturity at 15–20 years, and they may live as long as 70 years.

Until recently elephants occurred in most regions of tropical Africa. The savanna subspecies (*Loxodonta africana africana*) had a scattered distribution in savanna zones, and the smaller forest subspecies (*cyclotis*) occurred in the lowland forest region. Now, as a result of competition with man, elephants are found only in reserved areas and in regions remote from dense human habitation.

1.14   Perissodactyla

Two orders, the Perissodactyla and the Artiodactyla, embrace the very numerous and well-known African herbivores. The Perissodactyla are the 'odd-toed ungulates' because the weight of the body rests either on one digit (the 3rd) or on three digits (the 2nd, 3rd and 4th). There are three families of Perissodactyls, two of which are represented in tropical Africa.

The family Equidae includes the zebras and wild asses. These are large horse-like animals in which each foot terminates in a single digit which is protected by a hoof. These hooves, and the long slender limbs, are adaptations for fast and sustained running over firm terrain. Both zebras and wild asses are grazers although they may be forced to browse if good grass is unavailable. In some regions of East Africa, zebras have a regular annual migration, often with other species of ungulates, which follows the rains and the subsequent sprouting of new grass. Zebras are gregarious (Fig. 1.41) and are found in herds by themselves, or with wildebeest and other large artiodactyls. In the southern savannas, there are several subspecies of Burchell's zebra (*Equus burchelli*) which differ in the patterning of their black and white strips. Another species, the mountain zebra (*Equus zebra*), occurs in the hilly areas of the south-west zone, and is adept at climbing and scrambling over rocky country. The wild ass (*Equus africanus*)

Fig. 1.41   Equidae: Burchell's zebra (*Equus burchelli*), (Photo: D. C. D. Happold.)

Fig. 1.42   Rhinocerotidae: Black rhinoceros (*Diceros bicornis*). (Photo: C. A. Spinage.)

is a similar animal, adapted for the dry conditions of the arid regions of Somalia and Ethiopia.

The rhinoceroses (family Rhinocerotidae) are large heavily-built herbivores with short legs, naked skin and two horns composed of hardened hair on their snouts (Fig. 1.42). Rhinos have poor eyesight but good hearing. Although they are usually slow and lethargic, they are able to run short distances at surprisingly fast speeds. There are two species in Africa. The black rhino (*Diceros bicornis*) has two horns and is a browser. It has a scattered distribution in wooded savanna of the southern savanna and south-west arid zones, and in the eastern part of the northern savanna zone. In contrast, the white or square-lipped rhino (*Ceratotherium simum*) is a grazer which prefers open grassland savanna. It is limited to two discontinuous regions, one in the southern Sudan and northern Uganda and the other in Zululand, although it has recently been introduced, or reintroduced, into other parts of southern Africa.

1.15   Artiodactyla

The majority of the large African herbivores belong to the order Artiodactyla. These are the 'even-toed ungulates' as the weight of the body rests either on two digits (the 2nd and 3rd) or on four digits (the 2nd, 3rd, 4th and 5th). The reduction to two digits on each foot, together with the fusion of the elongated metatarsal bones, are adaptations for fast running. In suitable localities, some species of artiodactyls congregate in vast herds which are so characteristic of the African savannas. Some species are sympatric, but competition between them is reduced by various ecological mechanisms. The artiodactyls are extremely diverse in size, morphology and ecology. Consequently they have been separated into five families and the largest family, the Bovidae, has been divided further into nine subfamilies.

The pigs (family Suidae) are medium-sized solidly built animals with short slender legs terminating in four digits of which only two reach the ground. Pigs have relatively large heads and their canine teeth are enlarged to form tusks. These tusks are particularly noticeable in the warthog. Pigs are gregarious and are frequently seen in groups of up to 20 individuals. The three African species occur in different habitats and seldom overlap with each other. The warthog (*Phacochoerus aethiopicus*) is diurnal and occurs in the northern and southern savanna zones where it grazes on short grasses (Fig. 1.43). The bush pig (*Potamochoerus porcus*) lives only in the lowland forest zone

Fig. 1.43   Suidae: Warthog (*Phacochoerus aethiopicus*). (Photo: W. Leuthold.)

and in forest outliers; it is mostly nocturnal and it digs with its snout and is partly omnivorous. The third species is the rare giant forest hog (*Hylochoerus meinertzhageni*) which is restricted to certain dense forests in the lowland rain forest zone and in East Africa. The giant forest hog is also mainly diurnal and feeds on grasses, leaves, roots, fruits and berries.

The family Hippopotamidae is comprised of two species of hippopotamus. Hippos are the most amphibious of the artiodactyls, spending much of their time in freshwater. The common hippopotamus (*Hippopotamus amphibius*) is large and rotund with short stocky legs and occurs in most of the major rivers and lakes of tropical Africa (Fig. 1.44). Its special adaptations to life in water include the absence of hair, nostrils on the top of the snout which can be closed when the animal submerges, and the ability to remain submerged for up to five minutes. Secretions from special sebaceous glands protect the skin. Hippos tend to rest in the water during the day. At night they emerge and feed on grasses in the vicinity of the water. They are gregarious animals, and in reserves where they are protected they may become so numerous that virtually all the grass is removed in the vicinity of the shore line. As a result they destroy the environment both for themselves and for other herbivorous mammals. The second species, the pygmy hippopotamus (*Choeropsis liberiensis*), is smaller, more terrestrial in habit and less gregarious than the common hippo. It occurs in swampy areas in parts of the West African lowland rain forest zone.

The water chevrotain (*Hyemoschus aquaticus*) is the sole African representative of

Fig. 1.44 Hippopotamidae: Hippopotamus (*Hippopotamus amphibius*). (Photo: C. A. Spinage.)

Fig. 1.45 Tragulidae: Water chevrotain (*Hyemoschus aquaticus*). (Photo: U. Rahm, from Rahm, 1966.)

the family Tragulidae. It is a small semi-aquatic antelope, and its most characteristic feature is the development of its upper canines into tusks (Fig. 1.45). Unlike other artiodactyls, it is probably omnivorous but little is known of its habits. The water chevrotain occurs in the lowland rain forests of West and Central Africa.

The family Giraffidae comprises the giraffe (*Giraffa camelopardalis*) and the okapi (*Okapia johnstoni*). Giraffes are characterised by their extremely long necks and legs which enable them to browse on vegetation beyond the reach of other herbivores (Fig. 1.46). They can reach leaves up to 20 feet above the ground. Giraffes are usually found in small herds, and they have a scattered distribution in the northern and southern savanna zones. Giraffes from different areas can be distinguished by the patterning of their light and dark fur, and this has resulted in the recognition of several subspecies. Okapis have shorter necks and legs than giraffes. They are solitary and elusive and occur only in a small part of the lowland rain forest zone of eastern Zaire where they browse on leaves, twigs and fruits.

Fig. 1.46   Giraffidae: Giraffe (*Giraffa camelopardalis*). (Photo: H. B. Cott.)

The family Bovidae is the largest family in the order Artiodactyla. The bovids are very diverse in size, morphology, behaviour and ecology, and consequently the family is divided into nine subfamilies. They are the most conspicuous mammals of the African savannas. Many species are sympatric, and some of these form large herds of mixed composition. Herding is a characteristic of many bovids, but there are also many which are usually found singly, in pairs or in small family groups. All male bovids, and the females of some species, have horns. The horns are species-specific in structure, and are useful means of identifying different species. All bovids have a four-chambered stomach and ruminate their food – a behaviour pattern which is very noticeable when these animals are kept under observation.

The buffalos (subfamily Bovinae) are large cow-like animals with wide flattened horns or 'bosses' projecting sideways from the head (Fig. 1.47*a*). The single African species (*Syncerus caffer*) shows considerable subspecific variation in horn shape and coat colour throughout its range. Buffalos occur in the northern and southern savannas, and a subspecies which is smaller than the savanna buffalo occurs in the lowland forests. Buffalos are gregarious and frequently form large herds. They graze, often on tall grass, and live near water since they need to drink regularly.

The spiral-horned antelopes (subfamily Tragelaphinae) have long horns with 1–3 spirals along their length. These beautiful antelopes have patterns of white stripes or spots on their bodies, and some have a distinctive white pattern on their heads (Fig. 1.47*b*). Most species live singly or in small groups. None form large herds as do the Bovinae and some Antelopinae. Tragelaphinae are found in a variety of habitats including some of the Ethiopian mountains (mountain nyala, *Tragelaphus buxtoni*), the savannas (bushbuck *T. scriptus*, kudus *T. strepsiceros* and *T. imberbis*, elands *Taurotragus* spp.) and the lowland rainforest (bongo *Tragelaphus euryceros*). Bushbuck are usually found near water, and the sitatunga (*Tragelaphus spekei*) is semi-aquatic and has long spreading hooves which enable it to move over swampy habitats.

The duikers (subfamily Cephalophinae) are small dainty antelopes (Fig. 1.47*c*). Characteristically, a duiker has a rounded back, and its head is held close to its body. There is a suborbital gland with a slit-like opening below the eye, and several species have a small tuft of hair on top of the head between the horns. Some species graze, but the majority browse on leaves and shoots. There are two genera of duikers. *Sylvicapra* contains only one species (*S. grimmia*) which occurs in most areas of the northern and southern savanna. In the other genus (*Cephalophus*) there has been extensive speciation, especially in the lowland forests of West Africa. There are now 15 species, all similar in general appearance, but differing in size and coat colour. The largest is the yellow-backed duiker (*C. sylvicultor*, shoulder height 80 cm) and the smallest is the red-flanked duiker (*C. rufilatus*, shoulder height 35 cm). *Cephalophus* duikers occur in lowland forests and forest outliers in the savannas. Some species have very limited distributions, e.g. the zebra duiker (*C. zebra*) occurs only in the forests of Liberia, Sierra Leone and western Ivory Coast.

The subfamily Reduncinae comprises two groups of antelopes. One group are grazing savanna antelopes of medium size, which live close to water and are often associated with swamps. The males have large curved or S-shaped horns with well developed rings (Fig. 1.47*d*). These antelopes are gregarious and some species live in very large herds. This group of antelopes includes the kob (*Kobus kob*) in the northern savanna, the waterbuck (*Kobus ellipsiprymnus*) in northern and southern savannas, Nile lechwe (*K. megaceros*) in the Sudd area of southern Sudan, and the lechwe (*K. leche*) and puku (*K. vardoni*) in parts of central and southern Africa. The second group of Reduncinae are the reedbucks (*Redunca* spp.). These have small horns with a forward projecting hook at the terminal end. Unlike the other Reduncinae, they are

a

b

c

d

e

f

g

h   i

Fig. 1.47 Bovidae: (*a*) Bovinae: Buffalo (*Syncerus caffer*). (Photo: C.A. Spinage.)
     (*b*) Tragelaphinae: Lesser Kudu (*Tragelaphus imberbis*). (Photo: W. Leuthold.)
     (*c*) Cephalophinae: Common duiker (*Sylvicapra grimmia*). (Photo: C. A. Spinage.)
     (*d*) Reduncinae: Kob (*Kobus kob*). (Photo: W. Leuthold.)
     (*e*) Hippotraginae: Beisa oryx (*Oryx gazella beisa*). (Photo: W. Leuthold.)
     (*f*) Alcelphinae: Lichtenstein's hartebeest (*Alcelaphus lichtensteini*). (Photo: W. Leuthold.)
     (*g*) Antilopinae: Peter's gazelle (*Gazella granti petersi*). (Photo: C. A. Spinage.)
     (*h*) Neotraginae: Oribi (*Ourebia ourebi*). (Photo: C. A. Spinage.)
     (*i*) Caprinae: Barbary sheep (*Capra lervia*). (Photo: Copyright Bruce Coleman Ltd.)

not gregarious, but they do live near water in reeds and dense grasses. There are three allopatric species – the bohar reedbuck (*Redunca redunca*) in the northern savanna, the southern reedbuck (*R. arundinum*) in parts of the southern savanna and the mountain reedbuck (*R. fulvorufula*) in certain hilly regions of southern and eastern Africa and Cameroun. The ribbok (*Pelea capreolus*) is confined to southern Africa, and is sometimes placed in a separate subfamily, the Peleinae, by itself.

The subfamily Hippotraginae contains three genera of large 'horse-like' antelopes. Their horns are large, either straight or curved, and there is a striking white and dark pattern on their heads (Fig. 1.47*e*). They are usually found in small herds. The genus *Hippotragus* contains the roan antelope in wooded northern and southern savanna regions, and the sable antelope which is limited to certain areas of the southern savanna. The genera *Addax* (one species) and *Oryx* (three species) are adapted to arid conditions. They are nomadic and wander over large areas in search of food and *Oryx*, in particular, congregate in areas where rainfall has brought a flush of new vegetation. The addax (*Addax nasomaculatus*) and the scimitar-horned oryx (*Oryx dammah*) occur in areas of extreme aridity in the Sahara and in the Sudanese arid zone. Both species flourish in areas of scanty vegetation, and since there is no water to drink they survive on moisture extracted from their food. The gemsbok (*O. gazella gazella*) occurs in the south-west arid zone, and the beisa oryx (*O. gazella beisa*) in the Somali arid zone.

The subfamily Alcelaphinae are characterised by their heads which have a pedicel of bone on the forehead below the horns, and by their backs which slope downwards from the shoulders to the rump (Fig. 1.47*f*). These grazing antelopes occur in the northern and southern savannas and frequently live in very large herds. The genus *Damalicus* contains the widespread topi (*Damaliscus lunatus*) of the northern savanna and parts of the Sudanese arid zone, and *D. hunteri* with a limited distribution in East Africa. *Alcelaphus* contains two allopatric species. The hartebeest (*A. buselaphus*) has many subspecies and is found in the southern part of the northern savanna, in East Africa and in southern Africa (but is rarely sympatric with the topi). Lichtenstein's hartebeest (*A. lichtensteini*) is found throughout most of the southern savanna and is usually not sympatric with the bubal hartebeest. The blue wildebeest (*Connochaetes taurinus*) is a widespread gregarious species of the southern savanna and parts of the south-west arid zone.

The gazelles and their relatives (subfamily Antilopinae, Fig. 1.47*g*) are graceful medium-sized antelopes with heavily ringed horns in both sexes (except in impala). Several species are adapted to dry conditions, as in the Hippotraginae, although others are found only in savanna regions. Most species in the subfamily are browsers and grazers, and are gregarious. The impala (*Aepyceros melampus*) occurs in the southern savanna, often in large herds, and appears to be ecologically equivalent to the kob of the northern savanna. Two species of *Gazella*, Grant's gazelle (*G. granti*) and Thomson's gazelle (*G. thomsoni*) occur in vast numbers in the savanna of East Africa, and another six species occur in the Somali and Sudanese arid zones and in the Sahara. The latter are sparse in numbers because of the scanty resources of their arid habitats. The gerenuk (*Litocranius walleri*) and the dibatag (*Ammodorcas clarkei*) have long limbs and elongated necks. Gerenuk can stand on their hindlimbs and reach up into shrubs to feed, and in this manner they exploit vegetation which cannot be obtained by other mammals of similar size. The springbok (*Antidorcas marsupialis*) occurs in southern Africa including the south-west arid zone. This species browses and grazes, and frequently forms very large herds.

The subfamily Neotraginae contains several antelopes whose only common characteristic appears to be their small size. They are very varied in their habits and distributions. The klipspringer (*Oreotragus oreotragus*) is widespread but rare in the rocky areas of the southern savanna and on the Jos plateau in Nigeria. The oribi (*Ourebia ourebi*) is a slender, nimble, grazing antelope which is widespread and fairly common in the northern and southern savannas (Fig. 1.47*h*). Dik-diks (*Madoqua* spp.) have elongated hindlimbs and run in a characteristically erratic fashion when disturbed. They are found in bushy areas and thickets in the southern savanna. Grysbok and Steenbok (*Raphicerus* spp.) occur in parts of the southern savanna: the grysbok in hilly regions and the steenbok on the grassy plains. Two species of pygmy antelopes (*Neotragus* spp.) are allopatric in limited regions of West African lowland rainforest whilst the third species, the suni (*N. moschatus*), occurs in dry thicket country of eastern Africa.

The subfamily Caprinae includes three African species all of which are adapted for arid rocky regions. The rare Barbary sheep (*Capra lervia*) occurs on rocky hills in the Sudanese arid zone and the Sahara, and the ibex (*Capra ibex* and *C. walie*) are uncommon species in the Red Sea hills and limited areas of the Ethiopian mountains. All three species are very sure-footed, and jump from rock to rock with great speed and agility. They usually live in small groups. Their most obvious characteristic is the large thick horns which curl upwards, backwards and then downwards (Fig. 1.47*i*).

Chapter 2

Historical changes in Africa

The contemporary ecological scene has inevitably been greatly influenced by past geological, climatic and vegetational events which together have determined the types and variety of mammals existing today as well as the present environmental structure. To adequately appreciate how the present situation arose it is necessary to briefly trace the evolutionary trends displayed by the mammals and their habitats through the past 70 million years of the Tertiary and Quarternary. The early evolution of the mammals took place in the Mesozoic, and by the beginning of the Tertiary several distinct orders had already evolved.

The continental land mass of Africa has been one of the most stable in the world, having existed in its present or very similar form since the late Mesozoic. Information on fossil mammals has been obtained from numerous deposits occurring in many strata and from a wide range of localities (Cooke 1968). South Africa, East Africa and Egypt have been good sources of fossil material, the Sahara has provided many subfossils while the lowland areas of west and central Africa have been poor in fossils. There is considerable variation in the number of fossil deposits discovered from each geological period with a noteworthy shortage of material from the early Tertiary. For this period the main source has been the Eocene–Oligocene beds at Fayum in Egypt from which it is evident that mammals were by this time well established on the continent. Several orders having contemporary descendents were represented including Insectivores, primitive elephants (Proboscidea) and Primates. In addition, other groups were found, such as the Anthracotheriidae and the Hyaenodontidae, which were subsequently to become extinct. The former were short-legged Artiodactyls (Fig. 2.1) of a rather piglike form and the latter small to medium size slimly built carnivores whose dentitions were fundamentally different from those of living Carnivores.

The Miocene deposits from East Africa show a number of significant changes in the fauna. Artiodactyla, Carnivora, Lagomorpha and the antecedents of modern man (Hominidae) made their first appearance while the hyaenodonts, anthracotheres and Proboscidea became less numerous components of the fauna. About this time temporary connections were probably being established between Africa and Eurasia resulting in a limited faunal interchange. Ancestral giraffes (Palaeomerycidae), tragulids, shrews, hedgehogs, rhinoceroses and chalicotheres were among the immigrant groups to reach Africa from Europe. The last was a rather aberrant group of horselike forms possessing claws in place of hoofs. The first true giraffes had evolved in Africa by the late Miocene by which time hyaenas, horses and probably hippopotamuses had made their appearance from Asia. This was also a period of considerable migration from Africa to Europe and Asia. Among the groups whose representatives colonised other continents were the Primates, Proboscidea, pigs and antelopes (Fig. 2.2). Throughout the Tertiary, geological and faunal evidence suggests

Fig. 2.1   Reconstructions of some extinct African mammals. Vertical bars = 0.5 m.
A, *Megalohyrax* (Hyracoidea) Olig.;
B, *Bothriodon* (Anthracotheriidae, Suina, Artiodactyla), Olig. – Mio.;
C, *Hyaenodon* (Hyaenodontidae, Carnivora), Olig. – Mio;
D, *Mixtotherium* (Cebochoeridae, Suina, Artiodactyla), Olig.;
E, *Trilophodon* (Gomphotheriidae, Proboscidea), Mio.;
F, *Chalicotherium* (Chalicotheriidae, Perissodactyla), Mio.;
G, *Myorycteropus* (Orycteropodidae, Tubulidentata), Mio.;
H, *Aceratherium* (Rhinocerotidae, Perissodactyla), Mio.;
I,   *Dorcatherium* (Tragulidae, Artiodactyla) Mio.;
J,   *Notochoerus* (Suidae, Artiodactyla), Plies.;
K, *Deinotherium* (Deinotheriidae, Proboscidea), Mio-Pleis;
L, Machairodont (Felidae, Carnivora), Plio-Pleis. (After Cooke 1972). See also Fig. 2.2 for evolution of families to which these genera belong.

that faunal exchange of this type occurred irregularly and on a limited scale. There were no protracted periods of connection between Africa and either Asia or Europe that permitted a free and continuous movement. The evolution of the African fauna continued without interruption during long periods of isolation. The main periods of exchange were probably the late Oligocene, late Miocene and late Pliocene.

The Quarternary was a period of consolidation with a few groups such as camels, deer and bears reaching the continent for the first time. However, the more significant events of this period were the decline in richness of the fauna and the replacement of some of its more archaic forms by species surviving to the present. These changes resulted in the fauna of the Upper Pleistocene being very similar to that of the present day. The contemporary mammal fauna of Africa is rich compared to other continents and the fact that it is impoverished relative to its geologically recent antecedents is, at first sight, very surprising. Examples of the differences can be obtained from the Suidae and Bovidae (Cooke, 1968). At present there are four species of pigs from four genera; in the Pleistocene there were at least sixteen species from five genera. The alcelaphine Bovidae which includes the wildebeests, topi and hartebeests is currently represented by three genera and seven species. The Pleistocene fauna contained at least fifteen further species and more than eight genera. The cause of this decline is a matter of conjecture but as will be seen from the following pages the Pleistocene was a period of relatively rapid and dramatic climatic fluctuation. The direct and indirect effects of these changes could have been implicated in the extinction of many species.

At the same time as the mammals were evolving the continent of Africa experienced a series of geological and climatic changes. The Eocene to the late Miocene was a time of geological inactivity and stability. Most of the continent then consisted of an undulating plain with little land more than 600 m above sea level. World temperatures were warmer from the Eocene to the Pliocene than at present and as there were fewer mountains prior to the late Miocene much of the land surface of Africa probably afforded favourable climatic conditions for the evolution of lowland species. It is probable that evergreen forest, savanna and arid areas persisted from the early Tertiary to the Miocene even though their boundaries may have been subject to variation. The lack of high ground and its associated cooler conditions would have prevented the evolution of a montane fauna.

The present relief of Africa owes much to the major geological upheavals of the late Tertiary. At the end of the Miocene about 12 million years ago extensive areas of eastern and southern Africa were uplifted 1 200 m or more. In addition, the Ethiopian and Kenya Highlands were overlaid by volcanic outpourings which added further to their stature. More volcanic activity during the Pliocene was responsible for the formation of several high mountains including Kilimanjaro, Mt Kenya, Mt Elgon and Mt Cameroun. In eastern Africa tilting took place so that there was a further elevation occurring along the eastern edge of the recently formed massif. This resulted in the production of the Nguru and Uzungwa Mountains of Tanzania which rise to over 2 200 m. At this time a large lake filled the centre of the Congo Basin.

Change continued during the Pleistocene to produce many of the familiar contemporary features of the continent. Over the last million years rifting took place and Lakes Albert, Nyasa and Tanganyika became established. The Congo lake disappeared and Lake Victoria was formed. Continued volcanic activity resulted in the formation of new mountains. Among the more important were the Virunga Mountains on the Zaire–Rwanda border; others included Rungwe (2960 m) in Tanzania and Marsabit (1 704 m) in Kenya. The vast Rwenzori massif (5 109 m) is a mountain formed of hard ancient rocks which continued to rise during the Pleistocene.

These major physiographical changes were accompanied by appreciable

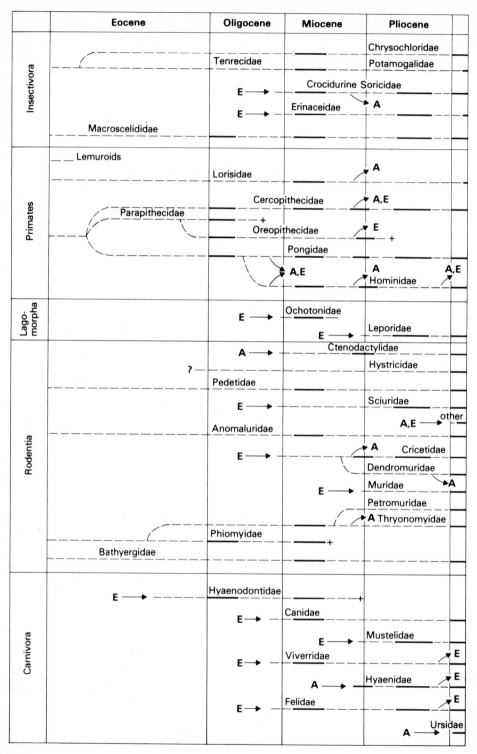

Fig. 2.2 Evolution of mammal families in Africa since the Eocene. A broken line indicates assumed, and a continuous line established, presence. Arrows suggest times of entry or spread of families from or to Europe

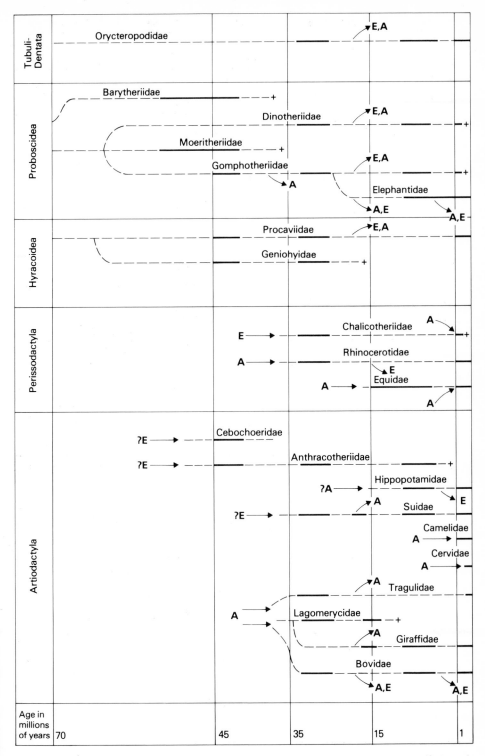

(E) or Asia (A). A cross (+) represents a group that has become extinct in Africa (After Cooke 1972).

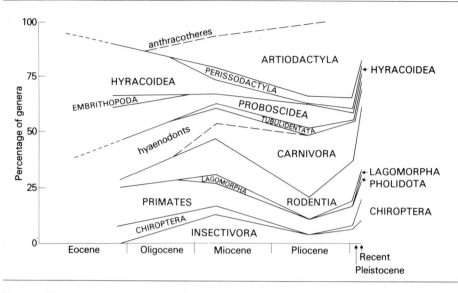

Fig. 2.3 Variation in the composition of the mammal fauna during the Tertiary and Quarternary. The number of genera in each order is expressed as a percentage of the total number of genera in the fauna at a particular period. The sudden change in the composition of the recent fauna is attributable to small numbers of fossil bats and insectivores (After Cooke 1968).

fluctuations in climate. During the Pleistocene there were four glacial periods and although the ice caps did not reach what is now tropical Africa the changes in world climate were sufficient to be felt over all the continent. Their effects were two-fold. First, temperature was lowest when the glaciation was at a peak with associated changes in atmospheric conditions affecting the rainfall regime. Second, there was an elaborate sequence of pluvial and interpluvial periods. Pluvials were times when rainfall at a particular site was higher than at present, and interpluvials were times when there was less. Correlation between pluvials and glaciations has been partially established for the last glaciation but not with the earlier ones.

Since the start of the Last Glaciation about 70 000 years ago there has been a continuously changing climate. In geological time these fluctuations in conditions have been extraordinarily rapid and while the main vegetation types such as forest and savanna have been in continuous existence throughout the glaciation the areas each covered has probably ranged between the extensive and the restricted. The most recent severe conditions of the glaciation were between 25 000 and 15 000 years ago during which time the mean temperature fell by 5 °C (Fig. 2.4). Two earlier cold spells of short duration occurred 52 000 and 35 000 years ago. Since the last cold spell the temperature increased to produce the warmest conditions of the cycle (hypsithermal) between 8 000 and 4 000 years ago. A temperature decline then occurred so that at present the mean temperature is 2 °C below the maximum at the hypsithermal (Fig. 2.4).

Moreau (1952, 1966) has drawn attention to the major vegetation changes that probably resulted from the coldest glacial conditions. He points out that with a decline of 5 °C in temperature the montane vegetation would descend from its present altitude of approximately 1 500 m to 500 m. There would then be an extremely large area of the continent covered by what is at present considered to be high altitude vegetation. It would further provide considerable vegetation uniformity across wide tracts of the

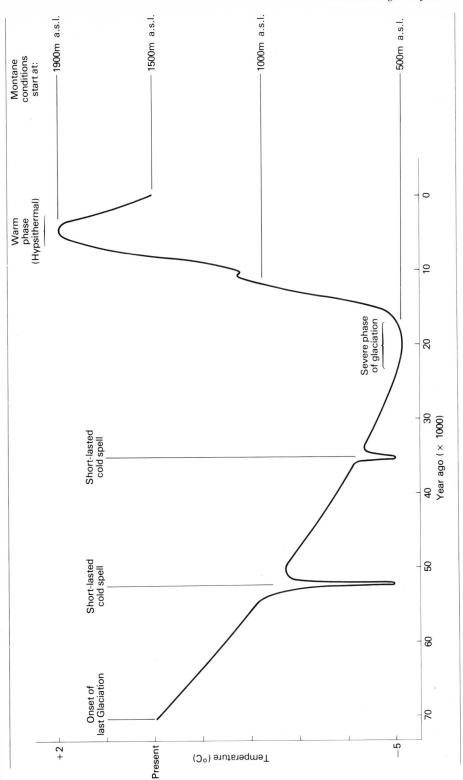

Fig. 2.4 Schematic representation of changing temperature conditions throughout the Last Glaciation.

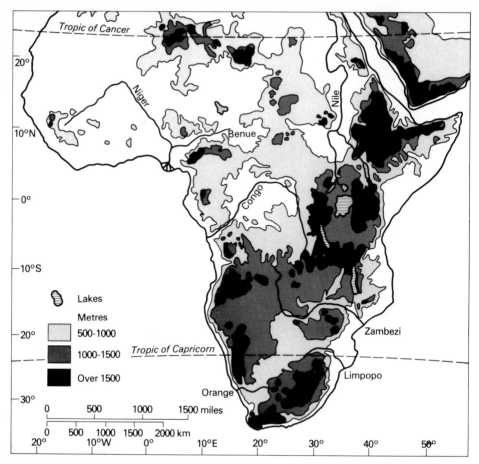

Fig. 2.5   Physical map of Africa.

continent. The Ethiopian, Saharan, East African, Angolan, Cameroun and South African mountains would have been floristically and faunistically interconnected (Fig. 2.5). The tropical lowland conditions would have been retained over a large area of West Africa west and north of the Niger River, the Congo Basin and a coastal belt up to 300 km wide in eastern Africa. The lowland species of plants and animals would have been confined to small areas compared to the present and, furthermore, were isolated into three main regions by intervening montane groups.

As conditions ameliorated and the temperature moderated there was a gradual recession of montane vegetation to higher ground, so that by 12 000 years ago, as a result of mean temperature increasing by approximately 2·5 °C, this vegetation would only be found above 1 000 m above sea level (Fig. 2.5). Its previous continuity was then lost and large isolated montane regions were created. The Cameroun Mountains were isolated, the Ethiopian massif separated from the Kenya ranges and the mountains of South Africa no longer connected with those further north. The recession of the montane vegetation was accompanied by a spread of both moist and dry lowland conditions.

The mildest phase of this glacial cycle occurred 6 000 years ago when higher temperature and increased evaporation would have raised the lower limit of the

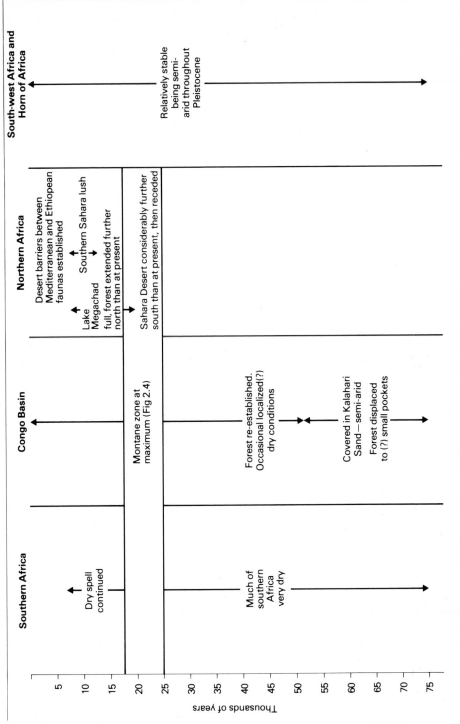

Fig. 2.6   Regional climatic and vegetational conditions during the Last Glaciation.

montane zone to 1 900 m and in consequence the montane faunas must have occupied more confined areas than at present. The overall effect would have been to create a larger number of smaller isolated mountains. Subsequent cooling of the climate once again lowered the level of these conditions to around 1 500 m (Figs. 2.4 and 2.5). The hypsithermal would have eliminated montane faunas from situations attaining an altitude of less than 1 900 m. If these localities had no connections above 1 500 m with other higher montane areas they could not be re-invaded by montane species as a result of the recent temperature decline even though the appropriate conditions prevailed. This circumstance accounts for the absence of montane vegetation in various parts of Africa at altitudes of more than 1 500 m.

Temperature has not been the only climatic variable during the Last Glaciation. Changes in rainfall have also exerted their influence on the distribution of the main types of lowland vegetation. Evidence of change in the vegetation boundaries is incomplete but is sufficient to illustrate the widespread extent to which it occurred. The persistence of semi-arid conditions in South West Africa and the Horn of Africa, their prevalence in southern Africa and the occurrence of dry spells in the early part of the glaciation in the Congo Basin (Fig. 2.6) all point to protracted periods of low rainfall in many parts of the continent.

Within the last 22 000 years considerable vegetation changes occurred within the Sahara–West Africa–northern Congo Basin belt which can be correlated with changes in rainfall and temperature. At the start of this period the Sahara Desert extended 300 to 600 km south of its present southern boundary in West Africa. This took it to within 50 km of the River Gambia and to the present location of Sokoto and Kano in northern Nigeria. A recession of the desert followed. The site of Lake Chad was occupied by a larger lake (Lake Megachad) covering at least three times the area of the present lake. This persisted until 8 500 years ago. Water drained into Lake Megachad from evergreen forests in the south, which at that time extended 500 km beyond their present northern limit. Eight thousand years ago there was vegetational continuity between the Mediterranean and West Africa. Northern species of tree such as oak (*Quercus*), lime (*Tilia*) and olive (*Olea*) penetrated much further south than today. These were accompanied by European faunistic elements which included primitive cattle (*Bos primigenius*) and a Cervid deer. Simultaneously, there was a northward extension of the African fauna as rhinoceros (*Ceratotherium*) and *Kobus* remains have been found at Ahaggar which is now 650 km north of the southern limit of the desert. All this points to considerable less aridity than at present and it is suggested that the most recent ecological separation of northern from tropical Africa commenced 5 000 to 6 000 years ago. The present configuration of the Sahara is thus very recent although in the light of information from the height of the glaciation this desert could then have been more extensive than at present.

The brief survey of the Tertiary and Quarternary history of Africa highlights the physiographic and climatic transformations that have occurred and the effects they have had on the distribution of the vegetation and the fauna it supports. In spite of the changes that have transpired it is probable that the major types of vegetation such as forest and savanna have persisted throughout this time. The mammals have thus been able to evolve in remarkably stable vegetation conditions and it has been the dynamic oscillations of the boundaries of the various vegetation types that has caused the perplexing distributional discontinuities, geographical variation, speciation and subspeciation that characterises much of the contemporary mammal fauna of tropical Africa.

Chapter 3

Comparison with other regions

The present faunal composition of a large area such as a continental land mass is the result of several historical events during the past 70 million years and the contemporary range of available habitats. The changes one continent experiences are not necessarily identical with those occurring elsewhere and in consequence the evolution of two continental faunas cannot be expected to follow precisely the same course. However, the three main tropical regions of South America, Africa and South-East Asia have a number of ecological features in common. For example, each supports large areas of tropical rain forests that display appreciable similarity in their gross structure or physiognomy even though the species of plants in each are quite distinct. Moreover, in South America and Africa there are large areas of tropical grassland. These similarities and differences can be accounted for as a result of uniformity and persistence of tropical conditions across the equatorial belt with relatively little floral inter-communication between them. Animals would be subjected to similar conditions and constraints. East–West connections were few and irregular so that evolution in at least partial isolation from each other was a feature of these continental faunas. Historical interchange was less frequent between some places than others which resulted in varying degrees of faunal affinity. This is manifested in the greater similarity between the mammal fauna of Africa and Asia than between Africa and South America.

Keast (1969) has compared the fauna of Africa with that of South America. The former includes the north African elements whose main affinities are with the temperate Palaearctica while the Neotropical region extends southwards from southern Mexico and incorporates both tropical and temperate South America. The main vegetational differences between the two continents (Table 3.1) are the high proportions of desert in Africa and rain forest in Neotropica. There is more than 90 per

Table 3.1 *Mammal faunas and vegetation features of Africa and Neotropica. (After Keast 1969.)*

	Africa	Neotropica
Area (million ha)	2968	1855
Latitudinal range	33 °N–34 °S	24 °N–55 °S
Area: in tropics (%)	78	70
above 1 500 m (%)	3·7	7
rain forest (%)	9	32
woodland and open forest (%)	31	22
savanna, grassland, steppe (%)	19	38
desert (%)	30	3
Number of families	51	50
Number of genera	240	278
Number of species	756	810

cent endemism at the species level in both continents and at a higher taxonomic rank 29 and 54 per cent of the families are endemic in Africa and Neotropica respectively. Both continents support large numbers of species. The Orders Marsupialia, Edentata, Pholidota, Tubulidentata, Proboscidea and Hyracoidea have representatives inhabiting only one of the two continents (Table 3.2).

Table 3.2   *Composition of the mammal faunas of Africa and Neotropica. (After Keast 1969.)*

	Africa			Neotropica		
	Families	*Genera*	*Species*	*Families*	*Genera*	*Species*
Marsupialia	—	—	—	2	14	60
Insectivora	5	20	95	2	2	10
Chiroptera	9	42	175	10	80	222
Primates	5	19	51	3	16	42
Edentata	—	—	—	3	14	26
Pholidota	1	1	4	—	—	—
Lagomorpha	1	2	13	1	1	2
Rodentia	12	75	212	17	112	378
Carnivora	6	36	66	5	26	47
Tubulidentata	1	1	1	—	—	—
Hyracoidea	1	3	10	—	—	—
Proboscidea	1	1	1	—	—	—
Perissodactyla	2	3	7	1	1	3
Artiodactyla	5	36	87	3	9	17
Totals	49	239	722	47	275	807

In South America many of the marsupials fill the niches occupied by the Insectivora in Africa. The bats and rodents are better represented in Neotropica where there are more species than in Africa. Furthermore, they also comprise a larger proportion of the total species represented. The African fauna contains more than four times as many ungulates as South America and is better represented by carnivores, lagomorpha and Primates. Differences in faunal composition are probably best appreciated in relation to the niches occupied by the species comprising the fauna. Analysis of the fauna in this

Table 3.3   *Percentage of species occupying major adaptive zones in Africa and Neotropica. (After Keast 1969.)*

	Africa	*Neotropica*
Small insect-eaters and predators (shrews, etc.)	9·1	2·2
Fossorial moles	1·7	—
Rodents in mole niche	—	0·1
Specialised ant and termite feeders	0·8	0·4
Small to medium-sized terrestrial omnivores	3·7	3·8
Typical muroid rodents	21·4	27·5
Miscellaneous rodents, non-muroid	2·8	12·6
Rabbit-sized herbivores	4·0	2·1
Medium to large terrestrial herbivores	12·6	2·8
Fossorial herbivores (underground feeding)	2·0	0·02
Arboreal herbivores, omnivores and insect-eaters	11·4	13·1
Carnivores, weasel to fox-size	4·8	4·0
Carnivores and scavengers, large	0·9	0·2
Bats, fruit and blossom-feeding	3·4	9·9
Bats, insectivorous	19·7	17·7

way (Table 3.3) illustrates the ways in which the environmental resources are exploited. Africa has more small insectivores and large terrestrial herbivores and less rodents and frugivorous and blossom-eating bats. Looked at in this way there is, with one or two exceptions, remarkable similarity in the spectrum of adaptation by the mammals in the two continents.

Comparisons between the African and tropical Asian and Australasian faunas are more difficult. The prodigious number of islands between the mainland of Asia and Australasia has encouraged island endemism among small species and has acted as a barrier to the dispersion and interchange of both large and small mammals. In view of this situation it is probably more appropriate to compare a circumscribed area of tropical mainland Asia such as Malaya with selected countries in tropical Africa. Malaya is a small country mainly covered by lowland and montane forest. Zaire and Zambia are two countries in tropical Africa whose faunas are well known. The former contains extensive belts of rain forest and northern and southern savanna, while Zambia is largely covered by wooded savanna. There are approximately the same number of species present in Zambia (Table 3.4) as in Malaya, but in Zaire there are almost twice as many. Both African countries extend over substantially larger areas than Malaya. The faunal richness of Zaire is greatly enhanced as a result of its vegetational variety. In all three areas the bats and rodents are the two orders containing the greatest number of species and between them account for more than

Table 3.4 *Number of species of terrestrial mammals.*

	Tropical Africa		*Tropical Asia*	*Temperate Europe*	
Country	Zaire	Zambia	Malaya	Europe	France and Switzerland
Area (ha × 1000)	235 690	74 498	13 126	*c.* 453 000	59 322
Authority	Schouteden (1948)	Ansell (1960, 1964, 1969, 1973, 1974)	Medway (1969)	Van den Brink (1967)	Van den Brink (1967)
Insectivora	49	16	7	17	14
Dermoptera	—	—	1	—	—
Chiroptera	116	55	81	31	26
Primates	32	7	13	1*	—
Carnivora	36	28	30	24	14
Pholidota	3	2	1	—	—
Lagomorpha	2	4	—	3	3
Rodentia	95	63	54	48†	23†
Tubulidentata	1	1	—	—	—
Hyracoidea	5	2	—	—	—
Proboscidea	1	1	1	—	—
Perissodactyla	3	2	3	1	1
Artiodactyla	42	28	9	13‡	7‡
Total	385	209	200	138	88

Meester and Setzer (1971–77) have been used to up-date nomenclature and faunal lists for the African species.

*The Barbary Ape (*Macaca sylvanus*), probably an introduction.

†Excludes the introduced grey squirrel (*Sciurus carolinensis*) and coypu (*Myocastor coypus*).

‡Does not include any of the following deer that have been introduced into Europe: Chinese water deer (*Hydropotes inermis*), muntjac (*Muntiacus muntjak*), sika deer (*Sika nippon*) and white-tailed deer (*Odocoileus virginianus*).

half the total number of species present. A major difference between the Asian and African localities is the appreciably greater abundance of ungulate species in the latter. This is probably accounted for by the extensive areas of grass and bush in Africa which afford suitable conditions for many larger grazers and browsers.

Temperate Europe with its considerable variety of terrain, vegetation and climate supports many less species than does any one of the three tropical countries. When a confined area of Europe is examined, such as France and Switzerland, the faunal depletion is still greater. As in the tropics, bats and rodents comprise the major element with carnivores, insectivores and artiodactyls occurring in substantial variety.

In these brief summaries of faunal composition it is evident that the number of species is higher in the tropics than in temperate Europe. To account for this state of affairs is a demanding task which requires a detailed comparison of past and present environment. From the preceding account of the African fauna it is obvious that the ecological complexity is such as to discourage broad generalisations. It does, however, appear probable that in some places, as a result of climatic uniformity and floral heterogenity, a greater range of niches are available. For example, fruit-eating, nectarivorous and blossom-feeding species can only survive in situations where there is continuous flowering and fruiting throughout the year. These conditions only prevail in parts of the tropics. It is also possible that evolution has so operated in the tropics to produce a large number of species having narrow ranges of ecological requirements. If this is so the incidence of numerous narrow-niche species accompanied by a wider range of available niches than in temperate areas would go a long way towards accounting for the greater tropical diversity. However, these ideas are largely speculative and do not explain the mechanisms by which the situation arose. A great deal more information is required on the history of the continental land masses and their climates as well as their floras and faunas before this problem can be adequately resolved.

PART II Ecology in the biotic zones

Chapter 4

The biotic zones of tropical Africa

In tropical Africa, variations in climate, geomorphology and altitude have resulted in many types of vegetation which have been described in detail by botanists (e.g. Keay 1959). The details of each vegetation type are too complex for present purposes, and therefore it is necessary to divide the vegetation types into a few basic regions, each of which has certain biologically important features in common. These regions are generally referred to as biotic zones. Within each zone there are many microhabitats and variations in vegetation which may be important for a particular species, even though such habitats are not referred to specifically in the description of the zone.

The tropics are one of the major climatic regions of the world, extending across the Equator from $23\frac{1}{2}°$N (the tropic of Cancer) to $23\frac{1}{2}°$S (the tropic of Capricorn). In the tropics, the sun's rays at noon are nearly vertical throughout the year, the lengths of day and night are almost equal and the sun's rays at noon are exactly vertical twice each year. Two other characteristics determine the tropical climate. Firstly, the monthly mean temperatures do not show much seasonal fluctuation, although daily fluctuations may be considerable in some localities. Secondly, the annual rainfall and frequency of precipitation is very varied, ranging from more than 1 500 mm per annum in 'wet' localities to less than 250 mm per annum in 'dry' localities. In the very dry 'arid' regions, rainfall may be as little as 50–100 mm per annum, and there may be several years between significant rain storms. In all these respects the tropics are totally different to temperate and polar regions.

It is not possible to classify the climates of tropical Africa using rainfall alone, as rainfall and temperature are closely linked. For example, an annual rainfall of 800 mm where the annual mean temperature is low (as in Europe) produces a mild wet climate, but the same rainfall where the annual mean temperature is high (as in tropical Africa) produces a dry semi-arid climate. The most widely accepted classification of climates is that by Koppen which has been modified to some extent by subsequent authors (see Trewartha 1968). In tropical Africa, there are three principal climatic zones (Table 4.1) based on the relationship of potential evapotranspiration to precipitation. The potential evapotranspiration (E_p) is a hypothetical figure of the amount of water that would be lost by evaporation and transpiration if there was an unlimited supply of surface and ground water. In many localities, water is limited and therefore the *actual* evapotranspiration is much less than the *potential* evapotranspiration; such localities always suffer a water deficit for some, or all, of the year. On the basis of the relationship between E_p and rainfall, tropical Africa may be divided into three climatic regions:

1. The 'arid' regions where E_p is at least twice as large as the average annual precipitation.
2. The 'tropical wet and dry' regions where the E_p is greater than the average annual rainfall, but not as great as in the arid regions. These regions may be termed semi-arid, as the rainfall will exceed E_p in some months.
3. The 'tropical wet' regions where the annual E_p is smaller than the average annual rainfall.

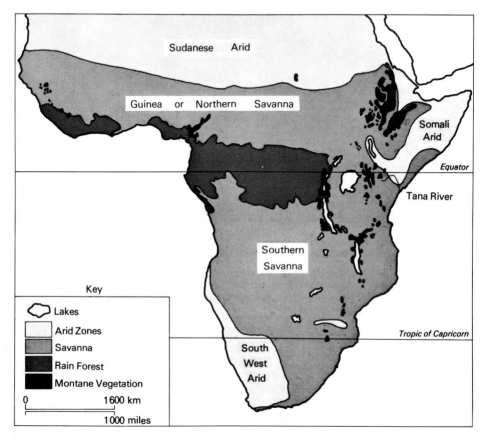

Fig. 4.1   The major types of vegetation from the Sahara to South Africa.

If the vegetation map of Africa (Fig. 4.1) is superimposed on the climatic map, several features are obvious. The 'arid zones' correspond roughly to the desert regions. The 'tropical wet and dry' climatic zone includes a wide variety of habitats which are classified botanically as 'savanna'. This climatic zone includes all the land between the arid zones and the tropical wet zones, except for the mountainous areas. In the following chapters, the term 'savanna' consists of all the country ranging from the dry 'Sahel savanna' with about 300 mm of rain per annum falling in 3–4 months to the relatively moist 'Guinea savanna' with up to about 1 600 mm of rain per annum falling in 8–9 months. On an annual basis, these habitats have a water shortage as the E_p is greater than the precipitation, although in some months of the wet season the situation may be reversed. The savannas are sometimes referred to as 'semi-arid', but this term is not used as it may be confused with the less arid parts of the 'arid zone'. Climatically,

Table 4.1 *The biotic zones of tropical Africa. (Compiled from data in Trewartha 1968 and Keay 1959.)*

Name	Synonyms	Climatic details	Annual rainfall	Evapotranspiration
Arid	Desert Sudanese semi-arid	Arid climate: average annual temperature over 18°C (64°F); rainfall irregular with high variability around annual mean; gradual transition to dry savanna	Under 300 mm	E_p at least twice as large as annual precipitation
Savanna	Steppe Sahel savanna Guinea savanna Forest-savanna mosaic (= derived savanna) Miombo woodlands Thorn bush	Wide range of climate from 'dry savanna' to 'moist savanna':		E_p higher than annual rainfall, but less than in arid zone
		Semi-arid; average annual temperature over 18°C; annual rain falls in 3–4 months; prolonged dry season; at least ten times as much rain as in driest month	300–900 mm	
		Tropical 'wet and dry' climate; annual rain falls in 4–10 months; marked seasonal rhythm of rainfall; at least one month has less than 6 cm of rain	900–1 600 mm	
Rain forest	Lowland forest Moist semi-deciduous rain forest Evergreen rain forest	Tropical wet climate; rainfall of driest month at least 6 cm; rainfall remains high throughout year; no 'dry season'; temperature uniformly high	1 600 mm or more	E_p less than annual rainfall

all the 'tropical wet and dry regions' of Africa are in continuity although zoogeographically it is convenient to distinguish the northern savannas from the southern savannas because in the past they were physically separate from each other (see Ch. 6). In some parts the arid zone penetrates the driest type of savanna, as along the western edge of the Ethiopian highlands, so that here the northern savanna is almost separated from the southern savanna at the present time. The southern savanna in Eastern Africa tends to be cooler than the northern savanna because of the higher altitude, and therefore rainfall effectively produces a more humid climate despite the low rainfall. The degree of aridity as far as plants are concerned is also related to the soil texture which influences the water-holding properties of the soil.

The 'tropical wet' climatic zone is not arid at any time of the year as precipitation is greater than E_p in all months of the year. This zone supports rainforest ranging from dry semideciduous rainforest near the forest–savanna margin to evergreen rainforest where the rainfall may be as high as 2 500 mm per annum.

Mountainous parts of tropical Africa are placed in a separate category mainly because of the lower annual temperatures, and low night temperatures which may fall below 0 °C. Rainfall is often high, but the cool temperatures prevent the establishment of vegetation typical of that rainfall at lower altitudes. The vegetation shows marked stratification with altitude, and the vegetation at higher altitudes in montane regions shows similarities to vegetation at higher and lower latitudes. The higher altitudes on African mountains are sometimes termed the 'Afro-alpine' zones.

Chapter 5

Rain forests

5.1 Distribution of lowland rain forest

The rain forest zone extends along the coastal regions of West Africa and across the lowlands of central Africa between the latitudes of 8 °N and 8 °S of the Equator (Figs. 4.1, 5.1). The rain forests form a more or less continuous forested area from Sierra Leone to eastern Zaire. All this region is less than 1 000 m above sea level and most of the West African forest is under 200 m. Small outliers of rain forest, isolated from the rain forest zone, may be found in suitable wet regions and along some rivers in other parts of tropical Africa. High rainfall is necessary for the maintenance of the rain forest; forest trees do not grow in permanently submerged and swampy soils although some species form freshwater swamp forests near large rivers which are seasonally flooded.

The forest zone may be divided into seven 'forest blocks', each of which has its own distinctive mammalian fauna (Booth 1958, Rahm 1972b). The forest blocks, from west to east, are the Liberian, Ghanaian, Western Nigerian, Eastern Nigerian, Gaboon, Congo and Central African forests, and the large rivers which are partly responsible

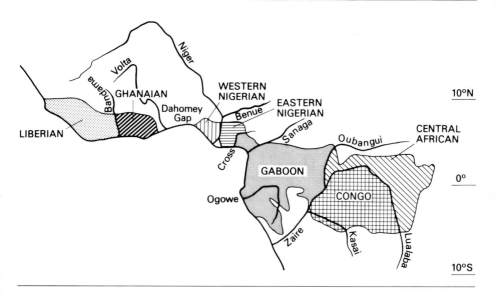

Fig. 5.1 The forest blocks and major rivers of the lowland rain forest zone of Africa. (Adapted from Booth 1958 and Rahm 1966).

73

for these divisions are the Bandama, Volta, Niger, Sanaga, Zaire (Congo) and Lualaba. Savanna grasslands extend southwards to the coast of the Gulf of Guinea at the 'Dahomey Gap' separating the Ghanaian and Western Nigerian forests (Fig. 5.1).

5.2 Climate

The distribution of the rain forest is largely determined by the relationship between potential evaporation and rainfall, the average annual rainfall and the duration of the rains. The mean annual rainfall is not less than about 1 600 mm, and in some areas it is as high as 2 500 mm. Rainfall is spread over most months of the year. There are at least six months with a minimum of 100 mm of rain each month, and not more than two or

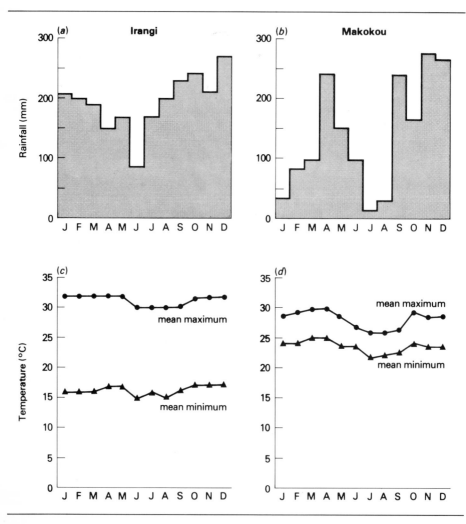

Fig. 5.2 The climate in the lowland rain forest at Irangi (950 m) and Makokou (400 m). (*a*) Mean monthly rainfall at Irangi. (*b*) Mean monthly rainfall at Makokou. (*c*) Mean monthly maximum and minimum temperatures at Irangi. (*d*) Mean monthly maximum and minimum temperatures at Makokou. (Data from Rahm 1967 and Charles-Dominique 1971).

three months with less than 25 mm of rain each month (Hopkins 1965). The climate is always moist and warm, and there are few daily and monthly fluctuations in temperature and humidity. At Irangi, Zaire, rainfall remains high in every month of the year except June, and at Makokou, Gabon, there are two wet seasons interspersed with two periods of lesser rainfall in January and in July–August (Fig. 5.2). The mean monthly temperatures, likewise, show little monthly variation; at Irangi the mean monthly maximum temperatures range from 29 °C to 32 °C and the mean monthly minimum temperatures range from 14 °C to 17 °C (Fig. 5.2). The mean monthly temperatures at Makokou also show little monthly variation. Relative humidity is rarely less than 60–70 per cent and often it is 90–100 per cent. In the rain forest zone close to the forest–savanna boundary, as at Gambari, Nigeria, there is a distinct 'dry

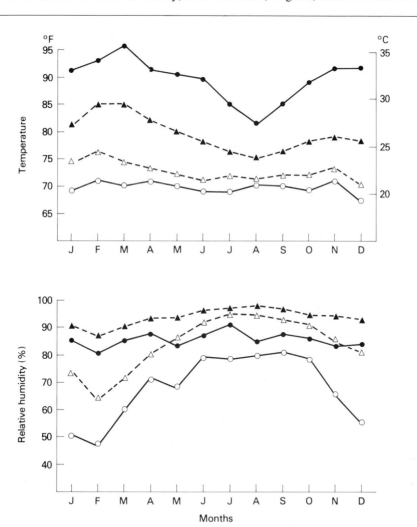

Fig. 5.3 The temperatures and relative humidities 10 cm above the ground (broken lines) and in the open (unbroken lines) in Gambari forest, Nigeria in 1969. Closed symbols record mean monthly maxima and open symbols record mean monthly minima (Happold, 1977).

season' when there is little or no rainfall for 2–3 months (Happold, 1977); at this time, mean monthly maximum temperatures are higher and the relative humidities are lower than at other seasons of the year (Fig. 5.3). The high temperatures and abundant vegetation result in a large water loss by evaporation and transpiration, but the high rainfall compensates for this so that in all rain forest localities, except those close to the forest–savanna boundary, precipitation exceeds evapotranspiration.

The climate inside the forest has a smaller range of daily and monthly temperatures and relative humidities than in the open air outside the forest, and there are slight differences in the climatic regime in each stratum or level in the forest (see Ch. 5.3 and Fig. 5.4). In a moist semi-deciduous forest in Nigeria, Evans (1939) showed that at

Fig. 5.4   Profile of lowland rain forest to show A, B, C, D and E strata (modified from diagram of profile in Shasha forest, Nigeria by Richards (1952)).

0·7 m above the ground (E stratum) there was a daily range of about 5·5 to 6·0 degrees Centigrade, whereas at 15–37 m above the ground (B stratum) the daily range was 9 to 10 degrees. The daily range of relative humidity showed considerable differences between the wet and the dry season. In the dry season the daily range was 18 per cent in the E stratum and 34 per cent in the B stratum, and in the wet season the equivalent figures were 4 per cent and 28 per cent. During the course of the year the lower strata of the forest have a smaller range of temperature and relative humidity compared with outside the forest. Climatic data from Gambari Forest, Nigeria (Happold, 1977) show that the shading effects of the dense upper layers result in a relatively even non-fluctuating climate, especially in the wet season (Fig. 5.3).

5.3   Vegetation

There are many sorts of rain forest, each with its own characteristic flora, depending

Table 5.1 *A comparison between the upper and lower strata in the rain forest to illustrate two contrasting habitats for mammals in the forest.*

	Upper strata (A and B)	Lower strata (D and E)
Temperature and relative humidity (see also Fig. 5.3)	Similar to that of the outside air. In the 'dry season', average daily maximum and minimum temperatures are 34 and 21 °C (range: 13 degrees); equivalent figures in the 'wet season' are 29 and 21 °C (range: 8 degrees). R.H. ranges from about 60 to 90 per cent. Climate is mostly warm and moist with some periods which are cooler and have moderate humidities	By comparison with the upper strata, the climate is always cool and moist with few extremes of temperature. In the 'dry season' average daily maximum and minimum temperatures are 29 and 24 °C (range: 5 degrees); equivalent figures in the 'wet season' are 24 and 22 °C (range: 2 degrees). Daily mean minimum R.H. is not usually less than 80 per cent
Light intensity during the daytime	High, except on cloudy days	Always low
Wind velocity	High during storms	Low, usually almost windless
Rainfall	Exposed to full force of raindrops, and total precipitation	Protected from full force of raindrops. Only about 35 per cent reaches the lower strata. Tree trunks often channel water to ground level
Availability of fruits	High. Most frugivores feed in upper strata	Less, as only some fruits fall to the ground in an edible state
Availability of flowers	High	Low
Availability of fresh green shoots	High, varying from month to month, and from tree to tree	Lower than in upper strata
Ease of movement for mammals	Special adaptations required for movement in higher strata (see text)	No special adaptations required, but movement may be difficult for large mammals

a

b

c   d

Fig. 5.5   Rain forest.
(*a*) The D and E strata showing herbs, creepers, saplings and the buttress roots of an A stratum tree (Gambari, Nigeria). (Photo: D. C. D. Happold.)
(*b*) A and B strata trees emerging through the lower strata on the edge of a forest clearing. The canopy, the shape of forest trees and tangles of climbing plants are well illustrated in this photograph. (Makokou, Gabon). (Photo: A. R. Devez, CNRS.)
(*c*) The D and E strata, with abundant growth of climbers. Trunks of B and C strata trees project upwards. (Makokou, Gabon). (Photo: A. R. Devez, CNRS.)
(*d*) A dense growth of climbing plants which have grown over the foliage of a forest tree (on right). These 'climbing columns' are used by small arboreal mammals when moving from one stratum to another (Makokou, Gabon). (Photo: A. R. Devez, CNRS.)

largely on the annual rainfall. One classification, among others, distinguishes three major types of rain forest, although there is a gradual transition between each type.

1. Dry semi-deciduous forest – with about 1 600 mm rain/year.
2. Moist semi-deciduous forest – with about 1 900 mm rain/year.
3. Moist evergreen forest – with about 1 900–2 500 mm rain/year.

Within the rain forest zone, the flora is also related to the soil type and geology of the area. Therefore in areas which are climatically similar, different soils result in different types of forest. Rain forest vegetation is very complex. It consists mostly of woody trees, shrubs and creepers and small herbs. The number of plant species is greater than in other tropical vegetation zones. In Shasha Forest, Nigeria, Richards (1952) records 115–155 tree species (with trunk diameters of 10 cm or more) on 1 ha (2·5 acre) plots, and there are probably two or three times this number of species if climbers, shrubs, herbs and saprophytic plants are also included. This abundance of species is reflected in the great variety of life forms in the forest (Richards 1952).

Forest trees may grow as high as 46 m, and on this vertical scale it is possible to recognise five horizontal strata (or storeys). The canopy, or A stratum, comprises the crowns of the tallest trees and is usually discontinuous because the crowns do not touch each other. The B stratum (15–37 m) is composed of trees with narrow crowns which are fairly close together but do not form a continuous layer, and the C stratum contains trees 5–15 m high which form an almost continuous cover. The D stratum (1–5 m) consists of shrubs and young trees, and the E stratum (less than 1 m) includes herbs, ferns, seedlings of all kinds, and grasses. The E stratum is often very sparse or completely lacking, except beneath openings in the canopy (see below). The structure of a forest can be shown by a 'forest profile' which gives a visual impression of the sizes of the trees and plants, their density and the amount of vegetation in each stratum (Fig. 5.4). The branches of many trees in the B, C and D strata intertwine and provide cross connections for arboreal mammals from one tree to another. Forest profiles vary greatly depending on the locality. The environment of the upper strata (A and B) is in marked contrast to that of the lower strata in the forest. As a result each provides a totally different environment for mammals (Table 5.1).

The rain forest is very heterogeneous in its habitats although it may appear rather homogeneous in structure. Large trees are blown down in storms so that openings are formed in the canopy. The increased light which now reaches the lower strata stimulates the growth of herbs and low shrubs so a new micro-environment, different from that of the typical forest, is formed. In time, new trees will grow and the 'clearing' will be restored gradually to its original condition. Rampant growth of herbs and climbers also occurs along the edges of rivers and tracks so that the canopy of the forest tends to be closer to the ground. Different associations of trees, determined by the locality and the past history of the forest, and seasonal changes in the forest, give rise to many habitats which can be exploited by forest mammals. After partial clearing and felling, 'secondary forests' are established; these have a different floral composition and climate to undisturbed 'primary forest', and therefore provide different habitats for mammals compared with primary forest. Differences in forest structure and composition, flowering and fruiting times of trees, and the seasonal availability of plant and animal foods, are some of the factors which determine the variety and numbers of forest mammals. Detailed descriptions of rain forest are given by Richards (1952) and by Longman and Jenik (1974).

5.4   Some adaptations of forest mammals

The abundance and variety of vegetation supports many species of mammals which possess adaptations for arboreal life. Monkeys can climb using their long powerful limbs and opposable fingers and thumb, squirrels have pointed claws and a long tail for balance, and climbing mice have special palms and digits which enable them to hold on to twigs. In flying squirrels a flap of skin (the patagium) extends between the fore and hindlimbs so that when it is stretched the flying squirrel can glide from tree to tree. Flying squirrels also have a row of backwardly projecting scales on the underside of the tail; these prevent the squirrel from slipping backwards when it lands and help it to climb upwards on a tree trunk. Pangolins have thickened prehensile tails, powerful limbs and long claws so they can climb on trunks and on small branches. The tree hyrax has no tail, no claws and a small rotund body, and appears to be unsuited for arboreal life; but moist flattened pads on the feet and strong back muscles allow it to climb from ground level to the canopy, and to jump from branch to branch.

The density of the D and E strata and the tangle of creepers hinder movement, and are some of the reasons why there are few large non-climbing forest mammals. The forest races of elephants and buffalos are smaller in size than those of the savanna. Large horns are disadvantageous in the forest because they may become tangled in low growing foliage. Bongo and duikers have small backwardly projecting horns which are held flat along the neck when the animal is walking and running. Okapis do not have horns, and forest pigs have solid bodies so they can push through the forest undergrowth.

Forest predators are hampered by the limited visibility in the forest. They tend to be fairly small in size and catch their prey by lurking and stalking rather than by chasing. Slow moving prey – frogs, insects, termites and young birds – are the staple diet of civets, genets and mongooses. The palm civet (*Nandinia binotata*) is unusual because it feeds mostly on fruits rather than on live prey. Shrews and elephant shrews, the smallest of the forest predators, feed on amphibians, insects and worms, and the forest herbs and dead leaves give them protection as they hunt on the ground. Insect-eating bats hunt in the canopy and in forest clearings, and are found infrequently in the lower strata of the forest.

5.5 Diversity of forest mammals

One of the most striking features of rain forest is the large number and diversity of mammalian species. There are several reasons for this:

1. The stratification of the forest results in many niches and habitats above the ground which have been exploited by forest mammals. This is in contrast to savanna and arid regions.
2. Forest resources are extremely varied so that many different resources are available for mammals. This is due to the numerous plant species which provide many sorts of leaves, shoots, fruits, seeds and bark for eating, different branch and twig structures for climbing on, and many places for domicile construction. The large number of invertebrate and vertebrate species provides a wide range of prey for mammalian predators.
3. Forest resources are abundant, and remain available throughout the year.
4. Because resources are abundant, several species can utilise the same resource, but not in *exactly* the same way, or at the same time, or in the same place.
5. There have been many opportunities for allopatric speciation due to the past history and distribution of the rain forest.

Stratification is one of the important characteristics of the rain forest as it results in a larger amount of environmental space which can be utilised by forest mammals, compared with savanna and arid habitats. This fact, amongst others, has led to the 'n-dimensional niche concept' which implies that the niche of a particular species varies according to spatial, temporal, trophic and behavioural parameters. Ecologists have suggested that this enlarged environmental space and the diversity of niches at different levels are two important reasons why so many species can coexist in the rain forest. Some species may be taxonomically closely related and overlap in their utilisation of forest resources (Section 5.7), but this does not appear to result in undue competition. The greatest number and diversity is found in the primary forest where stratification is well developed and there are numerous niches at all levels. There is less diversity in secondary forest where the trees are generally less tall, stratification is not so well developed and the ground layer has a greater density of shrubs and herbs. Small arboreal mammals and those that like to hide in dense cover are more common in secondary forest than in primary forest. The successional stages which culminate in secondary forest each have their own characteristics and their own typical mammalian fauna. The diversity and number of mammalian species at Irangi in Zaire and Makokou in Gabon illustrate this principle that a complex environment can support many species of mammals.

5.6   The mammals of Irangi and Makokou

Two areas of rain forest, at Irangi and at Makokou, have been selected to illustrate the relationships between the mammals and their environment, and the relationships between related sympatric species. Many of the examples in this chapter are taken from these two localities.

Irangi (28°27′ E, 01°54′ S) is situated on the eastern edge of the rain forest zone in eastern Zaire (Congo) at an altitude of about 950 m. It is a hilly region where the land slopes gradually downwards from the mountains bordering the western Rift Valley to the lowlands of the Congo and Lualaba rivers. Irangi is in a small river valley surrounded by forests dominated by *Gilbertiodendron dewevrei*, although there are many variations in the tree composition in nearby areas. The largest trees of the A stratum reach heights of 40 m and they form a relatively dense canopy. The D and E strata contain dense vegetation close to rivers and in some low lying parts of the forest. The annual rainfall is about 2500 mm and rain occurs in all months of the year. The temperature is very even throughout the year, and diurnal and seasonal fluctuations are small (Fig. 5.2). Mammals in the Irangi forest live in a remarkably constant environment, although the variations in monthly rainfall may result in seasonal variations in the food supply (Rahm 1970).

Makokou (13°0′E, 0°4′ N) is in the rain forests of north-east Gabon at an altitude of 300–500 m. There are extensive rain forests in the hilly regions, and swamp forests which are seasonally flooded border the rivers. The swamp forests are dominated by *Macrolobium* and *Gilbertiodendron*, and there are many climbers and small trees and shrubs in the D stratum (Gautier-Hion 1971; Fig. 5.5c). The total annual rainfall is usually less than 2000 mm and therefore is lower than at Irangi. There are two clearly defined periods with reduced rainfall compared with only one such period at Irangi (Fig. 5.2). The relative humidity averages 80–85 per cent.

Sixty-three species of mammals have been recorded from the Irangi forests (Rahm 1966). Some of these are common, but many of the larger species such as golden cats (*Felis aurata*), elephants (*Loxodonta africana*) and aardvarks (*Orycteropus afer*) are very rare. Some other species, which live in neighbouring forests, have not been recorded at Irangi. Each of the mammals at Irangi has its own particular habitat preference in the forest, and most of the obvious niches have been exploited (Table 5.2). The E stratum has the largest number of herbivores ranging in size from small mice to browsing antelopes, and carnivores ranging in size from shrews to mongooses. The E stratum, in particular, shows how the many species are distributed by size and feeding habit (Table 5.2). The smaller species, regardless of their food requirements, are generally more abundant than the large species which, with the exception of the duiker *Cephalophus monticola*, tend to be rare.

In the C and D strata are prosimians, arboreal mice and several species of squirrels and genets. The A and B strata contain the hyrax *Dendrohyrax*, two monkeys *Colobus* and *Cercopithecus*, two viverrids *Nandinia* and *Poiana* and the flying squirrels *Anomalurus* and *Idiurus*. The distribution of these flying squirrels is dependant on the presence of old trees with holes where they can rest during the day. The arboreal species are not necessarily confined to one stratum: monkeys, hyraxes and viverrids may move from one stratum to another.

Three other habitats may be distinguished (Table 5.2). First, there are aerial habitats along the forest edges above rivers and above the canopy which are utilised by insectivorous and frugivorous bats. Secondly, there are aquatic habitats which support otters (*Lutra* and *Aonyx*) and otter shrews (*Potamogale*) which feed on crabs, molluscs and fish, and also the water mongoose (*Atilax*) which is partially aquatic and feeds on fish, amphibians, millepedes and fruit (Rahm and Christiaenson 1963). Thirdly, there are banana plantations and farmlands in forest clearings which support several species of rodents, a squirrel and two species of viverrids, all of which are rare in the undisturbed forest and their presence at Irangi is due to these man-made habitats.

Each species has its preferred habitat in the forest which results in the ecological separation of closely related species; this is shown diagramatically for squirrels and viverrids in Fig. 5.6.

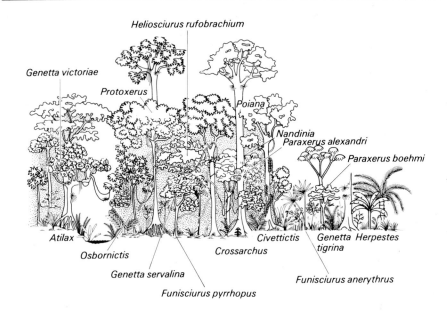

Fig. 5.6   Ecological separation of viverrids and squirrels in primary rain forest (left) and secondary rain forest (right) at Irangi (After Rahm 1972).

At Makokou, 118 species of mammals have been recorded (Charles-Dominique, pers. comm.) (Table 5.3). The separation of species by size and vertical strata is strikingly similar to that at Irangi. The richer fauna of Makokou is due mainly to the greater number of species of bats and large mammals. However, intensive sampling over a larger area at Makokou than at Irangi, as well as the greater variety of habitats at Makokou, may explain some of the differences between the two localities.

Both localities illustrate some general features of the ecology of rain forest mammals. The E stratum contains the largest number of genera distributed throughout all size groups. The number of species decreases with increasing height above the ground. There are virtually no very small, large and very large mammals in the D stratum, except for a few rodents at both localities and large primates at Makokou. The upper strata are inhabited mostly by small and medium sized primates, squirrels, flying squirrels and viverrids, all of which are very active and move between the strata. In both localities, plant-, fruit- and seed-eating mammals predominate in all strata. Meat and insect eaters comprise several species of pangolins, viverrids, shrews and prosimians, many of which are found on the ground. Bats are found in all strata. Comparison of the mammals at Irangi and Makokou suggests that the niches and

Table 5.2 *The genera of mammals at Irangi, Zaïre, to show feeding habits and habitat selection. H = essentially herbivorous and frugivorous, C = essentially carnivorous and insectivorous. Figures in brackets indicate number of species when more than one is present. (Data from Rahm 1966).*

Size		Vertical strata					Other habitats		
		A	B	C	D	E	Aerial	Water	Disturbed
Very small 5–100 g	H	Idiurus (2)	Idiurus (2)		Graphiurus Thamnomys Hylomyscus	Hybomys Praomys Colomys Lophuromys Deomys Stochomys			Rattus Mus (2) Lemniscomys Oenomys
	C					Scutisorex Crocidura (2)	Nycteris Hipposideros Myotis Glauconycteris Kerivoula Tadarida		
Small 100 g–5 kg	H	Anomalurus (2) Dendrohyrax	Anomalurus (2) Dendrohyrax Protoxerus	Galago (2) Perodicticus Heliosciurus	Galago (2) Paraxerus Funisciurus (2)	Cricetomys Atherurus	Hypsognathus		Paraxerus
	C		Manis (2)	Manis (2)	Manis (2) Perodicticus			Potamogale	

Table 5.2 —*continued*

Size		Vertical strata					Other habitats		
		A	*B*	*C*	*D*	*E*	*Aerial*	*Water*	*Disturbed*
Medium 5–15 kg	H	*Colobus* *Cercopithecus* (2)	*Colobus* *Cercopithecus* (2)			*Cercocebus* *Hyemoschus*			
	C	*Poiana*	*Poiana* *Nandinia*	*Nandinia* *Genetta* (2)	*Genetta* (2) *Felis*	*Felis* *Viverra* *Atilax* *Crossarchus*		*Lutra* *Aonyx* *Atilax*	*Genetta* *Herpestes*
Large 15–50 kg	H					*Orycteropus* *Cephalophus* (4) *Neotragus*			
	C					*Manis*			
Very large more than 50 kg	H			*Pan*	*Pan*	*Loxodonta* *Hylochoerus* *Potamochoerus* *Loxodonta, Pan*			
	C								
Totals		9	13	10	15	29	7	4	8

Table 5.3 *The principal genera of mammals at Makokou, Gabon to show feeding habits and habitat selection. H = essentially herbivorous and frugivorous, C = essentially carnivorous and insectivorous. Figures in brackets indicate number of species when more than one is present. (Charles-Dominique, pers. comm.)*

Size		Vertical strata					Other habitats	
		A	B	C	D	E	Aerial	Water
Very small 5–100 g	H	Idiurus	Idiurus		Thamnomys Hylomyscus (4) Graphiurus Dendromus	Oenomys Stochomys Deomys Lophuromys Hybomys Praomys (2) Mus		
	C					Sylvisorex (2) Crocidura (8)	23 spp Micro-chiroptera including Taphozous (2) Nycteris (4) Hipposideros (4) Rhinolophus (2) Pipistrellus (2)	
Small 100 g–5 kg	H	Anomalurus (2) Dendrohyrax	Anomalurus (2) Protoxerus Zenkerella Dendrohyrax	Heliosciurus	Myosciurus Paraxerus Funisciurus (4) Heliosciurus Epixerus	Atherurus Thryonomys Cricetomys	Megachiroptera (7)	
	C			Galago (2)	Manis (2) Galago (2)			Potamogale

Table 5.3 – *continued*

		Vertical strata					Other habitats	
Size		*A*	*B*	*C*	*D*	*E*	*Aerial*	*Water*
Medium 5–15 kg	H	*Colobus* (2) *Cercopithecus* (3)	*Colobus* (2) *Cercopithecus* (3)	*Cercocebus* (2) *Cercopithecus* (4)	*Cercocebus* (2) *Cercopithecus*	*Cephalophus* (5) *Cercocebus* (2)		*Lutra Aonyx Atilax Hyemoshus*
	C	*Poiana*	*Poiana Nandinia*	*Genetta* (2) *Nandinia*	*Felis Genetta* (2)	*Felis Viverra* ? *Bdeogale*		
Large 15–50 kg	H					*Orycteropus Cephalophus*		
	C					*Manis*		
Very large more than 50 kg	H			*Gorilla Pan Papio*	*Gorilla Pan Papio*	*Loxodonta, Hylochoerus Syncerus, Potamochoerus Tragelaphus* (2), *Gorilla Tragelaphus* (2), *Pan, Papio*		
	C							
Totals		10	13	15	28	43	30	5

utilisation of the environment are similar at both localities even though the species of mammals differ to a certain extent. The geographical range of many forest genera is continuous within the forest zone, and these genera tend to occupy the same niche at both localities. This is in contrast to the arid zones (Section 7.3) which are not in continuity with each other and where there is ecological replacement of species in different parts of the zone. Faunal lists from other rain forest localities confirm that the vertical separation, species composition and size range of mammals at Makokou and Irangi are typical of the rain forest zone as a whole.

5.7   Utilisation of forest resources

In a complex environment such as tropical forest many species can co-exist because each occupies a slightly different niche. There may be some overlap between certain parameters of the niches of different species, but not to the extent that competition excludes one of the two 'competing' species. Niche overlap is most likely to occur in relation to food, space, time and domiciles.

However, ecological separation can reduce competition between species (the so-called 'theory of competitive exclusion'). Even so, overlap in niche requirements will occur, and the survival of a species in a complex environment will depend on how much overlap it can tolerate with other species. The means of reducing niche overlap, and therefore competition between species, include:

1. Utilisation of the same general resources in slightly different ways (e.g. domiciles) and in different proportions (e.g. foods).
2. Differences in the times of utilisation of resources (i.e. different activity patterns).
3. Separation in different strata of the forest, and in different micro-environments within each stratum.

These methods of ecological separation are illustrated by five examples.

The food requirements of squirrels and murid rodents at Irangi

Rahm (1972*a*) examined the stomach contents of many squirrels, and his analysis showed that each species has its own food preferences. *Protoxerus stangeri*, *Heliosciurus rufobrachium* and *Funisciurus pyrrhopus* fed on shoots and a variety of fruits. Much more information is available for *Funisciurus anerythrus* and *Paraxerus boehmi* which live in the D and E strata and in secondary undergrowth. In these species, six types of food were identified: bananas, other plants, oil palm fruits, ants, termites and other insects. The percentage occurrence of the food types varied from month to month, and each species showed a preference for a particular food type. *Funisciurus anerythrus* ate mostly bananas from November to April, and other plants from May to October. Ants, termites and other insects were eaten at about the same rate throughout the year. In contrast, *Paraxerus boehmi* showed a strong preference for ants (50–70 per cent) from May to November. Both species of squirrel ate several genera of ants but avoided two genera of particularly aggressive ants. Although both squirrels live in the same habitat, they differ in their feeding habits and in the proportions of each food type in their diet.

There are nine species of small terrestrial rodents at Irangi, and each feeds on various combinations of the available vegetable materials, fruits and insects. Vegetable foods were the main diet of *Praomys*, *Malacomys*, *Hylomyscus*, *Stochomys* and *Oenomys*. Insects formed an important part of the diet of *Lophuromys*, *Malacomys*, *Hybomys*, *Hylomyscus*, *Colomys* and *Oenomys*, although the stomachs of some individuals of each of these species contained only vegetable material (Table 5.4). As in squirrels, this 'feeding spectrum' minimises the competition for a particular food resource. A similar situation has been shown for the small rodents in the rain forest of Ghana (Cole 1975).

Table 5.4   *The stomach contents of murid rodents at Irangi. The most important food item for each genus is in heavy type. (From Rahm 1972c.)*

Genus	n	Stomach contents			
		Vegetable remains only	*Vegetable remains with a few insects*	*Vegetable and insect remains in equal amounts*	*Insects only*
Praomys	38	**25**	6	5	2
Lophuromys	27	4	2	**18**	3
Malacomys	55	**35**	14	6	0
Hybomys	36	**15**	16	3	2
Praomys (Hylomyscus)	32	**28**	0	4	0
Stochomys	25	**21**	1	1	2
Colomys	5	1	0	2	2
Deomys	15	2	0	2	**11**
Thamnomys	4	**4**	0	0	0
Oenomys	9	**8**	0	1	0
Lemniscomys	6	2	2	2	0

The microdistribution of murid rodents at Irangi

The investigations of Rahm (1966, 1972*c*) showed that the relative abundance of nine species of murid rodents in hilly forest localities differed from that near to the forest rivers. In addition, each species showed differences in their feeding habits and times of activity (Table 5.5). *Malacomys, Colomys, Lophuromys* and *Stochomys* were relatively more abundant close to the rivers, whereas *Praomys, Hylomyscus* and *Deomys* occurred more frequently in the hilly parts of the forest. *Hybomys* was found with equal frequency in both habitats. These results suggest that each species tends to have a preferred environment, and that there is considerable variation in species abundance in similar, closely situated localities. The combination of many factors (Table 5.5), as well as differences in the sizes of the species, probably assists in the ecological separation of the nine sympatric species. Even so, some overlap may occur between *Hylomyscus* and *Thamnomys*, between *Praomys, Stochomys* and *Malacomys*, and between *Lophuromys* and *Hybomys*.

   Studies in Uganda (Delany 1971) and Nigeria (Happold, 1977) where the species composition differs from that at Irangi, suggest that the principles of micro-distribution elucidated at Irangi are applicable to rodents throughout the forest zone.

Bats of the rain forest at Makokou

There are five species of Megachiroptera and eleven species of Microchiroptera in the rain forest at Makokou (Brosset 1966). There are also many habitats besides the forest (houses, caves and secondary forests) which are domiciles for certain species of bats. The following account deals only with the true forest species (some of which also live elsewhere) and with those which live in caves in the forest.

   Much of the work on bats has been on those species which fly within 5 m of the ground because of the difficulties of seeing and capturing bats in higher strata in the forest. Three species (*Epomops franqueti*, *Megaloglossus woermanni* and *Hipposideros caffer*) are particularly common, but many other species may be observed (Table 5.6). The general indications of abundance vary depending on the exact locality and on the time of year. For example, *Myotis bocagei* is usually seen feeding and flying along the rivers, and fruit bats congregate at trees where the fruit is ripe. The nectar-feeding *Megaloglossus* is found where there are flowers.

During the daytime, bats hang by their hindfeet in shaded or darkened places. The forest bats exhibit a great variety of resting places. Fruit bats hang singly or in small

Table 5.5   *Ecological separation of murid rodents at Irangi. (Data from Rahm 1972c.)*

Genus	Per cent occurrence in forest near river n = 311	Per cent occurrence in hilly part of forest n = 235	Arboreal or terrestrial*	Activity†	Food‡
Praomys	14	20	GA	N	H
Lophuromys	8	0	G	ND	HI
Malacomys	20	8	GA	NN	HI
Hybomys	21	22	G	ND	H
Praomys (Hylomyscus)	12	20	A	NN	H
Stochomys	9	1	GA	NN	H
Colomys	2	0	G	NN	HI
Deomys	1	14	G	NN	II
Thamnomys	1	2	A	NN	HH

*G = Ground living, GA = Ground living and arboreal, A = Primarily arboreal.

†N = nocturnal and occasionally diurnal, NN = entirely nocturnal, ND = nocturnal and diurnal.

‡H = herbivorous, occasionally some insects, HH = entirely herbivorous, HI = about equal amounts of herbivorous and insectivorous foods, II = mostly insectivorous.

Table 5.6   *Bats of the rain forests of Gabon. (From Brosset 1966.)*

Species	Abundance	Domiciles
Megachiroptera:		
Epomops franqueti	A	Under vegetation near water
Scotonycteris zenkeri	R	?
Hypsignathus monstrosus	O	Under leaves over water
Myonycteris torquata	O	? forest, banana plantations
Megaloglossus woermanni	A	? forest, dry banana leaves
Microchiroptera:		
Hipposideros caffer	A	Large tree holes
Hipposideros commersoni	C	?
Hipposideros cyclops	R	Tree holes in living trees
Hipposideros beatus	O	Holes in fallen trees
Nycteris nana	R	Tree holes in living trees
Nycteris grandis	C	Tree holes in living trees
Nycteris hispida	O	Tree holes, human habitations
Mimetillus moloneyi	R	Holes in dead trees
Myotis bocagei	C	Flowering banana stems
Taphozous (Saccolaimus) peli	C	Tree holes in A and B strata
Kerivoula harrisoni	R	Dry leaves, old spherical birds nests

A = Abundant, C = common, O = occasional, R = rare.

groups on the undersides of small branches and leaves, often in dense vegetation, and some species take cover in banana trees near the forest. In contrast, most microchiroptera rest in darkened holes in trees and each species selects a hole of a certain size at a particular elevation. For example, *Hipposideros caffer* prefers holes where several individuals can rest together, *Hipposideros beatus* rests in holes of trees which have fallen and are lying on the ground, *Taphozous (Saccolaimus) peli* selects holes high up in the dead tree trunks and *Kerivoula harrisoni* spends the day under dead leaves or in abandoned spherical nests of birds. In Gabon, this last species also rests close to the ground among the extensive webs of an *Agelena* spider (Brosset 1966). In these examples, each species has its preferred domicile which it does not share with any other species.

In the forested areas of Gabon, there are several caves which are the domiciles of four species of bats: *Hipposideros commersoni, H. caffer, Miniopterus inflatus* and the fruit bat *Rousettus aegyptiacus* (Brosset 1969). For bats, caves have the advantage of darkness during the day, and an even temperature and humidity. Bats congregate in vast numbers in these caves, and in one cave there were an estimated 500 000 *Hipposideros caffer*. If more than one species inhabits the same cave, each species rests in a separate part of the cave (Fig. 10.11b).

At night, each bat species flies in its preferred stratum and habitat in the forest. *Epomops franqueti* is the commonest species of Megachiroptera in the lower strata, and *Hipposideros caffer* forms about 95 per cent of all the Microchiroptera. The use of the lower strata is rather surprising considering the problem of navigation and flying through the undergrowth, and the lack of fruit and flowers compared with the upper strata. Some species, such as *Pipistrellus nanus, Taphozous mauritanus,* and *Nycteris hispida,* fly in clearings and in the plantations near the human habitations where they roost (Fig. 5.7).

Fig. 5.7　Ecological separation of bats in the rain forest at Makokou (Data from Brosset 1966a).

Ant- and termite-eating animals

Four species of mammals which feed exclusively on ants and termites live in the forests near Makokou. The aardvark (*Orycteropus afer*) and the giant pangolin (*Manis gigantea*) are terrestrial, and the two small pangolins (*M. tricuspis* and *M. tetradactyla* are arboreal (Pagès 1970).

The aardvark and the giant pangolin feed on fungal termites which they dig out of the ground. The aardvark has hoof-like claws on its feet, and it uses its front feet to scrape and dig, and the hind feet help to kick away the loosened soil. It is an extremely quick and efficient digger, and it usually destroys each termite mound which it excavates. Aardvarks are uncommon animals because each individual requires a large area of rain forest to provide sufficient termites for its existence. They are nocturnal, and during the day they live in holes which they excavate in a termite mound.

The giant pangolin also feeds on termites but it is a less destructive animal. Giant pangolins have elongated claws on the front feet and a special articulation of the wrist enables them to dig channels and galleries in termite mounds (Fig. 5.8). The hind feet

Fig. 5.8 Excavations made by the giant pangolin while feeding on termites in a termite mound. This species feeds exclusively on ground-dwelling termites in rain forest. (Photo: A. R. Devez and E. Pages.)

are thick and stumpy with poorly developed claws but they give stability when the pangolin is digging. The termite mounds are not usually destroyed, and the pangolin can revisit each mound on a future occasion. Like aardvarks, giant pangolins are nocturnal and they spend the day in holes in excavated termite mounds.

The two species of arboreal pangolins are small and elongated with a long supple prehensile tail. The limbs have long claws so these pangolins can climb equally well on small branches and on thick tree trunks. They do not dig for food, but break into the nests of arboreal ants and termites. Both species rest in tree holes. *Manis tetradactyla* is entirely arboreal and lives in swamp forests close to rivers. The small scales on the body break up its outline so it is difficult to see as it hunts for *Crematogaster* ants during the daytime. Occasionally it rests in the sunshine on the topmost branches of a tree. This species is a good swimmer and can drop from overhanging branches into the water. Its proficiency in water is probably enhanced by the habit of swallowing air into the alimentary canal, so making it more buoyant. *Manis tricuspis* differs from *M. tetradactyla* as it sometimes descends to the ground, and it feeds on both ants and termites. It is also more adaptable as it lives in primary and secondary forests, and is generally a much more common animal.

These four species exploit ant and termite populations in the rain forest. Undoubtedly the abundance of ants and termites limits the numbers of each of these species, but the differences in activity times, the strata where they find their food, and their preferred prey tends to reduce competition between them.

The food requirements of primates at Makokou

The 12 species of primates near Makokou show differences in their food requirements. For some species, there are only a few observations on their natural foods, and therefore Table 5.7 only gives a general impression of how each species exploits the

Table 5.7 *Food eaten by monkeys in Gabon and Rio Muni. (From Gautier-Hion 1971, Gautier and Gautier-Hion 1969; and Jones 1970.)*

Species	Leaves	Fruits	Insects	Grasses
Cercopithecus talapoin	+	+ + +	+	
C. mona		+ + +	+ +	
C. cephus	+ +	+ +		
C. nictitans (R. Muni)	+ +	+ +	+ +	
(Gabon)	+ +	+ + +	+	
C. neglectus (R. Muni)	+ +	+ +		
(Gabon)	+	+ + +	+	
Cercocebus albigena	+ +	+ +		
C. galeritus		+ +	+	+ +
Colobus polykomos	+ + +			

+ + + = preferred food (highest percentage).
  + + = commonly eaten.
    + = occasionally eaten.

forest resources. Examination of stomach contents showed that, with one exception, all the *Cercopithecus, Colobus* and *Cercocebus* species ate leaves. *Colobus* ate only leaves, but the others, in addition, fed on fruits and seeds which comprised an important part of their diet. *Cercopithecus mona* consumed more insects than the other species of monkeys. The terms 'leaves' and 'fruits' are very general, and undoubtedly each species has its own preferences which vary on the time of year, and on the time of leaf formation and fruiting of each tree species. For most monkeys little is known of these preferences, but Gautier-Hion (1971) records a large variety of fruits which are eaten in different months by *Cercopithecus talapoin*.

Some prosimians are essentially insectivorous. *Arctocebus calabarensis* and *Galagoides demidovii* are more insectivorous than *Perodicticus potto, Galago alleni* and *Euoticus elegantulus* (Charles-Dominique 1971). *G. alleni* and *P. potto* feed mostly on fruits, and resinous gums are the favoured food of *E. elegantulus* (Fig. 5.9). In most forests, insects are available to a greater or lesser extent throughout the year (Fig. 5.11). Monkeys generally do not eat many insects and therefore they do not utilise the same foods as prosimians.

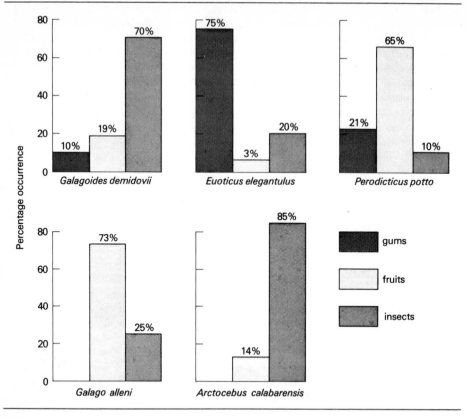

Fig. 5.9 Food specialisation in five sympatric species of prosimians in the rain forests of Gabon, as indicated by analysis of stomach contents and caecum contents (for vegetable gums). Top row: canopy species. Bottom row: undergrowth species. (After Charles-Dominique 1971.)

Gautier and Gautier-Hion (1969) suggest that sympatric species of monkeys eat the same sort of foods without competition because of the superabundance of fruits and leaves throughout the year, which implies that food resources do not regulate the numbers of monkeys in the rain forest. Conversely, Crook (1970) states that food supplies may be limiting although relatively constant throughout the year. Forest monkeys tend to live in groups of up to about 30 individuals, but because a group lives in a relatively small home range it is likely that only a few trees at a time are able to provide suitable food. The scattered dispersion of trees of the same species, and the variations in the times of shoot and fruit production of individual trees, may limit the food supply for monkeys despite the impression of food abundance. More information on food availability, competition for food and feeding preferences in many species is required to decide whether monkey abundance is determined by the availability of suitable foods or by social considerations or by a combination of both these factors.

5.8 Reproduction

Reproduction in rain forest mammals appears to be related to climate, especially rainfall, and the abundance and quality of available food. Daylength, which is an important factor regulating the breeding cycles of many temperate mammals, is unlikely to be an important regulating factor for mammals in African rain forests because daylength is fairly constant in this habitat. The importance of plant oestrogens is unknown, and there may be other factors which, as yet, have not been documented. In many species, reproduction is not generally confined to particular seasons although there are fluctuations in the level of reproductive activity during the year. In others, the breeding season is confined to a particular time of the year. These features are illustrated by the reproductive cycles of murid rodents and bats. A further example, the reproductive activity of two forest squirrels, is given on pp. 187 and 191.

Reproduction of murid rodents at Irangi and Makokou

At Irangi, the largest percentage of pregnant females of all species combined occurred towards the end of the wet season (January to April) although breeding females were

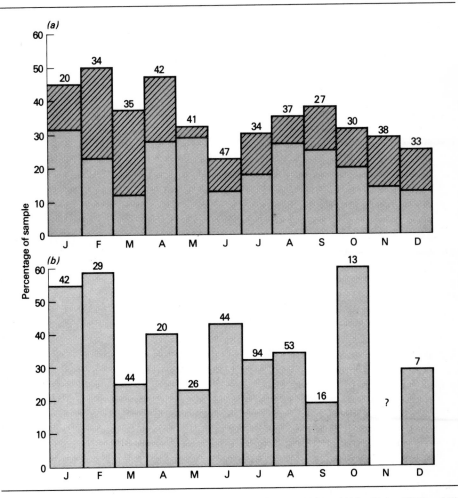

Fig. 5.10 Reproductive activity of murid rodents in the rain forest at (*a*) Irangi (After Rahm 1970) and (*b*) Makokou (After Dubost 1968). Shaded area show percentage of pregnant females in each monthly sample; striped area (Irangi) shows percentage of females with developing follicles in the ovaries. Numbers indicate the size of each monthly sample.

found in all months (Rahm 1970, Fig. 5.10). However, each species had its own breeding pattern. A large percentage of the herbivorous *Praomys* and *Hybomys* bred in April and May, but the termite-eating *Deomys* and the omnivorous *Malacomys* and *Lophuromys* bred regularly throughout the year. Although these results were based on a small sample, they showed that there was reproductive activity in all months. Rahm (1970) compared the breeding performances of populations of *Praomys*, *Lophuromys* and *Hybomys* in the rain forest with those in old plantations where there were bananas, manioc, sweet potatoes and other local crops. In the forest, there were marked fluctuations in reproductive activity whereas in the plantation the level of reproduction was fairly constant throughout the year (Table 5.8). This suggested that the level of nutrition was also a factor which initiated and maintained reproductive activity.

Table 5.8   *The reproductive rates of* Praomys, Lophuromys *and* Hybomys *in rain forest and in plantations in eastern Zaire. (After Rahm 1970.)*

	Months					
	Jan Feb	Mar Apr	May Jun	Jul Aug	Sep Oct	Nov Dec
Forest						
Number of females examined	15	30	20	12	21	18
Number pregnant	11	15	4	1	7	3
Per cent pregnant	73	50	20	8	33	17
Plantation						
Number of females examined	14	24	24	25	9	16
Number pregnant	8	7	10	9	5	8
Per cent pregnant	57	29	42	36	55	50

Dubost (1968) examined 390 individuals of 16 species of murid rodents during a 17-month survey at Makokou and found that pregnant females were present in every month of the year. The percentage frequency of breeding females varied from 20 to 25 per cent in March, May and September to 50 to 60 per cent in October, January and February (Fig. 5.10). Dubost (1968) suggested that in normal years there are three periods of maximum reproduction (January–March, June, October–November) and three periods of minimum reproduction. Rainfall and breeding activity did not correlate exactly although there was a relationship between the two. The percentage occurrence of pregnant females, regardless of the time of year, varied from 32 per cent in *Praomys* (*Hylomyscus*) *stella* (n = 113) to 56 per cent in *Stochomys longicaudatus* (n = 78). Dubost considered that litter size per female and the percentage fluctuations of females in breeding condition results in considerable variations in the abundance and population numbers of each species.

Other studies on reproduction in murid rodents in African tropical rain forests (Delany 1971, Happold 1977) have also shown correlations between seasonal variations in rainfall and reproductive activity. The exact relationship between these two parameters appears to vary from locality to locality. Despite these variations, the important features of murid reproduction in rain forests may be summarised as follows:

1. Murid rodents breed throughout the year.
2. The different levels of reproductive activity are probably related to seasonal fluctuations in rainfall, although the correlation between reproduction and rainfall differs according to the locality.

3. At Irangi, where the annual rainfall is higher and more evenly spread throughout the year, reproductive activity is generally at a lower level and more even than at Makokou where both rainfall and reproductive activity show greater fluctuations.
4. Each species has its own pattern of reproduction, which roughly follows that of the population as a whole, with periods of maximum and minimum activity.

Reproduction of bats at Makokou

The commonest fruit bat (*Epomops franqueti*) bred throughout most of the year (Brosset 1966). Young individuals and pregnant or lactating females were present whenever the species was caught. Non-seasonality of breeding in this species has also been recorded from Cameroun (Aellen 1953), Zaire (Vershuren 1957) and Rio Muni (Jones 1972).

Populations of the cave-dwelling *Hipposideros caffer* reproduced at different times of the year depending on the exact locality of their domiciles (Brosset 1969). Populations just north of the Equator bred mostly in April, and those just south of the Equator bred mostly in November. Populations from north and south of the Equator had different age structures. Brosset suggested that this unusual situation isolates the populations with the 'boreal' (northern) reproductive season from those with the 'austral' (southern) reproductive season. Different reproductive cycles occurred in *Miniopterus inflatus* and *Hipposideros commersoni* whose young were born only in October towards the end of the wet season. The differing breeding seasons of these bats suggests that each responds to the environmental stimuli in different ways, but the ultimate causes for these differences are unknown. Breeding in tropical bats is discussed further in Section 9.3.

5.9   Social organisations

Most species of forest mammals tend to be rather sedentary, living singly or in small groups dispersed throughout suitable areas within the forest. Species which generally have a dispersed organisation (see p. 236) are the terrestrial and arboreal rodents, hole-living microchiroptera, hyraxes, shrews, pangolins and duikers. Their overall distribution is fairly even throughout a suitable forest locality, and their biomass from one hectare to another is also fairly even. However, congregations of many individuals occur temporarily at suitable food sources; for example, monkeys, squirrels and fruit bats are attracted to fruiting trees, and *Megaloglossus woermanni* and other nectar-feeding bats come together at trees in flower. After feeding, the individuals disperse.

Some forest species live permanently in social groups, but these groups are never as large as herds and troops of savanna-living mammals. Forest resources tend to be rather scattered and a particular part of the forest normally contains only a few suitable food plants or insects at one time. Mammals living in groups may need to range widely in order to obtain sufficient food for all individuals in the group. The size of the range which can support the group partly depends on the feeding requirements of the species. A group belonging to a species which has a specialised food will have to range more widely than a species which is less selective. Forest elephants, buffalos, bush pigs and several species of monkeys often live in groups in the rain forest.

The ecology of forest monkeys near Makokou

The four species of monkeys at Belinga in north-east Gabon (Table 5.9) spend most of their time in the canopy 40–50 m above the ground. Gautier and Gautier-Hion (1969) suggested that movement for these large monkeys is easier in the canopy than in the lower denser vegetation, and possible sources of danger are detected more easily in the canopy. They sometimes descended to the ground to feed, and at night they slept in trees at least 10 m above the ground. The larger number of species at Ndjaddie (Table 5.9) is related to the swampy habitats which are seasonally flooded. *Cercopithecus*

Table 5.9   *The species composition of monkeys at Belinga and Ndjaddie in north-east Gabon. (From Gautier and Gautier-Hion 1969.)*

Species	Per cent occurrence	
	Belinga n = 90	Ndjaddie n = 24
Cercopithecus nictitans	37	25
C. cephus	29	12
C. mona	25	8
C. neglectus	0	21
C. talapoin	0	4
Cercocebus albigena	9	8
C. galeritus	0	8
Colobus polykomos	0	12

neglectus lives in the dense vegetation near the rivers, and this species as well as *Cercopithecus talapoin* and *Colobus polykomos* require a riverine habitat because of their preference for spending the night in branches which overhang water. Some species occur in bands of single species composition, or of mixed species composition. These bands probably confer a number of advantages to the individuals in the band, such as increased awareness, safety and greater efficiency during foraging. Within a 'polyspecific band', there may be segregation of each species. Gautier and Gautier-Hion (1969) cite an example where *Cercopithecus mona* monkeys headed the polyspecific band as it moved through the forest, and they were followed by *C. nictitans* and *C. cephus*. When the band stopped to feed, the monkeys were randomly dispersed and there was no segregation of the species. These bands varied in composition during the day: monospecific bands were more frequent in the morning, and polyspecific bands occurred more frequently in the evening.

5.10   Numbers and biomass of forest mammals

The resources of food, water and shelter in tropical rain forests appear to be comparatively stable throughout the year. The abundance of flowers, fruits and insects fluctuates from month to month (Fig. 5.11) but these resources may not be limiting at any time. Rainfall is sufficiently high and constant that water, in some form, is always available. These conditions are in marked contrast to the resources in dry savanna and arid zones (Chapter 6 and 7).

It is likely that the relative stability of resources is reflected in the relative stability of population numbers and biomass, and in the ratio between the number of organisms in different trophic levels. This is illustrated by the population numbers of one group of rain forest mammals (Fig. 12.13) which compares the numbers of small terrestrial rodents in a tropical rain forest in Nigeria (Happold 1977) with the numbers of rodents in a temperate English woodland (Southern 1970) over an equivalent length of time. There is little other information on populations of rain forest mammals. However, the very limited evidence suggests that populations of some rain forest mammals do not

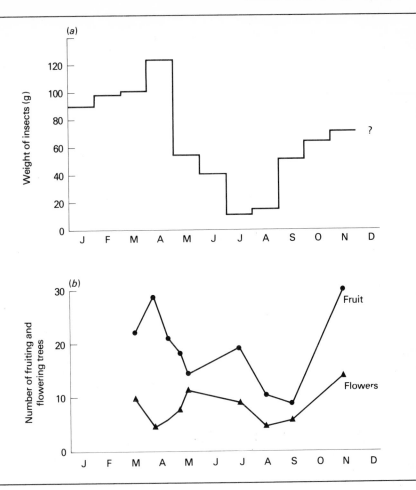

Fig. 5.11 Seasonal availability of insects, fruits and flowers in the rain forest at Makokou. (*a*) The monthly weight of insects caught in an ultra-violet light trap. (*b*) The numbers of fruiting and flowering trees on a 3 km transect line through the forest. (After Charles-Dominique 1971.)

fluctuate as greatly as those in less stable habitats. The relative stability may be due partly to the constancy of the environment, and partly to the larger number of species in the community.

Biomass is a measure of productivity of the habitat. On this basis, rain forest (with its high primary production) might be expected to have a high biomass of mammals compared with other habitats in tropical Africa. There appears to be no accurate measurements of the total biomass of mammals in rain forest. This is largely because it is difficult to evaluate the biomass of the largest mammals such as bush pigs, several species of primates, elephants and buffalos which spend only a small part of their time in a small sampled area. The few measurements that are available for selected animals suggest that the biomass of mammals in rain forest is considerably less than in the savannas (Table 11.14) despite the luxuriant vegetation and high primary production of the rain forest. For example, Collins (in Bourlière 1963*b*) recorded a biomass of only 5 kg km^{-2} for duikers in the forests of Ghana, and Happold (1977) has calculated that the small terrestrial rodents in a Nigerian rain forest (excluding squirrels, pouched rats and brush-tailed porcupines) is about 71 kg km^{-2}. The biomass of African rain forest mammals probably remains relatively stable with only minor fluctuations throughout the year, especially when compared with savanna and arid zone habitats.

5.11 Zoogeography

There are many patterns of distribution of mammals in the rain forest zone. For example, the ranges of five species of *Cercocebus* monkeys do not overlap except in parts of the 'Gaboon' and 'Central African' forest blocks (Fig. 5.12). Similarly, three of

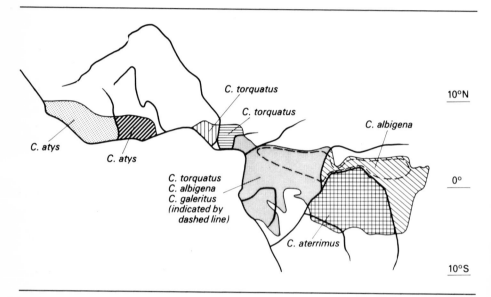

Fig. 5.12 The distribution of *Cercocebus atys*, *C. torquatus*, *C. albigena*, *C. aterrimus* and *C. galeritus* in the lowland rain forest zone. Subspecies are not shown. (Data from Booth 1956, Dorst and Dandelot 1970, Gartlan and Struhsaker 1972, Happold 1973*b*, Sabater Pi and Jones 1967; nomenclature follows Napier and Napier 1967.)

the four species of *Colobus* monkeys in the rain forest have non-overlapping ranges, and in the northern part of the 'Gaboon' forests, *Colobus satanus* overlaps with *Colobus guereza occidentalis* (Fig. 5.13). The eleven species of *Cephalophus* duikers show different patterns of distribution. The widespread *C. sylvicultor* occurs in all forest blocks; others occur in several, but not all, forest blocks; and *C. jentinki* and *C. zebra* are found only in the 'Liberian' forest block (Fig. 5.14). Similar sorts of patterns are found at the subspecies level, and it appears that quite small topographical barriers can result in subspecific differences. This is illustrated by the subspecies of *Cercocebus atys*, *Colobus* spp. (Fig. 5.13) and by *Helioscyurus rufobrachium* (Fig. 5.15).

The results of these different patterns is that the mammals of each forest block are made up of three components:

1. Widespread species which are found throughout the forest zone; e.g. elephant (*Loxodonta africana*), pouched rat (*Cricetomys gambianus*), and bushbuck (*Tragelaphus scriptus*).

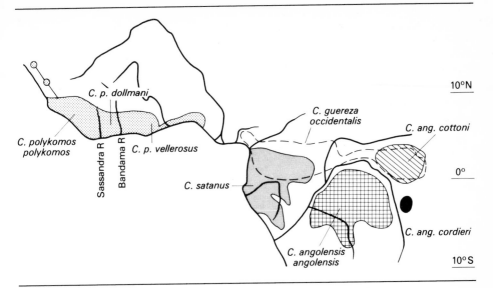

Fig. 5.13 The distribution of *Colobus polykomos, C. angolensis, C. guereza* and *C. satanus* and their subspecies in the lowland rain forest zone. (Data from Dorst and Dandelot 1970, Gartlan and Struhsaker 1972, and Rahm 1972*a, b, c*.)

2. Species which occur in several, but not all, forest blocks; e.g. black duiker (*Cephalophus niger*), bay duiker (*C. dorsalis*), golden cat (*Felis auratus*), several species of monkeys and rodents, and the pygmy hippopotamus (*Choeropsis liberiensis*).
3. Species which are restricted to one forest block, e.g. Jentink's duiker (*Cephalophus jentinki*) and zebra duiker (*C. zebra*).

Some forest blocks such as 'Gaboon' are rich in species, but others such as 'Western Nigeria' have relatively few species.

Relic patches of rain forest occur in the forest–savanna zone (or derived savanna) bordering the rain forest zone. These are either riverine forests or isolated forest patches which have survived due to special edaphic or climatic reasons or because of lack of human interference. Their presence indicates the probable extent of the rain forest zone in former pluvial times (see Ch. 2). Riverine forests are often in continuity with the rain forest zone, but isolated forest patches are normally completely surrounded by savanna. Relic forests need to be large enough to provide a typical forest climate, enough variation in plant species, and stability to prevent gradual encroachment of the savanna. Forest relics contain fewer mammal species than in the rain forest zone, and these are only the most adaptable forest species. For example, in the relic forests of western Nigeria are the rodents *Praomys tullbergi* and *Lophuromys sikapusi* (Happold 1975) and the monkeys *Cercopithecus mona* and *Cercocebus torquatus*; this is an impoverished fauna compared with that of the extensive rain forests to the south (Fig. 5.16).

The abundance of mammalian species (and species of other animals) reflects the extent to which speciation has occurred. A new species evolves allopatrically 'if a population which has become geographically isolated from its parental species acquires, during the period of isolation, characters which promote or guarantee reproductive isolation when external barriers break down' (Mayr 1942). It is most

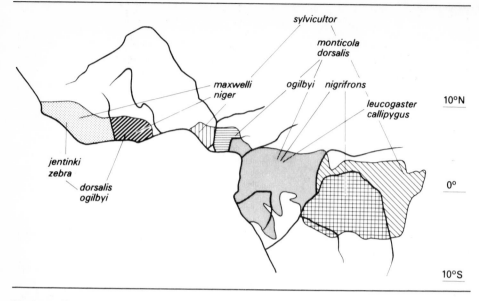

Fig. 5.14   The distribution of *Cephalophus* duikers in the rain forest zone. (Data from Dorst and Dandelot 1970, Happold 1973, Rahm 1966, 1972*a, b, c*.)

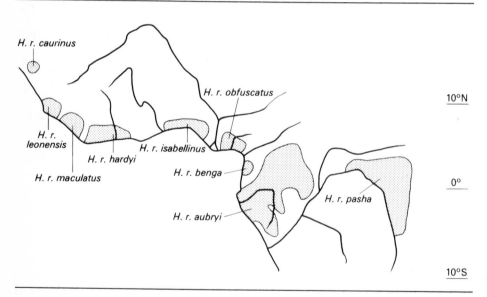

Fig. 5.15   The distribution of the subspecies of the squirrel *Heliosciurus rufobrachium* in the lowland rain forest zone (Modified from Rahm 1972*a, b, c*).

likely that populations of some species have been isolated from other populations during the past because of the changes that have occurred in the extent and distribution of the rain forest. It is generally agreed that the African rain forest expanded during the pluvial periods to form a much greater area of forest with continuity between the forest

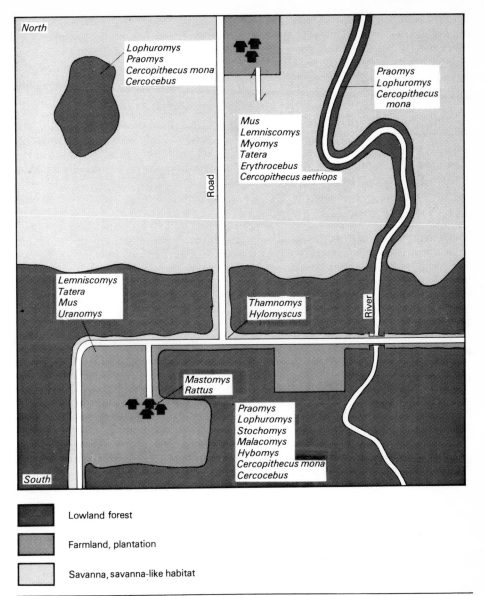

North

Lophuromys
Praomys
Cercopithecus mona
Cercocebus

Praomys
Lophuromys
Cercopithecus
mona

Mus
Lemniscomys
Myomys
Tatera
Erythrocebus
Cercopithecus aethiops

Road

Lemniscomys
Tatera
Mus
Uranomys

Thamnomys
Hylomyscus

River

Mastomys
Rattus

Praomys
Lophuromys
Stochomys
Malacomys
Hybomys
Cercopithecus mona
Cercocebus

South

Lowland forest

Farmland, plantation

Savanna, savanna-like habitat

Fig. 5.16   The ecological distribution of some murid rodents and primates in the rain forest, forest relics, savanna and farmland of western Nigeria. Some forest species occur in the riverine forest and relic forests of the savanna, and some savanna species have moved into savanna-like clearings and farmlands in the forest. There is an interchange of species between savanna farmlands and savanna grasslands. (Happold, unpubl.)

blocks; and that during the dry periods the rain forest was confined to a few isolated areas termed refugia (Moreau 1952). The subsequent dispersal of forest mammals from these refugia depended on the new limits of the forest and whether there were topographical features to prevent further dispersal. For West Africa, Booth (1958) has suggested that there were three refugia on the southernmost land tips of the West African coast (Fig. 5.1). The present distribution of forest mammals may be correlated with the past distribution of the rain forest, the ability of each species to disperse and the importance of different topographical features (rivers, mountains, savanna gaps in the forest) as barriers to dispersal. Each species dispersed to a different extent, and therefore the mammalian fauna of each forest block is related to its position relative to the former refugia and the ability of each species to disperse and overcome any potential barriers to dispersal.

The importance of sympatric speciation (speciation without geographical isolation) in rain forest is uncertain. However, it seems possible that isolation by vertical strata could have assisted in reproductive isolation. The most likely course of events is that the diversity of mammal species in the rain forest may have been achieved mostly by allopatric speciation during dry periods and subsequently reinforced by physical separation within each vertical stratum.

5.12   Tolerance of environmental change

Most rain forest mammals are unable to tolerate any alteration in the forest environment. When a forest is modified in any way, there is a change in the abundance and composition of the mammal fauna. Small environmental changes occur naturally in the forest all the time, as when a tree falls. This temporarily alters the environment; some species disappear and others, more suited to the new environment, replace them. In time, the original conditions are restored and the original mammal species return. This pattern of events is an indication of the narrowness of the niches of most forest mammals, and is one reason why there are so many mammal species. Any alteration or removal of niches results in the disappearance of the species that occupied such niches.

In recent years, there have been many man-made changes in the rain forest zone. Much of this zone is no longer forest because of clearing and felling, and the former forest has been replaced by farmland and plantations of cocoa, rubber, oil palm, teak and other exotic trees. Selected felling of commercially valuable indigenous trees has altered the structure and composition of many forests, rather similar to the effects of natural tree falls but on a much larger scale. The majority of forest mammal species, particularly the larger ones, are not able to live in these altered and disturbed habitats, and therefore many of them have become locally extinct and their geographic ranges are now limited to where there is undisturbed rain forest. Forest mammals, and indeed all forest animals, which are unable to adapt to any other habitat, will become more rare as forest clearance increases. Some species can withstand a small degree of change provided their particular niche remains unchanged; for example, tree hyraxes and flying squirrels can live in cocoa plantations where some of the tall forest trees have been left to give shade to the cocoa.

As the forest has been replaced by farms, grasslands and plantations, some savanna species have penetrated into the forest zone. Typical savanna rodents including *Thryonomys swinderianus*, *Arvicanthis niloticus*, *Lemniscomys striatus*, *Uranomys ruddi*, *Tatera valida* and *Mus minutoides* may be found in suitable habitats in the forest zone. These small species have probably moved into the 'savanna-like' habitats bordering roads, and then into adjacent farms and grasslands (Fig. 5.16). Commensal species such as *Rattus rattus* and *Praomys* (*Mastomys*) *natalensis*, are associated with human habitations in the forest zone. Plantations of exotic trees may contain some forest mammals, but the composition of the mammal fauna is usually very different to that of the undisturbed forest. Cocoa plantations in Nigeria, where some forest trees still remain, have a varied small mammal fauna (Everard 1966), but few mammals (if any) inhabit teak plantations. Some species of small mammals can live in oil palm plantations.

In eastern Zaire, Rahm (1967) found that some murid rodents' have successfully exploited the new habitats in the forest zone. Species inhabiting farmlands in the forest zone include the common forest species *Praomys* and *Lophuromys*, and *Oenomys*, *Lemniscomys* and *Mus* (which are normally associated with farms and grasslands and not with forest) are common. Some forest species, for example *Malacomys*, *Colomys*, *Deomys* and practically all the larger forest mammals, are unable to survive in destroyed forest lands.

Chapter 6

Savannas

Large areas of Africa south of the Sahara are covered by grasslands and woodlands which in many places support large multi-specific herds of ungulates and other large mammals. These and other similar types of vegetation are well known to the casual observer and have frequently been referred to as savanna. However, the term 'savanna' has defied uniform and consistent definition by different authorities. This has largely been due to uncertainty as to the range of plant communities that should be included within this common name. It is important to be clear how this term is used in the account that follows and for the reader to be aware of the vegetational types which are included by the authors under the general heading of savanna. We recognise it as encompassing virtually all types of grassland, bush, scrub and woodland including the extensions of these vegetation types into semi-arid areas. The savanna thus forms a natural association of related vegetation types having considerable similarities and overlaps of their faunas. With this composition the savanna corresponds closely to Lind and Morrison's (1974) rangelands. It is however more embracing than that adopted in Keay's (1959) widely used vegetation classification of Africa. This author distinguish between savanna, steppe, semi-arid bush, scrub and grassland, all of which are incorporated under the one heading here. The areas covered by tropical savanna are shown in Fig. 6.1, and to these have been added Keay's (1959) vegetation patterns. Savanna covers a larger area than any of the other biotopes.

The northern savanna is located north of the rain forest in west Africa and extends in a broad belt from Senegal to Sudan and then further eastwards into Somalia through an extensive area of low rainfall woodlands and steppe in northern Kenya and southern Ethiopia. The northern sector of this savanna is in the Sahelian zone and ultimately merges with the arid desert of the Sahara. Between the savanna and lowland forest is a region where the vegetation is either forest or savanna depending on local differences in topography, soil, climate and past history. The ecology of mammals in this mixed habitat has been considered previously (p. 104).

The southern savanna has its northern limits in Uganda and Kenya. It then extends in a broad south-westerly and southern sweep to South Africa. To the north-west, this great expanse is bounded by forest–savanna mosaic and in the south-west by the Kalahari Desert and its associated arid and semi-arid conditions.

6.1 Climate and vegetation

The equatorial rain forest receives and is dependent on a high annual precipitation dispersed evenly throughout the year. Moving north or south from the forest, rainfall becomes progressively less with vegetation changing accordingly. In West Africa there is a sequence of forest, forest savanna mosaic, wooded savanna, Sahelian savanna and finally desert from south to north which is related to a gradual decline in the annual

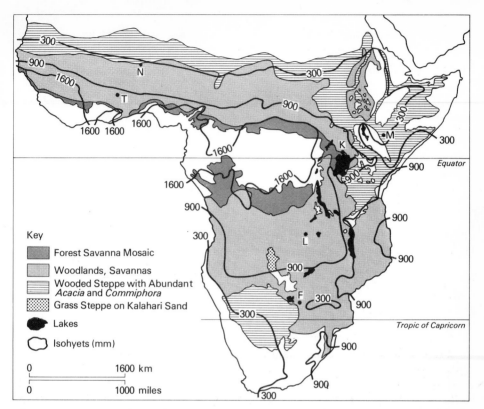

Fig. 6.1 Map showing the four major savanna vegetation types recognised by Keay (1959), viz.; (i) Forest savanna mosaic, (ii) Woodlands, savannas, (iii) Wooded steppe and (iv) Grass.

In this account most situations having an average annual rainfall of between 300 mm and 1 600 mm within these vegetation types are regarded as savanna. The main exceptions occur in the forest savanna mosaic around the 1 600 mm isohyet where local conditions determine whether woodland, grassland or forest are present. Around the 300 mm isohyet there is a gradual transition into semi-arid and arid conditions. The 900 mm isohyet broadly separates the moist from the dry savannas although transitions as in the arid areas are gradual and not abrupt. F, Francistown; K, Kampala; L, Lubumbashi; M, Moyale; N, Niamey; T, Tamale (see Fig. 6.2).

rainfall. As annual rainfall declines there is a reduction in the length of the wet season, and an increase in the dry season. Similar changes prevail in the savanna south of the lowland forest where the main difference in the rainfall regime is the period of its occurrence. North of the equator the wet season extends from approximately April to September and south of the equator from approximately November to March (Fig. 6.2). Parts of East Africa provide an exception to this pattern, having two annual wet and dry seasons. This unusual and locally very variable pattern is attributed to a variety of factors including oceanic influences, complex air currents and the presence of large lakes.

There are broad changes in savanna vegetation over large geographical areas and also variations on a more local scale. Altitude, edaphic factors, slope and water table level can, together with other influences, account for vegetation differences in very small areas as for example where areas of woodland and grassland are in juxtaposition. The savanna vegetation is frequently a complex mosaic and often provides a variety of conditions for animal life within quite small areas.

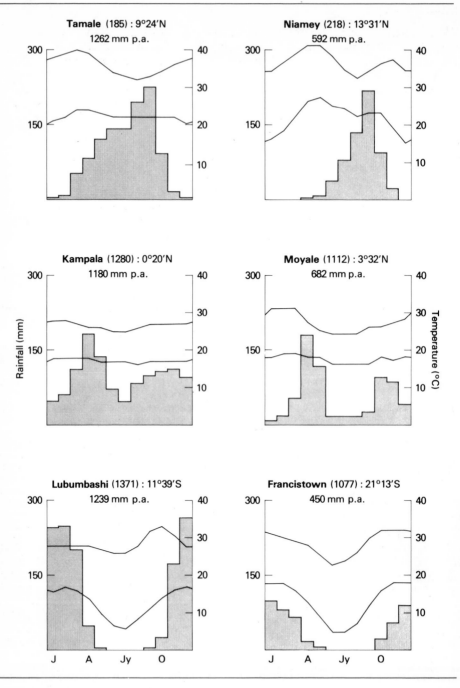

Fig. 6.2 Monthly mean rainfall (histograms) and minimum and maximum temperatures. Moist and dry localities have been selected from northern (Tamale and Niamey), East African (Kampala and Moyale) and southern (Lubumbashi and Francistown) savannas. Their locations are shown in Figure 6.1. Latitude, height above sea level (m) and average annual rainfall (mm) are given for each locality.

Moist savanna

The woodland savannas which cover much of the northern and southern areas have an annual rainfall of more than 900 mm (35 in) (Fig. 6.1). In the north it is frequently referred to as Guinea savanna. Here there is a gradual transition from a woodland dominated by *Lophira, Daniellia, Afzelia* and *Terminalia* in the south to one of *Isoberlinia, Monota* and *Uapaca* in the north. The latter attains heights of 10 m to 16 m with either the crowns almost touching or the trees more widely dispersed. The woodlands can thus be open or quite dense. *Isoberlinia* woodland is usually less dense than the southern Guinea woodlands where the growing season is longer. Both types of vegetation are accompanied by a variable grass cover.

In southern Africa *Brachystegia* and *Julbernardia* are dominant in much of the woodland. These are commonly referred to as 'miombo' woodlands, obtaining this name from a vernacular word for *Brachystegia*. The vegetation covers much of Tanzania, Zambia, Mozambique and Angola. These trees usually have slender trunks, much-branched crowns and leaves made up of numerous small leaflets. Like *Isoberlinia* they can also form dense woodland. The commonest grass in the miombo woodland is *Hyparrhenia filipendula*.

The forest–savanna mosaic or derived savanna has arisen as a result of felling, farming and burning of the climax forest community. Invasion by grasses follows and as a result of continuous suppression of the forest trees a savanna develops. This vegetation typically consists of a mixture of forest remnants, incoming savanna trees and a grass layer which in East Africa is often dominated by *Pennisetum*. In parts of west Africa the commonest entrant tree species are *Lophira, Butyrospermum, Burkea, Daniellia* and *Pterocarpus*. These are accompanied by forest remnants such as *Triplochiton, Terminalia* and *Chlorophora* (Hopkins 1965).

Fire is a regular feature of savanna during the dry season and burning of the dried grass results in a charred and blackened landscape. Fires travelling against the wind are slow and those carried by a following wind are fast. The former generate considerable heat at ground level as a result of more gradual progression and frequently kill many seeds and grass roots. The latter move rapidly across the surface and are relatively more destructive *above* ground level than slow burns. As a result they frequently scorch and burn young trees but are less effective in burning the bases of grasses and seeds. At the end of the dry season much of the herbaceous vegetation is dead. This makes it particularly vulnerable to fire and causes greater damage to the vegetation than burns early in the dry season when the moisture content of plants is higher. Frequently, grasses put on a new burst of growth immediately after the fire and prior to the onset of the rains. Trees in the woodlands show varying degrees of fire resistance. Over much of the moist savanna the combination of fire and heavy grazing by domestic or wild stock prevents re-growth of trees and shrubs and produces a derived grassland. These may be dominated by grasses such as *Hyparrhenia* and *Themeda* although many other species are frequently present. The uniformity of this grassland may be broken up by the growth of shrubs or trees on disused termite mounds. For example, in Rwenzori Park, Uganda, the shrubs *Capparis* and *Grewia* and the tree *Euphorbia candelabrum* are often found in such situations while in west Africa *Terminalia* is very characteristic of this situation.

The areas covered by grassland burns have been recorded in six dry seasons from July 1970 to July 1973 in Rwenzori Park (Eltringham, 1976). The most extensive burns occurred in January 1971, when they covered 32·7 per cent of the surface; only 1 per cent was burnt in the following dry season. These were the highest and lowest figures for the period of observation. There was a gradual increase in the area burnt at each dry

a

b

c

Fig. 6.3 (*a*) Northern Guinea savanna (Nigeria) in the dry season. Note small stature of trees which are sufficiently numerous to form an open woodland. The grasses and herbs are thinly dispersed and at this time of year provide little cover. (Photo: D. C. D. Happold.) (*b*) Grass and bush (*Capparis*) savanna in Rwenzori Park, western Uganda. This vegetation supports several species of large mammals (see text). (Photo: Ugandan Department of Information.) (*c*) Eland in dry, *Acacia tortilis* woodland in Kenya. Evergreen with browse are in middle foreground. (Photo: M. J. Coe.)

season from July 1971 to July 1973, when 29·7 per cent of the area caught fire. It was estimated that during the three years 55 per cent of the Park was burnt on at least one occasion.

Dry savanna

Where the annual rainfall falls below 900 mm conditions become more arid and the vegetation adapts accordingly. The dry woodlands and wooded steppe are found in areas with a mean annual rainfall of between 300 and 900 mm (Fig. 6.1). They spread across Africa from Senegal to Somalia, then through eastern Kenya and central Tanzania and reappear in Botswana and South West Africa and on a more limited scale in some of the hotter and drier river valleys of Rhodesia and Zambia. In the Sahelian zone of Senegal, open woodland supports a variety of trees including *Acacia*, *Adansonia*, *Balanites*, *Boscia*, *Commiphora* and *Grewia* which are accompanied by a variety of herbs and grasses, the latter including *Chloris*, *Zornia*, *Echinochloa*, *Eragrostis* and *Panicum*. The vegetation here can be very sparse with the ground cover varying considerably from one season to another and also from year to year in response to differing annual rainfall. In eastern Kenya and Tanzania there occurs a bushland of low woody shrubs (of which *Commiphora* is the most important) and small trees, particularly acacias. These are frequently deciduous and many are thorny or succulent. Such localities are sometimes referred to as thorn-scrub. Other trees include *Balanites*, *Lannea* and the baobab (*Adansonia*), which is one of the few really large trees occurring in this vegetation. *Acacia–Themeda* woodland occurs in considerable areas of the Kenya highlands where the rainfall is 500 to 750 mm per annum. This fairly open dry grass woodland is frequently used for ranching and is very vulnerable to the effects of heavy grazing which may encourage the growth of shrubs due to the absence of fire.

In Botswana the Kalahari Desert with an annual rainfall of 200 to 450 mm supports arid and dry savanna vegetation. Continuity with the more northerly savanna is achieved as a result of a gradual increase in rainfall to the northeast of the country. Here, where annual precipitation reaches 700 mm, the vegetation consists of various associations of woodland and scrub. As in similar situations elsewhere in Africa *Terminalia*, *Acacia*, *Combretum*, *Grewia* and *Adansonia* are important members of the plant community. The presence and importance of grass species such as *Cymbopogon*, *Sporobolus*, *Aristida*, *Eragrostis*, *Cynodon* and *Digitaria* indicates much in common with situations further north.

An important climatic feature of dry savanna (and arid regions, Ch. 7) having an average rainfall of less than 600 mm is the considerable variability in the amount of rain falling from year to year. This is well illustrated for St-Louis in Senegal (Bille 1974) (Fig. 6.4) where annual rainfall has ranged from 144 to 691 mm

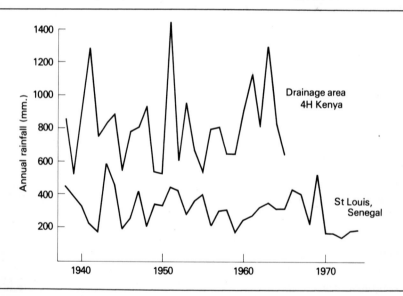

Fig. 6.4   Annual rainfall figures for St-Louis, Senegal and eastern Kenya.

during the last 100 years. The average is about 375 mm, but this figure has relatively little significance in view of the wide range around this average. Similar data were obtained from eastern Kenya and western Uganda. In both these localities Laws (1969*a*) obtained figures for large drainage areas which are, in fact, of more ecological value than single-station readings as they represent a far wider geographical area. Like the Sahelian readings they displayed very considerable fluctuations, although there was the greater fluctuation in the lower rainfall situation of eastern

Kenya (Fig. 6.4). Furthermore, the Sahelian minimum figure of 144 mm, is very substantially less than the Kenyan one of about 550 mm.

Rainfall influences the structure and productivity of the grasslands. In the Sahelian area, the availability of ground water to plants is very important. This depends on the total amount of rain falling as well as the time at which it falls. Thus widely interspersed heavy showers could be much less productive than the same amount of rain falling steadily over a more limited period. Rainfall can also affect the time when trees come into leaf, the quantity of leaves produced and the production of seeds and fruits (Fig. 6.5) (Poupon and Bille 1974). In years of exceptionally low rainfall grass seeds may not

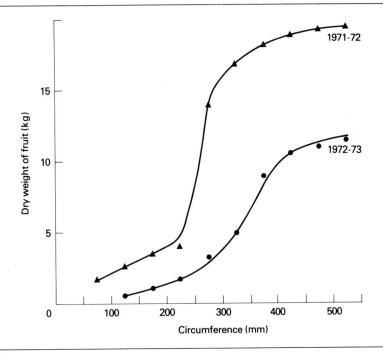

Fig. 6.5 Production of fruit in *Boscia senegalensis* in relation to circumference of the trunk in years of average (1971–2) and poor (1972–3) rainfall (After Poupon and Bille 1974).

germinate and the production of further seeds is negligible. Germination and growth take place in the year following if sufficient rain falls. Enough seeds will survive over almost two years to provide a good grass cover (Bille and Poupon 1974). These savannas of low and erratic rainfall pose unique and at times severe problems to their mammal inhabitants, and by virtue of these phenomena markedly differ from the higher rainfall savannas.

6.2   Mammals of selected savanna localities

A broad picture of the types of mammals inhabiting savanna can be obtained by the examination of the list of species known to live in one well-studied area. This does not mean that all savannas support similar faunas but rather that the range of forms in different localities have underlying similarities. These broad faunal characteristics can be seen in the savanna of Rwenzori Park, Uganda. Here, in this mixture of grass and woodland, the mean annual rainfall ranges in different parts of the park between 800 and 1 200 mm. This long narrow park is bounded to the west by Lake Amin (formerly Edward) and is transected by a belt of semi-deciduous medium altitude forest. The species list (Table 6.1) excludes those animals found only in forest. It may not be

Table 6.1 *Mammals living in the savanna of Rwenzori Park, Uganda.*

Insectivora
Crocidura bicolor
C. cyanea
C. flavescens
C. gracilipes
C. jacksoni
C. turba
Sylvisorex megalura

Chiroptera

Eidolon helvum	Straw-coloured fruit bat
Rousettus aegypriacus	Egyptian fruit bat
Epomophorus wahlbergi	Wahlberg's epauletted fruit bat
Epomops franqueti	Franquet's fruit bat
Hypsignathus monstrosus	Hammer-headed fruit bat
Taphozous mauritianus	Mauritian tomb bat
Nycteris hispida	Hairy slit-faced bat
Lavia frons	Yellow-winged bat
Rhinolophus landeri	Lander's horse-shoe bat
Hipposideros caffer	Sundevall's African leaf-nosed bat
Pipistrellus nanus	Banana bat
Scotophilus nigrita	Yellow house bat
Tadarida condylura	Angola free-tailed bat
T. pumila	Little free-tailed bat

Primates

Cercopithecus pygerythrus	Vervet
Papio anubis	Olive baboon

Pholidota

Manis gigantea	Giant pangolin

Tubulidentata

Orycteropus afer	Aardvark

Carnivora

Canis adustus	Side-striped jackal
Ictonyx striatus	Zorilla
Poecilogale albinucha	White-naped weasel
Mellivora capensis	Ratel
Lutra maculicollis	Spotted-necked otter
Viverra civetta	African civet
Genetta tigrina	Large-spotted genet
Atilax paludinosus	Marsh mongoose
Herpestes ichneumon	Egyptian mongoose
Herpestes sanguineus	Black-tipped mongoose
Ichneumia albicauda	White-tailed mongoose
Mungos mungo	Banded mongoose
Crocuta crocuta	Spotted hyena
Felis libyca	Wild cat
Felis serval	Serval
Panthera leo	Lion
Panthera pardus	Leopard

Table 6.1 – *continued*

Proboscidea

    Loxodonta africana ————————— Elephant

Artiodactyla

Hippopotamus amphibius —————	Hippopotamus
Phacochoerus aethiopicus —————	Warthog
Potamochoerus porcus ——————	Bush-pig
Hylochoerus meinertzhageni ————	Giant forest-hog
Tragelaphus spekei———————	Sitatunga
T. scriptus —————————	Bushbuck
Kobus ellipsiprymnus ——————	Waterbuck
Kobus kob —————————	Kob
Redunca redunca ———————	Bohor reedbuck
Damaliscus lunatus———————	Topi
Sylvicapra grimmia ——————	Common duiker
Syncerus caffer ———————	Buffalo

Lagomorpha

    Lepus crawshayi———————————— Crawshay's Hare

Rodentia

Tatera valida ————————	Bocage's Gerbil
Dendromus melanotis—————————	Tree mouse
Otomys irroratus ———————	Laminate-toothed rat
Thamnomys dolichurus —————	Tree rat
Mylomys dybowskyi———————	Three-toed grass-rat
Arvicanthis niloticus ——————	Unstriped grass-mouse or Nile rat
Lemniscomys striatus ——————	Punctated grass-mouse
L. macculus	
Aethomys kaiseri ——————	Bush rat
Praomys natalensis ——————	Multimammate rat
Zelotomys hildegardeae—————————	Broad-headed mouse
Mustriton ———————————	Pygmy mouse
Mus minutoides ———————	Pygmy mouse
Lophuromys sikapusi———————	Harsh-furred mouse
Graphiurus murinus ——————	Dormouse
Thryonomys gregorianus ————	Lesser cane-rat
Hystrix sp. —————————	Porcupine
Cricetomys gambianus —————	Giant pouched rat

exhaustive although it contains a reasonably balanced representation of the species inhabiting the Park and the omissions, if any, are probably rarities.

Such a list takes no account of the ecological requirements, size, abundance or habits of the animals, nor does it show the ecological role of each species. Even a preliminary glance shows some ecological separation with species such as the spotted-necked otter, hippopotamus and sitatunga, having adaptations to aquatic situations. Of further interest is the extent to which different groups are represented. The order Artiodactyla has several species, while in contrast the Primates, many of which are arboreal, are not so numerous. There is a rich variety of insectivores, bats, carnivores and rodents. Some of the smaller groups such as Lagomorpha and (not represented in Rwenzori Park) Perissodactyla are almost exclusively savanna dwelling.

The drier savanna in the vicinity of Fété Olé, Senegal, has an average annual rainfall of between 350 and 400 mm. On the slightly more elevated ground the sandy soils support a thin grass layer with a scattering of trees and shrubs while in the depressions which are less well drained there are patches of thick scrub. Poulet (1972) recorded 34 species (Table 6.2) in an area of 100 km^2. This is less than half the number recorded in

Table 6.2 *Mammals living in the Sahelian savanna near Fété-Olé, Senegal.*

Insectivora
  Crocidura sericea
  C. lusitania
  C. lamottei
  Erinaceus albiventris

Chiroptera
  Rousettus aegyptiacus ————————— Egyptian fruit bat
  Taphozous perforatus————————— Egyptian tomb bat
  Nycteris thebaica ————————— Egyptian slit-faced bat
  Asellia tridens————————— Trident leaf-nosed bat
  Tadarida major ————————— Lappet-eared free-tailed bat

Primates
  Cercopithecus patas ————————— Patas

Tubulidentata
  Orycteropus afer ————————— Aardvark

Carnivora
  Canis aureus ————————— Common jackal
  Canis adustus————————— Side-striped jackal
  Vulpes pallida————————— Pale fox
  Ictonyx striatus ————————— Zorilla

Artiodactyla
  Phacochoerus aethiopicus ————————— Warthog
  Gazella rufifrons————————— Red-fronted gazelle
  G. dorcas————————— Dorcas gazelle
  G. dama ————————— Dama gazelle

Lagomorpha
  Lepus crawshayi————————— Crawshay's Hare

Rodentia
  Heliosciurus gambianus ————————— Gambian sun squirrel
  Xerus erythropus ————————— Geoffroy's ground squirrel
  Praomys natalensis ————————— Multimammate rat
  Arvicanthis niloticus ————————— Nile rat or unstriped grass-mouse
  Taterillus pygargus
  Taterillus gracilis ————————— Slender gerbil
  Desmodilliscus braueri ————————— Brauer's dwarf gerbil
  Hystrix cristata ————————— Crested porcupine

Rwenzori, even though only two orders are totally absent (Proboscidea and Pholidota) at Fété Olé compared with Rwenzori. This reduction in faunal variety must be related to the more arid conditions producing a less rich and diverse vegetation and the over-exploitation of the area by man through intensive grazing of domestic stock. It is interesting that the two areas have a number of species in common, e.g. rousette fruit bat, side-striped jackal, aardvark, nile rat and warthog. In addition to these ubiquitous species there are also species such as gerbils, sand fox and dorcas gazelle which suggests affinities with the desert fauna. Mongooses are absent and ungulates poorly represented. The scarcity of ungulates reflects the poor supply of graze and browse throughout the year and indicates the proximity of this area to arid conditions.

Savanna vegetation does not contain the above ground diversity and vertical stratification of rain forest and in consequence offers the mammals a less varied situation to exploit. On the other hand its more open structure results in considerably greater production of ground vegetation in the form of grasses, herbs and shrubs. This has been a major factor in the evolution of the many ungulate species that characterise this vegetation. As well as showing considerable faunal diversity the ungulates can also be numerically abundant although the actual species present can vary from one locality to another. Thus in the dry savanna of Nairobi Park, wildebeest, Coke's hartebeest, Thomson's gazelle, Burchell's zebra, Grant's gazelle and impala are present but all absent from Rwenzori. In Kafue Park, Zambia, there are greater kudu, sable and roan antelope all of which are absent from the other two Parks. The size and uniformity of the ungulate fauna of five geographically separate areas of savanna from Zambia to Cameroun is clearly illustrated by the comparison in Table 6.3. Out of a total of 41

Table 6.3   *Number of ungulate species in various national parks.*

Park	Total no. of species	Species in common				
		Kafue	Serengeti	Rwenzori	Garamba	Bénoué
Kafue, Zambia	21	—	13	7	9	8
Serengeti, Tanzania	27	13	—	9	12	13
Rwenzori, Uganda	12	7	9	—	11	10
Garamba, Zaire	18	9	12	11	—	15
Bénoué, Cameroun	16	8	13	10	15	—

species the number in any one savanna area ranged from 12 to 27 with only 5 species (warthog, bushpig, hippopotamus, bushbuck and buffalo) common to all five places. There are varying degrees of difference. The species in Rwenzori are, with the exception of Kafue, well represented elsewhere. In contrast, less than half the species recorded from Serengeti occur in any one other area.

6.3   The large herbivores

Food and ecological separation

There are 13 species of large herbivores in the savanna of Rwenzori Park (Table 6.4). These range in size from the elephant weighing up to 5500 kg to the small common duiker of 10 to 15 kg. The inclusion of the duiker among the large herbivores may seem surprising but it is of a different order of size to most herbivorous rodents which are appreciably smaller and are normally considered to be small. Differences in size facilitate the exploitation of the habitat in various ways. Obviously, large browsers can utilise vegetation at higher levels than small ones. However, differences can be more subtle than this. Some smaller animals such as the common duiker can and will more readily penetrate into bushes, whereas most larger species will feed from their periphery. There can also be differences in food selection, with the smaller species better able to obtain discrete small items such as fruits, seeds and flowers. Some species have quite unique food sources or feeding habits which display little in common with other species. Thus the bushpig is an omnivorous digger feeding and living in thick bush and obtaining much of its food from the substratum; the sitatunga browses on semi-aquatic vegetation and the giant forest-hog is a grazer commonly found at forest edges.

However, more careful analysis is required to establish the precise feeding habits of other species and recognise the extent of separation and overlap between them. Field (1971, 1972) has made a detailed study of feeding in the short-grass/thicket areas of

Table 6.4   *Feeding habits of the larger herbivores in Rwenzori Park, Uganda.*

	Species	Food and feeding habit	Notes
Very large	Elephant	Grazer and browser	
Large	Hippopotamus	Grazer; short grasses	Near watercourses
	Buffalo	Grazer; short grasses/medium height pyrophilous grasses	
Medium	Kob	Grazer; medium height pyrophilous grasses	
	Topi	Grazer; medium height pyrophilous grasses	Southern sector of Park only
	Warthog	Grazer; short grasses	
	Waterbuck	Grazer; short grasses/medium height pyrophilous grasses	
	Bushpig	Omnivorous; roots and bulbs most important	Thick bush, much food obtained by digging.
	Giant forest hog	Grazer; grasses and herbaceous plants	Mainly forest edge
	Sitatunga	Browser; leaves, twigs and fruit	Semi-aquatic vegetation
	Bushbuck	Browser; leaves and shoots of bushes, grasses to a much lesser extent	
Small	Bohor reedbuck	Grazer; grasses	
	Common duiker	Browser; leaves, twigs, bark, young shoots, fruit, seeds	

Rwenzori Park where the most common grasses are *Sporobolus* and *Microchloa*. Other grass species are also present as well as many legumes, other herbs and *Capparis* bush. As far as the grazers are concerned the grasses are particularly important as a food source. There are clear seasonal differences in the diet of elephants which take less browse in the wetter months than the drier months. Over the whole period of the study from August to May elephants were observed eating grasses, sedges and herbs 79·4 per cent of the time and browse 20·6 per cent. The inflorences, fruits and stems of plants were all consumed in addition to the leaves.

In the same area, the stomach contents of six common sympatric species of grazers (buffalo, kob, warthog, waterbuck, topi and hippopotamus) were examined. These were then compared to the abundance of plant species in the areas from which they had been collected. Detailed analysis through the wet and dry seasons enabled Field (1972) to draw some important conclusions regarding the feeding ecology of these animals. This information is summarised in Fig. 6.6 where it can be seen that diets usually vary from one season to the next. It also appears that separation is very fine and that appreciable overlap exists. This may be an artefact of presenting the information in this rather condensed and simplified form. For example, in the wet season waterbuck and buffalo are shown as having similar diets. Detailed examination of the food they consumed showed that the commonest grasses in waterbuck, in order of abundance, were *Themeda*, *Sporobolus* and *Heteropogon*, and in buffalo were *Themeda*, *Chloris* and *Hyparrhenia*. Small differences such as these are probably of considerable importance and quite commonplace among the six closely related species. Field (1972) concluded that little competition for food occurs between them as a result of their specialised feeding habits. If it does occur at all it is most probably in the dry season as a result of reduction in food supply by the larger herbivores, particularly buffalo and hippopotamus.

The vegetation of the Tarangire Reserve in Tanzania is different to that of

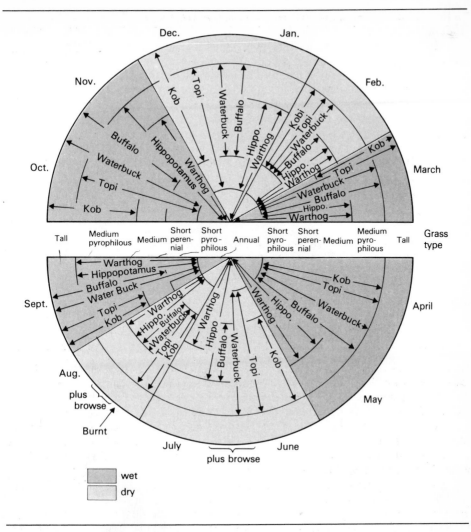

Fig. 6.6 Range of food preferences of six species of ungulates in the short grass areas of Rwenzori Park at different times of the year. The transitional periods from dry to wet seasons, i.e. February–March and August–September, are shown in greater detail. The name of each species covers the type of grassland most preferred, while arrows indicate the range of plant types that is tolerated. Examples of grass type are, tall: *Imperata*; medium pyrophilous: *Themeda*; medium: *Sporobolus*; short perennial: *Cynodon*; short pyrophilous: *Microchloa*; annual: *Eragrostis*. (After Field 1972.)

Rwenzori. It is dry savanna comprised mostly of a mixture and intergradation of grassland and dense to very open *Acacia* and *Commiphora* woodlands. Lamprey (1963) lists 14 common herbivores within the Reserve ranging in size from Kirk's dik dik (*Madoqua kirki*) to elephant. In the rainy season there is a dispersal of zebra, buffalo, wildebeest, eland and elephant from the Reserve into the adjacent Masai steppe followed by a gradual return after the rains finish. The remaining species may have a partial dispersal in the rains (warthog, dik dik, waterbuck and rhino) or the dry season (impala) or may have little or no dispersal in either wet or dry seasons (giraffe, Grant's gazelle, hartebeest and lesser kudu).

In considering the ecological requirements of these species Lamprey (1963) drew attention to the types of vegetation they typically occupied as well as their main feeding habits. The results of this analysis (Fig. 6.7) illustrate how so many herbivores are able to obtain separation when account is taken of seasonal movement and habitat occupation as well as feeding habits. The two species displaying greatest overlap are zebra and wildebeest, both of which are grassland grazers in wet and dry seasons. An indication of differences in feeding habits of these two species has been provided by Bell (1969), who pointed out that in Serengeti in the dry season wildebeest consumed the sheath and leaf of grasses while zebra ate mainly stem and leaf.

There are in the Tarangire and Masai areas four species of ungulates in addition to those included in Fig. 6.7. They are all uncommon and have specialised habitat

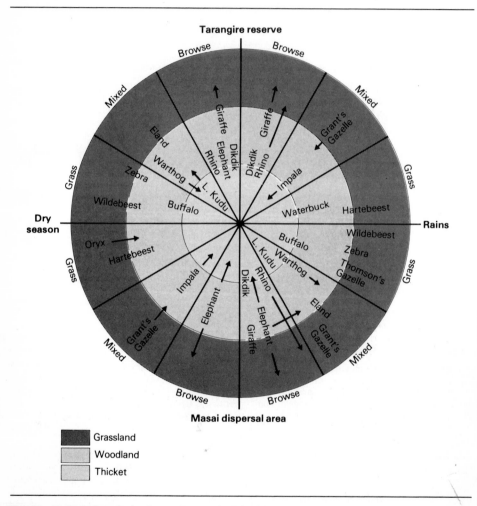

Fig. 6.7 Ecological separation in ungulate species inhabiting the dry savanna of the Masai and Tarangire areas. The diagram is divided horizontally to show spatial distribution and vertically for the rainy and dry seasons. The concentric circles indicate broad habitat preference. A species name is placed in a position relating to the bulk of the population, and arrows indicate some spread into adjacent categories. The position of each species in the quadrants indicates the proportion of grass and other foods taken (After Lamprey 1964).

requirements. Bohor reedbuck are found living in and feeding on grass bordering water in Tarangire. Bushbuck live in dense vegetation of water course ravines where they browse on shrubs. Klipspringer (*Oreotragus oreotragus*) is a browser and grazer of the vegetation of rocky outcrops and, finally, gerenuk (*Litocranius walleri*) feeds mainly on the foliage of *Acacia* in drier areas.

The studies of these large savanna herbivores in Uganda and Tanzania both independently suggest appreciable ecological separation among a group of species which display a gross uniformity of structure and function. This state of affairs probably has general application and has facilitated the great ungulate diversity in savanna and ensured an efficient utilisation of resources. However, these feeding studies do not show if the separations are maintained as a result of competitive exclusion. Nor can it be stated whether in the event of one species being absent which, if any, of these remaining would move into the vacant trophic niche. As a first step to obtaining this information it is necessary to establish the trophic versatility of a species as well as the foods that form the bulk of its diet at a particular location.

Certain favoured foods are often available only at certain times of the year and may then form a substantial part of the diet. Furthermore, some grazing and browsing ungulates are very selective and frequently only feed on vegetation of the preferred size, shape, height, tenderness and palatability. Leuthold and Leuthold (1972) have examined food selection by giraffe in Tsavo Park, Kenya. Most of the food species were trees or large shrubs (Fig. 6.8). Giraffe rarely fed on creepers, vines and small shrubs and never on herbs and grasses. All the common species of trees and large shrubs were

Fig. 6.8 Many species of browsing and grazing mammals affect the growth and life-forms of the plants they feed on. This large shrub has assumed a characteristic shape due to continuous browsing by giraffe. The lower part has been browsed; the growth is dense with smooth contours as in a regularly cut hedge. The upper part, which can not be reached by giraffe, is not dense and has long outward growing branches. (Photo: D. C. D. Happold.)

Table 6.5   *The availability of nineteen food plants and their consumption by giraffe in the dry season habitat of Tsavo Park, Kenya (from Leuthold and Leuthold 1972).*

Plant species	Frequency (%) in habitat (n = 710)	Frequency (%) in food (n = 1280)
Evergreen species providing food throughout the dry season		
Salvadora persica	27·5	10·5
Thylachium thomasii	13·5	22·0
Boscia coriacea	6·2	32·9
Acacia tortilis/elatior	4·9	10·2
Cadaba farinosa	4·2	0·9
Azima tetracantha	3·4	0·1
Balanites orbicularis	1·1	0·3
Capparis tormentosa	1·0	1·3
Acacia thomasii	0·7	0·9
Newtonia hildebrandtii	0·6	0·7
Dobera glabra	0·3	0·3
Species providing edible parts during only part of the dry season		
Cordia ovalis	11·7	0·0
Euphorbia scheffleri	8·0	8·7
Ehretia teitensis	5·9	0·1
Cordia gharaf	4·1	2·5
Calyptrotheca taitensis	3·8	1·2
Sesomothamnus rivae	1·7	2·3
Melia volkensii	1·0	3·2
Combretum ukambense	0·4	2·1
Total	100·0	100·1

Table 6.6   *The proportions of the five most important food plants eaten by giraffe during the wet and dry seasons in Tsavo National Park, Kenya. The values are expressed as the percentage of the total number of food records for each season. (From Leuthold and Leuthold 1972.)*

Plant species	Percentage of total in wet season	Corresponding percentage in dry season
Plant species prevalent in wet season		
Hymenodictyon parvifolium	15·4	1·0
Premna holstii/oligotricha	14·2	3·9
Premna resinosa	13·8	1·3
Calyptrotheca taitensis	10·9	0·8
Melia volkensii	9·2	2·1
Totals	63·5	9·1

Plant species	Percentage of total in dry season	Corresponding percentage in wet season
Plant species prevalent in dry season		
Boscia coriacea	21·4	1·1
Lawsonia inermis	16·8	1·1
Thylachium thomasii	14·3	1·9
Salvadora persica	6·8	0·2
Euphorbia scheffleri	5·6	0·3
Totals	64·9	4·6

eaten, but normally giraffe preferred particular species on which they fed more frequently. Table 6.5 shows how some species are selected and others ignored. Selection of particular food plants also varied with the season; a species such as *Boscia coriacea* had a frequency of 21 per cent in the dry season feeding records and of 1 per cent in the wet season (Table 6.6).

Buffalo also selected particular foods in Tsavo National Park (Leuthold, 1971). Here, 73 per cent of the diet consisted of two species of grass (*Digitaria macroblephara* and *Panicum maximum*) even though they comprised only 44 per cent of the available vegetation (Table 6.7). Dicotyledons were largely rejected while the remaining grasses

Table 6.7   *Food of buffalo in Tsavo Park, Kenya. (From Leuthold 1972.)*

The composition of food eaten by buffalo	
Plant type	Percentage of total food (n = 11 004)
Grasses (26 species)	94·91
Other Monocotyledons	2·72
Dicotyledons (32 species)	2·38
Total	100·01

Comparison of the available and consumed vegetation		
Plant type	Percentage abundance of plant types (n = 945)	Percentage of each food type eaten (n = 410)
Grasses		
Digitaria macroblephara	37·14	28·05
Panicum maximum	6·46	44·88
Other spp.	29·64	17·79
Subtotal	73·24	90·72
Other Monocotyledons	9·00	7·80
Dicotyledons	17·77	1·46
Totals	100·01	99·98

formed a relatively small element of the diet. As this study deals with feeding behaviour at one time of year (January–February) it is not possible to ascertain whether the Tsavo buffalo have seasonal changes in their food preferences.

Stewart and Stewart (1970) compared the feeding habits, by means of faecal analysis, of eight ungulate species with the abundance of grass species in six areas of *Acacia–Themeda* woodland in southern Kenya. The mammals examined were cattle, wildebeest, hartebeest, topi, Grant's and Thomson's gazelles, eland and zebra. Three to six of these species and eleven to twenty seven grass species occurred in each locality studied. From this complex set of conditions Stewart and Stewart (1970) found that two species of grass (*Themeda triandra* and *Cynodon dactylon*) were consistently eaten by most mammal species irrespective of the abundance of these grasses. These were, then, preferred species. Some grasses, e.g. *Aristida adoensis*, *Eragrostis* spp. and *Harpachne schimperi*, were taken on some occasions and ignored by the same animals at other times. These were neither favoured nor ignored species. Finally, some grasses, e.g. *Pennisetum mezianum*, were largely ignored even when abundant. These experiments demonstrate a broad similarity in the food preferences of these species of mammal. However, some differences in utilisation of dicotyledonous plants result from varying faunal compositions in the study areas and seasonal differences in diets. For example, Grant's gazelle and eland consumed appreciable quantities of dicotyledonous material while hartebeest, wildebeest and zebra ate much less.

These three studies from East Africa illustrate the selective factor in large herbivore diets and the ability of several species to vary the quality of their food intake in relation to availability. These animals have their favoured foods which will be their first choice, other things being equal. The occurrence of food selection and dietary flexibility make possible some degree of competitive exclusion. Thus when two consumer species favour the same food plant it is apparently possible for the less successful species to be deflected to an alternative source. The trophic relationships between different species inhabiting a common area are very intricate and these generalisations oversimplify the situation. Account has to be taken of factors such as seasonal behaviour and the parts of plants consumed before a precise interpretation can be made of the extent of competition.

Activity

The activity patterns of all mammals are adapted to their daily mode of life. They may be determined by a wide range of factors such as food availability, climatic conditions, nutritive demand and protection from predation. They can also serve to minimise competition for a common resource such as food or water, where species with similar requirements are active at different times of the day. Many species have a diurnal (daylight), crepuscular (twilight) or nocturnal (night) activity. Others may have any combination of these three. Generalisations concerning activity are obtained from the accumulation of information on several individuals.

The hippopotamus is a good example of a nocturnal species even though the occasional individual may be observed feeding in the daytime. During the day, hippopotamus rest in shallow water and are mainly inactive. At night they leave the water and come on to land to feed. Individuals will travel up to 7 km from the river or lake in which they pass the day. Warthog are active during the day and have some crepuscular and nocturnal activity until about 2000 hours when they return to their holes for the remainder of the night (Fig. 6.9). Lechwe also tend to be diurnally active

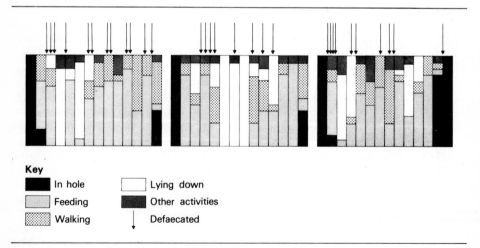

Key

■	In hole	□	Lying down
▨	Feeding	▰	Other activities
▦	Walking	↓	Defaecated

Fig. 6.9 Daily activity of a young male warthog on three successive days. Each vertical block combines one hour's reading; these commence at 0600 hours and terminate at 2000 hours. (After Clough and Hassan 1970).

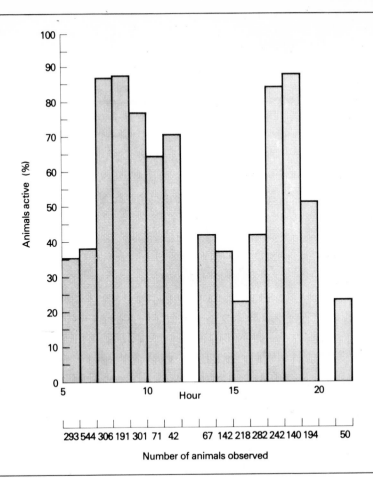

Fig. 6.10 Daily activity of the lechwe (*Kobus leche*) in Okavango Swamp (After Lent 1969).

and nocturnally inactive (Fig. 6.10), while elephant have a major resting period between 0400 and 0700 hours and a minor one from 1100 to 1400 hours (Fig. 6.11).

These examples illustrate several other features. The data recorded on three successive days on an individual warthog (Fig. 6.9) show how activities are not the same on each day. In this animal there was a much longer time spent lying down on the second day than on the first or third. The combined data on eighteen elephants (Fig. 6.11) suggest a peak of resting between 0300 and 0400 hours. In this species walking attains a peak between 1800 and 2100 hours and, apart from a short break between 0400 and 0700 hours, browsing and grazing occupy a considerable proportion of time. Lechwe (Fig. 6.10) show a bimodal peak of feeding and moving with more than 60 per cent of the members of the herd being active from 0700 to 1200 hours and again from 1700 to 1900 hours.

Co-ordination of activities occurs in species living in large groups. Herds of impala (Jarman and Jarman 1973) co-ordinate their feeding, lying down and ruminating–standing activities (Fig. 6.12). They feed mostly after dawn and before dusk although a few individuals feed at any time of the day or night. Similarly, movement occurs at most times of the 24-hour period with peaks from 0800 to 1100

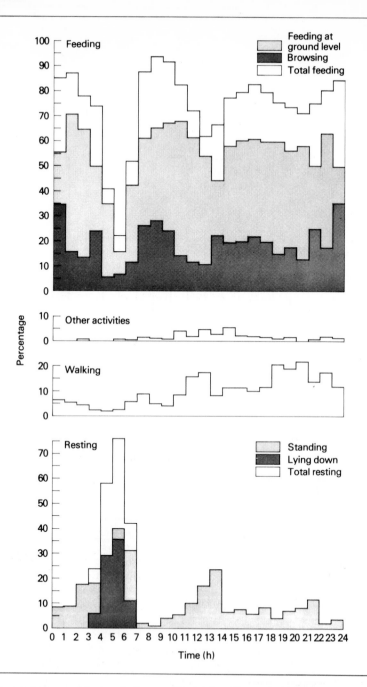

Fig. 6.11   Activity patterns of elephant in Rwenzori Park (After Wyatt and Eltringham 1974).

hours and at about 1800 hours. Lying down occurs almost exclusively at night and ruminating–standing is seen most frequently between the morning and evening peaks of feeding activity. Daytime co-ordination in female impala herds averaged 58 per cent

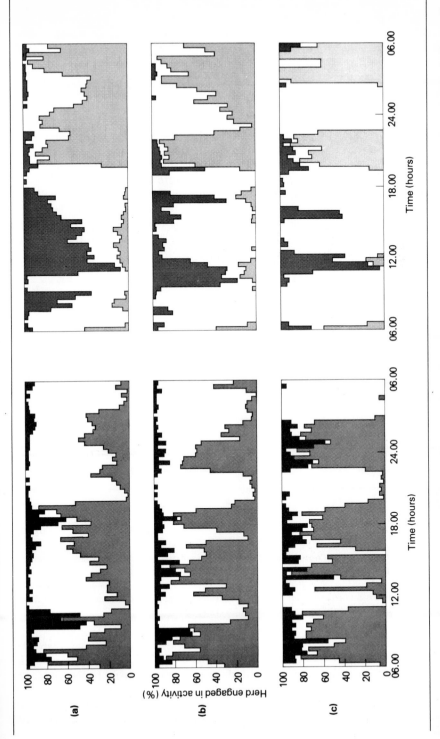

Fig. 6.12 Activities of female herds of impala at different times of the year in Serengeti (*a*) January, (*b*) May, (*c*) July. At the left are mobile activities; feeding (medium shading), moving (black) and at the right are static activities: lying down (light shading) and ruminating-standing (black shading). (After Jarman and Jarman 1973).

in January and 68 per cent in July, and night time co-ordination averaged 68 per cent in January and 76 per cent in July, although at many times the actual co-ordination was much higher than the average. Of particular interest is the way in which activity patterns are modified by environmental and social changes. When grasses are abundant, impala move less often, have feeding peaks in the morning and evening, and spend most of the night lying down. As food becomes less abundant in the dry season, they spend more time moving, feeding occurs throughout most of the day and many individuals feed from 2200 to 0300 hours. Increased feeding activity at night results in less time lying down (Fig. 6.12).

Similarities in the activity patterns of different species results in them undertaking the same activity at the same time and sometimes in the same place. The utilisation of mineral licks in northern Nigeria was maximal between 1000 and 1500 hours when western hartebeest, waterbuck, warthog and baboons were frequent visitors (Henshaw and Ayeni, 1971). In Tsavo Park, Ayeni (1975) noted that several species including warthog, impala, oryx, waterbuck, hartebeest, zebra, giraffe and eland made most of their visits to waterholes during daylight, rhinoceros came during the night and elephant and buffalo visited at all times (Fig. 6.13). Overlap in utilisation was reduced

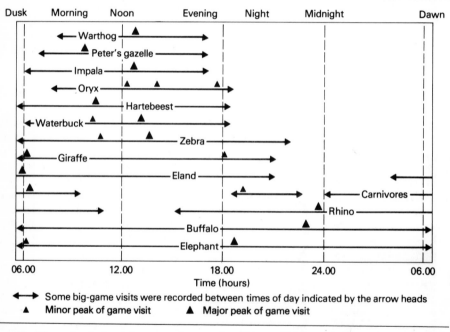

Fig. 6.13   Times of arrival and departure of mammals utilising artificial waterholes in Tsavo Park during dry weather. Peak periods of use are also indicated (After Ayeni 1975).

as a result of each species having its peak visit at different times. Even so, there was considerable use between mid-day and 1600 hours. The smaller species used the waterholes during daylight when as a result of enhanced vision their chances of escape from predators were greater. The larger ungulates and the carnivores used the waterholes more at night. Interspecific competition was further reduced as a result of some species spending relatively short periods at the waterhole. Thus herds of 250–500 buffalo drank in a closely packed group and moved off within a few minutes.

Furthermore, the utilisation of standing water is subject to considerable seasonal variation with the heaviest demands made towards the end of the dry season.

Interactions with the habitat

A mammal may modify its habitat through any of its biological activities such as feeding, drinking, defaecating, digging and physical destruction of plants and soil. Each species affects its habitat in a particular way. Usually, these are not obvious unless the population density of a species is sufficiently high to alter permanently its own habitat and those of other species. Such modification can result in detrimental results for some species and beneficial ones for others. In the savanna, there are several instances of habitat modification by the large herbivores.

Heavy grazing pressure can reduce plant cover and the production of seeds, harden the soil due to trampling and reduce the percolation of rain. Trampling of soil occurs along game trails, around water holes, salt licks and hippo wallows. This often leads to the formation of erosion gullies and a belt of land almost devoid of vegetation.

Elephants pull down branches, uproot small trees, remove the bark from some trees (e.g. *Terminalia*), pull up grass roots and trample soft soil into hard pans. These effects are normally localised, and in recent years the most striking effects of elephants have been in reserved areas where their populations have rapidly increased as a result of a series of man-induced changes in the surrounding areas. In Kabalega Park, Uganda, Buechner and Dawkins (1961) recorded a 55–59 per cent reduction in tree cover in the woodland and riparian forest from 1932 to 1956. This coincided with an increase in the elephant population and regular burning which between them restricted the regrowth of woody vegetation and produced a treeless grassland. Other effects of this habitat change were a reduction in shade and shelter and local alterations in the water level and the hydrological cycle. In creating these less favourable conditions for themselves the elephants invoke homestatic reproductive mechanisms (Laws 1968a) to reduce their numbers. They include delaying the onset of maturity and increasing the interval between calving. These are not always sufficiently rapid to bring the populations into a balanced equilibrium and as a result the elephant may become vulnerable to undernutrition (Section 12.5). The habitat modifications resulting from these increases in elephant numbers can influence the abundance of other species of large mammal. Over a fifteen-year period in the tall-grass savanna of Rwenzori Park, Uganda, an increase of 46·3 per cent in elephant numbers was accompanied by a decline of 80·3 per cent in buffalo (Field 1971).

Measurement of the effects of grazing and burning in Kabalega Park, Uganda, by Spence and Angus (1971) suggest that the absence of both these phenomena in *Combretum–Terminalia* woodland results in a rapid recovery of woody species. Even with continued grazing and the cessation of fires there is a significant increase in shrub cover and diversity. However, in the *Sporobolus–Setaria* grasslands, shrub regeneration and herb improvement are dependent on both fire protection and respite from grazing.

Hippopotamus are also capable of producing major habitat changes if their numbers are too high. They prefer short grass regions which are maintained in this condition by regular grazing. Normally other nearby grasslands are not utilised so that the habitat is a mosaic of short grass, long grass and bushy areas. If hippopotamus become too numerous (again in reserved areas) a number of changes are evident. There is a change in the species composition of the grasses, reduction of the grass cover, erosion of the soil and an increase in the number and density of scrubby bushes which previously were prevented from spreading by grass fires. Hippopotamus pluck the short grasses so many of the palatable loose-rooted species are pulled up while others such as the creeping stoloniferous species (e.g. *Chrysochloa orientalis*) become more numerous. The adverse effects caused by too many hippopotamus were very evident on the Mweya Peninsula in Rwenzori Park, but after many of the hippopotamus had been removed by cropping, there was a gradual improvement of the habitat. Many, but not all, grass species became more numerous and the total grass and litter cover increased.

The successional changes induced by elephants and hippopotamus not only affect these species, but other species as well as this habitat modification provides a different set of vegetational conditions to those prevailing previously.

Hippopotamus were completely removed from Mweya Peninsula during 1957 and 1958 and re-establishment prevented until 1966. From that time no further control was exercised over the peninsula population and invasives were permitted to take up residence. Surveys of the six commonest species of large mammals (Eltringham 1974) in 1956 and 1968 illustrates the rapid rate of re-establishment by hippopotamus as well as changes in densities of other mammal species (Table 6.8). Buffalo increased their

Table 6.8   *Changes in numbers of large mammals on Mweya Peninsula, Uganda. (From Eltringham 1974.)*

	1956–7	*1963–7*	*1968*
Buffalo	20·2	122·5	177·7
Bushbuck	16·4	13·6	10·5
Elephant	9·5	15·2	25·6
Hippopotamus	94·1	4·5	23·7
Warthog	41·4	37·7	29·6
Waterbuck	20·0	51·8	43·4

numbers dramatically, elephant and waterbuck to a much less extent. At the same time numbers of bushbuck and warthog slightly declined. The estimated biomass in 1968 was 20 per cent greater than that in 1956.

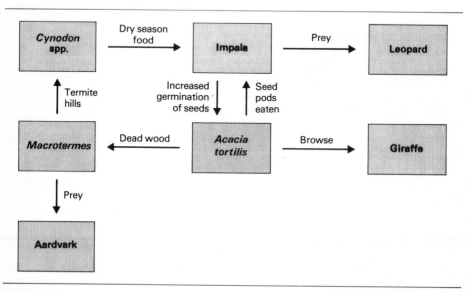

Fig. 6.14   The effects of impala on *Acacia tortilis* trees and *Cynodon* grass in the Tarangire area. Tanzania (After Lamprey 1963).

Some successional changes caused by one species are beneficial for other species, as in the grazing sequences in the Rukwa valley described on p. 202. The life forms of shrubs are often an indication of the amount of browsing by mammals. Heavy browsing by giraffes causes a 'browse line' on tall shrubs and trees, and the frequent nibbling of growing shoots results in a dense, hedge-like structure of many shrubs (Fig. 6.8). In fact, all browsing mammals will stimulate the growth of new shoots when they bite off apical stems.

A more complex inter-relationship between mammals and their environment has been described by Lamprey (1963) (Fig. 6.14). Impala feed on the seeds of *Acacia tortilis*, and the germination of the seeds is improved by the action of digestive juices in the gut of the impala. The resulting new *Acacia* trees produce more seeds for the impala to eat, and when the trees die the termite mounds which develop around the dead wood are suitable places for the growth of *Cynodon* grass. This grass is utilised by impala in the dry season and it may assist in the survival of the impala so that, in time, they will be able to eat more *Acacia* seeds. The behaviour of the impala indirectly results in the production of more *Acacia* trees and (with the help of *Macrotermes*) more *Cynodon* grass. Other mammal species also benefit from this association.

6.4   Rodents of moist savanna

The crater area of Rwenzori Park is characterised by dense swards of *Imperata*, *Cymbopogon* and *Themeda* one to two metres tall and accompanied by a variety of other less abundant grasses and herbs. There is a scattering of *Capparis* bushes while at the periphery of the area are some *Euphorbia* trees. Here the grasses afford particularly suitable habitat for small rodents as they provide excellent cover and abundant food. Twelve species of rodents have been recorded from this habitat. The smallest species are the grass-climbing *Dendromus melanotis* and the pygmy mouse (*Mus minutoides*), both weighing about 7 g. The larger species such as *Aethomys kaiseri* and *Mylomys dybowskyi* can weigh well in excess of 100–130 g. Examination of the feeding, microdistribution, burrowing habits and activity of the commoner species (Table 6.9)

Table 6.9   *Ecological habits of the commoner rodents in the dense grassland of Rwenzori Park, Uganda.*

Species	Size (approx. wt.)	Feeding habit	Burrows	Microdistribution	Activity
Aethomys kaiseri	Large (110 g)	Herbivorous	?	*Capparis* bush	N
Mylomys dybowskyi	Large (115 g)	Herbivorous	No	*Imperata-Cymbopogon*	C
Lemniscomys striatus	Medium (36 g)	Omnivorous	No	Widespread	C
Lophuromys sikapusi	Medium (80 g)	Insectivorous	No	*Imperata-Cymbopogon*	C
Praomys natalensis	Medium (42 g)	Omnivorous	Yes	Widespread	N
Zelotomys hildegardeae	Medium (60 g)	Insectivorous	?	*?Hyparrhenia*	N
Mus triton	Small (14 g)	Omnivorous	No	Widespread	N
Mus minutoides	Small (7 g)	Omnivorous	Yes	Widespread	N

Also present in relatively small numbers are *Dendromus melanotis* (7 g), *Arvicanthis niloticus* (80 g), *Tatera valida* (120 g) and *Otomys irroratus* (100 g).

N = Nocturnal.   C = Crepuscular.

indicates some of the ways in which they utilise their habitat (Delany 1964, Neal 1970, Cheeseman 1975). Ideally, more data are required on some of these aspects of their ecology. At present, there is insufficient information to detail seasonal variation in diet and the proportions of each food taken. However, the records of activity are sufficient to provide considerable insight into minor variations between species (Fig. 6.15). For

example, two nocturnal species such as *Aethomys* and *Praomys* differ in the former being much less active in the middle of the night. The absence of a diurnal species is a little surprising. Nevertheless, the overall picture is one of diversification of habit among the rodent species resulting, as with the large herbivores, in a highly effective exploitation of habitat resources.

Savanna fires have a considerable effect on these animals as unlike the large mammals they cannot so readily move away from this hazard. Fire modifies the habitat to such an extent as to make it unsuitable for certain species present before the burn to survive after it has passed. Both *Mylomys* and *Lophuromys* do not reappear in a burnt area until the elapse of several months. A similar situation prevails in derived savanna in Nigeria where *Mus minutoides* and *Praomys* (*Myomyscus*) *daltoni* take some time to return after a burn (Anadu 1973). This could be related to their feeding habits. *Mylomys* has been observed to feed on the central core of *Imperata* leaves. Should this be its principal food it will only be able to obtain it in quantity from mature stands of the grass. *Lophuromys* consumes large numbers of termites living in the dead grass litter which is rapidly destroyed by fire.

Comparisons have been made in Rwenzori Park between the rodent faunas of unburnt tall grass (*Imperata*, *Cymbopogon*, *Hyparrhenia*) and short grass (*Sporobolus*, *Bothriochloa*, *Chloris*) accompanied by patches of dense bush (Delany 1964). The short grass offers poor cover, less food and more open ground for the rodents. It also supports a smaller number of species and lower densities than the tall grass. The commonest species in short grass are *Arvicanthis*, *Lemniscomys* and *Praomys*; only *Arvicanthis* occurs at significantly higher densities in short grass than in long grass. Dense bush forms suitable refuges for *Arvicanthis* warrens whose inhabitants can forage in adjacent grassland. Within the Park savanna as a whole the large mammals are more numerous and better represented in the short grass where their grazing, as for example with hippopotamus, can almost eliminate the ground flora. Even with less rigorous grazing there is frequently appreciable reduction of the cover so important for the survival of small rodents. This apparent inverse relationship between rodent and large herbivore densities is important in so far as it illustrates how relatively small differences between habitats in juxtaposition may result in quite considerable differences in the character of faunas they support.

6.5   Small mammals of dry savanna

A detailed study of many species of small mammals inhabiting various types of dry savanna including woodlands, thickets and more exposed situations having a poor seasonal cover of grasses and herbs has been undertaken close to the Kerio River, near Lokari, in Turkana District of Kenya (Coe 1972*b*). This is a hot semi-arid area where the mean maximum and minimum temperatures are 34·9 °C and 23 °C respectively and the mean annual rainfall is about 400 mm. However, the headwaters of the River Kerio collect considerable quantities of rain water and so ensure the constant provision of a riverine vegetation in its lower reaches. Flooding from the river produces fertile alluvial flats.

The habitats in this area are either riverine or lava-derived (Fig. 6.16). The former include *Acacia tortilis* woodland and patches of *Salvadora* and *Cordia* thickets. The former are particularly important as they provide dense palatable foliage, a supply of fruit throughout the year and considerable shade. The lava-derived habitats include the fine gravel which supports a scant vegetation. The widely dispersed lava outcrops rise above the surrounding plain and vary in size from small individual mounds to areas of rolling hills.

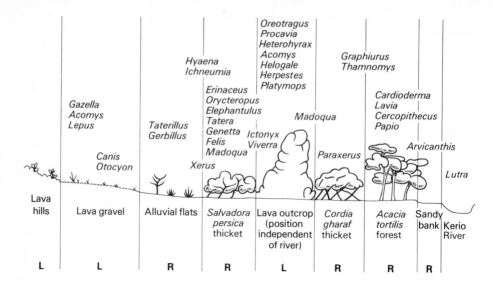

Fig. 6.16 Diagrammatic cross-section through the major habitat types in the dry savanna of Turkana showing segregation of small mammal genera. (After Coe 1972).

Bats are not common, probably due to the sparsity of insects in the long dry seasons. Of the five species recorded Peter's flat-headed bat (*Platymops setiger*) inhabit rocky outcrops, the heart-nosed big-eared bat (*Cardioderma cor*) and the yellow-winged bat (*Lavia frons*) roost in the *Acacia* and are active in the early evening or during daylight, and the banana bat (*Pipistrellus nanus*) and the hairy slit-faced bat (*Nycteris hispida*) roost in hollow trees from which they appear after dusk.

Spotted-necked otters (*Lutra maculicollis*) inhabit the river and its banks. Where sandy banks and open areas of *Acacia* woodland support grass and herbs there are abundant Nile rats (*Arvicanthis niloticus*). The trees provide suitable habitat for the arboreal tree rat (*Thamnomys dolichurus*) and dormouse (*Graphiurus murinus*) as well as roosting places for vervets (*Cercopithecus pygerythrus*) and baboons (*Papio anubis*). Both species of primates are common in the *Cordia* thickets where they feed on the seasonal crop of fruit. Genet (*Genetta genetta*) and wildcat (*Felis libyca*) are common and both feed on roosting birds. The bush squirrel (*Paraxerus ochraceus*) is seldom found outside these thickets. Aardvark (*Orycteropus afer*) feed on the numerous termites associated with the plant debris.

The *Salvadora* thickets and the tracks and paths that penetrate them form a suitable habitat for several species of mammal. The smallest species are the elephant shrew (*Elephantulus rufescens*), the gerbil (*Tatera robusta*) and the spiny mouse (*Acomys cahirinus*). The shrew feeds mainly on termites and to a lesser extent on other insects and the rodents consume seeds, leaves, flowers and other plant material. The diurnal unstriped ground squirrel (*Xerus rutilus*) lives in burrows located close to the *Salvadora* stems. During the warmest part of the day it feeds on fruits and seeds under the bushes while in the early morning or late afternoon it comes out into the clearings and tracks.

Guenther's dik dik (*Madoqua guentheri*) is a common browser of these thickets.

There are appreciable differences between the faunas of the *Salvadora* thickets and the adjacent alluvial flats. The latter offer a much less favourable habitat. Here the vegetation consists of scattered stands of *Acacia* on dust-like alluvium which produces an ephemeral ground vegetation in the wet season. The fauna here is poor and specialised. The only mammals exclusive to these flats are three species of gerbil (*Taterillus nubilus*, *Gerbillus pusillus* and *G. gerbillus*). They are herbivorous and nocturnal spending the days in their burrows with the entrances plugged with soil. The lava-derived gravel flats are also among the less favoured habitats with again few species present. Here are found the spiny mouse and the hare *Lepus capensis*. The lava outcrops are inhabited by two species of hyrax (*Heterohyrax brucei*, *Procavia* sp.) which are often found in the rock fissures, the nocturnal gregarious insectivorous pygmy mongoose (*Helogale hirtula*) and the diurnal, black-tipped mongoose (*Herpestes sanguineus*). The spiny mouse is also common.

There still remain a number of species that are relatively uncommon so that little is known of their ecology in this region. They include the hedgehog (*Erinaceus albiventris*), spring hare (*Pedetes capensis*), jackals (*Canis mesomelas*, *C. adustus*), bat-eared fox (*Otocyon megalotis*), zorilla (*Ictonyx striatus*), civet (*Viverra civetta*), white-tailed mongoose (*Ichneumia albicauda*) and oribi (*Ourebia ourebi*). The fauna of South Turkana is further enriched by the inclusion of several species of large mammal as well as a number of small mammals not found in the vicinity of Lokari. Coe (1972*b*) gives a total of 55 species. This compares favourably with the number recorded from the wetter savanna of western Uganda (p. 114). For the smaller mammals there is probably a greater heterogeneity of microhabitats in Turkana. In addition to the diversity of vegetation there are stable and unstable habitats, considerable variability in the quantity of ground water and appreciable differences in the structure of the substratum. These are accentuated as a result of the prevailing hotter and more arid conditions.

6.6 Insect eaters

Termites, ants and other insects are important components of the savanna ecosystem, and they are sufficiently abundant to support populations of several insect-eating species of mammal. There is a wide spectrum of size among these mammals. Many of the shrews weigh only a few grams and are amongst the smallest mammals, whereas the aardwolf (*Proteles cristatus*), giant pangolin (*Manis gigantea*) and ant bear or aardvark (*Orycteropus afer*) are very large in relation to the food source.

The aardwolf feeds exclusively on termites. As it is unable to dig into the soil or into hard nests it feeds on surface-living termites. An analysis of 97 faecal pellets from Serengeti National Park showed that *Trinervitermes bettonianus* was either the only or most abundant termite in 89 per cent of the samples (Kruuk and Sands 1972). In Serengeti this is the only species that forages on the surface in large numbers, a habit that has resulted in this being the most important source of food for the aardwolf. Termite concentrations are located by the aardwolf as it walks an irregular course over the grass plains, with head bent forwards and downwards. It appears that termites are found fortuitously although sound and scent may help in their location. The termites are licked up with the broad tongue (together with a lot of soil and loose vegetation) while the head is pushed forward and rotated from side to side. The aardwolf is a very selective feeder but of necessity it includes other prey (*Dorylus* ants and *Odontotermes badius* termites) in its diet during the rainy season.

The giant pangolin and ground pangolin (*Manis temminckii*) scrape the surface soil in their search for insect food. This is the principal method of feeding in the ground pangolin which is highly selective in the species of ants and termites it consumes. In Sudan it was observed (Sweeney 1956) to feed on the juvenile stages of certain ants and termites. The favoured genera were *Crematogaster*, *Odontotermes* and *Microcerotermes*; next in preference came *Microtermes*, *Amitermes* and *Ancistotermes*. The very common *Trinervitermes* and *Macrotermes* were generally avoided. The giant pangolin takes surface food but will also tear into termitaria (Kingdon 1971). The loosened earth is then kicked back with its hind legs. Little information is available on the species of insect consumed by this pangolin. The widespread aardvark also excavates termite mounds and may frequently visit a mound from which it regularly removes some of the inhabitants. *Macrotermes* is a favoured food in many areas although several other species including *Trinervitermes*, *Pseudocanthotermes* and *Basidentitermes* are consumed.

In Uganda, the aardvark takes mainly termites in the wet season and ants in the dry season (Melton 1976). This is attributed to the quiescence of termites in the dry season and not the aardvark's inability to dig under the driest of conditions.

There are a large number of small mammals for whom insects are the only or major source of food. These include the insectivorous bats, shrews, some rodents such as *Lophuromys sikapusi* and some carnivores like the banded mongoose (*Mungos mungo*). Little detailed information is available on the food of the small mammals. It is probable that many are opportunistic feeders taking such insects, carrion and any other animal food they may encounter. This has been confirmed in captive *Crocidura hirta* which ate ground beef, earthworms, mealworms, mantids, crickets, termites, beetles, grasshoppers and moths as well as the carcases of bats and rodents (Meester 1963).

6.7   Zoogeography

The broad sweep of savanna from the west African coast to the south of the continent provides a continuous stretch of this vegetation for its mammalian inhabitants. Although it may have existed in its present form for a relatively short time, this has probably been long enough to facilitate maximal dispersal and interchange from previously isolated sectors. However, the spread of mammals through the savanna has not been complete and, as a result, the geographical distribution of species within the savanna is far from uniform. Dispersal can be restricted by many contemporary biotic and abiotic factors such as vegetation, topography and climate. In addition evolution and history may operate as, for example, through competitive exclusion of sibling species which have evolved independently in isolation. It is the combination of historical and present events that accounts for present day distributions.

The recognition as long ago as the end of the nineteenth century of regional endemism resulted in the establishment (Sclater 1896) of two zoogeographical subregions within the Ethiopian savanna. Sclater's Cape subregion extended from South Africa to the Congo Basin in the west and to the River Tana watershed of Kenya in the east. It is in the vicinity of the Tana River watershed and eastwards into Uganda that the savanna from the south joins the huge northern savanna extending from Senegal eastwards across Africa to southern Sudan, Uganda and Kenya. The northern savanna was identified as the Saharan subregion. Davis (1962) has referred to the line of separation between the two subregions as the Sclater line. A further zoogeographical subregion which was previously part of the Saharan subregion has been recognised by Chapin (1923) on the basis of the distinctness of the avifauna of the area. This is located in the Horn of Africa (Eritrea, Somalia, part of Ethiopia and north-east Kenya) and referred to as the Somali Arid subregion. While these subregions provide a useful framework and basis for the comparison of faunas in different parts of the continent they cannot be regarded as zones with unique faunas and little intercommunication. There are no rigid and obvious boundaries between them and few natural constraints at the present time to the exchange of their faunas. In many places they extend into arid regions and in consequence embrace more than the typical savanna species.

The contemporary geographical distributions of certain genera and species reveal a variety indicative of a complex faunal history (Fig. 6.17) as well as providing information on the extent of faunal regionalisation. There are several genera, frequently monospecific, that are widespread through both northern and southern savannas. These include giraffe (*Giraffa*), common duiker (*Sylvicapra*), buffalo (*Syncerus*), elephant (*Loxodonta*), hippopotamus (*Hippopotamus*), wild dog (*Lycaon*), cheetah (*Acinonyx*) and white-tailed mongoose (*Ichneumia*) (Fig. 6.17a). Southern savanna genera include Selous' mongoose (*Paracynictis*), springbuck (*Antidorcas*), wildebeest (*Connochaetes*) (Fig. 6.17d), four-striped grass-mouse (*Rhabdomys*) and the pouched mouse (*Saccostomus*). There appear to be no endemic genera in the northern savanna. In the Somali subregion there are gerenuk (*Litocranius*), dibatag (*Ammodorcas*) (Fig. 6.17c), beira (*Dorcatragus*) and the gundi (*Pectinator*). In contrast to the latter genera of broadly regional distribution there are also genera having different species in northern and southern savanna. The elands of the genus *Taurotragus* (Fig. 6.17b) fall within this category. The giant eland (*T. derbianus*) has a discontinuous distribution from Senegal to Sudan over which range it is represented by two subspecies. In the south the eland (*T. oryx*) extends from Natal and northern Cape Province as far as the Tana River in Kenya, Rwanda and Uganda and is represented by three subspecies. Similarly, the kobs of the subgenus *Adenota* have two species (*Kobus* (*A*) *kob* and *K.* (*A*) *megaceros*) in the northern savanna and the puku (*K.* (*A*) *vardoni*) and lechwe (*K.* (*A*) *leche*) in the south. For the nine species of gazelle (*Gazella*) the situation is rather more complicated. Four species are northern, three Somali and two (Grant's and Thomson's – *G. granti* and *G. thomsoni*) traverse the boundary zone between north and south in East Africa.

There are some genera characteristic of dry savanna. If they are widely distributed over the continent then it is reasonable to expect their northern and southern populations to be widely separated. This is particularly obvious in the oryx (*Oryx*) (Fig. 6.17e) with its very interesting distribution. The gemsbok (*Oryx gazella*) is found in south and south-west Africa and Botswana. It is also present in Eritrea, Somalia, Sudan, Ethiopia, Uganda, Kenya and Tanzania. A second species (*O. dammah*) occurs in the Sahelian zone as far east as Sudan. This species is geographically much closer to the northern population of *O. gazella* than are the two populations of *O. gazella* which are separated from each other by about 2500 km. The striped hyaena (*Hyaena hyaena*) and brown hyaena (*H. brunneus*) are also animals of dry savanna. The former is found in the drier sahelian zone and Somali arid of the north extending into Tanzania and the latter is mainly found in south-west Africa.

The final distribution pattern concerns those genera having some species that are widely distributed and others that are more localised. The hares of the genus *Lepus* have two species, Crawshay's Hare (*L. crawshayi*) and the Cape Hare (*L. capensis*) which occur extensively in northern and southern savannas with the former more typical of moister situations and the latter of drier ones. The southern bush hare *L. saxatilis* occurs only on higher ground in southern South Africa and *L. habessinicus* is restricted to Ethiopia and Somalia. The zebras also come within this category. Burchell's zebra (*Equus burchelli*) is widespread in savanna south of the equator and extends north into southern Sudan, Ethiopia and Somalia. Of more restricted distribution are Grévy's Zebra (*E. grevyi*) from the Somali subregion and the

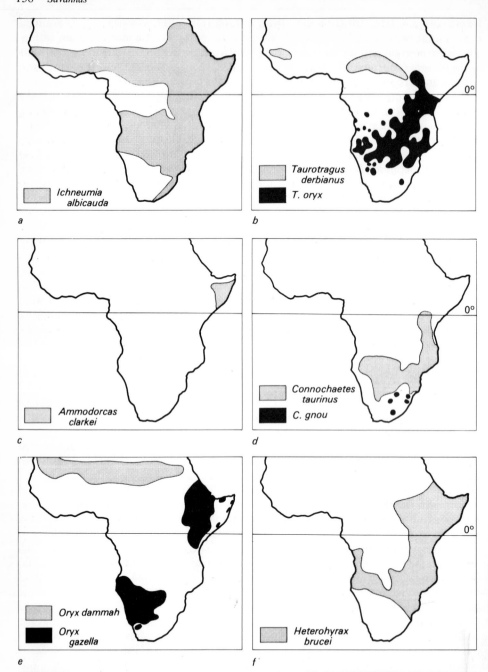

Fig. 6.17 The distribution of selected savanna genera. (*a*) The white tailed mongoose (*Ichneumia albicauda*), a widespread monotypic genus; (*b*) elands (*Taurotragus*) with one northern and one southern genus with two southern species; (*e*) oryx (*Oryx*), a genus of dry and semi-arid savannas having one of its species (*O. gazella*) in both northern and southern savanna; (*f*) yellow-spotted dassie (*Heterohyrax brucei*), a monotypic genus having a limited distribution in northern, southern and Somali subregions. (After Dorst and Dandelot 1970).

Mountain Zebra (*E. zebra*) which inhabits mountains in Cape Province, South West Africa and Angola.

The foregoing does not summarize all the distribution patterns of savanna mammals. If anything it simplifies the situation in an attempt to highlight recognisable faunal regionalisation at both generic and specific levels. The evolutionary interpretation is difficult and can only adequately be undertaken against a comprehensive background of all mammal groups. Many species do not readily conform to the distributions described and do not recognise the broad faunal boundaries. For example, the Nile rat (*Arvicanthis niloticus*) is very largely northern in its distribution extending across West Africa to Ethiopia and into Kenya, Uganda and Rwanda. It then ranges southwards across Sclater's Line as far south as Zambia. Here is an animal apparently typical of northern savanna with partial but incomplete penetration of southern savanna. This pattern is frequently repeated with varying degrees of range extension.

From an ecological viewpoint an appreciation of zoogeography is helpful in understanding the reasons for the presence of certain species and the absence of others. It can also be a valuable guide to the species that may be anticipated in uninvestigated localities. The fauna present within any one place is frequently an amalgam of species originating from different zoogeographical zones. This is particularly true in East Africa where northern, southern and Somali savanna faunas are in close proximity. In his study of mammals in northern Kenya, Coe (1972*b*) recognised 22 cosmopolitan species, 9 of northern savanna origin, 8 Somali arid and 10 East African endemic, i.e. species restricted to southern Sudan, Ethiopia, Somalia, Kenya and Uganda. This situation is typical of this and other parts of Africa and illustrates the obvious heterogeneity of origin of the mammal fauna.

Chapter 7

Arid zones

There are three arid regions in tropical Africa, referred to as the Sudanese, Somali and South-west Arid Zones (Fig. 4.1). The Sudanese and South-west arid zones extend beyond the limits of the tropics. The Sudanese arid zone lies north of about 12 °N and extends from Mauritania and Senegal in the west to the Sudan in the east, and includes the Sahara desert. The Somali arid zone comprises the coastal regions of Ethiopia, Somalia and Kenya and it connects with the Sudanese arid zone along the Red Sea coast. The third region, the South-west arid zone, comprises the Namib and Kalahari deserts of South Africa, South-west Africa and Botswana. At the present time, the South-west arid zone is isolated from the arid zones north of the Equator, but it is probable that it was linked with the Somali arid zone in the past along a 'drought corridor' (Balinsky 1962). The alternation of pluvial and dry periods since the Pleistocene (one million years ago) resulted in the drought corridor narrowing and closing when the rain forests expanded, and widening when the forests retreated (Moreau 1952, Balinsky 1962). There are sufficient similarities between the mammal faunas of the South-west arid zone and the Somali–Sudanese arid zones (Meester 1965) to suggest that there were connections in the not too distant past.

The arid zones are basically flat with some isolated granitic hill masses called jebels or inselbergs (in the north), or koppies (in the south). Some of the jebels are dissected with cracks and gullies, and some have deep crevices and caves. Large sand ridges occur in some localities. Water courses (wadis, khors) cross the sand plains, but they are usually dry except for a few hours after heavy rainstorms. The soils of the arid zones are normally shallow and almost entirely lacking in organic matter.

Two localities have been selected for detailed discussion in this chapter: the Sudanese sand plain near Khartoum in the Sudanese arid zone and the Kalahari Gemsbok National Park in the South-west arid zone. Near Khartoum (Fig. 7.1) the flat plain of sand and gravel is dissected by wadis and relieved by scattered jebels. There are a few large sand dune areas, locally known as 'qoz'. The river Nile flows northwards through the sand plain, but the mesic conditions of the river do not extend more than a few metres beyond the river bank. Temporary pools of water may be formed in depressions in the sand plain after heavy storms. The Kalahari Gemsbok National Park consists of extensive 'sandveld' of sand dunes interspersed with pans and depressions of hardened sand and soil (Fig. 7.2). This habitat covers about 90–95 per cent of the Park. The sandveld is dissected by the wide river beds of the Nossob and Auob rivers which contain a variety of soil types from course sands to soils with a high lime content. In some places on the river banks the underlying calcareous rock is exposed to form rocky outcrops. The river bed and banks form a wide depression, up to 4 km across, through the sandveld. The soil moisture content in the river beds and banks is higher than on the sandveld, and temporary pools of water occur in the river beds after heavy storms.

Fig. 7.1   The arid zone near Khartoum, Sudan.

(*a*) The sandplain with tussocks of dried grass and stunted *Acacia* trees. Distant jebels are visible on the horizon.

(*b*) A *Capparis* bush with windblown grass and seeds around its base. These will be buried gradually by windblown sand, and will provide food in the future for small rodents.

(*c*) Rocky jebels north of Khartoum. *Acomys cahirinus, Gerbillus campestris*, several species of microchiroptera, two species of *Vulpes* and *Procavia capensis* live in crevices and caves on the jebel; *Jaculus jaculus, Gerbillus pyramidum, Lepus* sp. occur in the sandplain at the base of the jebel. The line of a temporary watercourse, originating on the jebel, is indicated by the trees in the middle distance.

(*d*) The sandplain after the annual rains. Bushes and trees shoot new leaves, and green grasses and herbs form a dense cover over the ground. (Photos. D. C. D. Happold.)

a

b

c

7.1 Climate

Throughout the arid zones of tropical Africa, the annual potential evapotranspiration is at least twice as great as the annual rainfall (Fig. 7.3). Characteristically, the annual rainfall is very variable and in most arid regions long periods of drought are not uncommon. At Khartoum, the average annual rainfall is about 150 mm, but the actual rainfall has varied from 50 mm to 250 mm per year during the years 1940 to 1960 (Oliver 1965). Here the rain usually falls in a few heavy showers in July, August and September, and there is no rain for the remainder of the year (Fig. 7.3). Rainfall in arid regions is extremely localised, so that places a few kilometres apart may have differing amounts of rain and storms at different times. In the Kalahari Gemsbok National Park, the average annual rainfall is 226 mm, with the heaviest rain in February and April (Fig. 7.3). Although the average annual rainfall is higher than at Khartoum, the months of heaviest rainfall in the Kalahari Gemsbok National Park have less rain than the months of heaviest rainfall at Khartoum, and the rainfall is distributed more evenly throughout the year. However, rainfall is very sporadic, and although the average rainfall in April, for example, is 44 mm, the range varies from 0 mm to 100 mm (Maclean 1970).

Arid regions are also characterised by marked seasonal and diurnal fluctuations in temperature. The days are always hot in African arid regions and the nights are cool. The diurnal fluctuation in temperature is greatest during the 'dry season', and both maximum and minimum daily temperatures are lower than those in the 'wet season'. For example, at Khartoum in January (the coolest part of the dry season), there is an average daily range of 16 degrees from 32 °C to 16 °C (Fig. 7.3). In August (the wettest month of the year), there is an average daily range of 11 degrees from 36 °C to 25 °C (Oliver 1965). Extreme temperatures of 47 °C and 6 °C have been recorded at Khartoum which indicates considerable variation around the mean maximum and minimum. The months of highest rainfall are associated with a fall in temperature. The annual temperature fluctuations in the Kalahari Gemsbok National Park are similar to those at Khartoum except in two important respects (Fig. 7.3). The coolest months are in May to August, instead of in December to February, because the Kalahari Gemsbok National Park is in the southern hemisphere, and the mean temperatures are cooler in Kalahari Gemsbok National Park so that in the hot season the maximum temperatures are rarely above the lethal limit for mammals and in the cool season sub-zero temperatures are not uncommon.

Insolation (exposure to the rays of the sun) is usually very high due to the absence of clouds, and there is practically no shade because vegetation is scarce. Consequently the range of temperatures in the open is considerably greater than the range of shade temperatures recorded by conventional meteorological stations. The soil at ground level heats rapidly during the day, and loses heat rapidly at night. At Khartoum, the temperature 1 cm below ground level may fluctuate as much as 35 degrees from a maximum of 65 °C at about 1400 hours local time to a minimum of 30 °C just before sunrise (Oliver 1965) (Fig. 7.4). However, the soil is a good insulator and diurnal fluctuations decrease with depth. Many arid zone animals dig burrows which vary in depth from about 50 cm to more than 100 cm. At these depths, the diurnal fluctuation in temperature is less than one degree, but there are seasonal variations which follow

---

Fig. 7.2 The south-west arid zone in the Kalahari Gemsbok National Park. (*a*) Sand dune with colonising grasses. (Photo: National Parks Board, South Africa.) (*b*) Wildebeest grazing on *Aristida* grasses in a dune trough. (Photo: G. L. Maclean.) (*c*) Calcrete outcrops on the banks of the Auob river. (Photo: G. L. Maclean.)

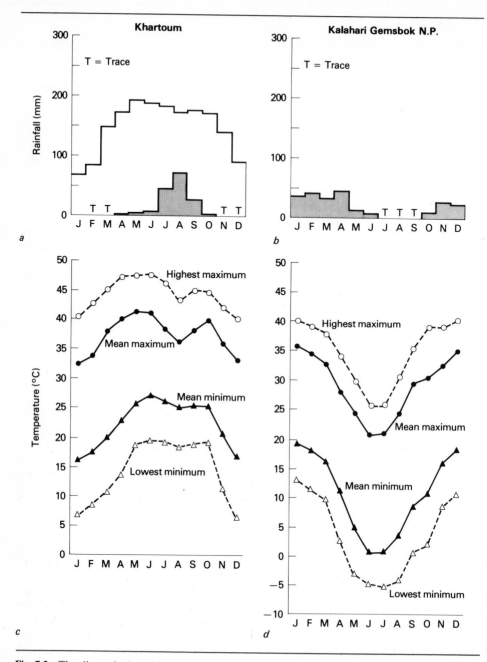

Fig. 7.3 The climate in the arid zone at Khartoum and Kalahari Gemsbok National Park. (*a*) Mean monthly rainfall (shaded histogram) and mean monthly potential evaporation (white histogram) at Khartoum. (*b*) Mean monthly rainfall at Kalahari Gemsbok National Park. (*c*) Mean monthly maximum and minimum temperatures, and highest maximum and lowest minimum temperatures at Khartoum. (*d*) Mean monthly maximum and minimum temperatures, and highest and lowest minimum temperatures at Kalahari Gemsbok National Park. (Data for Khartoum from Oliver (1965) for thirty years (1931–60), and for Kalahari Gemsbok National Park (Twee Rivieren) from G. L. Maclean (pers. comm.) for six years (1961–6).

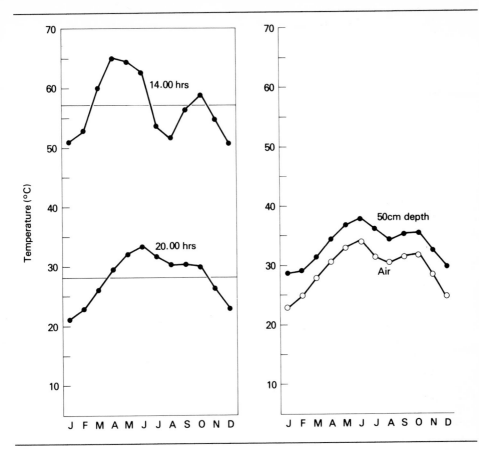

Fig. 7.4 Mean monthly temperatures at 1 cm below sand surface at 1400 and 2000 hr. The mean diurnal fluctuations are greater than indicated in the figure because the daily minimum temperatures occur just before sunrise at about 0600 hr. (Data from Oliver 1965.)

Fig. 7.5 The mean monthly soil temperatures at 50 cm depth. The temperatures at 0800, 1400 and 2000 hr each day do not vary more than one degree at this depth. The temperature at 50 cm parallels the mean monthly air temperature. (Data from Oliver 1965.)

the mean temperature of the air above the ground (Figs. 7.5, 7.11). The annual range of temperature also decreases with depth (Fig. 7.6).

Low relative humidities are characteristic of tropical arid climates, but there are seasonal variations related to the movements of the Inter-tropical Convergence Zone (ITCZ) and the occurrence of rain. Diurnal fluctuations inversely follow the diurnal fluctuations in temperature. The relative humidity is highest just before sunrise, and lowest at about 1600 hours. The annual regime of relative humidities at Khartoum and in the Kalahari Gemsbok National Park are illustrated in Fig. 7.7.

High temperatures and low relative humidities result in high rates of evaporation from open water or moistened soil. This, as well as the low unreliable rainfall and the absence of springs and rivers, results in the aridity which is the major problem for animals and plants in the arid zones. The monthly potential evapotranspiration at Khartoum, in relation to rainfall, is illustrated in Fig. 7.3. The daily evaporation is related to temperature and windspeed. Evaporation is usually minimal at about 0600

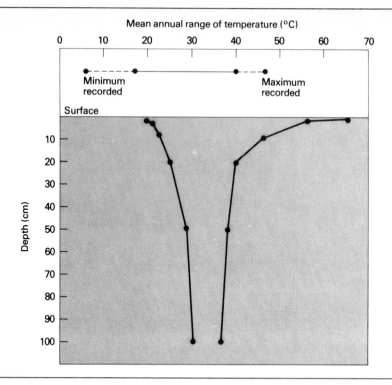

Fig. 7.6   The mean annual range of temperature at various depths in the sand near Khartoum. The annual range of temperature diminishes with increasing depth, and the temperatures in the top 10 cm of sand are often higher than the mean maximum air temperatures. (Data from Oliver 1965.)

hours, and maximal at about 1000 hours; 60–70 per cent of the total daily evaporation occurs during daylight hours (Oliver 1965).

7.2   Vegetation

Plants provide the mammals of the arid zones with food, water and shelter, and consequently the carrying capacity of the arid zones is primarily related to the state of the vegetation. Plant life is sparce in arid regions mainly because of the lack of water, and therefore the density and distribution of the vegetation is related to rainfall and geomorphology. Rainfall run-off collects at the bases of jebels, in depressions and in watercourses. These localities support xerophytic plants, whose deep roots draw moisture from the ground water many metres below the surface, and drought-enduring plants which are dormant in the dry season and begin growth from rootstocks or rhizomes after rain. In localities where water does not collect, there are many species of desert grasses and herbs which appear only after rainstorms. These ephemeral drought-evading plants germinate, grow, flower and set seed within three to four weeks before the upper layers of the soil dry again. Further details on the biology of plants in arid zones is given by Cloudsley-Thompson and Chadwick (1964).

In the arid regions near Khartoum, scattered *Acacia tortilis, A. nubica, A. ehrenbergia, Capparis, decidua* and *Ziziphus spini-christi* trees and bushes form a savanna-like woodland in some localities, and in others they are virtually absent. The

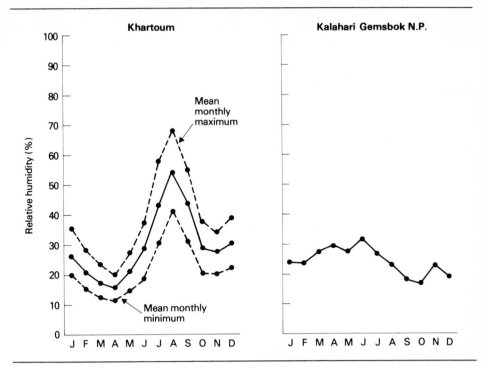

Fig. 7.7 Relative humidities at Khartoum and Kalahari Gemsbok National Park (Twee Rivieren). Solid lines: mean monthly relative humidities; broken lines: mean monthly maximum and minimum humidities (Khartoum only). The high relative humidities at Khartoum in July–September are due to the rainstorms of these months (Fig. 7.3*a*). (Data for Khartoum from Oliver 1965; for Kalahari Gemsbok National Park from Maclean 1970.)

wadis contain clumps of the perennial grasses *Panicum turgidum* and *Cymbopogon proximum*, and small trees of *Acacia* spp., *Balanites aegyptiaca* and *Commiphora africana*. Other shrubs, grasses and climbers may also be present (Kassas 1956, Halwagy 1961), but succulents are rare. From July to August, ephemeral grasses and herbs cover the sand plains in areas where rain has fallen, but these plants soon wither and their stems and seeds are buried by shifting sand or are blown by the wind to accumulate on the windward side of rocks, dunes and bushes. By December, there is little evidence of their existence. The scattered bushes of *Capparis* and *Ziziphus* consolidate sand around their roots and create stable mounds into which small mammals can burrow (Fig. 7.1*b*).

The vegetation of the Kalahari Gemsbok National Park varies greatly in composition and abundance depending on locality and topography (Fig. 7.2). On the sandveld, especially on the crests and rises of the dunes, there are scattered *Acacia*, *Grewia*, *Boscia albitrunca* and *Terminalia sericea* bushes and shrubs. Clumps of *Aristida*, *Eragrostis* and *Athenatherum* grasses grow on the dunes, but shrubs and grasses are absent or rare in the troughs between the dunes. The river beds and banks support an entirely different and richer flora due to the generally higher moisture content of the soils, and the mosaic of different soil types. Most parts of the river beds are dominated by *Acacia giraffae* and/or *A. haematoxylon*, and by the perennial grasses *Panicum coloratum* and *Eragrostis bicolor*. Ephemerals are common in the river beds after rains and many of them continue to grow into the beginning of the dry season; these include species in the genera *Chloris, Enneapogon, Tribulus, Eragrostis, Geigeria* and *Schmidtia*. The river banks, and most of the dune troughs with shallow sand, are covered by a shrub *Rhizogum trichotomum*, a perennial grass *Aristida obtusa* and an ephemeral grass *Schmidtia kalaharensis*. The river banks of the Auob have outcrops of calcrete, and the soils and sands in this region have a high lime content. *Enneapogon, Eragrostis* and *Schmidtia* are the commonest species around these outcrops and they, and other species, are heavily grazed. Succulent plants are generally uncommon in the park, but some grow on the rocky areas of the river banks. Plants which appear to be important sources of water, particularly in the dry season, are *Citrellus* spp. (fruits and seeds), *Cucumis* spp. (fruits), *Elephantorrhiza* (roots), *Crinum* (bulbs) and *Oxygonum delagoense* (stems and leaves). After rains, for example two showers of 12 mm or more within two or three weeks, ephemeral plants germinate and grow on the sandveld providing a luxuriant, though temporary, source of food for many mammals (Morris 1958, Brynard 1958, Leistner 1959, Parris 1971).

7.3   Mammals of the Sudanese plain and Kalahari Gemsbok Park

The mammals of the three arid zones have evolved under similar conditions and so there is a tendency for each zone to support mammals with ecological equivalents in other zones. However, each zone has several species of endemic mammals not found elsewhere. There are many features of arid habitats which have resulted in the evolution of special morphological features. For example, the terrain is often sandy and soft so mammals need broad feet (camel) or hairy soles (jerboa, some gerbils) to facilitate locomotion. The terrain is very open so that mammals, especially small ones, rely on sandy colouration, good eyesight, acute hearing and sustained erratic locomotion to avoid predators.

Fifteen species of mammals commonly occur on the sand plains near Khartoum (Table 7.1). There are also some non-arid zone species, e.g. Nile rat (*Arvicanthis niloticus*), white tailed mongoose (*Ichneumia albicauda*), genet (*Genetta genetta*) and fruit bat (*Eidolon helvum*), living in the Nile valley and, although they are not discussed in this chapter, their presence shows that non-arid species can penetrate into the arid zones if tracts of suitable habitat are present (Happold 1967a). Most mammals in the arid zones depend on plants for food. Near Khartoum, for example, shrubs are eaten by the dorcas gazelle, herbs and grass are eaten by the hare, and there are five species of small rodents which feed on grasses, herbs and seeds. Mammals which are not directly dependant on plants for food are small in size and comparatively uncommon. These include two species of insectivorous hedgehogs (*Erinaceus, Paraechinus*), two species of fox (*Vulpes*) and a striped weasel (*Ictonyx*). The foxes and weasel are probably insectivorous of necessity at some times of the year when rodents and lizards are rare or inaccessable. Insect-eating bats live in rocky crevices and caves and may be fairly abundant at some times of the year. The jebels near Khartoum support their own species of mammals, and these have feeding habits as diverse as those mammals on the sand plains. Neither the jebels nor the sand plains support any large carnivorous, insectivorous or seed-fruit eating mammals. Permanently fossorial mammals are also absent, probably because underground roots, rhizomes and bulbs are too scattered to provide adequate food.

The mammals of the Kalahari Gemsbok National Park may be divided into two groups (Table 7.2). First, there are species which live in the sandveld and are capable of surviving without free water or with only infrequent access to water, and secondly there are species which live near the riverbeds and which are dependant on vegetation

Table 7.1 Niche segregation of the mammals of the Sudanese plain near Khartoum on the basis of domiciles and feeding habits. Species confined to the mesic habitat along the Nile valley are not included. (Data from Happold 1967a.)

Domiciles	Feeding habits				
	Browsers	Grazers	Fruit and seed eaters	Carnivores	Insectivores
Live above ground level, large in size	Gazelle (*G. dorcas*) Goats	Addax* Oryx*			
Live above ground (G), or in holes and crevices (H). Medium size	Hare (*Lepus*) G	Hare G Ground squirrel (*Xerus*) H	Ground squirrel H	Foxes (*Vulpes pallida, V. rueppelli*) H	Foxes (*Vulpes pallida, V. rueppelli*) H
Live in burrows, small size, nocturnal		Gerbils (*Gerbillus* two spp.) Jeroba (*Jaculus*)	Gerbils (*Gerbillus* two spp.) Jerboa (*Jaculus*)	Weasel (*Ictonyx*)	Zorilla (*Ictonyx*) Hedgehogs (*Erinaceus, Paraechinus*)
Caves					Microchiroptera (several species)
Jebels	Barbary sheep*	Rock hyrax (*Procavia*) Rodents (*Acomys, Gerbillus campestris*)	Rock hyrax Rodents (*Acomys, G. campestris*)	Foxes (*Vulpes pallida, V. ruepelli*)	Microchiroptera (as in caves)

Note: the species indicated by an asterisk may not occur near Khartoum at the present time and quantitatively they are unimportant. However, there is good evidence that they occurred in recent historical times.

Table 7.2 *Niche segregation of the mammals of the Kalahari Gemsbok National Park on the basis of domiciles and feeding habits. Rare species are not included. Species confined mostly to the Nossob and Auob river beds are indicated by an asterisk. (Data from Rautenbach 1971, Davis 1968, Nel and Nolte 1965, Eloff 1961, Parris 1971, Leistner 1959.)*

Domiciles	Feeding habits				
	Browsers	Grazers	Fruit and seed eaters	Carnivores	Insectivores
Live above ground, large size	Gemsbok Steenbok	Gemsbok Steenbok Springbok Blue wildebeest* Red hartebeest* Eland*		Lion* Wildcat* Caracal*	
Live above ground (G), or in holes or crevices (H). Medium size		Hare (*Lepus*) G Springhare (*Pedetes*) H Porcupine (*Hystrix*) H*	Ground squirrel (*Xerus*) H* Porcupine (*Hystrix*) H*	Bat-eared fox Silver jackal Black-backed jackal Mongooses (three spp.)	Aardvark*
Live in burrows, small size		Mole rat (*Cryptomys*) Gerbils (three spp.) Karroo rat (*Parotomys*) Rodents (*Rhabdomys*, *Malacothrix*, *Thallomys*, *Mus*, *Saccostomus*)	As for grazers		Shrew (*Crocidura hirta*)*
Caves, crevices					Microchiroptera (two spp.)

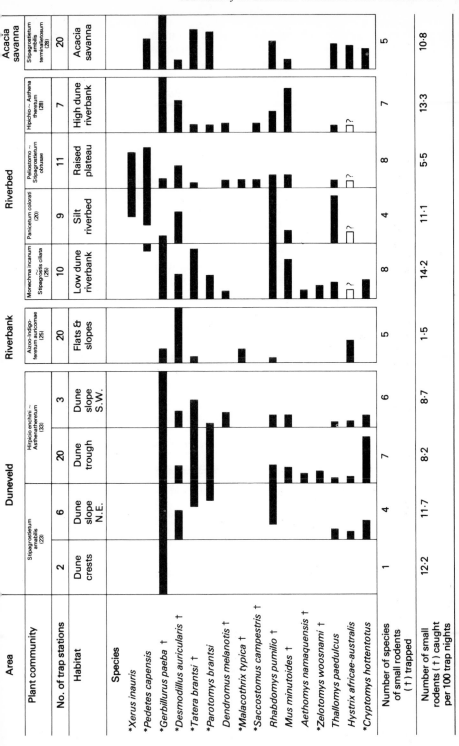

Fig. 7.8 Ecological distribution of rodents in the southern part of the Kalahari Gemsbok National Park. The number of trap stations (20 m apart) gives an indication of the width of each habitat sampled. The mean number of plant species in each community is given in parenthesis. An asterisk indicates species which burrow, and † indicates the small species of rodents which were trapped. (Adapted from Nel and Rautenbach 1975).

with a high water content or require water to a greater extent than the sandveld mammals. These two major habitats have resulted in a mammal fauna which contains more species than that at Khartoum; however, some species in the riverbed habitat may not be considered as arid zone mammals because of their dependance on this relatively mesic habitat. Blue wildebeest, red hartebeest and eland, whose presence is due to the mesic riverbed habitat, are elements of a fauna found further to the south and west (towards the inland escarpment of south-west Africa) but which does not extend further north and north-east into the more arid parts of the Kalahari desert. Some of these large ungulates move into the sandveld to feed on the ephemeral plants after rain storms. Gemsbok and springbok can survive in the sandveld for considerable periods of time. Niche selection in the arid environment of the Kalahari is well illustrated by the rodents (Nel and Rautenbach 1975). *Xerus* and *Pedetes* inhabit only the riverbed where there is fine soil. The other species live in a variety of habitats in the dune riverbanks, on the dune slopes and troughs, and in the surrounding *Acacia* savanna (Fig. 7.8); each has its own particular niche requirements. Only one species (*Gerbillurus paeba*) survives on the dune crests probably because it is the most widespread and most numerous of all the Kalahari rodents. The highest numbers of small rodents, and the greatest species diversity, are found in the low dune riverbanks (mostly *G. paeba* and *R. pumilio*), dune troughs (mostly *G. paeba*) and the silt riverbed (mostly *R. pumilio*). The least numbers and smallest species diversity are found on the dune crest and slopes (*G. paeba*) and the calcrete riverbed (*Desmodillus*).

Most of the niches occupied by mammals at Khartoum are occupied by similar mammals in the Kalahari Gemsbok National Park. There are some interesting ecological equivalents (Table 7.3) especially for the small rodents and the medium sized

Table 7.3   *Arid zone ecological equivalents in the Sudanese plain (Sudanese arid zone) and in the Kalahari Gemsbok National Park (south-west arid zone).*

Sudanese plain	Kalahari Gemsbok National Park
Dorcas gazelle (*Gazella dorcas*)	Springbok (*Antidorcas marsupialis*)
Pale fox (*Vulpes pallida*) Rüppell's fox (*Vulpes rueppelli*)	Bat-eared fox (*Otocyon megalotis*) Cape fox (*Vulpes chama*) Black-backed jackal (*Canis mesomelas*)
Jerboa (*Jaculus jaculus*)	Springhare (*Pedetes capensis*)
Gerbillus pyramidum *Gerbillus watersi*	*Gerbillurus paeba* *Tatera brantsi* Namaqua gerbil (*Desmodillus auricularis*) Karroo rat (*Paratomys brantsi*)
Scimitar-horned oryx (*Oryx dammah*) Addax (*Addax nasomaculatus*)	Gemsbok (*Oryx gazella*)

carnivores. The genera *Lepus, Ictonyx* and *Xerus* occur in both arid zones, but there are some genera which occur in one but not the other; for example, *Gazella, Jaculus, Gerbillus, Acomys, Procavia* and *Paraechinus* occur at Khartoum but not in the Kalahari Gemsbok National Park, and *Pedetes, Cryptomys, Gerbillurus, Tatera, Desmodillus, Paratomys, Otocyon* and *Canis* occur in the Kalahari Gemsbok National Park but not at Khartoum. The jebel habitats near Khartoum, and their associated mammals (Table 7.1) do not seem to have any direct equivalents in the Kalahari Gemsbok National Park. The large ungulates and carnivores which live mostly near the riverbeds and river banks in the Kalahari Gemsbok National Park have no equivalents in the arid zone at Khartoum.

The common mole-rat (*Cryptomys hottentotus*) which lives in the hardened soils of the river banks (Rautenbach 1971) also has no equivalent at Khartoum, nor has the shrew (*Crocidura hirta*). Owl pellet analysis suggests that this latter species is quite common in some localities in the Nossob river bed (Davis 1968). The four principal sandveld rodents (*Tatera brantsi, Gerbillurus paeba, Desmodillus auricularis* and *Paratomys brantsi*) all live in communal burrows (de Graaf and Nel 1965, Nel 1967) as do *Gerbillus pyramidum* and *Gerbillus watersi* at Khartoum (Happold 1967a). *Paratomys* is unusual in being dielactive (Davis 1958) like *Xerus*, whereas the other small rodents are entirely nocturnal.

7.4   Population numbers and biomass

The carrying capacity (p. 321) of the arid zones is determined mainly by the availability of food and water, and therefore is proportional to the extent of plant growth, seed production and prey abundance. These, in turn, are related to rainfall, and since rainfall is low and unpredictable, biomass is subject to large-scale fluctuations. Although sudden increases in the numbers of arid zone mammals has often been recorded, quantitative information to indicate the magnitude of these population fluctuations is rare.

Small non-migratory species remain in the same locality all the time and their numbers may fluctuate greatly. Jerboas, gerbils and hedgehogs at Khartoum increase

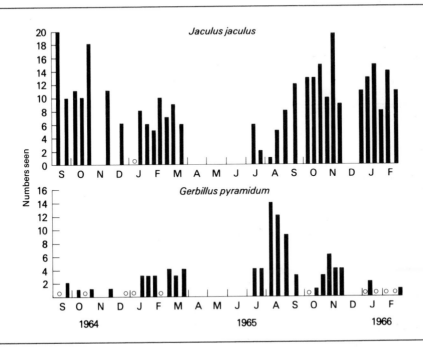

Fig. 7.9   The numbers of jerboas (*Jaculus jaculus butleri*) and gerbils (*Gerbillus pyramidum*) seen in the arid zone near Khartoum during standardised two-hour sampling periods. A zero indicates that no specimens were seen. There was no sampling in April, May, June and December 1965. (After Happold 1967b.)

in number during and immediately after the rainy season, and decrease during the main part of the dry season. Rainfall at Khartoum is seasonal (Fig. 7.3) and therefore the rise and fall of population numbers is predictable, although the level of population numbers depends on the actual amount of rainfall and the food resources. In more arid regions, rainfall is more sporadic and unpredictable, as are the population numbers. In severe dry periods, small non-migratory species may become very rare or locally extinct. The problem for these species is to ensure that enough individuals survive so they can reproduce when conditions become suitable again (Ch. 7.5).

The number of jerboas and gerbils seen during a standard drive of about two hours immediately after sunset at Khartoum (Happold 1967*b*) illustrates the variability of population numbers. The highest numbers of jerboas were seen after the wet season (September to December), although some individuals were seen in every month in which there was sampling (Fig. 7.9). Gerbils were not as numerous but their numbers remained fairly stable with an increase due to young animals after the wet season.

The biomass of large migratory species in a particular area may range from zero during a drought to a relatively high figure if a flush of new vegetation attracts many individuals. However, the biomass on a long term basis over a large area is generally small. Valverde (in Bourliere 1963*a*, *b*) records a biomass of ungulates in Rio del Oro of 0.3 kg/km^{-2}, and the four species of ungulates in the Oum–Chalouba district of Chad have a biomass of about 80 kg/km^{-2}. These biomasses are very low when compared with other tropical habitats.

7.5   Problems of life

The variability of the habitat, and the corresponding fluctuations in population numbers, has resulted in the natural selection of a number of adaptions which are characteristic of individuals and populations of arid zone mammals. Many of these characteristics are concerned with survival when food and water are scarce and when the environmental temperature reaches the upper limits of tolerance. Others are concerned with the ability to reproduce rapidly and to put the maximum energy into reproduction when conditions are favourable.

Fluctuations in the availability of food

Because the species of plants and their density vary depending on topography, rainfall and season, the amount of food available for mammals varies from time to time and from place to place. Arid zone mammals attempt to survive fluctuating food resources in several ways; some travel long distances from poor areas into richer ones, some store food and others change their diet.

Dorcas gazelle, addax, scimitar-horned oryx and gemsbok are examples of nomadic arid zone mammals. These antelopes can travel many miles in search of food and water. Addax are recorded as being able to detect changes in the humidity of the air so they can find areas where grass is sprouting after a rain storm. The ability to migrate and travel long distances is essential for the survival of these mammals because of the widespread, sporadic availability of suitable foods. Similarly, insect-eating bats are very mobile. Large flocks of the Trident leaf-nosed bat (*Asellia tridens*) inhabited a jebel cave several miles from the Nile river during the cool dry season when, presumably, there was inadequate food further away in the desert, but they did not live in this cave in the rainy season (Happold, unpublished). Small non-migratory mammals are unable to escape from harsh environmental conditions, and therefore their population numbers are subject to considerable fluctuations (Section 12.5).

Another method of overcoming fluctuating food resources is by hoarding food when supplies are plentiful. *Gerbillus pyramidum* at Khartoum (Happold 1968), and *Desmodillus auricularis* (Keogh 1973) and *Gerbillurus paeba* (Stutterheim and Skinner 1973) in the Kalahari Gemsbok National Park, hoard food for use in times of shortage. The ground squirrel (*Xerus erythropus*) which lives in the Sudanese and Somali arid zones also buries food for future use (Ewer 1965). Jerboas (*Jaculus jaculus*) do not store food and so it is likely that their population numbers fluctuate more than those of food-hoarding species. Food hoarding is a widespread behaviour pattern among rodents of arid regions, and has been recorded for many species of the North American and Australian deserts.

A third method of surviving fluctuating food resources is to change the diet or eat a wide variety of foods. This is especially true of the carnivorous and insectivorous mammals whose prey numbers fluctuate erratically. For example, insects are abundant at Khartoum in some months, and almost absent from December to June (Cloudsley-Thompson and Idris 1964). Foxes, weasels and owls which feed partly on small vertebrates are all faced with times when food is scarce. The feeding habits of desert predators have rarely been studied, but it is likely that they are not too selective in their feeding preferences because, at times, there may be little suitable food. Monad (in Schmidt-Nielsen 1964) found that fennec foxes have a mixed diet of insects, lizards, rodents and plant material.

Availability of water

Aridity is an equally important problem for arid zone mammals. The limited rainfall means that there is no free water for most or all of the year, and mammals have to obtain water from their food and by metabolism. Throughout most of their lives, arid zone mammals survive on very little water and many characteristics of their anatomy, physiology and behaviour facilitate conservation of body fluids.

Adaptations which have been recorded in African arid zone mammals include storage of water in the camel (Schmidt-Nielsen 1964), the ability to eat saline succulents in the rodent *Psammomys* (Schmidt-Nielsen 1964), reliance on the high water content of a succulent (*Trianthema*) which obtains its moisture from advective fog in the Namib desert (Louw 1972), migratory movements to search for green forage and/or water, and many physiological characteristics of the kidneys, skin and blood system. The methods of obtaining and conserving water are closely linked with temperature regulation, and each arid zone species possesses its own unique combination of adaptations to conserve water and maintain the correct body temperature under varying conditions of water deprivation and heat stress (see Schmidt-Nielsen 1964). Some of these problems, and solutions, in the jerboa and the dorcas gazelle are discussed further in Sections 7.6 and 11.1.

Arid zone carnivores obtain most of their water from the body fluids of their prey. In the Kalahari Gemsbok National Park, for example, the black-backed jackal (*Canis mesomelas*), bat-eared fox (*Otocyon megalotis*) and the spotted hyaena (*Crocuta crocuta*) feed extensively on the workers of harvester termites (*Hodotermes mossambica*) which emerge after rain (G. L. Maclean, pers. comm.). Probably some species of small rodents also obtain water by eating these termites.

Temperature

A third major problem confronting arid zone mammals is the high temperatures which approach, and sometimes exceed, the limits of tolerance. Large mammals, which because of their size have to remain on the surface of the ground, shelter in shady areas, and some (e.g. the camel) are able to withstand an increased body temperature provided this extra heat load can be lost during the night. Large mammals are usually inactive during the hottest and driest times of the day. Cooling mechanisms which depend on the evaporation of water, such as sweating, panting and licking, are infrequently used because water is scarce. However, water loss by evaporation may take place, for a short period of time, if the body temperature reaches a particular upper limit. This topic is discussed in more detail in Section 11.2.

Small mammals avoid the highest temperatures of the day by sheltering in burrows or caves where the maximum daily temperature, and the daily range of temperature, is less than that of the air (Figs. 7.4, 7.5 and 7.6). After sunset, as the air temperature is falling, foxes, weasels, hedgehogs, rodents and bats emerge from their resting places. They may be active until dawn, but this will depend on the species and the exact climatic conditions of the night. Their burrowing or cave-dwelling behaviour during the day, and nocturnal activity on or above the surface, reduces the range of temperatures to which they are exposed. This is a very essential behavioural characteristic for small mammals as they are unable to survive long exposures to the typically high temperatures of the surface sand and the air during the day.

The cold temperatures recorded in arid regions (Fig. 7.3), especially at night during the cool period of the year, may be lethal to small mammals. Rodents, in particular, tend to be rather inactive on cold nights, or they emerge from their warmer burrows for only short periods of time.

Reproduction

The population numbers of arid zone mammals tend to fluctuate in relation to climate and the availability of food. After a period of drought and limited (or non-existant) food resources, population numbers may be very low. It is advantageous for a species if the population numbers can be increased as rapidly as possible when there is a temporary abundance of food. Conversely, it is not an advantage to have a regular breeding season if the resources are irregular and unpredictable as young born during a drought are unlikely to survive. Characteristics which allow rapid reproduction when conditions are 'right' so as to produce the maximum number of weaned young in the minimum of time, will result in a population which is sufficiently large that some individuals should survive to breed again after the next drought. Such characteristics include a social organisation which reduces competition for mates, a short gestation period, rapid growth of the young to weaning age, a post-partum oestrus so a second litter can develop while the former litter is suckling, and the storage of food to supply readily available energy when reproduction begins. Arid zone mammals vary in their ability to reproduce rapidly. Some rodents, e.g. *Acomys*, *Gerbillus*, *Taterillus* and *Jaculus*, begin to breed as soon as new resources are available and the first young are weaned during the flush of new grasses and seeds. Populations of small mammals can recover quickly after drought periods due to their rapid reproductive rates.

Large mammals are less numerous in arid zones because of the scarcity of food, and because of their greater longevity they do not need to produce as many young in order for the population to survive. In addition, large mammals have much longer gestation periods compared with small mammals, and are unable to produce young quickly enough to take advantage of the temporary food abundance. Increases in population numbers may occur after years of food abundance when conditions are de-teriorating again, and the converse may also occur. Thus it does not follow that populations of large mammals will increase and decrease in exact synchrony with the carrying capacity. The populations of large species survive, not because of rapid reproduction, but because of their mobility to search for food, their longevity and because some food resources last for a long time due to a low rate of utilisation.

7.6   Comparative ecology of jerboa and dorcas gazelle

Although most of the mammals in the arid zones are exposed to similar sorts of environmental problems, they have not been exposed to identical selection pressures, and the problems of survival have been solved in several ways. This becomes very clear when the ecology of two sympatric species, the jerboa and the dorcas gazelle, are compared. The jerboa (*Jaculus jaculus*) is a small rodent weighing about 40 g, and the dorcas gazelle (*Gazella dorcas*) is an antelope weighing about 16 kg. Both species inhabit the sandplain near Khartoum.

Ecology of the Sudanese jerboa

The Sudanese jerboa (Fig. 1.23) strongly resembles the kangaroo rat (*Dipodomys*) of the North American deserts and the hopping mouse (*Notomys*) of the Australian deserts. The resemblance is due to convergent evolution, and each genus has evolved similar adaptations. Jerboas (and their ecological equivalents) are nocturnal and fossorial. When burrowing, they use their forelimbs to loosen sand and pile it underneath them, and their powerful hindlimbs kick the accumulated sand back and out of the entrance. Sand is also shovelled and packed down by the jerboa's blunt nose. Valve-like nostrils are another adaptation for burrowing in this species. Jerboas have elongated hindlimbs, short forelimbs, and long tails with a tuft on the tip; these are adaptations for sustained fast saltatorial and bipedal locomotion over open terrain. The thick fur on the soles of the hindfeet facilitate locomotion on soft sand. The ability to travel easily over long distances, at high speed if necessary (up to 20 km/h), enables jerboas to utilise scattered food resources without excessive loss of energy, and to avoid predators. Jerboas have large eyes, large ear pinnae and enormous tympanic bullae (Fig. 7.10) which help them to detect predators and other animals, and which give them maximum awareness of their surroundings. (In contrast, mice of similar size in non-arid vegetated habitats tend to have small ear pinnae, small eyes and short limbs. The vegetation obstructs their hearing, vision and locomotion, but provides cover.) The gerbils (*Gerbillus pyramidum* and *G. watersi*) (Fig. 1.22*b*), combine both sets of characteristics: short limbs and comparatively slow locomotion with large eyes and medium-sized ear pinnae and typanic bullae (Fig. 7.10). In contrast to jerboas, the gerbils utilise food close to bushes and shrubs, and they avoid predators by running into cover or into their burrows. Jerboas (unlike gerbils) do not store food in their burrows; consequently the number of jerboas are likely to decrease to a greater extent during long periods of drought and food shortage than those of gerbils.

  Both jerboas and gerbils eat seeds, leaves and the stems of herbs and grasses, and their food provides most of the water available to these species. For much of the year, these foods are air-dried and contain only a small percentage of water. During the dry season, jerboas obtain additional water by feeding on the bulbs of *Cyperus bulbosus* (53 per cent water) and corms of *Dipcadi* sp. (74 per cent water) (Ghobrial and Hodieb 1973). Jerboas can also obtain water by metabolism so that by deliberately eating more, they can increase their metabolic water to a significant extent. It is essential that jerboas conserve water in every possible way. Their kidneys are capable of excreting nitrogenous wastes in considerably less water then that required by non-arid zone mammals. Urine concentrations as high as 4320 mM/l have been recorded, compared

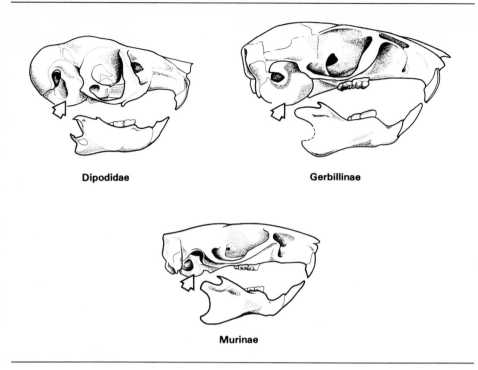

Dipodidae

Gerbillinae

Murinae

Fig. 7.10   Skulls of two arid-zone rodents, *Jaculus jaculus* (top left) and *Gerbillus gerbillus* (top right), and a savanna rodent, *Praomys natalensis* (below), to show the enlargement of the tympanic bullae (arrowed) characteristic of the Dipodidae and Gerbillinae.

with concentrations of 2160 mM/l for domestic rats (Schmidt-Nielsen 1964). It is uncertain whether jerboas produce a smaller bulk of faeces with a lower water content compared with non-arid zone rodents; faeces with a low water content help to conserve water although quantitatively this source of water loss is not important. Jerboas pant to cool themselves in emergencies (such as after being chased), but at other times they attempt to reduce evaporative water loss from their respiratory tracts. They do this in at least three ways.

1. During the day they shelter and sleep in deep burrows which are cooler and more humid than the air above ground. In the cool dry season, jerboas live in burrows close to the surface (25 cm), but in the hot season the burrows are much deeper (70 cm) where the mean daily temperature and daily temperature fluctuations are not as great as those close to the surface (Ghobrial and Hodieb 1973). At these depths, jerboas spend the day in temperatures of about 26–28 °C in the cool season and 37 °C in the hot season (Fig. 7.11). The relative humidities of burrows near Khartoum has not been measured, but burrows in the Egyptian desert near Abu Rawash had relative humidities ranging from 69–100 per cent (Yunker and Guirgis 1969).
2. Jerboas sleep with the head tucked under the abdomen, and Kirmiz (1962) suggested that in this way they inhale air which is already moist.
3. Jerboas usually plug the entrances of their burrows with sand, and it seems likely that this helps to raise the humidity inside the burrow because no dry air can enter

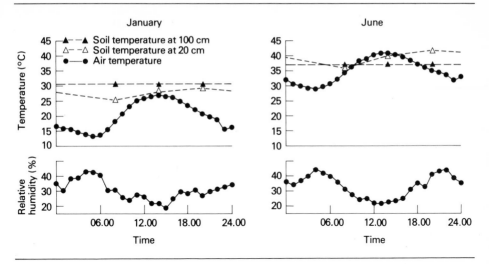

Fig. 7.11   The temperatures of the air, the soil at 20 cm and 100 cm depth, and the relative humidity of the air, during a 24-hour period in January (left) and June (right) at Khartoum. In January, soil temperatures are higher and have smaller daily fluctuations compared with air temperatures. Burrowing rodents are not exposed to low temperatures in their burrows. In June, air and soil temperatures are higher than in January, and at the hottest time of the day (1000 to 1600 hr) burrowing rodents are protected from the high air temperatures. By alternating between nocturnal activity (with frequent returns to the burrow in cool weather) and daytime resting in a burrow of suitable depth, rodents avoid the extremes of temperature. They are not exposed to temperatures above 40 °C which are potentially lethal (see text). (Data from Sudan Meteorological Service, and Oliver 1965.)

from outside, and because of evaporation from the moist sand surrounding the burrow. The occurrence of plugging in *Notomys alexis* (the ecological equivalent of the jerboa in the Australian deserts) has been correlated with relative humidities of less than 42 per cent, and the occupants of artificial burrows were able to raise the humidity by plugging the burrow entrance (Happold, M. 1975). The disadvantage of plugging lies in the concomitant increase of the carbon dioxide concentration, and to compensate for this *Notomys* has an oxygen dissociation curve shifted to the left of the normal mammalian position (Baudinette 1972). The same situation is likely to occur in *Jaculus* also.

The evolution of the jerboa, like all hot arid zone mammals, has been profoundly influenced by the high temperatures which occur in their habitats. Although no data are available for *Jaculus jaculus*, two related species (*J. orientalis* and *J. deserti*) can maintain their body temperature of 36–37 °C at environmental temperatures from 0 °C to 33 °C, but the body temperature increases when the air temperature is 33–35 °C and death occurs from heat exhaustion after one hour at 40 °C (Hooper and Hilali 1972). This range of tolerance is similar to that of non-arid zone rodents of similar size, and therefore the upper lethal temperature of the jerboa is not particularly high, and it would not be able to withstand the daytime temperatures above the ground (Figs. 7.4 and 7.6). Most non-arid zone mammals rely on evaporative cooling to prevent over-heating. Jerboas are unable to do this because of the need to conserve water (Section 7.5), so they avoid high environmental temperatures by remaining in their burrows during the day and emerging at night when the sand surface and air temperatures are neither too high or too low. Because food is often scarce, jerboas do not waste energy by metabolising it to produce heat on cold nights. It is more economical to remain in the burrow as the microclimate of the burrow can be modified to some extent by varying the depth, plugging the entrances, and by lining the nests with insulating materials such as grass. In cold weather, several jerboas huddle together in the same nest; each individual gains heat from the other individuals, and collectively they require less energy to remain warm. Burrowing has the added advantage of enabling small mammals like jerboas to avoid exposure to strong winds, sandstorms, rainstorms, intense solar radiation and daytime birds of prey.

To summarise, the principal adaptations of the jerboa to life in arid regions are:

1. Nocturnal activity to avoid the high temperatures and low humidities of the daytime.
2. Burrowing to suitable depths to avoid daytime air and subsurface temperatures. Burrowing provides the jerboa with a suitable microclimate which facilitates the maintenance of the correct body temperature and the conservation of body fluids.
3. Morphological features which allow easy locomotion over the sand (long hindlimbs, hairy hind toes, long tail), awareness of the open environment (large eyes, large tympanic bullae, long ear pinnae) and the conservation of water (specialised kidneys).
4. An ability to survive and grow on air-dried grasses, seeds and bulbs with a high water content, without any free water.
5. An ability to reproduce quickly after rainstorms when there is a temporary abundance of food and water.

Ecology of the dorcas gazelle

The dorcas gazelle has a wide distribution in the arid regions of the northern Sudan. These gazelles are lightly built so they can run quickly over the sand plains. The body is covered with long guard hairs (up to 3·5 cm long) and a short dense undercoat (Ghobrial 1970*a*). The hairs can be erected to form an insulating layer during cool dry nights, and when there is high insolation during the daytime. Ghobrial (1970*a*) suggests that the coat holds a layer of humid air which helps to prevent excess water loss through the sweat glands and the thin epidermis.

Gazelles cannot burrow like jerboas to escape from the high daytime temperatures, but observations show that they are active at night, in the early hours of the morning and at dusk. They rest in the shade of small bushes at the hottest time of the day. In the dry season, when the maximum daytime shade temperatures are usually less than 35 °C, gazelles may be active all day.

Gazelles need to maintain their body temperature within narrow limits as they can not tolerate an increase in their body temperature. During the day, the high ambient temperature and high insolation heats the body, and the gazelle begins to sweat when the ambient temperature is 22 °C and the body temperature is 38 °C. The ventilation rate (and therefore the loss of water from the lungs) increases as the ambient temperature rises. Because thermoregulation depends on the cooling effects of sweating and on evaporation from the respiratory tract, gazelles require an adequate daily supply of water to replace that lost during the hottest part of the day. The dependance of the dorcas gazelle on a regular supply of water for thermoregulation is an unexpected characteristic for an arid zone mammal. In this respect, the dorcas gazelle is less well adapted than two closely related species (*G. thomsoni* and *G. granti*) from less arid regions, which are able to tolerate hyperthermia for several hours during the hottest period of the day (Taylor, C. R. 1972) (Section 11.2).

Dorcas gazelles are very selective in their feeding habits. Despite the variety of shrubs and grasses available, they feed exclusively on the leaves of *Acacia tortilis*. This tree is found along the sides of wadis and in the open sand plains, and remains evergreen for 18 months after the last rainstorm (Carlisle and Ghobrial 1968). The leaves, whatever their age, contain an average of 48·7 per cent water and provide the gazelle with an abundant and easily obtainable supply of water and food. If rain does not fall for 18 months, the leaves drop from the trees, and the gazelles have to move to another area where rain has fallen more recently.

Dorcas gazelles have different food and water requirements in the cool dry season and in the hot (and probably wet) season. Experiments have shown that a gazelle requires about 590 ml water/day in the cool season, and only about 160 ml are lost by evaporation to prevent hyperthermia. The daily food intake provides more than enough water. However, in the hot season a gazelle requires about 840 ml water/day and it loses more water by evaporation, but because it eats less and therefore takes in less water, it must find sources of drinking water. There may be temporary pools of water after rainstorms, but if there is no rain gazelles move towards the Nile valley and the cooler Red Sea hills. Migrations of dorcas gazelle have been observed for many years, and it is now realised that these migrations are due to the increased water requirements in the hot season. The distribution of gazelles each month, therefore, is determined by the past pattern of rainfall, the distribution of *Acacia tortilis* leaves, and the present pattern of rainfall and temperature.

If dorcas gazelles do not obtain sufficient water, they lose weight rapidly (Ghobrial 1970*b*, 1974). When water is in short supply, they produce a smaller volume than normal of concentrated urine, and water loss in the faeces is reduced to about one third of normal. If deprived of drinking water during the hot season and fed on sorghum containing only 8 per cent water, gazelles die in four to five days. Consequently gazelles rely on behavioural mechanisms including mobility, selection of food with a high water content and activity rhythms to survive in arid regions.

All these characteristics suggest that dorcas gazelles appear to be less well adapted to arid regions then some other arid zone mammals. They are not found in extreme arid conditions, and their distribution is determined by the necessity to obtain sufficient water in the hot season.

The principal adaptations of the dorcas gazelle to life in the arid regions are:

1. Mobility to range widely over the sand plains in search of suitable food and water.
2. Activity is confined to the night and the coolest part of the day. Activity times are longer in the cool season then in the hot season.
3. The ability to migrate to cooler and wetter areas when necessary.
4. The ability to concentrate urine and to reduce the water content of the faeces, as a means of conserving water. (Conversely, the gazelle is not well adapted for arid regions because it requires a regular supply of water.)
5. A thick coat, sweating and increased ventilation, which enable the gazelle to withstand the high temperatures on the sand surface during the hottest hours of the day.

Chapter 8

Mountains

There are, across the continent of Africa, numerous high plateaux, mountain ranges and peaks that rise to considerable elevations above the rest of the continental land mass. Several high mountains are more than 4000 m above sea level (e.g. Kilimanjaro 5693 m, Kenya 5202 m, Rwenzori 5119 m, Karisimbi 4508 m, Ras Dedjen 4621 m and Cameroun 4070 m), while considerable expanses of land are above 2000 m. Figure 8.1 shows that the principal areas of mountain vegetation occupy vast stretches of east and central Africa as well as numerous small isolated locations across the continent. There

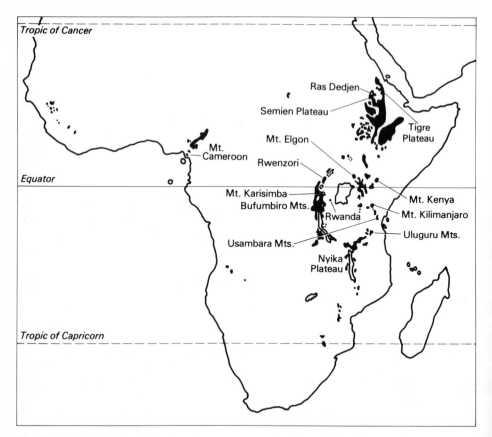

Fig. 8.1 The distribution of the areas of montane vegetation in tropical Africa. Locations are given of mountains referred to in the text.

are many similarities between the flora and fauna of mountain regions, although the separation and isolation of these regions from each other has led to many endemic species. The evolutionary implications of these similarities are of considerable interest and are discussed briefly on pp. 170–3.

8.1   Climate and vegetation

Climatic conditions, particularly temperature, are influenced by increasing altitude. This has been shown on Mt Cameroun where mean annual temperatures are 25 °C, 19·5 °C, 14 °C, 8·5 °C and 3 °C at 1 000 m intervals from sea level to 4 000 m. At higher altitudes, the mean annual temperature is still lower, with for example an estimated − 3 °C at 5 181 m on Mt Kenya. A further feature of these mountains is the relative constancy of the minimum night and maximum day temperatures throughout the year at altitudes above 3 000 m. At 3 300 m the mean annual minimum temperature has an amplitude of 1·6 °C to 2·8 °C and at 5 100 m this may reach 3·9 °C. The mean maximum temperatures have a slightly greater amplitude. This results in an appreciable temperature range within each twenty-four-hour period particularly at the higher altitudes (Table 8.1). The rainfall varies from one mountain to another as well as at

Table 8.1   *Temperatures (°C) on East African mountains.*

	Mt Kenya (4 191 m)	Kilimanjaro (4 135 m)
Mean maximum	5·4	5·2
Mean minimum	− 3·6	− 0·8
Mean range	8·9	10·0

different aspects and altitudes on the same mountain. Mt Kenya is one of the drier mountains; nowhere does the annual rainfall exceed 2 400 m. On the wet south-east aspect there are 750 mm p.a. of rain at the peak, 2 300 mm at about 1 800 to 2 400 m and 1 250 mm at 1 500 m. In contrast the annual rainfall in the south-west foothills of Mt Cameroun is 10 000 mm; this steadily declines to around 3 000 mm at the peak and continues falling in the leeward north-east to 2 000 mm at the base. Precipitation on the east of Rwenzori falls from over 2 000 mm at higher altitudes to 1 500 mm at 1 500 m.

These variations in rainfall and the very different temperature regimes to those prevailing in the tropical lowlands have considerable effects on the vegetation. In the areas where man has not modified the plant communities there is an obvious altitudinal stratification. Furthermore, it is usually different for each montane area. At lower altitudes there are gradual and sometimes imperceptible changes from montane to lowland vegetation. Demarcation between two vegetation types does not always occur at the same elevation and as a result altitude alone cannot be taken as a guide to where montane vegetation begins. The amount of cloud present varies with elevation and this, too, may influence the plant species present.

Montane vegetation includes montane evergreen forests, bamboo forests, grasslands, sub-alpine and alpine communities. Much of the lower mountain forests consist of broad-leaved trees superficially similar to the lowland evergreen rain forest but differing from it by having a less rich flora and trees of smaller stature. The floristic composition of the forests varies according to the annual rainfall (Fig. 8.2). In East Africa some of the wetter forests are dominated by *Aningeria adolfi-friederici*, some of those of intermediate rainfall by cedar (*Juniperus*) and some of the drier ones by *Brachylaena* and *Croton*. Bamboo (*Arundinaria*) forest (Fig. 8.3c) is found in wetter

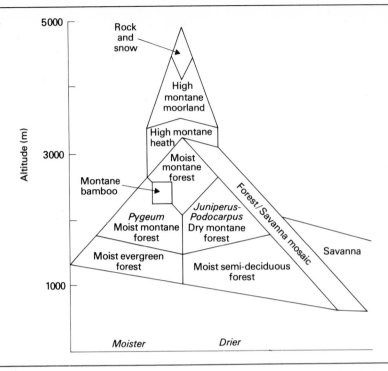

Fig. 8.2   Generalised profile of the major types of montane vegetation in East Africa. (Adapted from Langdale-Brown, Osmaston and Wilson, 1964.)

locations at slightly higher altitudes around 2 600 m where soils are deeper and slopes gentler. Above this is a low stature woodland of *Hagenia* and *Rapanea* in moist localities or *Afrocrania* and *Agauria* in drier localities on thin soils. Under natural conditions this woodland extends to 3 400–3 500 m, but the removal of vegetation and the introduction of cultivation leads to a forest–savanna mosaic through what was previously this broad woodland belt.

According to the mountain, upland forest usually gives way to the ericaceous woodland of giant heaths where *Philippia* and *Erica* are dominant at elevations between 2 500 m and 3 500 m. These woodlands are best developed on the wetter mountains where the trees are draped with the lichen *Usnea* and the ground carpeted with thick mosses. The only other trees on Rwenzori in this zone are *Rapanea*, *Senecio* and *Hypericum*. However, on the drier Mt Kenya *Adenocarpus*, *Anthospermum* and *Euryops* occur and *Philippia* may be replaced by stands of *Protea*. The *Dendrosenecio* woodland and wooded grassland at altitudes above about 3 500 m is referred to as the high montane grassland or the afro-alpine zone. It is in this association that we find the bizarre *Dendrosenecio* species attaining heights of 8 m and the giant *Lobelia*. The abundance of the former depends on the wetness of the mountain. On Rwenzori patches of dense woodland cover considerable areas. On Mts Elgon and Kenya the woodland is more open. The ground layer mainly consists of *Alchemilla*. Snow occurs above approximately 4 500 m.

In Ethiopia the high plateaux have been dissected and divided by rivers which originate in the northern extension of the east African Rift Valley. Man's activities have considerably modified the vegetation over much of the area and, as a result of cultivation and erosion, its original character in many places is extremely difficult to discern. Up to about 2 700 m on the Simien plateau there are undulating grasslands with remnants of *Hagenia* woodland and occasional cedars (*Juniperus procera*). The latter species occurs quite widely throughout the Ethiopian plateaux and probably formed extensive areas of woodland in earlier times. At 3 200 m there are giant *Hypericum* and *Erica* and red-hot pokers (*Kniphofia*), whilst between 3 350 m and 3 810 m there are open moorlands with *Helichrysum*, *Artemisia* and giant *Lobelia*. Further north and east on the Tigre plateau human activity has been most intense and the vegetational stratification of broad-leafed forest, cedar and olive woodlands and giant heath is virtually lost. In places where cultivation has been abandoned stunted *Acacia* grow and desert succulents such as aloes and euphorbias thrive.

The vegetation of Mt Cameroun is somewhat different (Eisentraut, 1963) (Fig. 8.4) from that of the highlands of eastern Africa and Ethiopia. The mountain forest extends down to 900 m and is characterised by an abundance of tree ferns. This is replaced at 1 600 m by cloud forest similar to the evergreen mountain forest of East Africa. The mountain savanna occurs at 2 100 m and is composed of a scattering of trees and mixed herb–grassland. This in turn gives way to a mountain grassland at 3 100 m, and bare, broken ground with some moss cover at 3 700 m.

The climate and vegetation of mountains provide a wide range of conditions for their mammalian inhabitants. In the montane evergreen forests there is a luxuriance of vegetation and a mildness of climate which favour occupation by numerous species. As altitude is increased temperatures decline and vegetation becomes less diverse so that within the highest vegetation zone conditions are much less favourable to animal life. Here, in the Afro-alpine zone, night temperatures are below freezing, vegetation cover is patchy, slow growing and nowhere as dense as in forest. Many plants have leaves that are leathery, hairy or reduced; spines are frequently present. These structures make many of the plants inedible to herbivores. Animals living in this zone are thus confronted by a harsh climate, low primary production and a considerable quantity of unpalatable vegetation. This contrasts markedly with conditions on the lower mountain slopes.

8.2 Mammals of the montane regions

At the present time little is known of the ecology of the high mountain faunas of Africa. The harsh and inclement climate has (fortunately) discouraged settlement in these areas by man so that no permanent bases exist for protracted periods of residence and continuous study. Instead, the faunas have largely become known as a result of scientific expeditions which spend only short periods at any altitude. However, collections of mammals in this way have provided a great deal of useful information on the species present in different types of vegetation. Unfortunately, expedition collection in this way has its shortcomings. The shortness of a stay at a particular station may result in inadequate trapping and thereby provide incomplete representation of the species present. The matter is further complicated by the varying abundance of species from one location to another making it even more difficult to assess whether the record is complete. However, in some areas at altitudes up to 2 500 m the mountain evergreen forest faunas are quite well known as is shown by Rahm (1966) and Rahm and Christaensen's (1963) detailed studies in eastern Zaire. Our comprehensive knowledge of both lowland and montane forest on Mt Cameroun is dependent on the collections obtained during the course of several expeditions (Eisentraut 1963) and for this reason is probably less complete than that from eastern Zaire. The results of these two investigations are summarised in Table 8.2.

a

b

c

Fig. 8.3 (*a*) Upper alpine zone of Mount Kenya at an altitude of approximately 4300 m. The large rosettes on stems are of *Senecio keniodendron* and the erect inflorences are of *Lobelia telekii*. Note the tussocks of *Festuca* in the foreground. Exposed rocks such as shown here may form refuges for the hyrax (*Procavia johnstoni*). (Photo: M. J. Coe.) (*b*) The Aberdare Mountains of Kenya at approximately 3200 m. Ericaceous scrub is in the background, elephants on *Carex* marsh and *Alchemilla* scrub in the foreground, (Photo: M. J. Coe.) (*c*) Inside bamboo forest (*Arundinaria alpina*). Pure stands of bamboo are accompanied by few other plant species except the grass *Oplismenus hirtellus*. Elephant, baboon and bush pig may be found in these forests, but the spectrum of species present is restricted. (After Lind & Morrison 1974.)

There is a gradual faunal change from the lowland to the montane forest. In many parts of Africa the two are separated by savanna or cultivation. The change generally involves a depletion of the total number of species because the range of many rain forest species does not extend into the mountainous areas or, for historical reasons, some species have not reached mountainous areas. This reduction is moderated in a number of localities by the presence of distinct mountain species. Some such as the mountain tree squirrel (*Funisciurus carruthersi*) in the Rwenzori and Kivu and Rwanda mountains and the bush squirrel (*Paraxerus lucifer*) in the Nyika Plateau occur only in the montane forest while others such as the harsh-furred mouse (*Lophuromys woosnami*) and the mountain climbing mouse (*Praomys (Hylomyscus) denniae*) are more widespread and extend their ranges beyond the forest into the bamboo and ericaceous zones. The complexities and patterns of species distribution are well illustrated by the rodents of western Rwenzori (Misonne 1963) (Fig. 8.5). As on Mt Cameroun and probably all other African mountains, the trend is to less diversity with increasing altitude. On Rwenzori the decline becomes most sharp in the transition from montane evergreen to bamboo forest at 2700 m.

These examples describe faunal change on individual mountains. There are,

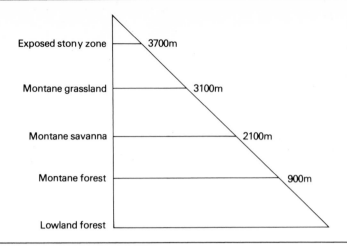

Exposed stony zone ——————⟍ 3700m

Montane grassland ———————⟍ 3100m

Montane savanna ——————————⟍ 2100m

Montane forest ——————————————⟍ 900m

Lowland forest

Fig. 8.4   Diagrammatic scheme of the vegetation types on the south face of Mount Cameroun (adapted from Eisentraut, 1963).

however, a few cases of individual species not having a uniform ecological distribution across the continent. The harsh-furred mouse, *Lophuromys sikapusi*, occurs in West Africa from the lowest elevations to 3500 m. In this area it is the only representative of this genus. In Uganda at the eastern limit of its range it does not occur above 1500 m. It may be that here the presence of two other species (*L. woosnami*, *L. flavopunctatus*), both occurring at high altitudes, competitively exclude *L. sikapusi*. The black-fronted duiker (*Cephalophus nigrifrons*) has a discontinuous distribution. The western sector of

Table 8.2   *Faunal stratification in west and central Africa (numbers of species)*

	Mount Cameroun (from Eisentraut 1963)					
	Lowland forest	*Tree-fern forest*	*Cloud forest*	*Montane savanna*	*Montane grassland*	*Bare ground*
Insectivora	9	4	3	2	—	—
Chiroptera	21	12	6	—	—	—
Primates	8	4	2	—	—	—
Carnivora	6	5	3	—	—	—
Rodentia	21	18	13	6	6	2

	Eastern Zaire (from Rahm 1966)		
	Lowland forest	*(Species common to both)*	*Montane forest*
Insectivora (excluding *Crocidura*)	4	(2)	3
Chiroptera	10	(1)	2
Primates	12	(8)	9
Carnivora	15	(10)	10
Rodentia	27	(14)	22
Hyracoidea	1	(0)	1
Proboscidea	1	(1)	1
Tubulidentata	1	(0)	0
Artiodactyla	13	(5)	5
Pholidota	3	(0)	0

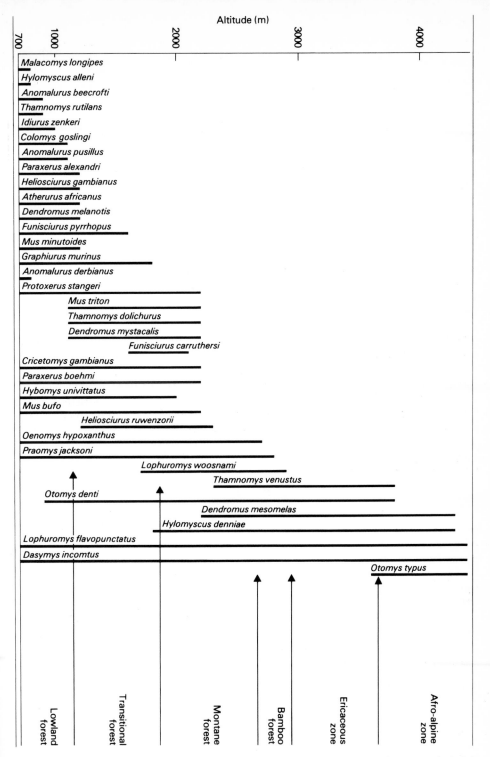

Fig. 8.5 The stratification of rodents on western Rwenzori. Lowland savanna species are not included. (Adapted from Misonne 1963.)

its range extends through the lowland forest of Cameroun, Zaire and north-east Angola. In the east it is found only in the montane forests of Kivu, Rwenzori, Elgon and Kenya where at least three quite distinct races are to be found. It is difficult to account for these changes in ecological habit and again one is tempted to consider the possible roles of competing species in different regions or to ask whether historical changes in habitat conditions have played a part in such anomalous geographical distributions.

A further intersting change in altitudinal distribution is shown by the four-striped grass-mouse (*Rhabdomys pumilio*). The discontinuous range of this species differs from the two preceding examples as its main axis of distribution is north–south. The northern limits of its range is Kenya and Uganda, where it is found in grassland above 1 800 m. In Tanzania it is mainly montane and has not been recorded below 1 100 m (Swynnerton and Hayman, 1950), whereas at the southern limits of its range in South Africa it is to be found on the veld and down to sea level. These changes may be associated with the species-adaptive physiology which possibly prevents it entering the uniformly warmer lowland tropical conditions.

The ecology of the afro-alpine mammals have been studied in greatest detail on Mt Kenya (Coe, 1967). Here the mammals are generally small in size and represented by few species. On Mt Kenya the three most abundant herbivores are the hyrax (*Procavia johnstoni*), the laminate-toothed rat (*Otomys typus*) and the common duiker (*Sylvicapra grimmia*). These three have an interesting and reasonably clear-cut microhabitat and trophic separation. The hyrax feeds on grasses, mosses and the leaves of *Alchemilla argyrophylla* and generally lives in burrows situated among the less dense vegetation. In contrast the laminate-toothed rat is found in the tussock grassland in wetter situations. These two species occur in quite high densities in their favoured localities. Coe (1967) estimated that the runs of the rats covered 30 to 40 per cent of the ground surface in some areas and that an individual hyrax foraged over an area of approximately 2 600 sq. m. The shy duiker spends much time in the *Dendrosenecio–Alchemilla* woodland and at lower altitudes in patches of *Erica* bush. This species is chiefly a browser feeding on the *Alchemilla* and other woody plants. Less is known of the habits of other animals living in this area. Shrews (*Crocidura allex*, *Myosorex polulus*) are present and at least two other species of rodent. These are the omnivorous harsh-furred mouse (*Lophuromys flavopunctatus*) and the subterranean and herbivorous mole rat (*Tachyoryctes splendens*). Leopard (*Panthera pardus*) inhabit the mountain and feed on hyrax, *Otomys* and the duikers. Packs of wild dog (*Lycaon pictus*) have been recorded as have the occasional lion (*Panthera leo*) and marsh mongoose (*Atilax paludinosus*). Compared to savanna and forest this is a relatively uncomplicated situation. However, it is worth stressing that even though there is not a wealth of species there is quite a high density of mammals which must collectively play a considerable role in the dynamics of this ecosystem.

8.3   Faunal affinities

During the course of his studies on the history and evolution of the bird faunas of Africa, Moreau (1966) investigated in some detail the previous climate of the continent (Ch. 2). He concluded that the present reduction and isolation of the land areas covered by montane vegetation has been due to the recent world-wide recession of the glaciers and the isolation of populations affords the opportunity for the evolution of mountain endemics. The distribution of the laminate-toothed rats (*Otomys*) probably sheds most light on previous faunal connections between the African mountains. The occurrence of *Otomys tropicalis* on Mt Cameroun and on much of the higher ground in eastern

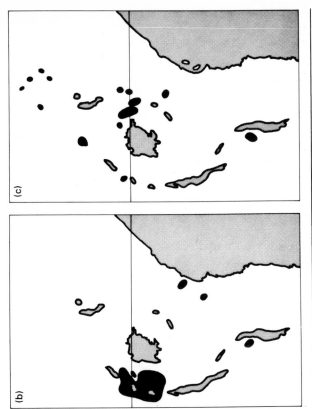

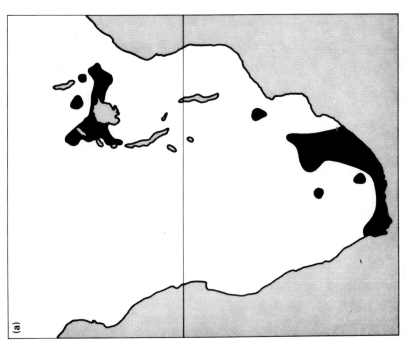

Fig. 8.6 The distribution of three species of laminate-toothed rats (*Otomys*). All three species have disjunct distributions. (*a*) *Otomys irroratus* (= *tropicalis*) is a widely distributed species; (*b*) *O. denti* and (*c*) *O. typus* are restricted to the mountains of East Africa. (Adapted from Misonne 1963.)

Zaire, Uganda and Kenya (Fig. 8.6) provides strong evidence of a former east–west faunal link. Should this species prove to be conspecific with *O. irroratus* in the south there is then evidence of a former very extensive range. Connections between other mountain blocks are reinforced from the distribution of *O. denti* (Fig. 8.5) which is found in Rwenzori, the Kivu mountains, western Rwanda, Nyika Plateau and the Usambara and Uluguru mountains of Tanzania. *Otomys typus* (Fig. 8.5) provides a link with the Ethiopian mountains. This species is usually found above 2300 m, and has been recorded from various mountains in Kenya, Uganda, Sudan, Zambia and Tanzania, in addition to Ethiopia. These three species have quite extensive geographical ranges. It is important to recognise that a montane species can be restricted in its spread and at its most confined it occurs only on one mountain. The remaining six species in this genus are generally southern African in their distribution. The present distribution of this genus highlights the faunal similarities between widely separated but ecologically similar geographical areas in east, west and southern Africa. It is also quite thought-provoking as to how the species of this genus evolved. The soft-furred rat, *Praomys delectorum*, is an example of a species living in a restricted

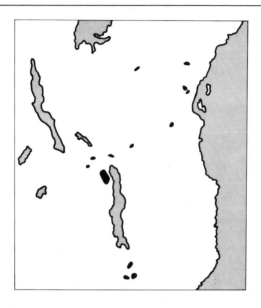

Fig. 8.7   The distribution of the soft-furred rat *Praomys delectorum*. This species has a discontinuous distribution in the mountains of the southern part of East Africa.

geographical area but nevertheless occurring in several isolated populations. This species is found only in the southern highland areas of East Africa (Fig. 8.7).

The three main blocks of the east African mountains (Ethiopia, central Kenya, Rwenzori–Kivu–Rwanda) have a number of species in common. The mole-rat (*Tachyoryctes splendens*) is a typical example while the maned rat (*Lophiomys imhausi*) is restricted to the first two. The presence in Ethiopia of other more widespread species with disjunct distributions such as the harsh-furred mouse (*Lophuromys flavopunctatus*) and the mountain reedbuck (*Redunca fulvorufula*) point to further links with the south. However, in Ethiopia there is an exceptionally large endemic element confined to the highlands and particularly the high montane grasslands. Corbet and Yalden

(1972) suggest there has been a long period of isolation from any similar lowland habitats due to the persistence of a continuous forest belt below the high grassland. The endemic species include the gelada baboon (*Theropithecus gelada*), Simien fox (*Canis simensis*), mountain nyala (*Tragelaphus buxtoni*), genet (*Genetta abyssinica*), giant mole-rat (*Tachyoryctes macrocephalus*) and the murid rodents *Stenocephalemys albocaudata*, *Muriculus imberbis*, *Dendromus lovati*, *Praomys albipes*, *Pelomys dembeensis* and *Lophuromys melanonyx*. In this list three genera (*Theropithecus*, *Stenocephalemys* and *Muriculus*) are endemic. This is a poorly studied fauna and further investigation may well bring to light more endemic species and genera. Excluding the bats and marine mammals, 8·9 per cent of the mammal species found in Ethiopia are endemic. Many of the species inhabiting lower ground occur elsewhere in the continent but in the mountainous regions 40 per cent of the species are endemic. This is an exceptionally high percentage and in marked contrast to any other African montane region.

Mountains such as Cameroun, Elgon, Kilimanjaro and Kenya support small numbers of endemic species. The only recorded endemic species from Mts Kenya and Cameroun are the shrews *Myosorex polulus* and *M. preussi* respectively. The Rwenzori–Kivu–Rwanda mountains come second to Ethiopia in the number of endemics. These include the shrew *Myosorex blarina*, the mountain tree squirrel (*Funisciurus carruthersi*), the mountain sun squirrel (*Heliosciurus ruwenzorii*), the harsh-furred mice (*Lophuromys woosnami* and *L. cinereus*), the mountain thicket rat (*Thamnomys venustus*) and Delany's swamp-mouse (*Delanymys brooksi*). The size of this area and the appreciable subdivision and isolation of its component mountains makes it an ideal situation for intraspecific variation. There are indications that this occurs in those species listed here which inhabit both the Rwenzori and Kivu mountains, as separate races characteristic of each of these mountain areas have been described. Confirmation of the reality of these races is required for at least some of the species as taxonomists in the past have often been prone to erect new races on rather slender evidence.

Misonne (1963) has examined the penetration by the Congo lowland forest fauna into the mountain forests of Rwenzori and into the mountains further east while Kingdon (1973) has discussed the possible routes and connections between these mountainous areas in the past. Both agree that the western forest fauna becomes a progressively smaller component of medium altitude and montane forest as one progresses further east. According to Misonne's (1963) data the montane forests of Kilimanjaro and the Usambara Mountains contain less than 20 per cent of these species present in the equivalent Rwenzori forest.

From this short account it is evident that diverse evolutionary processes, geological changes, past climates and present ecological conditions have combined to produce the contemporary faunas of these high African mountains. The available information is so incomplete as to permit only the most general conclusions. Fortunately, there is sufficient to promote speculation and this may provide the stimulus for the more active field investigations necessary to our clear understanding of the present distribution of these mammals.

PART III Ecological perspectives

Chapter 9

Life histories

The life history of a mammal is the sequence of events it passes through from fertilised egg to death. This includes embryonic and post-embryonic development, the time taken from fertilisation to birth, the ages at maturity and production of progeny, the number of young produced and the frequency of their production. Even within a fairly homogeneous group such as the placental mammals there can be considerable variation from one species to another as to the form the life history takes. From an ecological standpoint reproduction, which is an integral part of the life history, represents the population increase factor. But the precise ways in which additions are made depend on the life history of each species and how this manifests itself in a particular situation.

All species possess several characteristic reproductive attributes (Fig. 9.1) which

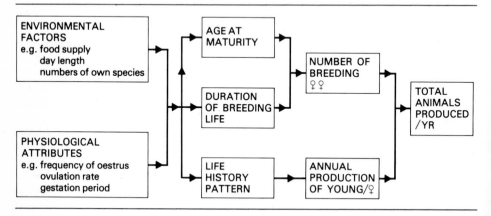

Fig. 9.1 Factors involved in determining pattern of a mammalian life history and the numbers of young produced.

determine the number of young that will be produced on one occasion and the frequency of production. This information indicates the reproductive capability of the species. However, the figure is likely to be much modified by environmental factors such as climate and food supply. Thus the interaction of environment with developmental and reproductive physiology produces a species-characteristic life history. This is flexible and capable of change in response to conditions although it is inevitably constrained within the inherent physiological limitations of the species. It is thus the prevailing, rather than the attainable, life cycle that is ecologically most relevant as it is this that accounts for the realised population increase. In this chapter the various components of the life history are looked at individually and their importance assessed in relation to population production.

9.1   Ecological significance of reproductive cycles

Female

In most species of mammals, the female regularly releases eggs from ovaries (*ovulation*). When this occurs ovulation is said to be spontaneous. There are, however, a few species amongst the carnivores, rodents and lagomorphs where eggs are shed from the ovary as a result of the stimuli provided by copulation. These species are referred to as induced ovulators. The female is particularly receptive to mating about the time of ovulation and it is then that fertilisation is most likely to result. This receptive period is the *oestrous* and usually lasts from one to several days. Whilst this ovarian activity is in progress the inner wall of the uterus becomes vascularised. This increases immediately after ovulation in anticipation of the implantation of recently fertilised eggs. Should there be no fertilisation the uterine walls regress and the cycle recommences after a short or long period. In non-primate mammals this regression does not involve bleeding resulting from the break-down of tissues. Here the cycle is called an *oestrous cycle*. In the primates, where bleeding occurs, the cycle is a *menstrual cycle*.

Some mammals have several oestrous cycles within the breeding season (*polyoestrous*) and others only one (*moneostrous*). A number of species, particularly rodents, have an oestrous within a few hours of giving birth (*post-partum oestrous*). If mating and fertilisation occur at this time, the mother is simultaneously pregnant and suckling. This situation can place a great strain on the animal's reserves especially at the immediate post-partum. The tree rat (*Thamnomys dolichurus*) adapts to this situation in an interesting way. Although there is a post-partum oestrous (Bland 1973) mating often does not take place at this time, being delayed until the next oestrous four or five days later, by which time lactation is well under way. A similar situation is probably found in the elephant where there is usually a two to two-and-a-half-year calving interval and a 22-month gestation period.

A modification of the reproductive cycle recorded in some species of Chiroptera, Edentata, Carnivora and Artiodactyla is seen where fertilisation is followed by a short period of embryonic development. Then for a time no development occurs and finally there is a continuation of growth and differentiation. The stage of inactivity precedes the formation of the placenta and is therefore before the embryo is implanted. This phenomenon is called *delayed implantation*.

The only recorded instances from tropical Africa is in the fruit bat (*Eidolon helvum*) in Uganda (Mutere 1967). In this animal mating occurs from April to June when the males are reproductively most active. Implanted embryos have only been evident from October onwards with births occurring in February and March at the beginning of the rainy season. Mutere (1967) was able to demonstrate that the unimplanted stage was the multicellular blastocyst.

The frequency of oestrous is obviously involved in various ways with the rate of population increase. In polyoestrous species the failure of mating at one oestrous may only delay the female's production of young by a few days because a further oestrous will appear after a relatively short time. Similarly, the occurrence of a post-partum oestrous can result in a rapid proliferation of young particularly in a species with a

Table 9.1 *Reproductive data of selected African mammals*

Species	Age at first conception	Polyoestrous (P) or Monoestrous (M)	Frequency of oestrous or menstruation (days)	Post-partum oestrous	Gestation period (days)	Lactation	Authority
Insectivora							
Elephant shrew (*Elephantulus myurus*)	6–10 months	P	?14	Yes	c. 56	4 weeks	Horst (1954)
Chiroptera							
Straw-coloured fruit bat (*Eidolon helvum*)	?1 year	M	—	No	c. 120*	1 month	Mutere (1967)
Sundevall's leaf-nosed bat (*Hipposideros caffer*)	2 years	M	—	No	c. 90	3 months	Brosset (1968, 1969)
Commerson's leaf-nosed bat (*H. commersoni*)	2 years	M	—	No	c. 150	5 months	Brosset (1969)
Primates							
Bushbaby (*Galago senegalensis*)	1 year	P	31·7	No	124–146	?3–5 months	Dukelow (1971)
Vervet (*Cercopithecus pygerythrus*)	?3–4 years	P	30	No	180–213	—	Dukelow (1971)
Grey-cheeked mangabey (*Cercocebus albigena*)		P	30	No	c. 175	c. 40 months	Rowell and Chalmers (1970)
Gelada baboon (*Theropithecus gelada*)	c. 4 years	P	c. 30	No	150–185	12–18 months	Dunbar and Dunbar (1974)
Chimpanzee (*Pan troglodytes*)	7–10 years	P	37	No	227	2–4 years	Dukelow (1971)
Gorilla (*Gorilla gorilla*)	?	P	c. 31	No	251–295	1·5 years	Schaller (1963)
Proboscidea							
Elephant (*Loxodonta africana*)	11–20 years	P	14–21	Unlikely	c. 670	2 + years	Laws (1969a), Sikes (1971)
Carnivora							
Spotted hyaena (*Crocuta crocuta*)	2–3 years	P	14	No	110	6–18 months	Kruuk (1972)
Lion (*Panthera leo*)	2–4 years	P	11–65	—	105–113	8 months	Schaller (1972)

Table 9.1 – *continued*

Species	Age at first conception	Polyoestrous (P) or Monoestrous (M)	Frequency of oestrous or menstruation (days)	Post-partum oestrous	Gestation period (days)	Lactation	Authority
Rodentia							
Climbing wood-mouse (*Praomys alleni*)	38 days	P	—	Yes	25–33	?30 days	Delany (1971)
Cameroun soft-furred rat (*Praomys morio*)	75 days	P	—	Yes	26–27	29 days	Eisentraut (1961)
Multimammate rat (*Praomys natalensis*)	53 days	P	6	Yes	23	21 days	Meester (1969)
Orange-toothed mole rat (*Tachyoryctes splendens*)	120 days	P	—	No	37–40	35–40 days	Jarvis (1973)
Tree rat (*Thamnomys dolichurus*)	80–100 days	P	4–5	Yes	24	24 days	Bland (1973)
Artiodactyla							
Warthog (*Phacochoerus aethiopicus*)	1–2 years	P	?42	No	171–175	c. 12 weeks	Clough (1969)
Hippopotamus (*Hippopotamus amphibius*)	9 years	P	20	—	c. 340	c. 12 weeks	Laws and Clough (1966)
Wildebeest (*Connochaetes taurinus*)	16 months	P	15	Unlikely	240–270	6–12 months	Watson (1969)
Eland (*Taurotragus oryx*)	28 months	P	21	Yes†	255–280	—	Treus and Kravchenko (1968)
Domestic cow (*Bos taurus*)	6–14 months	P	14–23	—	210–235	—	Cockrum (1962)
Domestic goat (*Capra hircus*)	8 months	P	21	—	135–160	—	Cockrum (1962)

*Excludes period of unimplanted blastocyst.   †15–30 days after parturition

short gestation period. In some species the frequency of oestrous is uncertain as in the elephant shrew (*Elephantulus myurus*) where fertilisation takes place at the first oestrous and is followed by further fertilisations at each post-partum until the termination of the season (Horst 1954). Failure to fertilise at the oestrous of a monoestrous species results in no young being produced in that season.

Determination of the reproductive potential of a population must take account of more than the frequency of oestrous and the number of ova shed (ovulation rate). Information is also required on the age at first breeding, the gestation period and the time spent lactating. Such comprehensive data are known for surprisingly few African mammals, with Table 9.1 summarising the situation in some better-known species. These are sufficient to illustrate the considerable differences that can occur. The potential population growth over a period of eight months can be estimated for two of these species. In making this calculation certain assumptions are made concerning their breeding. In the multimammate mouse (*Praomys natalensis*) an average litter size of twelve, equal numbers of each sex, no mortality and continuous breeding over the specified period are all assumed. Given these conditions one pair are capable of producing, through themselves, their progeny and their progeny's progeny over 6700 animals in eight months. In contrast, over the same period, as a result of longer gestation periods and smaller litter sizes a pair of wildebeest will produce one young and a pair of elephants only 0·3 young. The longer time taken to attain maturity and the protracted gestation periods of the larger mammals mitigate against rapid population replacement.

Male

Ecological interest in the male cycle centres around the time or age of attainment of sexual maturity and the subsequent continuity of production of spermatozoa to facilitate fertilisation. Puberty involves a number of changes in the male genitalia including an increase in the size of the epididymides, opening of the testis tubules and enlargement of their diameter. Then follows cellular division resulting in sperm formation. The testes may descend into a permanent scrotum or may occupy this position only at times of reproductive activity. The main changes are well illustrated by the warthog (Fig. 9.2) being most obvious between tooth wear age groups VI to IX, that is at approximately one to two years of age.

The males of some species are sexually active throughout their life from the time of sexual maturity while others typically have one or more inactive periods or *anoestrous*. In warthog, wildebeest and kob histological examination of the testes has shown that spermatozoa are produced continuously from the onset of maturity. There is no obvious quiescent phase although mating may be prevented by social factors rather than physiological inability. In the kob reproduction can only take place after a male has acquired a territory and this may not be until several years after his reproductive organs have started functioning. From their behaviour, it may be inferred that many other species are continually sexually active. This is supported by the frequent matings of individual lions and their readiness to mate whenever they encounter a lioness in oestrous. The same is probably true for many primates.

There are, by comparison, several other species which display very definite testicular regression. This has been demonstrated in adult males of the fruit bat *Eidolon helvum* (Mutere 1967). In this bat the mean monthly weights of the testes range from 5·2 g in April to 5·8 g in June and from 1·4 g in October to 2·4 g in November. The heaviest testicular weights coincided with the greatest abundance of spermatozoa in the epididymides. This was at the same time of year as mating took place and when

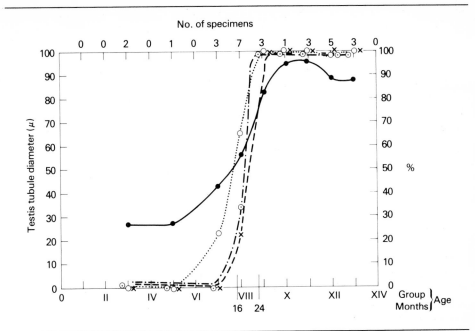

Fig. 9.2 Maturation of male warthog. ⊙ Per cent mature based on testis and epididymis weight; ● mean testis tubule diameter; × per cent testis tubules open; ○ per cent with spermatozoa in epididymis. Roman numerals refer to age groups based on tooth wear. (After Clough 1969.)

spermatozoa were present in the female genital tracts. A more detailed study has been made on the desert jerboa *Jaculus jaculus*. Ghobrial and Hobieb (1975) noted that in the fully mature active male, tubule diameter ranged from 100 to 300 μm, the average testes weights were 0·64 g and 80 to 100 per cent of the tubules were in full spermatogenesis. In the post-breeding season regression occurred; the tubules were 65 to 180 μm in diameter, the testes weighed 0·13 g and only 10 to 40 per cent were active. Complete cessation of spermatogenesis did not take place. Decline in activity and reduction in testicular size outside the breeding season may well characterise several other rodents, with data on the multimammate mouse (*Praomys natalensis*) and punctated grass-mouse (*Lemniscomys striatus*) supporting this. There is however also evidence of some species such as the gerbil *Tatera leucogaster* going into complete anoestrous for a few months of the year.

Perhaps one of the most interesting situations is found in rock hyraxes (*Procavia* and *Heterohyrax*) (Glover and Sale 1968). At any one time only a small proportion of the adults are sexually active having large, swollen testes and spermatogenesis in progress. Most adult males have small, flaccid testes displaying very little if any sperm formation. Even though there are few sexually active males some do maintain this condition throughout the non-breeding season. Hyraxes are gregarious animals having a complex social structure and it is possible that within a group only one male is sexually active and the remainder are rendered quiescent by this animal; some may remain quiescent for long periods. It has been demonstrated in captivity that a sexually active male can suppress the activity of other males. This example of social factors influencing male fertility differs from the situation in the kob where the males are continuously producing sperm. The difference may, however, only be one of degree, as

Table 9.2   *Gestation periods and number of young.*

Species	Gestation period (days)	Usual	Range
Insectivora			
Shrew (*Crocidura hirta*)	?18	4	1–5
Chiroptera			
Straw-coloured fruit bat (*Eidolon helvum*)	120	1	1
Egyptian fruit-bat (*Rousettus aegyptiacus*)	120	1	1–2
Primates			
Vervet (*Cercopithecus pygerythrus*)	213	1	1–2
Chimpanzee (*Pan troglodytes*)	202–261	1	1–2
Gorilla (*Gorilla gorilla*)	274	1	1
Rodentia			
Giant pouched rat (*Cricetomys gambianus*)	42	4	2–4
Peter's forest rat (*Thamnomys rutilans*)	25	1, 2, 3	1–3
Nile rat (*Arvicanthis niloticus*)	18	4	3–10
Punctated grass-mouse (*Lemniscomys striatus*)	28	5	1–8
Back-striped mouse (*Hybomys univittatus*)	29–31	2	1–4
Climbing wood mouse (*Praomys alleni*)	25–33	3	1–5
Jackson's forest rat (*Praomys jacksoni*)	34–37	3	1–8
Multimammate rat (*Praomys natalensis*)	23	12*	1–19
Harsh-furred mouse (*Lophuromys flavopunctatus*)	30–31	2	1–4
Spiny mouse (*Acomys cahirinus*)	36–40	1, 2	1–4
Tree mouse (*Dendromus melanotis*)	23–27	3, 4	3–6
Orange-toothed mole rat (*Tachyoryctes splendens*)	37–40	1	1–4
Crested porcupine (*Hystrix cristata*)	42–64	2	1–4
Brush-tailed porcupine (*Atherurus africanus*)	100–110	1	1–3
Cane rat (*Thryonomys swinderianus*)	?70	4	3–6
Carnivora			
Hunting dog (*Lycaon pictus*)	72–73	7	2–12
Civet (*Viverra civetta*)	c. 60 or c. 80	2	2–3
Banded mongoose (*Mungos mungo*)	60–62	3	3–5
Spotted hyaena (*Crocuta crocuta*)	c. 110	2	1–3
Lion (*Panthera leo*)	105–112	3, 4	1–6
Cheetah (*Acinonyx jubatus*)	90–93	4	3–4
Proboscidea			
Elephant (*Loxodonta africana*)	c. 670	1	1
Hyracoidea			
Southern tree hyrax (*Dendrohyrax arboreus*)	230	1	1
Bruce's hyrax (*Heterohyrax brucei*)	230	2	1–2
Johnston's hyrax (*Provavia johnstoni*)	214–222	2	1–3
Sirenia			
Dugong (*Dugong dugon*)	333	1	1
Perissodactyla			
Burchell's zebra (*Equus burchelli*)	361–390	1	1–2
Black rhinoceros (*Diceros bicornis*)	530–550	1	1
Artiodactyla			
Warthog (*Phacochoerus aethiopicus*)	171–175	3, 4	1–8
Giant forest hog (*Hylochoerus meinertzhageni*)	125		2–6
Hippopotamus (*Hippopotamus amphibius*)	227–240	1	1–2

Table 9.2 – *continued*

Species	Gestation period (days)	Number of young	
		Usual	Range
Giraffe (*Giraffa camelopardalis*)	400–480	1	1–2
Bushbuck (*Tragelaphus scriptus*)	180	1	1
Eland (*Taurotragus oryx*)	255–280	1	1–2
Buffalo (*Syncerus caffer*)	343–346	1	1
Common duiker (*Sylvicapra grimmia*)	123	1	1–2
Waterbuck (*Kobus ellipsiprymnus*)	272–287	1	1–2
Lechwe (*Kobus leche*)	215–248	1	1
Reedbuck (*Redunca arundinum*)	*c.* 215	1	1–2
Roan antelope (*Hippotragus equinus*)	*c.* 275	1	1
Sable antelope (*Hippotragus niger*)	261–271	1	1
Lichtenstein's hartebeest (*Alcelaphus lichtensteini*)	237	1	1–2
Blue wildebeest (*Connochaetes taurinus*)	239–243	1	1–2
Oribi (*Ourebia ourebi*)	210	1	1
Thomson's gazelle (*Gazella thomsoni*)	165–200	1	1
Springbok (*Antidorcas marsupialis*)	171	1	1

*Uganda figure, may vary regionally.

once social conditions alter, the quiescent hyrax may then soon come into breeding condition. In both these examples there is an apparent surfeit of sexually capable males who are available for breeding should they be required.

There is a further important issue concerning the male cycle. For those species having anoestrous or quiescence it might be asked whether it is the males through their sexual activity that control the onset and termination of breeding. This is a subject that has been little considered for African mammals and consequently requires far more detailed examination. As far as can be ascertained females apparently come into oestrous about the same time as the males start showing greatest sexual activity. The two events may coincide or there may be a causal relationship.

9.2 Litter size

A review of litter sizes and gestation periods appears in Table 9.2. This information endorses some of the generalisations made in the previous sections, and provides an insight into the range of litter sizes that exist. A more critical examination of the number of young produced shows that this can vary greatly within a species subjected to a range of environmental conditions. Embryonic mortality and resorption can also modify litter size. Occasional cases have been reported for large mammals such as elephant (Laws 1969a) but this phenomenon is apparently best known in rodents. Neal (1968) found the six commonest species of rodents in Rwenzori Park, Uganda, all had embryos resorbing (Table 9.3); these ranged from 0·9 to 11·9 per cent. The Nile rat, *Arvicanthis niloticus*, was of particular interest in this study having very different proportions of resorbing embryos at two localities a few kilometres apart. The mean numbers of implanted embryos (3·67 and 4·64) were significantly different between the two sites. However, as a result of the differential mortality the mean numbers of live embryos (3·60 and 4·09) were not significantly different statistically. From Kenya, Jarvis (1973) has information on the change in embryo number with embryonic age in the mole rat, *Tachyoryctes splendens*. She found that pregnant females from near Nakuru contained on average 1·3 early foetuses and that this figure dropped to 1·0 full term embryos. Here, the number of embryos in early pregnancy ranged from 1 to 3 with

Table 9.3   *Resorption of embryos in rodents in Rwenzori Park, Uganda. (After Neal 1968.)*

Species	Mean no. implanted ± S.E.	Range of litter size	Total gravid ♀♀ examined	Per cent embryos resorbing
Nile rat (*Arvicanthis niloticus*) (Crater Track)	3·67 ± 0·05	2–5	15	1·9
Nile rat (*Arvicanthis niloticus*) (Mweya Peninsula)	4·64 ± 0·04	3–10	44	11·9
Punctated grass-mouse (*Lemniscomys striatus*)	5·02 ± 0·15	3–8	58	4·8
Harsh-furred mouse (*Lophuromys sikapusi*)	3·24 ± 0·12	2–5	46	2·2
Pygmy mouse (*Mus triton*)	4·5 ± 0·13	2–6	14	6·4
Three-toed grass-rat (*Mylomys dybowskyi*)	4·33 ± 0·25	2–6	21	0·9
Multimammate rat (*Praomys natalensis*)	12·61 ± 0·21	7–19	41	4·0

usually only one surviving. From the examination of over a thousand pregnant females, representing several species of rodents in Zaire, Dieterlen (1967) found over 14 per cent contained one or more dead embryos. Full appreciation of the extent of embryonic mortality depends on the examination of large samples. Although this is

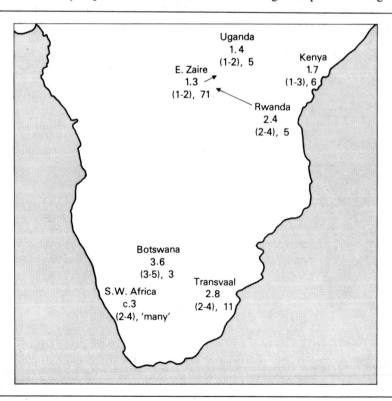

Fig. 9.3   Regional variation in mean embryo numbers in the laminate-toothed or vlei rat, *Otomys irroratus*. The figures in brackets indicate range; this is followed by number of pregnant females examined. (Data from Davis, R. M. 1972, Delany 1974, Dieterlen 1968, Hollister 1919, Misonne 1963, Shortridge 1934, Smithers 1971.)

apparently a common phenomenon in rodents, it has not so far been demonstrated to involve more than a small percentage of embryos.

Some, but by no means all, species of rodents display an increase in foetus number with increasing maternal size and age. In western Uganda, the punctated grass-mouse, *Lemniscomys striatus*, gradually increased its foetus number through the longer rainy season extending from September to December. During this time the monthly mean litter sizes increased from 4·75 to 5·38. As these young were produced from the same cohort of adult females the increase is attributed to higher production by older animals (Neal 1968). From the same area it was also found that harsh-furred rats (*Lophuromys sikapusi*) with clean body weights of less than 75 g had a mean litter size of 2·82 and those above this weight had one of 3·35.

In some species, the average number of foetuses in a pregnant female displays regional variation. Jarvis (1973) observed that *Tachyoryctes* litters averaged 1·0 at birth at Nakuru, Kenya whilst only 155 kilometres away at Nairobi the average was 1·3–1·5. Data are also available from wider geographical areas for the vlei or laminate-toothed rat (*Otomys irroratus*) and the multimammate rat (*Praomys natalensis*). The former has a disjunct but widespread distribution. It is however, best known from east and southern Africa. From Fig. 9.3 it appears that litters are smaller in equatorial localities than in the south. The Rwanda figure, although based on a small sample, is relatively high compared to the remainder from East Africa. Apart from this figure, the females in the south produce about twice as many young in each litter as those astride the equator. The multimammate rat has 12·61 foetuses per pregnant female in western Uganda, 10·0 in Botswana and Malawi, 9·8 in eastern Zaire and 9·46 in the Transvaal (Neal 1968, Smithers 1971, Hanney 1965, Dieterlen 1967, Coetzee 1965). The lowest of these figures is approximately 75 per cent of the highest. Foetal mortality is available only for the Uganda sample which reduces the figures of live embryos to 12·10 (Table 9.3). Variations possibly caused by the collections containing different proportions of old and young breeding females are not considered. Such information as is available is scant and conflicting. Hanney (1965) suggests that in Malawi there is increased size of litter with maternal size and presumably age (Table 9.4). On the other hand, examination of large numbers of these animals in Uganda does not support this

Table 9.4 *Variation in litter sizes of* Praomys natalensis *in Malawi according to maternal size. (After Hanney 1965.)*

Head-and-body length of mother (mm)	No.	Mean no. of embryos	Range
100–109	5	9·4	7–13
110–119	7	9·6	8–11
120–129	10	11·5	8–14
130–139	5	13·6	11–17

contention. It is interesting to note that in the laboratory, where conditions are probably optimal, the average litter size of this species is 7·32 (Oliff 1953). This information on these two species poses a number of interesting questions. Are the conditions in Uganda more severe for the multimammate rat than those in Transvaal? Is the vlei rat better adapted to tropical than south temperate conditions? Is litter size related in any way to the number of litters produced, or the length of breeding season?

In temperate regions there can be a steady increase in litter size as high mountains are ascended. This is associated with a more rigorous climate at higher altitudes and a shorter summer breeding season. In high tropical mountains these climatic conditions do not prevail and it would be interesting to know whether litter size or foetus number remain constant at all altitudes. Flux (1969) has obtained useful information on embryo numbers in the hare, *Lepus capensis*, in Kenya. At altitudes of 600 m (Magadi), 1 200 m (Olorgesaile) and 1 800 m (Akira) he found mean embryo numbers were 1·75, 1·45 and 1·24 respectively. This indicates a decline with increasing altitude. Apparently contradicting these results, Flux also found an increase in the number of juveniles present as altitude increased. This apparent anomaly could be resolved if there was a higher percentage of pregnant females in the higher altitude populations.

9.3   Duration and time of occurrence of breeding seasons

A great deal has been written concerning the breeding periods of wild mammals in temperate regions. Once maturity is attained, the reproductive organs are activated as a result of hormones secreted by the gonads which in turn are regulated by hormonal secretions from the anterior pituitary. The activity of the part of the brain known as the hypothalamus is controlled by an assortment of nervous stimuli. Some emanate from the animal itself and others from external factors. The hypothalamus has neural and vascular connections with the pituitary organ. In the female, hormones stimulate the ovarian follicles to grow, the corpora lutea to form and milk to be produced. The important question to be answered is what environmental factors are responsible for initiating and terminating seasonal breeding? In some temperate mammals there are indications that day length plays an important role in stimulating the pituitary via the hypothalamus. Other stimuli to breeding which can probably be equally important are nutrition and temperature (Amoroso and Marshall 1960). In the tropics where there is considerable thermal uniformity the latter is unlikely to be so important.

Whilst the physiological causes underlying seasonality of breeding in African mammals may not be well known considerable information is available on the times of year at which these animals give birth to their young. In examining this phenomenon it is probably important to place the time of breeding in relation to some climatic event rather than the months of the year when it occurs. In tropical Africa, the major climatic changes during the year are the result of seasonal rainfall. In rain forest there is a steady fall throughout the year but even here many places display some fluctuation within the twelve-month period. The savanna and more arid areas have distinct wet and dry seasons.

Of the other seasonal climatic changes day length (or photoperiod) is probably the most obvious although nothing like so striking in its effects on the habitat as rainfall. Near the equator day length is approximately twelve hours thoughout the year and at 20° North and South during the months of shortest day length (December and June respectively) it averages about eleven hours. Photoperiod fits into a regular geographical pattern of increasing summer day length and decreasing winter day length away from the equator.

Mother and young are likely to be making high nutritional demands on the habitat just prior to birth when the embryo is growing rapidly as it nears full term, and following birth when the mother is suckling. Thus the timing of births is quite critical in order to ensure maximum opportunity for survival of the young. In a seasonal situation such as found in a savanna this is probably at about the onset of the rains or soon after when there is often a new flush of herbaceous vegetation. However, the length of the gestation period varies from species to species and the sequence of reproductive events culminating in birth starts at an earlier time and possible under climatic conditions different from those prevailing when the young are born. Thus births in the wet season could be conceived in the dry season and determination of the factors regulating breeding then necessitates examination of the prevailing climatic and other conditions at the time of conception. However, it is probable that selection has operated to ensure that the young appear at the most propitious time and that reproductive mechanisms have adapted accordingly.

Information on periods of births and rainfall patterns in several localities and for a variety of species are given in Table 9.5. To present some of these data in a more uniform manner the breeding season has been expressed in relation to wet and dry seasons of standardised length in Figs. 9.4 and 9.5. Here, one of the most striking features is the apparent lack of uniformity within an order. For example, among the Primates the olive baboon (*P. anubis*) breeds throughout the year in western Uganda whilst the yellow baboon (*P. cynocephalus*) only gives birth in the middle of the dry season in Amboseli. Kenya. In examining these examples prime consideration must be given to the conditions afforded to mother and young at the time of birth. Sale (1969) observes how in two hyraxes one (*Heterohyrax brucei*) produces its young in the dry season preceding the rains and the other (*Procavia syriacus*) through the wet season. The latter feeds mainly on herbaceous vegetation, which is particularly rain-dependent; the former is semi-arboreal and is able to browse on leaves, shoots and buds of trees and shrubs in the dry season and then exploit the flush of herbs in the wet and early dry season. For many grazing herbivores the wet season is apparently a suitable time for the young to be born. Among these animals the lechwe (*Kobus leche*) has an anomalous pattern. This species breeds throughout the year, having a peak in births towards the end of the dry season. There must be suitable conditions throughout the year to sustain continuous breeding while the dry season peak in births may be attributed to aspects of its behaviour. This animal has a poor sense of smell; is not a particularly fast runner and prefers open country (Robinette and Child 1964). These dry season young are born at a time when grass cover is low; this affords a measure of protection as at this time the lechwe can use its visual acuity to best advantage to avoid predators. As the calves grow they soon find themselves in the wet season with its more plentiful supply of grass. The black and white colobus (*Colobus guereza*) is a continuous breeder without any distinct peak. This monkey inhabits situations, notably forest, where although there is seasonality in the rainfall there is a continuous supply of suitable food in the form of a fresh growth of leaves in the trees.

The foregoing examples are concerned with species from particular localities. When the breeding of one species is traced over a wide geographical area further interesting conclusions can be drawn. Data on reproduction in the multimammate rat (*Praomys natalensis*) have been obtained from as far south as Botswana and the Transvaal northwards to Uganda and then westwards to Sierra Leone (Table 9.5, Fig. 9.5). In some places breeding is continuous and in others restricted but in all cases the peak reproductive activity is in the wet and early dry seasons and nowhere has there been reported a peak in births at the end of the dry season. The adaptive nature of the pattern is illustrated by the occurrence of two short breeding seasons where there are two wet seasons and similarly one breeding season where there is only one wet season. More detailed consideration is given later (pp. 342–4) to the reasons for continuous breeding in seasonal situations but it is pertinent to point out that so far no reference has been made to the quantity of rain falling in the wet season and that similarly the 'dry season' can be a period of low precipitation or none at all.

The elephant (Table 9.5, Fig. 9.5) provides an example of a different type. Isolated populations north and south of the River Nile in Kabalega Park, Uganda, have different breeding cycles. In the north the time of maximum conception is associated with the early rains and south of the river with the later rains. The five-month

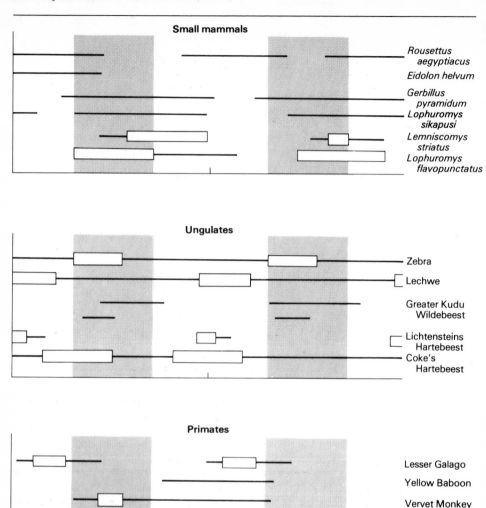

Fig. 9.4   Periods of births in relation to wet and dry seasons. The shaded areas represent rainy periods which have been given a standardised length. Where a locality has two wet seasons these are represented by the two cycles: if there is only one wet season, then the information is duplicated in the two cycles. The solid line represents the period of breeding except when births are particularly numerous in which case such times are represented by open blocks. Further information is provided in Table 9.5.

retardation in conception in the south bank population may be due to nutritional deficiency in this area where the diet is almost exclusively grass and not a balanced mixture of grass and browse (Laws 1969a). There could also be a density-dependent social effect. In Tsavo Park, Kenya, the time of peak conceptions coincides with or succeeds the two rainfall peaks. It appears then that the elephant cycles do correlate

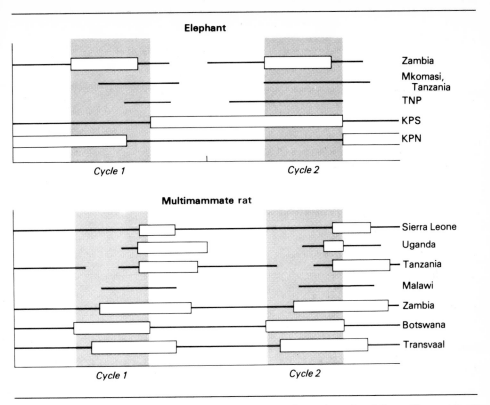

Fig. 9.5 Periods of births in two species, the elephant (*Loxodonta africana*) and the multimammate rat (*Praomys natalensis*), in different parts of Africa. Legend as for Fig. 9.4; further details are given in Table 9.5.

with rainfall but can under certain conditions be deflected from the anticipated pattern.

So much for the regions of markedly seasonal precipitation. The rain forest in eastern Zaire where Rahm (1970) undertook his work on the reproduction of Thomas's Tree Squirrel (*Funisciurus anerythrus*) and Boehm's Bush Squirrel (*Paraxerus boehmi*) has a high annual rainfall which is spread over the whole year. The wettest months are from September to April inclusive (Fig. 9.6). Pregnant females were present throughout the year (Fig. 9.6) and in *Funisciurus* their numbers were quite low between May and July. Perhaps of greatest significance is the percentage of adult females visibly pregnant at any one time. In the tree squirrel this ranges between a minimum of 8 per cent in March and a maximum of 44 per cent in October; the comparable figures for the bush squirrel are 10 per cent in May and 33 per cent in July.

These appear to be relatively low figures and at any one time a substantial proportion of the population capable of breeding apparently remains reproductively inactive. It would be interesting to know whether this is a general feature of tropical forest-dwelling mammals. Further support is forthcoming from Dubost's (1968) study of rain forest rodents at Makokou, north-east Gabon. The annual precipitation of around 1 600 mm falls in every month of the year with the period July to September receiving less than at other times. Dubost's monthly figures combined for all species of rodents show there was no month when less than 18 per cent (May, September) of the adult females were pregnant and none when there were more than 61 per cent (October).

Table 9.5 Periods of births in localities having seasonal rainfall.

Species	Births in whole (W) or part (P) of year	Time of births	Main periods of births	Rains	Locality	Authority
Chiroptera						
Straw-coloured fruit-bat (*Eidolon helvum*)	P	Feb.–March	—	March–May Oct.–Jan.	Kampala, Uganda	Mutere (1967)
Egyptian fruit-bat (*Rousettus aegyptiacus*)	P	Jan.–March July–Oct.	—	March–May Oct.–Jan.	Bukakata, Uganda	Mutere (1968)
Primates						
Bushbaby (*Galago senegalensis*)	P	Aug.–Dec.	Sept.–Oct.	Nov.–March	Zambia, S. Tanzania	Kingdon (1971)
Black-cheeked white-nosed monkey (*Cercopithecus ascanius*)	P	April–Oct.	June–Sept.	March–May Sept.–Nov.	Uganda	Haddow (1952)
Vervet (*Cercopithecus pygerythrus*)	P	Oct.–March	Nov.	March–April	Masai-Amboseli, Kenya	Struhsaker (1967b)
Black and white colobus (*Colobus guereza*)	W	—	—	March–May Sept.–Nov.	Uganda	Haddow (1952)
Olive baboon (*Papio anubis*)	W	—	—	March–May Sept.–Nov.	Ishasha, Uganda	Rowell (1966)
Yellow baboon (*Papio cynocephalus*)	P	May–Oct.	—	March–April Oct.–Dec.	Masai-Amboseli, Kenya	Altmann and Altmann (1970)
Hyracoidea						
Syrian hyrax (*Procavia syriacus*)	P	June–July	—	April–May	Rift Wall, Kenya	Sale (1969)
Syrian hyrax (*Procavia syriacus*)	P	June–Nov.	—	March–Dec.	Rift Floor, Kenya	Sale (1969)
Bruce's hyrax (*Heterohyrax brucei*)	P	Feb.–March	—	March–May	Lukenya, Kenya	Sale (1969)
Carnivora						
Spotted hyaena (*Crocuta crocuta*)	W	—	—	March–April Nov.–Dec.	Serengeti, Tanzania	Kruuk (1972)
Spotted hyaena (*Crocuta crocuta*)	W	—	Feb.–May	Jan.–May	Ngorongoro, Tanzania	Kruuk (1972)
Lion (*Panthera leo*)	W	—	Jan. Aug.–Sept.	March–April Nov.–Dec.	Serengeti, Tanzania	Schaller (1972)

Table 9.5 – *continued*

Species	Births in whole (W) or part (P) of year	Time of births	Main periods of births	Rains	Locality	Authority
Proboscidea						
Elephant (*Loxodonta africana*)	W	—	Dec.–April	March–May Aug.–Nov.	KPN, Uganda	Laws (1969*a*)
Elephant (*Loxodonta africana*)	W	—	June–Nov.	March–May Aug.–Nov.	KPS, Uganda	Laws (1969*a*)
Elephant (*Loxodonta africana*)	P	March–May Sept.–Dec.	—	March–April Nov.–Dec.	TNP, Kenya	Laws (1969*a*)
Elephant (*Loxodonta africana*)	P	April–June Oct.–Jan.	—	March–May Oct.–Dec.	Mkomasi, Tanzania	Laws (1969*a*)
Elephant (*Loxodonta africana*)	P	Aug.–May	Nov.–March	Nov.–April	Zambia	Hanks (1972)
Rodentia						
Egyptian gerbil (*Gerbillus pyramidum*)	P	June–Feb.	—	July–Sept.	Khartoum, Sudan	Happold (1966)
Harsh-furred mouse (*Lophuromys flavopunctatus*)	P	Feb.–Aug. Oct.–Dec.	March–June Oct.–Dec.	Feb.–June Sept.–Nov.	Mayanja Forest, Uganda	Delany (1971)
Harsh-furred mouse (*Lophuromys sikapusi*)	P	March–June Sept.–Jan.	—	March–May Aug.–Nov.	Western Uganda	Neal (1968)
Punctated grass-mouse (*Lemniscomys striatus*)	P	April–June Oct.–Dec.	May–June Nov.	March–May Aug.–Nov.	Western Uganda	Neal (1968)
Multimammate rat (*Praomys natalensis*)	W	—	Nov.–May	Oct.–April	Transvaal, S. Africa	Coetzee (1965)
Multimammate rat (*Praomys natalensis*)	W	—	Nov.–April	Nov.–April	Botswana	Smithers (1971)
Multimammate rat (*Praomys natalensis*)	P	Feb.–June	—	Nov.–May	Malawi	Hanney (1965)
Multimammate rat (*Praomys natalensis*)	P	March–Nov.	May–July	Nov.–May	Rukwa, Tanzania	Chapman et al. (1959)
Multimammate rat (*Praomys natalensis*)	W	—	Jan.–July June	Nov.–April	Kafue, Zambia	Sheppe (1972)
Multimammate rat (*Praomys natalensis*)	P	May–July Oct.–Dec.	Nov.	March–May Aug.–Nov.	Western Uganda	Neal (1968)
Multimammate rat (*Praomys erythroleucus*)	W	—	Nov.–Dec.	May–Nov.	Sierra Leone	Brambell and Davis (1941)

Table 9.5 – *continued*

Species	Births in whole (W) or part (P) of year	Time of births	Main periods of births	Rains	Locality	Authority
Orange-toothed mole rat (*Tachyoryctes splendens*)	W	—	Feb.–March	March–Dec.	Nakuru, Kenya	Jarvis (1969)
Orange-toothed mole rat (*Tachyoryctes splendens*)	P	Aug.–May	Jan.–Feb.	March–May Oct.–Dec.	Nairobi, Kenya	Jarvis (1969)
Artiodactyla						
Coke's hartebeest (*Alcelaphus buselaphus cokei*)	W	—	Feb.–April July–Sept.	March–May Nov.–Dec.	Nairobi, Kenya	Gosling (1969)
Lichtenstein's hartebeest (*Alcelaphus lichtensteini*)	P	July–Aug.	July	Nov.–March	Kafue, Zambia	Mitchell (1965)
Blue wildebeest (*Connochaetes taurinus*)	P	Dec.–Feb.	—	Nov.–May	Serengeti, Tanzania	Watson (1969)
Lechwe (*Kobus leche*)	W	—	July–Sept.	Nov.–March	Kafue, Zambia	Robinette and Child (1964)
Greater kudu (*Tragelaphus strepsiceros*)	P	Jan.–April	—	Nov.–March	Fort Jameson, Zambia	Wilson (1965)
Perissodactyla						
Burchell's zebra (*Equus burchelli*)	W	—	Jan.–March	Jan.–May	Ngorongoro, Tanzania	Klingel (1969)

KPN = Kabalega Park North.   KPS = Kabalega Park South.   TNP = Tsavo National Park.

This and much of the previous work reported here pose many interesting and unanswered questions. Do seasonal breeders have a high percentage of females pregnant at one time compared to continuously breeding species? How do total numbers of young produced by comparable species in different situations compare? Is the overall production of young per capita per year the same in seasonal and aseasonal localities?

The breeding of African mammals is apparently very much associated with seasonal factors of nutrition and water availability. The possibility of photoperiod acting as a proximate stimulus on ungulates has been considered by Spinage (1973), who noted

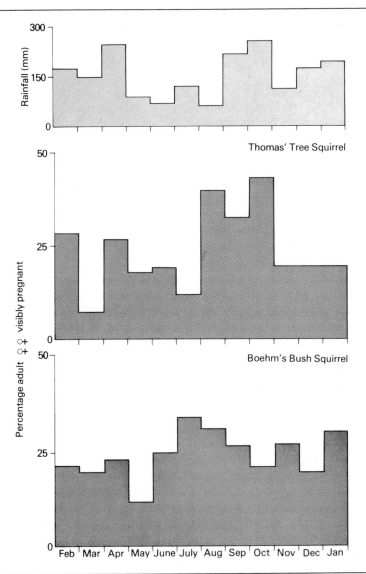

Fig. 9.6 Incidence of pregnancy in Thomas's Tree Squirrel (*Funisciurus anerythrus*) and Boehm's Bush Squirrel (*Paraxerus boehmi*) and occurrence of rainfall in eastern Zaire. (After Rahm 1970.)

that some species conceived at times of shortening days and others when days are lengthening. The zebra has most of its conceptions at times of increasing day length whereas the warthog, impala and wildebeest have peak conceptions at times of decreasing day length. These differences are adaptive and relate to the gestation period. In the thirteen remaining species he considered there was no clear correlation with photoperiod. If and when day length acts as a proximate stimulus to breeding it is likely that it functions in association with other factors such as the nutritional characteristics of the food supply at the time of conception. It is also possible that in these animals other factors exercise a much more influential effect on the cycle and sublimate the importance of light to a minor role. In South Africa, Miller and Glover (1975) found the duration of the copulatory period of male rock hyrax (*Procavia capensis*) increased as latitude decreased. The trend did not correlate with climatic conditions such as rainfall and temperature and here it was assumed that photoperiod was involved in the activation of the testes.

But perhaps one of the most interesting of all breeding cycles is found in the bat, *Hipposideros caffer*. Brosset (1968) described how within a population occupying eight caves in close geographical proximity in northern Gabon some colonies had young born in April and others in November. As females are monoestrous and the males are assumed to have seasonal anoestrous there must be sexual isolation between the two categories of colonies. Brosset points out that in close proximity to the equator (0°52'–1°08'N) typical northern or southern reproductive patterns can prevail. This explanation does not however account for the causative mechanisms.

9.3   Post-embryonic development

The post-embryonic development of all mammals displays several features relating to the ecology and survival of the young. However, the neonates of some species are more adapted than others. Compensation for limited adaptation may result in the production of greater numbers and more intensive maternal care during development. In many large mammals the neonate is active shortly after birth and very soon capable of walking with the mother. There is often a good covering of hair, and apart from the proportionate size of various organs, the absence of horns and tusks and the undeveloped reproductive system these animals resemble their parents in all but size.

Table 9.6   *The immediate post-embryonic development of Coke's Hartebeest (*Alcelaphus buselaphus*). (After Gosling 1969.)*

Activity	Minutes after birth
Movement of hind legs	1·30
Attempt to stand	9·10
Firm standing	30·50
Walking	34·30
Suckling attempt	32·00
Successful suckling	42·20
Following response	44·30
Appearance of gait faster than walking	38·35

The rapidity with which they acquire mobility is illustrated by Coke's hartebeest (Gosling 1969) (Table 9.6). Within an hour the young are able to walk without assistance. Like the hartebeest the young elephant is also soon able to stand and within an hour able to walk in a rather wobbly way (Sikes 1971). Subsequent growth is well illustrated by Sikes' (1971) sketches of stature and size of different ages (Fig. 9.7). Klingel (1969) found young zebra able to walk within fifteen minutes of birth. For these animals, often inhabiting open savanna, the rapid acquisition of motor co-ordination and movement is important to survival.

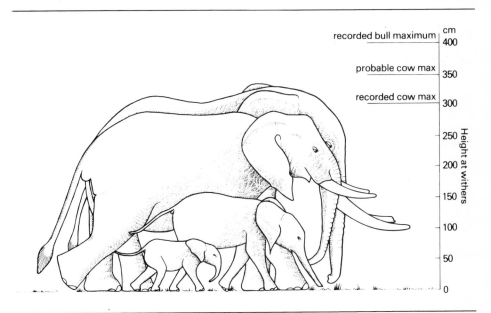

Fig. 9.7 Sizes of elephants from day of birth to adult. The sketches, originally based on photographs, show two bull calves, an adult cow and an adult bull. (Adapted from Sikes 1971.)

Carnivores usually have a covering of hair at birth and often have their eyes closed. They are born in a nest where they remain with their litter mates during a period of complete dependence on the mother. Their period of association with the parent is relatively long as the young have to learn the rather complex tasks of searching for and catching food. Ewer (1973) recognises three stages in the development of the young. These are the nestling period, the mixed nutrition period when both solid food and

Table 9.7 *Development of carnivores. (After Ewer 1973.)*

Species	Eyes open (days)	Eat solids (days)	Weaned (weeks)	Independent (months)
Civet (*Viverra civetta*)	0–4	*c.* 30	*c.* 20	
Large-spotted genet (*Genetta tigrina*)	5–18	42–91	8	
Banded mongoose (*Mungos mungo*)	10			$2\frac{1}{2}$–3
Lion (*Panthera leo*)	At birth	56	33	24
Cheetah (*Acinonyx jubatus*)	10–11	30–35	12–20	$15\frac{1}{2}$–18

milk are taken and the post-weaning dependence on the parent (Table 9.7). The first phase is absent or extremely brief in many of the large herbivores and is a period of considerable vulnerability to predation.

The rodents show considerable variation in patterns of post-embryonic development. At one extreme are those species such as the laminate-toothed rats (*Otomys*) which produce small litters and large young that are well covered in fur and have their eyes open at birth (Fig. 9.8). These animals are independent at a very early

Fig. 9.8   One-day-old laminate-toothed rat (*Otomys irroratus*). Note how it is well covered in fur, the eyes are open and the animal is apparently capable of locomotion. (From Dieterlen 1968.)

age and having no permanent nest are referred to as *nidifugous* species. They contrast with the *nidicolous* species such as the banana mice (*Dendromus*) where the young are born blind and hairless and leave the arboreal nest as well-formed independent individuals after the relatively long period of about thirty-five days (Dieterlen 1971). A thorough analysis of the post-embryonic development of a small rodent has been undertaken by Meester (1960) on the multimammate rat (*Praomys natalensis*) (Fig. 9.9). Among the Insectivora, the elephant shrews have precocious well-formed young at birth in contrast to shrews of the genus *Crocidura* where the neonates are blind and naked (Fig. 9.10). In *C. hirta* (Meester 1963) the young acquire hair by the seventh day (Fig. 9.11), toes become detached by the eighth day, all the teeth have erupted by the eighteenth day and the young are weaned by about the twentieth day.

Growth from birth to adult frequently passes through three phases. There is an initial phase of rapid growth followed by a second phase of slower growth and finally a period of size stabilisation or very gradual increase (Fig. 9.12). However, some individual organs, such as the hind foot of the gerbil, may attain their maximum size far in advance of the rest of the body. Such precocious developments are often adaptive. Well-formed functional limbs are important if the juvenile is to keep apace of the

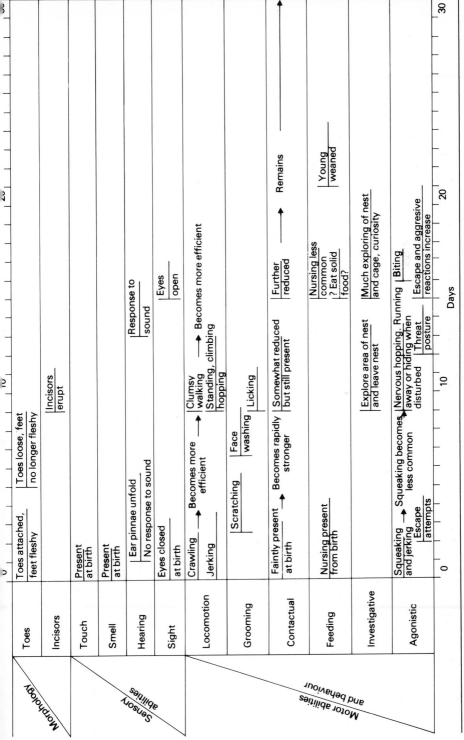

Fig. 9.9 The post-embryonic development of the multimammate rat (*Praomys natalensis*). After Meester 1960.)

Fig. 9.10   Three-day-old shrews (*Crocidura hirta*). Note the absence of a good covering of hair, the unseparated digits, the poorly developed ear pinnae and closed eyes. (From Meester 1963.)

Fig. 9.11   Seven-day-old shrews (*Crocidura hirta*). The digits and ear pinnae are well formed and there is a covering of hair. (From Meester 1963.)

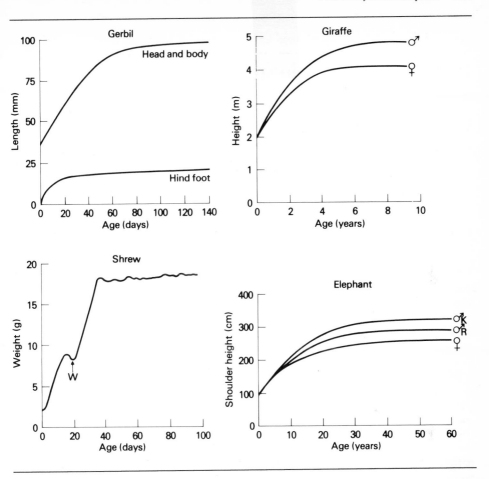

Fig. 9.12 Growth curves of a gerbil (*Gerbillus pyramidum*), shrew (*Crocidura hirta*), giraffe (*Giraffa camelopardalis*) and elephant (*Loxodonta africana*). W = time of weaning ♂$_K$, ♂$_R$ = males from Kabalega and Rwenzori Parks respectively. (After Happold 1968, Meester 1963, Foster and Dagg 1972, Laws 1966.)

movements of the mother or is to avoid enemies soon after leaving the nest when it assumes an independent existence. Growth patterns, like age to maturity, may also vary slightly in response to habitat conditions. This has been demonstrated in the bull elephants of Kabalega and Rwenzori Parks in Western Uganda (Fig. 9.12) where in the former they attain a larger size.

Chapter 10

Behaviour and ecology

If an organism is going to survive, it must be adapted to a particular niche. The nature of the niche partly depends on the environment, but also on the morphology, physiology and behaviour of the species which determines how the organism can utilise that environment. Although the environment in any locality has its own characteristics of vegetation, resources, climate and seasonality, the individual (through its behaviour) selects its own niche by using those components of the environment which are necessary for its survival. Consequently, the behaviour of a species determines, to a large extent, the ecological characteristics of the species.

For the purpose of this chapter the behaviour of an individual is divided into individual behaviour, intra-specific social behaviour and inter-specific behaviour. Individual behaviour is concerned with the behavioural patterns which the individual can perform in the absence of conspecifics. These include movements within the home range (section 10.1), domicile construction (section 10.2), postures, locomotion, grooming, feeding and selection of a niche. Intra-specific social behaviour includes all the behavioural interactions between conspecifics (section 10.3), the methods of communication between conspecifics, how individuals of the same species live together and how these intra-specific interactions affect the social organisations of the species (section 10.4). Inter-specific behaviour considers the behavioural interactions between individuals of different species, and is mostly concerned with predator and anti-predator behaviour, and the associations between different species (section 10.5).

The genetically determined behaviour patterns allow a species to utilise the environment in particular ways. For example, they determine how the species feeds, whether it migrates, whether territoriality is an established part of its way of life, how it rears its young and the length of time required by the young before before they become independent. The environmental conditions in which the individual or species lives can modify or alter the expression of the behavioural characteristics of the species so that a single species may show different behavioural patterns in different environmental conditions. For example, climatic variations and the subsequent changes in the availability of food, water and nutrients determine localised and migratory movements, where an individual can feed, drink and rest, and how large a home range is needed for its survival. Consequently behaviour and environment both determine the life style of each species.

10.1 Home range, migration and nomadism

The numbers of individuals in a particular area are related to the resources of that area, and the biomass may change seasonally depending on the conditions of the habitat (Ch. 7, and section 11.3). On this basis, relatively stable habitats such as rain forest contain species which are relatively sedentary. Unstable habitats with seasonal changes such as savannas and arid regions contain some species which are comparatively mobile. Where resources are clumped, either permanently or seasonally, the distribution of mammals will also be clumped and non-random. Resources of this kind include flushes of fresh vegetation, water holes, rocky outcrops and isolated forest patches. Very often one particular resource is limiting, and the lack of this resource prevents the dispersion of the species into those areas of the environment which would otherwise be suitable.

Decreases in food supply may affect mammals in one of two ways. Firstly, small mammals which are sedentary may be unable to obtain sufficient food. Many will die, and consequently the populations of such species will decrease. Secondly, species which can move away from temporarily unsuitable regions may be able to survive and their overall population numbers will not show much fluctuation. (This generalised situation may change after years of drought, or under certain unnatural conditions.) Local movements in response to fluctuating resource availability alters the dispersion of mammal species.

A consequence of these ecological characteristics is that every individual needs a particular restricted living space which contains all its requirements for survival. This space is the 'home range' and it can be defined as the area which is habitually used by the individual during its lifetime, and which contains all the resource requirements for survival and reproduction. An individual may move outside its home range occasionally and for short periods of time, but it returns to its home range again. Within the home range there may be a 'core area', 'centre of activity' or 'monopolised zone', all of which imply that one part of the home range is utilised more extensively and more frequently than other parts (Jewell 1966). The core area may be close to the domicile, an area of favourable grazing, or a particular association of resources required by the individual. Certain social and behavioural considerations may force an individual to leave its home range, and it will then have to re-establish itself elsewhere and form a new home range.

Home ranges vary in size from small to very large. Four principal factors which influence the home range size are:

1. The size of the individual and its mobility.
2. The quantity and availability of the resources.
3. The constancy, or lack of constancy, of the resources.
4. Behavioural considerations associated with territoriality and population densities.

The utilisation of the home range varies according to the species and the size of the home range. In shrews and small rodents, the home range tends to be small in size (1–5 ha), and most parts of it may be visited within a short period of time. A small home range suggests, in addition, that the resources are rather stable. Conversely, some large species have extensive home ranges but they utilise only a small part of the home range at a time. In localities where the resources fluctuate, it is necessary that the individual wanders over a large area from one food source to another. The actual movements depend on the spatial and temporal availability of these resources.

It is convenient to distinguish three types of movement within the home range, even though the same ecological principles apply to each type. The scale of movement is relative: the distances covered in daily localised movements of elephants could be larger than life-long movements of rodents.

1. *Localised movements* occur when the individual moves short distances within part (or all) of the home range during a limited period of time. Daily movements from

domicile to feeding and drinking areas are localised movements, and they are relatively predictable. Localised movements may occur in the same area throughout the year, as in sedentary species, or during part of the year when an essentially migratory species remains in the same locality for a limited period of time. Extended localised movements occur in 'catena movements' when individuals move from drier and higher ground into the moist river valley during the dry season, and then move back up the catena during the wet season.

2. *Migrations* are also predictable. They differ from localised movements because the migratory species move their domiciles, feeding and drinking areas during the course of the migration depending on the changing environmental conditions. Migratory species do not migrate continuously. When suitable conditions have been reached they are relatively sedentary until the deterioration of the habitat, or the advent of better conditions elsewhere, initiate a new migratory phase. The distances involved in migrations are usually measured in tens or hundreds of kilometres, although the mechanisms involved in migrations are similar to those of the larger localised movements.

3. *Nomadism* is unpredictable and irregular, and is exemplified by animals which live in unpredictable habitats. Large mammals of the arid zone and dry savanna are nomadic as they move over long distances to habitats where food and water are available. The degree of nomadism during the year is entirely dependent on the environmental conditions.

The concept of home range is quite different to that of territory (p. 227). There is no active participation by the individual to establish a home range, and other conspecifics may enter and use the individual's home range. In contrast, a territory is exclusive to one individual or to a particular group of individuals, and certain other conspecifics are not tolerated inside the territory. There are specific behavioural displays and characteristics which establish and maintain a territory, but these are not necessary to establish a home range. In most instances, the territory is a small area within the home range, and it is very rare for the area of the territory to equal that of the home range. In addition, a territory is generally, but not always, established for a specific reason for a short period of time and unlike the home range does not last for the whole life span of the individual.

Localised movements

Localised movements occur in all species during the day-to-day search for food, water and other requirements. These localised movements are often random and dependent on the exact location of the resource on a particular day, but many species habitually use preferred 'game paths', trails and runways within the home range. Fossorial species can only move within their burrow system. The extent of such movements (which are instrumental in determining the size of the home range) varies from small movements in rodents to extensive movements in many species of termite eaters, fruit bats, savanna primates, large herbivores and carnivores. Directional daily movements from a domicile to feeding and watering places have been observed in some species of primates, fruit bats and hippopotamus. The study of localised movements in large diurnal species is relatively easy, but extremely difficult in small nocturnal species. Any details on localised movements must include the actual distances moved during a specified time. All these localised movements result in the dispersion or aggregation of individuals, and the actual patterns of dispersion depend on the requirements of the individual and the dispersion of the resources.

Fig. 10.1   Herd of buffalo following a game trail to a water hole in Tsavo National Park. (Photo: W. Leuthold.)

Some species undertake much larger movements. These are most obvious in the large herbivorous species, and there appears to be a relationship between the tendency to have large localised movements (and migrations) and the feeding habit (Jarman 1974). Such movements are also related to the numbers of individuals living together and to the size of each individual, as these considerations determine the volume of food that is required. Antelopes which live in large herds and feed on seasonally growing grasses have regular large scale movements (Table 10.11) whereas savanna species which live in groups of two to twelve individuals and feed on grasses and browse tend to be fairly sedentary, although they may enlarge their home range when conditions are poor. The following examples illustrate different patterns of dispersion in relation to seasonal conditions and food availability.

Large mammals in the Rukwa valley exhibit catena movements in relation to rainfall, the level of water in the flood plain and the types of food which are available at different times of the year. All these factors are inter-related because any particular locality in the valley shows seasonal variations in the level of flooding and in the growth stages of different types of vegetation (Vesey-Fitzgerald 1960, 1965a). There is a succession of plant associations extending from the lake edge to the woodlands near the escarpment. Close to the lake are the flood plains which are flooded for up to seven months each year. Further away are the perimeter grasslands dissected by watercourses and depressions which form a mosaic of different habitat types, and finally there are the woodlands on the higher ground near the edge of the escarpment (Fig. 10.2). The annual cycle of growth in the vegetation can be illustrated by the *Vossia* and *Echinochloa* association in the watercourses (Fig. 10.3). The plants start to grow when the rains begin and growth continues as the floodplains are submerged by water. At the end of the rains, the water level subsides and the plants are trampled by large mammals. The tall grasses are flattened and begin to shoot upwards from the nodes to form a 'lawn'. They remain in this state due to continual grazing until the rains begin again.

The large mammals react in different ways to these seasonal changes in the habitats (Fig. 10.4). Hippopotamus always remain close to the water's edge, so that they follow the rising flood waters which gradually cover the flood plain. The semi-aquatic puku feed along the edge of the flooded areas during the rains while the flood plain is under water, and during the dry season they remain close to the dried watercourses where they rest in the shade during the heat of the day. Elephants, which cannot venture on to

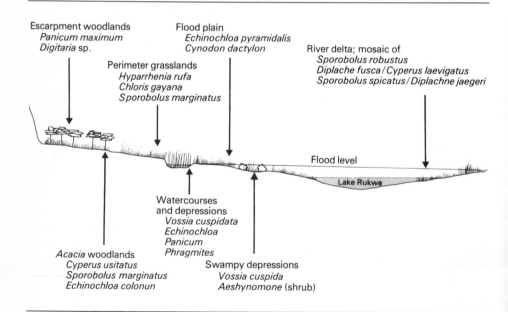

Fig. 10.2 Schematic profile of the Rukwa valley, Tanzania, to show the habitats utilised by large mammals. (Data from Vessey-Fitzgerald 1965*a*.)

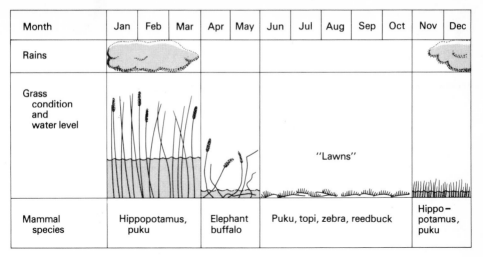

Month	Jan	Feb	Mar	Apr	May	Jun	Jul	Aug	Sep	Oct	Nov	Dec
Rains												
Grass condition and water level								"Lawns"				
Mammal species		Hippopotamus, puku		Elephant buffalo		Puku, topi, zebra, reedbuck					Hippo- potamus, puku	

Fig. 10.3   The annual cycle of the *Vossia* grasslands in the Rukwa valley in relation to the rains, water level and utilisation by large mammals. (Data from Vesey-Fitzgerald 1965*a*.)

the flood plain when the soil is soft or under water, remain in the *Acacia* woodlands until the rains have stopped and the floods are receding. Then they move into the tall *Vossia* grasslands in the watercourses, and as the dry season continues they feed on the *Vossia* in the depressions on the flood plain. A further inter-relationship is the modification of the habitat by some species so it becomes a suitable feeding area for other species. Elephant, hippopotamus and buffalo are particularly important in this respect as they trample the tall tough grasses which, in that condition, are unsuitable as food for the antelopes. When these grasses shoot again after trampling and flattening, the new shoots are soft and palatable and can then be eaten by several species of grazing mammals. All the species utilise the Rukwa valley habitats in different ways, and the movement of each species depends on its ability to move on the floodplain and on the location of the most suitable grazing.

A similar sort of relationship is shown by the behaviour of the mammals on the Kafue flats in Zambia (Sheppe and Osborne 1971) (Fig. 10.5). Here the Kafue river spreads out over the flood plains; the time of the greatest floods is at the end of the rains because most of the flood water comes from the higher reaches of the river. The flood plain consists of small lakes, some of which have water for most of the year, and 'water meadow grasslands' which have nutritious short grasses and herbs after the plain has been flooded and before the vegetation is burnt. At the margins of the flood plain, 5 to 20 (8–32 km) miles from the river itself, are extensive woodlands. The flood waters do not normally reach these woodlands although occasionally the termite mounds on the edge of the flood plain are partly submerged. The mammals of the Kafue flats may be divided into four classes (Table 10.1) on the basis of their utilisation of the flood plain at different stages of the flooding cycle. Each species behaves differently in relation to the water level, and some species never move out on to the flood plain even when it is dry and there is abundant suitable grazing.

Elephants require a large volume of food each day, and they have to look for suitable food sources over a wide area. Their large size and mobility allows them to travel considerable distances in a short time looking for food and water, and regular movements of elephants occur wherever there is seasonal variation in food supply. In the Kabalega Falls Park, Uganda, large herds of elephants feed on the tall grasses by

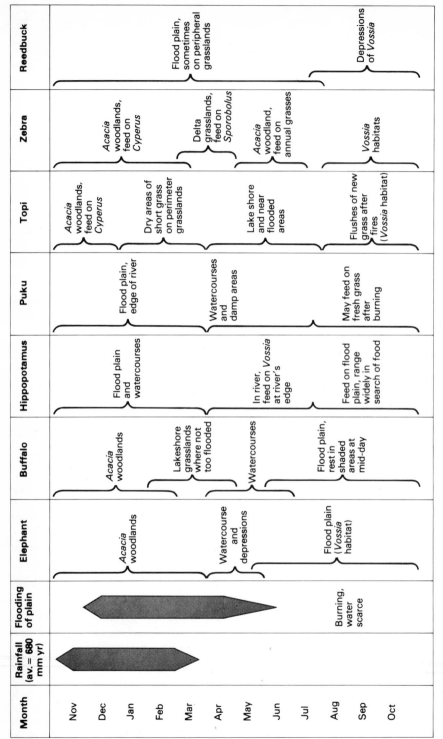

Fig. 10.4 The annual movements of seven species of large mammals in relation to flooding and food requirements in the Rukwa valley, Tanzania. (Data from Vesey-Fitzgerald 1965*a*.)

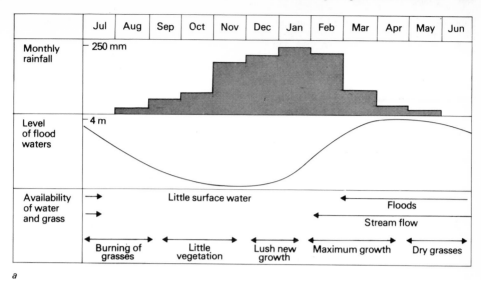

a

b

	Dry season and early rains	Rainy season	End of rains and dry season
River	Hippo	Hippo	
Flood plain (10-40 km)	Lechwe Zebra Wildebeest Eland Roan Buffalo	Lechwe Zebra Wildebeest (local flooding) Roan Buffalo	(Kafue river floods) Hippo Lechwe
Surrounding termite zone and woodlands	Eland, Buffalo	Eland	Buffalo, Zebra, Roan Eland, Wildebeest, Lechwe

Fig. 10.5 The annual cycles of rainfall, flood water level, availability of water and grass, and localised mammal movements on the flood plains of the Kafue river, Zambia.   (*a*) The annual cycle of rainfall, flood water levels, and the availability of water and grass.   (*b*) The distribution of large mammals in the river, flood plain and surrounding termite zone and woodlands during three periods of the year. The name of each species is indicated at its preferred habitat. (Data from Sheppe and Osborne 1971.)

the side of Lake Albert (or Mobutu) during the wet season, but as the grasses dry and become tough and unpalatable in November, the elephants move away from the lake and climb the escarpment into Budongo Forest (Fig. 10.6). Burning of the grasses near the lake probably accelerates the movements of the elephants because the habitat rapidly becomes unsuitable for them. They spend the dry season from November to March in the woodland forests, where they congregate near the headwaters of streams and rest under the trees during the hottest hours of the day. They feed on some woody vegetation, but more frequently on the unburnt grasslands which are interspersed between the woodlands. When the rains begin in April and new grasses sprout near the Lake, the elephants move back to their wet-season habitat (Buss 1961, Buechner *et al* 1963). This seasonal movement of elephants is related to the necessity of finding dry

Table 10.1   *Use of the flood plain by ungulates at Lochinvar and Blue Lagoon ranches on the Kafue Flats, Zambia. (From Sheppe and Osborne 1971.)*

Habitat	Species
Amphibious	Hippopotamus, sitatunga
Terrestrial	
Use flood plain extensively	
Feeding in water	Lechwe
Not feeding in water	Zebra, wildebeest, eland, buffalo, roan antelope, reedbuck, bushpig
Use flood plain marginally	Oribi
In woodlands and 'termite' zone	Common duiker, grysbok, bushbuck, kudu, reedbuck, impala

season feeding areas, and an adequate supply of water and shade. Similar sorts of movements have been observed in the Tsavo National Park in Kenya (Leuthold and Sale 1973) where elephant populations are well dispersed in the wet season, but are congregated near permanent water supplies in the dry season. It appears that the elephants are divided into 'subunits' each of which habitually stays within a certain area. During the dry season, they may travel up to 80 km to feed on new vegetation resulting from localised rainfall, and it is likely that localised elephant movements are determined primarily by food supply and the nutritive quality of the food. Inadequate food (in quantity and quality) will cause malnutrition which may have adverse effects on the population, as in the drought of 1970–71 (section 11.3). The behavioural aspects of finding food in sufficient quantity, and the limited dispersion of elephants because of

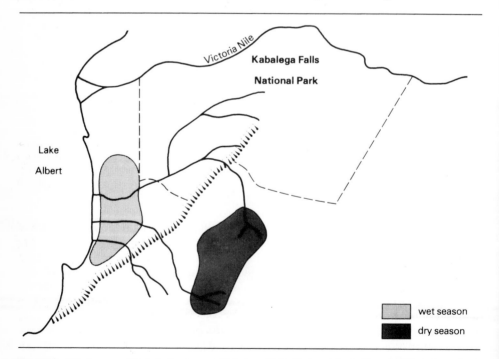

Fig. 10.6   The movements of elephants near Kabalega Falls National Park, Uganda. (Data from Buss 1961.)

the necessity to stay near water, can have important implications for population regulation (Ch. 12).

Migrations

The migrations of mammals in the Serengeti are probably the most spectacular of all migrations in Africa at the present time. Wildebeest (Fig. 10.7), Burchell's zebra and

Fig. 10.7   Migrating wildebeest. (Photo: Norman Myers. Copyright Bruce Coleman Ltd.)

Thomson's gazelle are the principal migratory species, and much of the recent study on migration and its causes has been on these three species. The necessity to migrate (and presumably the reason why the migration evolved) appears to be related to the very precise food requirements of each species. The amount of protein in different sorts of plants and in different stages of plant growth, as well as the protein requirements of each species, determines to a large extent where and how feeding will occur (Bell 1971, Gwynne and Bell 1968, Jarman pers. comm.). Therefore details on feeding behaviour are necessary to understand why wildebeest, zebra and Thomson's gazelle undertake extensive migrations.

Wildebeest eat short grasses 10–15 cm high with a large proportion of leaf and a small proportion of stem. The cell walls of grass leaves are easily broken down in the rumen, and this diet has a high percentage of protein in relation to the total volume of food consumed. When grasses are fully grown and their cell walls are lignified, breakdown and consequent assimilation is slower and less efficient and wildebeest are unable to extract sufficient food. So therefore they must either select only those parts of the grass with thin cell walls or they must find new feeding areas. Thomson's gazelle eat grasses 5–10 cm high which also contain a high proportion of protein. Thomson's gazelle (20–25 kg) are smaller animals than wildebeest (180–230 kg); they require only

20 per cent of the food required by wildebeest, and can survive on areas of short grass and dicotyledonous plants which are unable to support wildebeest. Thomson's gazelle are able to spend five times as long looking for an adequate supply of food compared with wildebeest, and they have time to be very selective. However, the daily requirement of protein per unit weight for a Thomson's gazelle is two to four times higher than that of a wildebeest, and therefore the quality of the food must be much better than that required by wildebeest. Zebra can eat taller grasses which are nutritionally of poorer quality than those required by the other two species. They do not have a rumen, and therefore extraction and breakdown of protein is less efficient than in ruminants. Zebra obtain sufficient protein because the passage of food through the alimentary canal is about twice as fast as in ruminants. As a result, zebra must ingest much more grass than wildebeest, but it can be of lower quality.

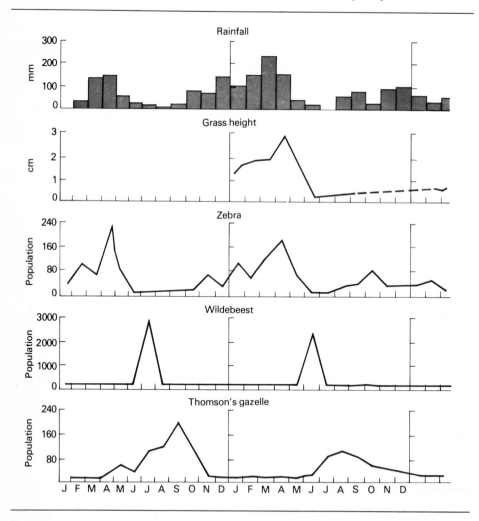

Fig. 10.8   The population numbers of zebra, wildebeest and Thomson's gazelle in relation to rainfall and grass length in the western Serengeti in 1966. Population numbers are based on daily counts on a 3000 m by 800 m transect (Adapted from R. H. V. Bell; 'A grazing ecosystem in the Serengeti'. Copyright © 1971 by Scientific American, Inc. All rights reserved.)

These differences in the grasses, selectivity of food, digestion and protein requirement are some of the reasons for the migratory behaviour of these species. The particular patterns of soil type, species of grass, absolute rainfall and length of the wet season determine where grasses of the 'correct' size and structure are to be found. The volcanic soils of the southern Serengeti plains do not hold soil moisture, and the short grasses wither and die soon after the rains end. The combination of soil type and low rainfall (600 mm per annum) results in a quick growth of short high-protein grasses which attract many animals during the rains. When the rains end, the productivity of the plains drops, and the animals have to find other pastures. The grass species in the western Serengeti grow taller than those on the plains, and as a result of higher rainfall (1 000 mm per annum), a longer wet season and increased moisture in the alluvial soil, they provide food for the migrating herds after the plains grasses have died. Several rivers run westwards into Lake Victoria, and abundant vegetation grows along the banks of these rivers. In the northern Serengeti the grass species are different to those in the western Serengeti. They are taller and grow for a longer period of time due to even higher rainfall (1 100 mm per annum) and the high moisture content of the soil. Each of the three areas provides, at some time during the year, suitable feeding conditions for the three migratory species.

When the rains begin in October–November on the Serengeti plains, herds of zebra, wildebeest and Thomson's gazelle congregate to feed on the new grasses. Zebra feed on the upper parts, wildebeest on the middle parts, and Thomson's gazelle on the parts closest to the ground. As the grasses dry out, the zebra move towards the taller grasses of the western Serengeti (Fig. 10.8). They are followed later by the wildebeest, and later still by the Thomson's gazelle who, because of their smaller size and because they have partly switched from poor quality grass to high protein browse, have been able to survive on the plains longer than the other species. By the late dry season, the zebra have moved to the northern Serengeti. They trample the grasses which then become suitable for the wildebeest and Thomson's gazelle which come later. Despite the abundance of grass, there is normally inadequate food to feed the enormous herds which congregate in the northern Serengeti during the late dry season, and considerable mortality may occur (e.g. up to 10 per cent of the wildebeest herds). When the rains begin again, the three species migrate south to the short grass plains, and the migratory cycle begins again. Migration occurs in a clockwise direction from the plains to the western Serengeti, then to the northern Serengeti woodlands and finally back to the plains, with zebra in the lead followed by wildebeest and Thomson's gazelle in the rear (Fig. 10.9). The exact migration paths of each species show some similarity and any differences are due to the exact requirements of each species and the available forage. Similarly, the pattern of distribution of each species within a particular area is related to the spatial distribution of food and the threat of possible predation. The annual differences in the pattern of wildebeest migration are related to the differences in annual rainfall (Pennycuick 1975), and to the spatial and temporal occurrence of grasses. In particular, rainfall determines the wildebeest movements on to, and away from, the plains and the extent to which they utilise the northern Serengeti.

Another aspect of grazing patterns and migratory movements is the effect of one species on another. The large herds of wildebeest reduce the green plant biomass of the Serengeti plains by about 85 per cent (400 g m^{-2}) of the initial standing crop. This heavy grazing stimulates new plant growth and therefore increases the annual primary production (see also section 11.3). Thomson's gazelle are significantly associated with areas previously grazed by wildebeest, and they remain in these areas during the early dry season after the wildebeest have migrated to the western Serengeti. The co-existence of these two species is an example of co-evolution rather than direct

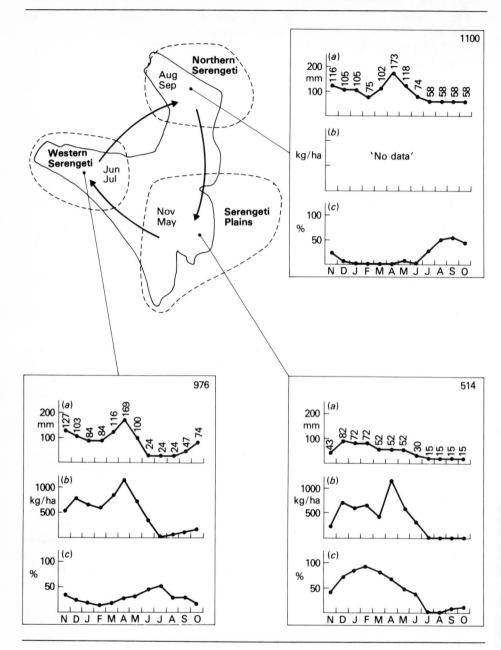

Fig. 10.9 The migrations of wildebeest in the Serengeti in relation to rainfall and primary production. Wildebeest move in a clockwise direction through the Serengeti, spending varying lengths of time in each of the three regions. (*a*) Mean monthly rainfall (mm); figure at top right of graph indicates mean annual rainfall (Norton-Griffiths *et al*. 1975). (*b*) Grass primary production (kg/ha) (Sinclair 1975). (*c*) Mean monthly number of wildebeest (Pennycuick 1975). Wildebeest utilise the grasses on the plains to the greatest extent, and only leave for the western and northern Serengeti (where the grasses are longer and are less heavily grazed) when grass growth on the plains has stopped.

competition; facilitation of energy flow through the Thomson's gazelle population is a consequence of the heavy grazing by the wildebeest (McNaughton 1976).

Migration is clearly not essential for all the large Serengeti mammals since topi and kongoni have much smaller seasonal movements, and buffalo and impala are more or less sedentary. These species must be considered briefly to indicate how the movements of the migratory species may affect these relatively sedentary species.

The semi-migratory and non-migratory Serengeti mammals can live in a limited area provided it contains a year-long supply of food. Buffalo can survive on tall course grasses of low protein content which grow in moist non-wooded regions, and they vary the proportion of different food items during the course of the year (Sinclair and Gwynne 1972). Even so, food may become scarce due to over-utilisation or poor growth and this may result in the mortality of some individuals. Topi and hartebeest are fairly mobile and they move within a large range, but they do not have regular predictable migrations. If wildebeest move into their range and, consequently, food supplies are reduced, they move into neighbouring areas. Similarly, impala stay in a limited region but the herds tend to spread out when food is scarce and, like Thomson's gazelle, their diet consists of a higher percentage of dicotyledonous plants than in the wet season. Instead of migrating, these species move down the catena during the dry season to habitats where suitable vegetation is more abundant.

Some energy relationships of the Serengeti ecosystem are discussed in section 11.3.

Nomadism

Unpredictable long-distance movements are not common in African mammals, and they occur only in the large species of the arid zones. Nomadism is unpredictable as the movements do not occur at any particular season of the year, or at yearly intervals, and the direction and extent of nomadic movements vary according to local conditions at a particular time. Scimitar-horned oryx, addax, several species of arid zone gazelles, and the Nubian ass are nomadic in the Sudanese and Somali arid zones. They travel quickly over enormous distances seeking suitable feeding areas. It is generally impossible to predict where individuals and herds may be found, although the growth of new grasses and vegetation after unpredictable rainstorms or flash floods usually results in the congregation of nomadic species. Gemsbok, springbok and eland in the south-west arid zone show similar nomadic movements (section 7.5).

These examples illustrate how the home range has to be extremely large for some species to survive throughout the year. The home range is determined by many features of the environment such as rainfall, soil type, plant species and nutritional characteristics of the forage, and by the behaviour of the species themselves.

10.2 Domiciles

Many species of African mammals in several families have the ability to build or construct domiciles. The term 'domicile' means 'a dwelling place', or 'a regular place of abode'. The smaller species of mammals show the greatest tendency to construct domiciles, probably because they are much more susceptible to environmental change than larger species. Consequently, domicile construction does not occur in the Perissodactyla, Artiodactyla (except some Suidae), Proboscidea and Sirenia. Some form of domicile is present in the other orders, though not in every species within an order, and in some species the domicile plays a very important part in the life and survival of the species.

There are several reasons why mammals use and build domiciles.

1. Domiciles protect the individual (or group of individuals) from possible sources of danger, e.g. predators, fire and sudden inclement weather conditions. This is undoubtedly the most widespread use of domiciles. Nocturnal insectivores, rodents, lagomorphs, prosimians, pangolins, hyraxes, bats and some carnivores all rest in domiciles during the day and emerge to feed and drink at night. During the day, they are protected from diurnal predators, daytime temperatures and humidities, and high light intensities. The pattern of daytime resting and nocturnal activity has evolved as a behavioural characteristic of these species. Other species, for example some squirrels and some mongooses, are diel active, and rest in their domiciles at night. In all these species, the domicile is essential for survival throughout their lives. Some species use domiciles at certain periods only, as for the birth and early development of the young (e.g. some felids).

2. Domiciles allow some species to escape from environmental extremes which are a normal part of the climatic regime. This is especially true in hot arid regions (Ch. 7). In arid-zones rodents, the individual, or group of individuals, is able to modify the temperature and humidity of the domicile. In others, e.g. bats in caves, there is no modification of the environment, but the domicile may be many degrees cooler than the ambient external temperature.

3. Domiciles may be used to store food during times of plenty for use at a later date. Several species of rodents which live in habitats where resources fluctuate have specialised in storage of seeds, fruits and dried grass. Species in the subfamilies Gerbillinae and Cricetomyinae and some squirrels (especially *Xerus*) exhibit food storing behaviour. Notable studies on food storing include Ewer's work (1965, 1967) on *Xerus* and *Cricetomys*.

4. Permanently fossorial species dig tunnels underground when searching for food. The resulting network of tunnels form a permanent underground 'domicile'. The individual utilises these tunnels, and digs new tunnels, when searching for food and some parts of this tunnel system are used as a domicile in the strictest sense of the word.

The nature of domiciles is very varied, ranging from those where the individual simply uses a natural environmental feature to those where the individual (or group) actively modifies the environment and constructs the domicile. On this basis, three types of domicile construction can be distinguished:

1. Natural domiciles, with little alteration of the environment.
2. Constructions on or above the ground using leaves, grasses, branches, etc.
3. Excavation and domicile building underground.

There is considerable variation in complexity and use of the environment in each of these types. Some species show morphological adaptations for domicile construction, but the complexity of construction is never as great as that found in some species of birds.

The most frequently used domiciles are natural ones in or under trees, in caves or under rock boulders. Many *Cercopithecus* monkeys, some Felidae and many fruit bats rest on tree branches where they are exposed to the climatic conditions surrounding the tree. Fruit bats usually hang under branches or leaf petioles where they are protected from rainfall. Other species rest in holes in trees, in hollow standing tree trunks, or caves where it is dark and where there is some protection from the climate (Fig. 10.10). For example, many squirrels, flying squirrels, dormice and prosimians climb into tree holes, and many microchiroptera fly into hollow tree trunks and caves where they rest

Fig. 10.10   A group of fruit bats (*Rousettus* sp.) in a cave in Rwenzori National Park. The bats can 'crawl' along the roof of the cave. (Photo: C. A. Spinage.)

during the day (Fig. 10.11). Trees which have fallen to the ground and are decaying offer a domicile to non-arboreal species such as shrews and terrestrial forest rodents. *Praomys tullbergi*, a West African forest rodent, frequently utilises crevices and cracks around the buttress roots of large forest trees (Happold, 1977).

Some species have the behavioural attributes to modify the environment by building a domicile where they can rest. Lagomorphs and cane rats (*Thryonomys*) construct the simplest sort of nest on the ground by scraping a small hollow in the soil and bending grass around the hollow. This gives a limited amount of protection, and helps to make the resting animal almost invisible. In other species, simple nests are built in the natural domiciles described above. Many species of ground-living rodents arrange leaves and grass to form a cup-shaped nest but this behaviour does not involve any complex nest-building behaviour (Fig. 10.12).

More elaborate domiciles are built by the tree-climbing mice *Thamnomys* and *Praomys* (*Hylomyscus*). *Thamnomys* lives in tangles of secondary growth in rain forest where many small branches form a network on which it can build its nest. It collects grasses which are cut and shredded into small strips which are interwoven to form a close-knit sphere with a hollow centre and an opening at the side. *Hylomyscus* and some dormice build nests of similar construction.

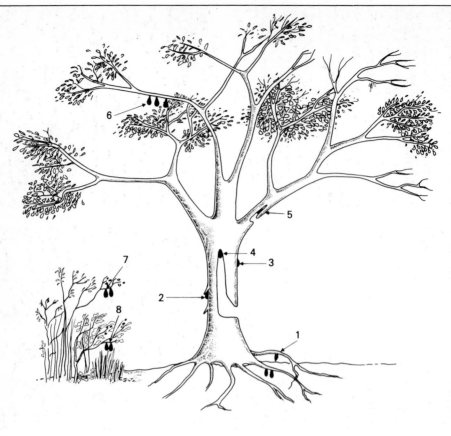

a

b

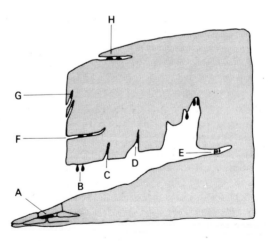

Fig. 10.11   Resting places of bats in (*a*) trees and (*b*) caves. 1 *Epomophorus, Hipposideros*; 2 *Eptesicus*; 3 *Taphozous*; 4 *Nycteris*; 5 Molossidae; 6 *Eidolon*; 7 *Lavia*; 8 *Nycteris*.
A *Myotis, Tadarida*; B Emballonuridae, *Rousettus*; C *Taphozous, Myotis*; D *Otomops*; E *Hipposideros, Rhinolophus*; F *Tadarida*; G *Taphozous*; H *Tadarida*. (After Brosset 1966*a*.)

Fig. 10.12 Nests of rodents. These nests were built in captivity by rodents which were given a large choice of naturally occurring nest materials. The savanna species (*a, b*) selected grasses which were chewed, shredded and interwoven to form nests which were characteristic of each species. Forest species selected dried leaves of particular sizes and shapes which were laid flat and unbroken (*c*), or were broken and piled to form a cup-shaped depression (*d*). (*a*) *Arvicanthis niloticus*; (*b*) *Tatera valida*; (*c*) *Malacomys edwardsi*; (*d*) *Praomys tullbergi*. (Photos: D. C. D. Happold.)

Most large species do not construct nests, although notable exceptions are the gorilla and chimpanzee (Fig. 10.13). The gorilla builds a tree nest of sticks and twigs which forms a platform where the animal rests at night. The nest is used for one night only, probably because gorillas range widely for food, and a new nest is built for the following night (Schaller 1963). Similarly chimpanzees usually, but not always, use a nest for a single night (Lawick-Goodall 1968).

Mammalian species which excavate a hole or a burrow and subsequently build a nest in the burrow, can modify their environment to a larger degree than those species which have been considered above.

The first group of species are those which excavate a domicile for resting and rearing young and which come to the surface to feed. The simplest sort of excavation is a large hole which may twist and turn several times before ending in a nest or 'den'. Aardvarks, canids and some mustelids and viverrids dig these sorts of burrows and they vary only in size and small details. Some species, e.g. warthogs, also use underground domiciles

Fig. 10.13   Tree nest of chimpanzee. (Photo: Helmit Albrecht. Copyright Bruce Coleman Ltd.)

but since they usually do not excavate themselves, they take over burrows which have been abandoned by other species. Many species of rodents are very accomplished burrowers. Burrowing species scratch at the soil with their forepaws and as the spill-heap accumulates, it is kicked backwards with the hindfeet. Some species use the nose or head to push earth in the burrow. The diameter of the burrow is slightly wider than the body diameter of the burrower, and therefore it is often possible to identify the species which has made the burrow by the size and characteristics of the burrow entrance. The length, complexity and depth of the burrow varies greatly, but it is usually fairly constant for each species (Fig. 10.14). *Lophuromys sikapusi* in West Africa, for example, lives in soft swampy ground and its burrow is very shallow, whereas species in savanna and arid regions dig deeper where they are protected from surface temperatures and humidities. Other interesting features of rodent burrows are:

(*a*) Many species have a nesting area in the burrow. The diameter of the nest area is usually greater than the burrow, and the floor (and perhaps the sides and roof depending on the species) is lined with plant materials. The nature of the nest is extremely varied.

(*b*) Some species store food in parts of their burrows. *Tatera, Taterillus, Gerbillus, Cricetomys* and *Uranomys* collect seeds, fruits and dried grasses which are deposited in the nest or in a special food store. In captivity, *Uranomys* places food in parts of the burrow which later becomes filled with soil again, and which, presumably, will be refound if the animal re-excavates. *Xerus* buries food in holes which may not be part of the domicile burrow.

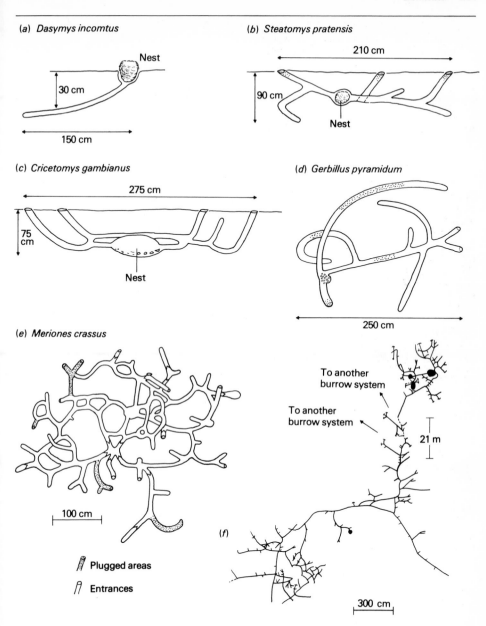

(a) *Dasymys incomtus*

Nest

30 cm

150 cm

(b) *Steatomys pratensis*

210 cm

90 cm

Nest

(c) *Cricetomys gambianus*

275 cm

75 cm

Nest

(d) *Gerbillus pyramidum*

250 cm

(e) *Meriones crassus*

To another burrow system

To another burrow system

21 m

100 cm

(f)

300 cm

⫪ Plugged areas

⫪ Entrances

Fig. 10.14 Rodent burrows and their characteristics. (*a*) *Dasymys incomtus*: surface nest; single shallow burrow often leading to stream. (After Hanney 1965.) (*b*) *Steatomys pratensis*: subterranean nest; several entrance holes, plugged with soil when not in use. (After Hanney 1965.) (*c*) *Cricetomys gambianus*: subterranean nest, often used as food store; several entrances, not plugged. (After Hanney 1965.) (*d*) *Gerbillus pyramidum*: subterranean nest; several burrows; entrances usually plugged; sections of burrow used as food store and filled with sand. (After Petter 1961.) (*e*) *Meriones crassus*: complex subterranean colonial burrow system, often used by many individuals; several entrances and nest areas. (After Petter 1961.) (*f*) *Heterocephalus glaber*: part of a large complex burrow system used for permanent residence and for food-searching; many 'mole-hills' of excavated soil on surface; no permanent entrance holes. (After Jarvis and Sale 1971.)

(c) Many species construct 'pop-holes' in their burrows. These are parts of the burrow which extend upwards towards the surface, but stop a few centimetres below the surface. They form an emergency exit so that if the occupant of the burrow needs to escape, it can push up through the pop-hole. These have been recorded, for example, in the burrows of *Jaculus, Tatera, Taterillus* and *Uranomys*.

(d) Some rodent species block up their burrow entrance with a plug of soil or sand. This is done when the animal has entered the burrow by pushing soil from the floor of the burrow into the burrow entrance. Similarly, soil from the spillheap is pushed into the burrow entrance when the animal leaves the burrow (Fig. 10.15). This behaviour has been observed in *Jaculus, Gerbillus, Taterillus* and *Tatera*, and is seen most often in species living in arid regions.

Fig. 10.15   Jerboa (*Jaculus jaculus*) plugging the entrance of the burrow with its flattened 'pig-like' nose. (Photo: D. C. D. Happold.)

Secondly there are those species which excavate and remain in their burrows practically all the time. The rodent families Rhizomyidae and Bathyergidae are almost entirely fossorial and are morphologically adapted for living underground (Jarvis and Sale 1971). When burrowing, the rhizomyid *Tachyoryctes splendens* braces itself against the side of the burrow with its fore and hind feet. The soil is loosened at the soil face by upward and forward sweeps with the large projecting lower incisors. The soil is then pushed backwards along the burrow with the side of the face and the forefeet (Fig. 10.16). As the burrow increases in length, branch burrows which go directly to the surface are constructed so newly excavated soil can be pushed in a plug to the surface where it forms a spill heap. After use, all holes to the surface are blocked so the burrow is predator- and water-proof. The burrow contains a nest chamber filled with nesting material where the animal sleeps, where food may be stored and where faeces are deposited. *Tachyoryctes* excavates foraging burrows where it feeds on tubers and roots

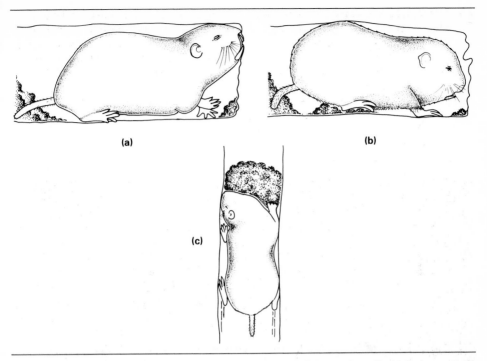

Fig. 10.16 Digging and transportation of soil by *Tachyoryctes*. (*a*) Excavating soil with incisor teeth (*b*) Kicking soil backwards (*c*) Pushing soil with side of head. (After Jarvis and Sale 1971).

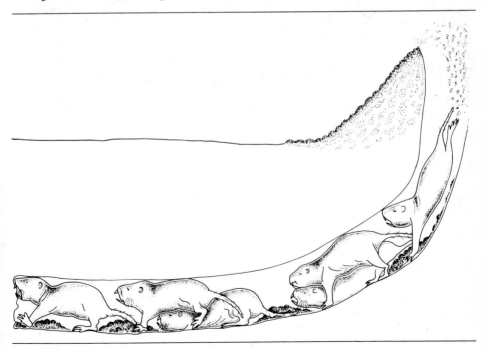

Fig. 10.17 Co-operative digging by six *Heterocephalus*. (After Jarvis and Sale 1971.)

exposed during excavation. This species of *Tachyoryctes* is so well adapted to subterranean life that it does not need to go to the surface; in fact it avoids showing itself above ground even when pushing soil on to spillheaps. A 'bolt-hole' leads to the deepest part of the burrow and the escape reaction in *Tachyoryctes* is to bury itself in the bolt-hole. This behaviour is very different to that of most rodents which escape by leaving the burrow.

The bathyergids show a number of differences in their burrowing behaviour and the type of burrows compared with *Tachyoryctes*. These differences are due mostly to the structure and function of the nest chamber, the methods of transport of soil to the surface and because several individuals co-operate in digging the burrow (Jarvis and Sale 1971) (Fig. 10.17).

The golden mole (*Chrysochloris stuhlmanni*, order Insectivora) builds a much more compact burrow compared with the fossorial rodents (Fig. 10.18). In the Rwenzori

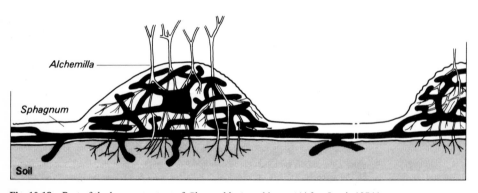

Fig. 10.18   Part of the burrow system of *Chrysochloris stuhlmanni* (After Jarvis 1974.)

Mountains, this species excavates burrows in the layers of dense sphagnum moss overlying the soil surface, although some burrows extend down into the soil (Jarvis 1974). Most of the burrows are in clumps of *Alchemilla* where the growth of sphagnum forms a large mound surrounding the roots of these plants. Large empty chambers, which may be for nesting, occur in some parts of the burrow system. Golden moles feed mostly on insects, snails and worms, and they probably find sufficient food by foraging in their extensive burrows. If insufficient prey is available, golden moles have to extend their burrow system.

10.3   Categories of social behaviour

Social behaviour can be defined as behaviour which has to do with two or more individuals (Tinbergen 1953). All mammals exhibit some degree of social behaviour since it is necessary for males to associate and interact with females at the time of mating, and for females to associate with their young prior to weaning. In theory it would be possible for a mammal to live the rest of its life without having any behavioural interaction with other conspecifics but in fact most mammals participate in a great deal more social behaviour than this. The majority live in pairs, family groups or in larger groups, and they interact with conspecifics most of the time. Although there are some species which live singly for most of their lives, social interactions of a different kind contribute to the establishment and maintenance of the distance between each individual.

The social behaviour of mammals falls broadly into six categories:

1. Communication and contacts for investigation.
2. Agonistic behaviour.
3. Amicable behaviour (not associated with sexual and parental behaviour).
4. Sexual behaviour.
5. Parent-offspring behaviour.
6. Social play.

Each category is not exclusive, and there is some overlap between different categories. This section discusses these six categories of social behaviour and section 10.4 shows how social organisations in African mammals can be described in terms of these categories.

Communication and contacts for investigation

The transmission of information from one individual to another requires actions or the use of structures to convey signals, and the appropriate receptors and behaviour to facilitate receiving these signals. Communication has become one of the most important and essential aspects of social behaviour in mammals and it is achieved to some extent through all the major sense organs – olfactory, auditory, visual and tactile. There is a tendency for communication to be most complex in species which live in large groups with complex intra-specific interactions. The intensity and frequency of communication between individuals varies according to the situation; some degree of communication occurs all the time, but it increases and is more obvious during sexual displays, in the presence of danger and in disputes between conspecifics.

The olfactory system of most land mammals is highly developed, and the production of odour signals and their reception by chemoreceptors is probably of great importance in the majority of orders (Table 10.2). Odours of communicatory significance are carried by secretions from the skin glands and reproductive tract, and by urine, faeces and expired air. Some of these odours are distributed by the every-day activities of the animal. Others are distributed by special behaviour patterns, such as glandular marking, urine marking and faeces marking, whose primary function is to place the odoriferous substance in specific places and sometimes on other individuals. Behaviour patterns which facilitate the detection of olfactory signals include sniffing the air, sniffing the substrate, smelling urine and faeces and sniffing other animals. The need to sniff conspecifics has resulted in the occurrence of many contact postures such as naso-nasal and naso-anal.

Auditory communication involves vocal and non-vocal signalling, and the use of activity sounds (Table 10.3). Through auditory communication, mammals are able to transmit information about species, sex, individuality, physiological status, motivation and spatial position (Tembrock 1968).

Visual communication operates through expressions, structures and movements (Table 10.4). Mammals show a great range of expressions as a result of movements of their ears, eyes, eyelids, nostrils, lips, jaws, hair, limbs, tail and penis. The position of the head in relation to the body can be varied to convey information (Figs. 10.25–10.27). Also some expressions convey distinct messages, while others convey

Table 10.2 *Olfactory communication in some African mammals. (From Tembrock 1968, Ewer 1968 and Ewer 1973.*

Order	Relative importance	Behaviour	Type of information conveyed
Insectivora	High	Glandular marking, Faecal marking, and salivation	Territoriality
		Glandular and investigatory contacts	Individuality, reproductive condition
Chiroptera	High	Glandular and investigatory contacts	Individual recognition
		Investigation of urine?	
Primates	Low?	Smelling (galagos)	Investigation
		Urine marking	
		Sternal gland marking	?
Pholidota	High		
Lagomorpha	High	Glandular marking	Reproductive condition and territoriality
Rodentia	High	Cheek and anal gland marking	Reproductive state and territoriality
		Urine marking	
		faecal marking	
		Investigatory contacts	Individuality, reproductive state
Carnivora	High	Anal and ano-genital marking, Faecal marking, urine marking, investigatory contacts	Range of information including individuality, territoriality, and reproductive state
Tubulidentata	High	Investigatory contacts	Unknown
Hyracoidea	Low	Dorsal gland display	?Threat
Proboscidea	?	Rubbing secretions from dermal gland	?Individuality
		Male smells female urine	Reproductive state
Perissodactyla	High	Glandular marking	Individuality
		Urine smelling	Reproductive condition
		Faecal smelling	Territoriality and individuality
Artiodactyla	High	Glandular marking	Territoriality, individuality
		Sniffing	Individuality
		Urine marking and faecal marking	Territoriality, individuality, reproductive condition

mood. The value of visual communication is related to the efficiency of the visual system, and this in turn is closely related to the environment and the animal's way of life. Eyesight is generally far inferior to the senses of smell and hearing, and visual communication is highly developed only in primates, some rodents, carnivores, equids and artiodactyla. In many of these and other mammals, parts of the pelage are distinctly coloured, often with contrasting colours, and these parts are used in highly conspicuous visual display; for example, the tree hyrax (*Dendrohyrax dorsalis*) turns its back towards a potential enemy, raises the hair along the back and displays a flash of

Table 10.3 *Auditory communication in some African mammals. (From Tembrock 1968, Ewer 1968, Ewer 1973, Altmann 1967.)*

Order	Relative importance	Behaviour	Type of information conveyed
Insectivora	High	Vocal signals, including high-pitched squeaks	Warning, threat, readiness for copulation
		Drumming with hindlimbs	Unknown
Chiroptera	High	Vocal signals, including sonic and ultrasonic squeaks	Cohesion between mother and young, territoriality, navigation and location
Primates	High	Vocal sounds (very varied), lip smacking, tooth chattering	Communication between individuals, warning, threat
		Beating ground and chest	Warning, threat, ?
Pholidota	?	Rattling and hissing	Defence
Lagomorpha	Low	Vocal signals	Alarm, territoriality
		Drumming with hindlegs	Warning
Rodentia	High	Vocal signals including squeaking, piping, growling, etc.	Parental care, threat, warning, reproductive state
		Tooth chattering	Fear, threat
		Drumming, tail banging, quill rattling (porcupines)	Threat
Carnivora	High	Vocal signals, including barking, growling, spitting, snarling, etc.	Threat, warning, parental care, individuality, inhibition of aggression, status
Tubulidentata	?	Squeaking	Unknown
Hyracoidea	High	Vocal screams (*Dendrohyrax*) Whistles (*Procavia*)	Contact between individuals and warning
		Foot stamping	Contact
Proboscidea	High	Vocal sounds including trumpeting Mechanical sounds (breaking branches, drumming tail)	Coherence of group, warning, threat, reproductive state
		Respiration and digestive 'rumbles'	Unknown
Perissodactyla	High	Vocal sounds, including grunts, squeaks, etc.	Contact, warning, cohesion
Artiodactyla	High	Vocal sounds (very varied)	Warning, threat, contact between individuals, territoriality

white fur and bare skin. Other examples of visual communication are given in Table 10.4.

Tactile communication operates through the senses of touch, temperature and pain (Table 10.5). All mammals touch conspecifics, for instance when males and females are mating, and when females and young are suckling. Mammals which live in pairs, family groups or larger groups frequently touch each other during resting and feeding and a great many elements of amicable behaviour (p. 228) such as social grooming, climbing-over, rubbing and lying in contact transmit information about mood, relationship,

Table 10.4 *Visual communication in some African mammals. (From Tembrock 1968, Ewer 1968, Ewer 1973.)*

Order	Relative importance	Behaviour	Type of information conveyed
Insectivora	Low	?	?
Chiroptera	Low	Head postures, wing fanning (Megachiroptera)	?
Primates	High	Facial expressions, postures	Communication, contact, warning, threat
		Display of coloured perianal region	Sexual condition
Pholidota	Low	?	?
Lagomorpha	High	Postures, flank patterns, gambolling	?
		White tail display	Alarm
Rodentia	High	Postures, expressions, pilo-erection, tail position	Varied, many types of information including status, sexual condition, threat
		Tail-lashing (*Thryonomys*)	Readiness to copulate
Carnivora	High	Postures, expressions, pilo-erection	Varied, including status, sexual condition, threat, communication between individuals
Tubulidentata	Low	?	?
Proboscidea	High	Head and trunk postures	Varied, communication between individuals, threat
Hyracoidea	?Low	Dorsal white patch display	Warning
Perissodactyla	High	Body, head, ear and neck postures Twitching of skin Ritualised displays	Communication, contact between individuals, threat
Artiodactyla	High	Head and body postures; many ritualised postures in male-male encounters and sexual displays	Varied, status, sexual condition, territoriality, communication between individuals, threat

reproductive state and the motivation for bonding. In general these signals convey comfort and amicability; in contrast, agonistic behaviour, when contactual and sometimes painful, conveys information about mood and relationships which repels individuals from each other.

In many instances, several means of communication are used simultaneously; for example, a male Uganda kob displays his status and intentions by smell, posture, movement, shape, colouration and vocal sounds, and female baboons indicate their sexual condition by smell, peri-anal displays, body movements and facial expressions.

Agonistic behaviour

Agonistic behaviour repels and/or keeps individuals apart, and has the opposite effects to amicable behaviour. It comprises attack, pursuit, fighting in contact, escape, threat

Table 10.5   *Tactile communication in some African mammals. (From Tembrock 1968, Ewer 1968, Ewer 1973.)*

Order	Relative importance	Behaviour	Type of information conveyed
Insectivora	Unknown	?	?
Chiroptera	Unknown	?	?
Primates	High	Mutual grooming, huddling	Social status, group cohesion, ?sexual stimulation, mother–young relationships
Pholidota	Unknown	?	?
Lagomorpha	Unknown	?	?
Rodentia	High	Sniffing, huddling, fighting in contact, social grooming	Varied, investigation, amicable and agonistic encounters, mother–young relationships
Carnivora	High	Huddling, play, sniffing, fighting in contact, social grooming	Varied, investigation, amicable and agonistic encounters, mother–young relationships
Tubulidentata	Unknown	?	?
Hyracoidea	Low	Sniffing, huddling	Investigation, mother–young relationships
Proboscidea	High	Intertwining trunks, rubbing	Investigation, amicable encounters, mother–young relationships
Perissodactyla	?High	Sniffing, rubbing, fighting in contact	Investigation, agonistic encounters
Artiodactyla	High	Sniffing, fighting in contact	Investigation, mother–young relationships, agonistic encounters

and submission. Agonistic behaviour occurs in the context of competition for, and defence of, food, water, territory, mates and young, and in some species in the establishment of status based on success or failure in aggressive encounters. Parents may promote weaning and the dispersion of the young by threatening and attacking their offspring, and parents may also establish discipline through mild forms of aggression. Agonistic behaviour may occur between individuals or between groups of individuals. It is normally observed intra-specifically, but it can occur inter-specifically.

When individuals or groups of individuals are involved in agonistic behaviour, one individual or group is usually defeated. Defeat is usually shown by submission either after a display of aggressive postures and threats, or after a bout of fighting in contact. Only rarely does it result in severe injury. In group-living species, selection against excessive aggression and injury has resulted in the ritualisation of many expressions (Fig. 10.19) and behaviour patterns which signify the intent to attack or not to attack. Selection has favoured behaviour which results in the settlement of disputes without physical combat.

Two particularly important social phenomena which result from victory or defeat in agonistic interactions are status hierarchies and territories. Status hierarchies are

Fig. 10.19   Ritualised fighting between two adult sable antelopes (*Hippotragus niger*). In this species, the contestants 'kneel' on the forelegs and interlock their horns. (Photo: R. D. Estes.)

formed when there are sustained aggressive–submissive relationships amongst animals which co-exist in one area (Wilson 1975). In contrast, territories are formed when the status of individuals or groups of individuals is determined by their positions relative to the boundaries of a discrete area marked out by the individual or group concerned. Status hierarchies and territoriality play major roles in the social behaviour and ecology of many African mammals.

Status hierarchies

Most hierarchies are composed of individuals of different ranks. The simplest hierarchy occurs when individuals of a particular sex or age-group are dominant to individuals of the opposite sex or another age-group. In this situation, an individual needs only to recognise the sex or age of other individuals to know his social relationship to these individuals. For example, age-based hierarchies occur in the bachelor herds of many species of ungulates where the older males are dominant to the younger males. In mixed herds of adult individuals, females are usually submissive to males. A more complex hierarchy occurs when the ranks are in linear sequence, and it is essential that *particular* individuals are recognised. Individual A dominates all others, individual B dominates all except A, so that a social scale (A, B, C, D, E, . . .) is established. The status of individuals is not necessarily constant; it may change with age, physical development and parenthood. Status is not always manifested through aggression. In many African primates (*Papio*, *Cercopithecus*), the rank order is revealed by the direction of mutual grooming so that C grooms B who grooms A. In other species, rank order is revealed through postures and expressions, and through auditory and olfactory signals. Burchell's and mountain zebras (*Equus burchelli* and

E. zebra) and baboons (*Papio* spp.) illustrate the principle of a linear hierarchy particularly well. Zebras live in small groups consisting of one adult stallion, several mares and their foals. The stallion is dominant over all, and a linear hierarchy occurs in the mares. Young males voluntarily form bachelor herds in which dominance does not appear to exist, and they do not join the stallion-mare-foal herd (Klingel 1967). Savanna-living baboons (*Papio anubis*) occur in large multi-male groups with many females and young. The dominant male is the leader of the group, but other males may remain in the group provided they show submissive behaviour towards the dominant male. Similarly a rank order exists within the females of the group. The hierarchy is established as a result of agonistic encounters between individuals of the group, but the social ranking so established is extended into many aspects of every-day life.

A much looser form of social stratification occurs in gorillas, buffalo, several species of antelopes during the non-breeding season, and some carnivores, where several males and females co-exist without overt signs of aggression and without any particular male being the dominant male. One male may assume the role of 'leader', and this individual usually leads the group in attack or is the aggressor if the group is threatened in any way. Most large herds of bovids do not establish a hierarchy system and yet agonistic behaviour is kept to a minimum within the herd; buffalo are an exception to this generalisation as the males have a rank hierarchy (see p. 258).

Elephants form 'female groups' which consist of females and their young, and 'male groups' which consist of males about 15 years of age or older. Groups join or separate according to environmental conditions, but male and female groups associate for only short periods of time. The social organisation within the group is flexible although low ranking individuals give way to high ranking individuals under conditions of stress (Douglas-Hamilton 1975).

Territoriality

The term 'territory' has been used in various ways and there is no general agreement on a precise definition. One reason is that territories and territorial behaviour differ considerably from species to species. One definition which appears to fit all species is that a territory is an area bounded by a 'line' across which there is a change in dominance (J. Nelson, pers. comm.), and another is that a territory is an area occupied more or less exclusively by one individual, or by a group of individuals, by means of repulsion of conspecifics through overt defence or advertisement (Wilson 1975). The concept of territory is complicated because it need not be a fixed geographical area: some migratory species move their territories with them. Territory size varies depending on the size of the species, its method of courtship and the area of the habitat needed to supply the resources necessary for life and reproduction, but it is normally fairly constant in size within a species. However, the sizes of territories may depend on the locality, and they are usually larger in marginal areas as in the 'peripheral' territories of Uganda kob. Territories are usually, but not always, established on the basis of an agonistic encounter, but once established the presence and status of the territorial holder may be advertised in many ways:

1. Other conspecifics which are not tolerated in the territory are chased away, at least as far as the territorial boundary.
2. The territory is marked by urination and defaecation (rhinoceros, pygmy hippopotamus) and by rubbing glandular secretions on to grasses and tree trunks and other prominent objects (many artiodactyls). Some species mark the territorial boundary in specific places so there is an accumulation of marking signals (e.g. defaecation in rhinoceros).

3. Soil or bush horning occurs in some antelopes, and is thought to be a method of marking (e.g. Grant's gazelle).
4. 'Static–optic' marking occurs when the territory holder adopts a recognisable stance, or silhouette, or stands on a piece of high ground within the territory (e.g. a broken-down termite mound) so he can see the limits of his territory, and other conspecifics can see that a territory has been established (e.g. Grant's gazelle, Blue wildebeest, bontebok (*Damaliscus dorcas*), western kob).
5. Ritualised postures and movements are displayed near the boundary of the territory, especially when a potential unwanted intruder is close by (e.g. many species of artiodactyls and primates).
6. Noises of many sorts are given to inform a potential intruder that a territory has been established.

A territory holder is intolerant of other conspecifics who may challenge his dominance within the territory. A male Uganda kob which has established a territory during the breeding season is intolerant of other males but not of females. Similarly, individuals of a group which hold a group territory, as in lions, are intolerant of other individuals from another group which enter their territory.

The function of a territory varies in different species, and is related to the requirements of the territory holder(s). Four types of territory are recognisable in African mammals.

1. Individual territories are held by the male or by the female on a more or less permanent basis. This type of territory is uncommon. It may occur in bushbuck and sitatunga (Estes 1974), and male white rhinoceros hold large territories for several years but allow non-territorial males and females to enter the territory (Owen-Smith 1974).
2. Pair territories are established on a more or less permanent basis by a male and a female together, and are used for all activities. The young of the pair use the territory until they are adult (e.g. Cephalophinae, Neotraginae).
5. Male reproductive territories are maintained by the male during the breeding season (Fig. 10.20). In some species the territory is held after the breeding season for varying lengths of time. The male may leave his territory temporarily to feed and drink.
4. Group territories are established by the individuals in the group. This form of territory is fairly permanent, and the size of the territory is related to the dispersion and abundance of food and other resources. Species which hold group territories include baboons, some forest monkeys, lions and hunting dogs.

Territorial behaviour occurs to the greatest extent in the orders Carnivora, Primates, Perissodactyla and Artiodactyla. It may also occur in other orders (including orders containing species of small size) but evidence for this is lacking. The family Bovidae has evolved the most varied and diverse forms of territorial behaviour which are associated with courtship and mating activities (Fig. 10.20). The size of the territory in relation to the habitat, the reaction of the territory holder to other males and females and the duration of territoriality show considerable variation. Territorial behaviour has a profound effect on the social organisations of many species (section 10.4). A further account of territory in African mammals is given in the journal *Zoologica Africana*, volume 7 of 1972.

Amicable behaviour

The term 'amicable' is used to denote any social behaviour which lacks agonistic

Thomson's gazelle
(Walther 1964, 1972)

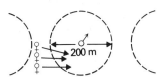

Females pass through territory.
No other males allowed to enter.
Duration: 1 week—5 months

Grant's gazelle
(in areas also occupied by
Thomson's gazelles)
(Walther 1965)

Harem (10-20 females, with
young) stay inside territory. No
males allowed to enter

Grant's gazelle
(in open plains) (Walther 1965)

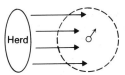

Herds (40-400) females, young
and non-territorial males
pass through territory. Territorial
male shows dominance to
non-territorial males

Wildebeest
(Non migratory in Ngorongoro
crater) (Estes 1966)

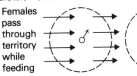

Females
pass
through
territory
while
feeding

Duration: up to 1 year

Wildebeest
(Migratory in Serengeti)
(Walther 1972)

Duration: few hours to 3 days;
during rut only

Uganda Kob
(Buechner 1961)

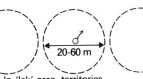

In 'lek' area, territories
clustered together; in other
areas territories spread out
(Leuthold 1966).
Duration: all year

Tssebbe
(Joubert 1972)
Kruger National Park

Harem of 6-8 females stay
within territory. No other males
allowed to enter

Topi
(Jewell 1972)
Queen Elizabeth Park

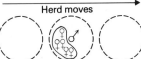

Male territory moves as herd
moves. Male attempts to contain
harem within territory, but some
females move from one harem to
another

Waterbuck
(Kiley-Worthington 1965,
Spinage 1959)

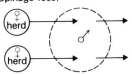

Area: up to 4 sq. km.
Duration: up to 2 years

Lechwe
(de Vos and Dowsett 1966)

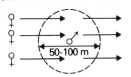

Females pass through territory
Duration: 14 days approx

White Rhinoceros
(Owen-Smith 1972)

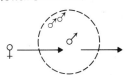

Subsiduary non-territorial bulls
remain in territory. Females
pass through.
Area: 1-2 sq. km

Fig. 10.20 Patterns of territoriality in eight species of Bovids and the white rhinoceros. The principal differences between these territories include the area of the territory, the degree of tolerance of the territorial holder towards other males, the duration of the territory, and whether the female(s) remain within the territory or move in and out at will.

elements. Therefore it should include sexual and parental behaviour, but it is convenient to treat these separately and to consider here amicable behaviour which appears to be independent of reproductive condition and age.

Amicable behaviour attracts and/or keeps individuals together and it establishes and maintains bonds between members of both sexes and all ages in social groups. Examples of amicable behaviour in African mammals include social grooming, huddling, rubbing, communal nesting, climbing over, mounting, pushing under and many examples of amicable expressions. Amicable behaviour and group living make it possible for mammals to co-operate in certain tasks for the achievement of a common goal; this may be effected by synchronisation of activities, as in hunting or digging a burrow, or through the division of labour as seen in monkey troops.

Sexual behaviour

Sexual behaviour concerns all behaviour between a male and a female during courtship and mating. Behavioural elements include sniffing, elaborate courtship displays, licking of the urine of the female by the male, displays of the genitalia, mounting and copulation. Sexual displays tend to be ritualised and stereotyped in many species, and closely related species show many similarities in their sexual behaviour. The Bovidae have particularly elaborate male sexual displays, and many behavioural elements are unique to this family but occur in many species within the family (Tables 10.6 and 10.7). Further details on sexual behaviour are given in section 10.4.

Parent–offspring behaviour

Parent–offspring behaviour is associated with the relationship between the mother and her young, and in some species between the father and his young. For convenience, maternal behaviour may be divided into three stages. Preparturant behaviour (before the birth of the young) includes nest-building as in rodents, and leaving the herd so the young can be born in seclusion as in many ungulates (e.g. Grant's gazelle). Parturant behaviour (during birth) includes breaking the membranes, eating the afterbirth, licking the neonate and cleaning the nest. Postparturant behaviour is all the behavioural activities after birth until the young become independent of the mother; this includes suckling, grooming, retrieving, protecting, bringing food, stimulating micturition and defaecation, warming and cooling and many other elements. Maternal behaviour in mammals has been reviewed by Rheingold (1963), and in ungulates by Lent (1974). The amount of parental care is greatest in species whose young are poorly developed at birth (altricial young) and are born in burrows or secluded places as in most rodents, insectivores and carnivores. It is least in those species whose young are well developed at birth (precocial young) and are not born in burrows as in hyraxes, lagomorphs, perissodactyls and artiodactyls. Elephants are exceptional as parental care lasts for several years after the birth of the precocial young. On a behavioural basis, precocial young are either 'hiders', 'followers' or 'riders'. Hiders remain hidden in a 'form' amongst tall grass or under bushes, and their safety depends on their camouflage and their ability to remain motionless when potential danger is nearby (e.g. lagomorphs, Grant's gazelle, Thomson's gazelle). The mother does not approach the young, except to suckle at particular times each day, as this might indicate the location of the young to a potential predator. The duration of the hiding response ranges from a few days in lagomorphs to 2–4 weeks in waterbuck (Spinage 1969) and 2–4 months in reedbuck (Jungius 1970). Followers are able to stand and walk within an hour or two of birth; they then follow their mothers and gain some protection by being surrounded by

Table 10.6 *Comparison of some behavioural elements in closely related species of Bovidae.*

	Grant's gazelle (Walther 1965)	Thomson's gazelle (Walther 1964)	Waterbuck (Kiley-Worthington 1967)	Impala (Jarman and Jarman 1963)	Topi (Jewell 1972, Walther, pers. comm.)	Tsessebe (Joubert 1972)	Uganda kob (Buechner and Sloeth 1965, Leuthold 1966)
Male displays							
Pawing ground	+	+	−	−	+	+	
Rubbing face on ground	−	−	−	−	−	+	
Rubbing grass with preorbital gland	−	+	−	−	?	+	−
Marking with urine	+	+	?	−	−	?	−
Marking with faeces	+ +	+ +	−	−	+ +	+	−
Weaving horns	+	+	−	−	−	−	?
Static optic marking	?	?	−	+	+	+	+
Horning ground	+	+	?	+	+	+	?
Male–male displays							
Males flank by flank (sometimes with circling)	+ +	−	?	−	+	+	?
Presentation of horns (Gehörnpräsentieren)	+	+ +	+	?	+	+	?
Head casting up and down	−	−	−	−	+	+	−
Male–female displays							
Head and neck stretched forward	?	+ +	+ +	+ +	+ +	+	?
High nose-tail erect	+ +	+ +	?	−	+ +	+ +	+ +
Mating kick (Laufschlag)	+	+ +	+ +	−	+ +	−	+
Male tests urine of female (Flehmen)	+ +	+ +	+ +	?	−	−	+
Laufschlag with pincers movement	−	−	+	−	−	−	+
Male rubs face on female	−	−	+	−	−	−	−
Female circles round male during Laufschlag and may poke or bite male	+	+	+	?	−	−	+
Other displays							
Stotting	+	+ +	−	−	?	−	−
Whistling by male	−	−	−	−	−	−	+

+ Clearly observed.   + + Especially pronounced.   − Not observed.
? Presence uncertain.   No symbol No information.

adults (e.g. elephants, rhinoceros, giraffe, zebra, wildebeest, buffalo, etc.). This behaviour pattern is typical of most large species, those which form large herds and those which migrate. Riders remain in physical contact with their mother as she continues her daily activities, either clasped to the chest near the nipples or riding on the back (e.g. most species of monkeys).

The duration of parental care is partly dependent on the development of the young at birth, but also on the average longevity of the species and its way of life. For example, young rodents are dependent on parental care for the first few weeks of life, but are entirely independent after weaning. In elephants, the young are precocial but they feed from their mothers up to three years of age, and are protected by their mothers for several years. In many primates (e.g. baboons and chimpanzees) the mother–offspring bond continues for 1–2 years or longer and young always return to their mothers at times of danger. The exact details of parental behaviour are species-specific.

Table 10.7   *A comparison of the behaviour between three species of the genus* Kobus *(family Bovidae, subfamily Reduncinae). (Mostly after de Vos and Dowsett 1966.)*

	Waterbuck	Puku	Lechwe
Stotting when alarmed	−	+	+ +
Lifts tail when alarmed	?	+	+
Rests in shade	+	−	−
Vocalisations	+	+ + + 'whistle'	+ + 'grunts'
Lambs are hidden in vegetation after birth	+	+	+
Number of lambs in 'lamb groups'	2–3	2–3	Up to 50
Ability to browse (all species are primarily grazers)	+ + +	+	−
Territorial behaviour by males			
Horning of grass	−	−	+
Pursuit of other males entering territory	+ +	?	+
Male–male displays			
Naso-nasal contact	+	+	+
Horn clashing or interlocking	+ +	+	+
Chasing	+	+	+
Male–female displays			
Male chases female in oestrus	+ ?	+	+
Head and neck stretch forward	+ +	−	−
Laufschlag	+ +	+	+
High nose-tail erect	−	+	+

− Not present.
+ Present.
+ + Well developed.
+ + + Very well developed, especially when compared with another species.
? Presence uncertain.

Young of similar ages may associate to form a creche, peer group or nursery herd. This association is most conspicuous when the majority of the annual production of young are born within a few weeks of each other. Nursery herds form when the young are weaned (or are in the process of weaning) and are less dependent on their mothers. In the Artiodactyls, nursery herds occur in, for example, impala (Schenkel 1966a, b, Jarman and Jarman 1973), Uganda kob (Leuthold 1967), waterbuck (Spinage 1969) and Thomson's gazelle (Walther 1964a or b). The numbers in the nursery herd range from a few individuals to several hundred, and the nursery herd may, or may not, be accompanied by one or more females. Baboons and some species of *Cercopithecus* monkeys form temporary nursery troops which are usually concerned with play activities.

In some species where there is a strong pair bond the father assists in caring for the young, and in some murid rodents where the male nests with the female the male assists with grooming and retrieving of the young. Indirectly many males which live in groups show parental care: a male which is guarding the group, or showing agonistic behaviour towards a source of danger, is showing parental care towards his own young as well as to other young in the group.

◀ **Fig. 10.21** Birth of an African elephant. The mother is surrounded by other females and young of her group, which take an interest in the new-born young. (a) The young is enclosed in the membranes immediately after birth, (b) the membranes are removed by the mother, (c) the young attempts to find the nipples of its mother. (Photos: W. Leuthold.)

There are a few species where other individuals (usually females) assist with the care of the young. In many African primates, a non-breeding female or 'aunt' looks after a young in the temporary absence of the mother. In the murid rodent *Acomys*, other females assist at the birth of the young (Dieterlen 1962, 1963, Fig. 10.22). In rodent species which live in groups, non-mother females and young of previous litters may assist in some aspects of parental behaviour as in *Praomys tullbergi* (Happold 1978). Young elephants are protected in the female-young herds by their mothers and by non-mother females, and female lions look after and feed the young of other females in the pride.

As the young grow older, the mother–offspring bond gradually breaks down. This is due to reciprocal changes in the behaviour and physiology of the mother and of her young. In many instances, the bond breaks at the time of weaning and the mothers may show agonistic behaviour toward their young by chasing them away. However, bond breakdown and weaning are not always concomitant; in elephants, the young associate with their mothers for many years after weaning.

Social play

Social play is seen most commonly in young mammals whose needs are looked after by their parents. Play behaviour can be distinguished from 'typical' adult behaviour by several characteristics (Ewer 1968, Loizos 1966).

1. There is a lack of motivation so that the behaviour patterns are not performed with any serious intent.
2. The sequence of behavioural patterns is normally re-ordered and fragmented, and there is a repeated interchange of roles.
3. Play behaviour is usually a less refined version of adult behaviour, even though it is performed with maximum efficiency for the age of the individual.
4. It is a daily part of routine activities as it is necessary for the young animal to experiment with the relationship between its own actions and the external world, and for the full development of its social behaviour.

Play, therefore, is a means whereby the young individual learns about its environment, and acquires skills and information necessary for later life. Usually play takes place between individuals which are at about the same stage of development. Most play is concerned with movements which are related to prey catching and to fighting and escape behaviour. In many species with complex communal social organisations (e.g. many primates, hunting dogs, hyaenas, some bovids), play also enables the young to learn many of the elements of social behaviour associated with cohesion, communication, courtship, dominance and submission. The play sequence appears to have no definite aim or goal, and play movements are often exaggerated. The types of play change with age; for example, young lions play at first with inanimate objects, later they play with other young lions and finally they show play-hunting behaviour (Schenkel 1966c).

Play behaviour is especially well developed in many species of communal carnivores especially the Felidae, Canidae and some Viverridae, and is mostly related to prey catching and hunting behaviour. In contrast, play behaviour in the aardwolf (*Proteles cristatus*) and the bat-eared fox (*Otocyon megalotis*) shows affinities to escape behaviour because both these species, as adults, tend to show escape behaviour rather than fighting behaviour (Ewer 1968). Young baboons indulge in many play activities, and in many nursery herds of antelopes the young jump up and down, chase and push each other. Some rodents also show play behaviour; young cane rats (*Thryonomys*

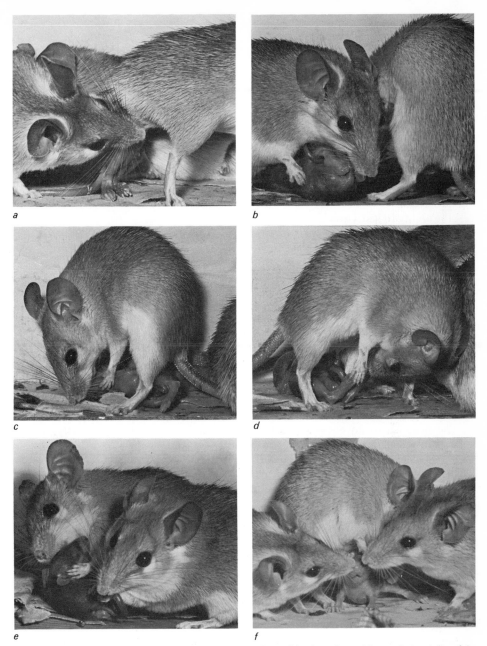

Fig. 10.22   Birth and maternal care in *Acomys cahirinus*. Parturition is prolonged due to the large size of the precocial young. Other females assist with the birth and look after the young.   (*a*) and (*b*) A non-mother female assists during the birth.   (*c*) Investigating the young after the birth.   (*d*) Cleaning the forepaws after the birth.   (*e*) Grooming the young.   (*f*) Several females investigating the young. (From Dieterlen 1962.)

swinderianus) show all the elements of adult fighting behaviour in play fights, and play in the ground squirrel (*Xerus erythropus*) shows many elements of escape behaviour (Ewer 1968).

Although play behaviour is prevalent in young, it also occurs in the adults of some species. Female lions play with their young and this enables the young to learn by imitation and by experience of adult behaviour. Several species of small carnivores 'play' with their prey before or after the prey has been killed. These observations suggest that play is not confined solely to young animals, and has a function in some adults.

Conversely, the young or adults of many species do not exhibit play behaviour. Ewer (1968) suggests that the development of play as a species characteristic is related to

(a) the necessity for quick accurate movements, especially in hunting and escape behaviour;
(b) the opportunity to play, as in young which need a long period of time under adult protection;
(c) the ability to learn quickly;
(d) the importance of integration into a communal social system.

10.4   Social organisations

Most social behaviour either attracts and/or keeps individuals together, or it repels and/or keeps individuals apart (Happold, M. 1975). The relative frequency of occurrence of these attracting and repelling elements, and the circumstances in which they occur, determines how the individuals in a population are dispersed and how they interact with each other. Dispersion and interaction are the two phenomena which give rise to the social organisations of species.

The relative frequency of attracting and repelling behaviour varies according to several parameters of space and time. These include:

1. The distance between individuals.
2. The position of an encounter between two individuals. This is clearly seen in territorial behaviour where the behaviour of individuals depends on their positions in relation to territorial boundaries. The behaviour of individuals may also depend on their positions in relation to the position of limited resources.
3. The physiological condition of the animal; for example its age, sex, health and reproductive condition.
4. The time of the encounter in relation to abiotic factors such as day, night and season of the year.
5. The genealogical relationship of the individuals.
6. The duration of an encounter, because relationships may change with time.

At any particular time, the relationships between individuals varies depending on the parameters listed above. Consequently, it is necessary to know the precise conditions in order to understand how and why an individual is interacting with another individual.

There are two other considerations which are related to the social organisations of species. Firstly, phylogenetic relationships are responsible for similarities in the social behaviour and social organisations of closely related species, and secondly, the distribution and occurrence of resources can result in variations within a species in different parts of its range. The primates illustrate an order where there are similar behaviour patterns in many closely related species, although similar species which live in different habitats may show divergent behaviour patterns. The antelopes exhibit similar characteristics, and they also show how large groups can live in regions of high primary production while closely related species live in smaller, more widely dispersed groups in regions of low primary production. A convenient way to illustrate social organisations is to compare the number of individuals which live together in a group (Table 10.8). African mammals show great variation in the size, composition and organisation of groups which is a reflection of the diversity of species and habitats.

Social organisations, therefore, are 'dispersed' with a high frequency of repelling behaviour (1, below), or 'communal' with a high frequency of amicable behaviour between two or more individuals (2, 3 and 4, below) (Eisenberg 1966).

1. *Dispersed.* Each individual shows repelling behaviour to conspecifics, except when males and females associate at the time of mating, and when mothers associate with their young prior to weaning. Leopards and pangolins exhibit dispersed organisations.

2. *Pair formation.* Individuals of the opposite sex are attracted to each other so that a bond (of variable duration) is established between the two individuals. Pair bonding is often of short duration in African mammals. However, some species (oribi, dik-dik) are usually seen in pairs which suggests a fairly permanent pair bond between a male and a female.

3. *Family groups.* Several individuals which are related to each other remain together as a group. Examples of family groups are seen in many monkeys, elephants, zebras, rock hyraxes, some carnivores and rodents. A dominance hierarchy (p. 226) is often present in family groups.

4. *Groups of unrelated individuals.* Individuals and families that are not related are attracted to each other. Group size ranges from small groups of a few individuals to very large herds consisting of many thousands of individuals. The disadvantages of living in groups such as the greater utilisation of resources, the rapid transmission of diseases and parasites and the chances of attracting more predators appears to be offset by many advantages which include:

(*a*) the possibility of co-operation between individuals and division of labour;
(*b*) protection from predators, because some individuals can 'watch', and there is less chance that a *particular* individual will be preyed upon;
(*c*) 'social facilitation', so that breeding is synchronised and less energy is spent in looking for a mate. When many young are born at about the same time in a group, there is a greater chance that a high percentage will survive, because predators will only be able to kill a small percentage of the young before the remaining young are old enough to evade predation. This pattern of reproduction is shown, for example, by all the Alcelaphinae.
(*d*) Better utilisation of food, because more individuals are looking for, and finding, food resources even though a greater volume of food is being consumed by the group and there may be less food for each individual.

These types of social organisation are not exclusive, and one type can merge into another, and a particular species may show more than one type of social organisation during its life or during the year. For example, some species with dispersed organisations for most of the year form pair bonds and/or family groups during the breeding season. Conversely, some species which live in large groups split up into small groups and single individuals during the breeding season. Very simplified descriptions of the social organisations found in each family are given in Table 10.9. Some large

Table 10.8   *Group size and social organisation in some African primates, Artiodactyla, Perissodactyla, Hyracoidea, Carnivora and Proboscidea.*

Species	Locality	Habitat	Average group size (range)	Organisation	Reference
Grey-cheeked mangabey (*Cercocebus albigena*)	Mabia, Uganda	Rain forest	17	Multi-male groups	Chalmers (1968)
Black and white colobus (*Colobus guereza*)	Mt Meru, Kenya	Rain forest	13	Multi-male groups	Ullrich (1961)
Baboon (*Papio anubis*)	Nairobi NP, Kenya	Wooded savanna	41 (12–87)	Multi-male groups	de Vore and Hall (1965)
	Amboseli, Kenya	Savanna	80 (12–185)	Multi-male groups	de Vore and Hall (1965)
Patas (*Cercopithecus patas*)	Kabalega Falls NP	Open grassland	15	Single-male groups, all male groups	Hall (1966)
	Waza NP, Cameroun	Sahel savanna	21 (7–27)	Single-male groups, all male groups	Struhsaker and Gartlan (1970)
Gorilla (*Gorilla gorilla*)	Kivu NP, Zaire	*Hagenia* forest	17 (5–27)	Single- or multi-male groups, some solitary males	Schaller (1965)
Chimpanzee (*Pan troglodytes*)	Gombe stream Reserve, Tanzania	Forest and savanna	2–20	Single- or multi-male groups, solitary males, male groups, female-and-young groups	Goodall (1968)
White-collared mangabey (*Cercocebus torquatus*)	Rio Muni	Rain forest	14–23	Multi-male groups	Jones and Sabater Pi (1968)
Vervet (*Cercopithecus pygerythrus*)	Amboseli, Kenya	Wooded savanna	16–50	Multi-male groups	Struhsaker (1967a)
Giraffe (*Giraffa camelopardalis*)	Nairobi NP, Kenya	Wooded savanna	2–7	Mixed herds, female-and-young herds, solitary males	Foster (1966)

Table 10.8 – *continued*

Species	Locality	Habitat	Average group size (range)	Organisation	Reference
Addax (*Addax nasomaculatus*)	Sub-sahara	Semi-desert	5–15	Mixed herds	Dolan (1966)
Oryx (*Oryx gazella*)	S.W. Africa, Kenya	Arid savanna	25 (2–100)	Mixed herds, single males, bachelor male herds	Estes (pers. comm.)
Impala (*Aepyceros melampus*)	Rhodesia	Savanna woodland	10–100	Mixed herds, territorial males, bachelor male herds	Dasmann and Mossman 1962, Schenkel 1966a,b
Wildebeest (*Connochaetes taurinus*)	Ngorongoro, Tanzania	Grassland	2–150 (>10000 during migration)	Female-and-young herds, territorial males, bachelor male herds (mixed herds during migration)	Estes 1969
Grant's gazelle (*Gazella granti*)	Ngorongoro, Tanzania	Grassland	?	Mixed herds, female herds, bachelor male herds, territorial males	Walther 1965
Topi (*Damaliscus lunatus*)	Rwenzori NP, Uganda	Grassland	Up to 50 (herds join to form aggregations of up to 1 000)	Female-and-young herds with one male, bachelor male herds	Jewell 1972
Waterbuck (*Kobus ellipsyprymnus*)	Zambia	Wooded savanna	2–15	Female-and-young herds with one male, bachelor herds, single males	de Vos and Dowsett 1966
Puku (*Kobus vardoni*)	Zambia	Grasslands	2–15	As for waterbuck	de Vos and Dowsett 1966
Black rhinoceros (*Diceros bicornis*)	Ngorongoro, Tanzania	Grassland	1–4	Pairs and young, solitary males	Klingel and Klingel 1966b
White rhinoceros (*Ceratotherium simum*)	Umfolozi, S. Africa	Savanna	1–3, up to 6	Female-young pair, solitary males	Owen-Smith 1972

Table 10.8 — *continued*

Species	Locality	Habitat	Average group size (range)	Organisation	Reference
Zebra (*Equus burchelli*)	Kenya	Savanna	Up to 20	One male with several mares and foals, bachelor male herds	Klingel 1967
Hyrax (*Procavia johnstoni*)	Mt Kenya, Kenya	Alpine grasslands		Female-and-young family group, with one dominant male	Coe 1962
Elephant (*Loxodonta africana*)	Tsavo NP, Kenya	Arid savanna	2–15, up to 90	Female-and-young family groups, male groups, solitary individuals, aggregations of family groups to form super-groups	Glover (1963)
Hunting Dog (*Lycaon pictus*)	Ngorogoro, Tanzania	Grassland	6–21	Multi-male groups of varied composition	Estes and Goddard (1967)
Lion (*Panthera leo*)	Serengeti, Tanzania	Grassland, wooded savanna	1–25	Mixed prides of 2–4 males, females, and young; composition of pride or part of pride varies frequently. Some solitary individuals	Schaller (1972)
Cheetah (*Acinoyx jubatus*)	Nairobi N.P., Kenya	Grassland	2–5	Mixed group, usually led by a single male	Eaton (1970b)
Banded mongoose (*Mungos mungo*)	Kafue NP, Zambia Rwenzori NP, Uganda	Grassland and bush savanna	15 (10–30) 14 (2–29)	Mixed groups Mixed groups	Simpson (1964) Rood (1975)

Table 10.9 *The social organisations of the families of African mammals.*
The information in this table is incomplete due to the lack of information for many families. The generalisations for most of the families should be regarded as tentative until further data is available. A more detailed account of mammal 'sociobiology' is given by Wilson (1975).

Order and family	Social organisation	References
Insectivora		
Tenrecidae	? Solitary or family groups (subfamily Potamogalinae only)	Dubost (1965)
Soricidae	Mostly solitary. The young of some shrews seize tails and form a chain behind the mother	
Erinaceidae	Mostly solitary	
Macroscelidae	Mostly solitary, small groups	Rathbun (1973)
Chrysochloridae	Solitary, although the burrow systems of different individuals may join up due to clustering of burrows at the bases of bushes	Roberts (1951), Jarvis (1974)
Chiroptera		
Pteropodidae	Varied; solitary and dispersed (*Megaloglossus, Epomops*), small groups (*Micropteropus, Nanonycteris*), large groups (*Eidolon, Rousettus*). Often form aggregations at suitable feeding sites	Rosevear (1965), Bradbury (1977)
Rhinopomatidae	Small to large groups of mixed sexes, sexes separate during parturition	Bradbury (1977)
Emballonuridae	Varied. No definite information on African species	Bradbury (1977)
Nycteridae	Monogamous families (*Nycteris*)	Bradbury (1977)
Megadermatidae	No information	
Hipposideridae	Large groups of mixed sexes (*Asellia, Hipposideros*)	Happold (1967a), Brosset (1969), Menzies (1973)
Rhinolophidae	Small to large groups, sometimes solitary	Menzies (1973)
Vespertilionidae	Varied, from solitary to monogamous families and groups. No definite information on African species	Bradbury (1977)
Molossidae	?, some groups of mixed sexes (*Tadarida*)	Bradbury (1975). Happold (1967a)
Primates		
Lorisidae and Galagidae	Solitary (*Arctocebus, Perodicticus, Galago*). Several *Galago senegalensis* may be seen in a single tree	Eisenberg *et al.* (1972), Charles-Dominique (1971)
Cercopithecidae	Varied, ranging from small and large single male troops with associated subordinate males (some *Colobus* spp., some *Cercopithecus* spp., *Papio hamadryas, P. leucophaeus, Theropithecus gelada*), to multi-male troops with a social hierarchy in the males (*Cercopithecus talapoin, Cercocebus torquatus*) and multi-male troops with no hierarchy in adult males (*Cercopithecus pygerythrus, Papio ursinus, P. anubis, P. cynocephalus*)	Eisenberg *et al.* (1972)
Pongidae	Small to medium groups with a social hierarchy in the males (*G. gorilla*), or with no hierarchy in the males (*Pan troglodytes*)	Eisenberg *et al.* (1972)
Pholidota		
Manidae	Solitary. Young carried on the back of the mother	Pagés (1970)

Table 10.9 – *continued*

Order and family	Social organisation	References
Lagomorpha		
Leporidae	? mostly solitary (*Lepus*). Little information on African species	
Rodentia		
Anomaluridae	Small family groups	McLaughlin (1967), Rahm (1969*a*)
Sciuridae	Little information on African species; probably solitary or small groups (*Xerus*)	Rosevear (1969)
Muridae	Very varied. Some live in groups (*Rhabdomys, Arvicanthis, Praomys, Acomys*). Others fairly solitary (?*Lophuromys*). African murid rodents have not been studied extensively from this viewpoint	Eisenberg (1967). Unpublished records of present authors
Cricetidae	Varied. As for Muridae	
Dipodidae	Uncertain, mostly dispersed, but will form small groups in burrows during cool weather	Happold (1967*b*)
Muscardinidae	? small family groups	Rosevear (1969)
Thryonomyidae	Small groups of one male and several females	
Ctenodactylidae	Small and large groups	George (1974)
Rhizomyidae	Generally solitary	Jarvis and Sale (1971)
Hystricidae	? Pairs and small groups	Starrett (1967)
Pedetidae	?	
Petromyidae	?	
Bathyergidae	Solitary (*Heliophobius*) and in groups (*Heterocephalus*)	Jarvis and Sale (1971)
Carnivora		
Canidae	Mated pairs (*Canis, Fennecus,* ?*Vulpes*), small groups (*Otocyon*), large co-ordinated groups (*Lycaon*)	Ewer (1973), Kleiman (1967)
Mustelidae	Probably most solitary. No definite information for African species	Ewer (1973)
Viverridae	Solitary or in pairs (*Nandinia, Genetta, Poiana*), small to large groups, possibly family groups (*Suricata, Crossarchus, Helogale, Mungos, Cynictis*)	Ewer (1973)
Hyaenidae	Solitary or small groups (*Proteles*), small to large groups or 'clans' (*Crocuta*)	Ewer (1973), Kruuk (1972), Kruuk and Sands (1972)
Felidae	Solitary (especially the small species of *Felis* and *Panthera pardus*), family groups (varying in composition and number (*P. leo* and *Acinonyx*))	Ewer (1973)
Tubulidentata		
Orycteropodidae	Solitary	Pagés (1970)
Hyracoidea		
Procaviidae	Solitary or family groups (*Dendrohyrax*), groups or 'colonies' of mixed sexes (*Procavia, Heterohyrax*)	Rahm (1969*b*), Coe (1962)
Sirenia		
Dugongidae	Small groups, may be family groups	Jones and Johnson (1967)

Table 10.9 – *continued*

Order and family	Social organisation	References
Trichechidae	Mostly solitary, loose aggregations	
Proboscidea		
Elephantidae	Small or large female and young groups, male groups, some solitary individuals. Groups divide into subgroups and join into supergroups.	Douglas–Hamilton (1975)
Perissodactyla		
Rhinocerotidae	Small family groups, occasionally loose aggregations, with territorial males (*Ceratotherium*). Basically solitary with male territories (*Diceros*)	Owen-Smith (1972, 1974), Klingel (1966)
Equidae	Family groups, which may join to form loose aggregations, bachelor-stallion herds, mare-and-foal herds; some species are territorial	Klingel (1972, 1974)
Artiodactyla		
Suidae	Solitary or family groups (*Hylochoerus*), small family groups (*Phacochoerus*), small to large groups up to forty (*Potamochoerus*)	Dorst and Dandelot (1970)
Hippopotamidae	Solitary (*Choeropsis*), small to large groups of mixed sexes (*Hippopotamus*)	Dorst and Dandelot (1970)
Tragulidae	Solitary (*Hyemoschus*)	Dubost (1965)
Giraffidae	Solitary (*Okapia*). Mixed herds of up to forty individuals, male herds, and female-and-young herds (*Giraffa*)	Foster (1966), Dorst and Dandelot (1970)
Bovidae	Very varied (see Table 10.11)	Jarman (1974)

species have been well studied, but information is almost non-existent for small and nocturnal species. There is great scope for investigation into the social behaviour and social organisations of these small species.

In orders and families with many species, there is usually a wide range of social organisations. Three orders (Primates, Carnivora and Perissodactyla) and one family (Bovidae) have been chosen to show the range of social organisations within groups of taxonomically similar mammals. These examples illustrate the categories of behaviour described earlier (section 10.3), and show how the social organisations may vary in space and time. Finally, the principal characteristics of the social organisations of African mammals are compared to illustrate the similarities and differences between these organisations.

Social organisation in primates

The prosimians are basically solitary, but the families Cercopithecidae and Pongidae are communal and show a great variety of social behaviour and organisation. Group size in the communal species ranges from a few individuals to groups (or troops) of up to 200 individuals. The social organisation of each species is fairly constant, although there may be slight changes in the number of individuals in the group, the group composition and the stability of the group from time to time. Eisenberg *et al.* (1972) have recognised five levels of social organisation in primates based on the numbers and composition of the group, and the relationship of the individuals in the group.

Table 10.10   *The social organisations of African primates, based on troop structure and feeding habits. (From Eisenberg* et al. *1972.)*

Solitary	Parental family	Uni-male troop*	Age-graded multi-male troop†	Multi-male troop‡
Insectivore-frugivore	No African examples (?)	Arboreal folivore	Arboreal frugivore	Semi-terrestrial frugivore-omnivore
Galagoides demidovii		*Colobus guereza*	*Ceropithecus talapoin*	*Cercopithecus pygerythrus*
Perodicticus potto		*Cercopithecus mitis*	Semi-terrestrial frugivore-omnivore	*Papio cynocephalus*
		C. campbelli mona	*Cercocebus torquatus*	*P. ursinus*
		Cercocebus albigena	Terrestrial folivore-frugivore	*P. anubis*
		Semi-terrestrial frugivore	*Gorilla gorilla*	*Pan troglodytes*
		Cercopithecus patas		
		Theropithecus gelada		
		Papio leucophaeus		
		Papio hamadryas		

*Troop with only one adult male which is very intolerant to maturing males.

†Troop with several adult males which are organised in an age-graded series with moderate male tolerance.

‡Troop with several adult mature males and high male tolerance. Males may be ranked in a dominance hierarchy.

Similarly, there appear to be relationships between social organisations, habitats and feeding preferences (Table 10.10). The five levels of social organisation are:

1. *Solitary species.*   These species are characterised by a minimal amount of direct social interactions. A mother and her young may live together as a social unit, but normally each female has her own separate home range. Males are solitary with non-overlapping home ranges, although the home range of one male often overlaps with the home range of several females.

2. *Parental families.*   These consist of a male, a female and their young. The male and female form a pair bond, do not associate with other males or females and they live in their own home range. This social organisation appears to be rare, and has not been recorded in any species of African primate.

3. *The uni-male troop.*   One adult male, several young males who show submissive behaviour to the dominant adult male, and females with their young comprise the uni-male troop. The adult male is very intolerant of the maturing males which, in time, are forced to leave the troop and join separate bachelor troops. Adult females are tolerant of each other. New uni-male troops are formed when a bachelor male entices sub-adult females away from an established troop.

4. *The age-graded male troop.*   This level of organisation differs from the uni-male troop in that the dominant male shows more tolerance to maturing males, and there may be more than one adult male in the troop. Age-graded male troops are often larger than uni-male troops, and may split into sub-troops which tend to minimise the chances of agonistic behaviour between males. There is a linear hierarchy, usually based on age, and an absence of several males within the same age bracket.

5. *The multi-male troop.*   This is probably the most highly evolved level of social organisation in primates. There are several adult males which exhibit a high degree of tolerance to each other and to the young maturing males. The adult males are arranged

in a linear hierarchy but this is not as pronounced as in the age-graded male troop. The adult males dominate the maturing males which themselves are arranged in an age-based rank order.

Eisenberg *et al.* (1972) consider that these five levels of social organisation represent an evolutionary series beginning with the primitive solitary (or dispersed) organisation and ending with the advanced multi-male social organisation. The large troops (numbers 3, 4 and 5, above) are gradations in social organisation based on the increasing tolerance and co-operation between the males in the group. There are other classifications of primate social organisations; for example, Crook (1970) suggested five levels of organisation in the communal primates based on male tolerance, group size and the environment.

The classification described above suggests that a single species can not be classified into more than one of the five levels of social organisation, and that there are no spatial and temporal changes in social organisation. However, *Colobus guereza* in Ethiopia have three distinct types of troop. These are small uni-male troops (3–5 individuals), large uni-male troops (6–10 individuals) and multi-male, or age-graded male, troops (8–12 individuals). The different troops are distinguished by their composition, type of leadership and territorial defence, and the frequency of agonistic behaviour (Dunbar and Dunbar 1976). Each type of troop may represent a different stage in the life cycle of the species, so there is a normal progression from one form of social organisation to another, and all three types of troop can exist in the population at the same time. Many species of Artiodactyla have spatial and temporal changes in their social organisations, and similar changes may be more widespread in the Primates than is realised at the present time.

Solitary species

Pottos (*Perodicticus potto*) are arboreal slow-moving prosimians which live in the lowland rain forest. Their social organisation is dispersed or solitary (Charles-Dominique 1971, 1974). Each female has a territory of about 7·5 ha, and there is only a slight overlap with the territories of adjacent females. Similarly, there is little overlap between the territories of adjacent males, but the male territory is about 12 ha and overlaps with the territories of several females. Thus females allow males into their territories, although they do not allow other females. There are limited contacts between individuals in the regions of overlap, but because of the nature of the habitat, the sedentary nature and slow movements of pottos, most interactions are those of mutual avoidance. Pottos advertise their presence and the extent of their territories by marking the branches with urine; and it is likely that the scent of the urine is a means of individual recognition. Vocal and visual communication between adults is rare.

In regions of overlap, pottos exhibit temporal separation from one another. For example, when a particular tree in an overlap region is in fruit, only one potto feeds at a time on the fruit, and a second potto will feed only when the first has moved away.

Contacts between males and females are discrete. During courtship, the male pursues the female in the region where their territories overlap. The pursuit lasts for about one hour each night over a period of weeks, but during this time there is no physical contact between the male and the female. Later the female allows the male to touch her, and they indulge in mutual grooming. A semi-permanent bond is established, but the two individuals remain independent for most of the time, and they communicate indirectly by urine marking. It is likely that pottos are polygamous because the male territory overlaps the territories of several females.

The young potto is weaned at 2–3 months but remains with its mother for up to one year. Prior to weaning, the female leaves her young each night and rejoins it in the morning. Most communication between mother and young is tactile, although the young emit some vocal sounds to re-establish contact with the mother in the early morning. Young males leave their mothers at about 6 months of age, probably as a result of agonistic interactions with the adult male. The young male becomes a wanderer until he establishes a territory of his own.

The social organisation of Demidoff's galagos (*Galagoides demidovii*) are similar in many (but not all) respects to that of the potto (Charles-Dominique 1972, 1974).

The uni-male troop

Mona monkeys (*Ceropithecus campbelli lowei*) are typical rain forest monkeys of the Ivory Coast. During a four-year study at Adiopodoume (Bourlière *et al.* 1969) the number in the troop under observation varied slightly but did not exceed fifteen individuals. At one time the troop contained one adult male, eight sub-adult males and six females. The adult male appeared to be the leader and spent a lot of his time watching, and was the only male to emit loud warning noises in response to situations that were potentially dangerous to the troop. Agonistic behaviour is rare in this species but when it occurs it is usually directed by the dominant male towards sub-adult males. There was no evidence of a status hierarchy in the sub-adult males or in the females. The troop slept in particular trees each night, and during the day they dispersed to look for food. The home range for this troop was about 3 ha and it is probable that most parts of the home range were visited each day. The mona monkeys spent most of their time in the middle and upper layers of the forest, but they descended to the ground to look for fallen fruits. The area where the troop regularly lived and fed was not entered by other mona monkeys and was probably a 'group territory'; the displays and loud vocalisations of the dominant male at the boundary of the territory probably helped to repel neighbouring troops. Splitting of the troop into two sub-troops occurred when a young male habitually rested by himself in a separate sleeping tree. Later he was joined by other monkeys from the troop. During the day, this sub-troop foraged independently, and returned to its preferred trees to sleep at night. Eventually the members of the sub-troop disappeared and presumably formed a new 'group territory' elsewhere.

The females of the troop acted as mothers and 'aunts'. Adult females took great interest in any new born infant and females other than the mother temporarily assisted in caring for the infant. Any agonistic behaviour that occurred occasionally between mothers and other females was limited to chin-thrusting and head bobbing. Care by several monkeys in the troop probably assisted the infants to become integrated as members of the troop and gave them a high chance of survival.

Mona monkeys are only one example of many monkeys which have a uni-male organisation; most species of the large genus *Cercopithecus* have this type of social organisation (see Table 10.10).

The age-graded male troop

Gorillas are large forest-dwelling apes which spend a lot of time on the ground. However, despite their size, they climb trees where they sit and feed, and build nests in the branches where they sleep at night. In Kivu, groups of mountain gorillas (*Gorilla gorilla beringei*) lived in closely co-ordinated groups. Group size ranged from 2 to 30 individuals (Schaller 1963, 1965). Each group was comprised, on average, of 1·7 silver-backed males (large males weighing 650–1 000 kg with silver hairs on the back), 1·5 black-backed males (weighing 330–550 kg with few or no silver hairs on the back), 6·2 females, 2·9 juveniles and 4·6 infants. In most groups the composition remained constant for long periods of time, in others there were frequent changes. In a stable group, the dominant silver-backed male with the females and young formed the main part of the group; other males were peripheral and frequently joined or left the group. Gorillas have a wide range of behavioural characteristics. Schaller suggested that posture and gestures, facial expressions, vocalisations and other noises, and physical discipline of infants were important co-ordinating elements. Other overt interactions including mutual grooming, sexual behaviour, and agonistic behaviour were rare even though members of the groups were close to one another all day. The greatest amount of contact behaviour was between mothers and their young and this persisted until the young were about 3 years old. Gorillas have extensive home ranges, but Schaller observed that they often spent many days in restricted localities within the range. Home ranges of different groups overlapped, so that sometimes different groups came into contact. Generally such contacts were peaceful, and each group kept aloof and detached from the other group. Occasionally individuals from different groups intermingled.

The multi-male troop

Two species of savanna-living monkeys which live in multi-male troops are the baboon (*Papio cynocephalus*) (Hall and de Vore 1965) and the vervet monkey (*Cercopithecus pygerythrus* (Struhsaker 1967a, b). The baboon group is based on a hierarchy with a dominant male as the leader of the troop. All other members of the group show submissive behaviour towards the dominant male, and he threatens or attacks potential enemies whenever the group is in danger. The mating frequency of the dominant male is higher than that of subordinate males and therefore the dominant male fathers most of the young in the group. The subordinate males exhibit a hierarchy amongst themselves, and the status of any male is a reflection of his fighting ability, and his ability to enlist the support of other males. This system of dominance ensures comparative peace and stability within the group, and it affords the greatest amount of protection to the individuals of the group, especially to the mothers with young. When baboons are on the move, or are foraging in the grass, they are spread out with the males looking after the troop. The most dominant males are in the centre and close to the females carrying young; the least dominant males are in front, at the sides and the back (Fig. 10.23). A 'sentinel' baboon is often observed in front of the troop, and if he barks to indicate possible danger, one of the dominant males comes forward to investigate. When feeding, a male at the side of the troop keeps watch and warns the troop of danger.

A social organisation which is as complex as that of baboons is only possible if there are many methods of communication between members of the troop. Hall and de Vore (1965) listed 14 types of vocalisation, 32 types of visual communications and expressions and 15 elements of tactile communication. Agonistic behaviour includes fighting in contact, many forms of threat, escape and 'fear' behaviour; amicable behaviour includes social grooming, lip smacking, 'greeting' behaviour and presentation. All these result in close integration between members of the troop and establishment of the hierarchy. As well as adaptability in their social organisation, baboons show great adaptability in their ecology.

The home range of baboon troops, like those of gorillas, overlap and different troops may come into contact. Most studies suggest that troops stay apart even when population densities are high. Different troops may meet at water holes; if this happens the larger troop tends to displace the smaller troop. Fighting and threat display between troops are rare.

Baboon troops tend to remain stable as co-ordinated cohesive units, and they have

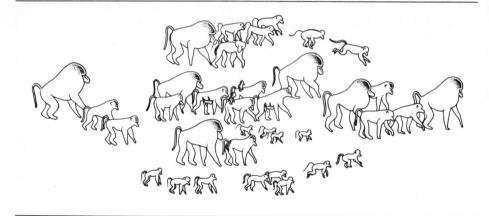

Fig. 10.23 The positions of individual members of a baboon troop during movement. Females with young are in the centre and surrounded by adult males, and groups of juveniles frolic around the periphery of the troop. Other adult males and females precede and follow the centre of the group, and two oestrous females (with dark hindquarters) are closely attended by adult males. (After Hall and de Vore 1965.)

regular feeding, drinking and sleeping times. This type of social organisation can only occur when food is abundant and sufficiently dispersed so that competition does not occur. Baboons feed on a variety of seeds, fruits, bulbs and insects, and they are sufficiently adaptable that they can take advantage of any abundant source of food that is present. An advantage of large troops in baboons is that it minimises the chances of predation. The variety of behavioural elements, complex social organisation and ecological adaptability have resulted in baboons being the most abundant and successful savanna primate. This adaptability is also shown by the flexibility of behaviour shown by baboons under different environmental conditions; forest-living *Papio anubis* do not appear to exhibit the dominance hierarchy (Rowell 1966) so typical of their savanna-living conspecifics.

The vervet monkey, *Cercopithecus pygerythrus*, is a common species in the savannas of Africa. A study in Masai Amboseli National Park (Struhsaker 1967*a*, *b*) showed that this species lives in mixed troops of 7 to 53 individuals composed of several males, adult females and young. They live in several types of woodland savanna but the highest densities of monkeys are found in areas where fever trees (*Acacia zanthophloea*) and shrubs (*Azima tetracantha* and *Salvadore persica*) are abundant, probably because of the abundance and variety of food associated with this habitat. Vervets inhabiting woodlands with scattered *Acacia tortilis* trees occur at lower densities. At night, the troop splits into sub-troops of 1–6 individuals. The composition of each sub-troop and the trees where the sub-troop sleeps are fairly constant which suggests that each sub-troop is not a random aggregation of monkeys, and that particular trees are selected as sleeping sites. In the morning the sub-troops join up again. The habit of selecting preferred sleeping trees is a common characteristic in cercopithecine monkeys and has been recorded for several species including *Cercocebus albigena*, *Cercopithecus mitis*, *C. mona*, *C. neglectus*, *C. ascanius* and *Papio anubis* (Lumsden 1951).

During the day the troop as a whole moves over its home range and sometimes there is overlap between the home ranges of neighbouring troops. Vervet monkeys are active all day, but they tend to move more often and over larger distances in the early morning and late afternoon. Like baboons, they feed on a wide variety of flower buds, stems, fruits and insects, but unlike baboons they do not venture into open grasslands to feed. They usually drink once every two days, mostly between 1100–1500 hrs, but this varies depending on the amount of water within the home range.

Within the troop, there is a dominance hierarchy as in baboons. Dominant individuals have priority in the choice of space, food and grooming relationships. Dominance is asserted by a confident walk, rapid glancing from side to side, lip smacking and teeth chattering, and the 'Red-white-and-blue' display when the dominant individual exposes his coloured genitalia and perianal region. Subordinate individuals including other mature males show typical submissive behaviour towards the dominant male.

A vervet troop forms a territory within its home range, but there appears to be no correlation between troop size and the size of the territory and home range. Probably the resources within the territory are a more important consideration. The relationships between neighbouring troops is rather variable. Vocalisations and chasing across the territorial boundaries occur frequently, but at other times parties of vervets sit within a few yards of each other on either side of the territorial boundary. The composition of any troop is not constant: young and immature males of different troops may play and groom each other and there may be an interchange of individuals from one troop to another.

Struhsaker (1967c) lists 60 different behaviour patterns in vervets including 46 which appear to communicate information from one individual to another. In addition, vervets make 36 vocal sounds but because many of the sounds intergrade with each other, an exact numerical estimate is unreliable. Adult males show 38 methods of communication. The other males, females and juveniles show 30–37, and infants show 19 methods of communication. This large repertoire enables vervets to have a complex and well integrated social behaviour which, as in baboons, confers many advantages. The efficient detection of potential predators by the troop enhances the chances of survival, and learned information about the environment also increases the efficiency of the troop during exploitation of its home range. As in other mammals, territoriality is presumably important for the spacing and dispersion of vervets throughout their range.

Social organisation in the Bovidae

There are many types of social organisation in the Bovidae, ranging from species which live in pairs or trios to those which live in large herds. Some species have well developed territorial behaviour, and in others territoriality is absent. Jarman (1974) has classified the Bovidae into five classes based on social organisation, the degree of territoriality, feeding habits and reaction to predators (Table 10.11). It is interesting that species within any class are identical or very similar in all these characteristics. Clearly the set of characteristics found within each of these classes act in association for the benefit of the species concerned, although the relationship between social organisation and any other character is uncertain. It appears that the varied social organisations in the Bovidae, as in the Primates, are due to a balance between phylogeny (which is responsible for similarities between closely related species) and adaptations to particular niches (which are responsible for differences between closely related species). It is likely that, at the present time, Bovidae are undergoing rapid speciation and ecological radiation, which may partly account for the immense variety in social organisations and the variety of horns which are used often to assert dominance in territorial males. The social organisations of African Bovidae are reviewed by Jarman (1974), Estes (1974) and Geist (1974).

Table 10.11 *Social organisation and feeding behaviour of African Artiodactyls. (From Jarman 1974.)*

Class	Examples	Group size	Food habit	Seasonal variation in food	Selectivity for particular food	Seasonal change in habitat	Reaction to predators	Territoriality
A	Duikers, royal antelope, klipspringer, grysbok	1–3 (pairs, and pairs with young)	Mostly browse on one vegetation type	None	Food spatially scattered; feeds selectively on particular items	None	Become inconspicuous	Both sexes establish permanent territories
B	Reedbucks, oribi, lesser Kudu ? beira	1–3 (occ. 1–12)	Browse and grasses	Varies seasonally	Feeds selectively in several vegetation types. Intermediate between Classes A and C	Lives in several vegetation types	Remains inconspicuous and motionless, flees when disturbed	Males of some species have territories
C	Waterbuck, kob, puku, lechwe, impala, ?most gazelles	6–60 (large aggregations up to 200, single males)	Grasses (wet season) and browse	Seasonal change in food	Feeds on wide variety of plants with wide dispersion. Not particularly selective	Changes in relation to food availability. Local movements	Freezes and then flees (woodland areas); watches predator and then runs (open areas)	Males highly territorial, associated with reproductive cycle of variable length
D	Hartebeest, wildebeest (?addax, oryx, roan antelope)	6 – several 100, single males	Grasses of correct size and palatability	None	No selection if grass condition is correct	Seasonal movements to find grass of correct size and palatability. Migrations	Moves slowly away, or may follow predator. Flees when attacked	Males have territories during reproductive season
E	Giant eland, buffalo	Herds of up to several 100	Grasses, grasses and browse (eland)	None	Grasses have continuous dispersion. Selection for certain favoured	None, provided suitable food available	Little reaction. May attack predator (buffalo)	No territoriality

The basic characteristics of the five classes of social organisation (Jarman 1974) are:

Class A: solitary or dispersed, territorial.
Class B: small groups, most adult males usually have permanent territories. Shows resemblances to Classes A and C.
Class C: small or large groups, a proportion of males hold territories.
Class D: small to large groups, usually migratory, a proportion of males hold territories.
Class E: medium to large groups, non territorial.

The boundaries between each class are not rigid, and there is certainly some overlap in the characteristics of each class of social organisation because the classes are based on a number of characteristics (see above).

The range of social organisations in the Bovidae is illustrated by one example from classes A, B, D and E. Three examples illustrate class C because this class contains some of the best studied antelope species.

Class A: Maxwell's duiker

Cephalophus maxwelli are duikers of the lowland rain forest. They are usually found singly or in pairs. They have exclusive territories which are held by one individual, or by a pair. Both sexes use scent marking as an important method of communication. They have well developed suborbital glands which produce a copious secretion which is rubbed on to twigs, bark and other prominent objects. Ralls (1971, 1974) has shown that the frequency of marking depends on the sex of the individual and on whether the neighbouring individual is a male or a female. In captivity, a male and a female rub their suborbital glands against each other's faces (Aeshlimann 1963, Happold, unpubl.) (Fig. 10.24), and it is likely that the suborbital secretions may be an important

Fig. 10.24 Face rubbing in *Cephalophus maxwelli*. The male (right) and female are rubbing secretions from the sub-orbital gland on to each other's faces. The long slit-like opening of the gland is visible between the eye and the nostril on the left side of the male's face. (From photo by D. C. D. Happold.)

means of individual recognition. This behaviour suggests that a male and a female may form a pair-bond. In addition, *Cephalophus* have pedal and inguinal glands, but the significance of these in their social organisation is not known.

In the rain forest, *Cephalophus* regularly use pathways which they have made. The scent marks of the individual along the pathways presumably advertise the extent of the territory. Vocal sounds and visual displays are not present in this species (cf. other classes), probably because of the need to remain inconspicuous.

Class B: lesser kudu
The lesser kudu (*Tragelaphus imberbis*) lives in thickets and bush country in the savannas of eastern Africa. Adult males are solitary; however, it is uncertain whether they have exclusive territories or whether mutual antagonism keeps them apart (Jarman 1974). Females live in small groups of two to ten individuals, and adult females are usually associated with one or more other females and immature males. Female groups are not territorial, and may enter the territory of a male. Bachelor herds of non-territorial males do not occur (cf. classes C and D), although young subadult males may leave the females and associate in separate groups.

The lesser kudu has a large repertoire of ritualised displays associated with male–male interactions and courtship which involve olfactory, visual and tactile communication. Interactions between two males begin with nasal–nasal sniffing, and are followed by pushing with the foreheads or the horns. Dominance is established when the winner pushes the loser away from the scene of the encounter (Walther 1958) (Fig. 10.25). Courtship displays begin when the male and female rub their necks together. Later the male follows or chases the female with his head and neck stretched forward and the horns lying along the neck and shoulders. During mating, the neck and chin of the male rest on the back of the female (Walther 1964a, 1965) (Fig. 10.25).

The social organisation of the lesser kudu differs from that of Maxwell's duiker in group numbers, the role of territoriality, the lack of scent marking and the importance of visual displays; and it differs from that of classes C and D in having permanent adult male territories and smaller numbers of individuals in female groups.

Class C: Thomson's gazelle, Grant's gazelle and Uganda kob
The species in this class are characterised by territoriality in only part of the adult male population at a time, the occurrence of bachelor herds of non-territorial males and elaborate ritual male displays associated with territoriality and courtship. The group size is large, both for female herds and for mixed herds when territories are not being defended.

Thomson's gazelle (*Gazella thomsoni*) live in herds on the open plains of East Africa. They form bachelor herds of young males and non-territorial adult males, and female herds containing females of all ages and their young. Herd size is extremely variable, and during migration the herds intermingle and form large aggregations of up to 1 000 individuals. Herd structure appears to be rather variable and individuals move from herd to herd, and often mixed herds are formed with impala and Grant's gazelle. Possibly because of the high intensity of predation on this species (p. 318), Thomson's gazelle have special behavioural signals which warn of potential danger; these include tail wagging and flicking of the flanks, and a curious stiff-legged bounding termed 'stotting' (Fig. 10.32). Adult males are territorial and they establish the limits of their territories by urinating and defaecating in succession on the same spot and by rubbing secretions from the preorbital glands on grasses and twigs. The territorial male defends his territory by chasing other males who cross the boundary, and by physical fighting with territorial neighbours. Walther (1964b) has described how vigorous fighting occurs when a male is establishing his territory. At first defeated rivals move well away but later, as the territory boundaries of adjacent males become more defined, fights simply reaffirm the exact location of the boundaries. Most males retain their territories

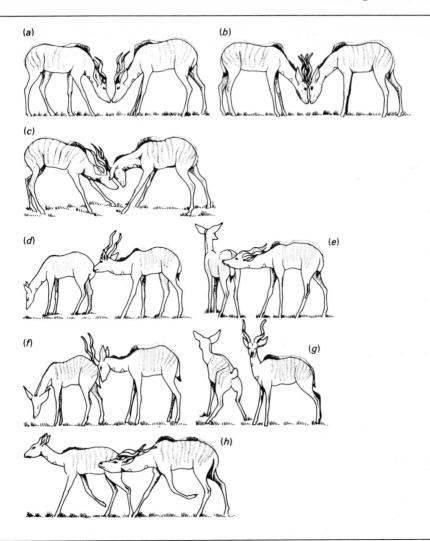

Fig. 10.25 Behavioural displays of lesser kudu (*Tragelaphus imberbis*). (*a*) Nose sniffing between males. (*b*) head-pressing between males, (*c*) horn-pressing between males, (*d*) male sniffing genital region of female, (*e, f*) male head-rubbing the genital region of female, (*g*) female urinates while the male shows 'Flehmen', (*h*) male with neck outstretched while chasing female. (From Walther 1964*a*.)

for two to eight weeks, by which time many of the Thomson's gazelle may have left the area because of changing grazing conditions. As the urge to defend the territory wanes, the territorial male may wander far from his territory although he will return later. The female herds can move into a male's territory at will, and when this happens, the male tries to keep them within his territory. The mating behaviour of the male is very characteristic, and is composed of several distinct behavioural elements (Fig. 10.26). The male approaches the female with his neck and head pointed forward and the horns lying parallel to the neck (low-stretch display); this is alternated with lifting the nose upwards and forwards. The male tests the reproductive state of the female by sniffing at her vulva; this stimulates urination and as the female urinates, the male tests the urine by

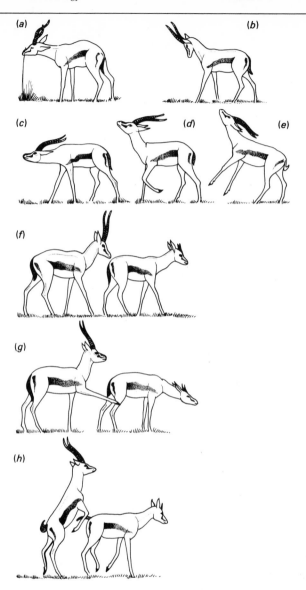

Fig. 10.26 Behavioural displays of Thomson's gazelle (*Gazella thomsoni*). (*a*) Male marking with pre-orbital gland, (*b*) male showing high head display (Gehornpräsentieren), (*c*) male showing low stretch display, (*d*) male showing lifted head position, (*e*) male showing symbolic 'Laufschlag' with high nose display, (*f*) 'pair-marching' of male and female, (*g*) 'Laufschlag', (*h*) mating. (From Walther 1964*b*.)

retracting his lips and wrinkling his nose. This grimace is referred to as 'Flehmen'. If the female is in oestrous, the male chases her and periodically touches her back leg with one of his extended forefeet ('Laufschlag'). The female walks slowly forward during copulation, forcing the male to walk bipedally behind her. Male gazelle do not grasp or rest upon the female during copulation.

In Grant's gazelle, territorial and mating behaviour show many similarities to that

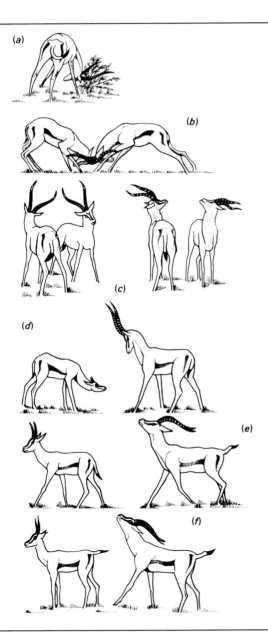

Fig. 10.27 Behavioural displays of Grant's gazelle (*Gazella granti*). (*a*) Horn-weaving by male, (*b*) males fighting, (*c*) flank to flank display of males, (*d*) high head display by male, (*e*) pair-marching of male and female, (*f*) simple 'Laufschlag'. (From Walther 1965*a*.)

of Thomson's gazelle (Fig. 10.27, Table 10.6). However, there are some differences: Grant's gazelle do not mark with the preorbital gland, and rival males display their necks and horns with 'threat circling' so that physical fighting is infrequent in this species (Walther 1965).

Uganda kob (*Kobus kob thomasi*) live in large herds in the grassland savannas of

Uganda and southern Sudan. There are herds composed of young males and adult non-territorial males, and female herds composed of females of all ages and young males up to the age of weaning. The male herds contain up to 500 individuals and female herds usually contain 30–50 individuals but may be as large as 1 000. Herd structure and number is varied, and partly depends on the grazing conditions from month to month. Small herds may join to form larger ones in regions of favourable grazing, and large herds may split into smaller herds at random. Uganda kob are not migratory, although males tend to move further than females when looking for fresh grazing.

One of the most distinctive features of the social organisation in Uganda kob is the formation of the 'lek' or territorial breeding ground by adult males in breeding condition (Buechner and Schloeth 1965, Leuthold 1966). Each lek has a central area, about 200 m in diameter, which contains up to 15 territories. These central territories are about 15–30 m in diameter. Surrounding each central area are larger peripheral territories so that the lek as a whole contains up to 40 territories. These are maintained throughout the year, although the individuals who hold the territories may change quite frequently. The central territories where most of the mating occurs may change ownership every few days. However, there is an increasing length of occupancy towards the peripheal territories, some of which may be held by the same individual for up to a year. This system is feasible because Uganda kob breed throughout the year. Males return to the bachelor herds when they are not breeding.

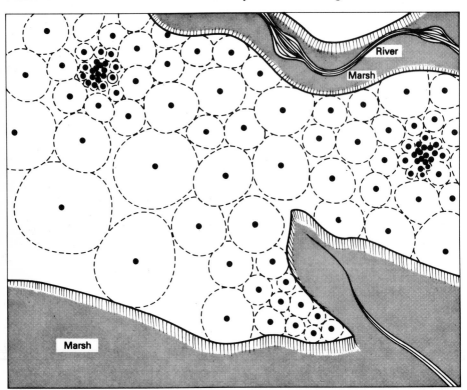

Fig. 10.28 Schematic representation of central (lek) territories and peripheral territories of Uganda kob. (Leuthold 1966.)

In addition to the lek territories, there are single territories which are found between the leks (Leuthold 1966) (Fig. 10.28). The actual position and size of these single territories is determined by the environment; the largest (and least favourable) single territories are normally in regions far removed from the leks, where visibility is poor and where the grasses tend to be less palatable. Although the central territories of the leks are the principal mating areas, a particular male which holds a central territory for a few days may only mate with a few females. Another male, which occupies a peripheral or single territory for a longer period of time, may mate with as many females as the central territory male but over a longer period of time. Thus, these two males could have equal genetic contributions to the next generation. There are no definite data to show the relative genetic contributions of males which occupy different types of territories, but Leuthold (1966) has suggested that the variations in the territorial behaviour may confer adaptability on the population which may be valuable if there are changes in environmental conditions.

All populations of kob show territoriality, but lekking appears to be more important to the Uganda kob than to kob from other regions (Leuthold 1966).

Class D: wildebeest

The wildebeest (*Connochaetes taurinus*) is a gregarious species whch alternates between two forms of social organisation (Estes 1966, 1969, Jarman 1974). In the sedentary phase (as in the Ngorogoro crater), a proportion of adult males hold exclusive territories. Large female herds pass through the territories (Fig. 10.20), and the females are continuously harassed as the male tries to retain them inside his territory. The male advertises his territory by depositing his dung inside the territorial boundary, and by his presence. Usually the male remains in the central part of the territory which is heavily grazed and trampled. He is extremely active as he chases the females inside the territory and has interactions along the territorial boundary. In marginal areas, the territories are larger than those in the most preferred areas and there are normally few, if any, females in these marginal territories. Non-territorial males form bachelor herds and are often driven into marginal areas by the aggressive territorial males. Nursery herds of young are present after the breeding season.

In migratory populations (as in the Serengeti), there are large mobile herds of mixed sexes. More or less permanent territories cannot be established, and the males form either temporary territories associated with a limited area of ground, or a defended area (not associated with a particular area of ground) in which the male confines his female herd. When a migratory herd stops, the males appear to establish a hierarchy amongst themselves; this results in the dispersion of the males which then begin to herd the females (Estes 1969). Possibly the dispersion and herding occur simultaneously (Jarman 1974). Bachelor herds accompany the mixed herds during migration, and the female herds may be segregated according to age and reproductive condition.

These two social organisations are interchangeable, as exemplified by the Ngorongoro population. Further details on the migrations of wildebeest in the Serengeti are given on pp. 207–11.

There are many characteristic behaviour patterns associated with territoriality and courtship in wildebeest. Territorial conflicts between males are ritualised and actual fighting is rare. An interesting feature of large aggregations is the dispersion of individuals in relation to each other. During migrations, wildebeest move in single file as an anti-predator precaution. When grazing or resting at night, each individual is orientated in the same direction with sufficient individual space between each individual to allow adequate movement (Estes 1966, 1969).

Class E: buffalo

Plains buffalo (*Syncerus caffer*) are large gregarious bovids which live in herds of 50–1000 individuals (Jarman 1974). They are relatively sedentary, and their social organisation differs from that of the other classes as there are many adult males in the herd, and a fixed female membership (Jarman 1974). Adult males remain in the herd for many years; they are arranged in a linear hierarchy and dominant males obtain most of the mating rights (Grimsdell 1969). Adult and sub-adult males tend to form sub-groups within the herd, although adult males freely associate with females. In the Serengeti, old males and adult males which are low in the hierarchy may leave the herd to form bachelor herds of up to 20 individuals, and in the dry season sub-groups of immature males leave the herd to form temporary bachelor herds (Sinclair 1974c). A few old males may become solitary.

Young buffalo associate with their mothers until they are 3 years old. Young males, 4–5 years old, associate in sub-groups within the herd until they are mature.

There are many behavioural characteristics which promote cohesion between members of the herd. Agonistic behaviour is rare between males of similar status, but individuals of low status are often chased and they may leave the herd to join bachelor groups. Sub-groups of immature males are tolerated by the adult males. In addition, group defence, group protection of the young, integration of the young into the herd from birth, social licking and minimal social distance ('individual distance') result in typical herd behaviour (Estes 1974).

There is no male or herd territoriality; the herd moves at will in its home range and there is only slight overlap between the ranges of adjacent herds. Buffalo exhibit simple postures as means of intra-specific communication (Sinclair 1974c), and they do not have elaborate displays associated with territoriality and courtship as in species of classes B, C and D.

Social organisation in the Perissodactyla

The four species of African Equidae are very similar, and are included in the single genus *Equus*. However, two separate social organisations have evolved in these species (Klingel 1972, 1974). Burchell's zebra (*E. burchelli*) and the mountain zebra (*E. zebra*) live in family groups consisting of one stallion, several mares and their foals. There is a status hierarchy in the members of the family group. These species are non-territorial, and each family group utilises a large home range which is shared with other family groups. Even when thousands of individuals converge on favoured grazing areas, the family groups remain intact. Agonistic behaviour is rare, and there is no fighting between adult males for the possession of mares. Young males stay with their family group until 2–3 years of age. Then they join bachelor stallion groups until they are 5–6 years of age when they attempt to form their own family groups. These bachelor stallion groups are also non-territorial and non-hierarchical, although the oldest male usually leads the group.

In contrast, Grevy's zebra (*E. grevyi*) and the wild ass (*E. africanus*) form loosely bonded, and non-hierarchical groups of varied composition. There are stallion groups, mare groups, mother and foal groups and mixed groups, all of which are non-territorial. In addition, some males form territories whose characteristics are in marked contrast to those of most bovids. In Grevy's zebra, for example, the territories have an average size of 5.75 km^2, and other males are allowed into the territory provided they do not interfere with the owner's mating activities. The territorial boundaries are marked with piles of dung. There is rarely any fighting at the boundaries unless a female in oestrous is nearby. As in the Bovidae, territorial behaviour facilitates mating because when an oestrous female is in neutral ground outside a territory, several males fight for her and frequently none of them succeed in mating.

In the non-territorial species, the family groups are together all the time and breeding occurs throughout the year, even though the groups migrate from one grazing ground to another. In the territorial species, the territories are established in the wet season grazing grounds, and each stallion remains on or close to his territory even when the mares, young and non-territorial stallions have moved to dry season grazing grounds. The territorial stallion leaves his territory only to drink but he does not abandon his territory unless ecological conditions become very severe. In these species, the mares are separated from the breeding stallions for a large part of the year, and therefore the duration of the reproductive season is much shorter than in the non-territorial species. This is the reverse of the usual situation in which year-round territoriality is associated with year-round breeding (e.g. Uganda kob).

White rhinoceros (*Ceratotherium simum*) usually live in small groups of up to six individuals, although larger groups aggregate temporarily at favoured grazing grounds. Territorial males occupy territories of 1–2 km², but as in territorial equids, other males are permitted to enter the territory. Females are also allowed to enter the territory, and the territorial male forms an association with them for up to three weeks. Reproduction is non-seasonal, but most mating takes place at the beginning of the rains when there is a flush of green grass. Except when coming into oestrous, the females (accompanied by a calf) have home ranges of 10–15 km² which overlap extensively with those of other females, and include the territories of several males (Owen-Smith 1972, 1974).

Social organisation in the Carnivora

There are two basic types of social organisation in the Carnivora: (1) The majority of species are solitary or live in pairs, and are sometimes accompanied by their young, and (2) a smaller number of species live in groups of related (or unrelated) individuals (Table 10.12). Some species of group-living carnivores have been well studied, but very

Table 10.12   *The social organisations of African carnivores. Many species are not included as definite information is lacking. See also Table 10.9. (Data from Ewer 1973.)*

Solitary, pairs, family groups	Large groups, individuals probably unrelated
Many species of mongooses*	*Lycaon pictus*
*Panthera pardus**	*Panthera leo*
*Proteles cristatus**	*Crocuta crocuta*
Vulpes spp.	*Mungos mungo*
Canis spp.	*M. gambianus*
Acinonyx	*Crossarchus obscurus*
Genetta spp.*	*Helogale parvula*
Poiana richardsoni	*Suricata suricatta*
	Cynictis penicillata

*Tendency to be solitary and not in pairs/family groups.

little is known about the social organisations of the smaller species, many of which are nocturnal.

Olfactory communication is common in the solitary species. Urine and faeces marking, and secretions from the anal glands which are rubbed on to prominent objects in the environment, convey information about territorial boundaries and the status and condition of individuals (Ewer 1975). Individuals of solitary species meet infrequently, and most communication is indirect. Visual and vocal communication is not well developed in solitary species (except when young are present), but is of much greater importance in group living species.

There are clearly advantages and disadvantages of group living for predators. For the smaller species which feed on insects, group living is feasible because insects are usually common and abundant. Several small species of viverrids and mustelids are diel-active, whereas many of the larger mongooses are solitary and nocturnal and feed on larger prey (Rood 1975). For large species, the disadvantages of obtaining only a small meal from the prey are probably offset by the enhanced ability of a group to capture prey, provided the prey species is numerous. Group hunting may increase the size of the prey which can be taken. The area of the hunting range is determined by the number of predators and by the availability of prey.

A detailed account of communication, hunting behaviour and social organisation in the carnivores is given by Ewer (1973).

Solitary species, pairs and family groups
The majority of the Mustelidae and Viverridae are solitary except when breeding and rearing their young, although there are some viverrids which are notable exceptions. Many species of African canids, for example *Vulpes* spp. and *Canis* spp., live singly or in pairs, and the aardwolf (*Proteles cristatus*) is solitary probably because of its unusual hunting methods and because it feeds almost exclusively on termites (Kruuk and Sands 1972). Most species of Felidae are solitary, including the African wildcat (*Felis libyca*), caracal (*Felis caracal*) and leopard (*Panthera pardus*).

Large groups
Several species of viverrids live in groups. For example, the Gambian mongoose (*Mungos gambianus*) hunts in parties of up to 25 individuals during the daytime (Booth 1960), and the banded mongoose (*Mungos mungo*) and the dwarf mongoose (*Helogale parvula*) live in small colonies (Dorst and Dandelot 1970) (section 1.9).

Banded mongooses live in packs (Fig. 10.29) which are relatively stable social units. On Mweya Peninsula in Rwenzori National Park (Rood 1975), the average number of individuals in a pack was 14 (n = 16), with a range of 2–29. Each pack consisted of several males, females and their young, and there was no interchange of individuals between neighbouring packs. A large pack may split voluntarily to form two packs which in time may become independent social units. The home ranges of mongoose packs overlap and there are frequent encounters between neighbouring packs. After visual contact has been made, the level of agonistic behaviour between packs depends on the relative sizes of each pack. Small packs usually retire when they encounter a large pack. However, when two packs of approximately equal size meet, the individuals chase each other uttering loud vocalisations, mark with secretions from the anal glands and occasionally indulge in physical fighting. Familiarity and frequent contact probably establishes a dominance hierarchy between neighbouring packs.

Within a pack there is no clearly defined hierarchy. No individual is dominant, although males tend to be more aggressive than females, and males are mostly responsible for guarding the young in the den. Banded mongooses are diel-active, and the members of a pack forage together with individuals spread out over an area of about 60 m by 40 m. While foraging, individuals in the pack maintain contact with each other by a nearly continuous series of chirrups, twitters and grunts. Group foraging has several advantages for banded mongooses (Rood 1975). The group detects

Fig. 10.29   Group of foraging banded mongooses (*Mungos mungos*), (Photo: E. G. Neal.)

potential predators more easily than an individual, and clustering together is a form of anti-predator behaviour. An abundant source of food is shared because the excited vocalisations of the finder attract other individuals in the pack. Occasionally, banded mongooses in a pack drive away another small predator from freshly killed prey. Group foraging in diel-active mongooses is probably a means of protection and is advantageous to all individuals in the group, whereas it is of little (or no) advantage to nocturnal mongooses. Consequently, diel-active mongooses have evolved many characteristics essential for maintaining contact and communication between individuals, including social grooming, living together in a den, and care of the young by all individuals in the pack.

In addition two species of the South African meercats (*Cynictis penicillata* and *Suricata suricatta*) are diel-active and live in colonies. They either dig their own warrens, or take over burrows dug by ground squirrels (Dorst and Dandelot 1970), and in some instances they live in burrows with the ground squirrels. In *Suricata*, much of the behaviour of the species is related to promoting social contact and cohesion between the individuals in the colony (Ewer 1963). Strange individuals are not accepted into the colony. Vocal sounds expressing threat, alarm, feeding satisfaction and intention to huddle are of particular importance in the life of the meercat colony. Similarly, mutual grooming undoubtedly strengthens the bond between individuals, and the parent–young relationships have social-bonding functions. Despite these characteristics which have evolved for a colonial life, meercats show behavioural elements which are also seen in non-colonial viverrids (Ewer 1963).

Fig. 10.30   A pack of hunting dogs. (Photo: C. A. Spinage.)

The hunting dog (*Lycaon pictus*) is the most social of the canids. Hunting dog packs (Fig. 10.30) may contain as many as twenty-one dogs, and each pack is usually led by an adult male. The other members of the pack are not arranged in any order of dominance and behavioural interactions between these individuals are mostly amicable. A greeting ceremony (consisting of face licking and poking the nose into the corner of the mouth), food solicitation and appeasement are frequent behaviour patterns within the pack, all of which probably strengthen the social bonds between the individuals. Similarly, several vocalisations assist in pack cohesion. The hunting dog is a very efficient predator, and when hunting the pack works as a co-ordinated team. This probably increases the chances of success and gives a better opportunity to feed regularly with the minimum expenditure of energy (Estes and Goddard 1967). Hunting dogs maintain a territory around the burrows where their young are reared, and they range over 100–200 km² looking for prey. Home ranges of separate packs may overlap. When packs meet, dogs bark but rarely fight, and the smaller pack withdraws (Kuhme 1965).

Lions (*Panthera leo*) live in 'prides' which are usually family groups and typically contain an adult male, several females and their young. Lion groups tend to be larger in grassland areas than in bushy country. The group as a whole lives within a territory in which it does most of its hunting, and is intolerant of any trespassing lions. A group may split into two, but the resulting sub-groups are relatively tolerant of each other. At a later date, one of the groups may have to leave the original territorial area and stake out a new territory for itself. The success of this will depend on the area required for the territory (which will be related to prey abundance) and the density of other lions nearby. Territorial boundaries are established by urination and roaring, but rarely by fighting. As young males become adolescent they leave the family group, or they are driven out by the adult male. Females move away from the group to give birth to their young, but subsequently both parents feed and care for the young. Females play with their young and teach them to hunt and kill prey; this is of great importance for the survival and social life of young lions.

The social organisation of lions is flexible. Although co-operation is advantageous, lions are quite capable of killing and living by themselves and they do not have to rely on other individual lions once they are weaned and can fend for themselves (Ewer 1968). In this respect, they are very different to the social African Canidae where co-operation is necessary for survival. Social behaviour, and many other aspects of lion ecology, have been described in great detail by Schaller (1972) and Rudnai (1973, 1974).

Comparison of social organisations

This chapter has discussed the variety of social behaviour and social organisations in selected African mammals, and the ways in which these behavioural characteristics are integrated with ecological characteristics to give the many life styles seen in African mammals. The behaviour of several orders and families has not been mentioned, mainly due to lack of adequate detailed information, but an indication of the range of social organisations in each family is given in Table 10.9. The classification and naming of communal social organisations is difficult and controversial. A logical classification should take each of the following parameters into consideration:

1. The group size and composition in terms of age, sex and genealogical relationships between individuals.
2. The male–female mating ratios, hierarchies and organisation within the group.
3. The function of territoriality (if present).
4. Seasonal changes in these parameters and the reasons for any change.
5. Other ecological information which may be related to behavioural characteristics.

These considerations are partly taken into account if the social system is divided on the basis of structure and function into three 'subsystems', each of which deals with a particular aspect of social organisation (Crook *et al.* 1976):

1. Mating subsystem (e.g. monogamy, polygamy, duration of male–female bond).
2. Rearing subsystem (e.g. duration of male participation, mother–young bond, parent–young bond).
3. Resource exploitation subsystem (e.g. group size, group stability, environmental exploitation, range exclusiveness, predator–prey relationships).

According to Crook *et al.* (1976), any social organisation can be analysed in relation to each subsystem. Differences between the characteristics and environments of related species may result in variations in social organisation.

The social behaviour and organisation of a species is a product of many ecological and evolutionary considerations, and each behavioural characteristic must have some adaptive significance. Examples of the relationships between behaviour, ecology and evolution have been given for a few species in the preceding pages. However, there are several basic concepts of social organisation, and a comparison of each of these concepts illustrates differences and similarities between orders and families.

The range of social organisations in an order or family
Orders with few species do not show a great range of social organisations (e.g.

Pholidota, Sirenia, Tubulidentata, Proboscidea). In contrast, orders and families which have evolved into diverse environments tend to have a large range of social organisations. For example, dispersed organisations and a great variety of communal organisations are exemplified by the orders Chiroptera, Carnivora, and Artiodactyla, and the families Pteropodidae, Bathyergidae, Viverridae, Cercopithecidae, Bovidae, Felidae, Giraffidae, Procaviidae and Hippopotamidae.

The occurrence of dispersed organisations
There are some orders and families in which all, or almost all, of the species have dispersed organisations; these include the Pholidota, Tubulidentata, Sirenia, Insectivora, Lorisidae, Rhizomyidae and Tragulidae. Unlike other orders and families, these do not have any species with complex communal organisations.

Changes in the social organisation with time
Some species have seasonal changes in social organisation, e.g. wildebeest (p. 257), Uganda kob (p. 256), Thomson's gazelle (p. 252) and Grevy's zebra (p. 258). Seasonal changes are usually associated with changing environmental conditions, or with separation of the population into different reproductive categories. In contrast, many species do not show any seasonal change in social organisation.

Changes in social organisation associated with population density
In natural populations, increase in density may result in dispersion of indivduals into marginal areas which were not colonised previously. Consequently, group size tends to be smaller, and home range is larger, in marginal areas than in preferred areas (e.g. elephants, many species of artiodactyls). In territorial species, territories in marginal areas tend to be larger than those in preferred areas (e.g. wildebeest, Uganda kob).

The occurrence and role of individual territories
Individual territories are usually associated with reproductive activities or with 'living space' (p. 228). Some species exhibit individual territorial behaviour (e.g. many species of artiodactyls, some perissodactyls and some carnivores), but many others do not. Territorial behaviour varies according to space and time:

(*a*) *Space.*   Most territories are associated with a fixed geographical region (e.g. 'lek' territories of Uganda kob, male reproductive territories of Grant's gazelle, Thomson's gazelle, impala, white rhinoceros, Grevy's zebra, sedentary wildebeest, potto). Other territories are not associated with a fixed geographical area, as when the species is constantly moving or migratory (e.g. migratory wildebeest, topi).

(*b*) *Time.*   Most male reproductive territories are held for a few days or weeks during a clearly defined breeding season, and a large amount of energy is required to establish and maintain the territory (e.g. Uganda kob, Thomson's gazelle, Grant's gazelle, impala, sedentary wildebeest). Some species, however, maintain a more or less permanent territory for many months or even years (e.g. Grevy's zebra, white rhinoceros). In these species, agonistic behaviour and territorial boundary disputes are much less frequent than in temporary territories.

Communal territories
Communal territories are held by a pair, family group or large group of individuals. They are usually maintained for long periods of time and are related to the area needed by the group for survival. Pair territories occur in may duikers (*Cephalophus*) and

Neotragus spp, some elephant shrews (Rathbun 1975), cane rats (*Thryonomys swinderianus*) and possibly in some species of foxes (*Vulpes*), jackals (*Canis*) and bushbuck (*Tragelaphus scriptus*). Prides of lions, uni-male monkey troops and possibly some viverrids live in communal family territories. Large group territories occur in, for example, age-graded and multi-male monkey troops, hunting dogs and spotted hyaenas. Mutual antagonism between the holders of adjacent communal territories is usually sufficient to maintain the territory without direct interactions which are typical of individual territories.

The adult male in communal organisations

The number and role of reproductively-mature males varies in communal social organisations. This feature of social organisation is significant as the general evolutionary principle is that only the 'best adapted' males have the opportunity to mate to ensure the genetic fitness of the population. Three types of male participation can be recognised:

1. In pairs or family groups there is only one adult male, and he has the exclusive mating rights to the female. Young males, which are the offspring of the pair, leave their parents and establish their own pair bonds when they become mature. This situation may, or may not, be associated with territoriality.
2. In large groups there may be several adult males. When there are no marked seasonal changes in the male social organisation and no individual male territoriality, there are four types of relationship between the males:
    (*a*) One adult male is dominant. He does not allow other adult males to live in the group, and he is intolerant of young immature males (e.g. uni-male monkey troops).
    (*b*) Several adult males co-exist in the group. The males are arranged in a linear dominance hierarchy so that the most dominant male(s) have the right to mate (e.g. age-graded and multi-male monkey troops, lion, buffalo).
    (*c*) There are many males in the group, and all appear to have equal status (e.g. communal bats, communal rodents, hunting dogs, rock hyrax).
    (*d*) The males remain separate from the females most of the time in exclusive male groups which associate with females only for reproductive activities and under special circumstances (e.g. elephants).
3. In large groups where there are many adult males and seasonal changes associated with territoriality, the males alternate between temporary antagonism towards each other during the reproductive season, and tolerance outside the reproductive season. Non-territorial males associate in bachelor herds during the reproductive season and show moderate tolerance towards each other (e.g. Uganda kob, Grant's gazelle, Thomson's gazelle, Grevy's zebra).

Open membership and closed membership groups

In open membership groups, other conspecifics may join the group on a temporary or permanent basis. Therefore the composition and numbers of the group change with time. Individual recognition of members of the group does not occur (e.g. communal bats, several species of antelopes). Closed (or stable) membership groups are those in which the number and composition of the group is relatively constant, and individual recognition is necessary for group stability. A few individuals may leave temporarily or permanently, and new individuals may enter if accepted by the group (e.g. age-graded and multi-male monkeys troops, Burchell's zebra, elephants, hippopotamus, giraffe, lion, hyaena and possibly communal viverrids).

Group size and composition
Group size and composition show extreme variation. The average size of the group depends on the species, its phylogeny, the exact environmental conditions and the season of the year. Examples are given in Table 10.8.

Co-operation and division of labour
Several conspecifics may co-operate in a particular task for the benefit of all the individuals concerned. For example, hunting dogs co-operate in hunting, the bathyergid *Heterocephalus* co-operate in digging tunnels and elephants assist an injured companion. Some species exhibit group defence against a predator either by massing together (e.g. buffalo) or by giving species-specific visual displays and vocal sounds (e.g. artiodactyl anti-predator behaviour, warning sounds of many species).

Individuals of the group may perform different tasks for the good of the group as a whole. For example, baboons and several other primate species usually have sentinels to warn the group of potential danger while the remainder of the troop feeds or sleeps.

Groups of mixed species composition
Some species associate with other species to form mixed, or polyspecific, groups. This habit is seen in only a few species; some examples are given on p. 271.

10.5   Inter-specific behaviour

Predator and anti-predator behaviour

Carnivores hunt and kill their prey in many different ways. Hunting behaviour depends partly on the size and form of the predator, the size of the prey and whether the predator hunts by itself or in a group of conspecifics. Each species of predator has its preferred prey, although when food is short most predators change their prey to some extent. This necessitates changes in the predator's hunting behaviour. Kruuk and Turner (1967) studied the prey of four large predators in the Serengeti National Park (Table 10.13). Each predator showed different feeding preferences, and employed different hunting methods in order to obtain its preferred prey. The interaction between predator and prey is an example of interspecific behaviour in which the behavioural characteristics of the predator help it to catch its prey, and the behaviour of the potential prey assists it to escape ('anti-predator behaviour').

Predator behaviour
Hunting dogs (*Lycaon pictus*) hunt in packs of up to twenty-one individuals. They have great stamina and endurance and are able to run after their prey for up to 3 km until the prey is almost exhausted. The pack begins by walking towards a herd of potential prey. They get as close as possible before the herd takes fright and runs away. It appears that no particular individual is selected as prey until the dogs begin to run, and even then the pack often divides and each dog selects and follows a different individual before they all converge on one which is usually the slowest animal in the herd. Some packs, such as those in Ngorongoro crater (Estes and Goddard 1967), allow the leader of the pack to select the prey and the rest of the pack follows the leader. There are many variations in the hunting methods of these dogs, so it is likely that each pack modifies the basic hunting methods to suit its own conditions and habitat. Eventually the prey is taken and pulled to the ground. Hunting dogs often pull the prey apart before it dies, and there is no specific killing bite as in the felids (Leyhausen 1965).

Cheetahs also catch their prey by running, but in contrast to hunting dogs, they

Table 10.13 *The prey species of lion, leopard, cheetah and hunting dog in the Serengeti National Park, Tanzania. (From Kruuk and Turner 1967.)*

	Lion	Leopard	Cheetah	Hunting dog
	n = 39	55	23	42
Prey species				
Large (500 + kg)				
Buffalo	3	—	—	—
Medium (100–350 kg)				
Zebra (adult)	10	—	—	—
Wildebeest (adult)	19	1	1	5
Hartebeest	1	—	1	—
Ostrich	2	—	—	—
Topi	—	1	—	2
Small (10–100 kg)				
Zebra (juvenile)	—	4	1	—
Grant's gazelle	2	2	—	4
Thomson's gazelle	2	15	12	27
Impala	—	9	—	1
Reedbuck	—	6	—	—
Wildebeest (juvenile)	—	2	5	3
Other	—	4	1	—
Very small (less than 10 kg)				
Hare	—	—	1	—
Thomson's gazelle (juvenile)	—	—	1	—
Other	—	9	—	—

The numbers indicate the number of kills known to be killed by each species of predator.

chase the prey at great speed (100 km/h) over a distance of up to 300 m. Cheetahs give up the chase if the prey has not been overtaken within this distance. A cheetah begins the chase by stalking so as to approach the prey, usually a small herd of Thomson's

Fig. 10.31 A pack of hunting dogs (*Lycaon pictus*) running towards a small group of wildebeest which are not, as yet, running away. This 'curiosity' or 'behaviour of fascination' is typical of many prey species when potential predators are nearby (see p. 270). (Photo: R. D. Estes.)

gazelle, as closely as possible. The cheetah appears to select a particular gazelle but it does not rush towards it until the gazelle is facing away. The gazelle usually twists and turns to evade the cheetah, and if the hunt is successful the gazelle is knocked over and grabbed by the throat. The cheetah kills its prey by strangulation, so it may take several minutes before the prey is killed (Schaller 1968).

Lions are heavily built carnivores and therefore they cannot run as fast or for as long as hunting dogs and cheetahs. A lion approaches its prey using cover to conceal its movements so that the final chase is not more than 100–150 m. The lion clutches the neck, back or flank so that the prey is dragged down and falls towards the lion. The prey is killed by suffocation and/or a neck bite. Alternatively, the prey is knocked over by the lion so that it breaks its neck in falling. Hunting behaviour is rather varied (Schaller 1972). Lions may hunt singly, although often several lions belonging to the same pride will share in the kill, or two or three lions will participate in chasing the prey. Co-operation in hunting and killing is not necessary in large felids, and any 'co-operation' may be fortuitous. Leopards habitually hunt and kill their prey by themselves.

The principal differences in hunting behaviour of six predators in the Serengeti are summarised in Table 10.14.

Anti-predator behaviour
Anti-predator behaviour, other than running away or disappearing into a subterranean burrow, is virtually non-existent in small mammal prey species. The prey of larger predators (lion, leopard, hunting dog, cheetah and hyaena) show many forms of anti-predator behaviour which include freezing, flight, attraction towards the predator, following and mild aggression. Anti-predator behaviour is correlated with the diet, prey selection and hunting methods of the predator (Kruuk 1972). Anti-predator behaviour has been studied most extensively in the species which are the staple diet of the large savanna predators.

The flight distance of Thomson's gazelle increases in relation to the importance of the gazelle as prey to the predator. The principal predators, and the flight distances elicited in gazelle by each predator, are jackal (less than 50 m), hyaena (50–100 m), lion (100–300 m), cheetah (100–500 m) and hunting dog (500 m or more) (Walther 1969). Similarly the flight distance increases when more than one predator is seen together,

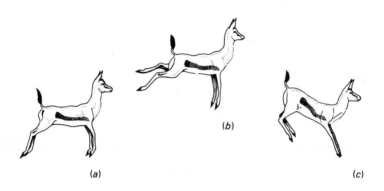

(a)   (b)   (c)

Fig. 10.32 'Stotting' by Thomson's gazelle. (Walther 1969.)

Table 10.14 *Some behavioural comparisons of Serengeti predators. (From Schaller 1972.)*

Characteristic	Lion	Leopard	Cheetah	Hyaena	Hunting dog	Jackal (2 species)
Av. weight of adult (kg)	110–180	35–55	35–55	45–60	17–20	5–9
Most commonly used habitat	Open woodlands	Thickets and riverine forest	Plains	Plains	Woodlands and plains	Woodlands (1 species) Plains (1 species)
Main activity time	Nocturnal	Nocturnal	Diurnal	Nocturnal	Diurnal	Nocturnal
Fastest running speed km/hr	60±	60±	95±	65±	70±	60±
Main hunting method for ungulates	Stalk, then fast brief rush	Stalk, then fast brief rush	Often stalk; very fast run of 200–300 m	No stalk; long chase of 1 + km	Stalk rare; long chase of 1 + km	Stalk infrequent; moderately long chase
Usual size of hunting group	Solitary or groups of 2–15	Solitary	Usually solitary	Solitary or groups of 2–30±	Groups of 2–30±	Solitary or groups of 2
Usual maximum prey size (kg)	900	60	60	300	250	5
Average hunting success for Thomson's gazelle	26%	?	70%	33%	57%	33%
Main killing method	Usually neck-bite; often strangulation	Usually neck-bite; often strangulation (?)	Strangulation	Evisceration	Evisceration	Evisceration
Maximum no. meals from prey	Several	Several	One	Usually one; occasionally several	One	Usually one
Method of catching meat	Lies by it; drags it into thicket	Hangs it in tree; drags it into thicket	None	Occasionally submerges it in water	None	Hides small pieces of meat

and therefore a pack of hunting dogs elicits the greatest flight distance. The behavioural attitudes of the predator also affect flight distance as the gait, speed of movement and number of individuals communicate the intentions of the predator(s) to the prey. When predators are not hunting, Thomson's gazelle show a strange reversal of their anti-predator behaviour; instead of fleeing, they are attracted towards the predator, especially towards cheetahs and leopards. This 'behaviour of fascination' (Walther 1969) includes looking and staring at the predator, and sometimes the predator is followed as it passes through the herd of gazelle, although there is always an 'empty circle' around the predator as the gazelle maintain a critical distance between the predator and themselves. The greatest fascination is shown towards the potentially most dangerous predators (except for packs of hunting dogs which always elicit immediate flight). When the predator(s) have been sighted but are still far away, gazelle show stotting behaviour (Walther 1969) bouncing up and down with all four legs held stiffly under the body as they move forward (Fig. 10.32). Stotting occurs most frequently at the beginning and end of flight when the gazelle are in a state of excitement, and presumably it is a communication signal between gazelle before and after flight. If a predator suddenly appears in a herd of gazelle, individuals 'explode' in all directions, making it more difficult for the predator to single out one individual which can be followed and caught. Most species in the Antelopinae and Neotraginae show stotting behaviour (Walther 1964*b*), and many prey species show some form of fascination behaviour with slight differences depending on the different sorts of predators.

Wildebeest also show curiosity towards large predators. As in Thomson's gazelle, the flight distance increases with the increasing potential danger of the predator. Lion elicit the greatest flight distance (40 m), followed by, in decreasing order, cheetah (20 m), hunting dog (20 m), hyaena (10 m) and jackal (less than 10 m). This order corresponds to the importance of the wildebeest as prey for each of the predators (Table 10.13). Wildebeest, like gazelle, do not show flight behaviour when the predators are not hunting.

Zebra form one of the main prey of lions, but they are unimportant in the diets of hunting dogs, hyaenas and cheetahs. Zebra show similar flight distances to those of wildebeest but they show far less curiosity or fear in the presence of a predator. Usually zebra stand and stare, except when being chased.

Herds of buffalo react to a predator by bunching and facing the predator so it is confronted by a solid mass of horns. This behaviour, and the size and weight of buffalo, makes adult buffalo in a herd practically immune from predation.

Despite these varied behaviour patterns towards predators, and the danger of the predator to the prey, it is surprising that the Bovidae show so little aggression towards predators. Many bovids have horns which could be used as very effective weapons, as they are in intraspecific agonistic behaviour. Thomson's gazelle sometimes attack jackals which threaten their young, and female wildebeest with calves show some aggression towards predators. Similarly, zebra families with young may show aggression and attack predators. However, aggression is not shown by single adult prey individuals when caught or injured. The importance of defence against a predator is partly related to the relative sizes of the predator and the prey; defence rarely occurs unless the prey is at least three times heavier than the predator (Schaller 1972). For example, adult elephants, rhinos and hippos, by virtue of their size, are almost immune from predation. The importance of defence is also partly related to the efficiency of the armour or weapons of the potential prey. Some mammals, for example porcupines with their quills and oryx with their rapier-like horns, are seldom preyed upon for this reason.

The relationship between predator and prey must be very finely adjusted because it is important that the prey are not continuously harassed by the mere presence of the predator, and also the predator must be capable of catching its prey with a reasonably high percentage of successful chases if it is to survive. Changes in the hunting methods of the predator which make it more successful must be offset by changes in the anti-predator behaviour of the prey. For example, hyaenas, which are the most abundant predators in grassland savannas, prey extensively on wildebeest (Kruuk 1972). If the wildebeest took flight every time a hyaena was sighted, they would not have time for feeding and all the social interactions which are essential for their survival. Therefore wildebeest take little notice of hyaenas most of the time, because they can discern behavioural differences which distinguish non-hunting hyaenas from hunting ones. Thus the behaviour patterns of wildebeest and hyaenas are well adjusted to each other. Hyaenas would have to hunt in a different way if wildebeest reacted to them as they do to other carnivores (Kruuk 1972). All predator–prey systems must work in this way if both predator and prey are to survive and co-exist.

Other interspecific interactions

Behavioural interactions between sympatric species, other than those associated with predation, are bound to occur under certain conditions. Such interactions are either neutral, or are advantageous to one or more of the species concerned, or disadvantageous to one of the species concerned.

'Chance or neutral associations' (Estes 1967) occur frequently when two or more species aggregate to feed on the same fruits, or in the same grazing area. For example, fruit bats aggregate on flowering and fruiting trees, although sometimes one species gives way when another species arrives (Baker and Harris 1959). Several species of cave-dwelling bats rest in the same cave (Fig. 10.11). Plains ungulates may intermingle when feeding in the same general area, or on a flush of new grass, and several species may come close together when drinking at a waterhole (Fig. 10.33). In these examples, there do not appear to be any particular advantages in the association, but equally there do not seem to be any particular disadvantages, and agonistic behaviour, if present, is very mild and inconsequential.

In contrast, 'positive associations' (Estes 1967) are associations or interactions which are advantageous for one (or all) of the species concerned. Baboons are often seen feeding amongst herds of Grant's and Thomson's gazelle; this association is probably mutually advantageous, and the awareness of the baboons may assist in warning the gazelle of potential danger. However, baboons sometimes kill and eat small gazelle calves, but presumably the risk of such predation must be considerably outweighed by the advantages that the gazelle gain by the presence of the baboons. Vervet monkeys and bushbuck may be seen close together (Elder and Elder 1970, Henshaw 1972), and both species probably gain advantage from their combined sensory perception. Scavengers such as jackals and hyaenas steal some of their food from large predators, which is advantageous for them but may be disadvantageous to the large predator. The opposite situation occurs in the Ngorogoro crater where lions frequently steal from hyaena kills (Kruuk 1972). Several species are characteristically seen together which indicates a positive association and not a chance encounter. For example, zebra, wildebeest, Thomson's gazelle and Grant's gazelle frequently form mixed herds of varying composition, and some rain forest primates form polyspecific bands. These bands vary in composition depending on the locality; in Gabon, *Cercopithecus nictitans*, *C. cephus* and *C. mona* frequently formed polyspecific bands (Gautier and Gautier-Hion 1969) whereas at Southern Bakundu, Cameroun,

Fig. 10.33   A 'neutral association' of large mammals at a waterhole. (Photo: Jane Burton. Copyright Bruce Coleman Ltd.)

Cercopithecus nictitans, C. erythrotis and *C. pogonias* were the most frequently associated species (Gartlan and Struhsaker 1972). Occasionally, two or more species co-exist in a burrow at the same time; *Xerus* ground squirrels and the small viverrid *Cynictis penicillata* share the same burrow system (Dorst and Dandelot 1970).

A positive association between a mammal and another vertebrate is a rare but interesting situation. Oxpecker birds (*Buphagus* spp.) perch on the back, neck and head of elephants, rhinoceroses and many species of artiodactyls and they remove the ectoparasites from the skin (Fig. 10.34). Fish of the genus *Labeo* congregate around hippopotamus resting in water, and feed on the micro-organisms and algae attached to the skin of the hippopotamus. In both these examples, the mammals and the symbionts benefit from the association.

There are two main situations when agonistic behaviour occurs between different species: (1) when predators interact with their potential prey (as described above), and (2) when one species disrupts the activities of other species without necessarily intending or causing harm. Elephants often disrupt the activities of grazing species by physically walking through a herd which is feeding, or by shaking the head while approaching other animals. Henshaw (1972) records several instances of elephants disturbing hartebeest, waterbuck and buffalo in Yankari Game Reserve in northern Nigeria to the extent that the ungulates discontinued their activities and ran away. These elephants lived mostly in a narrow strip of riparian vegetation, and their aggressive behaviour

Fig. 10.34   Oxpecker birds feeding on the back of a white rhinoceros. (Photo: C. A. Spinage.)

may have been due to the effects of overcrowding during the dry season when many ungulates moved from the open woodlands into the riparian vegetation.

Finally, there are situations where there is no direct inter-specific interaction, but rather the behaviour of one species subsequently influences the behaviour and ecology of another species. Warthogs feed on *Balanites* fruits which have been shaken down from the trees by elephants, black rhinoceros feed on *Acacia mellifora* leaves when the trees have been pushed down by elephants (Lamprey 1963, 1967) and duikers feed on fruits dropped from trees by baboons (Wilson 1966). Elephants dig waterholes in dry river beds and provide a source of water for themselves and also for other species. Burrows and holes dug by aardvarks are used as domiciles by warthogs, bat-eared foxes and hyaenas (De Vos 1969). In the grazing sequences described on p. 203 and 209, one species alters the habitat to the subsequent advantage of other species.

Chapter 11

Ecophysiology and energetics

Many environments in tropical Africa are characterised by extreme climatic conditions which fluctuate greatly from day to night, or from season to season. Temperatures may alternate between very high in the day and cold at night, water may be abundant at some seasons and very scarce at others, and food resources may fluctuate in abundance and nutritional quality. The extent and magnitude of these environmental changes depend on the locality; they are greatest in arid and dry savanna regions (annual rainfall less than 300 mm), less in moist savannas (rainfall 900 mm to 1 600 mm) and least in lowland rain forest habitats (rainfall more than 1 600 mm). African mammals, especially those living in harsh fluctuating environments, have evolved many adaptations to ensure that the individual can survive during periods of environmental stress. These include:

1. The ability to maintain the body temperature within physiologically determined limits, in spite of high or low ambient temperatures.
2. The ability to remain in water balance when free drinking water is scarce or absent.
3. The ability to survive the seasons of the year when food is in short supply, or when food is low in calories and protein.

The mechanisms of each of these adaptations vary according to the size, volume and phylogeny of each species. The most remarkable adaptations are generally found in species which live in habitats where there are high environmental stresses at some times of the year; conversely, species which live in comparatively stable habitats are less able to withstand high or low temperatures, a wide range of daily fluctuations in temperature, lack of water or reduction in food availability. This chapter describes a few selected examples to show how some species of African mammals cope with environmental extremes, and how their ecology is partly determined by variations in water availability, temperature and quality and abundance of food.

11.1 Water

During the dry season of the year in arid and dry savanna regions, free drinking water is scarce or absent, and the percentage volume of water in grasses is less than in the wet season. Many species therefore, suffer shortages of free drinking water and water in the food. Body fluids have to be conserved because a reduction of body fluids below about 80 per cent of normal is lethal for most species. In hot arid regions where water shortage is most likely to occur, the individual also has to cope with high ambient temperatures in the day time. An obvious way to cool the body is by evaporation of water from the body surface provided the individual is able to spare body fluids for this purpose.

Thus water conservation, and maintenance of a stable body temperature (T_B) are conflicting demands for an individual in hot arid environments, and the individual has to 'balance' the two demands according to its environmental and physiological conditions at any particular time. If water is scarce, many mammals can reduce their daily minimum water requirements so that the turnover rate of fluids in the body (i.e. the rate at which fluids are eliminated and then replaced) is also reduced.

Body fluids may be conserved by several means:

1. Production of concentrated urine so that only a small volume of water is lost during the elimination of urea.
2. Reduction of the volume of water in the faeces.
3. Reduction of evaporative water loss by
   (a) the ability of the individual to survive an increase in its body temperature so that water need not be used to maintain a constant body temperature;
   (b) activity rhythms and behaviour patterns which enable the individual to remain in the coolest and most moist micro-environment in its habitat.
4. The ability to withstand desiccation and reduction in the extracellular and intracellular fluids in the body.
5. The ability to locate sources of free drinking water, to change the diet as conditions require and to eat saline foods if necessary.

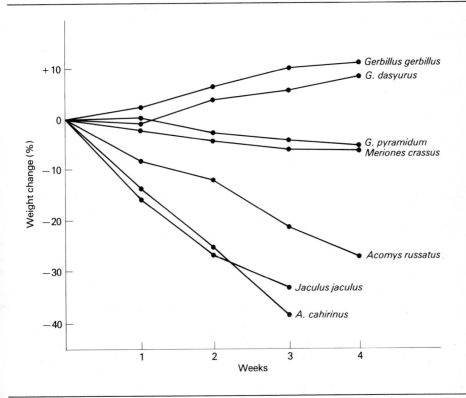

Fig. 11.1 The effects of water deprivation on the body weights of several species of arid zone rodents. During the experiment, the rodents were kept at 30 °C and 30 per cent RH, and fed on dry barley. (After Schmidt-Nielsen 1964.)

Many species which are subjected to water stress at some time of the year utilise several of these means to conserve water. The importance of any one of them varies according to the species.

Water metabolism of some rodent species in African arid regions has been well studied, and there are considerable differences in the ability of species to withstand desiccation (Shklonik and Borut 1969). Some rodents can survive for long periods without drinking. When deprived of drinking water and fed on dry barley at 30 °C and 30 per cent relative humidity (RH), *Gerbillus gerbillus* and *G. dasyurus* gained weight slowly, whereas *G. pyramidum*, *Meriones crassus*, *Acomys russatus* and *A. cahirinus* lost weight (Fig. 11.1). The ability to gain weight in the first two species reflects their ability to survive on very limited amounts of water, not to use water for evaporative cooling and to produce concentrated urine and dry faeces. Increases in the environmental temperature and decreases in relative humidity appear to reduce the ability of rodents to maintain weight when fed on dry barley in the absence of water. *Acomys cahirinus*, for example, lost 10 per cent of its body weight in 28 days when the ambient temperature (T_A) was 18–26 °C and the relative humidity (RH) was 60–75 per cent, 20 per cent of its body weight in 28 days when T_A was 26 °C and RH was 50–60 per cent, and 40 per cent of its body weight in 21 days when T_A was 30 °C and RH was 30 per cent (Fig. 11.2). The closely related *A. russatus* was better at maintaining its weight under

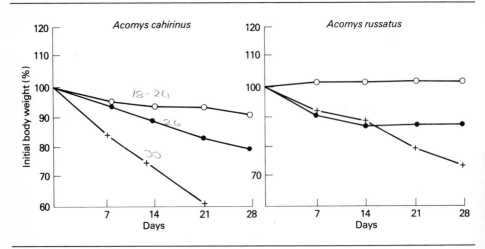

Fig. 11.2   Weight changes in (*a*) *Acomys cahirinus* and (*b*) *Acomys russatus* kept without water on a diet of dry barley at different environmental conditions. Open circles: 18–24 °C, 60–75 per cent RH. Closed circles: 26 °C, 50–60 per cent RH; + = 30 °C, 30 per cent RH. Each point represents the mean of seven mice. (After Shkolnik and Borut 1969.)

these conditions. In both species, evaporative water loss was low up to 25 °C but increased significantly at temperatures above 30 °C. Clearly these species suffer heat stress and evaporative water loss above 30 °C but they are rarely, if ever, exposed to such conditions in nature. In this respect they differ from other rodents (see below) but they are able to maintain their water balance due to two important characteristics. First, they produce an exceedingly high urea concentration in the urine (up to 4700–4800 mM/l) which is among the highest recorded for rodents, and second, they feed extensively on land snails which provide water as long as the large amounts of urea resulting from this high protein food can be eliminated (Shklonik and Borut 1969). This strategy is obviously successful since spiny mice are widely distributed, and often very common, in arid areas of Africa north of the Equator.

The sand rat (*Meriones crassus*) is another rodent species which lives in arid sandy areas of Africa north of the Equator. When deprived of water in captivity, sand rats lost up to 26 per cent of their initial weight in two weeks (Kulzer 1972). This reduced weight was maintained for up to 10 days, and then the body weight started to increase (Fig. 11.3). When free water is not available, sand rats conserve water by producing a

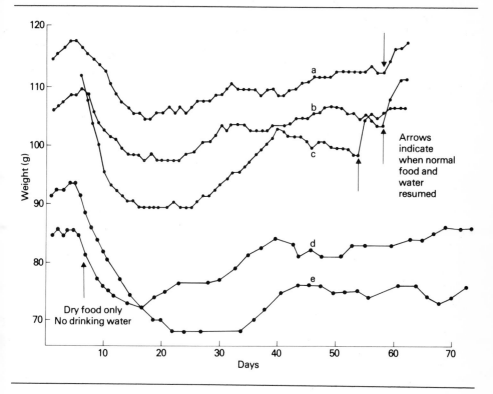

Fig. 11.3 Weight changes in *Meriones crassus* when deprived of water. This species can survive without water for many weeks; animals *a*, *b*, and *c* were given water after 50–60 days (arrows); animals *d* and *e* survived without water for 160 days. (After Kulzer 1972.)

small volume of urine which is about three times the concentration of normal urine. This species can maintain a constant weight when fed on dry seeds when $T_A = 20$–$25\,°C$ and RH = 20–40 per cent. Some other rodents have similar capacities in this respect. The jerboa (*Jaculus jaculus*) can be kept in captivity without drinking water when fed only on sunflower seeds (Happold, unpubl., Kirmiz 1962). It, too, is capable of producing a very concentrated urine (up to $4\,300\,\text{mM/l}$) if necessary (Schmidt-Nielsen 1964).

Another way of quantifying the adaptations of arid-zone rodents is to measure the amount of water which each species drinks after a period of water deprivation (Table 11.1). The species best adapted to (seasonal) absence of water do not need to drink after water deprivation; the less adapted species drink varying amounts after water deprivation and are able to survive in arid regions only because they utilise a local supply of preformed water (e.g. snails in *Acomys*, bulbs in *Jaculus* (p. 157), and saline plants in *Psammomys*.

An unusual method of maintaining water balance is illustrated by the sand rat (*Psammomys obesus*), which has the ability to feed on juicy saline plants of the family Chenopodiaceae. The distribution of sand rats in the arid regions in Africa north of the Equator is determined, to a large extent, by the presence of these plants. Sand rats are able to eliminate the excess salts in the urine which is at least as concentrated as the sap in the plants (Schmidt-Nielsen 1964). The urine is about four times as saline as sea water, and although the urea concentration is not particularly high, the urine electrolytic concentration (1 920 mEq/l) is the highest recorded from any mammalian kidney (Table 11.2). The sand rat, therefore, can utilise a source of water in arid regions because of the extreme ability of its kidney to excrete salt. It has no competition for this water supply as other sympatric species are not able to drink the saline sap of these plants.

Table 11.1 *Water consumption of arid zone rodents after one month without water at 30 °C and 30 per cent RH. (Shklonik, in Schmidt-Nielsen 1964.)*

Species	Water consumed (per cent of body weight)
Acomys cahirinus	11·38
Acomys russatus	9·26
Jaculus jaculus	4·30
Meriones crassus	0·0
Gerbillus pyramidum	0·0
Gerbillus dasyurus	0·0
Gerbillus gerbillus	0·0

Table 11.2 *Maximal urine concentrations recorded in rodents. (Schmidt-Nielsen, 1964.)*

Species	Urine urea mM/l	Urine electrolyte m Eq/l	Urine osmotic concentration Osm/l
Gerbillus gerbillus	3410	1 600	5·5*
Jaculus jaculus	4320	1 530	6·5*
Psammomys obesus	2850	1 920	6·34
White rat	2 160	760	2·9

*Estimated.

Water is conserved by the reduction of evaporative water loss and the production of concentrated urine. The kidneys of *Jaculus jaculus* and *Gerbillus gerbillus* have long renal papillae which project into the ureter; this gives maximum re-absorbtion of water in the kidney and helps to produce a concentrated urine (Schmidt-Nielsen and O'Dell 1961, Khalil and Tawfic 1963). In *Jaculus jaculus* there is a special arrangement between the cortical and juxtamedullary glomeruli which results in a large filtration area (Munkácsi and Palkovitzs 1965) and therefore the production of highly concentrated urine. Other means of conserving and obtaining water include nocturnal activity, burrowing feeding on bulbs and succulents. Further details for *Jaculus jaculus* are given in section 7.6.

The water requirements of rodents which live in mesic environments where water is usually abundant have rarely been investigated. It is unlikely that these rodents possess any special adaptations for water conservation since water is always available, in some form, in their natural habitat. Observations on several species in the rain forest zone (*Praomys tullbergi, Lophuromys sikapusi, Malacomys edwardsi*) suggest that these species require large volumes of water each day, and that water deprivation results in rapid loss of weight and finally death in 3–5 days (Happold, unpubl.).

Ungulates, like rodents, show a wide variation in their water requirements, and the methods by which water can be conserved. Most studies on ungulate water metabolism have been confined to measurements on the minimum amount of water needed for survival, the volumes of water lost in the urine and faeces and by evaporation, the rate of water turnover in the body, and how these parameters vary when water is scarce or absent. Water metabolism in East African ungulates has been reviewed by Maloiy (1973*a*).

The water requirements of ungulates vary according to the time of the year. During the wet season, free and preformed water are abundant, the climate is relatively cool and the individual does not have to lose water for evaporative cooling. In contrast, the dry season is hot during the day, water is scarce and the individual may lose considerable quantities of water due to evaporative cooling. The size of the animal, its behavioural characteristics and its ability to tolerate a change in its body temperature, determine its ability to survive in arid, or seasonally arid, habitats.

Minimum water requirements at a constant T_A of 22 °C, when demands for evaporative water loss are minimal, are shown in Table 11.3. Oryx (*Oryx gazella beisa*)

Table 11.3 *The minimum amounts of water (litres of water/100 kg body weight/day) required by some East African bovids at 22 °C and 22/40 °C. (Taylor (1968), Maloiy and Hopcraft (1971), Maloiy (1973b).)*

Species	n	Temperature	
		22 °C	22–40 °C
Thomson's Gazelle (*Gazella thomsoni*)	3	2·20	2·74
Impala (*Aepyceros melampus*)	2	2·49	2·93
Grant's Gazelle (*Gazella granti*)	3	2·08	3·86
Hartebeest (*Alcelaphus buselaphus*)	2	2·98	4·04
Oryx (*Oryx gazella*)	3	1·88	3·00
Wildebeest (*Connochaetes taurinus*)	3	2·99	4·81
Waterbuck (*Kobus ellipsiprymnus*)	3	5·98	—
Buffalo (*Syncerus caffer*)	3	3·43	4·58
Eland (*Taurotragus oryx*)	3	3·74	5·49
Dik-dik (*Madoqua* spp.)	4	5·59	7·72

are much better adapted for living in the arid zone than the other species. Waterbuck (*Kobus ellipsiprymnus*) require more water than other species of similar size, and consequently this species must always remain close to water. Dik-diks (*Madoqua* spp.) have a much greater surface area/volume ratio than the larger species, and this is reflected in their relatively higher water requirements (Maloiy 1973*b*). When these species are subjected to an alternating temperature regime of 22 °C for 12 hours and then 40 °C for 12 hours (22/40 °C), to simulate a heavy heat load during the day, the minimum water requirement is increased by up to 38 per cent.

When water is in short supply, ungulates reduce their food intake. This reduces the volume of available preformed water taken in with the food, but it also conserves water because the smaller amount of metabolic waste products (together with an increase in the urine concentration) require less loss of water in the urine and faeces. At 22 °C, and at 22/40 °C, restriction of water caused a drop in the food intake in all species which have been investigated (Table 11.4). However, when the food intake of different species

Table 11.4   *The food intake (kg food/100 kg BW/day ± SE) in some East African bovids during different conditions of temperature and water availability. (Maloiy 1973a.)*

Species	n	Ambient temperature and experimental conditions			
		22°C, water ad lib	22°C, water restricted	22/40°C, water ad lib	22/40°C, water restricted
Thomson's Gazelle (*Gazella thomsoni*)	3	2·65 ± 0·08	1·67 ± 0·04	2·56 ± 0·07	1·02 ± 0·06
Impala (*Aepyceros melampus*)	2	2·58 ± 0·06	1·99 ± 0·02	2·85 ± 0·04	2·15 ± 0·03
Grant's Gazelle (*Gazella granti*)	3	2·22 ± 0·05	1·53 ± 0·08	1·97 ± 0·08	1·51 ± 0·07
Hartebeest (*Alcelaphus buselaphus*)	2	3·18 ± 0·02	2·70 ± 0·04	2·63 ± 0·04	1·99 ± 0·02
Oryx (*Oryx gazella*)	3	2·23 ± 0·08	1·33 ± 0·05	2·25 ± 0·09	1·76 ± 0·10
Wildebeest (*Connochaetes taurinus*)	3	2·09 ± 0·07	1·67 ± 0·04	1·80 ± 0·08	1·47 ± 0·05
Waterbuck (*Kobus ellipsyprymnus*)	3	1·90 ± 0·90	1·61 ± 0·10	2·05 ± 0·09	

is compared during water restriction at these two temperatures, there are considerable differences between the species. Food intake was reduced by 2–29 per cent in Thomson's gazelle, Grant's gazelle, hartebeest and wildebeest, and it was increased in impala and oryx. Waterbuck are unable to withstand water restriction at 22/40 °C; at 40 °C they lose about 12 per cent of their body weight in 12 hours and are unable to tolerate this rate of water loss for long periods (Taylor, Spinage and Lyman 1969).

Water is lost from the body in the urine and faeces, and through evaporation by panting and sweating. The relative importance of each form of water loss depends on the species, the amount of available water and the level of heat stress during the day. During the wet season when water is abundant, ungulates produce a large volume of urine which has low osmolarity and a low urea concentration. When water is scarce, the urine is reduced in volume and increased in concentration. For example, the eland can produce urine which has twice the concentration and one half to one third the volume of 'normal' urine (Taylor and Lyman 1967) (Table 11.5). The camel also produces a concentrated urine and reduces the urine volume to about one half of normal (Schmidt-Nielsen 1964). Under some circumstances, the kidneys of ruminants re-absorb urea which is then resynthesised into protein by bacteria in the rumen (Maloiy 1973a); this serves the double purpose of conserving water and supplying the individual with additional protein. There is little information on urinary water loss and urine concentration for most species of African ungulates; this aspect of water metabolism has been studied less extensively than in rodents.

The ability of a species to reduce water loss in the faeces is also a good indication of its ability to survive periods of water shortage. Species which normally live in habitats with periodic water shortage produce relatively drier faeces, even when normally hydrated, than species which live in mesic habitats. Similarly, the ability to reduce the water content of the faeces when necessary ranges from 3 per cent in hartebeest to 69 per cent in camel (Table 11.6).

Table 11.5 *Water gain and loss (litres/100 kg body wt/day) in the eland during different conditions of temperature and water availability. (Taylor and Lyman 1967, Taylor, C. R. 1969b.)*

Conditions	Water gain				Water loss			
	Metabolic	Preformed	Drinking	Total	Faeces	Urine	Evaporation	Total
22 °C, water *ad lib*	0·32	0·21	4·85	5·38	1·74	1·76	1·89	5·39
22 °C, water restricted	0·38	0·21	3·15	3·74	1·54	0·56	1·63	3·73
22/40 °C, water *ad lib*	0·32	0·19	7·11	7·62	1·50	1·57	4·53	7·60
22/40 °C, water restricted	0·39	0·19	4·91	5·49	1·19	0·73	3·56	5·48

Evaporative water loss is the major source of water loss in most ungulates during periods of heat stress. At 22 °C, when water is abundant, all species lose some water by evaporation but the amount is doubled or trebled when a 12-hour heat load is imposed (Table 11.7). At 22 °C, when dehydrated, evaporative water loss is reduced although it increases at 22/40 °C. Evaporative water loss is always less in dehydrated animals than in hydrated ones regardless of the temperature conditions. The differences between species is partly dependent on whether there is an increase in the body temperature during the day, as a higher T_B is a means of reducing evaporative water loss (e.g. eland and oryx).

Table 11.6   *Water content of the faeces (g/100 g dry faecal matter) of some East African ruminants. (Schmidt-Nielsen et al. 1956, Taylor and Lyman 1967, Taylor, Spinage and Lyman 1969, Maloiy and Hopcraft 1971, Maloiy 1973a.)*

Species	Normal hydration	Dehydration
Camel (*Camelus dromedarius*)	109 ± 5	76 ± 2·5
Eland (*Taurotragus oryx*)	195 ± 4	160 ± 5
Waterbuck (*Kobus ellipsyprymnus*)	281 ± 15	212 ± 9
Hartebeest (*Alcelaphus buselaphus*)	140 ± 3	136 ± 2
Impala (*Aepyceros melampus*)	148 ± 4	128 ± 3
Dik-dik (*Madoqua kirki*)	94 ± 2	64 ± 2

Table 11.7   *Evaporative water loss (litres/100 kg body weight/day ± SE) during different conditions of temperature and water availability. (Taylor 1970a, Maloiy and Hopcraft 1971.)*

Species	Normal hydration		Dehydration	
	22 °C	22/40 °C	22 °C	22/40 °C
Grant's Gazelle (*Gazella granti*)	2·74 ± 0·18	4·68 ± 0·22	1·41 ± 0·07	3·25 ± 0·06
Thomson's Gazelle (*Gazella thomsoni*)	3·65 ± 0·31	6·50 ± 0·28	1·71 ± 0·10	2·38 ± 0·04
Oryx (*Oryx gazella*)	2·01 ± 0·22	3·74 ± 0·23	0·91 ± 0·07	2·15 ± 0·12
Wildebeest (*Connochaetes taurinus*)	1·36 ± 0·14	4·59 ± 0·30	1·10 ± 0·09	3·34 ± 0·07
Eland (*Taurotragus oryx*)	1·89 ± 0·29	4·53 ± 0·24	1·63 ± 0·12	3·56 ± 0·24
Buffalo (*Syncerus caffer*)	1·81 ± 0·14	4·10 ± 0·19	1·23 ± 0·09	3·07 ± 0·09
Hartebeest (*Alcelaphus buselaphus*)	2·60 ± 0·23	5·97 ± 0·18	1·45 ± 0·08	3·16 ± 0·13
Impala (*Aepyceros melampus*)	2·25 ± 0·14	3·94 ± 0·24	1·34 ± 0·06	1·92 ± 0·07

Evaporative water loss in ungulates is either cutaneous (through the sweat glands) or respiratory (through the respiratory tract and nasal passages, and often associated with deep breathing or panting). Evaporative water loss is mostly by sweating in camel, eland and waterbuck, and mostly by panting in hartebeest, wildebeest, impala, Thomson's gazelle, Grant's gazelle and oryx (Taylor, C. R. 1970*b*, 1972).

Many species of ungulates appear to be very flexible with the amount of water they can afford to lose through evaporative cooling. In dehydrated Grant's gazelle, Thomson's gazelle, oryx, wildebeest and buffalo, sweating does not begin until ambient temperatures are higher than those which initiate sweating in hydrated individuals. Panting and sweating rates were lower in dehydrated animals compared with hydrated ones, because most species can tolerate a *small* increase in body temperature during the hottest period of the day. The ability to tolerate any increase in body temperature varies greatly in different species (pp. 296–303).

The differences in water metabolism described above show that species differ in their daily water requirements and their efficiency in conserving body fluids when water is scarce. The rate of water turnover in the individual is a measure of the speed at which water passes through the body, and therefore the water requirements of the individual. The turnover rates, expressed as ml water/kg body weight/24 hours for four species, are: eland 78, wildebeest 53, hartebeest 52 and oryx 29 (Maloiy 1973*a*). These different rates indicate variations in water metabolism similar to those shown by the other methods described above.

Experiments under laboratory conditions can show the ability of a species to survive dry conditions, but do not show how the individual remains in water balance under natural conditions. Ungulates can obtain sufficient water, and reduce water loss, by daily and seasonal variations in their behaviour and ecology such as:

1. Selecting food items which contain adequate water supplies. This entails seasonal changes in diet.
2. Modification of activity times and remaining in the shade during the hottest time of the day in order to reduce heat load and evaporate water loss.
3. The ability to find moist food and water if they are available.
4. Seasonal changes in the frequency of drinking water.

Each species varies in all these characteristics, and consequently each has its typical ecological requirements and behaviour patterns. Broadly, ungulates can be divided into mesic, savanna non-migratory, savanna migratory, and arid zone species on the basis of their water metabolism and on their behaviour and ecology in relation to water availability.

The following examples illustrate the differences in water metabolism of four species of ungulates, and they show how these differences determine the habitats of each species. In semi-captive impala, the daily intake of drinking water is directly related to the water content of the food (Jarman 1973). Decrease in the water content of the food is correlated with an increase in the consumption of free drinking water. When the food contains more than 67 per cent water, impala do not require any free drinking water. They can survive on a minimum water intake of 2·5 l/100 kg body weight/day, or about 1·25 l/animal/day (Table 11.3). However, when fed on grass of known water content, and given access to drinking water under natural conditions but not exposed to direct sunlight, total daily water intake was about 3·41/100 kg/day (n = 2). In the dry season, impala do not drink each day as they are capable of drinking a large volume of water (more than one day's requirement) at each visit to a drinking place. Thus selection of suitable food, changes in the frequency of drinking and the amount drunk, changes in the pattern of activity as well as physiological considerations, enable impala to remain in water balance throughout the year without the need to migrate in the dry season.

Waterbuck can remain in water balance if they remain close to a permanent supply of drinking water. Cutaneous water loss is increased three times and respiratory rate is increased up to ten times when $T_A = 40$–$45\,°C$ in order to maintain a constant body temperature. They can reduce faecal water loss by about 25 per cent if necessary (Table 11.6), but they can not reduce urine volume or evaporative water loss if dehydrated during the hottest period of the day. Waterbuck require a regular daily intake of water to replace that lost in the urine and by evaporation (Taylor, Spinage and Lyman 1969).

Eland are very large antelopes which live in moderately dry regions. When water is available, eland drink freely but when it is scarce they can live without drinking. This is possible because of several water-obtaining and water-saving characteristics which enable them to remain in water balance (Taylor, C. R. 1969 *a*, *b*).

1. Eland feed mostly on leaves of several species of *Acacia* which contain, on average, 58 per cent water. These leaves provide the daily requirements of 5·5 l water/100 kg body weight/day in hot weather, and more than is required in cool and moderate temperatures.

2. The body temperature of eland rises as the ambient temperature increases up to 40 °C regardless of whether the individual is hydrated or dehydrated. Eland do not need to cool themselves by evaporative cooling until T_A is 40°C because they are able to 'store' heat by allowing the body temperature to increase. Therefore they save considerable quantities of body fluids. The stored heat is lost during the cool nights (see p. 297).

3. In the hottest season of the year eland do not feed between 1000 hours and 1900 hours. Instead they remain in the shade, thus reducing the heat load on the body and the necessity to lose water by evaporative cooling. Feeding at night in regions which cool rapidly after sunset, and yet are not too arid, has a further advantage. As the ambient temperature falls, the RH rises and plants which have wilted during the day absorb moisture and increase their water content. If climatic conditions are correct, water may condense to form dew which is then ingested with the food.

4. When water is scarce, urine volume is reduced to a half or a third of normal, and the concentration is doubled. There is a reduction in faecal water loss (Table 11.5).

Oryx are even better adapted for life in arid regions than are eland. They are able to obtain sufficient water for survival in the most arid regions of Africa, and many of their characteristics are similar to those of the eland but are developed to an even greater extent (Tables 11.3, 11.4 and 11.7). The oryx requires only about half as much water as the eland (Taylor, C. R. 1969a, b) so that by feeding at night, selecting the preferred food plants (mostly *Disperma* shrubs), reducing water loss in the urine and faeces, and by their ability to tolerate hyperthermia so that there is no heat gain from the environment, oryx can remain in water balance without free drinking water in extremely arid environments.

11.2   Temperature

The body temperature (T_B) of most resting mammals are normally within the range of 36–38 °C. The skin and the body extremities may become hotter or cooler than the internal 'core' temperature and there may be a daily fluctuation within narrow limits. Each species must maintain its body temperature within these limits regardless of the environmental ambient temperature (T_A). A mammal gains heat from three sources: metabolic heat from the combustion of food, radiation heat from the sun and air, and convection heat from the soil and its immediate surroundings. Heat loss (or thermal conductance) depends on body size (i.e. size/volume ratio), insulation and the difference between T_B and T_A. The methods of temperature regulation and the necessity for precise regulation varies according to the species and the environment in which it lives.

Most mammals are homeothermic because the core body temperature when the individual is resting does not normally vary more than 1–2° regardless of the ambient temperature. In contrast, other species are heterothermic because the body temperature undergoes regular daily or seasonal changes which are associated with changes in metabolic rate and body temperature. A specialised form of heterothermy is shown by a few species of large African mammals which are normally homeothermic; these species exhibit hyperthermia when the body temperature increases for a short period of time to a temperature which would be lethal for most mammals. This unusual characteristic enables large species to survive in arid regions with high daytime temperatures. Whereas homeothermic species can tolerate only a small range of body temperature, heterothermic species can tolerate a much greater range of body temperature. The actual range of body temperature is species-specific, and in heterothermic species is related to the ambient temperature of the environment (or micro-environment) where the species live. The body temperature is also related to the overall energy budget of the individual because homeothermy requires a constant expenditure of energy.

A slightly different situation occurs during strenuous exercise when the body temperatures of large homeothermic mammals may increase by as much as 4–7° for short periods of time without ill effects. Large carnivores, for example hunting dogs and cheetahs, have body temperatures as high as 44 °C when running. After exercise, the body temperature returns to normal due to evaporative heat loss and changes in activity patterns and behaviour (see below). It is likely that most large mammals can survive a rise in body temperature of 4–7 ° (due to either exercise or increased ambient temperature) provided it returns to 'normal' in a limited period of time (C. R. Taylor, pers. comm.).

The variety of African mammals and climatic conditions has resulted in many different strategies for regulating the body temperature:

1. When the ambient temperature increases or decreases beyond physiologically tolerable limits, some species shelter in a more equable microclimate (e.g. caves, burrows, under vegetation).
2. Behaviour and activity patterns reduce the effects of stress resulting from high or low ambient temperatures, e.g. times of rest, movement into water, activity cycles, seasonal and daily changes in behaviour and activity.
3. Some species can tolerate very high ambient temperatures (40 °C or more) by allowing the body temperature to rise above normal for several hours at a time. (This has the further advantage of reducing water loss through evaporative cooling, and is in contrast to the typical homeothermic condition.)
4. Other species can tolerate a widely fluctuating body temperature which changes in relation to the ambient temperature. This is most evident when the ambient temperature is low; some African mammals enter torpor or aestivation, and have considerably reduced metabolic rates at low ambient temperatures.
5. Excess load is usually dissipated by evaporative water loss, either by sweating (cutaneous evaporation) or by panting (respiratory evaporation) provided that there is an adequate supply of water and body fluids.
6. The density and colour of the hair or fur determine the amount of heat which is absorbed through the body surface. It also regulates heat loss by thermal conductance away from the body surface.
7. Many species have emergency methods of cooling the body (salivation, licking the fur, exposing the maximum body surface to the surrounding air).

Mammals normally combine several of these strategies to regulate their body temperature, and the physiological and environmental conditions at any particular time decide which strategy or strategies are utilised to the maximum extent. Desert rodents, bats, bathyergid rodents and ungulates illustrate the range of strategies which are used, and show how size, activity patterns and environmental requirements modify the methods of temperature regulation. In all mammals the methods of temperature regulation are closely associated with the availability of water (pp. 274–284) and it is often difficult to discuss temperature regulation independently from water metabolism.

Rodents

Small rodents which live in hot regions of Africa could be exposed to daytime air temperatures of up to 45 °C and surface soil temperatures up to 70°. Maintenance of a

T_B of 36–38 °C under these conditions would be possible only if rodents had a very high lethal T_B, or if they could tolerate hyperthermia, or if they could afford to use large volumes of water for evaporative cooling. There is no evidence that rodents of hot regions have a higher lethal body temperature than other mammals of similar size: water is normally scarce and there is insufficient for evaporative cooling in arid regions and seasonally hot dry areas. However, nocturnal activity, burrowing into the soil and living in rocky crevices enables rodents to avoid the extremes of daytime temperatures (Fig. 7.11). Experiments on small rodents have shown that most rodents rely on behavioural characteristics to maintain a constant body temperature.

Meriones crassus lives in the arid sandy regions of northern Africa, and maintains a T_B of 36 ± 0.8 °C when T_A is 18–25 °C (Kulzer 1972). When *Meriones* are active, their body temperature may rise to 39 °C. However, when exposed to an ambient

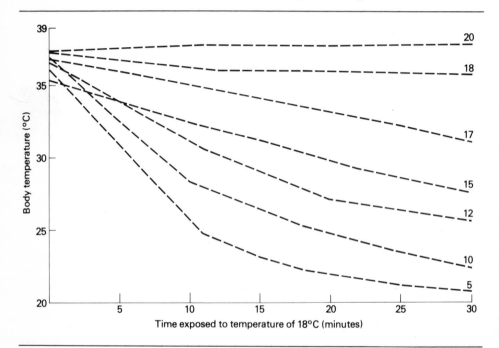

Fig. 11.4   The body temperatures of young *Meriones crassus* when exposed to an ambient temperature of 18 °C for 30 minutes. The age in days of each individual is indicated on the right of the graph. The ability to thermoregulate improves with age; it is least good at five days old (and younger) and is fully developed by twenty days old. (After Kulzer 1972.)

temperature of 44 °C for one hour, the body temperature increases to 42–43 °C. Salivation occurs when T_A is 37 °C or above, and saliva is licked over the fur so that the body temperature is reduced by evaporative cooling. This is an emergency measure which is used only when the body temperature approaches the lethal limit. When overheated, *Meriones* stretch the body and legs to give a large surface area for evaporative cooling. At low ambient temperatures (5 °C), *Meriones* curl into a sleeping position, but they do not aestivate or enter torpor as the body temperature remains at 36–38 °C. Temperature regulation in *Meriones* (and most other small rodents) is undeveloped at birth, but fully developed by about 3 weeks of age when the young become independent (Figs. 11.4, 11.5).

A smiliar pattern of temperature regulation has been observed in *Acomys cahirinus* (Shlonik and Borut 1969) (Fig. 11.6). When the ambient temperature is 10–30 °C, the body temperature is maintained at 36–38 °C. At low temperatures (5 °C), there is a fall in the body temperature of some individuals to 35 °C, and at high temperatures (35–40 °C), the body temperature rises to 41 °C. The deaths of some individuals when the ambient temperature is 40–45 °C indicates that this temperature is close to the lethal limit of the species. *Acomys russatus* show less ability to regulate the body temperature precisely, and they maintain a T_B of 36–38 °C only when T_A is 22–35 °C (Shklonik and Borut 1969) (Fig. 11.6). Hyperthermia occurs when T_A is 32·5 °C in *A. cahirinus*, and when T_A is 35 °C in *A. russatus*. Both species show similar behaviour to *Meriones* at high temperatures; they lie on the abdomen with the legs outstretched and salivate copiously.

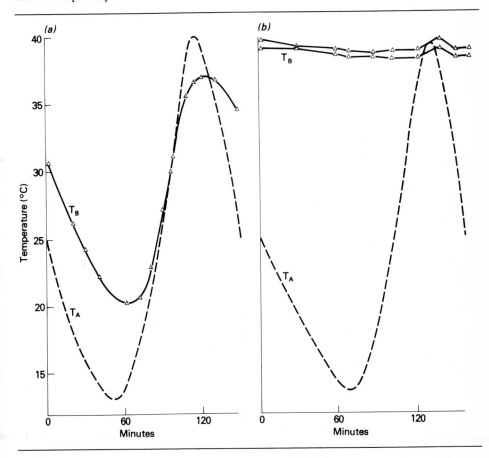

Fig. 11.5 The effects of low and changing temperatures on the body temperatures of young *Meriones crassus*. (*a*) At seven days old the body temperature fluctuates greatly and tends to follow the ambient temperature. (*b*) At 23 days old, steady body temperature is maintained regardless of the fluctuations of the ambient temperature. (After Kulzer 1972.)

Jaculus deserti and *J. orientalis* have a T_B of 37 ± 0.9 °C when T_A is 20–25 °C (Hooper and Hilali 1972). The body temperature is maintained at 36–38 °C when T_A is 0–33 °C, but when the ambient temperatures rises to 40 °C, T_B increases to 44 °C, which

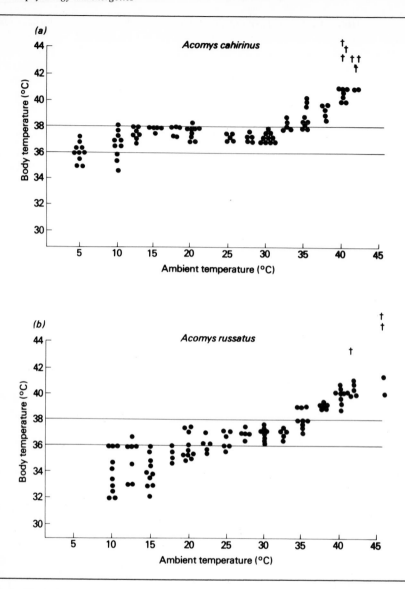

Fig. 11.6 The body temperature of (*a*) *Acomys cahirinus* and (*b*) *Acomys russatus* at different ambient temperatures. Crosses indicate animals which died. These graphs show that *Acomys cahirinus* maintains a more constant body temperature over a wider range of ambient temperatures than does *Acomys russatus*. (After Shkolnik and Borut 1969.)

appears to be the lethal limit of both species (Fig. 11.7). At low and high temperatures jerboas behave in characteristic ways. At low temperatures, they curl their bodies with the head tucked under the abdomen, retract the hindfeet under the body and erect the hairs. Prolonged cool temperatures of 5–10 °C in the laboratory and under natural conditions results in torpidity in *J. orientalis*; the body temperature drops to 9–11 °C, but it returns to normal again when the ambient temperature returns to 15–17 °C (Hilali and Veillat 1975). At high temperatures, they are restless at first and later show

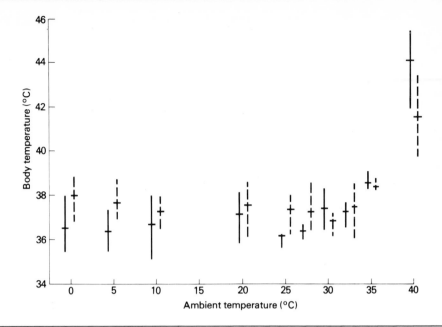

Fig. 11.7 The body temperatures of *Jaculus orientalis* (solid line) and *Jaculus deserti* (broken line) at different ambient temperatures. The mean and range of body temperature of eight animals is indicated for each ambient temperature. (After Hooper and Hilali 1972.)

behaviour similar to that of *Meriones* under similar conditions. The almost naked tail and hindfeet become red in colour due to increased blood flow and this probably increases heat loss. *Jaculus jaculus* shows similar behavioural characteristic (see section 7.6) and there is some evidence that this species also enters torpor because the body temperature drops to 11–13 °C during prolonged cool weather (Petter 1955).

The arid zone rodents of Africa regulate their body temperatures in similar ways to small rodents in other dry hot areas of the world. However, there is virtually no information on temperature regulation of rodents found in less arid and mesic environments in Africa. Preliminary studies (Happold, unpubl.) on several species of savanna and lowland rain forest indicate that these rodents can maintain a constant body temperature over a greater range of ambient temperatures than are encountered in their natural environments, and that the lethal limit is similar to that of other small rodents (40–44 °C). Some genera (*Lophuromys*, *Lemniscomys*, *Hybomys*) are partially diel-active and may be exposed to temperatures which approach the lethal limit. Normally, however, these species are exposed to high temperatures for only a few minutes at a time (so heat stress is minimal), and/or water is freely available for evaporative water loss if necessary.

Several species of large rodents are diel-active. They are exposed to high temperatures at the hottest times of the day, although they may be sheltered in the shade of trees (squirrels) and long grass (cane rats), or activity is alternated with rest periods in a cooler microclimate (ground squirrels). No information is available on temperature regulation in those species although their larger bulk (and therefore smaller surface/volume ratio) enables them to absorb a larger heat load without ill effects compared with small rodents.

Aestivation is a rare characteristic in tropical African rodents probably because few habitats (except high mountain areas and arid regions in the cool season) experience low environmental temperatures for long periods. Partial aestivation when the body temperature falls to 32 °C has been recorded in *Gerbillus campestris* and *Pachyuomys duprasi* (Petter 1955). The 'fat mouse' (*Steatomys*) appears to have a cycle of daily temperature fluctuations which are related to ambient temperature. The body temperature falls to about 14 °C without any adverse effects on the individual, and normal T_B is regained quickly when the ambient temperature rises to 30–36 °C. The body temperature remains at 33–34 °C when the animal is active, which is lower than that of other rodents of similar size. *Steatomys* usually have large deposits of fat which can be used to provide energy and metabolic heat during the dry season. Reduction of the body temperature, associated with fat deposits, is one way of surviving periods of reduced food resources and unfavourable climate.

Bats

The bats show two distinct methods of temperature regulation; Megachiroptera are homeothermic*, whereas Microchiroptera show varying degrees of heterothermy depending on the species and the climatic conditions (Kulzer 1965). Both Mega- and Microchiroptera show fluctuations in their T_B during a 24-hour period, although the fluctuations for microchiroptera are much greater than those of megachiroptera (Fig. 11.8, Table 11.8). The body temperature of microchiroptera is at its lowest during the daytime when the bats are resting. In experimental conditions, when T_A is 23–25 °C,

*The only known exceptions are two very small species (less than 30 g) from New Guinea which are heterothermic (Bartholomew *et al.* 1970).

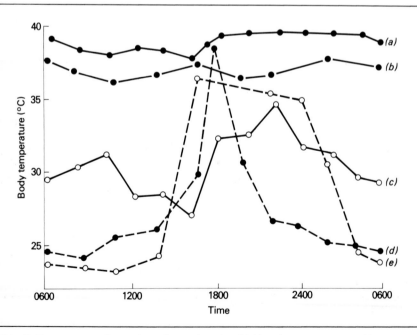

Fig. 11.8 Daily temperature fluctuations of several species of African bats at constant ambient temperature (23–26°C). (*a*) *Rousettus aegyptiacus*, (*b*) *Epomophorus anurus*, (*c*) *Rhinopoma microphyllum*, (*d*) *Tadarida condylura* and (*e*) *Eptesicus fuscus*. (After Kulzer 1965.)

Table 11.8 *Maximum and minimum body temperatures of several species of African bats during a 24-hour period. The actual time at which each species attains its maximum and minimum temperature is very varied. (From Kulzer 1965.)*

Species	T_A (°C)	T_B (max) (°C)	T_B (min) (°C)	T_B (max) less T_B (min)	T_B (min) less T_A
Rousettus aegyptiacus	27	39·0	34·9	4·1	7·9
Epomophorus anurus	24	37·5	36·0	1·5	12·0
Tadarida condylura	23	36·5	23·2	13·3	0·2
Tadarida pumila	23	38·7	33·0	5·7	10·0
Rhinopoma microphyllum	25	33·8	27·0	6·8	2·0
Rhinopoma hardwickei	25	34·3	27·6	7·6	2·6
Asellia tridens	26	38·5	33·0	5·5	7·0

the body temperature falls almost to the ambient temperature. Body temperature rises during the late afternoon prior to nocturnal activity; this rise is spontaneous and is not regulated by the ambient temperature. The energy requirements of microchiroptera are reduced when the body temperature is lowered. This is especially important in small species which would have to expend relatively large amounts of energy due to their high surface/volume ratio if they attempted to maintain a constant body temperature. Energy loss is reduced by sheltering in caves, hollow trees and holes where the ambient temperature is comparatively stable and usually lower than that of the air. However, Microchiroptera do not necessarily have to enter torpor: some (non-African) species show only small daily fluctuations in body temperature which are similar to those of Megachiroptera (Morrison and McNab 1967). There is great variation in the ability of microchiroptera to regulate the body temperature which is probably related to other aspects of the ecology of each species.

Rousettus aegyptiacus and *Epomophorus anurus* (Megachiroptera) maintain a T_B of 35–39 °C when T_A is 0–30 °C (Kulzer 1965) (Fig. 11.9). Probably this degree of homeothermy is typical for most Megachiroptera. *Rousettus* can only survive exposure to low temperatures (5–10 °C) for short periods of time (Kulzer 1963). At first, it maintains its normal body temperature, but after several hours T_B gradually falls (Fig. 11.12), and the individual dies when T_B is 15 °C. *Rousettus* have no mechanisms for increasing the body temperature if the cool conditions continue, but body temperature returns to normal after artificially rewarming or exposure to a warm ambient temperature. At low temperatures, *Rousettus* shiver and increase the respiratory rate as do all other homeothermic mammals. They become inactive, but not torpid. Hypothermia is less likely, and is delayed, in individuals which are adequately fed, and in adults compared with young individuals (Kulzer 1963). At high ambient temperature (40 °C), *Rousettus* increase their evaporative water loss by three to four times that at 25–30 °C (Laburn and Mitchell 1975). Under these conditions, *Rousettus* show several behavioural characteristics associated with cooling the body including open-mouthed panting, salivation, licking the body and lowering of the testes. Under normal conditions *Rousettus* are not exposed to such high ambient temperatures as they shelter in caves; similarly many of the smaller solitary and non-gregarious species which hang from branches and are shaded by leaves are not exposed to particularly high ambient temperatures during the daytime. In contrast, *Eidolon helvum* roosts in large colonies in the higher branches of dead trees and is exposed to high ambient temperatures for several hours, especially on cloudless days. This species must either have a very efficient mechanism for dissipating heat or it must rely on a higher rate of evaporative cooling than in other fruit bats. There is little information on how *Eidolon* regulates its body temperature, except that it has a T_B of 34·4–39·1 °C when T_A is

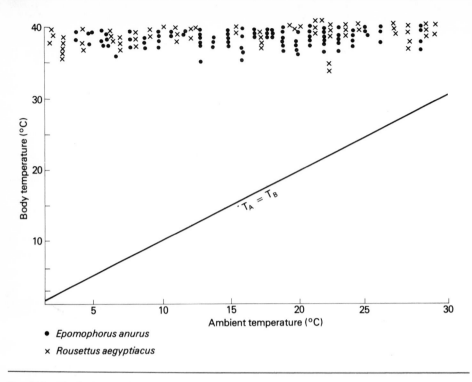

Fig. 11.9 The body temperatures of the fruit bats *Rousettus aegyptiacus* and *Epomophorus anurus* at different environmental temperatures. (Adapted from Kulzer 1963.)

4·5–38·0 °C, spreads its wings and pants during heat stress, and shivers when T_A is 13–15 °C (Kulzer, pers. comm.).

The body temperature of most Microchiroptera which live in tropical and subtropical regions falls with decreasing T_A (Fig. 11.10) but when T_A is 15–20 °C they exhibit an 'alarm reaction' (Kulzer 1965), or stress response. This results in spontaneous elevation of the body temperature associated with an increase in the metabolic rate which is maintained for as long as possible, although extended exposure to cool temperatures leads eventually to hypothermia and death. Hypothermic individuals of tropical microchiroptera are not able to warm up spontaneously or after stimulation, but only when the ambient temperature increases. These species do not show the deep torpor which is characteristic of related species in temperate latitudes.

Species in the families Rhinolophidae and Vespertilionidae show a different reaction to cold temperatures. They can enter torpor even in the tropics when the weather is cool, and their body temperature falls as the ambient temperature falls so that T_B is 1–8 °C above T_A (Fig. 11.11). At low temperatures, species in these families are lethargic but do not enter deep torpor as do some bats of temperate regions. Kulzer (1965) considers that the ability to enter torpor was necessary in order for tropical microchiroptera to enter and colonise the cool temperate zone. These two families comprise the majority of bats in temperate regions to the north of Africa, whereas the other families of African bats which do not enter torpor live only within the tropical and subtropical regions.

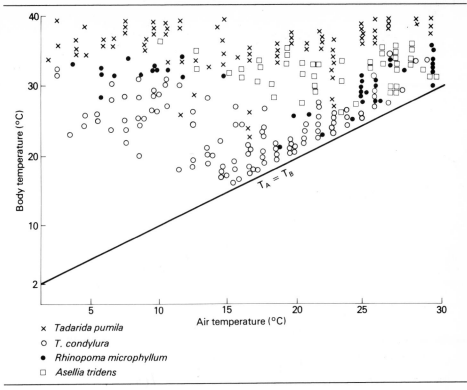

× *Tadarida pumila*
○ *T. condylura*
● *Rhinopoma microphyllum*
□ *Asellia tridens*

Fig. 11.10 The body temperatures of microchiroptera at different environmental temperatures. – *Asellia tridens, Rhinopoma microphyllum, Tadarida condylura, Tadarida pumila.* (Adapted from Kulzer 1965.)

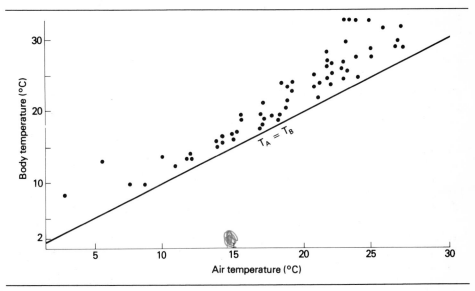

Fig. 11.11 The body temperatures of *Pipistrellus pipistrellus* (Vespertilionidae) at different environmental temperatures. (Adapted from Kulzer 1965.)

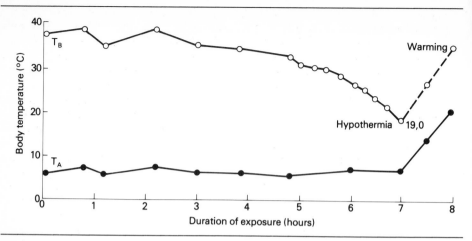

Fig. 11.12   The body temperature of *Rousettus aegyptiacus* during prolonged exposure to a low ambient temperature (5 °C). A fairly constant body temperature is maintained for the four hours, but there is a gradual fall in body temperature to 19 °C during the following three hours. Body temperature increases again as ambient temperature rises. (After Kulzer 1963.)

In summary, the chiroptera exhibit three strategies of temperature regulation:

1. Homeothermy over a wide range of ambient temperatures with no torpor or lethargy (most Megachiroptera).
2. Moderate heterothermy, with an 'alarm reaction' at cool temperatures so the body temperature does not vary greatly and a moderate metabolic rate is maintained. Slight lethargy occurs at cool temperatures (most tropical and subtropical Microchiroptera).
3. Definite heterothermy in which body temperature falls with decreasing ambient temperature although the body temperature is always at least a degree higher than the ambient temperature. Torpor and lethargy occur at cool temperatures (Rhinolophidae and Vespertilionidae).

With the possible exception of *Eidolon helvum* and microchiroptera which roost in the roofs of houses, African bats are rarely exposed to high ambient temperatures because of their behaviour and ways of life. More probably, arid, dry savanna and montane species are exposed to low ambient temperatures at night during some season of the year. The net results of these three strategies, as far as African species are concerned, is that all strategies allow bats to live in warm tropical regions. Strategy 3 is most suitable in habitats which are always or seasonally cool; strategy 1, and, to a lesser extent, strategy 2 are suitable only in habitats which are continuously warm. The situation is, in fact, more complex than this as migrations, availability of food resources and domiciles must all be considered in order to understand the distribution of each species. Certainly, the ability to regulate the body temperature, or the lack of it, is partly responsible for the major patterns of distribution of the higher taxa of bats.

Fossorial rodents

Fossorial mammals, as might be expected, have rather unusual mechanisms for thermoregulation because they live mostly, or entirely, below ground level in a relatively non-fluctuating microclimate. *Tachyoryctes splendens, Heliophobius argenteo-*

cinereus and *Heterocephalus glaber* are three spp. of rodents in the families Rhizomyidae and Bathyergidae which live in East Africa. Each has a slightly different distribution related to the annual rainfall and the nature of the soil where they make their burrows. Temperatures within the burrows probably remain fairly constant throughout the year, although differences occur between individual burrows depending on altitude, depth of the burrow and soil type. In March, the average temperatures were 23°C (range 21–25) in *Tachyoryctes* burrows, 26°C (range 23–27) in *Heliophobius* burrows, and 30°C (29–30) in *Heterocephalus* burrows (McNab 1966). Relative humidities were 90–100 per cent in *Heterocephalus* burrows; no data is available for the burrows of the other species althouth they are likely to be similar.

Tachyoryctes and *Heliophobius*, both of which have a dense covering of fur, show well developed homeothermy (McNab 1966). When T_A is 10–30 °C, T_B is 36 °C in *Tachyoryctes* and 35 °C in *Heliophobius* (Fig. 11.13). When T_A is 35 °C and above, both species show hyperthermia; T_B rises to 38 °C in *Tachyoryctes* and to 37 °C in *Heliophobius*, and the lethal T_A is 35–37 °C in *Tachyoryctes* and 37·5–38·5 °C in *Heliophobius*. The average body temperatures and the lethal temperatures are low compared with those of other small mammals.

In contrast, *Heterocephalus* has a completely naked skin. It is heterothermic, and the body temperature is a few degrees above ambient temperature when T_A is 10–30 °C (Fig. 11.13). At low temperatures, *Heterocephalus* is lethargic and its body is stiff. The

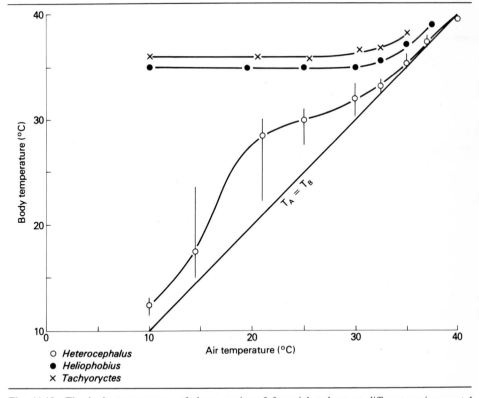

○ *Heterocephalus*
● *Heliophobius*
× *Tachyoryctes*

Fig. 11.13 The body temperatures of three species of fossorial rodents at different environmental temperatures. – *Tachyoryctes* (Rhizomyidae), *Heliophobius* (Bathyergidae), *Heterocephalus* (Bathyergidae) (McNab 1966). Each point represents the mean body temperature at each ambient temperature; range of readings is shown for *Heterocephalus*.

fall in body temperature is not completely linear, as *Heterocephalus* shows an attempt at homeothermy when T_A is 25–30 °C. The lethal temperature of this species is 39–40 °C and is higher than for the preceding species. *Heterocephalus* does not increase its body temperature when T_A is 30 °C or above to the same extent as does *Tachyoryctes* and *Heliophobius*, and is therefore better at tolerating higher burrow temperatures than these species (cf. burrow temperatures). The characteristics of temperature regulation in *Heterocephalus* is mostly due to its small size, poor insulation and high average burrow temperatures.

It is also of interest that these fossorial rodents have lower metabolic rates than might be expected for their sizes (McNab 1966): 84 per cent in *Tachyoryctes*, 76 per cent in *Heliophobius* and 40 per cent in *Heterocephalus*, and that they have higher rates of heat loss than expected: 118 per cent in *Tachyoryctes*, 121 per cent in *Heliophobius* and 281 per cent in *Heterocephalus*. The combination of these two sets of characteristics results in the typical body temperatures and extent of homeothermy in each species. Emergency cooling, if the ambient temperature becomes too high, is hampered by the high relative humidities in the burrows. None of these species appears to sweat or pant. *Tachyoryctes* and *Heliophobius* salivate and spread saliva on the fur when T_A is 30 °C or above, but when the atmosphere is saturated, there is no way of reducing the body temperature. This probably explains the rapid rise in body temperature when T_A is 32 °C and above. *Heterocephalus* does not sweat, pant or salivate, and its emergency temperature regulation is probably associated with the rapid conductance of heat from its poorly insulated body. The lack of evaporative cooling obligates all three species to live in habitats where ambient temperatures are fairly constant and do not rise above 32–34 °C. Similarly, the typical average body temperatures and upper lethal temperatures have been modified to conform with the requirements imposed by the environment and way of life (McNab 1966).

Large mammals – Artiodactyla

Unlike the small species, large mammals are unable to escape from the high ambient temperatures during the day. Consequently they stand a much greater chance of overheating; this is avoided or minimised by several characteristics which vary in their relative importance for each species.

1. The size of the individual determines the rate at which it gains heat from its surroundings. Small species (e.g. gazelles) gain heat (and also lose heat) more rapidly than large species.
2. Most species maintain their body temperature within confined limits, but others allow it to rise during the hottest period of the day without apparent ill-effects. Maintenance of a constant body temperature entails the loss of evaporative water, whereas hyperthermia is a means of saving body fluids.
3. Heat may be lost either by panting (respiratory evaporation) or by sweating (cutaneous evaporation), or by a combination of both forms of evaporative water loss. The exact means of heat loss is species specific.
4. Lack of water and dehydration of the body fluids affects the methods and precision of temperature regulation. Dehydrated individuals, in comparison with hydrated individuals, generally have a higher tolerance of increased body temperature, do not sweat so freely and do not respire so quickly.
5. The density and colour of the fur affects the absorbtion and reflectivity of radiant heat. Thick fur prevents rapid heating of the skin, but it also prevents rapid heat loss from the skin surface. Reflectivity and radiation of heat dissipates much of the effective heat load of the body.

There are two principal strategies of temperature regulation in African ungulates although many species show intermediate forms of temperature regulation (Taylor, C. R. 1970*a*):

1. Some species allow their body temperature to rise (slowly or quickly depending on the species) during the the day if dehydrated. They are able to tolerate hyperthermia when ambient temperature rises above the body temperature (i.e. when heat flows from the environment to the body), and the 'stored heat' is lost during the night. Water loss due to evaporation is minimal as there is no attempt to maintain a constant body temperature. If water is freely available, these species do not necessarily exhibit hyperthermia, and therefore their temperature regulation depends on whether or not they need to conserve water.
2. Other species maintain a more or less constant body temperature regardless of the ambient temperature but at the expense of losing large volumes of evaporative water.

However, during exercise the body temperatures of most of these herbivores rises to 44–45 °C for short periods of time. When the body temperature is high, the temperature of the blood going to the brain is regulated independently by a special cooling mechanism. This mechanism has been investigated in detail in gazelles (Taylor 1972) and is likely to be similar in other herbivores.

Thermoregulation mechanisms have been investigated in seven species (eland, oryx, Grant's gazelle, Thomson's gazelle, wildebeest, hartebeest, buffalo) and these species exemplify the various methods listed above.

The eland is a very large ungulate which lives in dry savanna regions where it is exposed to a high heat load during the day. The eland allows its body temperature to fluctuate; in the early morning it is as low as 33·9 °C and it may rise to 41 °C at the hottest period of the day (Fig. 11.14). Because the increase in body temperature is slow due to the large size of the eland, the highest body temperature is not reached until the hottest period of the day is over and when the ambient temperature is falling. When T_A is above 40–45 °C, eland maintain a T_B of 41 °C mostly by cutaneous water loss. Although sweating begins at 32–34 °C, only small volumes of water are lost; but sweating increases four to five times when T_A is 38–40 °C (Finch 1972). There is also an increase in the respiratory rate but water loss by this means is relatively unimportant (Fig. 11.15). The ability to tolerate hyperthermia enables eland to withstand high ambient temperatures without expending evaporative water except at very high ambient temperatures. Under natural conditions, eland rest in the shade during the hottest time of the day so that heat stress is reduced; this, in turn, keeps the skin temperature low, and prevents increases in sweating and in the respiratory rate. These remarkable adaptations allow eland to live in very hot climates where water is often scarce.

Oryx live in regions which are even more arid than those of the eland. Their methods of thermoregulation are similar to those of the eland except that when dehydrated (probably a common occurrence in arid regions), oryx allow their body temperature to rise so that it is *always* higher than the ambient temperature (Taylor 1969) (Fig. 11.15). The difference between T_A and T_B is always large enough that the oryx can lose metabolic heat (as well as heat derived from the environment) by conduction and radiation without loss of evaporative water. Oryx do not seek shade in the middle of the day and they appear to be able to withstand a T_A of 45 °C for at least 8 hours (Taylor 1969*a, b*). Undoubtedly the reflectivity of the pale coloured fur reduces absorbtion of radiant heat. The ability to survive such a degree of hyperthermia prevents the loss of large volumes of evaporative water which would otherwise be lost

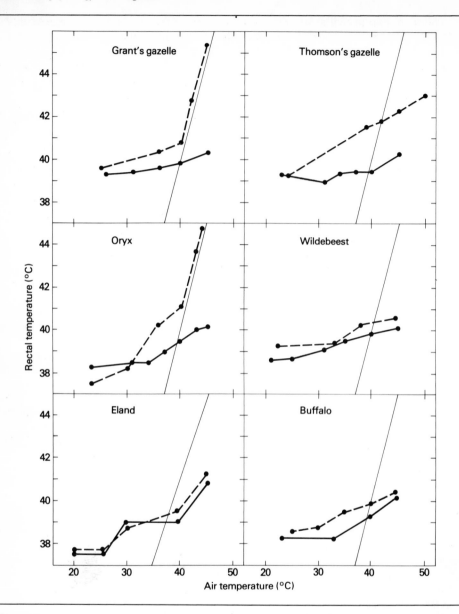

Fig. 11.14   Body temperatures of hydrated (solid lines) and dehydrated (broken lines) ungulates at different environmental temperatures. Waterbuck and buffalo cannot tolerate hyperthermia so in both hydrated and dehydrated individuals T_B remains fairly constant as T_A increases; this requires evaporative water loss. Eland can tolerate hyperthermia to a limited extent, so T_B rises when T_A is higher than T_B in both hydrated and dehydrated individuals. In dehydrated Grant gazelle and Oryx (and Thomson's gazelle to a lesser extent) T_B equals T_A when $T_A = 40°C$ or above. This figure should be interpreted in conjunction with Figs. 11.16 and 11.17. (After Taylor, C. R. 1969*b*, 1970*b*.)

by evaporative cooling – a condition which could not occur due to the shortage of water in arid regions. These adaptations enable oryx (and probably addax) to live in regions which are more arid than can be tolerated by other species of Artiodactyl.

Grant's gazelle live in hot dry savanna. The body temperature is maintained at 39–40 °C when T_A is 25–45 °C provided the animal is hydrated (Fig. 11.14). However, when dehydrated, the body temperature rises so that it is always slightly above the ambient temperature when T_A is 40–45 °C, so therefore there is no heat flow into the body. Thus Grant's gazelle are able to remain in a hot climate without the necessity for excessive water loss. The respiratory rate and the respiratory water loss increases rapidly when T_A rises above 35 °C (Fig. 11.16). Dehydrated individuals respire at about one seventh the rate of hydrated ones when T_A is 40 °C or above, but as they show hyperthermia they can survive in hot climates even when water is scarce. Measurements of water loss when T_A is 40 °C and water is limited, have shown that Grant's gazelle lose more water (Table 11.7) than Thomson's gazelle which live in generally wetter habitats. However, when exposed to ambient temperatures of 45 °C

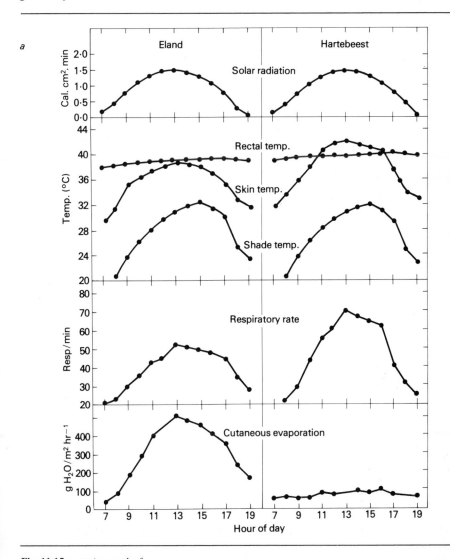

Fig. 11.15 *caption overleaf.*

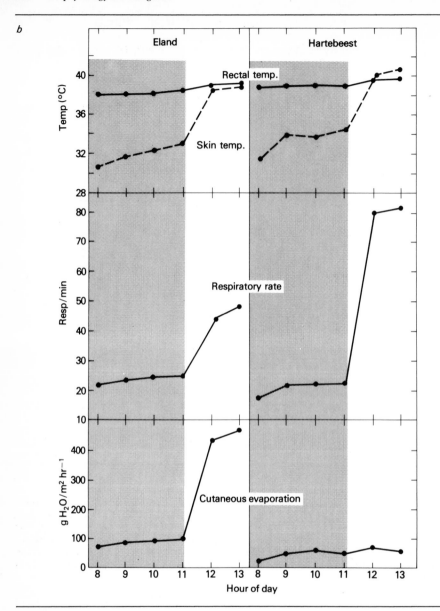

Fig. 11.15 Thermoregulation in eland and hartebeest. (*a*) The relationships of skin and rectal temperatures, respiration rate and cutaneous evaporation to solar radiation and shade temperature. (*b*) The effects of shade followed by solar radiation on skin and rectal temperatures, respiration rate and cutaneous evaporation. These graphs show how eland rely mostly on cutaneous evaporation to maintain a steady body temperature, whereas hartebeest rely mostly on respiratory evaporation associated with increased respiratory rate, high skin temperatures and very low cutaneous evaporation. (After Finch 1972*b*.)

for a short time, the body temperature of Grant's gazelle increases to 46 °C so that extensive evaporative water loss is avoided. Under similar conditions, Thomson's gazelle have a T_B of 42·5 °C so evaporative water loss is essential. As arid zones often

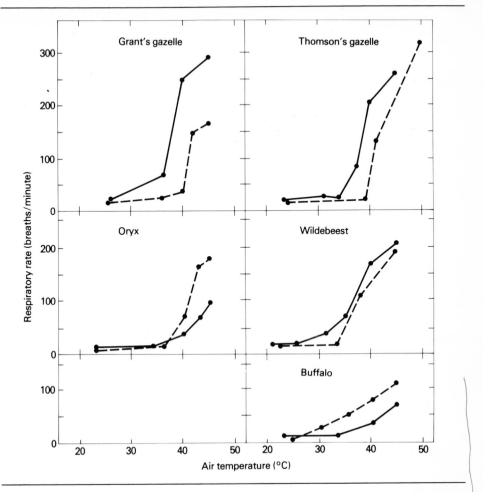

Fig. 11.16 Respiratory rates of hydrated (solid lines) and dehydrated (broken lines) ungulates at different environmental temperatures. In Grant's gazelle, Thomson's gazelle and wildebeest, hydrated individuals respire more quickly at any temperature compared with dehydrated individuals, because they lose heat mostly by respiratory evaporation. Oryx and buffalo mostly lose heat by cutaneous evaporation, and therefore an increased respiratory rate is not required in hydrated animals as the ambient temperature rises. If dehydrated, oryx and buffalo supplement cutaneous evaporation with respiratory evaporation. (After Taylor 1970*b*.)

have daytime sunshine temperatures of at least 45 °C, Grant's gazelle can survive in such regions on limited water resources, whereas Thomson's gazelle cannot (Taylor 1972).

Thomson's gazelle, like Grant's gazelle described above, maintain a T_B of 39–40 °C provided the individual is hydrated. When dehydrated, the body temperature rises. Thomson's gazelle cannot tolerate hyperthermia to the same extent as Grant's gazelle, and when T_A is 42 °C there is a sudden rise in the respiratory rate and respiratory water loss to prevent any further rise in body temperature (Taylor, C. R. 1970*a*, *b*). The pattern of respiratory rates is very similar to that of Grant's gazelle, but the main difference between the two species is that water loss in dehydrated animals is much higher in Thomson's gazelles when T_A is 45 °C or above (Fig. 11.16) because they

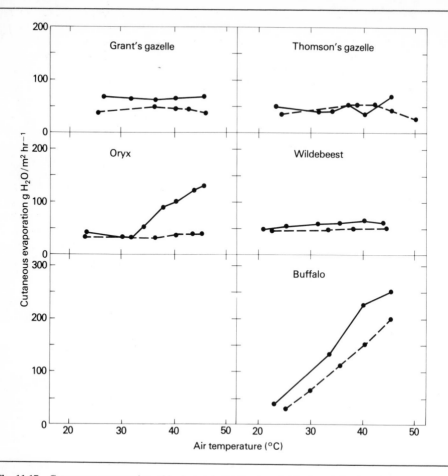

Fig. 11.17 Cutaneous evaporation of hydrated (solid lines) and dehydrated (broken lines) ungulates at different environmental temperatures. Oryx and buffalo mostly use cutaneous evaporation to lose heat, and they have much higher rates of cutaneous evaporation at any temperature compared with the other species. Rates of cutaneous evaporation in Grant's gazelle, Thomson's gazelle and wildebeest remain constant regardless of ambient temperature. (After Taylor 1970*b*.)

cannot tolerate hyperthermia (Fig. 11.14). As a result, Thomson's gazelle must live in regions where they are not exposed to ambient temperatures of 45 °C when water is scarce.

Hartebeest rely almost entirely on respiratory water loss as a means of evaporative cooling (Fig. 11.15). Under normal daytime conditions, T_B remains constant at 38–40 °C whether the animal is in the shade or in the sun. Cutaneous water loss remains low whereas the respiratory rate increases up to four times from 20 to 80 breaths/minute (Fig. 11.15). Respiratory water loss accounts for 62 per cent of the total evaporative heat loss. Finch (1972*a, b*) has shown that the light coloured dense fur of the hartebeest reduces heat gain through radiation. Approximately 42 per cent of the incident radiation is reflected, and of the absorbed heat about 80 per cent is reradiated due to the thick dense fur. Consequently the fur temperature varies from 37 to 46 °C and considerable quantities of heat are lost without ever heating the body. Cutaneous water loss is difficult with a thick fur, and consequently it accounts for only about one third of the total heat loss. The onset of evaporative water loss appears to be regulated by the temperature of the skin, and this is related to the amount of solar radiation and to the ambient temperature. Hartebeest begin to pant as soon as the skin temperature reaches 36 °C even though the respiratory rate begins to increase at lower temperatures (Finch 1972*b*). When T_A is 40–50 °C, the respiratory rate may rise to 200/minute and the animal pants with the mouth open (Maloiy and Hopcraft 1971). The combination of light coloured dense fur, evaporative water loss by panting and high reradiation of solar radiation allows hartebeest to live in hot areas of high solar radiation. However, the necessity to maintain a constant body temperature means that hartebeest cannot live in such severe arid conditions as can oryx and addax.

Wildebeest, like hartebeest, cannot tolerate hyperthermia. Although they have functional sweat glands, cutaneous water loss is slight, and most of the heat load is lost by increased respiratory rate and panting. In hydrated and dehydrated animals, T_B is maintained at 39–40 °C, with a slight increase in body temperature in dehydrated animals when T_A is 45 °C (Fig. 11.14). The respiratory rate remains fairly constant when T_A is 35 °C or less, but it increases three to four times when T_A is 40–45 °C (Taylor, C. R. 1970*b*) (Fig. 11.16). Panting begins when T_A is 28 °C (Taylor, Robertshaw and Hofman 1969) and air is inhaled and exhaled through the nostrils. Wildebeest have large spacious nasal cavities (hence their elongated faces) and most of the evaporation takes place from the surfaces of these nasal cavities. The large cavities also allow a rapid passage of air, with little resistance to air flow. When panting, the volume of air actually going into the lungs is similar to that at cooler temperatures; the extra air (due to the fourfold increase in ventilation) is taken into the nasal passages where the evaporative water loss occurs. The increased respiratory rate simply speeds up the transfer of heat away from the body.

Buffalo maintain a T_B of 38–40 °C when T_A is 20–45 °C. Like eland, buffalo are large and heavy so that it is difficult to lose heat rapidly. Buffalo do not show hyperthermia. Heat loss is mostly by cutaneous evaporation which increases from $50\,\mathrm{g\,m^{-2}\,h^{-1}}$ when T_A is 20 °C to $250\,\mathrm{g\,m^{-2}\,h^{-1}}$ when T_A is 40–45 °C (Fig. 11.17). Buffalo pant at high ambient temperatures even though heat loss through panting is small. Dehydrated buffalo can tolerate only a slightly higher body temperature, and they sweat less compared with hydrated individuals (Taylor, C. R. 1970*a, b*). Like waterbuck (see below), buffalo are dependent on a regular supply of water.

Waterbuck are able to maintain a T_B of 38–41 °C when T_A is 10–40 °C (Taylor, Spinage and Lyman 1969). As the ambient temperature rises, there is an increase in cutaneous water loss and respiratory rate. At low ambient temperatures (20–22 °C), respiratory water loss is slightly higher than cutaneous water loss, but when there is a periodic heat load of 40 °C, waterbuck sweat profusely so that cutaneous water loss is nearly double the respiratory water loss. The rate of evaporation in waterbuck during experimental conditions of 20–40 °C (p. 280) was about 40 per cent higher than in eland. This is probably because waterbuck maintain a more or less constant body temperature regardless of the ambient temperature, and this requires the expenditure of large volumes of water when T_A exceeds T_B. Consequently, waterbuck need to drink large quantities of water (Table 11.3) in order to maintain a constant body temperature.

11.3   Energy utilisation

For survival, energy income must be equal to, or greater than, energy expenditure. The necessity to balance energy income and expenditure places restraints on the individual, and on populations of individuals, because the parameters which determine the available energy are different from those which determine the rate of energy expenditure (McNab 1974). The energy available to herbivores, and ultimately carnivores, is obtained from plants which are the primary producers. The quantity of energy they produce is determined by the soil, geology, vegetation, temperature, sunshine and rainfall of the environment. Consequently, primary production varies temporally and spatially and, as a result, so does the energy available to mammals. The energy requirements of a mammal are greater during growth, pregnancy and lactation than at other times. Obviously, many aspects of the life histories of mammals and of populations will be determined by the available energy in the environment over relatively short periods of time. Ecological energetics is a comparatively new discipline, and as yet there are few studies on the energy relationships of African mammals.

Energy requirements

The minimum energy required to maintain a constant body temperature is the Basal Metabolic Rate (BMR), usually expressed in kcal/day. The energy requirements of an individual is related to its size, the environment in which it lives and (to a lesser extent) its phylogeny.

Size

The BMR is related in a constant way to the weight of the individual (BMR $= 70 \, W_{kg}^{0.75}$ kcal/day). Small mammals have a higher BMR in relation to their

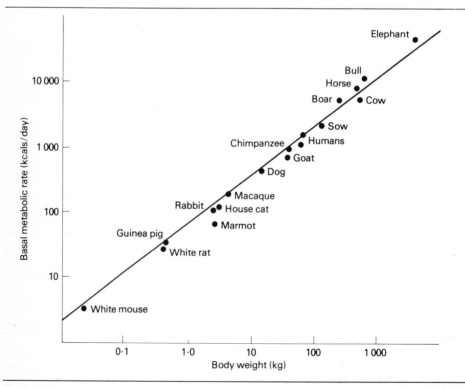

Fig. 11.18   The relationship between Basil Metabolic Rate and Body Weight in mammals, (After Kleiber, M. (1961) *Hilgardia*, **6**, 1932.)

size than large mammals because of their larger surface/volume ratio (Fig. 11.18). A high BMR is a consequence of size in small mammals because the relatively large surface area loses heat (energy) rapidly due to high thermal conductance, and this loss must be balanced by a high metabolic rate. This is extremely costly in energy and under some conditions it may be impossible for a small mammal to obtain sufficient food to provide enough energy. The energy budget of small mammals may be regulated to some extent by reducing the thermal conductance to conserve energy (thick fur, subcutaneous fat, small extremities, avoidance of low temperatures), or by raising the BMR (ingesting more food of high calorific content). An alternative is to allow the body temperature to fall slightly at particular times of the day or year so that less energy is expended. This form of heterothermy occurs, to varying degrees, in several African mammals such as fruit and insectivorous bats, shrews, mole-rats and possibly some very small rodents (section 11.2). In practical terms, small mammals in comparison with large mammals require more food/kg BW, which constitutes a higher percentage of their body weight (Table 11.12); and they cannot take in too much low calorie food or 'roughage' which would fill the alimentary canal and only supply a limited amount of energy. Large mammals have relatively lower metabolic rates in relation to their weight, although the actual rates per animal are higher. Their small surface/volume ratio, especially in warm tropical regions, could lead to overheating unless there are adequate means of losing heat when necessary (p. 296). Elephants which have been immobilised are in danger of rapid overheating as they are unable to lose heat by flapping their ears; consequently the ears of immobilised elephants must be splashed frequently with cool water to increase the rate of heat transfer from the body to the air (Douglas-Hamilton and Douglas-Hamilton 1975).

Physiologists can measure the BMR and this can be compared to the predicted value on the weight of the individual. Some species have lower BMRs than predicted; this is due probably to reduced heat loss associated with good insulation and a warm constant microenvironment (some desert rodents), or to extreme heterothermy (some mole-rats. Ant- and termite-eaters tend to have low BMRs, possibly due to their specialised feeding habits (pp. 92 and 136).

Size, volume and thermal conductance are, therefore, important factors regulating the energy requirements of mammals.

Climate
Climatic factors also affect energy requirements, in particular lower ambient temperatures are associated with the higher energy requirements of homeotherms. Tropical mammals require less insulation (i.e. they have a higher thermal conductance) than mammals of temperate and arctic environments which are exposed to very cold temperatures during the winter months. Tropical species, especially large species, lose less heat to their surroundings due to the generally small difference between the ambient temperature and the body temperature than mammals of cooler climates. More important for tropical species is the necessity to lose heat actively when the ambient temperature is high and there is a danger of overheating (p. 285). Low fat deposits, sparse hair, elongated extremities and many behavioural characteristics are common features in large tropical mammals which facilitate rapid loss of heat and a flow of energy away from the body. These characteristics are especially noticeable if tropical species are compared with cold-climate counterparts of similar size, e.g. African buffalo and bison, eland and elk, and African elephant and mammoth. Investigations on (non-African) rodents has shown that the BMR is similar in species from arctic, temperature and tropical regions (McNab 1974); therefore the energy

budget is balanced through adjustment of energy loss (rather than on energy gain) by means of variations in insulation, microclimate and behaviour.

Food

The principal source of energy for mammals is food, and therefore the type of food and feeding habits might be expected to impose restrictions on the energy expenditure of the mammal. The relationship between food habits and energetics is uncertain (McNab 1974), although the volume and weight of food ingested each day/kg BW depends on the calorific value of the food. Herbivores require a greater volume of food/kg BW because of the lower calorific value of herbage and the difficulties of digestion and assimilation of energy from plants. In contrast, carnivores require less food/kg BW because meat is easily digested and has a high calorific value. Obviously, energy derived from food must be adequate if the individual is to survive. Food may vary temporally and spatially in abundance, calorific value and availability, and any such variations may be important for the distribution, survival and recruitment of mammals. Each species differs in its efficiency of digestion and assimilation, and in the amount of food required (both in calories and constituents) for maintenance of the body tissues. Many herbivorous and insectivorous species in African savannas may have difficulty in obtaining adequate energy in the dry season when plants are dormant, insects are scarce and the effects of burning are severe. This does not matter unduly provided alternative (and usually less preferred) food sources are available. If the individual can utilise fat and other reserves in the body, a short period of food shortage does not normally lead to starvation. It is important to distinguish between total energy requirements, and the requirements of particular minerals and molecules. During the dry season, an individual may obtain adequate energy but inadequate protein; for example, buffalo which died in Serengeti during the dry season had full stomachs but because of the low protein content of the grass, they did not obtain adequate protein for body maintenance (Sinclair 1975).

Table 11.9   *The average chemical compositions (per cent dry weight) of grasses, legumes and browse in Kenya. (From Dougall 1963.)*

| | Grasses | Legumes | Browse | |
			Leguminous	Non-leguminous
Silica	4·11	1·18	0·59	1·60
Calcium	0·40	1·17	2·03	1·89
Phosphorus	0·23	0·29	0·17	0·22
Crude protein	11·60	21·86	13·76	12·95
Crude fibre	30·28	21·90	30·32	28·78

Analysis of the chemical composition of plants has shown that species vary in their protein, crude fibre, calcium and phosphorous content. Plants of the family Leguminaceae are particularly rich in protein, and calcium is more abundant in browse than in grasses and herbs (Dougall 1963, Table 11.9). There are marked differences in the various anatomical parts and stages of growth; for example, the young green leaves of grasses and shrubs of all species contain higher percentages of protein than dead leaves and stems (Field 1976). Different parts of the same plant may show considerable variation in chemical composition; for example, there is at least twice as much protein and a much smaller amount of silica in the leaves of *Acacia sieberiana* than in the green pods and in pods with seeds (Table 11.10). Herbivorous mammals can vary the quality of their food by selective grazing and browsing, and therefore they are able to obtain a diet of higher nutritive value than if they were non-selective. In most instances, food

Table 11.10 *The chemical composition (per cent dry weight) of different parts of selected grasses and browse utilised by buffalo in Uganda. (From Field 1976.)*

	Crude fibre	Crude protein	Silica
Acacia sieberiana			
leaves	20·08	27·47	0·08
green pods	30·34	11·12	0·42
green seeds	13·70	19·31	0·39
pods with seeds	39·82	11·73	0·22
Capparis tormentosa			
stems	29·48	19·12	0·32
leaves	12·06	36·02	0·30
growing points	7·54	38·43	0·22
flower buds	12·55	31·90	0·09
Chloris gayana			
green leaf	30·51	8·74	5·76
dead leaf	32·49	4·71	11·17
steam	42·22	3·96	3·07
Hyparrhenia filipendula			
green leaf	29·86	8·51	7·22
dead leaf	30·60	4·79	12·63
stem	42·23	3·04	7·38
Sporobolus pyramidalis			
green leaf	34·42	6·96	3·67
dead leaf	35·27	4·02	7·14
stem	40·08	4·14	2·97

with a high protein content is selected if available although plants of lower nutritive value may be eaten if they are especially palatable. Feeding habits and digestive ability determine to some extent the quality of the food which is eaten. Small browsing antelopes with weak jaws tend to feed on small protein-rich leaves lacking silica. Elephants and other large herbivores eat food which has a lower protein content and a higher proportion of crude fibre, but the large quantities ingested by these mammals ensures that normally there is adequate protein in the diet. The variations in food and feeding habits, and the effects of these variations on the ecology of each species, may be understood in relation to the composition and nutritive value of plant foods.

Species which have specialised on foods which are climatically limited are faced with particular problems (McNab 1974). Fruit, nectar, insect- and termite-eaters rely on foods which are periodically available, and which may be low in calorific value. Foraging for some foods may require considerable energy expenditure due to their wide dispersion and infrequent availability. Bats, hedgehogs, ant- and termite-eaters rely mostly on these types of food, and their low and variable metabolic rates may be due to the necessity to conserve energy when food is scarce and widely dispersed.

There are other strategies to overcome periods of food shortage associated with the dry season, cool temperatures and the effects of burning. Torpor, or aestivation, is shown by a few species of small African mammals although it is generally uncharacteristic of tropical mammals. *Steatomys* (Petter 1955), *Gerbillus* spp. (Petter 1955), *Jaculus* (Petter 1955, Hilali and Veillat 1975, Happold, unpubl.) and *Heterocephalus* (McNab 1966) enter torpor at low temperatures and/or when food is in short supply. Migration and nomadism (section 10.1) is shown by several large species and enables individuals to move from an unfavourable area where there is a reduction in available energy to one where energy is more easily obtained.

When food is in short supply and available energy and essential requirements are limited, there may be sufficient energy only for body maintenance. If conditions are not severe, most individuals will survive, but if conditions are severe a large proportion of the populations may die. Such adverse conditions normally last for only a few weeks or months during the dry season. However, the alternation of dry (energy limited) and wet (energy unlimited) seasons has determined many features of the life cycles of African mammals, such as times of pregnancy, lactation and the rates of mortality. The precise effects of food abundance and energy availability (and the absence of them) on the life cycle depends on the environment and on species requirements. Rain forest species are less likely to be affected than savanna species, as indicated by their extended reproductive seasons and lesser fluctuations in population numbers (section 12.4). In contrast, the biomass of mammals in rain forest is less than that of the savanna and is presumably due to the lesser amount of energy available to them in the rain forest. Precise details of the energetics of rain forest mammals and rain forest ecosystems are subjects for future investigation.

Growth rates and food consumption

In young mammals, food is converted into energy for growth. The rate at which a young mammal grows is dependent on: (a) the species and its ultimate adult size, (b) its efficiency at converting food into animal protein. Small species have a higher rate of weight increase, a smaller actual weight increase and take a shorter time to reach adult weight than do large species. For example, the West African forest mouse (*Praomys tullbergi*) increases its weight at an average of 0·3 g/day or at 0·78 per cent of adult BW/day, whereas an elephant increases at about 300 g/day or 0·007 per cent adult BW/day (Table 11.11). It takes *Praomys* 3–4 months, and an elephant takes about 240 months, to attain adult weight. Herbivorous species intermediate between these two extremes exhibit growth rates proportional to their size.

These relative growth rates are partly a function of the varying efficiency of each species to convert plant material into animal protein. Small species are more efficient in this respect than large species because they take in relatively more food each day and because they assimilate more energy from the food. There is also the problem of the practicability of finding and ingesting food. A shrew ingests 20–50 per cent of its body weight of food each day (Table 11.12); the larger ungulates ingest only 1–2 per cent/day, and it would be physically impossible for them to ingest and digest amounts similar in proportion to their adult weight as do shrews and other small mammals. As it is, larger mammals spend a considerable proportion of their day looking for, and ingesting food (section 6.3). Small mammals require more energy for each kilogram of their body weight in order to remain homeothermic; therefore they need relatively large amounts of food and their metabolic processes have evolved to be more rapid than in larger species.

A practical aspect of these growth rates is which species of African mammals utilise their environment in the most efficient way, and which are the most suitable for meat production. The answer to the controversy of whether cattle or wild ungulates are the best protein producers in the savanna depends partly on the growth rates and efficiency of utilisation of food. Small antelopes grow and produce protein more quickly than domestic cattle and breed at an earlier age (Table 11.11). On this basis alone, small African ungulates are better than domestic cattle for meat production; however, other considerations such as carcass composition, ease of handling, total cost of production

Table 11.11   Growth rates of selected African herbivores. *(From Talbot et al. 1965, Petersen and Casebeer 1971, Phillipson 1975 and Happold 1978.)*

Species	Live weight gain/day (g)	Duration of observations (months)	Average adult male weight (kg)	Age when adult weight attained (months)	Daily gain as per cent adult weight
West African forest mouse (*Praomys tullbergi*)	0·3	6	0·038	4	0·78
Thomson's gazelle (*Gazella thomsoni*)	40–60	10–15	24	18	0·25
Impala (*Aepyceros melampus*)	90–120	10–18	60	24	0·2
Grant's gazelle (*Gazella granti*)	100–190	10–18	66	24	0·28
Topi (*Damaliscus lunatus*)	150–200	12–24	133	30	0·15
Hartebeest (*Alcelaphus buselaphus*)	180–230	12–24	151	30	0·15
Wildebeest (*Connochaetes taurinus*)	190–240	12–30	210	45	0·11
Eland (*Taurotragus oryx*)	260	48	400	?	0·06
Buffalo (*Syncerus caffer*)	90–410	66	750	?	0·05–0·01
Elephant (*Loxodonta africana*)	300	Several years	4000	240	0·007
Domestic cattle	130	60	227	60	0·05

Table 11.12   Food consumption in African mammals.

Species	Average adult weight (kg)	Daily food intake (kg)	Food intake as per cent BW	Reference
Shrew (*Crocidura bottegi*)	0·0037	0·0021	56·0	Hunkeler and Hunkeler (1970)
Shrew (*C. flavescens*)	0·033	0·006	18·0	Hunkeler and Hunkeler (1970)
Grant's gazelle (*Gazella granti*)	50	1·1	2·2	Taylor and Maloiy (1969)
Thomson's Gazelle (*Gazella thomsoni*)	20	0·5	2·5	Taylor and Maloiy (1969)
Impala (*Aepyceros melampus*)	50	1·3	2·6	Maloiy and Hopcraft (1969)
Wildebeest (*Connochaetes taurinus*)	200	4·0	2·0	Taylor and Maloiy (1969)
Buffalo (*Syncerus caffer*)	750	8·0	1·0	Sinclair (1975)
Hippopotamus (*Hippopotamus amphibius*)	1400	18·0	1·3	Petrides and Swank (1965)
Elephant (*Loxodonta africana*)	3327	41·6	1·4	Phillipson (1975)
Lion (*Panthera leo*)	200	5–10	2·5–5	Kruuk and Turner (1967)
Cheetah (*Acinonyx jubatus*)	55	4·0	7·0	Schaller (1968)

and the carrying capacity of the environment also influence the feasibility of game ranching (section 13.5, Talbot *et al.* 1965, Talbot 1966).

A comparison of the relative growth rates, and utilisation of food, in impala and elephants indicates how size influences these parameters (Table 11.13). Although the

Table 11.13 *A comparison of food consumption and secondary production in young impala and young elephants. For this comparison, young are assumed to eat one half of the adult food requirement and to weigh half adult weight.*

	Impala (20 kg)	*Elephant (1 000 kg)*
Number of individuals	50	1
Total weight of individuals	1 000 kg	1 000 kg
Weight of food supplied	1 000 kg	1 000 kg
Food consumption/day	0·4 kg/ind/day*	17 kg/ind/day†
Total food consumption/day	20 kg/day	17 kg/day
Weight gain	0·1 kg/ind/day‡	0·3 kg/ind/day§
Total weight gain/day	5·0 kg/day	0·3 kg/day
Total weight gain after all food consumed	250 kg	17·3 kg
Ratio biomass produced : food consumed	1 : 4	1 : 57

*Adult food consumption: 0·7 kg/ind/day (Sinclair 1975).
†Adult food consumption: 34 kg/ind/day (Sinclair 1975).
‡Talbot, Ledger and Payne (1962) in Talbot *et al.* (1965).
§Phillipson (1975).

accuracy of the data used in this comparison is subject to considerable variation, the magnitude of the difference between the two species is evident. A given weight of impala produce a biomass about fourteen times as great as do a similar weight of elephant from the same quantity of food. This comparison is similar to that of rabbits and cattle (Phillipson 1963) which showed that the smaller species are much more efficient producers of animal protein.

Another way of indicating the production efficiency is by comparing production in relation to total biomass. The production : biomass ratio (P : B) is a measure of energy turnover in the population, which is itself related to the efficiency of energy utilisation and to the size and reproductive rates of the individuals in the population. In the Serengeti, the P : B ratio for several large ungulates combined (excluding elephants) was 1 : 5 or, expressed in another way, the secondary production was about 20 per cent/annum of the large ungulate biomass (Sinclair 1975). Elephants are less efficient with a P : B ratio of 1 : 18 (Phillipson 1975). In contrast, small mammals have a P : B ratio of 2 : 1 (Sinclair 1975) since there is a complete turnover of the total biomass two times each year. In some localities the P : B ratio for small mammals may be greater than 2 : 1; for example, in the crater area of Rwenzori National Park the annual production of the 10 species of small rodents was 5 681 g/ha giving a P : B ratio of 4·1 : 1 (Cheeseman 1975). These P : B ratios confirm that small mammals utilise energy more efficiently than large mammals, and that the energy flow and turnover of individuals in their populations is faster. Studies on population dynamics (Ch. 12) confirm that most small species breed more rapidly, have more young/litter and faster population increase than large mammals.

Energy and populations

The total available energy in a particular habitat ultimately determines the biomass of organisms which may be supported by that environment. This is achieved through the sequence:

$$\text{Energy} \rightarrow \text{Primary Production} \rightarrow \text{Carrying Capacity} \rightarrow \text{Biomass}$$

Each of these steps is influenced by many factors which operate in time and space. The net result is that primary production and biomass vary greatly in a single locality at different times, and between different localities. A small primary production supports a small biomass (as in arid, dry savanna and probably the afro-alpine zone) and a higher primary production supports a larger biomass (as in moist savanna but not in rain forest) (Table 11.14). Primary production on an annual basis (as compared with a

Table 11.14   *Biomass (kg km^{-2}) of selected species and communities of African mammals.*

Species/ community	Habitat	Locality	Biomass	Reference
Taterillus pygargus	Arid, dry savanna	Senegal	7·2–21·6	Poulet (1972)
Four spp. ungulates	Arid	Rio del Oro	0·3	Valverde, in Bourliere (1963b)
Four spp. ungulates	Arid, dry savanna	Oum-Chalouba, Tchad	80	Valverde, in Bourliere (1963b)
Four spp. rodents	Moist savanna	Nigeria	24–40	Anadu (1973)
Seven spp. rodents	Rain forest	Nigeria	23·4–122·9	Happold (1977)
Fourteen spp. rodents	Moist savanna	Rwenzori NP, Uganda	62·7–221·1	Cheeseman (1975)
All large herbivores	Moist savanna	Rwenzori NP, Uganda	19928*	Field and Laws (1970)
All large herbivores	Moist savanna	Ngorongoro Crater, Tanzania	7561*	Turner and Watson (1964)
All large hervibores	Dry savanna	Lake Rudolf, East Kenya	405*	Stewart (1963)
All large herbivores	Moist savanna	Manyara NP, Tanzania	19189*	Watson and Turner (1964)
Thirteen spp. large herbivores (including elephants)	Dry savanna	Tsavo East NP, Kenya	4115–4454	Leuthold and Leuthold (1976)
All large herbivores	Moist savanna	Tarangire GR, Tanzania	1050–12300 (dry) (wet)	Lamprey (1963)
All large herbivores	Moist savanna	Nairobi NP, Kenya	4500–9800	Foster and Coe (1968)
All large herbivores	Moist savanna	Serengeti plains, Tanzania	8352*	Sinclair (1972)
All large herbivores	Moist savanna	Albert NP, Zaire	7500–20400	Bourlière and Verschuren (1960)

*Biomass recalculated from original authors by Coe *et al.* (1976).

monthly basis) can give a misleading impression of the biomass it is capable of supporting. In habitats where seasonal changes are conspicuous, the least productive season supports the lowest number of animals and the lowest biomass. A regular reduction in this way may limit the total biomass of animals which can be supported over a longer period. The precise influence of fluctuating primary production on populations of mammals depends on the size, numbers, mobility, rate of increase and trophic level of the species. Populations of small primary consumers living in environments which have large fluctuations in primary production will be affected to the greatest extent (e.g. rodents). Large primary consumers (ungulates, elephants), and secondary and tertiary consumers will be less affected, and mammals regardless of their trophic level which live in habitats such as rain forests in areas of high rainfall, with a more or less constant primary production will be least affected.

The wealth of vegetation in tropical Africa, especially during the wet season, suggests there is an abundance of food and energy for primary consumers. However, much of this primary production is not available as a source of energy for several reasons:

(*a*) Lignification of plant growth is a means of storing energy, and in this form it can not be ingested by most herbivores;

(*b*) Leaves, grasses and stems become unpalatable to mammals with age due to coarseness and changes in chemical composition;

(*c*) Most primary consumers are selective in their choice of food, although they may ingest less preferred foods when necessary (p. 306);

(*d*) Some vegetation is physically unobtainable by mammals;

(*e*) Savanna burning of the grass destroys a high percentage of the annual primary production.

Primary production cannot, therefore, be equated with food (Sinclair 1975) as only a (small) proportion is available and suitable for ingestion. During assimilation in the alimentary canal, 40–80 per cent of the energy is absorbed (depending on the species and the condition of the food) which reduces still further the transfer of energy to the herbivore. Two studies which have investigated the energy relationships between African mammals and their food supply (Sinclair 1975, Phillipson 1975) have shown that suitable food is not nearly as abundant for the herbivore as it seems.

It is well known that there is a relationship between annual rainfall and primary production in arid and savanna habitats, although this relationship has rarely been quantified. By using measurements of monthly and annual rainfall, and the rates of grass production after different amounts of rain, Sinclair (1975) calculated the monthly grass production in three areas of the Serengeti National Park (Table 11.15). Primary production ranged from 0 kg/ha in the driest months to about 1 100 kg/ha in the wettest

Table 11.15 *Monthly grass production, calculated from mean monthly rainfall, in three regions of the Serengeti National Park. (Sinclair 1975.)*

	Tall grasslands and koppies		Short grasslands	
	Mean monthly rainfall (mm)	Mean monthly production (kg/ha)	Mean monthly rainfall (mm)	Mean monthly production (kg/ha)
Nov.	98·7	555	54·7	218
Dec.	101·8	781	92·5	709
Jan.	87·0	668	77·7	597
Feb.	82·5	633	87·4	670
March	111·7	857	84·9	427
April	150·2	1 154	88·1	1 135
May	92·3	706	47·4	610
June	44·3	340	26·2	337
July	15·9	0	5·2	0
Aug.	31·2	37·5	11·5	0
Sept.	38·3	92	17·2	0
Oct.	46·4	154	20·4	0
Annual totals	900·3	5977·5	613·2	4703

months. There were four months each year when the short grasslands on the Serengeti plains had zero production; during these months (July–October) they barely supported the few resident species because the heavy grazing by migrant herds in the wet seasons had removed all the former primary production. In contrast, the tall grasslands in the north-east had a limited production in July–October in addition to the accumulated production of earlier months when grazing pressure was small and migrant herds were absent.

In the tall grasslands in the dry season, the food requirements of the migrant herds were always in excess of the available food (Table 11.16). The mammals survived in the tall grasslands only because of the primary production 'carried over' from earlier months, and because the heavy grazing pressure lasted for only a few months until the rains began and the migrant herds departed. In the dry season, large ungulates

Table 11.16 *Mean monthly food availability and requirement (kg/ha) in the tall grasslands of Serengeti National Park. (Sinclair 1975.) Invertebrate food requirement is not included.*

Month	Monthly production	Food requirement			Available food	Remaining food
		Ungulate	*Small mammal*	*Total*		
Nov.	555	111·33	3·33	149·56	589·8	440·3
Dec.	781	29·22	8·87	94·59	1277·8	1183·3
Jan.	668	45·04	8·87	110·41	1907·8	1797·3
Feb.	633	48·07	8·87	113·44	2486·8	2373·4
March	857	48·07	8·87	113·44	3286·9	3173·4
April	1154	48·07	4·95	109·52	4384·0	4274·4
May	706	43·95	4·95	105·40	5036·9	4931·5
June	340	129·50	4·95	190·95	5328·0	5137·6
July	0	124·60	4·95	139·55	0	0
Aug. Dry	37·5	164·60	3·33	173·83	38·4	0
Sept. season	92	164·60	3·33	172·53	92·9	0
Oct.	154	164·60	3·33	172·53	154·9	0
Totals	5978	1121·65	68·60	1645·25		

Note: During wet months (Dec.–June) grass that remained uneaten at the end of month has been added to the production of the subsequent month. During the dry months (July–Oct.) any remaining grass dried rapidly and was unavailable in a subsequent month.

Table 11.17 *Total annual production, consumption and removal of grasses in two areas of Serengeti National Park. (Sinclair 1975.)*

	Tall grasslands		Short grasslands	
	kg/ha/yr	*Per cent of total*	*kg/ha/yr*	*Per cent of total*
Ungulate consumption	1122	18·8	1597	34·0
Small mammal consumption	69	1·2	4	0·1
Grasshopper consumption	456	7·6	194	4·1
Subtotal herbivore consumption	1647	27·6	1795	38·2
Removal by burning	3185	53·3	586	12·5
Removal by detritus feeders	1146	19·2	2322	49·5
Total annual grass production	5978	100	4703	100

consumed 95 per cent of the available forage: small mammals were few in number and grasshoppers (which were very abundant and important consumers in the wet season) were rare so their food requirements and consumption was minimal. The tall grasslands supplied good quality forage although it barely lasted during the last two months of the dry season. However, not all of the *annual* primary production was utilised by the large ungulates; they consumed 19 per cent of the overall annual production and the remainder was consumed by grasshoppers (7 per cent) and detritus feeders (19 per cent) or lost to the ecosystem by burning (53 per cent) (Table 11.17). In the short grasslands, there was no production during the dry season, but in the wet season they provided good forage (Table 11.18). As in the tall grasslands, not all the

Table 11.18   *Mean monthly food availability and requirement (kg/ha) in the short grasslands of Serengeti National Park. (Sinclair 1975.) Invertebrate food requirement is not included.*

Month	Monthly production	Food requirement			Available food	Remaining food
		Ungulate	Small mammal	Total		
Nov.	218	10·99	0·3	12·19	218·9	206·7
Dec.	709	183·59	0·3	210·89	942·7	731·8
Jan.	597	280·04	0·3	307·34	1 355·8	1 048·5
Feb.	670	280·04	0·3	307·34	1 745·5	1 438·1
March	427	280·04	0·3	307·34	1 892·1	1 584·8
April	1 135	280·04	0·3	307·34	2 746·8	2 439·4
May	610	280·04	0·3	307·34	3 076·5	2 769·1
June	337	21·93	0·3	49·23	3 133·1	3 083·9
July	0	0·5	0·3	1·7	0	0
Aug.	0	0·5	0·3	1·7	0	0
Sept.	0	0·5	0·3	1·7	0	0
Oct.	0	0·5	0·3	1·7	0	0
Totals	4 703	1 596·78	3·6	1 793·88		

See: Note for Table 11.16.

annual primary production was utilised by herbivores; ungulates (mostly migrants) consumed 34 per cent, small mammals 0·1 per cent and grasshoppers 4·1 per cent (Table 11·17). The remaining 60 per cent was burned or removed as detritus. This study illustrates a number of important features on the primary production and its utilisation in this savanna habitat:

(a) The annual production of available food varies from place to place and from month to month.
(b) The mammal biomass (and that of other organisms in the ecosystem) is related to, and dependent on, the spatial temporal distribution of the primary production.
(c) The total primary production is not available as food for herbivorous mammals due to changes with age in the texture, lignification, chemical composition and palatability of the forage, and to the selection of suitable food by the herbivores.
(d) Utilisation of suitable, available food by grazing ungulates (as a percentage of the total herbivore utilisation) in the Serengeti is high (80 per cent).
(e) The primary production of the least productive month(s) may act as a limiting factor to the annual biomass supported by the environment. The effects of short-term variations in primary production are species-specific.

Similar differences in primary production have also been recorded in Tsavo (East) National Park (Phillipson 1975). Rainfall and productivity were closely correlated, and rainfall patterns were used to estimate monthly and regional changes in primary production. In the four years 1969–72, the annual primary productivity in the Park as a whole ranged from 186 g dry weight/m² to 535 g dry weight/m², a threefold increase above the least productive year. The park was divided into nine productivity regions from those of low productivity and low rainfall to those of high productivity and high rainfall. In the drought years of 1970 and 1971, areas of low productivity covered about 80 per cent of the park, and there were about eight months when primary production was almost zero. In more 'normal' years, areas of low productivity were confined to small regions in the west and north of the park, and there were only three to four months of zero production.

Elephants are one of the most numerous mammals in the park and because of their large food requirements, periods of low production are likely to affect their distribution and survival. Distribution patterns of elephants in the drought years showed that elephants clustered in areas of highest primary production and that the maximum numbers of deaths (Fig. 12.22) occurred in the low productivity areas (Corfield 1973). Many of the elephants which died had full stomachs and were close (25–30 km) to water; death was apparently due to starvation by the low quality diet and not to lack of water (see also p. 353). Calculation of the total food consumption by Tsavo elephants, and the total monthly primary production, showed that in some months of each year there was inadequate food to support the elephant population. There may be a delayed effect as the protein content of fresh forage can be maintained for up to a month (Stanley-Price, in Phillipson 1975). Consequently, if primary production is reduced or non-existent for only a month at a time, this does not cause any hardship for the elephants. However, if primary production is less than the minimum requirement for two or more consecutive months, elephants will suffer an increasing level of starvation. The high mortality and obvious effects of starvation in 1970 and 1971 were due to the reduced primary production for a period of eight to nine months and the consequent shortage of high quality food in relation to the elephants' requirements. The situation was intensified by the large elephant population which had increased dramatically during the years preceding the drought. The highest number of deaths occurred in regions where the annual primary production was less than 100 g DW/m², and the distribution of elephant deaths correlated with regions where the annual primary production was 200 g DW/m² or less. Thus the elephant numbers and distribution in Tsavo (East) National Park appear to be governed by the temporal and spatial variations in primary production. Further analysis of the relationships between elephant numbers, primary production and population dynamics are given by Phillipson (1975).

These two studies illustrate the important principle that biomass and production may be predicted in relation to the pattern of rainfall and primary production, at least in the savanna. This relationship has been analysed for twenty-four wildlife regions in east, central and southern Africa (Coe *et al.* 1976). Accurate estimations of biomass, rainfall and primary production are essential if any relationship between them is meaningful. The estimation of animal numbers and biomass is difficult due to seasonal variations in visibility, and seasonal and regional variations in population structure. Rainfall data are often inadequate in many localities. Despite these difficulties, Coe *et al.* (1976) estimated the biomass and secondary production of large (800 kg), intermediate (100–750 kg) and small (5–9 kg) herbivores. In most savanna regions, especially those where the annual rainfall is less than 700 mm, biomass increases with increases in the annual rainfall, and there is a statistically significant linear relationship between annual rainfall and herbivore biomass (Fig. 11.19). Such a relationship must be taken with caution as *monthly* rainfall and biomass may not show such a definite

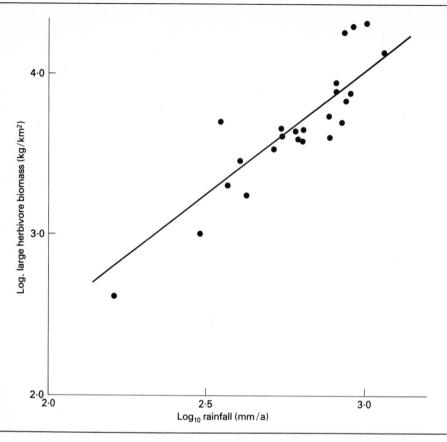

Fig. 11.19   The relationship between large herbivore biomass and mean annual rainfall in 24 wildlife areas of southern and eastern Africa. (After Coe, Cummings and Phillipson 1976.)

relationship. Rainfall and biomass are causally linked by primary production which varies depending on the amount and pattern of rainfall (Coe *et al.* 1976).

This relationship between rainfall and biomass refers to the total large mammal community and not to particular species within that community. Thus species composition, and the abundance of any particular species, may vary in environments of identical rainfall and primary production as a result of different biogeographical distribution patterns, competitive interaction between species in the community and the composition of the vegetation. Differences in species composition result in different levels of secondary production because of variations in production efficiency and assimilation between species. This does not invalidate the relationship (for large species) but emphasises that similar levels of secondary production can be achieved by mammal communities which differ in numbers and composition. Prediction of biomass by rainfall data in savanna habitats appears to have a more general application than prediction by vegetation analysis although, in general, rainfall influences the major vegetation zones of Africa. The importance of using rainfall data is that it allows an assessment of the carrying capacity (and hence the biomass) of an environment by a mixed community of herbivores over a long period of time, regardless of any short term changes in vegetation, rainfall and annual numbers.

Trophic levels

Ecological studies in many communities have established such well-known ecological phenomena as trophic levels, food webs and pyramids of numbers (e.g. Odum 1971, Krebs 1972, Whittaker 1975). The numbers of individuals and/or biomass diminishes at each successively higher trophic level during the energy transfer from primary production to primary consumer and from primary consumer to secondary consumer. Information on biomass and energy transfer at different trophic levels for African mammals is scant. Table 11.17 indicates that in the Serengeti grasslands only 20–34 per cent of the total primary production/annum was utilised by mammals (Sinclair 1975). In Tsavo (East) in 1969, the net primary production was 545 g/m^2; elephants consumed 22 g/m^2 (4 per cent), other large mammals 4 g/m^2 (less than 1 per cent), small mammals is scant. Table 11.17 indicates that in the Serengeti grasslands only 20–34 492 g/m^2 (90 per cent) (Phillipson 1975). In both these localities, the proportion of energy passing from primary production to mammalian herbivores (the largest and most obvious of all the herbivores) is small.

Phillipson (1973) has suggested a tentative model of energy flow in the Serengeti ecosystem (Fig. 11.20). His figures, like those of Sinclair (1975), show that herbivorous mammals utilise only a small percentage of the annual primary production (large mammals 10·4 per cent, small mammals 4·4 per cent), and that ecological efficiency decreases dramatically above the primary consumer level. Invertebrate plant feeders utilise a high proportion of the primary production, and it is unlikely that these

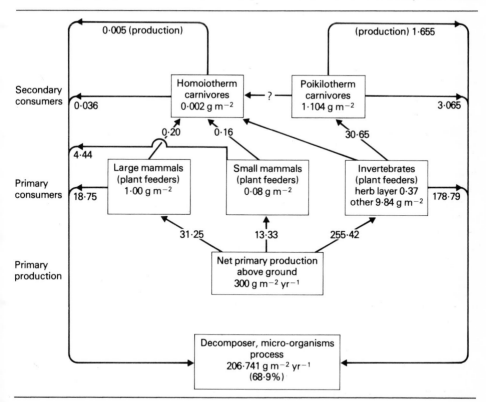

Fig. 11.20   A tentative model of the Serengeti plains ecosystem. Figures outside the boxes are in g m^{-2} per annum. (Phillipson 1973.)

invertebrates limit the food supply of mammals. Similarly burning does not markedly affect the available food supply of large grazing mammals because most grasses are no longer suitable as food by the time they can be burnt. However, energy flow at different trophic levels is modified in savannas which are burnt annually (as is evident in Table 11.17 but not in Fig. 11.20) because energy is lost to the system by burning. Small herbivorous and carnivorous mammals are temporarily affected to the greatest extent after burning because seeds, grass stems and invertebrate foods may be in short supply.

The energy relations of a predator to its prey in Africa are poorly understood, although there are some data on the numbers of prey required by predators. The food required to support one cheetah is indicated in Table 11.19. One cheetah requires about

Table 11.19   *Annual food requirement to support one cheetah (60 kg)*

Prey species (adult wt in kg)	Number killed each year*	Total weight killed/year (kg)	Food requirement of each prey animal (kg DW/ind/day)	Total food requirement for all prey (kg DW/yr)
Impala (50 kg)	19	950	1·3†	9015
Grant's gazelle (50 kg)	23	1150	1·1‡	9234
Thomson's gazelle (20 kg)	30	600	0·5§	5475
Hartebeest (150 kg)	4	600	4·8¶	7008
Totals	76	3300		30732

*Kruuk and Turner (1967).
†Maloiy and Hopcraft (1969) – 2·58 kg DW/100 kg BW/day.
‡Taylor and Maloiy (1969) – 2·2 kg DW/100 kg BW/day.
§Taylor and Maloiy (1969) – 2·65 kg DW/100 kg BW/day.
¶Maloiy and Hopcraft (1969) – 3·18 kg DW/100 kg BW/day.

76 prey/annum, and these prey require about 30000 kg/dry weight food/annum. On a weight basis, 30000 kg DW of vegetation supports 3300 kg of herbivores which, in turn, supports 60 kg of cheetah, or the cheetah : herbivore : vegetation ratio is 1 : 55 : 512. The maintenance of predators in an ecosystem, therefore, is extremely costly in terms of energy. Consequently predators are always few in number compared with their prey. Although a cheetah kills, on average, about 10 kg of prey/day (Kruuk and Turner 1967), it ingests only about 4 kg/day. The remainder supports smaller carnivores and scavengers.

The relationship between cheetah and its prey is probably representative of all carnivores. Lions, for example, kill at the rate of about 30 prey/lion/annum, and ingest about 3400 kg meat/lion/annum (Rudnai 1970 in Petersen and Casebeer 1971). Makacha and Schaller (1969) estimated a lower consumption of about 1800 kg meat/lion/year in Manyara National Park, and Kruuk and Turner (1976) calculated that 700 lions in the Serengeti required about 7800 prey/annum. In Seronera, Tanzania, an average lion kills and scavenges about 2500 kg of prey/annum which is equivalent to about 32 prey animals/annum (Schaller 1972). In all areas where the numbers of predators and their prey have been studied (Table 11.20) the total prey biomass greatly exceeds the predator biomass. For example, the 2000 lions in the Serengeti consume about 5 million kg of prey/annum, which is only 0·25–0·3 per cent of the prey biomass. Although the energetics of this predatory system are unknown, it is probable that the numbers of predators are ultimately limited by the abundance and availability (see pp. 345–9) of their prey, and that an African ecosystem (even where there are large herds of prey as in the Serengeti) can support only a limited number of large predators.

Table 11.20 *Predator biomass (in kg/km²) in 5 African reserves. (Schaller 1972.)*

Reserve	Lion		Leopard		Cheetah		Spotted hyaena		Hunting dog		Total predator biomass	Total prey biomass	Kg prey per 1 kg of predator
	No	Biomass	No	Biomass	No	Biomass	No	Biomass	No	Biomass			
Ngorongoro	70	25·3	20*	2·3	v.o.	—	479	68·1	v.o.	—	95·7	10 363	108
Manyara	35	37·7	10*	3·3	—	—	10*	4·0	—	—	44·7	7 785	174
Serengeti	2 000–2 400	7·6–9·2	800–1 000	0·9–1·2	200–250	0·3–0·4	3 500	5·1	250–300	0·1–0·2	14·0–16·1	4 222	262–301
Nairobi	25	21·3	10*	2·6	15	4·9	12*	3·8	v.o.	—	32·4	3 052	94
Kruger	1 120	5·7	650	1·0	263	0·5	1 500*	2·9	335	0·3	10·4	1 034	100

* = estimate   v.o. = visitor only to reserve.

Chapter 12

Populations

The study of numbers of animals is a particularly useful aspect of ecology as it makes possible the description of many events in an exact way. Furthermore the individual animal is an easily recognisable and well-defined unit providing the basic information required for population studies. Through the wise use of numerical analysis authoritative statements can be made on the abundance of animals in a particular location such as the number of wildebeest in Serengeti. As a result of more extensive analysis comparisons can be made between localities so that, for example, it can be established whether there are more buffalo in Serengeti than Rwenzori Park and whether they are of the same of different densities in the two places. A further precision can be obtained from numerical data by the application of rigorous and refined statistical techniques.

The same population can be estimated at different times and changes in its numbers recorded. The reasons for such changes comprise an important aspect of population ecology. The density of a population at any one time is the result of various factors operating upon it. Broadly, these can be divided into those favouring increase (mostly concerned with additions through reproduction) and those favouring decrease which are mostly associated with various causes of mortality. The effects of these components can be quantified so as to ultimately produce a comprehensive and numerically accurate breakdown of the factors involved in the maintenance of a species population.

These introductory remarks superficially outline the rationale for studying mammal populations with the closer examination of population phenomena elaborated in this chapter. There is, however, one aspect of population ecology not dealt with in the following account which should be briefly mentioned. This concerns the methods of assessment of populations in the field. The pursuit of accurate data makes this a particularly difficult exercise demanding the application of the appropriate methods for the species or group of species under study. Repeated observation is frequently desirable as are the application of alternative confirmatory techniques. Population assessment is often labour-intensive and time consuming but it is the acquisition of accurate data that provides the foundation for subsequent analysis and interpretation.

12.1   Population growth

One of the earliest studies on population increase was made by Gause (1934) on laboratory populations of the protozoan *Paramecium*. He observed that if a culture, in which food was maintained at a constant level, was inoculated with a few *Paramecium* the population increased in numbers until a certain level was reached (upper asymptote) at which point there was an equilibrium between food and number of organisms and the population remained stable. In growing to this level the population

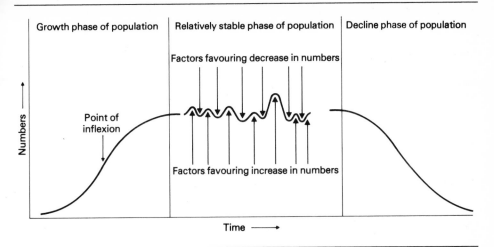

Fig. 12.1 The theoretical growth, stable and decline phases of populations. The relatively stable phase is most frequently encountered but is subject to considerable fluctuation.

curve assumed a characteristic S-shape (Fig. 12.1), known as the logistic curve. The growth of the population shows a number of features. Initially, as a result of there being only a few organisms the population increases slowly, then as they become more numerous there is a more rapid increase. Up to now the food supply has been far in excess of requirements and there has been no shortage of food. However, a time is reached when food becomes less readily available and a constraint is placed on the growth of the population. This constraint becomes more intense as the population grows with an inevitable slowing up in the increase in numbers until the supportable maximum is reached. The constraining effects of the environment are being felt when the curve changes from a progressive cumulative increase to a gradual tailing off. This point is called the point of inflexion (Fig. 12.1).

The upper asymptote of this curve approaches what is referred to as the *carrying capacity* of the habitat. Carrying capacity has been defined by Petrides and Swank (1965) as the *maximum number or mass of organisms which can be sustained by the environment for an indefinite period*. This definition takes account of variations in ecosystem productivity over long periods and emphasises the importance of density being related to available resources. Whether it can be applied to all habitat conditions, such as sporadic cataclysmic events like drought, is more debatable.

The logistic curve is rarely encountered among natural and semi-natural mammal populations mainly due to the infrequency of the appropriate circumstances. However, these could prevail when, for example, large mammals are translocated to new habitats or populations recover from dramatic reduction as a result of some temporary major disturbance such as flooding. From Africa there is, as yet, little relevant information, but useful data on north American mammals illustrates the principles which are equally applicable to African conditions.

The introduction of six white-tailed deer (*Odocoileus virginianus*) into the 485-hectare George Reserve of the University of Michigan in 1928 resulted in a population increase between then and 1934 which showed little sign of the attainment of the upper asymptote and at the same time habitat damage was very obvious. For some reason there was no effective constraint on this population so that it increased dramatically and unchecked. Predators were absent from the Reserve and man's intervention to cull the animals resulted in the population reduction (O'Roke and Hamerstrom, 1948). The introduction of reindeer (*Rangifer arcticus*) on the two Islands of St George and St Paul situated between the United States and Russia took place in 1911 (Scheffer 1951). The habitat was apparently suitable and similar to that of Alaska where wild reindeer ranged and from which source an estimate of the carrying capacity of the islands could be obtained. On St George the population never attained its anticipated maximum. On St Paul the population behaved in a completely different manner. The rate of increase was unexpectedly slow until about 1930 when there was a dramatic increase in numbers which continued until the population was far in excess of the supportable level. Deterioration of the habitat ensued and this was followed by population decline. The final example concerns the natural colonisation of Isle Royale in Lake Superior by moose (*Alces alces*) and wolf (*Canis lupus*) (Jordan *et al.* 1971, Mech 1966). Moose reached the island about 1900 and at first their numbers increased slowly. Then, between 1928 and 1930, there was an increase to well above the carrying capacity of the island, accompanied by a subsequent deterioration of the habitat and followed by a decline in moose numbers, finally resulting in a very low population in 1943. The moose populations then began to increase with the availability of plenty of food. Wolves reached Island Royale about 1948 and by 1959 had apparently attained a fairly stable density. This carnivore feeds on moose and an intimate predator–prey relationship developed between the two species. This may have accounted for the rapid stabilisation of the wolf population. These examples (Fig. 12.2) illustrate how for

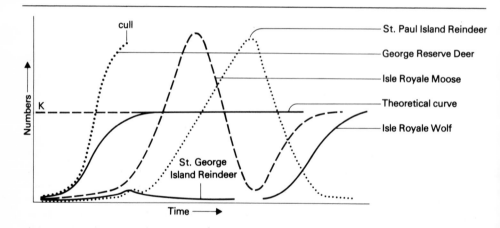

Fig. 12.2 Schematic representation of population growth patterns in North American mammals. The scales do not permit comparisons between densities. The figure illustrates how some populations have failed to follow the anticipated theoretical curve. K = upper asymptote.

colonising large mammals there appear to be considerable problems associated with the attainment of optimal densities. Furthermore, there is little uniformity of response to the environment by newly established populations.

In Africa, Grimsdell and Bell (1972) have recorded changes in an isolated population of semi-aquatic red lechwe (*Kobus leche leche*) in the Busanga Plain, Zambia. This plain covers an area of 700 km^2 of the Kafue National Park. Prior to 1946 there was intensive hunting of these animals which probably resulted in keeping the population at a very low level. Numerous natural predators including lion, leopard, cheetah and spotted hyaena have continuously inhabited the area. The removal of hunting pressure has given the lechwe an opportunity to increase their numbers to a new high density in balance with the changed environmental conditions (Fig. 12.3).

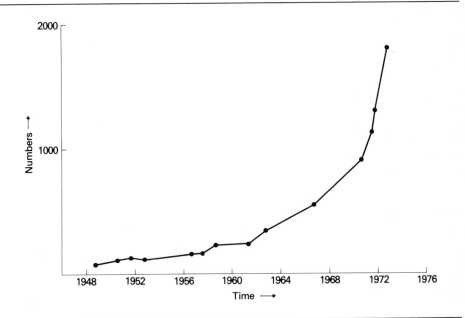

Fig. 12.3   Population growth of red lechwe (*kobus leche leche*) in Busanga Plain, Zambia, 1948–73. (After Grimsdell and Bell 1972.)

The available data show that there was a slow start to the main increase phase of population growth and in 1973 at the time of the last census the population was still growing rapidly giving no indication of an inflexion in the curve. It is therefore not possible to predict when the upper asymptote may be achieved.

Periodic epidemics of rinderpest occurred in the Serengeti buffalo population during the 1950s when the disease killed large numbers of animals. Thereafter, the population increased quite rapidly through the mid 1960s and later the rate of increase slowed down. Here (Fig. 12.4) the removal of a continuing adverse population factor (rinderpest) gave the opportunity for population growth which corresponded to the logistic curve (Sinclair 1973a). In both the buffalo and lechwe population suppression has been maintained by two different factors, man and rinderpest. These African examples are slightly different to those cited from America as in the latter animals had been introduced into areas or to conditions which may not have been identical with those from which they originated.

12.2   Numerical abundance

There are two ways of expressing numerical abundance; firstly, abundance can be space-relative and the density of mammals expressed as numbers per unit area as, for example, 12 rodents/acre or 4 elephants/hectare. Secondly, population comparisons can be made on a time relative basis provided that precisely the same method of obtaining the estimate is applied at the time of each census. In this method a relative measure or index of abundance is obtained between successive censuses. This can be

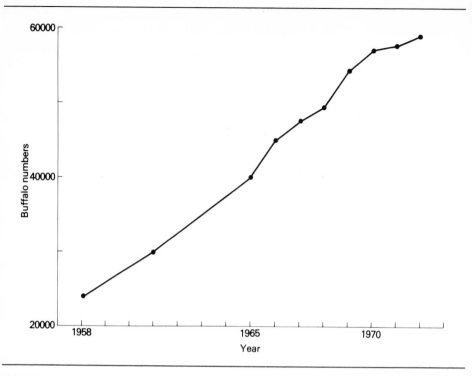

Fig. 12.4 Population growth of buffalo in Serengeti after disappearance of rinderpest epidemic in the 1950s. (After Sinclair 1973*a*.)

useful when applied to mammals such as small rodents with their secretive habits and posing particular problems of density estimation. This was undertaken by Neal (1970) who set traps for small rodents inhabiting grassland before and after burning in western Uganda (Table 12.1). The obvious differences in the catches probably reflect changes in densities even though the space-relative density cannot be derived from these data.

Table 12.1   *Catches (in 1000 trap nights) of selected species of small rodents inhabiting grassland before and after burning, in western Uganda 1965. (After Neal 1970.)*

	Unburnt *28 June–3 July*	*Burnt* *4 July–8 July*
Nile rat (*Arvicanthis niloticus*)	15	0
Punctated grass-mouse (*Lemniscomys striatus*)	103	44
Harsh-furred mouse (*Lophuromys sikapusi*)	21	0
Multimammate rat (*Praomys natalensis*)	49	67
Three-toed grass-rat (*Mylomys dybowskyi*)	21	0

The space-relative population estimate is usually a far more useful parameter. In obtaining this figure the area under consideration must be large enough to ensure it adequately embraces the ranges of the animals being censused. If not, the appropriate statistical adjustment must be incorporated into the estimate. The numbers of animals may vary considerably from habitat to habitat as well as at different times within the same habitat. During the past ten years ecologists have expended tremendous effort on

Table 12.2   *Densities of carnivores and primates.*

Species	Locality	Nos/km²	Authority
Carnivores			
Lion (*Panthera leo*)	Nairobi NP, Kenya	0·261	Rudnai, 1974
Lion (*Panthero leo*)	Manyara NP	0·385	Schaller and Lowther, 1969
Leopard (*Panthera pardus*)	Serengeti, Tanzania	0·036	Schaller, 1972
Leopard (*Panthera pardus*)	Nairobi NP, Kenya	0·063	Rudnai, 1974
Cheetah (*Acinonyx jubacus*)	Meru, Kenya	0·015	Adamson, 1969
Cheetah (*Acinonyx jubatus*)	Serengeti, Tanzania	0·012	Schaller, 1970
Spotted hyaena (*Crocuta crocuta*)	Nairobi NP, Kenya	0·035	Kruuk, 1966
Spotted hyaena (*Crocuta crocuta*)	Ngorongoro, Tanzania	1·622	Kruuk, 1966, 1968
Wild dog (*Lycaon pictus*)	Serengeti, Tanzania	0·115	Kühme, 1965
Banded mongoose (*Mungos Mungo*)	Rwenzori, Uganda	17·4	Rood, 1975

Species	Vegetation	Country	Nos/km²	Authority
Primates				
Angwantibo (*Arctocebus calabarensis*)	Primary forest	Gabon	2	Charles-Dominique (1971)
Demidov's galago (*Galagoides demidovii*)	Primary forest	Gabon	50	Charles-Dominique (1971)
Potto (*Perodicticus potto*)	Primary forest	Gabon	8	Charles-Dominique (1971)
Patas monkey (*Cercopithecus patas*)	Savanna	Uganda	3·5	Hall (1966)
Olive baboon (*Papio anubis*)	Gallery forest	Uganda	11	Rowell (1966)
Chimpanzee (*Pan troglodytes*)	Semi-deciduous forest	Uganda	6·7	Sugiyama (1968)
Gorilla (*Gorilla gorilla*)	Mountain forest	Zaire	1·1	Schaller (1963)

Table 12.3   *Densities of large mammals (nos/km².*

Locality:	Albert NP	Garamba NP	Lake Nakuru, NP
Country:	Zaire	Zaire	Kenya
Habitat:	Short grass, savanna	Mixed savanna	Woodland, grassland
Area surveyed (km²):	600	4800	28·4
Year(s):	1956	1963	1970
Reference:	Bourlière (1965)	Bourlière (1965)	Kutilek (1974)
Elephant (*Loxondonta africana*)	1·8	1·2	—
Burchell's zebra (*Equus burchelli*)	—	—	—
Black rhinoceros (*Diceros bicornis*)	—	—	—
Square-lipped rhinoceros (*Ceratotherium simum*)	—	0·3	—
Hippopotamus (*Hippopotamus amphibius*)	8·0	>0·1	—
Wart hog (*Phacochoerus aethiopicus*)	1·2	0·1	—
Giant forest hog (*Hylochoerus meinertzhageni*)	0·1	—	—
Giraffe (*Giraffa camelopardalis*)	—	0·1	—
Bushbuck (*Tragelaphus scriptus*)	0·1	—	0·8
Roan (*Hippotragus equinus*)	—	—	—
Waterbuck (*Kobus ellipsiprymnus*)	1·3	0·3	31·1
Kob (*Kobus kob*)	9·3	0·3	—
Puku (*Kobus vardoni*)	—	—	—
Reedbuck (*Redunca redunca/R. fulvorufula/R. arundinum*)	0·1	—	8·9
Hartebeest (*Alcelaphus buselaphus/ A. lichtensteini*)	—	0·3	—
Topi (*Damaliscus lunatus*)	2·1	—	—
Blue wildebeest (*Connochaetes taurinus*)	—	—	—
Impala (*Aepyceros melampus*)	—	—	9·0
Dama gazelle (*Gazelle dama*)	—	—	—
Red-fronted gazelle (*Gazella rufifrons*)	—	—	—
Thomson's gazelle (*Gazella thomsoni*)	—	—	8·9
Duikers (*Cephalophus* spp.)	—	—	—
Bay duiker (*Cephalophus dorsalis*)	—	—	—
Blue duiker (*Cephalophus monticola*)	—	—	—
Royal antelope (*Neotragus pygmaeus*)	—	—	—
Oribi (*Ourebia ourebi*)	—	—	—
Dik dik (*Madoqua kirki*)	—	—	0·7
Buffalo (*Syncerus caffer*)	13·9	1·0	0·9
Total:	37·9	3·5	60·2

the estimation of numbers of large mammals in the savannas of East and Central Africa. This information has been obtained as a preliminary to further research and the implementation of management practices. A sample of these large mammal densities is given in Table 12.3. These figures have been selected as representative of fairly static populations within the areas under survey. Localities experiencing mass movement of their populations are not supporting them throughout the year and therefore not comparable with the counts included in Table 12.3. Several points emerge from these data. Firstly, populations can be high and their biomass very considerable as in Kivu, Lake Manyara and Rwenzori Parks. In contrast, densities are relatively low at Garamba, Ngoma and Comoe. In Comoe Park the recent prevention of human interference may result in considerable increase. Nakuru National Park supports a relatively large number of smaller ungulates. But all these figures are very high

Table 12.3 – *continued*

Ngoma, Kafue Zambia Grassland 31 1965 Dowsett (1966)	Fété Olé Senegal Sahelian savanna 100 1969 Poulet (1972)	Rwenzori NP Uganda Grassland savanna 133* 1963–67 Field and Laws (1970)	Tano Nimri Ghana Rain forest 250 1954 Bourlière (1963a)	Comoe Valley Ivory Coast Woodland savanna 37 1968 Geerling and Bokedam (1973)
—	—	2·1	—	—
0·4	—	—	—	—
—	—	—	—	—
—	—	10·4	—	1·0
0·3	Infrequent	2·2	—	0·1
—	—	—	—	—
—	—	—	—	—
—	—	0·6	—	0·1
0·2	—	—	—	0·2
1·0	—	3·5	—	0·2
—	—	9·0	—	14·1
0·1	—	—	—	—
2·4	—	70·1	—	—
1·5	—	—	—	1·7
—	—	—	—	—
1·7	—	—	—	—
—	—	—	—	—
—	V. few	—	—	—
—	Infrequent	—	—	—
—	—	—	—	1·4
—	—	—	0·15	—
—	—	—	0·31	—
—	—	—	0·03	—
1·7	—	—	—	2·0
—	—	—	—	—
—	—	14·6	—	0·1
9·3	?	42·5	0·5	20·9

*Eight study areas north of Kazinga Channel.

especially when compared with the approximate estimate for the Tano Nimri Forest Reserve in Ghana (Bourlière 1963a). This is in any event quite a low estimate for forest (Bourlière 1973) as there must be many places supporting a wider range of forest species. It is unfortunate that no other figures exist for rain forest. Such numbers as are available for the Sahelian zone are also very low.

The Carnivores are generally not numerous (Table 12.2). This might be expected in view of their feeding habits, with the larger species being mostly dependent on the large herbivorous mammals. The primates present a rather different picture with the tiny Demidov's galago attaining quite appreciable numbers in the rain forest of Gabon. The wide ranging patas monkey in the savanna of Kabalega Park, Uganda, occurs at a relatively low density while the large mountain gorilla is also quite sparse.

Under suitable conditions rodents can be extremely numerous (Table 12.4). Dieterlen (1967) obtained staggeringly high densities in a mixture of elephant grass (*Pennisetum*) and bush close to agricultural land in eastern Zaire. This is one of the highest rodent population estimates obtained from any locality in the world. There is no evidence of it being a temporary high population as the figure is based on eight counts made at different times of the year. The total is made up from a large number of species. The habitat with its thick mixed vegetation must offer very suitable conditions as none of the remaining examples, which are probably much more typical of large areas of savanna and forest, approach this density. Rodent populations can fluctuate dramatically over a few months. The figures in Table 12.4 mask such fluctuations as

Table 12.4   *Densities of small rodents and insectivores.*

Habitat/locality	No. of counts	No. of species	Nos/km^2	Authority
Rodents				
Sahelian, savanna, Senegal	20+	1	300	Poulet (1972)
Elephant grass/bush, Zaire	8	13	36 200	Dieterlen (1967)
Unburnt savanna, Ivory Coast	11	11	1 200	Bellier (1967)
Tall grass savanna, Uganda	19	11	3 000	Cheeseman (1975)
Rain forest, Nigeria	33	7	2 260	Happold (1977)
Insectivores				
Elephant grass/bush, Zaire	8	5	2 300	Dieterlen (1967)
Primary forest, Gabon	1	10	57	Brosset (1966c)
Unburnt savanna, Ivory Coast	11	?	600	Bellier (1967)

they represent a mean value of all the counts obtained. Of the few studies available on shrews it appears that their densities are appreciably lower. Compared to the numbers of large mammals, the densities of these small ones are very high. But by virtue of their small size their biomass is still quite low. Delany (1972) estimated the biomass of Dieterlen's eastern Zaire population to be considerably less than any of the total large mammal figures. However, the energy demands per unit weight of a small mammal are relatively greater than a large one and they also utilise more energy in reproduction. It thus seems probable that the total energy requirements per unit area of large and small herbivorous mammals may be closer to each other than their biomass figures might suggest (see Section 11.3).

12.3   Population structure, survivorship and life tables

The structure of a population is its composition at a particular time in terms of the numbers of animals of each sex, and the frequency of the various age groups expressed in time intervals such as month or year classes. Alternatively, classification can be on the basis of such broad categories as immature, sub-adult and adult or on a series of relative measures of age as provided by tooth wear or attrition. When an index like this is used it is frequently desirable that it should be related to a time interval as it is possible that these arbitrarily defined stages may not all be of equal duration.

A rich literature exists (see Spinage 1973) on the determination of age in ungulates by means of teeth. In these animals the dental characters used include the eruption and replacement of certain teeth, the formation of cementum lines by calcification rings in secondary dentine and the attrition of the tooth. The last involves recording the decreasing height of the tooth, the progressive flattening and the increasing dentine exposure. After deciding on a number of recognisable categories, it is then desirable to compare these to live animals of known age. From this information the rates of change in tooth structure can be assessed and, by extrapolation, the ages of animals in each of the categories. Spinage (1967) adopted this approach in his study of waterbuck populations. He constructed various categories of eruption and attrition and converted these to time intervals with information obtained on wear rates in field immobilised animals. Supplementary and confirmatory information was provided from the cementum lines and growth of horns.

These and similar approaches have been applied to a variety of large mammals including black rhinoceros (Goddard 1970), buffalo (Grimsdell 1973), zebra (Klingel and Klingel 1966, Spinage 1972) (Fig. 12.5), elephant (Laws 1966) (Fig. 12.6),

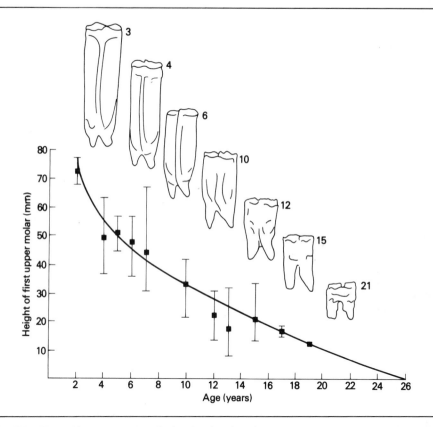

Fig. 12.5 Wear of first upper molar of zebra. Vertical lines show range and the drawings the appearance of the molar tooth at different ages. (After Spinage 1972.)

hippopotamus (Laws 1968*b*) and impala (Spinage 1971). In several of these examples, a method additional to dental characters has been used. These have included eye lens weight (hippopotamus, Laws 1968*b*), shoulder height (elephant, Laws 1966) and cranial measurement (rhino, Goddard 1970). The results of Laws, (1969*b*) age determination in two elephant populations from Tsavo and Kabalega National Parks are shown in Fig. 12.7. Here the data are based on animals cropped between 1965 and 1967. They provide a clear indication of the structures of these two populations and the ways in which they resemble and differ from each other. There are troughs in the numbers of certain age groups at approximately six- to eight-year intervals which are

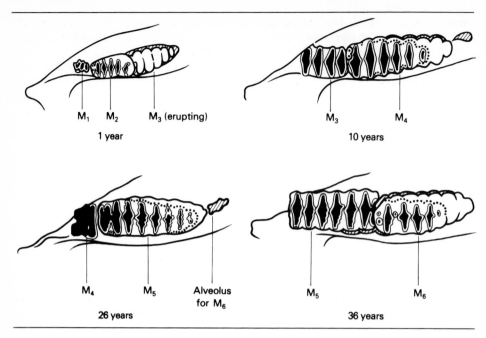

Fig. 12.6   Four stages in the eruption, attrition and elimination of the lower molar teeth of the elephant. (After Laws 1966.) New molars are erupted from the posterior of the maxilla and are worn away from the anterior of the jaw. Dentine is black in these figures; it becomes more apparent as wear progresses. Stage III (1 year) M_1 is very eroded and will shortly be lost, M_3 is erupting and has not yet developed a grinding surface; Stage IX (10 years) M_1 and M_2 have been replaced by M_3 and M_4, the former is well worn; Stage XVI (26 years) M_4 very eroded, site of appearance of M_6 apparent; Stage XXI (36 years) M_5 eroding, M_6 partially erupted and wearing anteriorly.

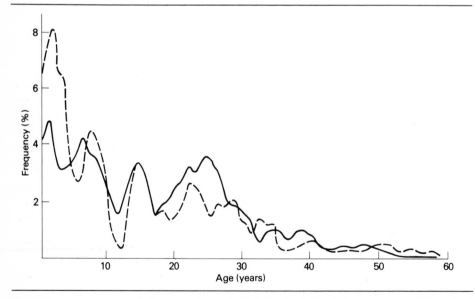

Fig. 12.7   Age structure of elephant populations in Kabalega Park North (————) and Tsavo Park (— — — —) in 1966. (Adapted from Laws 1969a.)

probably associated with low recruitment or mortality soon after birth. The existence of these troughs also means that the relatively few animals in these age groups can only make a small reproductive contribution to the population as a whole.

Various categories of molar tooth attrition and dental exposure have been utilised for assessing relative ages of rodents (Neal 1968, Delany 1971, Happold 1967*b* and Ansell and Ansell 1973). Delany (1971) took the analysis further by comparing patterns (Table 12.5) in wild animals with those reared in the laboratory. From this

Table 12.5 *Age and tooth wear in rodents reared in the laboratory. (From Delany 1971.)*

Age class	Hylomyscus Age (days)	Lophuromys Age (days)	Praomys Age (days)
I	15–28	15, 22	16–31
II	31–93	31	48–91
III	61–184	92–215	96–199
IV	242		199–297

information it was apparent that a broad spread of age could be found in any one tooth wear category. As with the larger mammals it is also uncertain whether teeth wear at the same rate in wild as in captive animals. In spite of the limitations to these methods, there have been some important results from studies making use of them. In his field study in Western Uganda on the multimammate rat (*Praomys natalensis*) Neal (1968) observed the monthly changes in population structure over a year (Fig. 12.8), and even though he was not able to accurately assign ages to his tooth wear categories it was possible to infer a great deal about the dynamics of the population. The appearance of young mice in June coincided with the end of the rains. The method of trapping was such that nestlings and young animals up to about one month old were caught infrequently or not at all. This meant that relatively small numbers were obtained in wear category I which was probably a short-lasted stage. The cohort appearing in May/June can be traced over the months until by November it is forming the group of larger animals that are the parents of the newly appearing young. A decline in numbers can be traced through this cycle as the animals become older and only a very small percentage of the population survives as long as a year.

It is also useful to know the numbers of animals in each age group at a particular time. This indicates the proportion of animals surviving to a particular age. However, this information is based on numbers of live animals and to know how many die from one time interval to the next it is necessary to calculate the proportional change between consecutive age groups. The calculation of this information demands equal catchability of all stages of the life-history. This is a simple concept which is a measure of mortality at different ages and is referred to as survival or survivorship. One method used to estimate age at death in wild populations has been to collect the skulls and lower jaws of large mammals that have died of natural causes. Under natural conditions the breakdown of bone is quite rapid and for this reason the samples will have come from animals dying over a fairly limited period. This method has been employed on black rhinoceros (Goddard 1970) and elephant (Laws 1966). The collected jaws are then aged and the total number in each class recorded. This is an estimate of the proportion of animals attaining the various age classes. It is also a measure of survivorship which is assumed to be representative of the population as a whole.

Survivorship is usually expressed by taking a cohort of 1 000 newly born individuals

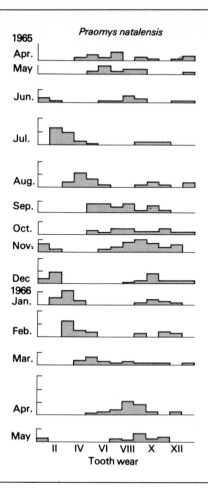

Fig. 12.8 Age structure of *Praomys natalensis* populations in Rwenzori Park. (After Neal 1968.)

and noting how many are still alive after regular time intervals. Thus at the same time as measuring survival to different ages, mortality rates are also obtained. Of the four survivorship curves shown in Fig. 12.9, three refer to actual ages of the animals. The fourth on the mole rat expresses the number of female survivors after the production of different numbers of litters. As these rats are not continuous breeders an estimate has to be obtained of the average time between litters. This was 173 days. There was considerable mortality up to the production of the first litter but thereafter the mortality rate declined. The black rhinoceros and wildebeest have high mortality in early life. This is apparently not the case in the baboon, where according to Berger (1972) the mortality rate was low until the animals reached what he referred to as the juvenile stage at 35 months. The mortality rate then increased up to the adult age of 57 months and thereafter decreased sharply. These examples illustrate the lack of uniformity in survivorship curves and the variability of ages of highest and lowest mortality.

The *death rate* is the number of animals dying within a particular time period divided by the total animals alive at the beginning of that period. For example, in

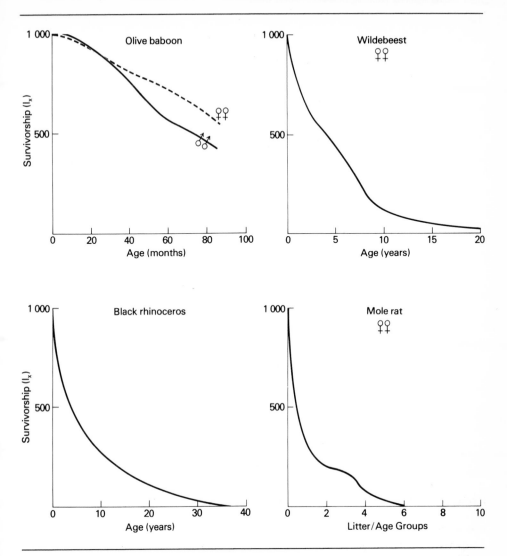

Fig. 12.9 Survivorship curves of olive baboon (Berger 1972), black rhinoceros (Adapted from Goddard 1970), female wildebeest (Watson 1969) and female mole rats (Jarvis 1973).

wildebeest 254 females of every 1 000 die in their first year. The death rate is thus 254/1 000. Were the curves in Fig. 12.9 linear, the death rates would be steadily increasing as the same number would die at each time interval while the number alive at the beginning of each interval would be declining. The life table is an extension of the survivorship curve and also incorporates survival and death rates, includes information on reproductive rates and predicts the replacement rate of the population. In constructing a table information is also required on the numbers of young produced by females of all ages. An example of a life table is provided on the wildebeest (Table 12.6). The essential information is the number of animals alive (survivors) at each interval, the number dying and the death rate. The *average life expectancy* of the animals in each group can then be obtained. The number of females produced by each

Table 12.6   *Life table of female wildebeest (*Connochaetes taurinus*) in Serengeti, Tanzania. (After Watson 1969.)*

Female age (years)	Survivors (l_x)	Deaths (d_x)	Death rate (q_x)	Average life expectancy p_x	Mean no. of ♀ produced/ adult ♀ (m_x)	$l_x m_x$
Birth	1 000	—	—	4	0·00	0·000
1	746	254	0.25	5	0·00	0·000
2	660	340	0.12	5	0·19	0·125
3	571	429	0.14	4	0·42	0·239
4	523	477	0.08	4	0·48	0·251
5	450	550	0.14	3	0·48	0·216
6	379	621	0.16	3	0·48	0·181
7	306	694	0.19	3	0·48	0·147
8	217	783	0.29	2	0·48	0·104
9	160	840	0.26	2	0·48	0·077
10	87	913	0.47	2	0·48	0·042
11	79	921	0.09	4	0·48	0·038
12	71	929	0.10	5	0·48	0·034
13	63	937	0.11	5	0·48	0·030
14	47	953	0.26	5	0·48	0·023
15	39	961	0.17	5	0·48	0·019
16	39	961	0.00	4	0·48	0·019
17	39	961	0.00	3	0·48	0·019
18	31	969	0.21	2	0·48	0·015
19	23	977	0.26	1	0·48	0·011
20	8	992	0.65	1	0·48	0·004
21	0	1 000	1.00	$\frac{1}{2}$	0·48	0·000

$$\Sigma l_x m_x = 1,594$$

female is required for each age class. The product of this figure and the number of female survivors provides an estimate of the number of young being produced by each age class.

This figure takes account of the fact that not all females reach maturity at the same time and similarly of those that cease breeding when relatively young. The sum of the $l_x m_x$ column is the net reproductive rate (R_0) or *finite rate of increase* and represents the number of animals that will replace the existing cohort. In the wildebeest this means that the original 1 000 adult females (Table 12.6) will be replaced by 1 594. This figure takes account of the age structure, survival, and reproductive rate of the population and assumes that conditions remain the same over the period of population replacement. It is possible to convert this increase to rate of increase per year. This is the intrinsic (annual) rate of increase r. In the wildebeest this is 0.073/head/year.

The annual production of young and the steady removal through death of all age groups inevitably produce a constant change in the animals comprising a population even though its structure may remain unaltered. Survivorship, replacement and structure are important interrelated parameters of animal populations and it is relevant to consider how they interact to produce different patterns of population turnover. The way in which replacement occurs is determined to a large extent by the life history pattern of the species concerned. By selecting two species with markedly different life histories and survivorship charactistics it is possible to examine how rates and patterns of population replacement can vary. Models can be constructed to compare short life cycle species such as the punctated grass-mouse (*Lemniscomys striatus*) (Neal 1968, Cheeseman 1975) and the long life cycle species such as the wildebeest. In the grassland of Rwenzori Park, Uganda, these mice, like the multimammate rats considered earlier, are born in one rainy season, breed in the next and the majority are dead by the one following. This is a very rapid turnover (Fig. 12.10) which contrasts with that of the wildebeest where there is a longer life

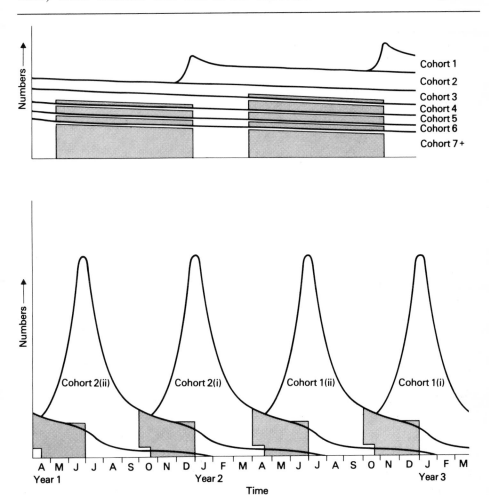

Fig. 12.10 Models illustrating the effects of two life history and survival patterns on the short term fluctuations in population numbers. The data are based on females only; shaded blocks represent pregnant animals. The upper diagram is derived from data on a long-lived species (wildebeest in Serengeti) and the lower a short-lived species (the punctated grass-mouse in Rwenzori). The figures show a steadily increasing wildebeest population and a stable mouse population. The former has one breeding season in the year, the latter two.

expectation and maturity is attained in two to three years. In both species a very high percentage of the adult females produce offspring during the seasonal breeding period. The mouse's habitat with its two short wet seasons probably accounts for the two breeding seasons in the year. The mouse has a mean litter size of 4·8 and an average production of 1·87 litters in the season. Assuming no adult female mortality during the breeding season this results in 9·0 young added to the population by each female, or with a 1 to 1 sex ratio, a female replacement of 4·5. In this species there are a few females breeding in their season of birth. The wildebeest data are given in Table 12.6. Here is a much longer lived species (up to 21 years) maturing at a later age (2–3 years) and producing only one young at each birth.

These two models (Fig. 12.10) show how strikingly different the population processes are in the wildebeest and *Lemniscomys*. The consequences of these two patterns, which are of wide application, can be considered further. The mouse with its high productive capability over the short term is capable of very volatile population fluctuations so that rapid recovery from low densities is quite possible. The wildebeest on the other hand exemplifies a species with a far more stable density. It does not have the ability to increase at anything approaching the rate of the mouse and if for any reason it experienced a sudden dramatic reduction in numbers recovery would take longer. In this particular model the population is increasing in numbers. According to Watson (1969) the wildebeest could rapidly regulate its density by delaying the age of first reproduction as the younger animals make a large contribution to the intrinsic rate of increase. These observations suggest relatively small fluctuations in large mammal populations within the twelve-month period. In this example for wildebeest, the high is of the order of a 25–35 per cent above the low. In contrast, many field studies on rodents reveal much greater increases. In Senegal, Poulet (1972) estimated that in 1971 the high population of the gerbil *Taterillus pygargus* was 1 250 per cent above the low, whilst in Malawi, Hanney (1965) recorded a high catch of the multimammate rat 1 670 per cent above the low. Furthermore, in many small mammals the density at the population peak may be subject to appreciable variation from year to year and is unlikely to be as constant as shown in Fig. 12.10.

The life history patterns of *Lemniscomys* and wildebeest apparently correspond to the *r* and *K* selection strategies proposed by MacArthur and Wilson (1967). Features of the former are variable population density, often well below carrying capacity of the environment, rapid development, and high reproductive rate at an early age. This strategy leads to high production. The *K* selection life history strategy leads to fairly constant population densities at or near the carrying capacity of the environment. Animals in this category generally have a slower development, delayed reproduction, larger body size and greater competitive ability. The high productivity of the *r* selectors would make them the better colonisers.

All species of mammal cannot be assigned to one or other of these models, as several assume different patterns. Life history phenomena and environmental conditions ultimately determine the pattern. On theoretical ground it is possible for the the density of a species to remain unaltered indefinitely but this could only prevail if rates of recruitment continually matched losses. In practice this is unlikely as the occurrence of fluctuations is in harmony with the typical temporal variation in environmental conditions.

12.4   Population fluctuations

Fluctuations in mammal populations over several years have been investigated in a number of localities. A regular census of the large mammals has been undertaken in most months of the year in the 122 km² of Nairobi Park, Kenya (Foster and Kearney 1967, Foster and McLaughlin 1968, McLaughlin 1970, Rudnai 1973) from 1961 to 1963 and 1966 to 1974. The annual figure is the mean of these monthly counts. The Park comprises a mixture of grassland, wooded valleys and a small forested area. To the south there is broad continuity with the Athi-Kapiti plains with which there is free interchange of large mammals. This movement between the two areas can account for large monthly variations in the counts. Within the Park artificial water sources have been provided so in the dry season mammals move into this more favourable habitat from the adjacent plain. During the wet season mammals disperse away from the Park to the plain. Poor rains in 1960 followed by a drought in the first half of 1961 resulted in an accumulation of animals in the Park followed by a dramatic mortality (Fig. 12.11).

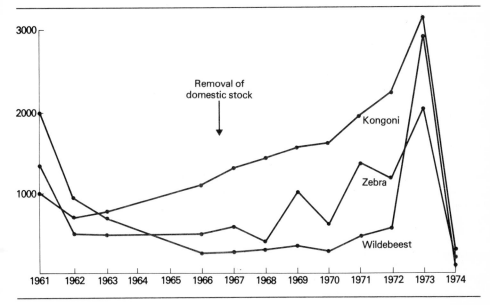

Fig. 12.11 Annual population fluctuations obtained from the mean of monthly counts of hartebeest (or kongoni) zebra and wildebeest in Nairobi Park, Kenya. (Adapted from Foster and Kearney 1967, Foster and McLaughlin 1968, McLaughlin 1970, Rudnai 1973.)

By 1962, there were on average less than 1 000 each of wildebeest, hartebeest and zebra in the Park. While numbers of the last two steadily increased from then until 1973 the fall in the wildebeest continued until a gradual recovery commenced in 1967. A considerable increase was observed in 1973 largely as a result of the Park accommodating massive numbers (over 8 000) in two of the eight months when counts were made. The high mortality on the plains and in the Park in early 1974 resulted from severe drought as well as serious poaching of zebra in areas adjacent to the Park. During the survey period there was a further major ecological modification involving the removal of 1 350 resident domestic cattle and sheep from the Park in May 1967.

Taking an example from the Primates, three troops of olive baboon inhabiting gallery forest in Western Uganda were monitored for six years (Rowell 1969). During the first three years (1963–5) there was a steady increase in numbers (Fig. 12.12) but from 1965 to 1968 there was a slight increase although the population remained fairly stable with 150 to 170 animals. The stabilisation of this population is associated with an increase in mortality after 1964 of young animals in the period from late pregnancy to a short time after birth. This Rowell (1969) refers to as perinatal death. Apparently, in one of the troops 25 per cent of known pregnancies did not produce young. It was estimated that animals surviving the perinatal period then had a life expectancy of about 33 years. There was little evidence of predation on these baboons even though predator species were known to be present.

The buffalo of Rwenzori Park, Uganda, have been counted at irregular intervals

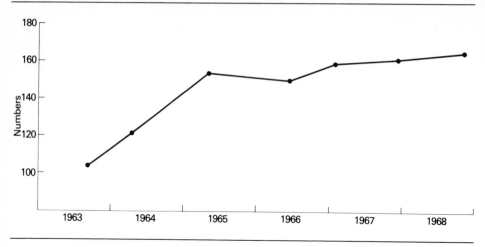

Fig. 12.12 Population densities of a baboon troop at Ishasha, Rwenzori Park. (From Rowell 1969.)

between 1963 and 1972 (Eltringham and Woodford 1973). This long narrow Park extends much further along its north–south axis (110 km) than its east–west, which seldom exceeds 30 km. The vegetation of most of the Park consists of grassland and woodland. There is, however, a broad strip of semi-deciduous forest separating the northern and southern sectors of savanna. Some buffalo apparently move into this forest in the dry season, and as counts could not be made within the forest the estimates are only for the savanna areas. This makes it most appropriate to compare fluctuations for wet and dry seasons separately. The mean number of animals recorded was 14760 on five dry season censuses (range 13499–17953) and 16715 on seven wet seasons censuses (range 14313–18040). Eltringham and Woodford (1973) consider that if allowance is made for underestimates in the counting techniques the number of buffalo within the Park has remained stable for at least the period 1970 to 1972 at around 18000 animals in addition to some animals in the forest. The total counts since 1963 indicate there have not been any large fluctuations. The buffalo probably never leave the Park but do display movements in response to wet and dry conditions. As well as the herds entering the forest in the dry season they also, at this time, move closer to water.

Seven species of ground-living rodents inhabiting Gambari Forest, Nigeria, were censused at the middle and end of each year from 1968 to 1975 (Fig. 12.13) (Happold 1977). Numbers ranged about a mean figure of 13·3/ha from 4·95/ha in mid 1973 to 22·7/ha in mid-1968.

The fluctuation in the tropical rain forest appears very modest when compared with that of a temperate woodland (Fig. 12.13). The difference may be partly accounted for by the greater uniformity of conditions in the former with a consequent trend to greater population stability. This more clearly emerges through detailed examination of one species (*Praomys tullbergi*) from November 1967 to November 1970. These data (Fig. 12.14) indicate monthly recruitment and a fluctuation having a 2·9 fold increase from 18 to 48 animals known to be inhabiting the grid in the months of lowest and highest numbers.

The seasonal movement of large mammals (section 10.1) may have considerable effects for a limited period of the year on the environments where it occurs. Within these locations there are very short term fluctuations in numbers. A good example of

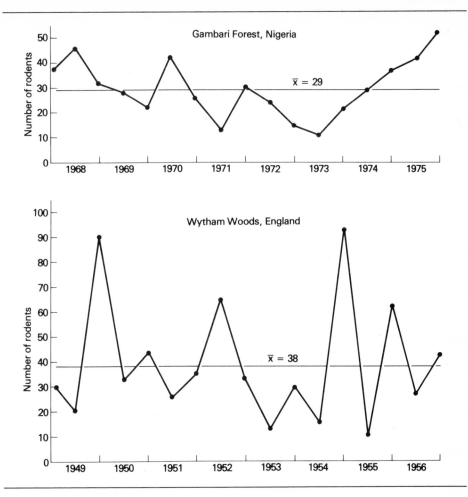

Fig. 12.13   Number and fluctuations of rodents in 2ha of Gambari Forest, Nigeria, and Wytham Woods, England. In the former there were seven species and the latter two. (After Happold 1977 and Southern 1970.)

density changes within an area as a result of movement is seen in the Tarangire Game Reserve in Northern Tanzania (Lamprey 1964). Here, in this acacia savanna bordering the Tarangire River there are large dry season congregations of ungulates. Many of these animals come from the adjacent Masai steppe where there is high stocking with domestic cattle and an indifferent water supply. The Reserve temporarily supports high numbers without any evidence of habitat deterioration. The fluctuations witnessed from 1958 to 1961 (Fig. 12.15) are mostly accounted for by movement in and out of the area. The five different movement patterns of the major species of ungulates further complicates the overall picture. Firstly there are the dry season immigrants including buffalo, zebra, wildebeest, eland and elephant. These animals enter the Reserve at the end of the rains and leave at the onset of the wet season and they account for a major portion of the overall fluctuation. The precise times of movement vary slightly from year to year in response to the rainfall. The warthog, waterbuck, dik-dik and rhino are resident and have a partial dispersal from the concentration area in the rains. Some species such as the giraffe, Grant's gazelle, hartebeest and lesser kudu have

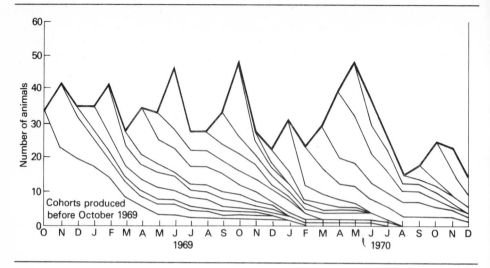

Fig. 12.14   Monthly population fluctuations in *Praomys tullbergi*. New cohorts are shown for each month. The heavy line indicates the population total. (Adapted from Happold 1977.)

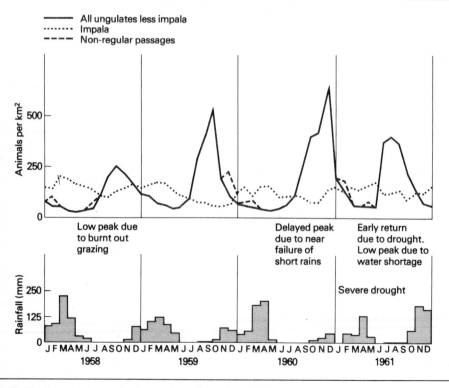

Fig. 12.15   Seasonal changes in the numbers of ungulates in Tarangire Reserve, Tanzania. Most species move out of the study area for the wet season. (Adapted from Lamprey 1964.)

little or no dispersal in wet or dry seasons. A fourth category is the passage migrants of buffalo, zebra and elephant. These species have irregular concerted migrating movements through the areas as part of their normal dispersal activity. Finally, there is the impala which has a partial dispersal from the Reserve during the dry season.

12.5 Factors involved in the regulation of populations

There are a large number of factors involved in the regulation of mammal populations including climate and food supply, predation, floods, fire, undernutrition, disease, parasitism and inter-specific competition. The intra-specific behavioural factors are considered elsewhere in the chapter on ecology and behaviour. These, together with all the other factors, can be variable in their effects within the same population at different times. They can be density-dependent or density-independent. They are sometimes ill-defined. And finally, several factors can operate simultaneously on a population.

Climate and food supply

In Chapter 9 attention was drawn to the variability that can occur in the time and duration of breeding periods not only between species but also within the same species living in different geographical locations. Climate, with particular reference to the seasonality of rain and its effects on vegetation growth, has been implicated as an important component of discontinuous breeding. Thus the chain of climate, vegetation and reproduction are interrelated and best considered together. Furthermore, by reference to a small selection of examples patterns can be illustrated and the various regulatory factors considered. Hanks (1972) studied the reproduction of elephant from 1964 to 1969 in the wooded and grassland savanna of Luangwa Valley, Zambia. From 1964 to 1968, 88 per cent of the conceptions occurred from November to May with a peak in February and March. These closely corresponded to the wet season when on average about 80 cm of rain falls between November and March. After a 22-month gestation period the young are born shortly before or during the wet season. The elephant changes its diet from browse and dry grass at the end of the dry season to fresh green grass during the rains. Monthly changes in the protein content of grass (Table 12.7) in the same general area suggest that it is sufficient during the rains to stimulate

Table 12.7 *Percentage crude protein in grass under repeated mowing at Mazabuka, Zambia. (Hanks 1972.)*

Nov.	3·35	May	2·2
Dec.	11·01	June	2·1
Jan.	6·13	July	1·08
Feb.	5·15	Aug.	0·86
March	4·6	Sept.	0·68
April	4·3	Oct.	0·64

ovulation and its subsequent decline may prove inhibitory. However, in 1969 for some undetermined reason, conceptions were appreciably out of phase with the rains, taking place from January to August and having a peak in the dry season month of June.

Study of the food and reproduction of Thomson's gazelle, hartebeest and giraffe on the Akira Ranch in the Kenya Rift Valley by Field and Blankenship (1973*b*) has produced some interesting results. Here there are three main vegetation types. Grassland dominated by the red oat grass (*Themeda triandra*) occurs on the plains, while elsewhere there are two types of bush, either the whistling thorn (*Acacia* *drepanobium*) or the dense Ol'Leleshwa (*Tarchonanthus camphoratus*). This area is rather drier than Luangwa Valley, having a mean annual rainfall of around 59 cm. Field and Blankenship measured the standing crop biomass of the vegetation, the conception rate of the ungulates and the survival of their young from 1970 to 1971. They also obtained mean annual rainfall data. Their work was both thorough and extensive with surveys being made in all three vegetation types. The analysis of their data was complicated by temporary movement of some of the animals off the ranch and by the irregular occurrence of fire. In spite of these complications some useful results were forthcoming (Table 12.8). The conception rate was obtained from animals that were culled and the survival of young measured by counting the relative abundance of young and immature animals in the population each year. The higher rainfall in 1970 was responsible for the richer vegetation growth and higher protein content and therefore a greater quantity of food than in 1969 and 1971. This resulted in the adults attaining good condition in 1970 and the conception of larger numbers in 1971. Similarly the presence of a good food supply in 1970 accounted for a higher survival of the young in 1971.

In the semi-arid grass-woodland of northern Senegal the average rainfall is 37 cm per annum although from 1969 to 1973 this figure was not attained. It is here that Poulet (1972, 1974) studied the population dynamics of the granivorous gerbil, *Taterillus pygargus*. In this area of low precipitation, Bille (1974) has drawn attention to an extremely important climatic phenomenon. The growth of vegetation is determined by both the quantity of rain falling in the wet season and the duration of the period which ground water is available to the plants. The latter can vary between 50 and 110 days per year and the upper extreme results in a standing crop production of plants of more than twice the lower value. The population figures of *Taterillus* and the relevant rainfall data (Table 12.9) are very revealing. The rains commence about July

Table 12.9   *Rainfall and population fluctuations in* Taterillus pygargus. *(After Poulet 1972, 1974, Bilke 1974.)*

Year commencing July	1969	1970	1971	1972	1973
Rain (cm) (July–Sept.)	32·1	20·8	20·2	3·3	20·6
Max. pop./ha. (Quadrat QR)	5·5	4·9	0·5	0·5	
Efficiency of rains	Good	Moderate	Poor	Zero	

so the population figures are probably a response to the plant growth induced by these rains. 1969 was a relatively good year even though it was below the average. There was a substantial drop in rainfall the following year. However, as this was spread over neither too long nor too short a period the consequent growth of plants was sufficient to produce enough seeds for the population to closely approach that of 1969. In contrast, the same quantity of rain fell in 1971 as in 1970 but the season was appreciably shorter and the rodent population, in consequence of poor primary production, much reduced. These studies more than the two preceding examples highlight the delicacy of the relationship between breeding and rainfall. This example deals with a much more fragile ecological situation with wide and frequent deviations from the mean rainfall figure.

The population recruitment of the desert-dwelling jerboa, *Jaculus jaculus*, in the vicinity of Khartoum is apparently relatively little influenced by rainfall. This is particularly important as this animal lives in an area of very low annual rainfall. In 1971 the total rainfall of just over 10 cm was rather below the annual mean rainfall of 15 cm. When Ghobrial and Hodieb's (1973) figures of the percentage of adult females

Table 12.8 *Plant biomass and conception rate and survival of young on Akira Ranch, Kenya. (After Field and Blankenship 1973.)*

	1969	1970		1971		
Rain (cm)	39·91	92·14		56·90		
Standing crop biomass vegetation (kg/ha.)	No data	5891 (June)	4375 (Sept.)	2493 (Jan.)	1241 (April)	3612 (Aug.)
Conception rate:						
Thomson's gazelle (*Gazella thomsoni*)		12		18		
Hartebeest (*Alcelaphus buselaphus*)		15		18		
Giraffe (*Giraffa camelopardalis*)		9		10		
Survival of young:						
Thomson's gazelle (*Gazella thomsoni*)		7·4		11·5		
Hartebeest (*Alcelaphus buselaphus*)		8·8		16·5		
Giraffe (*Giraffa camelopardalis*)		14·3		26·5		

Table 12.10   *Pregnancy and litter sizes in* Jaculus jaculus *in 1971. (After Ghobrial and Hodieb 1973.)*

	Jan.	Feb.	March	April	May	June	July	Aug.	Sept.	Oct.	Nov.	Dec.
Rain (cm)	—	—	—	—	trace	trace	3·8	3·5	2·8	—	—	—
Per cent adult ♀♀ pregnant	40	55	22	10	48	27	8	30	78	60	58	17
Mean litter size	4·0	3·5	2·2	3·4	3·2	1·8	2·3	3·5	4·8	3·7	2·8	3·0

pregnant and mean litter size are examined (Table 12.10) it can be seen that whilst there is a peak in both incidence of pregnancy and mean litter size towards the end of the rains and into the dry season there is also a considerable proportion of females pregnant throughout the year. The rains therefore appear to exert only a limited influence on the reproduction of this animal. The food of the jerboa is mainly derived from the subterranean bulbs of *Cyperus bulbosus* and corms of *Dipcadi* which also provide its water supply. During the cool wet season it also eats the stems and foliage of these plants. The availability of a subterranean supply of uniform quality must facilitate continuous breeding. These findings are not in complete accord with Happold's (1967*b*) earlier work on this species. He concluded that from mid 1964 to early 1966 this animal displayed more seasonal breeding.

Analytical studies on climate and the relations between food supply and reproduction have been undertaken on the rodents in Uganda and Kenya by Field (1975) and Taylor and Green (1976). The omnivorous punctated grass-mouse (*Lemniscomys striatus*) was examined in Rwenzori Park (Field 1975). This research covered only a few months and made use of small samples of animals. Field obtained monthly records of the percentage of females lactating or pregnant, the major food, rainfall and the fat content of the liver (Table 12.11). In 1972 the wet and dry seasons in

Table 12.11   *Rainfall, breeding, food and liver fat in* Lemniscomys striatus *in 1972. (After Field 1975.)*

	Jan.	Feb.	March	April	May	June
Per cent pregnant and/or lactating	?	16	24	13	87	81
Mean liver fat/liver wt (%)	2·2	3·2	1·5	6·4	2·3	2·3
Main food	Grass	?	Fruits	Insects	Insects	Grass
Rain (mm)	?	70	102	164	64	71

this locality were less distinct than usual. The maximum breeding was in May and June. The rains built up to a peak in April at the same time as insects became the most important component of the diet. These would have been a rich source of dietary protein which presumably had an important role in sustaining breeding. The high fat content of the liver also corresponded to the wettest month. In this mouse the situation is clearly very complex with considerable scope provided for speculation on possible causative and terminating mechanisms. A more extensive study has been undertaken by Taylor and Green (1976) on the granivorous Nile rat *Arvicanthis niloticus* in the Kenya Highlands (Fig. 12.16). Here, increase in testis size and the incidence of pregnancy coincide with the occurrence of large quantities of cereal and other seeds in the diet. Fat is laid down towards the end of the rains with this reserve up at the end of the dry and beginning of the wet season when leaves and stems are forming the bulk of the diet. The Nile rat apparently differs from the punctated grass-mouse in having the maximum accumulation of fat at a different time in its breeding cycle. However, differences in the diets and climatic regimes may account for these apparent inconsistencies.

These examples illustrate how rainfall, through food supply, indirectly effects the

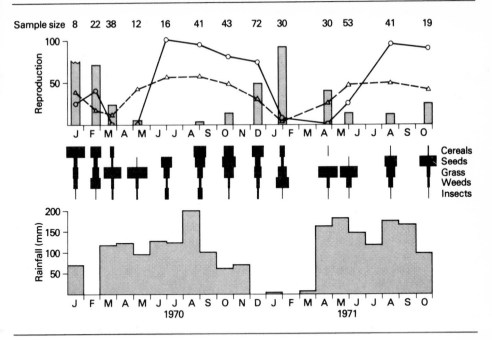

Fig. 12.16 Seasonal relations between reproduction, food and rainfall in *Arvicanthis niloticus* from Kitale, Kenya. (O — O) per cent adult females pregnant or lactating; (△- – △) index of testicular activity; (▨) fat index. Width of diet blocks provides an index of food consumed. (After Taylor and Green 1976.)

duration of breeding, numbers of young produced and survival of young animals. The nutritional quality as well as the quantity of available food is also important. Furthermore, the quantity of vegetation produced is not determined solely by precipitation but rather by its availability to the plants. There can be no doubt that this is a complex and very finely adjusted system, and that the recruitment of animals into a population is greatly influenced by these factors.

Predation

The effects of predators on mammal populations have been studied in great detail in the National Parks of East and South Africa where estimates have been obtained of the numbers and biomass of the larger prey species and their principal food sources (Table 11.20). This information gives a general picture of the relative weight of large carnivore to herbivore without in itself providing an indication of the interractions between them. The most striking feature is the uniformly low density and biomass of the predators which are never greater than one ninety-fourth the weight of the herbivores and can be as little as one three-hundredth. In Ngorongoro, Nairobi and Kruger the relative abundance of carnivores is much the same, in Manyara it is somewhat lower and in Serengeti very much lower than the first three.

The feeding habits of the spotted hyaena (*Crocuta crocuta*) have attracted the detailed study of Kruuk (1972) in Serengeti and Ngorongoro. From field observations he ascertained that the annual percentage of the hyaena's three major food species (wildebeest, zebra and Thomson's gazelle) were not the same in the two reserves (Table

Table 12.12   *Annual percentage of prey population killed and scavenged in Serengeti and Ngorongoro by spotted hyaena. (From Kruuk 1972.)*

	Serengeti		Ngorongoro	
	Killed and scavenged	Killed only	Killed and scavenged	Killed only
Wildebeest adult	1·9–3·1	1·6–2·6	11·2	11·0
Zebra adult and foal	2·2–1·7	1·0–0·8	9·4	9·0
Gazelle adult and foal	6·5–2·1	3·5–1·1*	3·4	1·8

*Possibly underestimated.

12.12), with hyaenas taking a greater proportion of the total herbivore population in Ngorongoro. There is an important fundamental difference in the behaviour of the prey in Serengeti and Ngorongoro resulting from the occurrence in the former of large scale annual migrations. Hyaenas follow their migratory prey in Serengeti and continue to feed on them throughout the year. In doing this the adults may have to be away from their cubs for several days at a time and as a result the young may on occasion die of starvation. This is a vicissitude not encountered in Ngorongoro. In Serengeti the hyaena population is unable to attain densities that might be anticipated in the light of the available food. Expressed in another way the hyaena population is taking a relatively small proportion of the prey and is not in consequence exercising an effective regulation of its density. The situation is very different in Ngorongoro where the high mortality (11 per cent) of wildebeest due to hyaena predation approximately matches recruitment. Here there is much greater evidence of the predator regulating the population.

The age groups of wildebeest killed in Serengeti and Ngorongoro (Fig. 12.17) are different. In Serengeti, fewer very young animals and more old animals are taken but this only reflects differences in age structures of wildebeest in the two populations. The larger number of calves killed in Ngorongoro is associated with a greater pressure on these animals for the relatively short period of the year when they are available for the hyaenas. There is also considerable pressure in Serengeti. However, the greater availability of older animals here than Ngorongoro may account for such a large proportion being taken.

In Serengeti there is considerable evidence that the availability of the prey regulates the numbers of predators. At Ngorongoro, the hyaenas display great competition for food and die younger than in Serengeti and it could well be that they have reached the carrying capacity of their habitat. Are they then regulating or regulated? Kruuk believes that ultimately hyaena numbers are controlled by food supply and that their regulatory capability lies in adjusting the prey numbers rather than exercising a dominant control.

The ecology and behaviour of lions have been investigated by Schaller (1972) in Serengeti. In this area there is a variety of vegetation including woodland and grassy plains. Most prides of lion are found in woodlands and along their edges where food and a constant supply of water are available throughout the year. Most of the Serengeti prides live in territories whose size is related to prey density. The densities of lion populations are fairly stable over long periods as has been shown in Nairobi Park where numbers remained around 20 to 25 adults for at least 20 years. In Serengeti the pride lions, which comprise most of the population, do not follow the migratory herds of wildebeest, zebra and gazelle. Instead they retain and remain within their territories. This means that for a large portion of the year the high densities of prey are not

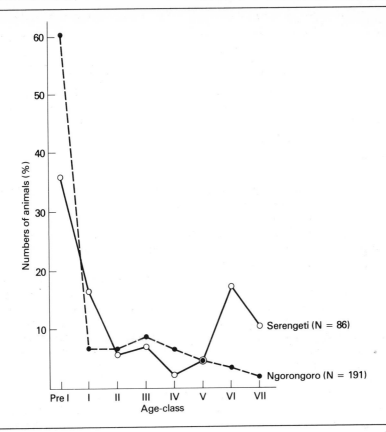

Fig. 12.17 Age-class distribution of wildebeest killed by hyaenas in Serengeti and Ngorongoro. (After Kruuk 1972.)

available to them. For example, the high wildebeest population is only available for about one third of the year. The newly born calves of this species suffer very little predation as a result of being born in the plains, where few lions are found. Schaller (1972) estimates that lions consume between 2·2 and 3·3 per cent of the wildebeest population each year. This is hardly sufficient to exercise a regulatory control on numbers. All species of predators collectively consume 9–10 per cent of the available prey biomass annually. The lion in Serengeti provides the interesting example of a static predator in a situation where a large segment of the prey is mobile. Schaller concludes that the size of a pride area is determined by the amount of prey available and is so adjusted to allow for the leanest time of the year and also, most importantly, for the leanest of years. This is a very important finding. In Serengeti lion numbers are low in relation to total prey biomass (Table 11.20) and in comparison with other Parks. This low density is probably imposed as a result of the migratory habits of large numbers of the prey. Expressed differently, the evidence suggests that food supply and availability exercise a regulation over the numbers of predators. The situation is not quite as simple as this as there are intra-specific factors at work, e.g. cub mortality through abandonment, violence, determining pride size. There is also a small loss of lion due to poaching round the boundaries of the Park.

In Nairobi Park following the drought of 1961 the populations of large herbivores

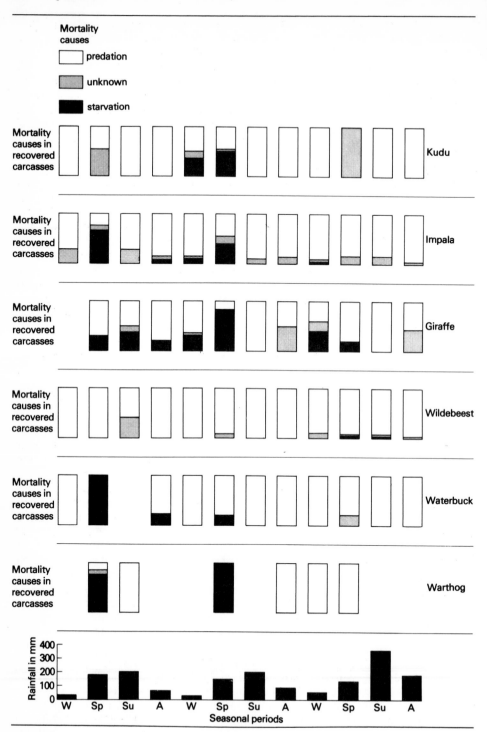

Fig. 12.18 Mortality of large mammals in Timbavati Nature Reserve, Transvaal. Mortality causes are expressed in percentages. W–Winter, Sp–Spring, Su–Summer, A–Autumn. (Adapted from Hirst 1969.)

showed a number of trends and it has been shown (Foster and Kearney, 1967) that from then until 1966 the lions were taking proportionally more wildebeest in a declining population. Were then the lions actually responsible for this decline? Whether this was true or not, Rudnai (1974) has shown how from 1968 to 1972 the percentage of wildebeest in lion kills has dropped appreciably and that of hartebeest has increased considerably. The predation rates on other major food species such as zebra and warthog have not changed to any marked extent. So it appears that once the wildebeest reached a certain critical low level, and at the same time the numbers of hartebeest increased, the lion moved to the alternative food source. Here then is adaptability in diet apparently responding to changing prey densities but very doubtfully regulating them.

The research of Hirst (1969) on the causes of death of wildebeest in Timbavati Reserve in South Africa may shed a different light on the regulatory role of predators. The study extended from 1964 to 1967 and of the 304 deaths due to predators, 291 were caused by lion. He categorised mortality into predation, starvation and 'unknown' and based his findings on the causes of death from recovered carcasses (Fig. 12.18). The almost complete absence of death from starvation, the reduction of the population from 3044 in April 1965 to 2087 in May 1966 mainly as a result of predation and the predilection of lion for wildebeest may all point to a predator regulated population. On the other hand the wildebeest population did not experience any dramatic fluctuation throughout the period of investigation which could suggest a population balance between this animal and the lion.

There is an alternative method of viewing predation. This involves identifying man as a predator in a situation where he regularly removes a portion of the population. This occurred during a tsetse fly control programme within 518 km of Chipengali in eastern Zambia when common duiker (*Sylvicapra grimmia*) were removed by shooting. This operation continued uninterrupted for two years (Wilson and Roth 1967). Two hundred and twenty-nine duiker were shot in the first year and 193 in the second year. The population density was not estimated although regular and carefully controlled observation sighting frequencies were recorded and used to provide an indication of duiker abundance. Sightings were continued for a whole year following the end of the shooting.

Duiker can mature at as young as eight months (Ansell 1963) so it is quite possible for rapid population replacement to occur. The removal of duiker did not appear to have any effect on their total numbers (Fig. 12.19) neither during the hunting

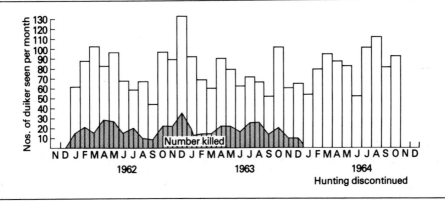

Fig. 12.19   Effect of hunting on the abundance of common duiker. (After Wilson and Roth 1967.)

programme nor in the year after it was over. Post-mortem examination of the shot animals showed that in 1963 the percentage of calves in the population had almost doubled to 14 per cent whereas juveniles and subadults had not increased significantly. In contrast to 1962 there was increased breeding activity in the juvenile components of the population in 1963. Thus although there was no shift in the age structure of the post-calf population there was taking place within the short period of two years a reproductive compensation for predator loss. At the same time as these reproductive changes were taking place, there was also gradual alteration in the animal's behaviour with a change to greater activity in the afternoon (Fig. 12.20).

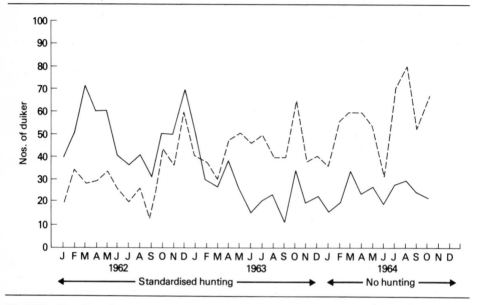

Fig. 12.20   The effect of hunting on the activity of common duiker illustrated by the number seen per month during the morning 0600–1200 hrs (solid line) and during the afternoon, 1200–1800 hrs (broken line). (After Wilson and Roth 1967.)

This study raises several relevant issues. A prey species will apparently adjust its reproductive processes to a change in sustained predator pressure upon it so as to increase production of young. But any such mechanism will inevitably have its limits so that if predation was continuously very intense then compensation by the prey could prove beyond its reproductive capabilities. Whilst this situation is unlikely to occur with a natural predator it could happen as a result of man overexploiting the population. The converse is equally important: a sustained and moderate cull may be undertaken without lasting deleterious effects on the population.

Floods and fire

There are a number of habitats such as the grass-covered plains of the Kafue Flats in Zambia where regular flooding takes place (Sheppe 1972). Here, water inundates an area of up to 5 500 km^2 to a depth of 5 m. The first shallow floods may occur as a result of local rainfall at the height of the wet season sometime between December and March. But the greatest source of floodwaters is from the upper Kafue basin where there is a higher rainfall than on the flats. The accumulation of water in the river system and its movement downstream results in its gradual horizontal spread on to the flats where it attains a maximum in May as the rains are terminating. There then follows a steady reduction of water and re-exposure of the flats. The flood plain has a rich grass cover accompanied by herbs, the vegetation being most dense along the edges of the permanent water courses. Plant growth takes place during the rains with many species continuing to grow under the water and subsequently emerging through it. As a result of the dense growth of plants through the water there is relatively little water visible. The regular enrichment of the flats results in a high annual primary production of herbs and grasses. These plains offer a mixture of conditions for most mammals. The flooding if sufficiently deep makes some habitat unavailable to mammals which tends to counterbalance the advantages of a rich growth of plants.

With the large mammals these regular floods are not responsible for heavy mortality (section 10.1). For the small mammals many of which are unable to escape the waters the situation is different (Sheppe 1972). The main breeding of rodents takes place in the rains and preceding the most extensive flooding. Their populations rapidly build up at this time and as the water gradually spreads from the main stream of the river they must either move ahead of it or succumb to it. High populations can be found in the islands or levées close to the river. Here Sheppe (1972) found a qualitative change taking place as the water level rose. Initially, in the early rains there were large numbers of the multimammate rat (*Praomys natalensis*) present. As the water level rose numbers of this species fell and those of the swamp rat (*Dasymys incomtus*), creek rat (*Pelomys fallax*) and two species of shrew (*Crocidura mariquensis* and *C. flavescens*) increased substantially. These species are better adapted to wetter conditions than *Praomys natalensis* but they are less well suited to the dryer conditions that inevitably follow. The land exposed by the receding flood is recolonised by animals moving from the periphery and from the islands that have not been completely flooded. However, the initial phase of this dispersion is at a time when these animals are not breeding and until this takes place densities must be quite low. The effects of flood on mortality have not been quantified so that it is difficult to precisely assess the role of this factor as a regulator of rodent populations although it must be of considerable importance.

Fire is of widespread, frequent and irregular occurrence over extensive areas of savanna. It is essentially a dry season phenomenon and can spread rapidly over large areas resulting in a charred and blackened landscape. Fire can cause mortality. Fires follow routes that are determined by such factors as wind, the situation of wetter areas and other barriers such as roads and tracks. They do not cover vast areas uniformly at the same time, and there are always places of retreat.

For small ground-dwelling mammals such as rodents and insectivores the spread of fire imposes serious problems. They have been witnessed (Cheeseman 1975) to move away from the leading edge of a fire several metres ahead of it and seek refuge in small unburnt clumps of vegetation. Many others disappear into holes and emerge after the fire has passed. A considerable post-burn survival has been observed by Bellier (1967) in Ivory Coast, Anadu (1973) in Nigeria and by Delany (1964) and Neal (1970) in Uganda. But these animals are then vulnerable to predators in their newly exposed habitat. This situation has been examined in detail by Neal (1970) in the *Imperata* and *Cymbopogon* grassland of Rwenzori Park. He found (Fig. 12.21) as a result of trapping immediately prior to the fire and continuously for several months afterwards that there was a selective response to the burn conditions by the various species of rodents. Some, such as the three-toed grass-rat (*Mylomys dybowskyi*), the Nile rat (*Arvicanthis niloticus*) and the harsh-furred mouse (*Lophuromys sikapusi*) did not return to the area for at least five months. In contrast, the numbers of the multimammate rat (*Praomys natalensis*) and the punctated grass-mouse (*Lemniscomys striatus*) built up very rapidly

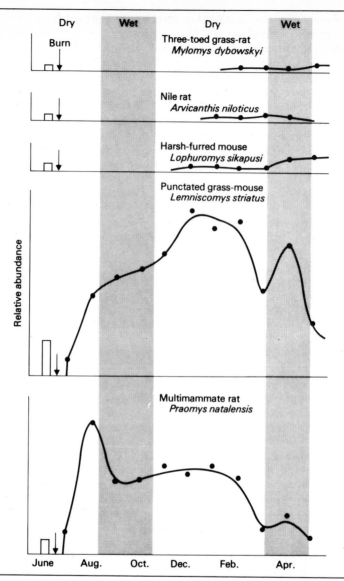

Fig. 12.21 The recolonisation of savanna grassland in Rwenzori Park by rodents following a burn. (Adapted from Neal 1970.)

as a result of both immigration and reproduction, attaining populations of much higher density than in the immediate pre-burn period. It must be stressed that fire as such does not apparently kill large numbers of animals. It is nevertheless a factor which through its indirect action by modification of habitat exerts a very considerable influence on the numbers of these animals.

Undernutrition

Inadequate food or undernutrition results, in its most extreme form, in the death of animals through starvation. Examples of this are found at times of adverse climatic conditions resulting in a low production of vegetation and an inadequate food supply. A most striking example of this in recent years has been witnessed in the elephant population of Tsavo Park, Kenya. In this locality the mean annual rainfall is about 50 cm. This figure is liable to appreciable fluctuation with a drop considerably below this figure at about ten-yearly intervals, as happened in 1970 and 1971. In these two consecutive years the average rainfall was low and the long dry season was unusually prolonged. The low rainfall reduced the primary productivity which combined with a long dry season resulted in a high mortality (p. 315).

Under these conditions, Corfield (1973) found that approximately 6000 elephants died out of a total population of about 21000. Mortality was not evenly spread throughout the Park with some of the highest concentrations of carcasses found in the vicinities of permanent water (Fig. 12.22). Under normal conditions elephants tend to congregate near water courses which accounts for higher densities in these places. Examination of the carcasses of elephant revealed the major cause of death to be starvation with no evidence of disease or abnormally high parasitic infections. There was a heavier mortality of adult females than males. This was believed to be due to the strength of the mother–calf bond limiting the area of search for food to the range of the young animals. Elephants cannot survive without drinking and the area available for exploitation would be controlled by the distance the calf could move. Adult males were not subjected to this constraint and were able to move further.

Attention should be drawn to the main incidence of mortality within the 10 inch 10 per cent isohyet which only encompasses part of Tsavo East (Fig. 12.23). This more arid vegetation zone is the most susceptible to reduced production from irregular rainfall with consequent dramatic effects on the elephant. In more general terms this suggests that mortality from this cause is only likely to occur in particular situations. Furthermore, there is considerable evidence of appreciable increases in the elephant population in the decade preceding 1971 partly from sources outside the Park so it seems quite probable that by 1971 the population was high relative to the carrying capacity of the habitat.

This sudden dramatic drop in numbers is a crude method of regulating population density and is certainly not unique. High mortality of large mammals occurred in Nairobi Park in 1961 and 1974 under similar conditions of low rainfall. Sudden changes of this type cannot be predicted by the animal which is unable to make a gradual adjustment to this temporary adversity. Mortality through starvation in other circumstances may not operate on the scale witnessed here. For example, hyaena cubs (p. 346) as well as wildebeest, zebra, hartebeest and buffalo (Sinclair 1974b) in Serengeti all suffer some deaths from starvation. In buffalo it was found that the older animals were more susceptible to death from starvation, with all but one of sixteen carcasses examined over ten years old having a very low marrow fat content. Most of the older buffalo died of undernutrition in the dry season when the quality of food was poorest and in shortest supply. This was not found in animals of less than ten years. In addition, undernutrition of the mother also caused some calf mortality, presumably through an inadequate food supply to the foetus.

In the Transvaal lowveld Hirst (1969) examined the causes of death in impala, wildebeest, zebra, giraffe, kudu, waterbuck and warthog from 1964 to 1967. In wildebeest and zebra there was a negligible number of deaths due to starvation throughout the study period. However, for the remaining species death from this cause occurred irregularly but not infrequently (Fig. 12.18). For most of them the South African spring and winter were the most vulnerable times. Apparently, the giraffe is far more susceptible to death from starvation than any of the other species; the kudu,

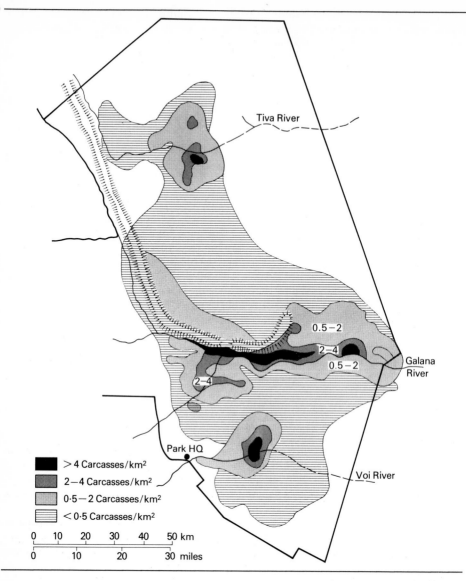

Fig. 12.22 Spatial distribution of elephant mortality in Tsavo Park East during 1970–1. Seasonal rivers are indicated by broken lines. (After Corfield 1973.)

waterbuck and warthog experience undernutrition more erratically although in the last two species it can be a major cause of death at certain times as in spring 1964. In kudu, starvation is an important population regulator being largely responsible for reducing the population within the Timbavati Reserve from 800 in autumn 1965 to less than 500 in summer 1966.

Diseases and parasites

Numerous records exist of mammals supporting a wide variety of ecto- and endo-

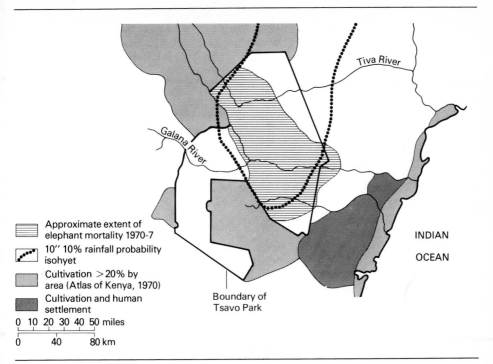

Fig. 12.23   Settlement, cultivation, elephant mortality in 1970–1 and rainfall in Tsavo Park. (After Corfield 1973.)

parasites including ticks, fleas, roundworms, flatworms and protozoa. Similarly, there is also considerable information on infection with pathogenic bacteria, viruses and other micro-organisms. However, when it comes to assessing the magnitude of mortality due to these organisms there are such less precise quantitative data. Of the diseases recorded from wild animals some are caused by agents that are endemic to Africa whilst others are exotic. Among the latter is the virus causing rinderpest which can be responsible for the dramatic reduction of ungulate populations particularly buffalo.

Large-scale mortality due to rinderpest has been recorded from much of Africa in the late 1890s. The disease was present almost continuously in Kenya and Tanzania from the 1930s to the early 1960s. From 1959 to 1961 it accounted for the death of an

Table 12.13   *Potentially important diseases of Serengeti buffalo. (From Sinclair 1974b.)*

	No. examined	Per cent affected	Per cent immune*	Age group affected
Rinderpest	62	0	10	Calf, adult
Theileriasus	40	n.e.	74–90	Calf
Babesiasis	27	n.e.	78	—
Anaplasmosis	27	n.e.	78	Calf
Allerton-type Herpes virus	46	n.e.	96	Calf
Brucellosis	98	6	29	Foetus
Foot-and-mouth	30	n.e.	60	Calf

*Immunity was determined from serum antibody tests.
n.e. = none examined.

estimated 40 per cent of wildebeest calves in the Narok district of Kenya (Talbot and Talbot 1961). Furthermore, a serious outbreak occurred in the Northern Frontier Province of Kenya in 1959 and persisted until at least 1962. There was considerable mortality of giraffe, bongo, bushpig and warthog (Stewart and Stewart 1964). Subsequent outbreaks occurred in this area in 1966 and 1967. More recently, as a result of cattle vaccination in the areas surrounding Serengeti, this disease has largely disappeared from the area. Anthrax is another disease that can cause large-scale mortality as has been illustrated by the death of 1000 wild mammals in Kruger National Park within four months. A survey of some of the potentially important diseases of buffalo (Table 12.13) showed a low level of immunity to rinderpest. In contrast, for several other diseases there were a large number of animals displaying immunity. This suggests that these diseases are continually present in the population even though they do not produce high host mortality. However, it is possible that if the population were subjected to very adverse conditions these diseases might become more evident.

Plague in man is caused by *Yersinia pestis*. This bacterium lives in several species of flea and can be transmitted from one flea to another through their rodent hosts. Under certain conditions there can be a rapid spread of plague through wild rodent populations with considerable mortality resulting. This phenomenon was investigated in the Orange Free State of South Africa from 1940 to 1942 where the affected rodent was the gerbil *Tatera brantsi* and the flea, *Xenopsylla philoxera*. During the first half of 1940 the gerbil colonies were censused and the extent of their occupation and activity measured. As plague swept through the population during this year the state of the colonies was monitored. By early 1941, only three of the original 34 colonies contained gerbils (Fig. 12.24). The plague epidemic had by then taken a dramatic toll

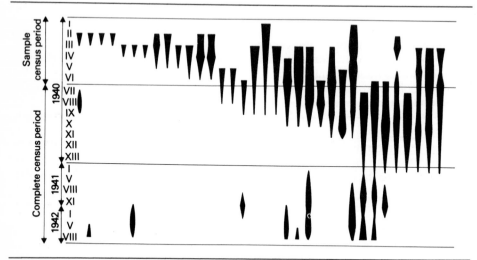

Fig. 12.24 The fate of thirty-four colonies of the gerbil *Tatera brantsi* in the Rooiwal Study Area, South Africa, during a plague outbreak in 1940. Each vertical band represents a colony and the width illustrates relative changes in density. Recovery from the 1940 epizootic is seen from the 1942 data. (After Davis 1953.)

of these rodents. There were then signs of recovery in 1942 but there were further extensive plague outbreaks in 1948 and 1954. The last year was apparently very similar to 1940. In 1955 extensive DDT-dusting and poisoning of gerbils apparently disrupted the host population and eradicated the bacterium.

This detailed investigation measured the effect of a disease outbreak in a wild population and demonstrated how the causative organism could exert no detectable control in some years and then make erratic, unpredictable and devastating reappearances at other times.

Parasitic infections have been widely recorded in large mammals. They can be found in a variety of situations (Table 12.14) within their host and may cause death if present in sufficient numbers. Instead of killing an animal they may debilitate it to such an extent as to render it more vulnerable to predators. Similarly, predators may suffer from debilitating diseases which make them unable to hunt and cause them to die of starvation; this phenomenon has been observed by Schaller (1972) in lions in Serengeti. In general, the magnitude of death from parasitism and disease is not well known. It is interesting to record that for the mountain gorilla Schaller (1963) stated, 'Diseases – especially viruses, bacteria and various blood and intestinal parasites – are probably the major cause of death in gorillas'. He then elaborated on the records of various parasites that have been found associated with this animal. But no quantitative estimate of death due to any one could be given. Lack of knowledge of mortality due to parasites is not uncommon and highlights the need for greater co-operative research between the veterinarian and field ecologist.

Interspecific competition

Competition between two species is most likely to occur when they are both making use of a common resource which would be population limiting to either species in the absence of the other. The resource could include a wide range of factors and conditions such as living space, breeding sites and food supply. It is, however, important to stress that competition does involve a common demand for precisely the same resource and should not be confused with the concept of niche where the precise ecological requirements of a species are being defined. In previous chapters where the ecological requirements of closely related genera and species have been examined it has often been found that they are such as to minimise competition and ensure maximum exploitation of the habitat. This is not to say that two competing species may not temporarily occupy the same niche. It is quite possible to envisage a situation where for example two species may live for most of their lives in different micro-habitats but come together to live off a common food. The niches are then different but competition would be taking place.

It is often difficult to recognise whether competition is actually in progress (section 6.3). This can only be resolved through careful observation, in situations where several closely related species are found together. Furthermore, if competition is occurring it is important to assess how it operates to limit the numbers of one or more species. An excellent example of this situation is provided by Sinclair (1974c) for buffalo and wildebeest in Serengeti. From rumen analyses of both species it was found that they were both exclusively grazers (Table 12.15) with the wildebeest eating a narrower range of grass sizes than the buffalo. There is considerable overlap in the diet with regard to the species of grass consumed and the parts of these plants eaten. During the dry season from July to October wildebeest preferred the open *Themeda triandra* grassland. At this time buffalo avoided this habitat and were found instead in the riverine grassland and forest. Examination of these riverine habitats showed that both species occupied the riverine grassland while only buffalo entered the forest. However, the forest could only support a small buffalo population.

The dry season numbers of buffalo and wildebeest from 1967 to 1969 within Sinclair's study area (Table 12.16), where these habitats were located, showed a high

Table 12.14   *Some parasites found in large mammals from East Africa. (From Sachs and Debbie 1969.)*

Location	Common name of nature of parasite	Generic name of parasite	Host animal
in eye cavity	eye worm	*Thelazia*	buffalo, kudu, bushbuck
in nasal cavity and frontal sinuses	oestrid larvae (nasal fly maggots)	*Oestrus, Kirkioestrus Gedoelstia, Rhinoestrus*	wildebeest, topi, hartebeest, zebra, giraffe
in nasal passage	Y-shaped nasal worm	*Mammomonogamus*	waterbuck, puku, kob, buffalo
in nasal passage	adult tongue worm	*Linguatula*	carnivores, mainly hyaena
on membranes in brain case	small oestrid larvae	*Gedoelstia*	wildebeest
in trachea	medium-sized oestrid larvae	*Oestrus, Rhinoestrus*	topi, giraffe
in trachea and bronchi	common lung worm	*Dictyocaulus*	wildebeest, topi, hartebeest, zebra
in lung tissue	lungworm nodules	*Protostrongylus*	wildebeest, topi, hartebeest
	very small lungworms	*Pneumostrongylus*	wildebeest, topi, hartebeest
		Protostrongylus	impala, Grant's and Thomson's gazelle
in and on lung and surrounding fat tissue	bladderworms (large cysts)	*Echinococcus*	wildebeest, puku, warthog
	smaller cysts	*Cysticercus*	almost all antelopes
in lung lymph nodes	tongueworm larvae	*Linguatula*	many antelopes and buffalo
heart: in musculature	measles (small bladderworm cysts)	*Cysticercus*	almost all antelopes
	long white filarial worm	*Cordophilus*	kudu, bushbuck
free in heart lumen	tongueworm larvae	*Linguatula*	many antelopes and buffalo
in aorta and main blood vessels	very large nematode	*Elaephora*	buffalo
liver: in bile ducts and gall bladder	liver flukes	*Fasciola*	wildebeest, topi, hartebeest, buffalo
	liver tapeworms	*Stilesia*	impala, eland, waterbuck
	liver nematodes	*Cooperioides*	impala
		Monotondella	giraffe
		Grammocephalus	elephant
in liver tissues	roundworms	*Strongylus*	zebra
	bladderworms	*Echinococcus*	giraffe, warthog
	tongueworm larvae	*Linguatula*	almost all antelopes and buffalo
on liver	bladderworm cysts	*Cysticercus*	many antelopes
free in abdominal cavity	large white roundworms	*Setaria*	many antelopes, buffalo, zebra
in mesentery blood vessels	blood flukes	*Schistosoma*	Uganda kob, sitatunga, buffalo
in mesentery lymph nodes	tongueworm larvae	*Linguatula*	many antelopes, mainly buffalo
in mesentery fat tissue	large bladderworms	*Cysticercus*	many antelopes

Table 12.14 – *continued*

Location	Common name of nature of parasite	Generic name of parasite	Host animal
in rumen	conical stomach flukes	*Paramphistomum, Calicophoron, Cotylophoron*	almost all antelopes and buffalo
kidney	tongueworm larvae	*Linguatula*	many antelopes
in musculature of whole body	measles (small bladderworms)	*Cysticercus*	almost all antelopes and buffalo
inside sacrum bone (in epidural space)	bladderworm cysts	*Cysticercus*	hartebeest, topi, wildebeest
hock region, connective tissues and muscles	tape-like worms or calcified patches	*Spargana*	many antelopes, warthog, carnivores
under the skin, in subcutis and connective tissues	thin whitish roundworms	*Filaria, Pseudofilaria*	many antelopes, giraffe, carnivores
inside abdominal wall and in kidney fat	nodules or calcified patches	*Strongylus*	zebra

overall density of wildebeest. With only an average of 7·1 per cent of the total population occupying the riverine grassland this nevertheless comprised 1 030 animals. The metabolic requirements of one wildebeest are equivalent to 0·459 buffalo so that their population can be equated with 472 buffalo. At this time of year there was a shortage of food for the buffalo and no alternative locations they could move to which could compensate for the energy loss due to wildebeest. Had wildebeest not been present, the buffalo population could have risen by a further 18 per cent for the area as a whole. This situation arose where preferred habitats were in juxtaposition with a third habitat both species could exploit. Among the carnivores Kruuk (1972) has witnessed appreciable competition between hyaena and other species. There is reciprocal competition between hyaena and lion with the latter sometimes moving in on hyaena kills and vice versa with occasionally the hyaenas chasing lions off their kills. The diets of these two species in Serengeti are broadly similar with wildebeest, zebra and gazelle comprising the main food. Some differences do occur; for example, very large animals may be consumed by lions and large bones by hyaenas. Even though there is considerable similarity in their diets, in other respects the ecology of these two species differ and as has been pointed out previously (p. 346) competition for food is probably not a major population limiting factor. Hyaenas have considerable competitive contact with other predatory species by taking their kills (Table 12.12). Kruuk (1972) summarised these findings by stating. 'Hyaenas clearly profit from the presence of leopards, cheetahs, wild dogs and man. Relations with lions, jackals and vultures are more ambiguous, and hyaenas probably more often provide food than take it.'

Table 12.15 *Comparison of buffalo and wildebeest diet. (From Sinclair (1974c), Lamprey (1963), Gwynne and Bell (1968) and Bell (1969).)*

Food component	Buffalo	Wildebeest
	(Sample size in parentheses)	
Grass (%)	99 % (124)	98 % (150)
Leaf (%)	11 % (52)	17 % (10)
Stem (%)	49 % (52)	30 % (10)
Height range of preferred grass (cm)	5–80	3–40

Table 12.16 *Numbers and density of buffalo and wildebeest occupying Sinclair's (1974b) Northern Study Area in the dry season.*

Year	Buffalo		Wildebeest			
	No.	Density/km²	No.	Density/km²	No. in riverine grassland	Per cent in riverine grassland
1967	2900	15·7	15000	82	1300	8·7
1968	1750	9·5	11300	61	800	7·1
1969	2500	13·5	17300	94	1000	5·8
Mean	2380	12·9	14500	79	1030	7·1

A quite different competitive interaction has been proposed for two species of rodent inhabiting the Transvaal highveld. In his study area, which consisted of a mixture of hydrophilous vegetation and grassland, Brooks (1974) found the two competing species were the four-striped grass mouse (*Rhabdomys pumilio*) and the laminate-toothed rat (*Otomys irroratus*). During the winter of 1970 *Rhabdomys* favoured the moister vlei vegetation. With the onset of breeding in late 1970 there was dispersal of these animals. They spread out from their favoured vlei vegetation extending their range into the grassland within and beyond the study area. The overall effect of this movement was to reduce the population density within the study area (Fig. 12.25) although a small recovery was staged towards the end of the breeding

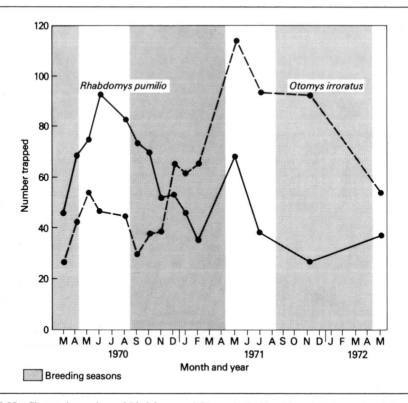

Fig. 12.25 Changes in numbers of *Rhabdomys* and *Otomys* in the Van Riebeek Nature Reserve, Transvaal. Shaded areas indicate breeding seasons. (After Brooks 1974.)

season. However, by this time the *Otomys* numbers were very high so that the relative abundance of the two species in May 1971 had been reversed for the study area as a whole over those of twelve months previously. At the critical period from November 1970 to January 1971 of change in relative abundance the *Rhabdomys* population was decreasing and the *Otomys* increasing.

Rhabdomys is mainly granivorous but also consumes green plant material and insects. *Otomys* feeds almost exclusively on the green shoots, stems and leaves in the wetter areas. *Rhabdomys* is a more catholic species in respect of the habitat conditions it occupies and its feeding habits. In autumn and winter 1970, the wetter vlei habitat probably provided better cover and greater quantities of seed than the grassland thereby offering a very suitable adverse season refuge. Competition for food with *Otomys* was probably minimal as a result of dietary differences. Although 1970–1 was wetter than 1969–70 there was no indication that this itself affected the survival of *Rhabdomys*. At the onset of the breeding season in 1970 adult male *Rhabdomys* displayed adrenal hypertrophy which suggests they were experiencing stress. In the wetter situation there was considerable sharing of runways between the two species; here, burrows were not constructed and it is probable that resting and breeding sites were at a premium. These greater demands on space at the onset of breeding may have resulted in the dispersion of the *Rhabdomys* which was more versatile and less specialised than *Otomys*.

From laboratory studies there is no evidence of agonistic behaviour between the species so this in itself was unlikely to cause the dispersion. *Otomys* is an appreciably larger species than *Rhabdomys* which may be an important asset in a crowded situation. The higher rainfall in 1970–1 may have consolidated the position of the highly adapted *Otomys* and sustained its higher density. In this situation the relative numbers of two closely related species have been transposed and the evidence points to a competitive interaction for space as a major causative element.

These three examples, ungulates, carnivores and rodents, illustrate how interspecific competition can operate in different ways with different end results. However, in the case of the lions and hyaenas although competition for food is a very real occurrence it is not of primary importance in regulating numbers. In contrast, the competition between buffalo and wildebeest for food and between *Rhabdomys* and *Otomys* for space have important effects on their densities.

12.6   Natural regulation of mammal populations

It is when all the data are assembled on the population regulation of a single species that the combined effects of the regulatory factors examined individually above begin to emerge. In providing a model of the regulation of buffalo populations (Fig. 12.26) Sinclair (1974*b*) categorised various regulatory agents into those that were primarily extrinsic, e.g. food supply, secondarily extrinsic, e.g. predation, endemic disease, and secondarily intrinsic, e.g. social factors, as well as extrinsic disruptive agents which include climate and physical conditions of the habitat. What this work demonstrates very clearly is the interactions which the various factors may have on each other. For example, the greater the undernutrition of the herds the more vulnerable they are to predation and disease and a consequent increase in mortality of young and adults can be anticipated. Conversely, higher rainfall results in higher plant production and the greater availability of more food. Density could thus be limited by food supply operating through climate.

During the past twenty years various views have been expressed as to the basic processes involved in the regulation of vertebrate populations. Probably among the

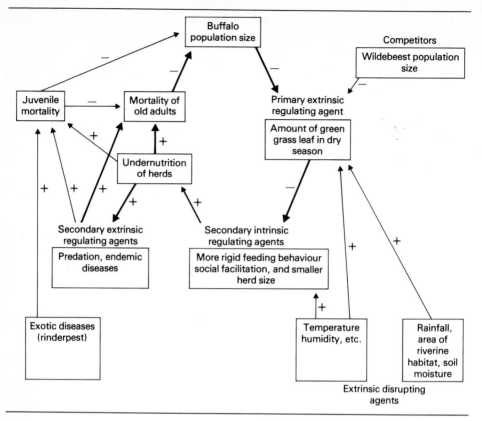

Fig. 12.26 Regulation of buffalo populations in Serengeti. Heavy lines indicate more important interactions. Minus signs indicate that a higher intensity has negative results; plus signs indicate positive results. (After Sinclair 1974*b*.)

more significant and certainly the most thought-provoking are those advanced by Lack (1954) and Wynne-Edwards (1962). Both believe in the density-dependent regulation of animal numbers. Their views are not in agreement on how this is achieved. Lack considers that the size of the breeding population is largely density-regulated as a result of food availability and that the number of progeny produced has so evolved as to ensure a maximum number of juveniles are reared under the average environmental conditions. Wynne-Edwards on the other hand maintains that competition and social behaviour ensure a spacing and dispersal of adults thereby controlling the birth rate in a density-dependent way. This maintains populations at optimal densities and does not involve them in high mortality from starvation. These ideas were developed against the background of studies in temperate regions and while they should have equal applicability in the tropics relatively few opportunities have been available for their examination in this situation.

As can be seen from the preceding account many factors operate on a single population to increase and decrease its numbers or to ensure its relative stability. For this reason it is difficult to generalise about regulation for all species of African mammals particularly as for the vast majority little is known of their population ecology. Thus in discussing what is known on how populations are apparently regulated in relation to general ecological theory the substance of the arguments must depend on a relatively small sample of material. This is obviously not an ideal situation. The remedy lies in the acquisition of more information.

Food supply clearly exerts an important influence on the maintenance, increase and decrease of populations. It has a role in the initiation, intensity and duration of breeding which is apparently stimulated by some as yet undefined ecophysiological factor(s). For some species, particularly those with long gestation periods, this may occur as infrequently as once a year. For those with short gestation periods successive pregnancies may occur until a change in environmental conditions inhibits further reproduction. This cessation may, for example, be caused by seasonal physiological and biochemical changes in the food, it may be caused by the quantity available or it could stem from changing behavioural patterns resulting from increased numbers. In other words the physiological change may be induced by the habitat conditions or the species itself. No matter what the cause the population certainly appears to respond to the slightest environmental change.

These aspects of population regulation are in accord with Lack's views. Food availability does set a limit on population densities with these limits rarely being attained or surpassed. A noteworthy exception is the mass mortality witnessed in large mammals, e.g. Tsavo elephants in years of drought. This interesting exceptional, but by no means isolated, incident is the result of a climatic variability and the occurrence of one or more periods of very low rainfall. The elephant is demonstrably able to adjust its numbers to inadequate food supply by various reproductive mechanisms. In the catastrophic drought conditions the change is too violent and too sudden for the reproductive processes to effectively adapt.

Many species of mammal adopt some form of social behaviour. This has been considered in detail in Chapter 10 although it is relevant here to draw attention to its possible role in population regulation. Territories, hierarchies and groups (whether comprised of individuals having numerous or few overt behavioural interactions), are organisational systems which probably facilitate a better use of resources than would prevail if animals were not organised into these systems. Territories may ensure a spacing appropriate to food supply (e.g. Maxwell's duiker, vervets) and regulation of breeding by territorial males (e.g. Thomson's gazelle, Uganda kob). The co-ordination of activities within a group can result in a more efficient exploitation of food supply. This has been recorded in groups with (e.g. baboons) and without (e.g. banded mongooses), status hierarchies. Group co-ordination can also provide a protective mechanism against predators. The examples and many more described in Chapter 10 support Wynne-Edwards' views on the importance of social behaviour in population regulation.

Evidence from a wide range of sources suggests that populations are regulated by a complex multiplicity of factors. The operative factors can differ from species to species as well as at different phases of the life cycle of one species. As a result it is difficult to accept the ubiquity of either Wynne-Edward's or Lack's views. Both can be highly relevant in certain situations and both have a great deal to contribute to thinking on regulatory mechanisms in African mammals. But it will be through the detailed examination and quantification of the full range of factors operating on individual species that a comprehensive picture will emerge of the major and most consistently operative factors in population regulation.

PART IV   Interactions with Man

Chapter 13

Man and mammals

Africa is a continent of change. During as short a period as the past half century there have been rapid developments in many of man's spheres of activity that have profoundly changed the landscape of Africa and in so doing greatly modified the habitats available to mammals. Originally, there was an ecological relationship between the indigenous populations and wildlife. But the colonisation of Africa by western man accompanied by his technology has been responsible for many fundamental changes observed in recent times. The sequence of events that have occurred is well known and need only be outlined here. The introduction of modern medicine saved lives and permitted a massive increase in human populations. Concurrently, there was greater utilisation and exploitation of renewable and non-renewable resources. These early developments sowed the seeds for change in a part of the continent whose social development at the turn of the century was vastly behind that of western Europe. It is essential that the relationships of mammals to man be considered in the context of these dramatic and rapid changes. Man and mammals frequently impinge upon one another and as will be seen in the more detailed accounts that follow these interactions operate in a wide range of quite different and unrelated ways. Mammals can be sources of food and other products such as skins and horns if properly nurtured, they can be pests and carriers of disease, and can be sources of considerable economic return through their attractions to tourists. They are also part of complex natural ecosystems which inevitably have as yet unrealised potential for man's wise exploitation.

Both colonial and independent governments have recognised the need to develop sound economies and increase gross national products, for by so doing the living standards of the ever increasing populations can be improved. Development programmes, whose objectives often include increasing agricultural production, make allowance for the predicted changes in human population numbers over the periods of the plans. According to United Nations statistics (UN 1973) the total population of West, East and Middle Africa has increased from 151 million in 1950 to 254 million in 1973 (Fig. 13.1). The annual rate of population increase in 1973 was 2·53. This means that if this population maintains its 1973 growth rate it will double the 1973 figure by the year 2002. The density and rate of increases of the Middle Africa zone are less than the other two. The populations of individual countries display similar trends to those of their zone as a whole (Fig. 13.1), although, as might be expected, there are slight deviations from the mean annual rate of increase. This population increase is thus a

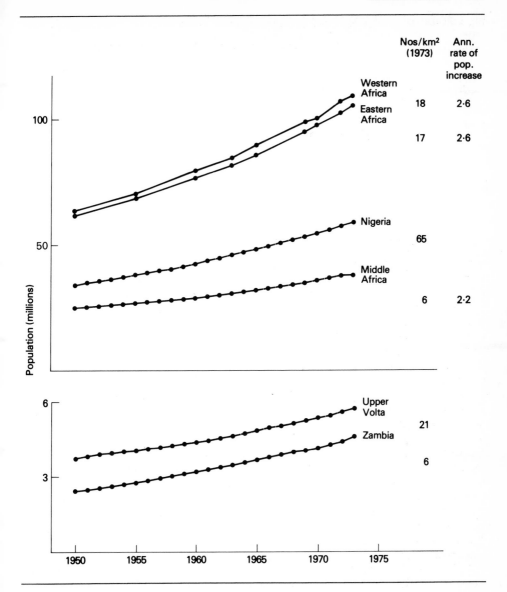

Fig. 13.1 Human populations of selected regions and countries of Africa. (Data from UN 1973.) Western Africa = Cape Verde Is., Dahomey, Gambia, Ghana, Guinea, Ivory Coast, Liberia, Mali, Mauritania, Niger, Nigeria, Port Guinea, St. Helena, Senegal, Sierra Leone, Togo, Upper Volta. Eastern Africa = Burundi, Ethiopia, Afars and Issas, Kenya, Madagascar, Malawi, Mauritius, Mozambique, Reunion, Seychelles, Somalia, Rhodesia, Uganda, Tanzania, Zambia. Middle Africa = Angola, Cameroon, Central African Republic, Chad, Congo, Guinea, Gabon, São Tomé, Zaire.

trans-continental phenomenon and not a feature of a particular region or country. These populations are growing exponentially and as a result the increased demand they make on the environment becomes greater every year.

Most of the population of tropical Africa is engaged in or directly dependent on agricultural or associated occupations. Agricultural enterprises vary considerably from large-scale undertakings such as ranches, tea estates, sugar plantations and large farms to the small-scale peasant farmer and pastoralist who frequently engage in traditional practices which have changed little over the past few hundred years. The extent of agricultural expansion in large and small-scale farming can be seen in the increases of areas harvested (Table 13.1). From 1962 to 1972 the areas of cassava, tea,

Table 13.1   *Areas of selected crops harvested in Africa (FAO 1974).*

| | *Area harvested (× 1000 ha)* | | | | |
| | | | | | *Per cent increase* |
	1961–5	*1970*	*1971*	*1972*	*1961–5/1972*
Whole continent					
Cassava	4464	5843	5943	5996	+ 34·3
Sugar	495	712	743	755	+ 52·5
Coffee	2692	3064	3060	3102	+ 15·2
Tea	77	117	124	140	+ 81·8
Ground nuts	6528	7171	7240	7208	+ 10·4
Selected countries					
Ground nuts (Niger)	325	357	394	400	+ 18·7
Tea (Kenya)	21	40	44	55*	+161·9
Coffee (Ivory Coast)	548	650	650	670	+ 18·2
Ground nuts (Senegal)	1059	983	1011	950*	− 10·3

*FAO estimate.

coffee, sugar and ground nuts harvested increased between 10 and 82 per cent. For individual countries (Table 13.1) there can be appreciable deviations from the continental trend but only occasionally, as with ground nuts in Senegal, is the trend downward. Records are also available for areas under cultivation over longer periods. For example, in Uganda the land under coffee increased from 22000 ha in 1939 to 3367000 ha in 1966 and over the same period the area under tea increased from 1093 to 12424 ha (Jameson 1970). These increases in land under cultivation inevitably result in a diminution in natural vegetation. There is a further effect on natural habitats that these statistics do not fully reveal. This concerns the widespread practice of shifting agriculture. Under this system one or more crops are grown for a limited period. Their cultivation is then moved elsewhere with the original site not used again for several years. An example of this practice can be seen in Liberia (Schulz 1975) where trees and other vegetation are removed in order to grow rice in the first year and cassava in the second. The land is then left and becomes covered in a regenerating low bush for anything from 6 to 15 years after which time it is once more cultivated. Schulz (1973) estimated that in 1970 2·9 per cent of the land in Liberia was under cultivation compared to 56·6 per cent which was regenerating. There is here an ecological disturbance over a much larger area than that being tilled at one time.

There have been contemporaneous changes in the numbers of cattle (Table 13.2) and goats with an increase in the former throughout the continent of over 20 per cent in 10 years. This is due to various factors including disease control, larger areas being ranched and larger pastorialist stocks. Examination of numbers in individual countries (Table 13.2) shows that cattle populations have increased at approximately the same rate in countries with moist savanna such as Uganda as those with drier savanna such

Table 13.2 *Numbers of cattle (× 100) in Africa (FAO 1974).*

	1961–5	1970	1971	1972	Increase per cent 1961–5/1972
Whole continent	132311	156766	158843	159252	+20·4
Upper Volta	1956	2500	2550	2400*	+22·7
Kenya	7253	8600	8900*	9200*	+26·8
Ivory Coast	301	408	420	440	+46·2
Botswana	1514	1650	1693	1800	+18·9
Uganda	3485	4145	4280	4600*	+24·2

*FAO estimate.

as Upper Volta. Longer term observations show considerable increases in cattle numbers although these may to some extent be the result of regeneration following large-scale reduction. In Rhodesia (Fig. 13.2) the numbers of African-owned cattle have not greatly increased in recent years; however, the increase since the rinderpest outbreak at the end of the last century has been enormous. In northern Ghana, Hill

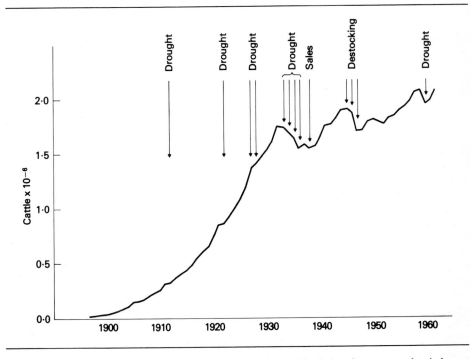

Fig. 13.2 Recovery of the African-owned cattle population in Rhodesia subsequent to the rinderpest outbreak in 1895. Various factors influencing the population growth are included. (Adapted from Ford 1971.)

(1970) recorded an increase from 110000 cattle in 1931 to 170000 in 1941 and then to 400000 in 1964. The overall picture is one of a relentless increase in numbers of cattle with little indication of voluntary restraint.

Agricultural practices either modify the natural vegetation or eliminate it with increasing human populations making the changes more rapid. Some of the more measurable consequences of these changes are considered in this chapter. There are, however, certain aspects of habitat modification that are difficult to quantify precisely in terms of how they influence mammal species diversity and numbers even though their gross effects are very apparent. These involve the gradual and often indiscriminate encroachment by man into virgin habitats. This is particularly obvious in lowland and montane forests where trees are felled to provide fuel and building materials, and where cultivation and domestic animals move into the cleared forests. The same process can and does occur in savanna. Frequently, little attention is paid to the suitability of the land for the husbandry being practised. As a result of these activities, deterioration of the habitat and soil erosion often occur and their effects are often dependent on the intensity of the activities. Thus patchy settlement with cultivated areas interspersed with semi-natural vegetation may still support natural associations of the fauna. As human populations increase the patches enlarge and finally coalesce with deleterious effects on much of the fauna.

The establishment and growth of modern cities in Africa has been incredibly rapid. In Kenya, the annual growth rates have been 6·7 per cent for Nairobi, 5·5 per cent for Mombasa and 8·2 per cent for Kisumu. Many of Africa's coastal towns have existed several hundred years. Inland the situation is very different with most cities and towns being major developments of the present century. Their siting has been both strategic and fortuitous; in some places they have replaced older and smaller settlements. Human habitations have always attracted a characteristic mammal fauna and the large city as the contemporary successor to the small hutted village is no exception to this.

The major changes described here are important in several respects. They have been simultaneous so that African ecosystems have experienced the effects of several different land use practices at the same time. The wild mammals are affected directly as a result of these changes as well as through the habitats being modified. Finally these pressures on natural ecosystems show few signs of lessening. The immediate and longer term prospects are of their continuation probably with greater intensity.

13.1   Effects of change in land use

Urban development

The close association of certain mammals with man's habitations is a well-documented phenomenon. Rodents can be widespread in houses and other buildings and bats may often be found in roofs. In Africa, the multimammate rat (*Praomys natalensis*) is a frequent dweller of huts and being a good climber will often occupy the mud walls and thatch roof. This omnivorous savanna species is highly adaptable and will readily range between cultivated fields and adjacent buildings. Two exotic species of rat have entered and become well established in Africa as a result of man's activities. They are the brown or Norway rat (*Rattus norvegicus*) and the black rat (*Rattus rattus*). They were first brought by ships and initially became established in ports. These species thrive and multiply in cities, towns and villages but it is unusual for them to be found in natural or artificial vegetation except in the vicinity of the human dwellings and other buildings that provide them with shelter and sustenance.

Both black and Norway rats, as well as the multimammate rat, have caused serious health problems as a result of carrying a flea which transmits the plague bacterium (p. 356) and have as a result been intermittently subjected to rigorous control measures. In one such operation Buxton (1936) obtained over 146 000 rats from Lagos between February 1931 and December 1934. Of these, just over 5 per cent were Norway rats. However, in Douala there was a gradual change in abundance of the two species from 1954 to 1959 (Voelkel and Varieras 1960). Here the percentage of Norway rats trapped increased from 60 per cent to 98 per cent of the total. Rosevear (1969) suggests this change may have been due to the construction of more substantial dwellings and the gradual introduction of underground sewage systems both of which may have created conditions favouring the Norway rat. The black rat is more arboreal, preferring above-ground situations such as roofs, particularly those that are thatched so that improved housing would offer it less suitable conditions. This rat would also have difficulty competing with the Norway rat in the subterranean sewage channels.

From East Africa, there is considerable information on the spread of *Rattus rattus* inland from the coast. This species was probably introduced into the port of Mombasa well before the beginning of this century and completion of the railway from the port to Kisumu on Lake Victoria in 1901 provided a dispersal route for black rats into the interior of East Africa. By 1919, Hollister (1919) reported that in Kenya '... it is found only along the railroad or about the older settlements and highways of trade'. It probably first appeared in Uganda very early in the present century having been recorded at Muhokya, in the eastern Rwenzori foothills in 1906 (Thomas and Wroughton 1910). It was recorded in Jinja in 1914 but as recently as 1917 it was very scarce in Entebbe (Hopkins 1949). The eastern part of Uganda was penetrated by 1921 (Fig. 13.3) and by 1938 it was widespread in most of the south of the country. In the east it reached Masindi Port in 1930, Butiaba in 1938 and was then probably transported by Lake Albert steamer to Kasenyi where it was first recorded in 1947. Dispersal from here to other parts of eastern Zaire followed (Fig. 13.3) (Misonne 1963).

The spread of *Rattus rattus* has resulted in the discontinuance of the commensal association of *Praomys natalensis* with man in places where the two species meet. The greater aggression and larger size of the introduced species are among factors responsible for its competitive supremacy.

Another exotic found in built-up areas is the house mouse (*Mus musculus*). Rosevear (1969) reports how relatively uncommon but quite widely dispersed this species is in West Africa having been obtained from several localities from Sierra Leone to Cameroun. In East Africa, Hollister (1919) commented on the absence of material in the collections he examined from Kenya and Uganda. Swynnerton and Hayman (1950) only recorded this species from a few coastal locations in Tanzania. Further inland the first records of this species in Uganda and Zambia are as recent as 1965 (Ansell 1966, Delany 1975). All this information points to very slow colonisation and suggests that this species encounters considerably greater ecological barriers than does the black rat. This species has, however, penetrated the Nile valley as far as Khartoum where it has become established in houses (Happold 1967a).

Areas under cultivation

A common and important ecological feature of cultivated areas is the extensive land coverage by a single crop species. Here, all plants and animals that are not beneficial to the crop are discouraged which, as far as mammals are concerned, usually involves the elimination of the larger species. However, similar control of small mammals is far more difficult. Furthermore, cultivation often provides small mammals with particularly favourable habitats so that in some situations they may attain higher densities than they do in natural vegetation. Under these circumstances they often do considerable damage to the crops themselves.

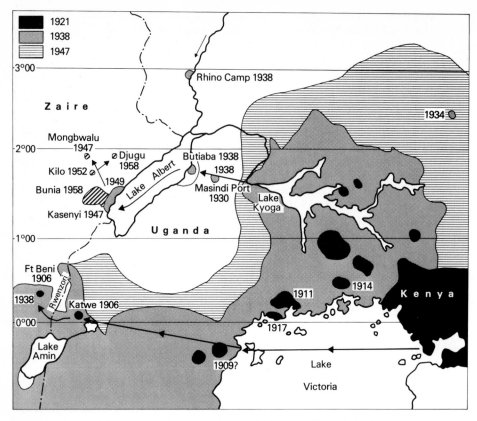

Fig. 13.3   Spread of the black rat (*Rattus rattus*) through Uganda to Zaire. (After Misonne 1963.)

Several species of rodents are known to be involved in the destruction of cocoa pods in Nigeria and Ghana. At Gambari, in Nigeria, in 1960–1 it was estimated that 4·6 per cent of the crop of pods had been damaged (Fig. 13.4) and from 1954 to 1960 there was an average yearly loss of crop in the Eastern Region and Ashanti of Ghana of 2·27 per cent (Taylor, R. D. 1961). Among the more important species responsible for this damage were Thomas' tree squirrel, *Funisciurus anerythrus*, in Nigeria and the green squirrel, *Paraxerus poensis*, in Ghana. These squirrels did not live in the cocoa trees but made regular forays from their nesting areas in adjacent vegetation. This habit resulted in greater damage round the periphery of the plantation. Giant rats, *Cricetomys gambianus*, excavated burrows all over the plantations where they lived permanently. This species is not as good a climber as the squirrels and is probably more dependent on vegetation at ground level. Other rodents implicated in the damage were *Stochomys longicaudatus* in Nigeria and *Stochomys defua* and *Praomys morio* in Ghana. The first and last of these are known to be good climbers.

In Sierra Leone, the main damage to cocoa was caused by several species of monkeys including the smoky mangabey. Here, for religious reasons, many of the people living in the cocoa-growing areas were reluctant to kill monkeys with the result that at the time of Taylor's (1961) study they were extremely numerous. Eight species of monkey including the smoky mangabey (*Cercocebus atys*), green (*Cercopithecus sabaeus*), white-nosed guenon (*C. petaurista*) and Campbell's mona (*C. campbelli*) were

Fig. 13.4 Young giant pouched rat (*Cricetomys gambianus*) eating cocoa pod. (Photo: K. D. Taylor.)

recorded from Kenema and Pujehun districts and some if not all of these periodically raided cocoa plantations. As with the rodents, damage was greatest at the edges of the plantations even though the monkeys were sufficiently wide ranging to penetrate to the interior.

The establishment of oil palm plantations in Ahoada, Nigeria, involved the planting of young nursery stock in rows. This was accompanied by a leguminous cover-crop, *Peureria*, sown between the rows whose function was to suppress weed growth. The annual oil palm plantings between 1960 and 1964 recorded losses of up to 80 per cent of the crop sown. Of this, all but 1 per cent was due to rodent damage (Greaves 1964). The succulent apical bud was chewed at ground level and this, in time, resulted in the death of the palm. Sixteen species of rodent were collected from the estate and of these six were common (*Tatera valida, Dasymys incomtus, Oenomys hypoxanthus, Lophuromys sikapusi, Praomys morio* and *Mus minutoides*). As far as could be ascertained most were prepared to eat the palm. Rodents were numerous within these plantations and it appeared probable that *Peureria* provided good cover and a source of food. The growth of the young palms was uninterrupted if they were enclosed in wire mesh cages. Alternatively, the rodent populations could have been reduced by not using a cover-crop and making certain no other vegetation became established. Similar problems have been encountered in Ivory Coast (Bellier 1965) where the common rodent species were *Dasymys incomtus, Lemniscomys striatus, Lophuromys sikapusi* and *Uranomys ruddi*. Other rodents invading these plantations included both savanna, e.g. *Tatera, Lemniscomys*, and forest, e.g. *Praomys, Oenomys* species.

Agricultural crops in the Kenya Rift Valley have been irregularly subjected to heavy loss by rodents (Taylor 1968). Here, massive outbreaks of rodent numbers are erratic with reports of their occurrence in 1951 and 1962. Maize, wheat and barley were among the damaged cereals (Fig. 13.5) in some instances accounting for as much as 34 per cent of the crop. Three species (*Praomys natalensis, Arvicanthis niloticus* and *Rhabdomys pumilio*) were responsible for most of the damage. Only *Praomys* climbed

Fig. 13.5   Damage to maize cob by *Praomys natalensis*. The rat climbed the plant in order to attack the cob. (Photo: K. D. Taylor.)

the maize stems to consume the cobs. The reasons for these outbreaks are not known. It has, however, been tentatively suggested that the exceptionally high rainfall of 1961 prevented much of the crop being harvested while at the same time weeds grew profusely. The combination of unharvested crops and dense weeds provided exceptionally suitable conditions for an increase in rodent numbers which manifested itself in the population explosion of 1962.

Damage to crops by rodents is probably far more widespread than has been recorded in the literature. In addition to the examples cited above serious depredations have been made by these animals on cotton in the Sudan (*P. natalensis*, *A. niloticus*) (Taylor, K. D. 1968) and maize in Tanzania (*P. natalensis* and *Arvicanthis* sp.) (Taylor, K. D. 1962).

The readiness with which rodents become established on peasant smallholdings where several crops are cultivated has been demonstrated by Delany and Kanseriimuhanga (1970) in a plot of 0·42 ha on the outskirts of Kampala. This was subdivided into compartments, some very small, of ten recognisable vegetation types. Coffee with an understory of cassava covered the largest area (42 per cent). Sweet potato (2 per cent), banana (2 per cent) and eucalyptus (6 per cent) were the remaining cultivated plants. The rest of the plot comprised grass and herb patches that had not been tended for several months. The whole plot was subjected to intensive rodent live-trapping from August to November 1967. During that time sixty-seven animals representing ten species were obtained (Table 13.3). This is a high and diverse rodent

Table 13.3 *Rodents obtained in the cultivated sectors of a plot of 0·42 ha in Kampala. (From Delany and Kanseriimuhanga 1970.)*

Plants:	Coffee–cassava	Sweet Potato	Banana	Eucalyptus
Area (per cent):	42	2	2	6
Rodents obtained:	*Thamnomys dolichurus* *Oenomys hypoxanthus* *Arvicanthis niloticus* *Aethomys hindei* *Rattus rattus* *Praomys natalensis* *Mus minutoides* *Lophuromys flavopunctatus*	*A. niloticus*	*P. natalensis*	—

Lophuromys sikapusi, Tatera valida were present elsewhere on the plot and *Otomys irroratus, Lemniscomys striatus* and *Mylomys dybowskyi* in the immediate vicinity.

fauna for so small an area and the catch of thirty-five animals in the cassava-coffee mixture draws attention to the potential seriousness of these pests to the smallholder.

Livestock production and habitat degradation

One of the most widespread causes of greater numbers of cattle is the increasing size of herds belonging to pastoral tribes. Many of these people inhabit regions of low rainfall where annual primary productivity is never very high. Natural ecosystems are adapted to these conditions and resilient to temporary and irregular adversities such as drought. However, when large numbers of cattle are introduced into such an area there is marked deflection of the ecosystem from its normal equilibrium.

Langdale-Brown, Osmaston and Wilson (1964) have described the cycle of events in Karamoja, Uganda, that have resulted from an increase in the cattle population. The sequence is broadly similar to what happens in other parts of tropical Africa having annual rainfalls of 500 to 900 mm providing, as with this Karamoja example, they are free from tse-tse flies (*Glossina* spp.). Much of the natural vegetation when not subject to heavy grazing consists of mixtures of *Combretum* and *Acacia* woodlands accompanied by various grasses including *Cymbopogon, Heteropogon, Hyparrhenia, Themeda* and *Setaria*. Overgrazing, trampling, exposure of the soil to sun, rain and wind and reduction of fire result in colonisation by woody and succulent species to form a modified savanna vegetation in which small trees become more common and perennial grasses are replaced by sparse annuals and herbs. The habitat is then liable to suffer from extensive erosion and if grazing persists dry thicket vegetation will move in. This consists of short well-branched trees and shrubs occurring together in dense and extensive clumps and separated by bare ground. Grasses are sparse and succulents, e.g. *Sansevieria*, become more abundant. The succession from savanna to bushland induced by overgrazing represents an end point in land deterioration. Little

Fig. 13.6 Effect of heavy grazing on vegetation near Khartoum, Sudan. Ground vegetation has virtually disappeared. These conditions are worsened in years of low rainfall. (Photo: J. L. Cloudsley-Thompson.)

suitable grazing then remains and attempts to ameliorate the problem by the construction of dams only exacerbates it further by encouraging further over-population by cattle.

Such vegetation changes are not necessarily uniform over extensive areas. They vary in accordance with soil type, topography and intensity of cattle grazing. Furthermore, the process of degradation is not necessarily irreversible as continual erosion can ultimately leave an exposed residual rock. This is resistant to further erosion and being permeable offers a favourable habitat for colonisation by savanna species such as *Sehima nervosum, Heteropogon, Acacia hockii* and *Combretum transvaalense*. Regeneration will, however, be impeded by continual heavy grazing.

These changes have considerable impact on the large mammals. Large numbers of cattle within an area can be responsible for displacing the wild mammals. This process is frequently assisted by the herdsmen accompanying the cattle. Casebeer and Koss (1970) have shown considerable similarity in the diets of hartebeest, zebra and cattle in Kenya Masailand and there can be little doubt that in Karamoja the habitats with large numbers of cattle will be less favourable to these wild species. Other grass-eating species such as topi and Grant's gazelle are likely to be similarly adversely affected while the ranges of elephant and black rhinoceros have retreated considerably during this century (Watson 1949).

Overstocking has taken place in the marginal lands of West Africa, in Somalia and northern Kenya as well as western Kenya and northern Tanzania. Many of these savannas have a lower rainfall than Karamoja. This can result in rapid deterioration of the vegetation particularly when increasing numbers of stock coincide with years of exceptionally low rain. This is well illustrated in Kenya Masailand where the drought of 1961 reduced the number of cattle from 973 000 to an estimated 673 000 (Simon 1962).

Over large areas of dry savanna and arid regions overgrazing and utilisation of trees for firewood have combined to have disastrous effects. Here goats as well as cattle have contributed to the reduction of vegetation (Fig. 13.6). Adult plants and seedlings

Fig. 13.7 Damaged *Acacia-Delonix-Terminalia* woodland in Tsavo East, Kenya. High populations of elephant are responsible for the transformation from woodland to scrub. (Photo: M. J. Coe.)

are eaten and in the dry season branches of *Acacia* and other trees may be cut down by herdsmen to provide leaves and fruit (Hemming 1966). Reduction and elimination of vegetation accompanied by trampling loosen the soil so that it is more readily dispersed by wind while the increasing amount of bare ground less readily absorbs the little rain that falls than does ground with a vegetation cover.

The overgrazing in the sahel savanna has been particularly serious in recent years as from 1920 to 1958 the region experienced higher than average rainfall in 27 of the 39 years (Winstanley 1973). As a result the region sustained a far higher population of men and cattle than it could sustain from the primary productivity to be anticipated from rainfall figures extending over a longer period. With the occurrence of several years of low rainfall in the 1960s and 1970s the inevitable result of gross overpopulation manifested itself through habitat devastation and dramatic mortality of humans and livestock.

Increased farming and settlement in the vicinity of national parks can result in artificially high concentrations of large mammals within their boundaries. Under these conditions appreciable habitat modification can result (Fig. 13.7; pp. 388–9).

Livestock production and tse-tse fly

Attempts to provide increased pasture suitable for cattle have led to concérted eradication programmes of several species of tse-tse fly (*Glossina*). The importance of tse-tse to cattle lies in its ability to transmit protozoan blood parasites of the genus *Trypanosoma* from wild game particularly large ungulates when the fly takes blood meals from more than one host. While trypanosomes usually, but not invariably, have little adverse effect on wild mammals they frequently cause debilitation, lassitude and death in domestic stock. This means that cattle and wild animals cannot survive in close proximity to each other in areas inhabited by these flies.

There are three groups of *Glossina* species each containing several closely related species. The *fusca* group includes forest-dwelling species, the *palpalis* group contains species living along the shores of lakes and rivers draining into the Atlantic and Mediterranean and the *morsitans* group contains wooded and bush savanna species. The life cycles of these flies bypass the egg stage and the adult female deposits an advanced larva under bushes or alternative shaded situations. The larva burrows into the ground and pupates.

Three methods have been used, frequently in combination, to control tse-tse fly. These have been game eradication, bush clearance and insecticidal spraying. The first destroys the reservoir for the trypanosomes, the second removes all suitable sites for larval deposition by the adult fly and the third makes the sites chemically toxic to the larvae. Drugs are available that prevent and cure trypanosomiasis but their use has been considered appropriate only where infection rates are relatively low. Various aspects of tse-tse control programmes are relevant to the ecology of wild mammals not least the massive eradication programmes that have taken place in several parts of Africa.

The *morsitans* group does not occur throughout all tropical savanna (Fig. 13.8) nor are its boundaries static. Its present distribution has been influenced by past outbreaks of rinderpest, an exotic viral disease of cattle and wild ungulates (p. 355), which has on a number of occasions dramatically reduced their numbers. The species of ungulate highly susceptible to rinderpest are also favoured food to the tse-tse fly (Ford 1971). Examination of the feeds of flies in East and West Africa shows that between 78 and 93 per cent of the former and 73 and 75 per cent of the latter are taken from species of ungulates most susceptible to rinderpest. Among the more susceptible ungulates are buffalo, eland, kudu, bushbuck, reedbuck, duiker, warthog and bushpig and those less affected are sable, roan antelope, wildebeest and impala. Thus, a major outbreak of rinderpest will particularly adversely affect the tse-tse on account of the selectively high mortality of many of its favoured hosts. In this way severe epidemics of rinderpest have reduced the ranges of tse-tse. The contraction is then followed by a phase of expansion of host and flies after the disease has declined.

A good example of tse-tse–game–cattle interaction is seen in the spread of the fly in the region west of Lake Victoria. Here, as elsewhere in Africa the rinderpest epidemic

Fig. 13.8   Geographical distribution of tse-tse flies of the *Glossina morsitans* group. (Adapted from Ford 1971.)

of 1889–90 resulted in high mortality of wild ungulates and cattle. At the same time the distributional limit of *Glossina morsitans*, apart from three small foci, shifted southwards to a position at the same latitude as the southern end of the Lake (Fig. 13.9). In its northward recolonisation the fly probably re-entered Uganda in the early part of the present century, reached Lake Kijanebalola (Fig. 13.9) by 1913 and spread north of this lake and Lake Nakivali by 1920. In 1919 there was a further serious outbreak of rinderpest in Ankole which checked the advance of tse-tse. After a pause the favoured hosts began to multiply and trypanosomiasis was able to continue its spread northward until by 1959 it had nearly reached the Katonga River. From Ford's (1971) data the rate of spread from 1920 to 1959 was approximately 2·5 km per annum. The rate was far from uniform as the extension from 1920 to 1944 covered only 32 km.

With this advance of tse-tse, control measures were introduced in Uganda in the 1930s. Early attempts at control by the creation of barriers of cleared ground and large-scale discriminative bush clearance did not arrest the advance of the fly. In 1958 hunting for reservoir hosts was commenced in northern Ankole and subsequently complemented by insecticidal spraying. Game eradication continued for seven years and by 1965 an estimated 440 000 ha had been reclaimed for grazing. From 1942 to 1962 there was considerable movement of cattle within Ankole resulting from tse-tse control and the need to shift these animals from areas of high trypanosomiasis infection. This was made easier by the fly not spreading into extensive areas of western Ankole. Between 1942 and 1962 there were from 180 000 to 220 000 head of cattle in this district. By 1966 the number had increased to 313 000.

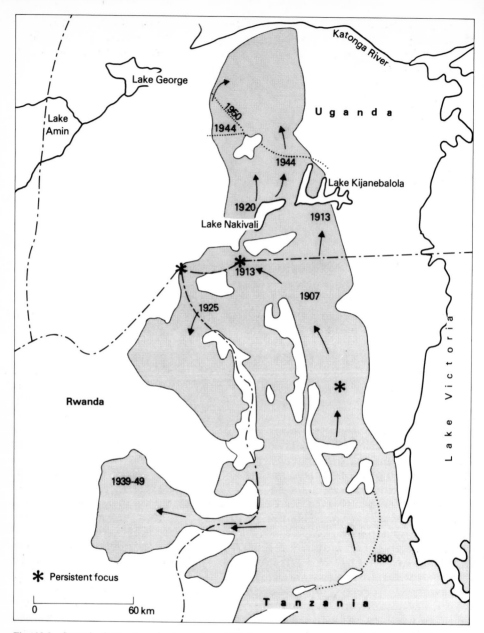

Fig. 13.9 Spread of *Glossina morsitans* since 1890 from eastern Tanzania into Rwanda and Ankole, Uganda (Adapted from Ford 1971.)

The game control measures involved the shooting of 45 000 animals between 1958 and 1965 (Table 13.4). Some species such as zebra were not shot as tse-tse do not feed on them. The development of cattle ranching in part of this area and the exclusion of larger game has resulted in the rapid regeneration of short woody plants, such as *Acacia hockii*, in the former grassland. This habitat modification is the result of the replacement of several species of large mammal by a single grazing species. Providing tse-tse is successfully prevented from re-entering this area these first results are encouraging as the cattle population now approaches the crude estimated total of 330 000 in 1915. This predates the 1919 rinderpest epidemic and the later spread of trypanosomiasis.

Table 13.4 *Game eliminated from Ankole, Uganda 1958–65. (From Wooff 1968.)*

Species	No. shot
Baboon	66
Bushpig	505
Giant forest hog	343
Warthog	1 973
Buffalo	2 144
Eland	646
Bushbuck	14 256
Duiker	14 455
Waterbuck	2 846
Reedbuck	6 683
Topi	176
Oribi	879

Game eradication has been practised elsewhere in Africa probably on its greatest scale in Rhodesia where an estimated 750 000 animals were shot before the large scale use of this method was stopped in 1961. The main campaign took place in a strip south of the River Zambezi where the tse-tse approaches the southern limit of its range (Fig. 13.8). A carefully planned control experiment was implemented at Nagupande in 1962. First an area of 52 000 ha was fenced and the elephant, buffalo and rhinoceros driven out or killed. Then intensive hunting of warthog, bushpig, kudu and bushbuck was commenced and continued uninterrupted until late 1965. From then until early 1967 there were three periods when hunters were withdrawn. These resulted in substantial recovery of the mammal populations (Fig. 13.10) that were soon reduced following reintroduction of shooting. Throughout the experimental period the numbers of tse-tse steadily declined (Fig. 13.10) except for a small temporary increase after cattle were introduced. This experiment took account of the preferred blood foods of tse-tse so that on termination impala, zebra, reedbuck, eland, roan, sable, duiker, grysbok, baboons and hyaena were as numerous as previously. Even though the fly was not completely eliminated its numbers were reduced by about 99·3 per cent.

Child, Smith and von Richter (1970) examined the results of game removal in a strip known as the Maun Front in close proximity to the Okavango Swamp, Botswana. This game-free corridor covered an area of 777 sq km. Tse-tse control hunting records from 1942 to 1964 provided the opportunity for the detailed analysis of the effects of an extended and continuous game removal campaign. During this period 60 000 animals were shot including buffalo, warthog, kudu, reedbuck, impala, tsessebe, wildebeest, duiker, sable, roan, eland, bushbuck, steenbok, lechwe, zebra and various other small mammals.

In most years there were between 40 and 60 hunters operating; in 1945 and 1946 there were many more than this (86 and 102) and from 1950 to 1955 the figure fell to between 21 and 35. The need to sustain hunting for so long a period indicates that the method failed to eliminate mammals from the area. This is confirmed by the final year's shooting producing the largest kill of 4 702 animals. Child, Smith and von Richter (1970) point out that after 23 years of hunting no species was eliminated as a result of this activity. The disappearance of one species (roan) and the decline of three others

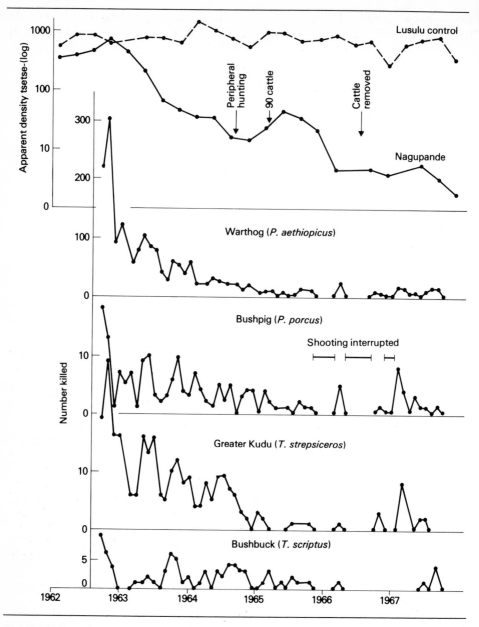

Fig. 13.10 Control of tse-tse fly in the Nagupande experiment. The mean quarterly densities of flies are given for the experimental and control areas and the numbers of game species removed. (Adapted from Ford 1971.)

(tsessebe, wildebeest and kudu) were probably due to population fluctuations over a far wider area than the Maun Front. The annual kills of the remaining species all showed progressive increases over the years.

Hunting was thus removing a proportion of the total fauna whose density was dependent on habitat conditions. This tse-tse control operation had inadvertently demonstrated that an annual resource was available without apparent permanent reduction in the population. In 1964, 324378 kg of meat were obtained from this control shooting (Table 13.5). In this exercise it should be recognised that the numbers

Table 13.5   *Dressed carcass weight of animals shot during tse-tse fly control on the Maun Front, Botswana in 1964. (From Child et al. 1970.)*

Species	No. shot	Total dressed weight of carcases (kg)
Buffalo	618	182591
Kudu	385	43750
Wildebeest	50	5977
Tsessebe	40	3455
Impala	617	16827
Reedbuck	531	20516
Warthog	916	29145
Duiker	1067	10185
Steenbok	376	1965
Lechwe	28	1387
Zebra	38	7220
Other large antelope	13	1359
Total	4679	324377

of hunters were insufficient to rigorously control the game. Furthermore, an important consideration is the proximity of a very large area of little disturbed game populations supplying animals into the area from which they were being removed. In the Maun Front the feasibility of tse-tse control by this method is obviously questionable and attention could well be directed to the undesirability of reclamation of land for cattle. Alternatives include the exploitation of game as a natural and renewable resource.

The relationship between tse-tse control measures and the ecology of large mammal populations are closely interlinked and demand careful appraisal in each situation. In some areas the replacement of game by cattle is in ecological and economic terms of dubious value. Elsewhere it may be more justifiable. It can be seen from the examples cited here that control of tse-tse by game elimination can have measures of success and failure. There can be no doubt that the tse-tse fly has had a dramatic impact on African ecology through its adverse effects on man and his cattle. In this account the main emphasis has been its bearing on the large mammals. This comprises only one aspect of a complex problem having very significant ramifications in many areas of agriculture, health, land use practices and conservation.

13.2   Hunting and poaching

Hunting for food has been widespread in Africa for a long time. This practice has often been tacitly regarded as acceptable as hunters have been following a traditional mode of livelihood and have not been obtaining animals for economic gain. This attitude attracted some credence at the turn of the century but since that time with human populations steadily increasing and the land available for mammals steadily decreasing uncontrolled hunting has accounted for very considerable reductions in mammal populations. This type of hunting has frequently ignored game laws, has been indiscriminate and has had no regard for the status of the species hunted or the age, sex or numbers of animals taken. Local hunters use all possible methods at their disposal for catching animals. These include firearms, snares, nets, arrows, spears, fire, traps and any other practicable technique.

As human populations have increased former centres of low population have become densely populated with the surroundings becoming subject to more intensive hunting. There has also been improved mobility resulting from extensive road construction and easier access to remote areas by vehicles. These developments have inevitably led to more and more animals being removed. Furthermore, as local hunting is an ongoing activity its continuity ensures a constant pressure on the species removed. Places where large mammals were probably never very numerous are most susceptible to the effects of hunting and it is here where they are most vulnerable to extermination. The main factor responsible for the low numbers of large mammals in West Africa is illegal local hunting (Happold 1973*a*).

There is a further type of hunting which is damaging to the existence of certain species. This is poaching for economic gain. The most vulnerable species are those having marketable products such as the skins of leopard and zebra, the tusks of elephants and horns of rhinos. For products such as these there has to be a demand and all too frequently this is not in their country of origin. The financial rewards are considerable which makes the risks worth taking. In recent years there has been an upsurge in this type of poaching in several African states. All steps should be taken to apprehend the culprits whether they are peasants, business men or close relatives of a Head of State (Tinker 1975).

Few precise data have been published on the extent of illegal removal of game animals whether for consumption or sale. This is due to the difficulty in obtaining accurate information for an extended period. National Parks frequently keep records of poaching incidents, quantities of poaching equipment confiscated and the number of poached animals retrieved but these may provide little more than a general indication of the extent of the activity. Edroma (1973) examined the poaching situation in Rwenzori Park in 1972 and 1973 and drew attention to the likelihood of it increasing in the future as a result of population growth within the Park villages, which here are small enclaves within the Park. For each year from 1971 to 1973 there was a monthly average of between 32 and 56 illegal entries recorded while in 1972 and 1973 there were 20·2 and 26·1 large mammals known to have been illegally killed each month (Table 13.6). Further, extremely useful information has been obtained on the reduction in recent years of elephant populations in East African Parks (p. 391).

Table 13.6 *Mean monthly numbers of animals known to have been killed by poachers in Rwenzori Park. (From Edroma 1973.)*

	1972	1973
Buffalo	4·9	4·4
Elephant	2·0	6·6
Giant forest hog	2·7	1·5
Hippopotamus	8·7	8·5
Uganda kob	1·0	0·2
Waterbuck	0·9	1·6
Warthog	?	3·3

The foregoing may appear to contradict some of the findings from tse-tse control schemes where continuous hunting failed to eradicate the large mammal species being hunted. However, success primarily depends on the intensity of hunting and where tse-tse game eradication schemes have been unsuccessful their failure can be attributed to insufficient sustained hunting effort. This contrasts with intensive, efficient, illegal hunting in localities accessible to high density human populations. It is from such places that many species of large mammals have been eliminated. Legal hunting does not have adverse long-term effects on large mammal numbers as this activity is subject to some form of control.

A detailed study of legal hunting has been undertaken by Marks (1973) on the Valley Bisa hunters who inhabit an area between the two sectors of the Luangwa Valley National Park in Zambia. Marks (1973) concentrated his study on hunting in the vicinity of Nabwalya where villages ranged in size from 4 to 73. There were 244 adults and 222 children in 21 villages covering an area of 155 sq. km. This area consisted of mopane woodland and open grassland. The study extended over twelve months during which time as a result of seasonal movements the relative abundance of large mammals was subject to fluctuation. For example, buffalo were an important component of the fauna in the wet months and impala were numerous for much of the year being the commonest species from August to October. Hunting was for larger mammals including elephant, buffalo, zebra, impala, waterbuck and warthog. Most hunts lasted for four hours or less and mainly took place in the mornings. In the wet season from November to May the hunts were generally of longer duration (Fig. 13.11). The

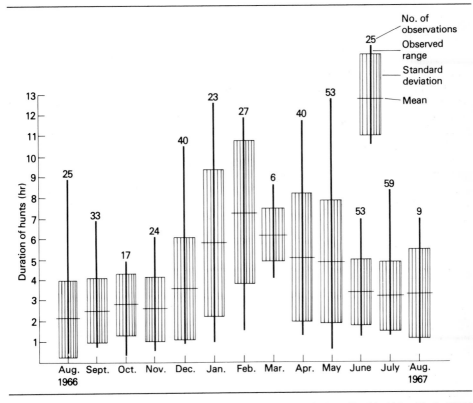

Fig. 13.11 The frequency and duration of hunts in the Nabwalya Study Area, Zambia. (After Marks 1973.)

effectiveness of individual hunters is shown in Table 13.7. Most hunters possessed muzzle-loading rifles which were slow to reload and lacking in accuracy, killing power and range. Hunter inaccuracy is not recorded in Table 13.7 which summarises actual

Table 13.7   *Success and yields for resident and official hunters in Nabwalya, Zambia, 1966–7. (From Marks 1973.)*

Classification individual	Weapon*	No. hunts	Time (hr)	Success† (%)	Mammals killed or retrieved	Biomass‡ (kg)	Yield = biomass/hr
Residents							
Paksoni	m	9	51·5	0	0	0	0
Lubeles	m	32	174·75	12·5	4	816	4·7
	s, r	42	150·25	45·2	20·5	4317	28·8
Chizola	m	43	178·5	23·2	12	2006	11·3
Kabuswe	m	16	50·25	18·8	3	138	2·8
Chando	m	24	109·5	12·5	3	496	4·6
Chibinda	m	40	141	12·5	5	1202	8·5
Timothi	m	49	276·25	28·6	13	2490	9·0
Jamesi	m	11	26	9·1	1	636	24·0
Official							
Pilsoni	s, r	6	24	50·0	3	691	28·8
Milandi	s	30	95	46·6	18	704	7·4
Game Guards	r	14	37·75	57·1	8	10896	286·7

*m = muzzle loader, s = shotgun, r = rifle.
†Success = successful hunts/total hunts × 100.
‡Carcass yield.

Transient and occasional visitors are omitted.

yields. Marks (1973) observed that 26 buffalo were wounded in addition to the 33 killed and retrieved.

During the year 27451 kg of meat was made available to the inhabitants of Nabwalya. This was made up of 1 elephant, 39 buffalo, 23 impala, 17 warthog, 8 waterbuck, 7 zebra, 2 puku, 2 bushbuck, 1 hippopotamus and 1 eland. Of these 79 were known to be adult. Game guards contributed 40 per cent of the yield. The total meat available amounted to the considerable figure of 91·5 kg per adult per year. After considering the abundance of large herbivorous mammals and the demands of their carnivore predators Marks (1973) concluded that the level of hunting in this situation was not damaging to the game herds.

This example provides very relevant information on the relationships between traditional hunting and ecological and social problems. In Nabwalya the human population density was low at three persons per square kilometer and the game populations were high. (Their densities were not estimated; instead the number of mammals seen per hour of hunting were recorded. The mean monthly figure never fell below 23.) The intensity of hunting was quite remarkable, there being throughout the year more than one hunt a day from a community of 82 resident adult males. The very high per capita consumption of meat reflects the African's taste for this food and his preparedness, given the opportunity, to consume far more than his nutritional requirements. In Nabwalya these habits were apparently of little consequence to the game. However, the retention of these attitudes, traditions and practices in higher density human populations have led to the reduction and elimination of large mammals from many areas. The difficult task is to change cultural attitudes so that it is appreciated that benefits accrue from not eliminating these animals and by seeking alternative sources of protein.

Brief mention should be made of legal hunting for sport. This is on a limited scale and is carried out within the game ordinances in selected localities. The numbers of animals taken by each hunter is carefully controlled. Sport hunting is regulated so as to ensure it has no adverse long-term effects on the ecology of the species being hunted or the habitats they occupy. There can be appreciable economic benefits to game departments, suppliers of safari kit, taxidermists and transport agencies (Clarke and Mitchell 1968) through this activity.

13.3   Endangered species

The foregoing account has drawn attention to changes in land use and management that have had an impact directly or indirectly on wild mammal populations. For most species this has resulted in the establishment of less hospitable habitats. The possible exceptions include several species of small rodents for whom there has been some environmental improvement. For many large mammals poorer habitat conditions have resulted in range contraction and dwindling numbers.

In an attempt to draw attention to this decline in numbers of certain species the International Union for the Conservation of Nature and Natural Resources has prepared a Red Data Book. In this it lists, on a continental basis, those species and subspecies that are endangered, vulnerable, rare, out of danger and indeterminate. These five categories are described (IUCN 1975) as follows:

1. *Endangered.*   Taxa in danger of extinction, the survival of which is unlikely if the causal factors now at work continue operating.

2. *Vulnerable.*   Taxa believed likely to move into the endangered category in the near future if the causal factors now at work continue operating.

3. *Rare.*   Taxa with small world populations which are not at present endangered or vulnerable but which are at risk.

4. *Out of Danger.*   Taxa formerly included in one of the above categories but which are now considered relatively secure because effective conservation measures have been taken or the previous threat to their survival has been removed.

5. *Indeterminate.*   Taxa which are suspected of belonging to one of the first three categories but for which insufficient information is available on which to base a decision.

There are thirteen endangered species or subspecies (Table 13.8) in mainland Africa south of the Sahara. Most have restricted geographical ranges, e.g. Simien fox, Tana River monkey, Cameroun clawless otter, mountain gorilla. There are some subspecies on this list. In the vulnerable category are several well-known species of widespread distribution including hunting dog, leopard, cheetah, black rhinoceros, chimpanzee and the aquatic manatee and dugong. The presence of lowland gorilla here means that the two subspecies of this species are either vulnerable or endangered. Furthermore, with the inclusion of chimpanzee all the African Pongidae are experiencing a precarious existence.

On the credit side, Africa can boast two taxa out of danger. These are the black wildebeest and bontebok which have survived and increased in numbers in South Africa as a result of active conservation measures. The species listed as indeterminate are Temminck's giant squirrels (*Epixerus ebii ebii, E. e. wilsoni*) from West Africa. There may be more species among the smaller mammals that could appropriately be included

Table 13.8　*International Union for the Conservation of Nature and Natural Resources. Mammals listed in the Red Data Book (1973) from mainland Africa south of the Sahara.*

Endangered

Cercocebus galeritus galeritus	Tana River monkey
Gorilla gorilla beringei	Mountain gorilla
Aonyx congica microdon	Cameroun clawless otter
Canis simensis	Simien fox
Equus africanus	African wild ass
Ceratotherium simum cottoni	Northern square-lipped rhinoceros
Taurotragus derbianus derbianus	Western giant eland
Cephalophus jentinki	Jentink's duiker
Alcelaphus buselaphus tora	Tora hartebeest
Alcelaphus buselaphus swaynei	Swayne's hartebeest
Aepyceros melampus petersi	Black-faced impala
Gazella dama lozoni	Rio de Oro Dama gazelle
Gazella leptoceros	Slender-horned gazelle

Vulnerable

Pan troglodytes	Chimpanzee
Gorilla gorilla gorilla	Lowland gorilla
Lycaon pictus	Hunting dog
Hyaena brunnea	Brown hyaena
Acinonyx jubatus	Cheetah
Panthera pardus	Leopard
Dugong dugon	Dugong
Trichechus senegalensis	West African manatee
Equus zebra	Mountain zebra
Diceros bicornis	Black rhinoceros
Kobus leche	Lechwe
Addax nasomaculatus	Addax
Oryx dammah	Scimitar-horned oryx
Dorcatragus megalotis	Beira antelope

Rare

Colobus rufomitratus gordonorum	Gordon's bay colobus
Colobus rufomitratus rufomitratus	Tana River bay colobus
Colobus verus	Olive colobus
Choeropsis liberiensis	Pygmy hippopotamus

in the rare or indeterminate categories. Lack of information on their ecology, numbers and taxonomy often makes their status difficult to ascertain.

These IUCN listings are not necessarily static. Improvement of environmental conditions can remove a species from the endangered list. Similarly, greater pressures can result in species being added. It is unfortunate that such listings do not adequately recognize regional differences in the status of a species or subspecies so that by the time an animal is placed on the list it has already reached a critical level over all its range.

13.4　National parks and game reserves

The problem of declining mammal habitats and numbers was both recognised and anticipated by colonial governments as long as fifty years ago. In order to deal with the problem various legislative programmes were introduced for the protection of wildlife. These measures were mainly aimed at species of large mammals and took cognizance of opposing considerations such as the need to prevent damage to smallholdings by elephant and the protection of this species from overhunting. This resulted in the establishment of several categories of conservation areas. Each area differed in the amount of protection given to its wildlife and to the habitat. These included controlled hunting areas, game reserves and national parks. In addition game laws were often enacted that had nationwide application. The national park afforded the greatest protection as hunting was illegal and human settlement was controlled.

Wildlife legislation has, for the most part, been the responsibility of national governments. The times of the establishment of national parks and other conservation areas have differed in each country due to government attitudes as well as the need to introduce protective legislation. Comparison of the dates of establishment of national parks in East Africa, Belgian Congo (now Zaire) and Rwanda (Fig. 13.12) shows how

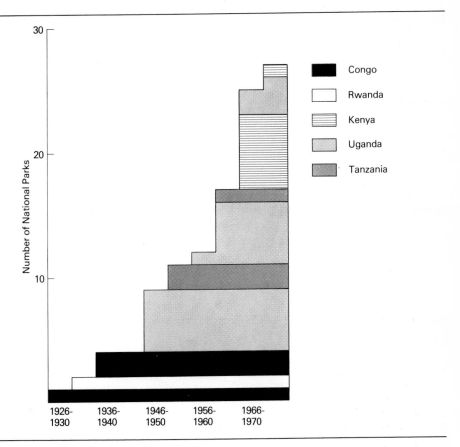

Fig. 13.12 Number of National Parks gazetted in Kenya, Uganda, Tanzania, Rwanda and Congo (now Zaire), 1926–75. Included here are only parks concerned with wildlife conservation. Dates refer to the times areas were gazetted as National Parks; they may previously have been established as a different type of conservation area, e.g. controlled hunting area.

countries under former Belgian administration (Zaire, Rwanda) were very early in setting up a national park system with the formation of the Albert (now Kivu) National Park in 1929. By 1940 three more parks were established in the Congo and Rwanda. In the immediate post-war period five parks were gazetted in Kenya to be followed by eight parks in Tanzania and Uganda between 1951 and 1975. By 1975, these five countries had twenty-seven national parks devoted to the conservation of wildlife.

There are numerous reasons why mammals and all other forms of wildlife should be conserved. It is important that all the components of natural ecosystems should be retained so that in the first instance their inter-relationships can be studied and understood. Only then is man in a position to manipulate natural environments in order to exploit them to his own advantage, as for example in agriculture and forestry, and at the same time not incur permanent damage or disharmony to the system. The elimination of a species creates a void which probably cannot be adequately filled by any other single species. Some other reasons for conserving wildlife are extensions of this concept. There is the possible potential of many mammals as food sources. These are far from fully realised at present although some progress has been made through the limited domestication of the cane rat (*Thryonomys*) and eland. There are aesthetic and educational values of wildlife which are difficult to quantify. For many people a considerable satisfaction obtains from the observation and casual study of fauna and flora. Finally wildlife, particularly the viewing of large mammals and birds in national parks, can offer economic rewards through tourism.

In Kenya, tourism earns more foreign exchange than any other industry and the attractions of this source of national income is receiving greater recognition from an increasing number of African states. However, a luxury trade such as this which is highly dependent upon visitors who have travelled from other continents is likely to be vulnerable to world economic conditions. It is also sensitive to domestic disturbances within the host country. The smallest political event can be reflected in a fall in the number of visitors to the national parks while major disturbances such as the expulsion of Asians from Uganda in 1972 and a resultant deterioration in tourist services have caused a fall in numbers to between a fifth and quarter those of 1971–2 (Fig. 13.13).

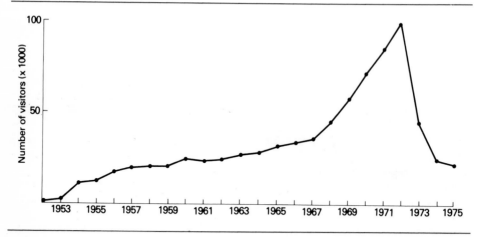

Fig. 13.13   Annual number of visitors to Uganda National Parks, 1952–75. (Source: Uganda National Parks.)

Over the same period the parks in Kenya have increased their attendance steadily, having possibly benefitted from a decline in the number of visitors to Uganda (Fig. 13.14). For these reasons it is desirable that national parks should aim in the long term to obtain their support from the endemic population under whose control they are maintained.

There has been considerable debate in recent years as to the extent to which national parks should be scientifically managed. The arguments mainly revolve around whether there should be controlled habitat modification, whether an ecological *status quo*

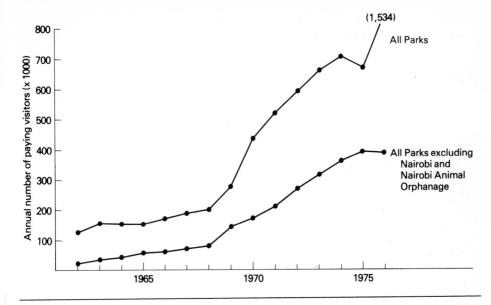

Fig. 13.14　Annual number of paying visitors to Kenya National Parks, 1962–76. The Nairobi National Park and the Animal Orphanage are very close to Nairobi City and in consequence attract a large number of visitors. As these may bias the data from the Parks as a whole numbers are given which include and exclude these two. (Data from Kenya Central Statistical Office.)

should be enforced or whether there should be virtually no interference with natural processes within the parks in which case man should do no more than observe and record any changes that may occur. This dilemma has largely been created by one species of mammal – the elephant. The evidence suggests that elephant numbers in the parks of East Africa have increased considerably over the past twenty years and that this has been due in part to immigration from peripheral areas where they have often been subjected to harassment and disturbance. Not only have existing populations increased their numbers as in Kabalega and Tsavo Parks. In Serengeti, no elephants were present for at least 40 years prior to 1955. Invasion then commenced so that ten years later (Lamprey *et al.* 1967) there were 2 000 established in the Park.

High populations of elephant are accompanied by considerable tree reduction, resulting in a gradual replacement of woodland by grassland and scrub (Figs. 13.7, 13.15). This process has been reported in Rwenzori (Field 1971), Kabalega (Buechner and Dawkins 1961), Tsavo (Glover and Sheldrick (1964) and Kruger (Wyk and Fairall 1969) Parks. Laws (1968*a*) pointed out that these changes lower elephant-carrying capacity and modify the composition of the ungulate fauna. In dryer areas such as Tsavo Park there are periodically years of low rainfall (p. 353) when the habitat experiences an abrupt temporary drop in carrying capacity. When this coincides with high elephant populations a dramatic mortality can be anticipated as the elephants' homeostatic regulatory mechanisms could not be invoked with sufficient rapidity to effect natural regulation.

In 1969 Laws predicted that this would occur in due course in Tsavo Park and would be accompanied by extensive habitat degradation. The latter, he believed, could be sufficient to lower the carrying capacity dramatically and continuously beyond the period of severe adversity (Fig. 13.16). Dry years in 1970 and 1971 resulted in the death

Fig. 13.15 Habitat changes induced by elephants in Tsavo Park. The area around the waterhole is devoid of vegetation and the surrounding country has changed from wooded savanna to thorn bush. (Photo: **W.** Leuthold.)

of just under 6000 elephants (Corfield 1975). Following this mortality it was suggested that the elephant population very rapidly came into equilibrium with the habitat's lower carrying capacity and that continuing vegetation degradation predicted by Laws (1969b) in one of his models (Fig. 13.16b) was not attained. On the other hand there is no suggestion from Corfield's (1973) data that the habitat would return to its former carrying capacity. In this respect Laws' views on permanent modification are confirmed and the prospect of further droughts may reduce populations still further.

The management issues posed by these elephant studies merit further consideration. Should elephants have been culled prior to the predicted mortality in 1970 and 1971? Had this been undertaken there would have been lower mortality from undernutrition and less habitat modification. The significance of habitat modification has provoked much discussion. The protagonists of non-culling have suggested that the vegetation changes witnessed in Tsavo are part of a natural or semi-natural long term cycle and have questioned whether *Commiphora* woodland is the climax vegetation of the area (Sheldrick 1972). This argument apparently loses some of its force when it is remembered that the cause of change is recent and man-induced through the inadvertent creation of high-density elephant populations. The new vegetation resulting from habitat modification by the elephants has a different floral structure, productivity and spectrum of mammal species and numbers with elephants a much smaller component than previously. It is a value judgement which is to be preferred.

If animals are to be culled what number should be removed? To answer this, information is required on numbers, distribution and various other population parameters as well as their impact on their habitat. Is there the prospect of a sustained

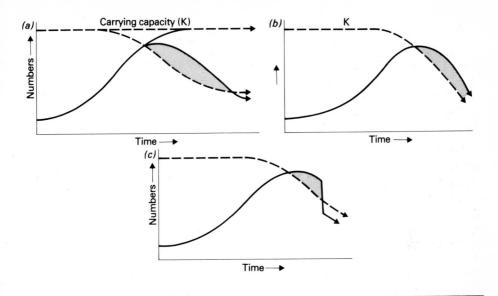

Fig. 13.16 Hypothetical responses of elephants to decreased carrying capacity. (After Laws 1969 and Corfield 1973.)   (*a*) Increase in population results in reduced carrying capacity and re-establishment of a balance at a lower population density.   (*b*) Increase in population results in steadily deteriorating habitat, declining carrying capacity and a drop in population density. Carrying capacity and population are not coming into equilibrium.   (*c*) Increase in population is followed by an abrupt fall in numbers. Carrying capacity and population density re-establish an equilibrium.

yield from elephant and other game species? This may be possible although there must be careful reappraisal of parks' policies and objectives if regular cropping is to be implemented.

The problems of management are peculiar to each park and must be considered in the light of prevailing local conditions. For example, while in many parks there is extensive tree destruction by elephants, in the vicinity of Seronera in Serengeti this is not on a scale sufficient to transform woodland to grassland (Croze 1974).

Unfortunately, much of this discussion is becoming academic as in recent years up to the time of writing (1976) elephant poaching throughout East Africa has attained enormous proportions. It is estimated that in 1973 12000 elephant were illegally killed in Kenya and at the 1974 rate of poaching elephants would be eliminated from Tsavo in four years. In Uganda, the population in Kabalega Park fell from 14309 in 1973 to 6030 in 1974 and then down to 2246 and in 2448 in 1975 and 1976 respectively (Anon 1977). This very abrupt decrease illustrates the administrative difficulties involved in parks management when confronted with a lucrative illegal activity directed against them. Poaching is not uniformly widespread throughout the continent with very high elephant populations persisting in some areas e.g. Selous Park, Tanzania (Anon 1976).

Management, involving an activity which favourably modifies the habitat or numbers of animals it contains, is generally recognised as desirable by national parks authorities. This may be little more than the erection of a boundary fence or ditch. In contrast more significant practices would be the extensive cropping of large mammals, the excavation of water holes and the construction of vehicular tracks which act as fire breaks. These should be undertaken only against the background of sound scientific knowledge so that their effects can be accurately predicted. The provision of amenities for visitors to parks should be to an extent which does not adversely disturb the wildlife to be conserved. These and many other considerations are the ingredients of sound management policies which should be implemented in a knowledgeable and responsible way.

13.5　Game ranching

The exploitation of African mammals for food and by-products such as horns, skins and hides has been proposed on a number of occasions (Dasmann and Mossman 1961, Harthoorn 1958, Hopcraft 1969, Roth 1966, Ruhweza 1968, Savory 1965, Talbot *et al.* 1965). Arguments favouring game ranching suggest that wild mammals are better adapted to utilising some types of natural vegetation particularly in semi-arid areas than are cattle and that in consequence the annual yield per unit area is likely to be greater if game are cropped instead of cattle. There can also be situations where game and cattle occur together so that it is feasible that both may produce an economic return. Under a cropping regime man intercalates himself as a predator removing animals before they die from other causes. The aim of such a programme must be to obtain a regular yield and thereby a sustained profitability. It is also feasible that some species of African mammals could be domesticated and, as a result, more readily harvested. This has hardly been attempted even though eland have been farmed in the USSR for more than 80 years (Treus and Kravchenko 1968) and elephant have been domesticated in the former Belgian Congo (Phillipson 1934).

A preliminary experiment in game ranching was undertaken by Dassman and Mossman (1961) on a 13 000 ha study area of the 333 600 ha Henderson Ranch in Rhodesia. From estimates of the numbers of mammals present they recommended a cropping plan that was duly implemented (Table 13.9). They considered, but did not demonstrate, that this crop amounting to 50 600 kg could be sustained on an annual

Table 13.9　*Game populations and yield from the 13 000 ha study area of Henderson Ranch, Rhodesia. (After Dassman and Mossman 1961.)*

Species	Estimated numbers	Recommended crop	Weight of dressed carcass (adult) (kg)	Total meat yield (kg)
Impala	2 100	525	23·6	12 390
Zebra	730	146	115·9	16 921
Steenbok	200	40	5·5	220
Warthog	170	85	31·8	2 703
Kudu	160	48	102·3	4 910
Wildebeest	160	32	118·2	3 782
Giraffe	90	15	454·5*	6 817
Duiker	80	28	9·1	255
Waterbuck	35	7	90·9*	636
Buffalo	30	5	259·1	1 296
Eland	10	2	272·7*	545
Klipspringer	10	3	6·4	19
Bushpig	10	5	31·8*	159
				50 653 kg

*Estimated.

The ranch also supported elephant, grysbok and bushbuck. Their numbers were too low to obtain meaningful estimates from the sampling method.

basis. The same area was capable of producing 42 900 kg of beef. At this ranch beef was more expensive to rear and market than wild game so that the financial return for the latter was appreciably more. This short-term experiment demonstrated the possibilities of game providing a sustained yield.

Croppings have since been undertaken on private farms, ranches and government land elsewhere in Africa. On the Kekopey Ranch in Kenya 1 000 Thomson's gazelle and 700 impala were taken in one year from a total standing crop of 3 000 of each species (Parker 1972). At Akira Ranch also in Kenya, Field and Blankenship (1973*a*) suggest an annual crop of 350 Grant's gazelle, 560 Coke's hartebeest, 750 Thomson's gazelle and 60 giraffe. On this 31 566 ha ranch there are on average (the game is subject to considerable movement) 695 Grant's gazelle, 1 605 hartebeest, 990 Thomson's gazelle, 280 giraffe and 4 340 cattle. These cropping rates assume optimal conditions of good nutrition, high survival of young, control of predators and low incidence of disease. The lack of uniformity in the percentage of each species to be taken recognises differences in breeding rates and age to maturity. From their study, Field and Blankenship (1973*a*) were able to advocate the continued exploitation of the compatible game and domestic stock, a domestication programme of some of the wild ungulates particularly the fast-breeding gazelles, and the introduction of limited sport hunting.

Sustained yield cropping has been carried out at two localities in Western Uganda (Field 1974). A mean annual crop of 774 Uganda Kob averaging 135 594 kg of dressed meat was removed from the Semliki Valley from 1963 to 1972 and in western Acholi 475 Uganda kob, 368 buffalo, 116 hartebeest and 82 other mammals mainly waterbuck, warthog and oribi were removed over a two-and-a-half-year period between 1965 and 1967. These produced 60 000 kg of dressed meat per annum.

The number of animals to be harvested will depend on the carrying capacity of the land in question. This has already (Ch. 12) been demonstrated to vary in relation to climatic and other conditions. In comparing the merits of game cropping and cattle ranching as meat sources account must be taken of the relative suitability of land for these methods of protein production. Data on the standing crop biomass of cattle in different situations provides comparative information on the level of supportable populations. In Kenya, savanna tribal grazings support 1 960–2 800 kg/km^2 of domestic stock (Talbot and Talbot 1963) and European-owned cattle ranches 3 728–5 600 kg/km^2 (Talbot, Ledger and Payne 1961). A commercial ranch in Ankole, Uganda, supports 23 000 kg/km^2 and this figure can be raised to 40 000 kg/km^2 with improvement of grazing (Eltringham 1974). The twenty-fold difference between the lowest and highest of these estimates reflects differences in management practices as well as carrying capacity and furthermore takes no account of the relative abundance of game. Nevertheless, attention is focussed on obvious differences in land suitability for cattle. It is debatable whether the highly productive cattle localities could make more than a small contribution of meat from game whereas those situations supporting less cattle may prove more suitable for game cropping on ecological as well as economic grounds. Each case must be subjected to analysis in these terms. Game ranching has still to be extensively developed in tropical Africa having up to the present hardly extended beyond an experimental stage.

13.6   Mammal ecology and human disease

Diseases such as yellow fever, sleeping sickness, malaria and plague are well known to the African continent where since historic times they have been known to inflict very high mortality on the human population. Over the years control measures have greatly improved but have not yet succeeded in complete eradication. Occasionally, in comparatively recent times epidemics have caused large numbers of deaths. This happened in Ethiopia between 1960 and 1962 when 30 000 persons died of yellow fever (Haddow 1968). The control of disease remains an urgent task in tropical Africa.

Many diseases of man are caused by micro-organisms such as viruses, bacteria and protozoa and their symptoms are usually manifested after the organism has become established in this host and has increased to large numbers. The causative organisms are frequently transmitted from host to host by another animal, frequently an arthropod, feeding on infected and uninfected individuals. Transmission can take other routes. The rabies virus can be passed from one host to the next through the bite of an infected animal. In contrast, schistosomiasis (which is caused by a trematode worm) is transmitted in a far more complex fashion having an aquatic snail as an intermediate host and a subsequent free swimming stage which penetrates the skin of the primary host.

Wild mammals are often reservoirs for disease organisms and thereby provide a locus from which infection into human populations can take place. Furthermore, there are some species of mammal that are largely immune to the micro-organism. The yellow fever virus is found in several species of primate (e.g. redtail monkey, *Cercopithecus ascanius*, blue monkey *C. mitis*, mona monkey *C. mona* and greater bushbaby *Galago crassicaudatus*) which may display no external manifestations of the disease. This is also true of the sleeping sickness trypanosome (*Trypanosoma brucei*) which has been recorded from several large mammals (e.g. impala, hartebeest, topi, warthog, waterbuck, wildebeest, zebra, lion). It is difficult to generalise about immunity to these diseases in their mammal hosts as this can vary within the same species at different geographical locations as well as between individuals in the same population.

There are several diseases of man whose causative organisms are found in wild mammals (Table 13.10). Numerous orders of mammals are implicated and some of the

Table 13.10   *Some human diseases found in mammals.*

Disease in man	Causative organism	Mammalian host(s)	Transmission organism (vector)
Lassa fever	Lassa fever virus	*Praomys natalensis*	Unknown at present
Malaria	*Plasmodium* spp.	Rodents (Anomaluridae, *Atherurus*, *Thamnomys*)	Anopheline mosquito
Plague	*Yersinia pestis*	Several rodents, notably *Tatera*, *Praomys*, *Rattus*	Several fleas
Rabies	Rabies virus	Numerous, particularly carnivores	None
Relapsing fever	*Spirochaeta duttoni*	Shrews, bats, primates, Muridae	Ticks
Schistosomiasis	*Schistosoma* spp.	Several rodents	Complex life cycle of parasite involving an aquatic snail
Sleeping sickness	*Trypanosoma brucei*	Bats, primates, ungulates, lion	Tse-tse fly (*Glossina* sp.)
Yellow fever	Yellow fever virus	Primates, hedgehog (*Erinaceus*), rodent (*Thryonomys*)	Mosquito (*Aedes simpsoni*)

species listed are abundant and widespread. If preventative measures are not in operation the likelihood of transmission from mammals to man depends on the proximity of infected animals to human populations and the presence of the appropriate vector. The former is obviously related to the ecology of the species in question. This can result in some diseases being more readily communicable than others.

The geographical distribution of a disease does not necessarily correspond to that of its host. Lassa fever is restricted to a few sites in west Africa while plague although known from a much wider geographical area is only found at a restricted number of sites within that area. A further factor in limiting the distribution of a disease is the efficacy of control measures.

An intricate relationship between the ecology of a species of mammal and the spread of a disease is to be found in plague transmission in South Africa (Davis 1964). Here there is a complex transfer mechanism of the plague bacterium *Yersinia pestis* between three rodent hosts. The main reservoir of the bacterium is the high veld gerbil, *Tatera brantsi* and its flea *Xenopsylla philoxera*. There is virtually no contact between the gerbil and man. When a severe outbreak of plague occurs there is extensive mortality amongst the *Tatera*. Its burrows are then inhabited by *Praomys natalensis* and the gerbil's flea then introduces the plague bacterium into the species. The spread of plague through the *Praomys* population results in the disease being close to human habitations as this rat is a common occupant of fields and farms. Plague can then be transmitted to the house rat, *Rattus rattus*, which will bring the disease still closer to man. The sequence is rather more complex than outlined here as several species of flea are also involved.

The importance of certain species of mammal in the transmission of disease is far from clear. Little is known of the incidence of infection of humans with malaria from rodents or whether rodents form epidemiologically important reservoirs for schistosomiasis. Schwetz (1953, 1954, 1956) and Nelson, Teesdale and Highton (1962) found heavy infection rates of *Schistosoma rodhaini* in *Dasymys, Pelomys* and *Lophuromys flavopunctatus*. These species are typical of moist situations and could play an important role in sustaining parasite numbers.

The role of wild mammals in the spread and maintenance of human disease should not be underestimated. However, it must also be appreciated that once an epidemic in man is under way the most rapid method of spread is from human to human. The significance of the wild mammal in this cycle can then become negligible. A knowledge of mammal ecology is very relevant in the control of disease but it is only one facet of a complex picture in which human ecology, parasitology and medical science all have equally important roles.

Postscript

In this account we have endeavoured to provide a balanced account of the ecology of all groups of African mammals from the diverse range of habitats they occupy. However, it is quite evident from our researches into the literature that there has been more intensive study in some parts of Africa and that considerably more attention has been given to certain orders. The species inhabiting a particular ecosystem are essential components of that system and inevitably, directly or indirectly, interact with each other. Thus the extensive investigation of one group and the neglect or lack of study of another inevitably provides an unbalanced and incomplete picture of the functioning of the whole system.

It is relevant, in understanding how this state of affairs has come about, to reflect on the course that the study of mammals in Africa has followed. The abundance, variety and size of the large mammals have attracted travellers to Africa since the times of the earliest explorations. During the latter part of the last century and the first decade of the present century many explorers, travellers, administrators, naturalists and others were gradually accumulating and despatching specimens of large and small mammals to the museums of Europe and America. This was the period of the collector and a time when museum zoologists were having a heyday with the description of new genera, species and subspecies. As a result of their efforts the taxonomic foundations were being laid for more advanced ecological study. Field naturalists of this period frequently lived under indifferent conditions totally unsuitable for the meticulate work they frequently undertook. Enthusiasm and dedication were not to be dampened by physical and climatic adversity. One such naturalist was Emin Pasha, who in 1883 and 1884 was Governor of Equatoria Province which covered what is now part of southern Sudan, northern Uganda and north-west Zaire. Of his efforts Thomas (1888) of the British Museum of Natural History wrote, 'When the cares and anxieties of a person in the position of a responsible governor of a large and turbulent African province are considered, it seems wonderful that Emin should have been able to make any collections at all, and still more should have made such a collection as the present, nearly every specimen of which has been very carefully labelled in his own handwriting with the date, sex and exact locality, particulars which add enormously to its scientific value.' Emin was but one of many whose combined efforts paved the way for further investigative and analytical research.

The period between the two world wars is noteworthy insofar as little attempt was made to study mammals in the field. This is not altogether surprising. At that time the professional zoologist was becoming particularly involved with experimental studies in the laboratory while in the tropics the attention of governments was being directed to the establishment of research laboratories whose efforts were particularly directed to the development of agriculture and fisheries and the improvement of human health. As a result wild mammals were viewed in the light of how they impinged on these practices, as for example in the eradication of sleeping sickness and the control of rodent pests. At this time there was little need for widespread concern about the conservation and extinction of animals. In many places they were numerous and if through man's activities they were locally reduced in numbers then they were still plentiful elsewhere. Nevertheless, the need for conservation was just beginning to be appreciated as it was during this period that the first national parks were created and some of the earlier game laws enacted.

Since the Second World War there has been a progressive awareness of the social and economic value of mammals. On the negative side they can destroy crops, carry and spread disease in man and his domestic stock, and cause considerable disturbance to inhabitants of rural areas. To their credit they can provide food, hides, ivory and as a result of easier and cheaper air travel a very considerable foreign income through the tourist trade. In many countries mammals form an important element in the national economy as a result of these detrimental and beneficial effects although it is probably in relatively few that the latter are maximised.

During the last thirty years there have been dramatic increases in the indigenous human populations which have directly or indirectly been responsible for the reduction of many wild mammal populations. Concurrently, biologists throughout the world have become more conscious of the relevance and need for ecological study. In Africa, this interest manifested itself in the establishment of field stations for the study of terrestrial ecology in Senegal, Ivory Coast, Gabon, Uganda, Kenya, Tanzania and Zambia. As a result of the efforts of their scientific staffs a great deal of work has appeared. There have been numerous studies additional to these. Universities in the tropics have been expanding and their staffs have been making their contribution while scientists at agricultural, veterinary, and medical research institutes, as well as visitors from overseas including those attached to special projects, have all made their impact. The last fifteen years has, mainly through these agencies, seen more ecological study than the preceding hundred years.

What of the future? There is not a single aspect of the ecology of African mammals that through further study could not produce new, valuable and relevant information. Furthermore, equally useful contributions can be obtained from the amateur naturalist as the professional biologist. The subject can benefit just as much from straightforward observational study as from more sophisticated and elaborate research. Every interested person has a potential contribution. There is also a need to communicate as widely as possible (and preferably to as young audiences as possible) the virtues and delights of natural history, for it is in this way that an awareness of the importance of wildlife is appreciated and future ecologists are bred. Such communication can be through the classroom, the media, wildlife societies and clubs, and literature such as introductory guides, manuals, pamphlets and booklets. The responsibility for advancing knowledge and education on African wildlife is coming to rest, quite appropriately, on the shoulders of the people of Africa. For a time yet they may be assisted by expatriate scientists and teachers but as their role diminishes we hope to see them replaced by a new generation of dynamic African ecologists.

References

Adamson, J. (1969) *The Spotted Sphinx*, Collins and Harvill, London.

Aellen, V. (1953) Contributions l'étude des Chiroptères du 'Cameroun. *Mem. Soc. Neuchateloise des Sc. Nat.*, **8** (1), 1–118.

Aeschlimann, A. (1963) Observations sur *Philatomba maxwelli* (Hamilton-Smith) une antelopé de la forêt eburnèenne. *Acta trop.*, **20**, 341–68.

Altmann, S.A. (1967) (ed.) *Social Communication among Primates*. University of Chicago Press, Chicago.

Altmann, S. A. and Altmann, J. (1970) Baboon ecology: African field research. *Biblthca primatol.*, **12**, 1–220.

Amoroso, E. C. and Marshall, F.H.A. (1960) External factors in sexual periodicity, pp 707–831. In Parkes, A. S. (ed.) *Marshall's Physiology of Reproduction*, Vol. 1. 3rd edn. Longman, London.

Anadu, P. A. (1973) *The Ecology and Breeding Biology of Small Rodents in the Savanna Zone of South-western Nigeria*. Ph. D. thesis, University of Ibadan.

Anderson, S. and Jones, J. K. (eds.) (1967) *Recent Mammals of the World*. Ronald Press, New York.

Anon. (1976) 80000 elephant alive and well in Selous. *Africana*, **6** (3), 17–19.

Anon. (1977) Further facts on Uganda elephants. *Africana*, **6** (4), Suppl. (i).

Ansell, W. F. H. (1960) *Mammals of Northern Rhodesia*. Government Printer, Lusaka.

Ansell, W. F. H. (1963) Additional breeding data on Northern Rhodesian mammals. *Puku*, **1**, 9–28.

Ansell, W. F. H. (1964) Addenda and corrigenda to 'Mammals of Northern Rhodesia'. *Puku*, **2**, 14–52.

Ansell, W. F. H. (1966) *Mus musculus* at Livingstone. *Puku*, **4**, 188.

Ansell, W. F. H. (1969) Addenda and corrigenda to 'Mammals of Northern Rhodesia', No. 3. *Puku*, **5**, 1–48.

Ansell, W. F. H. (1973) Addenda and corrigenda to 'Mammals of Northern Rhodesia', No. 4. *Puku*, **7**, 1–20.

Ansell, W. F. H. (1974) Some mammals from Zambia and adjacent countries. *Puku Suppl.*, **1**, 1–48.

Ansell, W. F. H. and Ansell, P. D. H. (1973) Mammals of the north-east montane areas of Zambia. *Puku*, **7**, 21–70.

Ayeni, J. S. O. (1972) Notes from a hide overlooking a lick at Yankari Game Reserve, North-eastern State of Nigeria. *J. W. Afr. Sci. Assn.* **17**, 101–12.

Ayeni, J. S. O. (1975) Utilisation of waterholes in Tsavo National Park (East). *E. Afr. Wildl. J.*, **13**, 305–24.

Baker, H. G. and Harris, B. J. (1959) Bat pollination of the silk cotton tree, *Ceiba pentandra* (L.) Gaertn. (sensu lato), in Ghana. *J. W. Afr. Sci. Assn.*, **5**, 1–9.

Balinsky, B. I. (1962) Patterns of animal distribution on the African Continent. *Ann. Cape Prov. Mus.*, **2**, 229–310.

Bartholomew, G. A., Dawson, W. R. and Lasiewski, R. C. (1970) Thermo-regulation and heterothermy in some of the smaller flying foxes (Megachiroptera) of New Guinea. *Z. vergl. Physiol.*, **70**, 196–209.

Baudinette, R. V. (1972) The impact of social aggregations on the respiratory physiology of Australian hopping mice. *Comp. Biochem. Physiol.*, **41**, 35–38.

Bell, R. H. V. (1969) *The Use of the Herb Layer by Grazing Ungulates in the Serengeti National Park, Tanzania*. Ph.D. thesis, University of Manchester.

Bell, R. H. V. (1971) A grazing ecosystem in the Serengeti. *Sci. Amer.*, **225**, 86–93.

Bellier, L. (1965) Evolution du peuplement des rongeurs dans les plantations de palmier'à huile. *Oleagineaux*, **20**, 573–6.

Bellier, L. (1967) Recherches écologiques dans la savane de Lamto (Côte d'Ivoire): densité et biomasses des petits Mammifères. *Terre Vie*, **3**, 319–29.

Berger, M. E. (1972) Population structure of olive baboons (*Papio anubis* (J. P. Fischer))in the Laikipia District of Kenya. *E. Afr. Wildl. J.*, **10**, 159–64.

Bigalke, R. C. (1972) The contemporary mammal fauna of Africa, pp. 141–94. In Keast, A., Erk, F. C. and Glass, B. (eds.) *Evolution, Mammals and Southern Continents*. State University of New York, Albany.

Bille, J. C. (1974) Recherches écologiques sur une savane sahélienne du Ferlo septentrional, Sénégal; 1972, Année sèche au Sahel. *Terre Vie*, **28**, 5–20.

Bille, J. C. and Poupon, H. (1974) Recherches écologiques sur une savane sahélienne du Ferlo septentrional,

Sénégal: la régénération de la strate herbacée. *Terre Vie*, **28**, 21–48.

Bland, K. P. (1973) Reproduction in the female African tree rat (*Grammomys surdaster*). *J. Zool., Lond.*, **171**, 167–76.

Booth, A. H. (1956) The Cercopithecidae of the Gold and Ivory Coasts: geographic and systematic observations. *Ann. Mag. nat. Hist.* **12**, 476–80.

Booth, A. H. (1958) The Niger, the Volta and the Dahomey Gap as geographic barriers. *Evolution*, **12**, 48–62.

Booth, A. H. (1960) *Small Mammals of West Africa*. Longman, London.

Bourlière, F. (1963a) Observations on the ecology of some large African mammals. *Viking Fund Publication in Anthropology*, **36**, 43–54.

Bourlière, F. (1963b) The wild ungulates of Africa: ecological characteristics and economic implications. *IUCN Publ.* n.s., **1**, 102–5.

Bourlière, F. (1965) Densities and biomasses of some ungulate populations in Eastern Congo and Rwanda, with notes on population structure and lion/ungulate ratios. *Zool. Afr.*, **1**, 199–207.

Bourlière, F. (1973) The comparative ecology of rain forest mammals in Africa and tropical America: some introductory remarks, pp. 279–92. In Meggers, B. J., Ayensu, E. S. and Duckworth, W. D. (eds.), *Tropical Forest Ecosystems in Africa and South America: A Comparative Review*. Smithsonian Institute, Washington.

Bourlière, F., Bertrand, M. and Hunkeler, G. (1969) L'écologie de la Mona de Lowe (*Cercopithecus campbelli lowei*) in Côte d'Ivoire. *Terre Vie*, **23**, 135–63.

Bourlière, F. and Verschuren, J. (1960) *Introduction a l'Ecologie des Ongules du Parc National Albert*. Institut des Parcs Nationaux du Congo Belge, Brussels.

Bradbury, J. (1977) Social organisation and communication, pp. 1–72. In Wimsatt, W. (ed.) *Biology of Bats*. Vol. 3 Academic Press, London.

Brambell, F. W. R. and Davis, D. H. S. (1941) Reproduction in the multi-mammate mouse (*Mastomys erythroleucus*) of Sierra Leone. *Proc. zool. Soc. Lond.*, **111B**, 1–11.

Brooks, P. M. (1974) *The Ecology of the Four-striped Field Mouse*, Rhabdomys pumilio (*Sparrman, 1784*) *with Particular Reference to a Population on the Van Riebeeck Nature Reserve, Pretoria*, D.Sc. thesis, University of Pretoria.

Brosset, A. (1966a) *La Biologie des Chiroptères*. Masson et Cie, Editeurs, Paris.

Brosset, A. (1966b) Les chiroptères du Haut-Ivindo, Gabon. *Biol. Gabon*, **2**, 47–86.

Brosset, A. (1966c) Recherches sur la composition qualitative et quantitative des populations de vertebres dans la forêt primaire du Gabon. *Biol. Gabon*, **2**, 163–77.

Brosset, A. (1968) La permutation du cycle sexuel saisonnier chez le Chiroptère *Hipposideros caffer*, au voisinage de l'équateur. *Biol. Gabon.*, **4**, 325–41.

Brosset, A. (1969) Recherches sur la biologie des chiroptères troglophiles dans le nord-est du Gabon. *Biol. Gabon.*, **5**, 93–116.

Brynard, A. M. (1958) Verslag insake voorlopige ondersoek rakende toestande in die nasionale Kalahari-gemsbok park. *Koedoe*, **1**, 162–83.

Buechner, H. K. (1961) Territorial behaviour in the Uganda kob. *Science*, **133**, 698–9.

Buechner, H. K., Buss, I. O., Longhurst, W. M. and Brooks, A. C. (1963) Numbers and migration of elephants in Murchison Falls National Park, Uganda. *J. Wildl. Mgt.*, **27**, 36–53.

Buechner, H. K. and Dawkins, H. C. (1961) Vegetation change induced by elephants and fire in Murchison Falls National Park, Uganda. *Ecology*, **42**, 752–66.

Buechner, H. K. and Schloeth, R. (1965) Ceremonial mating behaviour in Uganda Kob (*Adenota kob thomasi* Neumann). *Z. Tierpsychol.*, **22**, 209–25.

Buss, I. O. (1961) Some observations on food habits and behaviour of the African elephant. *J. Wildl. Mgt.*, **25**, 131–48.

Buxton, P. A. (1936) Breeding rates of domestic rats trapped in Lagos, Nigeria, and certain other countries. *J. Anim. Ecol.*, **5**, 53–66.

Carlisle, D. B. and Ghobrial, L. I. (1968) Food and water requirements of the dorcas gazelle in the Sudan. *Mammalia*, **32**, 249–56.

Casebeer, R. L. and Koss, G. G. (1970) Food habits of wildebeest, zebra, hartebeest and cattle in Kenya Masailand. *E. Afr. Wildl. J.*, **8**, 25–36.

Chalmers, N. R. (1968) Group composition, ecology and daily activities of free-living mangabeys (*Cerocebus albigena johnstoni*) in Uganda. *Folia primatol.*, **8**, 247–62.

Chalmers, N. R. (1973) Differences in behaviour between some arboreal and terrestrial species of African monkeys, pp. 69–100. In Michael, R. P. and Crook, J. H. (eds.) *Comparative Ecology and Behaviour of Primates*. Academic Press, London.

Chapin, J. P. (1923) Ecological aspects of bird distribution in tropical Africa. *Am. Nat.*, **57**, 106–24.

Chapman, B. M., Chapman, R. F. and Robertson, I. A. D. (1959) The growth and breeding of the multimammate rat *Rattus* (*Mastomys*) *natalensis* (Smith) in Tanganyika Territory. *Proc. zool. Soc. Lond.*, **133**, 1–9.

Charles-Dominique, P. (1971) Eco-ethologie des Prosimiens du Gabon. *Biol. Gabon.*, **7**, 121–228.

Charles-Dominique, P. (1972) Ecologie et vie sociale de *Galago demidovii. Z. Tierpsychol.*, **9**, 7–41.

Charles-Dominique, P. (1974) Vie sociale de *Perodicticus potto* (Primates, Lorisidae). Etude de terrain au forêt equatoriale de l'ouest Africain au Gabon. *Mammalia*, **38**, 355–79.

Charles-Dominique, P. and Martin, R. D. (1972) Behaviour and ecology of nocturnal prosimians. *Z. Tierpsychol. Suppl.*, **9**, 1–91.

Cheeseman, C. L. (1975) *The Population Ecology of Small Rodents in the Grassland of Rwenzori National Park, Uganda.* Ph.D. thesis, University of Southampton.

Child, G., Smith, P. and von Richter, W. (1970) Tsetse control hunting as a measure of large mammal population trends in the Okavango Delta, Botswana. *Mammalia*, **34**, 34–75.

Clarke, R. and Mitchell, F. (1968) The economic value of hunting and outfitting in East Africa. *E. Afr. agric. for. J.*, **33**, 89–97.

Cloudsley-Thompson, J. L. and Chadwick, M. (1964) *Life in Deserts.* Foulis, London.

Cloudsley-Thompson, J. L. and Idris, B. E. M. (1964) The insect fauna of the desert near Khartoum: seasonal fluctuations and the effects of grazing. *Proc. R. ent. Soc. Lond. (A)*, **39**, 41–6.

Clough, G. (1969) Some preliminary observations on reproduction in the warthog, *Phacochoerus aethiopicus* Pallas. *J. Reprod. Fert., Suppl.*, **6**, 323–38.

Clough, G. and Hassan, A. G. (1970) A quantitative study of the daily activity of the warthog in the Queen Elizabeth National Park, Uganda. *E. Afr. Wildl. J.*, **8**, 19–24.

Clutton-Brock, T. H. (1974) Primate social organisation and ecology. *Nature*, **250**, 539–42.

Cockrum, E. L. (1962) *Introduction to Mammalogy.* Ronald Press, New York.

Coe, M. J. (1962) Notes on the habits of the Mount Kenya hyrax (*Procavia johnstoni mackinderi* Thomas). *Proc. zool. Soc. Lond.*, **138**, 639–44.

Coe, M. J. (1967) *The Ecology of the Alpine Zone of Mount Kenya.* Junk, The Hague.

Coe, M. J. (1972*a*) Defaecation by African elephants (*Loxodonta africana africana* (Blumenbach)). *E. Afr. Wildl. J.*, **10**, 165–74.

Coe, M. J. (1972*b*) The South Turkana Expedition. IX. Ecological studies of the small mammals of South Turkana. *Geog. J.*, **138**, 316–38.

Coe, M. J., Cummings, D. H. and Phillipson, J. (1976) Biomass and production of large African herbivores in relation to rainfall and primary production. *Oecologia*, **22**, 341–54.

Coetzee, C. G. (1965) The breeding season of the multimammate mouse *Praomys* (*Mastomys*) *natalensis* (A. Smith) in the Transvaal Highveld. *Zool. Afr.*, **1**, 29–40.

Cole, L. R. (1975) Foods and foraging places of rats (Rodentia, Muridae) in the lowland evergreen forest of Ghana. *J. Zool., Lond.* **175**, 453–71.

Cooke, H. B. S. (1968) Evolution of mammals on southern continents. 2. The fossil mammal fauna of Africa. *Q. Rev. Biol.*, **43**, 234–64.

Cooke, H. B. S. (1972) The fossil mammal fauna of Africa. pp. 89–139. In Keast, A., Erk, F. C. and Glass, B. (eds.) *Evolution, Mammals and Southern Continents.* State University, New York.

Corbet, G. B. and Yalden, D. W. (1972) Recent records of mammals (other than bats) from Ethiopia. *Bull. Brit. Mus. (Nat. Hist).*, *Zool.*, **22**, 211–52.

Corfield, T. F. (1973) Elephant mortality in Tsavo National Park, Kenya. *E. Afr. Wildl. J.*, **11**, 339–68.

Crook, J. H. (1966) Gelada baboon herd structure and movement – a comparative report. *Symp. zool. Soc. Lond.*, **18**, 237–58.

Crook, J. H. (1970) The socio-ecology of primates, pp. 103–6. In Crook, J. H. (ed.) *Social Behaviour in Birds and Mammals.* Academic Press, London.

Crook, J. H., Ellis, J. E. and Goss-Custard, J. D. (1976) Mammalian social systems: structure and function. *Anim. Behav.*, **24**, 261–74.

Croze, H. (1974) The Seronera bull problem. II. The trees. *E. Afr. Wildl. J.*, **12**, 29–47.

Darlington, P. (1957) *Zoogeography.* Wiley, New York.

Dasmann, R. F. (1964) *African Game Ranching.* Pergamon, Oxford.

Dasmann, R. F. and Mossman, A. S. (1961) Commercial use of game animals on a Rhodesian ranch. *Wildlife*, **3**, (3), 7–14.

Dasmann, R. F. and Mossman, A. S. (1962) Population studies of impala in Southern Rhodesia. *J. Mammal.*, **43**, 375–95.

Davis, D. H. S. (1953) Plague in South Africa; a study of the epizootic cycle in gerbils (*Tatera brantsi*) in the northern Orange Free State. *J. Hygiene*, **51**, 427–49.

Davis, D. H. S. (1962) Distribution patterns of Southern African Muridae, with notes on some of their fossil antecedents. *Ann. Cape Prov. Mus.* **2**, 56–76.

Davis, D. H. S. (1964) Ecology of wild rodent plague, Ch. 21, pp. 301–14. In Davis, D. H. S. (ed.), *Ecological Studies in Southern Africa.* Junk, The Hague.

Davis, D. H. S. (1968) Notes on some small mammals in the Kalahari Gemsbok National Park, with special reference to those preyed upon by owls. *Koedoe*, **1**, 184–8.

Davis, R. M. (1972) Behaviour of the vlei rat, *Otomys irroratus* (Brants 1827). *Zool. Afr.*, **7**, 119–40.

De Graaf, G. and Nel, J. A. J. (1965) On the tunnel system of Brant's karro rat, *Paratomys brantsi*, in the Kalahari Gemsbok National Park. *Koedoe*, **8**, 136–319.

Dekeyser, P. L. (1956) Le Parc National du Niokolo-Koba. III. Mammifères. *Mem. I.F.A.N.*, **48**, 35–77.

Delany, M. J. (1964) An ecological study of the small mammals in Queen Elizabeth Park, Uganda. *Revue Zool. Bot. afr.*, **70**, 129–47.

Delany, M. J. (1971) The biology of small rodents in Mayanja Forest, Uganda. *J. Zool. Lond.*, **165**, 85–129.

Delany, M. J. (1972) The ecology of small rodents in tropical Africa. *Mammal. Rev.*, **2**, 1–42.

Delany, M. J. (1974) *The Ecology of Small Mammals.* Edward Arnold, London.

Delany, M. J. (1975) *The Rodents of Uganda.* British Museum (Nat. Hist.), London.

Delany, M. J. and Kanseriimuhanga, W. D. (1970) Observations on the ecology of rodents from a small arable plot near Kampala, Uganda. *Revue Zool. Bot. afr.*, **81**, 417–25.

De Vore, I. and Hall, K. R. L. (1965) Baboon ecology, pp. 20–52. In De Vore, I. (ed.) *Primate Behaviour.* Holt, Rinehart and Winston, New York.

De Vos, A. (1969) Ecological conditions affecting the production of wild herbivorous mammals on grasslands. *Adv. Ecol. Res.*, **6**, 137–83.

De Vos, A. and Dowsett, R. J. (1966) The behaviour and population structure of three species of the genus *Kobus. Mammalia*, **30**, 30–55.

Dieterlen, F. (1962) Geburt und Geburtshilfe dei der Stachelmaus, *Acomys cahirinus. Z. Tierpsychol.* **19**, 191–222.

Dieterlen, F. (1963) Verleichende Untersuchungen zur Ontogenese von Stachelmaus (*Acomys*) und Wanderratte (*Rattus norvegicus*). Beiträge zum Nesthocker-Nestfluckter-Problem bei Nagetieren. *Z. Säugetierk.*, **28**, 193–227.

Dieterlen, F. (1967) Jahreszeiten und Fortspflanzungsperioden bei den Muriden des Kivusee-Gebietes (Congo). I. Ein Beitrag zum Problem der Populationsdynamik in Tropen. *Z. Säugetierk.*, **32**, 1–44.

Dieterlen, F. (1968) Zur Kenntnis der Gattung *Otomys* (Otomyinae: Muridae: Rodentia). Beiträge zur Systematik, Ökologie und Biologie Zentralafrikanischer Formen. *Z. Säugetierk.*, **33**, 321–52.

Dieterlen, F. (1971) Beiträge zur Systematik, Ökologie und Biologie der Gattung *Dendromus* (Dendromurinae, Cricetidae, Rodentia), insbesondere ihrer zentralafrikanischer Formen. *Säugetierk. Mitt.*, **19**, 97–132.

Dolan, J. Jr. (1966) Notes on *Addax nasomaculatus. Z. Säugetierk.*, **31**, 23–31.

Dorst, J. and Dandelot, P. (1970) *A Field Guide to the Larger Mammals of Africa.* Collins, London.

Dougall, H. W. (1963) Average chemical composition of Kenya grasses, legumes and browse. *E. Afr. Wildl. J.*, **1**, 120.

Douglas-Hamilton, I. (1973) On the ecology and behaviour of the Lake Manyara elephants. *E. Afr. Wildl. J.*, **11**, 401–3.

Douglas-Hamilton, I. and O. (1975) *Among the Elephants.* Collins, London.

Dowsett, R. J. (1966) Wet season game populations and biomass in the Ngoma area of the Kafue National Park. *Puku*, **4**, 135–46.

Dowsett, R. (1966) Behaviour and population structure of hartebeest in the Kafue National Park. *Puku*, **4**, 147–54.

Dubost, G. (1965) Quelque renseignements biologiques sur *Potamogale velox. Biol. Gabon.*, **1**, 257–72.

Dubost, G. (1968) Aperçu sur le rythme annuel de reproduction des Muridés du nord-est du Gabon. *Biol. Gabon.*, **4**, 227–39.

Dubost, G. (1968) Le rythme annuel de réproduction du chevrotain aquatique, *Hyemoschus aquaticus* Ogilby, dans le secteur forestier du nord-est du Gabon, pp. 51–65. In Canivenc, R. (ed.) *Cycles Genitaux Saissonier de Mammifères Sauvages.*

Dukelow, W. R. (1971) Reproductive physiology of primates. *Lab. Primate Newsletter*, **10** (2), 1–15.

Dunbar, R. I. M. and Dunbar, P. (1974) The reproductive cycle of the gelada baboon. *Anim. Behav.*, **22**, 203–10.

Dunbar, R. I. M. and Dunbar, E. P. (1976) Contrasts in social structure among black-and-white colobus monkey groups. *Anim. Behav.*, **24**, 84–92.

Eaton, R. L. (1970a) The predatory sequence, with emphasis on killing behaviour and its ontogeny, in the cheetah (*Acinonyx jubatus*). *Z. Tierpsychol.*, **27**, 492–504.

Eaton, R. L. (1970b) Group interactions, spacing and territoriality in cheetahs. *Z. Tierpsychol.*, **27**, 481–91.

Eaton, R. L. (1974) *The Cheetah.* Van Nostrand Reinhold, New York.

Edroma, E. L. (1973) Poaching and human pressure in Rwenzori National Park. *Uganda J.*, **37**, 9–18.

Eisenberg, J. F. (1966) The social organisation of mammals. *Handbuch der Zoologie*, **10**, 1–92.

Eisenberg, J. F. (1967) A comparative study in rodent ethology with emphasis on evolution of social behaviour. *Proc. U.S. Nat. Mus.*, **122**, 1–51.

Eisenberg, J. F., Muckenhirn, N. A. and Rudran, R. (1972) The relation between ecology and social structure in primates. *Science*, **176**, 863–74.

Eisentraut, M. (1961) Gefangenschaftsbeobachtungen an *Rattus* (*Praomys*) *morio* Trouessart. *Bonn. zool. Beitr.*, **12**, 1–21.

Eisentraut, M. (1963) *Die Wirbeltiere des Kamerungebirges.* Paul Parey, Hamburg.

Eisentraut, M. (1973) Die Wirbeltierfauna von Fernando Poo und Westkamerun. *Bonn. zool. Monogr.*, **3**, 1–428.

Elder, W. H. and Elder, N. L. (1970) The social grouping and private associations of the bushbuck. *Mammalia* **34**, 356–62.

Eloff, F. C. (1961) Observations on the migration and habits of the antelopes of the Kalahari Gemsbok Park. III. *Koedoe*, **4**, 18–30.

Eltringham, S. K. (1974) Changes in the large mammal community of Mweya Peninsula, Rwenzori National Park, Uganda, following removal of hippopotamus. *J. appl. Ecol.*, **11**, 855–65.

Eltringham, S. K. (1976) The frequency and extent of uncontrolled grass fires in the Rwenzori National Park, Uganda. *E. Afr. Wildl. J.*, **14**, 215–22.

Eltringham, S. K. and Woodford, M. H. (1973) The numbers and distribution of buffalo in the Rwenzori National Park, Uganda. *E. Afr. Wildl. J.*, **11**, 151–64.

Estes, R. D. (1966) Behaviour and life history of the wildebeest (*Connochaetes taurinus* Burchell). *Nature, Lond.*, **212**, 999–1000.

Estes, R. D. (1967) The comparative behaviour of Grant's and Thomson's gazelles. *J. Mammal.*, **48**, 189–209.

Estes, R. D. (1969) Territorial behaviour of the wildebeest (*Connochaetes taurinus* Burchell 1823). *Z. Tierpsychol.*, **26**, 284–370.

Estes, R. D. (1974) Social organisation of the African Bovidae. *I.U.C.N. Publ. n.s.* **24**, 167–205.

Estes, R. D. and Goddard, J. (1967) Prey selection and hunting behaviour of the African wild dog. *J. Wildl. Mgt.*, **31**, 52–70.

Evans, G. C. (1939) Ecological studies on the rainforests of southern Nigeria. II. The atmospheric environmental conditions. *J. Ecol.*, **27**, 436–82.

Everard, C. O. R. (1966) A report on the rodent and other vertebrate pests of cocoa in Western Nigeria. Unpublished report of Res. Div. Min. Agric. Nat. Res., West Nig., 123 pp.

Ewer, R. F. (1963) The behaviour of the meerkat, *Suricata suricatta* (Schreber). *Z. Tierpsychol.*, **20**, 570–607.

Ewer, R. F. (1965) Food burying of the African ground squirrel, *Xerus erythropus*. *Z. Tierpsychol.*, **22**, 321–7.

Ewer, R. F. (1967) The behaviour in the African giant rat (*Cricetomys gambianus* Waterhouse). *Z. Tierpsychol.*, **24**, 6–79.

Ewer, R. F. (1968) *Ethology of Mammals.* Logos Press, London.

Ewer, R. F. (1973) *The Carnivores.* Weidenfeld and Nicolson, London.

FAO (1974) *Production Yearbook, 26.* Food and Agriculture Organisation, Rome.

Field, A. C. (1975) Seasonal changes in reproduction, diet and body composition of two equatorial rodents. *E. Afr. Wildl. J.*, **13**, 221–36.

Field, C. R. (1971) Elephant ecology in the Queen Elizabeth National Park, Uganda. *E. Afr. Wildl. J.*, **9**, 99–124.

Field, C. R. (1972) The food habits of wild ungulates in Uganda by analyses of stomach contents. *E. Afr. Wildl. J.*, **10**, 17–42.

Field, C. R. (1974) Scientific utilisation of wildlife for meat in East Africa: a review. *J. sth. Afr. Wildl. Mgmt. Ass.*, **4**, 177–83.

Field, C. R. (1976) Palatability factors and nutritive values of the food of buffalos (*Syncerus caffer*) in Uganda. *E. Afr. Wildl. J.*, **14**, 181–201.

Field, C. R. and Blankenship, L. H. (1973*a*) On making the game pay. *Africana*, **5**(4), 22–23 et seq.

Field, C. R. and Blankenship, L. H. (1973*b*) Nutrition and reproduction of Grant's and Thomson's gazelles, Coke's hartebeest and giraffe in Kenya. *J. Reprod. Fert. Suppl.*, **19**, 287–301.

Field, C. R. and Laws, R. M. (1970) The distribution of the larger herbivores in the Queen Elizabeth National Park, Uganda. *J. appl. Ecol.*, **7**, 273–294.

Finch, V. A. (1972*a*) Energy exchanges with the environment of two East African antelopes, the eland and the hartebeest. *Symp. zool. Soc. Lond.*, **31**, 315–26.

Finch, V. A. (1972*b*) Thermoregulation and heat balance of the East African eland and hartebeest. *Amer. J. Physiol.*, **222**, 1374–9.

Flux, J. E. C. (1969) Current work on the reproduction of the African hare, *Lepus capensis* L., in Kenya. *J. Reprod. Fert. Suppl.*, **6**, 225–7.

Ford, J. (1971) *The Role of Trypanosomiasis in African Ecology: a study of the Tsetse Problem.* University Press, Oxford.

Foster, J. B. (1966) The giraffe of Nairobi National Park: home range, sex ratios, the herd and food. *E. Afr. Wildl. J.*, **4**, 139–48.

Foster, J. B. and Coe, M. J. (1968) The biomass of game animals in Nairobi National Park. *J. Zool. Lond.*, **155**, 413–25.

Foster, J. B. and Dagg, A. I. (1972) Notes on the biology of the giraffe. *E. Afr. Wildl. J.*, **10**, 1–16.

Foster, J. B. and Kearney, D. (1967) Nairobi National Park game census 1966. *E. Afr. Wildl. J.*, **5**, 112–20.

Foster, J. B. and McLaughlin, R. (1968) Nairobi National Park game census 1967. *E. Afr. Wildl. J.*, **6**, 152–4.

Gartlan, J. S. and Struhsaker, T. T. (1972) Polyspecific associations and niche separation of rain forest anthropoids in Cameroon, West Africa. *J. Zool. Lond.*, **168**, 221–65.

Gause, G. F. (1934) *The Struggle for Existence*. Williams and Wilkins, New York.

Gautier, J. P. and Gautier-Hion, A. (1969) Les associations polyspecifiques chez les Cercopithecidae du Gabon. *Terre Vie*, **23**, 164–201.

Gautier-Hion, A. (1971) L'ecologie du Talapoin du Gabon. *Terre Vie*, **25**, 427–90.

Geerling, C. and Bokdam, J. (1973) Fauna of the Comoé National Park, Ivory Coast. *Biol. Conservation*, **5**, 251–7.

Geist, V. (1974) On the relationship of ecology and behaviour in the evolution of ungulates: theoretical considerations. *I.U.C.N. Publ. n.s.* **24**, 235–46.

Geist, V. and Walther, F. (eds.) (1974) The behaviour of ungulates and its relation to management. *I.U.C.N. Publ. n.s.*, **24**, 1–940.

George, W. (1974) Notes on the ecology of gundis (F. Ctenodactylidae). *Symp. zool. Soc. Lond.* **34**, 143–60.

Ghobrial, L. I. (1970*a*) A comparative study of the integument of the camel, Dorcas gazelle and jerboa in relation to desert life. *J. Zool. Lond.*, **160**, 509–21.

Ghobrial, L. I. (1970*b*) The water relations of the desert antelope, *Gazella dorcas dorcas. Physiol. Zool.*, **43**, 249–56.

Ghobrial, L. I. (1974) Water relations and requirements of the dorcas gazelle in the Sudan. *Mammalia*, **38**, 88–107.

Ghobrial, L. I. and Hodieb, A. S. K. (1973) Climate and seasonal variations in the breeding of the desert jerboa *Jaculus jaculus* in the Sudan. *J. Reprod. Fert. Suppl.*, **19**, 221–33.

Glass, B. P. (1965) The mammals of Eastern Ethiopia. *Zool. Afr.*, **1**, 177–179.

Glover, J. (1963) The elephant problem at Tsavo. *E. Afr. Wildl. J.*, **1**, 30–39.

Glover, T. D. and Sale, J. B. (1968) The male reproductive tract in the rock hyrax. *J. Zool. Lond.*, **156**, 351–61.

Glover, P. E. and Sheldrick, D. (1964) An urgent research problem on the elephant and rhino populations of the Tsavo National Park in Kenya. *Bull. epizoot. Dis. Afr.*, **12**, 33–38.

Goddard, J. (1970) Age criteria and vital statistics of a black rhinoceros population. *E. Afr. Wildl. J.*, **8**, 105–22.

Goodall, J. van Lawick (1968) The behaviour of free-living chimpanzees in the Gombe Stream Reserve. *Anim. Behav. Monogr.* **1** (3), 161–311.

Gosling, L. M. (1969) Parturition and related behaviour in Coke's Hartebeest, *Alcelaphus buselaphus cokei* Günther. *J. Reprod. Fert. Suppl.*, **6**, 265–86.

Greaves, J. H. (1964) Report on rodent damage to oil palms on an estate in eastern Nigeria. MAFF unpublished report, 19 pp.

Grimsdell, J. (1969) *The Ecology of the Buffalo*, Syncerus caffer, *in Western Uganda*. Ph.D. thesis, Cambridge University.

Grimsdell, J. J. R. (1975) Age determination of the African buffalo, *Syncerus caffer* Sparrman. *E. Afr. Wildl. J.*, **11**, 31–54.

Grimsdell, J. J. R. and Bell, R. H. V. (1972) Population growth of red lechwe, *Kobus leche leche* Gray, in the Busanga Plain, Zambia. *E. Afr. Wildl. J.*, **10**, 117–22.

Grubb, P. (1972) Variation and incipient speciation in the African buffalo. *Z. Säugetierk.*, **37**, 121–44.

Gwynne, M. D. and Bell, R. H. V. (1968) Selection of vegetation components by grazing ungulates in the Serengeti National Park, *Nature, Lond.*, **220**, 390–3.

Haddow, A. J. (1952) Field and laboratory studies on an African monkey *Cercopithecus ascanius schmidti* Matschie. *Proc. zool. Soc., Lond.*, **122**, 297–394.

Haddow, A. J. (1968) The natural history of yellow fever in Africa. *Proc. R. Soc. Edin.* **B, 70**, 191–227.

Hall, K. R. L. (1966) Behaviour and ecology of the wild Patas monkey, *Erythrocebus patas* in Uganda. *J. Zool. Lond.*, **148**, 15–87.

Hall, K. R. L. and De Vore, I. (1965) Baboon social behaviour, pp. 53–110. In De Vore, I. (ed.) *Primate Behaviour*. Holt, Rinehart and Winston, New York.

Halwagy, R. (1961) The vegetation of the semi-desert north east of Khartoum, Sudan. *Oikos*, **12**, 87–110.

Hanks, J. (1972) Reproduction of elephant, *Loxodonta africana*, in the Luangwa Valley, Zambia. *J. Reprod. Fert.*, **30**, 13–36.

Hanney, P. (1965) The Muridae of Malawi. *J. Zool., Lond.*, **146**, 577–633.

Happold, D. C. D. (1966) Breeding periods of rodents in the Northern Sudan. *Revue Zool. Bot. afr.*, **74**, 357–63.

Happold, D. C. D. (1967*a*) Guide to the natural history of Khartoum Province. III. Mammals. *Sudan Notes Rec.*, **48**, 111–32.

Happold, D. C. D. (1967*b*) Biology of the jerboa *Jaculus jaculus butleri* (Rodentia, Dipodidae) in the Sudan. *J. Zool. Lond.*, **151**, 257–75.

Happold, D. C. D. (1968) Observations on *Gerbillus pyramidum* (Gerbillinae, Rodentia) at Khartoum. *Mammalia*, **32**, 43–53.

Happold, D. C. D. (1973*b*) The red-crowned mangabey, *Cercocebus torquatus torquatus*, in western Nigeria. *Folia primat.* **20**, 423–8.

Happold, D. C. D. (1973*a*) *Large Mammals of West Africa*. Longman, London.

Happold, D. C. D. (1975) The effects of climate and vegetation on the distribution of small rodents in western Nigeria. *Z. Saugetierk.* **40**, 221–42.

Happold, D. C. D. (1977) A population study of small rodents in the tropical rainforest of Nigeria. *Terre Vie*, **31**, 385–457.

Happold, D. C. D. (1978) Reproduction, growth and development of a West African forest mouse, *Praomys tullbergi* (Thomas). *Mammalia*, **42**, 73–95.

Happold, M. (1975) *The Social Organisation of Conilurine Rodents*. Ph.D. thesis, Monash University, Australia.

Harris, C. J. (1968) *Otters*. Weidenfeld and Nicolson, London.

Harthoorn, A. M. (1958) Some aspects of game cropping. Unpublished report of Inst. Conf. Land Use Management, Lake Manyara, Tanganyika.

Hemming, C. F. (1966) The vegetation of the northern region of the Somali Republic. *Proc. Linn. Soc. Lond.*, **177**, 173–250.

Henshaw, J. (1972) Notes on conflict between elephants and some bovids, and on other interspecific contacts in Yankari Game Reserve, N.E. Nigeria. *E. Afr. Wildl. J.*, **10**, 151–3.

Henshaw, J. and Ayeni, J. (1971) Some aspects of big-game utilisation of mineral licks in Yankari Game Reserve, Nigeria. *E. Afr. Wildl. J.*, **9**, 73–82.

Hilali, M. El. and Veillat, J. P. (1975) *Jaculus orientalis*: a true hibernator. *Mammalia*, **39**, 401–4.

Hill, P. (1970) *Rural Capitalism in West Africa*. University Press, Cambridge.

Hinton, H. E. and Dunn, A. M. S. (1967) *Mongooses; their Natural History and Behaviour*. Oliver and Boyd, Edinburgh.

Hirst, S. M. (1969) Predation as a regulating factor of wild ungulate populations in a Transvaal Lowveld nature reserve. *Zool. Afr.*, **4**, 199–230.

Hollister, N. (1919) East African mammals in the United States National Museum. II. Rodentia, Lagomorpha and Tubulidentata. *Bull. U.S. Nat. Mus.*, **99**, 1–184.

Hooper, E. T. and Hilali, M. (1972) Temperature regulation and habits in two species of jerboa, genus *Jaculus*. *J. Mammal.*, **53**, 574–93.

Hopcraft, D. (1969) Experiment. *Africana*, **3** (9), 4–9.

Hopkins, G. H. E. (1949) *Report on Rats, Fleas and Plague in Uganda*. Government Printer, Entebbe.

Hopkins, B. (1965) *Forest and Savanna*. Heinemann, London.

Horst, Van der C. J. (1954) *Elephantulus* going into anoestrous; menstruation and abortion. *Phil. Trans.*, **238B**, 27–61.

Hunkeler, C. and Hunkeler, P. (1970) Besoins énergétiques de quelques crocidures de Côte d'Ivoire. *Terre Vie*, **24**, 449–56.

International Union for the Conservation of Nature (IUCN) (1973) *Red Data Book*. IUCN, Morges.

Jameson, J. D. (1970) *Agriculture in Uganda*. University Press, Oxford.

Jarman, M. V. and Jarman, P. J. (1973) Daily activity of impala. *E. Afr. Wildl. J.*, **11**, 75–92.

Jarman, P. J. (1973) The free water intake of impala in relation to the water content of their food. *E. Afr. agric. and for. J.*, **38**, 343–51.

Jarman, P. J. (1974) The social organisation of antelope in relation to their ecology. *Behaviour*, **48**, 215–67.

Jarman, P. J. and Jarman, M. V. (1973) Social behaviour, population structure and reproductive potential in impala. *E. Afr. Wildl. J.*, **11**, 329–38.

Jarvis, J. U. M. (1969) The breeding season and litter size of African mole-rats. *J. Reprod. Fert., Suppl.*, **6**, 237–48.

Jarvis, J. U. M. (1973) The structure of a population of mole-rats *Tachyoryctes splendens*. (Rodentia: Rhizomyidae). *J. Zool., Lond.*, **171**, 1–14.

Jarvis, J. U. M. (1974) Notes on the golden mole, *Chrysochloris stuhlmanni* Matschie from the Rwenzori mountains, Uganda. *E. Afr. Wildl. J.*, **12**, 163–6.

Jarvis, J. U. M. and Sale, J. B. (1971) Burrowing and burrow patterns of East African mole rats *Tachyoryctes*, *Heliophobius* and *Heterocephalus*. *J. Zool. Lond.*, **163**, 451–79.

Jewell, P. A. (1966) The concept of home range in mammals. *Symp. zool. Soc. Lond.*, **18**, 85–109.

Jewell, P. A. (1972) Social organisation and movements of topi (*Damaliscus korrigum*) during the rut at Ishasha, Queen Elizabeth Park, Uganda. *Zool. Afr.*, **7**, 233–55.

Jones, C. (1972) Comparative ecology of three pteropid bats in Rio Muni, West Africa. *J. Zool. Lond.*, **167**, 353–70.

Jones, C. and Sabater Pi, C. (1968) Comparative ecology of *Cercocebus albigena* (Gray) and *C. torquatus* (Kerr) in Rio Muni, West Africa. *Folia Primat.*, **9**, 99–113.

Jones, J. K. and Johnson, R. R. (1967) Sirenians, pp. 366–72. In Anderson, S. and Jones, J. K. (eds.) *Recent Mammals of the World: a Synopsis of Recent Families*. Ronald Press, New York.

Jordan, P. A., Botkin, D. B. and Wolfe, M. L. (1971) Biomass Dynamics in a moose population. *Ecology*, **51**, 147–52.

Joubert, S. C. J. (1972) Territorial behaviour of the tsessebe (*Damaliscus lunatus lunatus* Burchell) in the Kruger National Park. *Zool. Afr.*, **7**, 141–56.

Jungius, H. (1970) Studies on the breeding biology of the reedbuck (*Redunca arundinum* Boddaert 1785) in the Kruger National Park. *Z. Säugetierk.*, **35**, 129–46.

Kassas, M. (1956) Landforms and plant cover on the Omdurman Desert, Sudan. *Bull. Soc. Geog. d'Egypte*, **29**, 41–58.

Keast, A. (1969) Evolution of mammals on southern continents. 7. Comparisons of the contemporary mammalian faunas of the southern continents. *Q. Rev. Biol.*, **44**, 121–67.

Keay, R. W. J. (1959) *Vegetation Map of Africa South of the Tropic of Cancer*. University Press, Oxford.

Keogh, H. J. (1973) Behaviour and breeding in captivity of the Manaqua gerbil, *Desmodillicus auricularis* (Cricetidae, Gerbillinae). *Zool. Afr.*, **8**, 231–40.

Khalil, F. and Tawfic, J. (1963) Some observations on the kidney of the desert *J. jaculus* and *G. gerbillus* and their possible bearing on the water economy of these animals. *J. exp. Zool.*, **154**, 259–72.

Kiley-Worthington, M. (1965) The waterbuck (*Kobus defassa* and *Kobus ellipsiprymnus*) in East Africa: spatial distribution. A study of the sexual behaviour. *Mammalia*, **29**, 177–204.

Kingdon, J. (1971) *East African Mammals. An Atlas of Evolution in Africa. I.* Academic Press, London.

Kingdon, J. (1973) *East African Mammals. II.* Academic Press, London.

Kirmiz, J. P. (1962) *Adaptation to Desert Environment*. Butterworth, London.

Kleiber, M. (1961) *The Fire of Life*, John Wiley and Sons, New York.

Kleiman, D. G. (1967) Some aspects of social behaviour in the Canidae. *Amer. Zool.*, **7**, 365–72.

Klingel, H. (1967) Soziale Organisation und Verhalten freilebender Steppenzebras. *Z. Tierpsychol.*, **24**, 580–624.

Klingel, H. (1969) The social organisation and population ecology of the plains zebra (*Equus quagga*). *Zool. Afr.*, **4**, 249–63.

Klingel, H. (1972) Social behaviour of African Equidae. *Zool. Afr.*, **7**, 175–85.

Klingel, H. (1974) A comparison of the social behaviour of the Equidae. *I.U.C.N. Publ. n.s.*, **24**, 124–32.

Klingel, H. and Klingel, U. (1966a) Tooth development and age determination in the plains zebra (*Equus quagga boehmi* Matschie). *Der Zool. Garten N.F.*, **23**, 34–54.

Klingel, H. and Klingel, U. (1966b) The rhinoceroses of Ngorongoro Crater. *Oryx*, **8**, 302–6.

Krebs, C. J. (1972) *Ecology: the Experimental Analysis of Distribution and Abundance*. Harper and Row, New York.

Kruuk, H. (1966) Clan-system and feeding habits of spotted hyaenas (*Crocuta crocuta* Erxleben). *Nature, Lond.*, **209**, 1257–8.

Kruuk, H. (1968) Hyaenas, the hunter nobody knows. *Nat. Geog. Mag.*, **134**, 44–57.

Kruuk, H. (1972) *The Spotted Hyaena*. University of Chicago Press, Chicago.

Kruuk, H. and Sands, W. A. (1972) The aardwolf (*Proteles cristatus* Sparrman, 1783) as predator of termites. *E. Afr. Wildl. J.*, **10**, 211–27.

Kruuk, H. and Turner, M. (1967) Comparative notes on predation by lion, leopard, cheetah and wild dog in the Serengeti area, East Africa. *Mammalia*, **31**, 1–27.

Kühme, W. (1965) Freilandstudien zur Soziologie des Hyänenhundes (*Lycaon pictus lupinus* Thomas 1902). *Z. Tierpsychol.*, **22**, 495–541.

Kulzer, E. (1963) Temperaturregulationen bei flughunden der Gattung *Rousettus* Gray. *Z. vergl. Physiol.*, **46**, 595–618.

Kulzer, E. (1965) Temperaturregulation bei fledermausen (Chiroptera) aus verschiedenen Klimazonen. *Z. vergl. Physiol.*, **50**, 1–34.

Kulzer, E. (1972) Temperaturregulation und Wasserhaushalt der Sandratte *Meriones crassus* Sund., 1842. *Z. Säugetierk.*, **37**, 162–77.

Kutilek, M. J. (1974) The density and biomass of large mammals in Lake Nakuru National Park. *E. Afr. Wildl. J.*, **12**, 201–12.

Laburn, H. P. and Mitchell, D. (1975) Evaporative cooling as a thermo-regulatory mechanism in the fruit bat *Rousettus aegyptiacus*. *Physiol. Zool.*, **48**, 195–202.

Lack, D. (1954) *The Natural Regulation of Animal Numbers*. University Press, Oxford.

Lamprey, H. F. (1963) Ecological separation of the large mammal species in the Tarangire Game Reserve, Tanganyika. *E. Afr. Wildl. J.*, **1**, 63–92.

Lamprey, H. F. (1964) Estimation of the large mammal densities, biomass and energy exchange in the Tarangire Game Reserve and the Masai steppe in Tanganyika. *E. Afr. Wildl. J.*, **2**, 1–46.

Lamprey, H. F. (1967) Notes on the dispersal and germination of some tree seeds through the agency of mammals and birds. *E. Afr. Wildl. J.*, **5**, 179–80.

Lamprey, H. F., Glover, P. E., Turner, M. I. and Bell, R. H. V. (1967) Invasion of the Serengeti National Park by elephants. *E. Afr. Wildl. J.*, **5**, 151–66.

Langdale-Brown, I., Osmaston, H. A. and Wilson, J. G. (1964) *The Vegetation of Uganda and its Bearing on Landuse.* Government Printer, Entebbe.

Largen, M. J., Kock, D. and Yalden, D. W. (1974) Catalogue of the mammals of Ethiopia. I. Chiroptera. *Monit. Zool. Ital.*, **16**, 221–98.

Lawick-Goodall, J. van (1968) The behaviour of free living chimpanzees in the Gombe Stream Reserve. *Animal Behav. Monogr.* **1**, 161–311.

Laws, R. M. (1966) Age criteria for the African elephant. *E. Afr. Wildl. J.*, **4**, 1–37.

Laws, R. M. (1968*a*) Interactions between elephant and hippopotamus populations and their environments. *E. Afr. agric. for. J.*, **33**, 140–7.

Laws, R. M. (1968*b*) Dentition and ageing of the hippopotamus. *E. Afr. Wildl. J.*, **6**, 19–52.

Laws, R. M. (1969*a*) Aspects of reproduction in the African elephant, *Loxodonta africana. J. Reprod. Fert., Suppl.*, **6**, 193–218.

Laws, R. M. (1969*b*) The Tsavo Research Project. *J. Reprod. Fert., Suppl.*, **6**, 495–531.

Laws, R. M. (1970) Elephants as agents of habitat and landscape change in East Africa. *Oikos*, **21**, 1–15.

Laws, R. M. and Clough, G. (1966) Observations on reproduction in the hippopotamus (*Hippopotamus amphibius* Linn). *Symp. zool. Soc. Lond.*, **15**, 117–40.

Laws, R. M. and Parker, I. S. C. (1968) Recent studies on elephant populations in East Africa. *Symp. zool. Soc. Lond.*, **21**, 319–59.

Ledger, H. P., Payne, W. J. A. and Talbot, L. M. (1961) A preliminary investigation of the relationship between body composition and productive efficiency of meat producing animals in the dry tropics. *VIIIth Int. Congr. Animal Prod.*, Hamburg.

Leistner, O. A. (1959) Notes on the vegetation of the Kalahari Gemsbok National Park with special reference to its influence on the distribution of antelopes. *Koedoe*, **2**, 128–51.

Lent, P. S. (1969) A preliminary study of the Okavango lechwe (*Kobus leche leche* Gray). *E. Afr. Wildl. J.*, **7**, 147–58.

Lent, P. C. (1974) Mother–infant relationships in ungulates. *IUCN Publ. n.s.*, **24**, 14–55.

Leuthold, W. (1966) Variations in territorial behaviour of Uganda kob. *Behaviour*, **27**, 214–57.

Leuthold, W. (1967) Beobachtungen zum Jugendverhalten der Kob-Antilopen. *Z. Säugetierk.* **32**, 59–62.

Leuthold, W. (1971) Freilandbeobachtungen an Giraffengazellen (*Litocranius walleri*) in Tsavo National Park, Kenya. *Z. Säugetierk.*, **36**, 19–37.

Leuthold, W. (1972) Home range, movements and food of a buffalo herd in Tsavo National Park. *E. Afr. Wildl. J.*, **10**, 237–43.

Leuthold, B. M. and Leuthold, W. (1972) Food habits of giraffe in Tsavo National Park, Kenya. *E. Afr. Wildl. J.*, **10**, 129–41.

Leuthold, W. and Leuthold, B. (1976) Density and biomass of ungulates in Tsavo East National Park, Kenya. *E. Afr. Wildl. J.*, **14**, 49–58.

Leuthold, W. and Sale, J. B. (1973) Movements and patterns of habitat utilisation of elephants in Tsavo National Park, Kenya. *E. Afr. Wildl. J.*, **11**, 369–84.

Leyhausen, P. (1965) Über die Funktion der relativen Stimmungshierarchie. *Z. Tierpsychol.*, **22**, 412–94.

Lind, E. M. and Morrison, M. E. S. (1974) *East African Vegetation.* Longman, London.

Loizos, C. (1966) Play in mammals. *Symp. zool. Soc. Lond.*, **18**, 1–9.

Longman, K. A. and Jenik, J. (1974) *Tropical Forest and its Environment.* Longman, London.

Louw, G. N. (1972) The role of advective fog in the water economy of certain Namib desert animals. *Symp. zool. Soc. Lond.*, **31**, 297–314.

Lumsden, W. H. R. (1951) The night resting habits of monkeys in a small area on the edge of the Semiliki Forest, Uganda. *J. anim. Ecol.*, **20**, 11–30.

MacArthur, R. H. and Wilson, E. O. (1967) *The Theory of Island Biogeography.* Princeton University Press, Princeton.

Maclean, G. L. (1970) An analysis of the avifauna of the southern Kalahari Gemsbok National Park. *Zool. Afr.*, **5**, 249–73.

McLaughlin, C. A. (1967) Aplodontoid, Sciuroid, Geomyoid, Casteroid and Anomaluroid rodents, pp. 210–25. In Anderson, S. and Jones, J. K. (eds.). *Recent Mammals of the World: a Synopsis of Modern Families.* Ronald Press, New York.

McLaughlin, R. T. (1970) Nairobi National Park cansus, 1968. *E. Afr. Wildl. J.*, **8**, 203.

McNab, B. K. (1966) The metabolism of fossorial rodents: a study of convergence. *Ecology*, **47**, 712–33.

McNab, B. K. (1974) The energetics of endotherms. *Ohio J. Sci.*, **74**, 370–80.

McNaughton, S. J. (1976) Serengeti migratory wildebeest; facilitation of energy flow by grazing. *Science*, **191**, 92–4.

Makacha, S. and Schaller, G. B. (1969) Observations on lions in the Lake Manyara National Park, Tanzania. *E. Afr. Wildl. J.*, **7**, 99–103.

Maloiy, G. M. O. (1973*a*) Water metabolism of East African ruminants in arid and semi-arid regions. *Z. Tierzüchtg. Züchtgsbiol.*, **90**, 219–28.

Maloiy, G. M. O. (1973*b*) The water metabolism of a small African antelope: the dik-dik. *Proc. R. Soc. Lond.*, **184B**, 167–78.

Maloiy, G. M. O. and Hopcraft, D. (1969) Thermoregulation and water relations of two East African antelopes: the hartebeest and impala. *East Afr. Vet. Res. Org., mimeographed report.* (quoted by Petersen and Casebeer 1971).

Maloiy, G. M. O. and Hopcraft, D. (1971) Thermoregulation and water relations of two East African antelopes, the hartebeest and impala. *Comp. Biochem. Physiol.*, **38A**, 525–34.

Marks, S. A. (1973) Prey selection and annual harvest of game in a rural Zambian community. *E. Afr. Wildl. J.*, **11**, 113–28.

Mayr, E. (1942) *Systematics and the Origin of Species.* Colombia University Press, New York.

Mech, L. D. (1966) The wolves of Isle Royale. U.S. Nat. Park Serv., Fauna ser. 7.

Medway, Lord (1969) *The Wild Mammals of Malaya and Offshore Islands Including Singapore.* Oxford University Press, Kuala Lumpur.

Meester, J. (1960) Early post-natal development of multimammate mice *Rattus (Mastomys) natalensis* (A. Smith). *Ann. Trans. Mus.*, **24**, 35–52.

Meester, J. (1963) *A Systematic Revision of the Shrew Genus* Crocidura *in Southern Africa.* Transvaal Museum, Pretoria.

Meester, J. (1965) The origins of the southern African mammal fauna. *Zool. Afr.*, **1**, 87–93.

Meester, J. and Setzer, W. H. (eds.) (1971–7) *The Mammals of Africa. An Identification Manual.* Smithsonian Institution, Washington.

Melton, D. A. (1976) The biology of the aardvark (Tubulidentata-Orycteropodidae). *Mammal Rev.*, **6**, 75–88.

Menzies, J. I. (1973) A study of leaf-nosed bats (*Hipposideros caffer* and *Rhinolophus landeri*) in a cave in northern Nigeria. *J. Mammal.* **54**, 930–45.

Miller, R. P. and Glover, T. D. (1973) Regulation of seasonal sexual activity in an ascrotal mammal, the rock hyrax *Procavia capensis. J. Reprod. Fert. Suppl.*, **19**, 203–20.

Misonne, X. (1963) Les rongeurs du Ruwenzori et des régions voisines. *Explor. Parc. Natn. Albert Deux. Ser.*, **14**, 1–164.

Mitchell, B. L. (1965) Breeding growth and ageing criteria of Lichtenstein's Hartebeest. *Puku*, **3**, 97–104.

Monard, A. (1951) Resultats de la mission zoologiques Suisse au Cameroun: mammifères. *Mem. I.F.A.N. (Centre Cameroon), ser. Sci. Nat.*, **1**, 13–57.

Moreau, R. E. (1952) Vicissitudes of the African biomes in the late Pleistocene. *Proc. zool. Soc. Lond.*, **141**, 395–421.

Moreau, R. E. (1966) *The Bird Faunas of Africa and its Islands.* Academic Press, London.

Morris, D. (1965) *The Mammals: a Guide to Living Species.* Hodder and Stoughton, London.

Morris, J. J. (1958) Veld aangeleenthede en beweging van wild in die Kalahari-gemsbok park. *Koedoe*, **1**, 136–42.

Morrison, P. and McNab, B. K. (1967) Temperature regulation in some Brazilian phyllostomid bats. *Comp. Biochem. Pysiol.* **21**, 207–21.

Moss, C. (1975) *Portraits in the Wild: Animal Behaviour in East Africa.* Hamish Hamilton, London.

Munkásci, I. and Palkovitzs, M. (1965) Volumetric analysis of glomerular size in kidneys of mammals living in desert, semi-desert or water-rich environments in the Sudan. *Circulation Res.*, **17**, 303–11.

Mutere, F. A. (1967) The breeding biology of equatorial vertebrates: reproduction in the fruit bat *Eidolon helvum* at latitude 0°20′N. *J. Zool. Lond.*, **153**, 153–61.

Mutere, F. A. (1968) The breeding biology of the fruit bat *Rousettus aegyptiacus* E. Geoffroy living at 0°22′S. *Acta trop.*, **25**, 97–108.

Napier, J. R. and Napier, P. H. (1967) *A Handbook of Living Primates.* Academic Press, London.

Neal, B. R. (1968) *The Ecology of Small Rodents in the Grassland Community of the Queen Elizabeth National Park, Uganda.* Ph.D. thesis, University of Southampton.

Neal, B. R. (1970) The habitat distribution and activity of a rodent population in western Uganda, with particular reference to the effects of burning. *Revue Zool. Bot. afr.*, **81**, 29–50.

Nel, J. A. J. (1967) Burrow systems of *Desmodillus auriculari* in the Kalahari Gemsbok National Park, *Koedoe*, **10**, 118–21.

Nel, J. A. J. and Nolte, H. (1965) Notes on the prey of owls in the Kalahari Gemsbok National Park, with special reference to the small mammals. *Koedoe*, **8**, 75–81.

Nel, J. A. J. and Rautenbach, I. L. (1975) Habitat use and community structure of rodents in the southern Kalahari. *Mammalia*, **39**, 9–29.

Nelson, G. S., Teesdale, C. and Highton, R. B. (1962) The role of animals as reservoirs of bilharziasis in

Africa, pp. 127–49. In Wolstenholme, G. E. W. and O'Connor, M. (eds.), *Bilharziasis*, Churchill, London.

Norton Griffiths, M., Herlocker, D. and Pennycuick, L. (1975) The patterns of rainfall in the Serengeti ecosystem, Tanzania. *E. Afr. Wildl. J.*, **13**, 347–74.

Odum, E. P. (1971) *Fundamentals of Ecology*, 3rd edn. W. B. Saunders, Philadelphia.

Oliff, W. D. (1953) Mortality, fecundity and intrinsic rate of natural increase of the multimammate mouse, *Rattus (Mastomys) natalensis* (Smith) in the laboratory. *J. anim. Ecol.*, **22**, 217–26.

Oliver, J. (1965) Guide to the Natural History of Khartoum Province II. The climate of Khartoum Province. *Sudan Notes Rec.*, **46**, 1–40.

O'Roke, E. C. and Hamerstrom, F. N. (1948) Productivity and yield in the George Reserve deer herd. *J. Wildl. Mgnt.*, **12**, 78.

Owen-Smith, R. N. (1972) Territoriality: the example of the white rhinoceros *Zool. Afr.*, **7**, 273–80.

Owen-Smith, R. N. (1974) The social system of the white rhinoceros. *IUCN Publ. n.s.* **24**, 341–51.

Pagés, E. (1970) Sur l'écologie et les adaptations de l'oryctérope et des pangolins sympatriques du Gabon. *Biol. Gabon.*, **6**, 27–92.

Parker, I. C. (1972) The theory is: wildlife should earn its keep! *Africana*, **4** (10), 12–3.

Parris, R. (1971) The ecology and behaviour of wildlife in the Kalahari. *Botswana Notes and Records*, Sp. Edn. **1**, 96–101.

Pennycuick, L. (1975) Movements of the migratory wildebeest population in the Serengeti area between 1960 and 1973. *E. Afr. Wildl. J.*, **13**, 65–87.

Petersen, J. C. B. and Casebeer, R. L. (1971) A bibliography relating to the ecology and energetics of East African large mammals. *E. Afr. Wildl. J.*, **9**, 1–23.

Petrides, G. A. and Swank, W. G. (1965) Population densities and the range-carrying capacity for large mammals in Queen Elizabeth National Park, Uganda. *Zool. Afr.*, **1**, 209–25.

Petter, F. (1955) Notes on aestivation and hibernation in several species of rodents. *Mammalia*, **19**, 444–6.

Petter, F. (1961) Repartition geographique et écologie des rongeurs desertiques. *Mammalia* **25**, (spec. number) 1–222.

Petter, F. (1966) La lethargie de *Steatomys opimus*. *Mammalia*, **30**, 511–13.

Phillipson, J. (1963) *Ecological Energetics*. Edward Arnold, London.

Phillipson, J. (1973) The biological efficiency of protein production by grazing and other land-based systems, pp. 217–35. In Jones, J. G. W. (ed) *The Biological Efficiency of Protein Production*, University Press, Cambridge.

Phillipson, J. (1975) Rainfall, primary production and 'carrying capacity' of Tsavo National Park (East), Kenya. *E. Afr. Wildl. J.*, **13**, 171–201.

Phillipson, P. (1934) Domesticity the African elephant: experiments in the Belgian Congo. *Field*, **163**.

Poulet, A. R. (1972) Recherches écologiques sur une savanne sahélienne du Ferlo septentrional, Sénégal: les mammifères. *Terre Vie*, **26**, 440–72.

Poulet, A. R. (1974) Recherches écologiques sur une savanne sahélienne du Ferlo septentrional, Sénégal: quelques effects de la sécheresse sur le peuplement mammalien. *Terre Vie*, **28**, 124–30.

Poupon, H. and Bille, J. C. (1974) Recherches écologiques sur une savanne sahélienne du Ferlo septentional, Sénégal: influence de la sécheresse de l'année 1972–1973 sur la strate ligneuse. *Terre Vie*, **28**, 49–75.

Rahm, U. (1966) Les mammifères de la forêt equatoriale de l'Est du Congo. *Ann. Mus. Roy. Afr. centrale. Ser. 8°*, **149**, 39–121.

Rahm, U. (1967) Les muridés des environs du Lac Kivu et des regions voisines (Afrique centrale) et leur écologie. *Rev. Suisse Zool.*, **74**, 439–519.

Rahm, U. (1969a) Dokumente über *Anomalurus* und *Idiurus* des östlichen Kongo. *Z. Säugetierk*, **34**, 75–84.

Rahm, U. (1969b) Notes sur le cri du *Dendrohyrax dorsalis* (Hyracoidea) *Mammalia*, **33**, 68–79.

Rahm, U. (1970) Note sur la reproduction des Sciuridés et Muridés dans la forêt equatoriale au Congo. *Rev. Suisse Zool.*, **77**, 635–46.

Rahm, U. (1972a) Note sur la repartition, l'écologie et le régime alimentaire des sciuridés au Kivu (Zaire). *Rev. Zool. Bot. afr.*, **85**, 321–39.

Rahm, U. (1972b) Zur Verbreitung und Ökologie der Säugetiere des Afrikanischen Regenwaldes. *Acta trop.*, **29**, 452–73.

Rahm, U. (1972c) Zur Oekologie der Muriden in Regenwaldgebiet des östlichen Kongo (Zaire). *Rev. Suisse Zool.*, **79**, 1121–30.

Rahm, U. and Christiaensen, A. (1963) Les mammifères de la region occidentale du Lac Kivu. *Ann. Mus. Roy. Afr. centrale Ser. 8°*, **118**, 1–83.

Ralls, K. (1971) Mammalian scent marking. *Science*, **171**, 443–9.

Ralls, K. (1974) Scent marking in captive Maxwell's Duikers. *IUCN Publ. n.s.* **24**, 114–23.

Rathbun, G. B. (1973) Territoriality in the golden-rumped elephant shrew (*Rhynchocyon chrysopygus*). *E. Afr. Wildl. J.*, **11**, 405.

Rautenbach, I. L. (1971) Notes on the small mammals of the Kalahari Gemsbok National Park. *Koedoe*, **14**, 137–43.

Rheingold, H. F. (ed.) (1963) *Maternal Behaviour in Mammals*. Wiley, New York.

Richards, P. W. (1952) *The Tropical Rain Forest*. University Press, Cambridge.

Roberts, A. (1951) *The Mammals of South Africa*. Trustees of 'The Mammals of South Africa' Book Fund, Johannesburg.

Robinette, W. L. and Child, G. F. T. (1964) Notes on biology of the lechwe (*Kobus leche*). *Puku*, **2**, 84–117.

Rood, J. P. (1975) Population dynamics and food habits of the banded mongoose. *E. Afr. Wildl. J.*, **13**, 89–112.

Rosevear, D. R. (1965) *The Bats of West Africa*. British Museum (Nat. Hist.), London.

Rosevear, D. R. (1969) *The Rodents of West Africa*. British Museum (Nat. Hist.), London.

Roth, A. H. (1966) Game utilisation in Rhodesia in 1964. *Mammalia*, **30**, 397–423.

Rowell, T. E. (1966) Forest-living baboons in Uganda. *J. Zool. Lond.*, **149**, 344–64.

Rowell, T. E. (1969) Long-term changes in a population of Uganda baboon. *Folia Primat.*, **11**, 241–54.

Rowell, T. E. and Chalmers, N. R. (1970) Reproductive cycles of the mangabey, *Cerocebus albigena*. *Folia Primat.*, **12**, 264–72.

Rudnai, J. (1973) Reproductive biology of lions (*Panthera leo massaica* Neumann) in Nairobi National Park. *E. Afr. Wildl. J.*, **11**, 241–54.

Rudnai, J. (1974) The pattern of lion predation in Nairobi Park. *E. Afr. Wildl. J.*, **12**, 213–26.

Ruhweza, S. (1968) Game management practices in Uganda. *E. Afr. agric. for. J.*, **33**, 275–6.

Sabater Pi, J. and Jones, C. (1967) Notes on the distribution and ecology of the higher primates of Rio Muni, West Africa. *Tulane Stud. Zool.* **14**, 101–9.

Sachs, R. and Debbie, J. G. (1969) A field guide to the recording of parasitic infestation in game animal. *E. Afr. Wildl. J.*, **7**, 27–38.

Sale, J. B. (1969) Breeding seasons and litter size in Hyracoidea. *J. Reprod. Fert. Suppl.*, **6**, 249–64.

Savory, C. R. (1965) Game utilisation in Rhodesia. *Zool. Afr.*, **1**, 321–37.

Schaller, G. B. (1963) *The Mountain Gorilla*. University of Chicago Press, Chicago.

Schaller, G. B. (1965) The behaviour of the mountain gorilla, pp. 324–67. In De Vore, I. (ed.) *Primate Behaviour*, Holt, Rinehart and Winston, New York.

Schaller, G. B. (1968) Hunting behaviour of the cheetah in the Serengeti National Park, Tanzania. *E. Afr. Wildl. J.*, **6**, 95–100.

Schaller, G. B. (1970) This gentle and elegant cat. *Nat. Hist.*, **79**, 31–9.

Schaller, G. B. (1972) *The Serengeti Lion. A Study of Predator–Prey Relations*. University of Chicago Press, Chicago.

Schaller, G. B. and Lowther, G. R. (1969) The relevance of carnivore behaviour to the study of early hominids. *Southwest J. Anthrop.*, **25**, 307–41.

Scheffer, V. B. (1951) The rise and fall of a reindeer herd. *Sci. Monthly*, **73**, 356–62.

Schenkel, R. (1966a) On sociology and behaviour in impala (*Aepyceros melampus* Lichtenstein). *E. Afr. Wildl. J.*, **4**, 99–115.

Schenkel, R. (1966b) On sociology and behaviour of impala (*Aepyceros melampus suara* Matschie). *Z. Säugertierk.*, **31**, 177–205.

Schenkel, R. (1966c) Play, exploration and territoriality in the wild lion. *Symp. zool. Soc. Lond.*, **18**, 11–22.

Schenkel, R. and Schenkel-Hulliger, L. (1969) *Ecology and Behaviour of the Black Rhinoceros*. Paul Parey. Hamburg.

Schmidt-Nielsen, B. and O'Dell, R. (1961) Structure and concentrating mechanism in the mammalian kidney. *Amer. J. Physiol.*, **200**, 1119–24.

Schmidt-Nielsen, B., Schmidt-Nielsen, K., Houpt, T. R. and Jarnum, A. S. (1956) Water balance of the camel. *Amer. J. Physiol.* **185**, 185–94.

Schmidt-Nielsen, K. (1964) *Desert Animals. Physiological Problems of Heat and Water*. University Press, Oxford.

Schouteden, H. (1948) Faune du Congo Belge et du Ruanda-Urundi. I. Mammifères. *Ann. Mus. Congo Belge Terv., 8° Zool.*, **1**, 1–331.

Schulz, W. (1973) *A New Geography of Liberia*. Longman, London.

Schwetz, J. (1953) On a new schistosome of wild rodents found in the Belgian Congo, *Schistosoma mansoni* var. *rodentorum* var. nov. *Ann. trop. Med. Parasit.*, **47**, 183–6.

Schwetz, J. (1954) On two schistosomes of wild rodents of the Belgian Congo: *Schistosoma rodhaini* Brumpt, 1931; and *Schistosoma mansoni* var. *rodentorum* Schwetz 1953; and their relationships to *S. mansoni* of man. *Trans. R. Soc. trop. Med. Hyg.*, **48**, 89–100.

Schwetz, J. (1956) Role of wild rats and domestic rats (*Rattus rattus*) in schistosomiasis of man. *Trans. R. Soc. trop. Med. Hyg.*, **50**, 275–82.

Sclater, W. L. (1896) The geography of mammals. IV. The Ethiopian region. *Geogr. J.*, **7**, 282–96.

Sheldrick, D. (1972) Tsavo the hard lessons of history. *Africana*, **4**, (10) 14–15 et seq.

Sheppe, W. (1972) The annual cycle of small mammal populations on a Zambian floodplain. *J. Mammal.*, **53**, 445–60.

Sheppe, W. and Osborne, T. O. (1971) Patterns of use of a flood plain by Zambian mammals. *Ecol. Monogr.*, **41**, 179–205.

Shkolnik, A. and Borut, A. (1969) Temperature and water relations in two species of spiny mice (*Acomys*). *J. Mammal.*, **50**, 245–55.

Shortridge. G. C. (1934) *The Mammals of South West Africa*. William Heinemann, London.

Sidney, J. (1965) The past and present distribution of some African ungulates. *Trans. zool. Soc. Lond.*, **30**, 1–397.

Sikes, S. K. (1971) *The Natural History of the African Elephant*. Weidenfeld and Nicolson, London.

Simon, N. (1962) *Between the Sunlight and the Thunder. The Wildlife of Kenya*. Collins, London.

Simpson, C. D. (1964) Notes on the banded mongoose, *Mungos mungo* (Gmelin). *Arnoldia*, **19**, 1–8.

Sinclair, A. R. E. (1972) Long term monitoring of mammal populations in the Serengeti: census of non-migratory ungulates. *E. Afr. Wildl. J.*, **10**, 287–97.

Sinclair, A. R. E. (1973*a*) Population increases of buffalo and wildebeest in the Serengeti. *E. Afr. Wildl. J.*, **11**, 93–108.

Sinclair, A. R. E. (1973*b*) Regulation and population models for a tropical ruminant. *E. Afr. Wildl. J.*, **11**, 307–16.

Sinclair, A. R. E. (1974*a*) The natural regulation of buffalo populations in East Africa. III. Population trends and mortality. *E. Afr. Wildl. J.*, **12**, 185–200.

Sinclair, A. R. E. (1974*b*) The natural regulation of buffalo populations in East Africa. IV. The food supply as a regulating factor, and competition. *E. Afr. Wildl. J.*, **12**, 291–311.

Sinclair, A. R. E. (1974*c*) The social organisation of the East African buffalo (*Syncerus caffer* Sparrman). *IUCN Publ. n.s.*, **24**, 676–89.

Sinclair, A. R. E. (1975) Resource limitations in tropical grasslands. *J. anim. Ecol.*, **44**, 497–520.

Sinclair, A. R. E. and Gwynne, M. D. (1972) Food selection and competition in East African buffalo. *E. Afr. Wildl. J.*, **10**, 77–89.

Smithers, R. H. N. (1971) *The Mammals of Botswana*. National Museums of Rhodesia, Salisbury.

Southern, H. N. (1970) The natural control of a population of tawny owls (*Strix aluco*). *J. Zool. Lond.*, **162**, 197–285.

Spence, D. H. N. and Angus, A. (1971) African grassland management – burning and grazing in Murchison Falls National Park, Uganda. *Symp. Brit. ecol. Soc.*, **11**, 319–32.

Spinage, C. A. (1962) *Mammals of East Africa*. Collins, London.

Spinage, C. A. (1967) Ageing the Uganda defassa waterbuck *Kobus defassa ugandae* Neumann. *E. Afr. Wildl. J.*, **5**, 1–17.

Spinage, C. A. (1969) Territoriality and social organisation of the Uganda defassa waterbuck *Kobus defassa ugandae*. *J. Zool. Lond.*, **159**, 329–61.

Spinage, C. A. (1971) Geratodontology and horn growth of the impala (*Aepyceros melampus*). *J. Zool. Lond.*, **164**, 209–25.

Spinage, C. A. (1972) Age estimation of zebra. *E. Afr. Wildl. J.*, **10**, 273–7.

Spinage, C. A. (1973) A review of the age determination of mammals by means of teeth, with especial reference to Africa. *E. Afr. Wildl. J.*, **173**, 165–88.

Spinage, C. A. (1974) Territoriality and population regulation in the Uganda Defassa waterbuck. *IUCN Publ. n.s.*, **24**, 635–43.

Starret, A. (1967) Hystricoid, Erethrizintoid, Cavoid and Chinchilloid rodents, pp. 254–72. In Anderson, S. and Jones, J. K. (eds.) *Recent Mammals of the World: a Synopsis of Recent Families*. Ronald Press, New York.

Stewart, D. R. M. (1963) Wildlife census – Lake Rudolf. *E. Afr. Wildl. J.*, **1**, 121.

Stewart, D. R. M. and Stewart, J. (1963) The distribution of some large mammals in Kenya. *J. E. Afr. nat. Hist. Soc.*, **24**, 1–52.

Stewart, D. R. M. and Stewart, J. (1970) Food preference data by faecal analysis for African plains ungulates. *Zool. Afr.*, **5**, 115–29.

Stewart, D. R. M. and Talbot, L. M. (1962) Census of wildlife on the Serengeti, Mara and Loita Plains. *E. Afr. agric. for. J.*, **29**, 56–60.

Struhsaker, T. T. (1967*a*) Social structure among vervet monkeys (*Cercopithecus aethiops*). *Behaviour*, **29**, 83–121.

Struhsaker, T. T. (1967*b*) Behaviour of vervet monkeys (*Cercopithecus aethiops*). *Univ. Calif. Publs. Zool.*, **82**, 1–74.

Struhsaker, T. T. and Gartlan, J. S. (1970) Observations on the behaviour and ecology of the Patas monkey (*Erythrocebus patas*) in the Waza Reserve, Cameroon. *J. Zool., Lond.*, **161**, 49–63.

Stutterheim, C. J. and Skinner, J. D. (1973) Preliminary notes on the behaviour and breeding of *Gerbillurus paeba paeba* in captivity. *Koedoe*, **16**, 127–48.

Sugiyama, Y. (1968) Social organisation of chimpanzees in the Budongo Forest, Uganda. *Primates*, **9**, 225–58.

Sweeney, R. C. H. (1956) Some notes on the feeding habits of the ground pangolin *Smutsia temminckii* (Smuts). *Ann. Mag. nat. Hist.*, **12(9)**, 893–6.

Swynnerton, G. H. and Hayman, R. W. (1950) A checklist of the land mammals of the Tanganyika Territory and the Zanzibar Protectorate. *J. E. Afr. nat. Hist. Soc.*, **20**, 274–392.

Talbot, L. M. (1966) Wild animals as a source of food. *Bureau Sport Fisheries and Wildl. Special Sc. Rep.*, **98**.

Talbot, L. M. and Talbot, M. H. (1961) Preliminary observations on the population dynamics of the wildebeest in Narok District, Kenya. *E. Afr. agric. for. J.*, **27**, 108–16.

Talbot, L. M. and Talbot, M. H. (1963) The wildebeest in Western Masailand, East Africa. *Wildl. Monogr.*, **12**, 1–88.

Talbot, L. M., Ledger, H. P. and Payne, W. J. A. (1961) The possibility of using wild animals for animal production. *Int. Congr. Anim. Prod.*, **8**, 205–10.

Talbot, L. M., Payne, J. A., Ledger, H. P., Verdcourt, L. D. and Talbot, M. H. (1965) The meat production potential of wild animals in Africa. A review of biological knowledge. Commonwealth Agricultural Bureaux.

Taylor, C. R. (1968) The minimum water requirements of some East African bovids. *Symp. zool. Soc. Lond.*, **21**, 195–206.

Taylor, C. R. (1969*a*) The eland and the oryx. *Sci. Amer.*, **220**, 88–95.

Taylor, C. R. (1969*b*) Metabolism, respiratory changes, and water balance of an antelope, the eland. *Amer. J. Physiol.*, **217**, 317–20.

Taylor, C. R. (1970*a*) Strategies of temperature regulation: effect on evaporation in East African ungulates. *Amer. J. Physiol.*, **219**, 1131–5.

Taylor, C. R. (1970*b*) Dehydration and heat: effects on temperature regulation of East African ungulates. *Amer. J. Physiol.*, **219**, 1136–9.

Taylor, C. R. (1972) The desert gazelle: a paradox resolved. *Symp. zool. Soc. Lond.*, **31**, 215–27.

Taylor, C. R. and Lyman, C. P. (1967) A comparative study of the environmental physiology of an East African antelope, the eland and a Hereford steer. *Physiol. Zool.*, **40**, 280–95.

Taylor, C. R. and Maloiy, C. M. O. (1969) The effect of dehydration and heat stress on intake and digestion of food in some East African bovids. *Trans. 8th Int. Cong. Game Biol.*, Helsinki 1967. (quoted by Petersen and Casebeer 1971).

Taylor, C. R., Robertshaw, D. and Hofmann, R. (1969) Thermal panting: a comparison of wildebeest and zebu cattle. *Amer. J. Physiol.* **217**, 907–10.

Taylor, C. R., Spinage, C. A. and Lyman, C. P. (1969) Water relations of the waterbuck, an East African antelope. *Amer. J. Physiol.*, **217**, 630–4.

Taylor, K. D. (1961) An investigation of damage to West African cocoa by vertebrate pests. MAFF unpublished report, 35 pp.

Taylor, K. D. (1962) Report on a two-day visit to the northern region of Tanganyika. MAFF unpublished report, 3 pp.

Taylor, K. D. (1968) An outbreak of rats in agricultural areas of Kenya in 1962. *E. Afr. agric. for. J.*, **34**, 66–77.

Taylor, K. D. (1969) The need for ecological research on rodent pests of agriculture in the Gezira. MAFF unpublished report, 10 pp.

Taylor, K. D. and Green, M. G. (1976) The influence of rainfall on diet and reproduction in four African rodent species. *J. Zool. Lond.*, **180**, 367–89.

Tembrock, G. (1968) Communication in land mammals, pp. 338–404. In Sebeok, T. A. (ed.) *Animal Communication*. Indiana University Press, Bloomington, Indiana.

Thomas, O. (1888) On a collection of mammals obtained by Emin Pasha in equatorial Africa, and presented by him to the Natural History Museum. *Proc. zool. Soc. Lond.*, **1888**, 3–17.

Thomas, O. and Wroughton, R. C. (1910) Ruwenzori Expedition reports. 17. Mammalia. *Trans. zool. Soc. Lond.*, **19**, 481–518.

Tinbergen, N. (1953) *Social Behaviour in Animals*. Methuen, London.

Tinker, J. (1975) Who's killing Kenya's jumbos? *New Scientist*, **66**, 452–5.

Treus, V. and Kravchenko, D. (1968) Methods of rearing and economic utilisation of eland in the Askaniya – Neva Zoological Park. *Symp. zool. Soc. Lond.*, **21**, 395–411.

Trewartha, G. T. (1968) *An Introduction to Climate, 4th edn.* McGraw-Hill, New York.

Turner, M. and Watson, R. M. (1964) A census of game in Ngorongoro Crater. *E. Afr. Wildl. J.*, **2**, 165–8.

Ullrich, W. (1961) Zur Biologie und Soziologie der Colobusarten. *Zool. Gart.*, **25**, 305–68.

UN (1973) *Demographic Yearbook 1972*. United Nations, New York.

Van den Brink, F. H. (1967) *A Field Guide to the Mammals of Britain and Europe*. Collins, London.

Verschuren, J. (1957) Exploration du Parc National de la Garamba: Chiroptera. *Institut des Parcs Nationaux du Congo Belge*, 7, 1–465.

Vesey-Fitzgerald, D. F. (1960) Grazing succession among East African game animals. *J. Mammal.*, **41**, 161–72.

Vesey-Fitzgerald, D. F. (1965a) The utilisation of natural pastures by wild animals in the Rukwa Valley, Tanganyika, *E. Afr. Wildl. J.*, **3**, 38–48.

Vesey-Fitzgerald, D. F. (1965b) Lechwe pastures. *Puku*, **3**, 143–7.

Voelckel, J. and Varieras, G. (1960) Le répartition des espèces *R. norvegicus* et *R. rattus* à Douala (3° note). *Med. Trop. Marseille,* **20**, 625–9.

Walther, F. (1958) Zum Kampfund Paarungsverhalten einiger antilopen. *Z. Tierpsychol.* **15**, 340–80.

Walther, F. (1964a) Verhaltensstudien an der Gattung *Tragelaphus* De Blainville, 1816 in Gefangenschaft, unter besonderer Berucksichtigung des Sozialverhaltens. *Z. Tierpsychol.*, **21**, 393–467.

Walther, F. (1964b) Einige verhaltensbeobachtungen an Thomsongazellen (*Gazella thomsoni* Gunther 1884) in Ngorongoro-Krater. *Z. Tierpsychol.*, **21**, 871–90.

Walther, F. (1965) Verhaltensstudien an der Grantgazelle (*Gazella granti* Brooke, 1872) in Ngorongoro-Krater. *Z. Tierpsychol.*, **22**, 167–208.

Walther, F. (1969) Flight behaviour and avoidance of predator in Thomson's gazelle (*Gazella thomsoni* Guenther 1884). *Behaviour*, **34**, 184–221.

Walther, F. (1972) Territorial behaviour in certain horned ungulates with special reference to the examples of Thomson's and Grant's gazelles. *Zool. Afr.,* **7**, 303–7.

Walther, F. (1973 Social groupings of Grant's gazelle (*Gazella granti* Brooke, 1872) in the Serengeti National Park. *Z. Tierpsychol.*, **31**, 348–403.

Watson, J. M. (1949) The wild mammals of Teso and Karamoja. III. *Uganda J.*, **13**, 182–201.

Watson, R. M. (1969) Reproduction of wildebeest, *Connochaetes taurinus albojubatus* Thomas, in the Serengeti Region and its significance to conservation. *J. Reprod. Fert. Suppl.*, **6**, 287–310.

Watson, R. M. and Turner, M. I. M. (1964) A count of large mammals of the Lake Manyara National Park; results and discussions. *E. Afr. Wildl. J.*, **3**, 95–8.

Weir, J. S. (1970) The effect of creating additional water supplies in a central African National Park. *Symp. Brit. ecol. Soc.*, **11**, 367–86.

Whittaker, R. H. (1975) *Communities and Ecosystems.* 2nd edn. Macmillan, New York.

Wilson, E. O. (1975) *Sociobiology: the New Synthesis.* Harvard University Press, Cambridge, Mass.

Wilson, V. J. (1965) Observations on the greater kudu (*Tragelaphus strepsiceros* Pallas) from a tsetse control hunting scheme in Northern Rhodesia. *E. Afr. Wildl. J.*, **3**, 27–37.

Wilson, V. J. (1966) Notes on the food and feeding habits of the common duiker, *Sylvicapra grimmia*, in Eastern Zambia. *Arnoldia*, **14**, 1–19.

Wilson, V. J. (1975) *Mammals of the Wankie National Park, Rhodesia.* Nat. Mus. Rhodesia, Salisbury.

Wilson, V. J. and Roth, H. H. (1967) The effects of tsetse control operations on common duiker in Eastern Zambia. *E. Afr. Wildl. J.*, **5**, 53–64.

Winstanley, D. (1973) Rainfall patterns and general atmospheric circulation. *Nature, Lond.*, **245**, 190–4.

Wooff, W. R. (1968) The eradication of the tsetse *Glossina morsitans* Westw. and *Glossina pallidipes* Aust. by hunting. 12th Meeting of the International Scientific Council for Trypanosomiasis Research.

Wyatt, J. R. and Eltringham, S. K. (1974) The daily activity of the elephant in the Rwenzori National Park, Uganda. *E. Afr. Wildl. J.* **12**, 273–90.

Wyk, P. van and Fairall, N. (1969) The influence of the African elephant on the vegetation of the Kruger National Park. *Koedoe*, **12**, 57–89.

Wynne-Edwards, V. C. (1962) *Animal Dispersion in Relation to Social Behaviour.* Oliver and Boyd, Edinburgh and London.

Yunker, C. E. and Guirgis, S. S. (1969) Studies of rodent burrows and their ectoparasites in the Egyptian desert. I. Environment and micro-environment; some factors influencing acarine distribution. *J. Egypt. Publ. Hlth. Assn.*, **44**, 498–542.

Bibliography

Books and Guides on African Mammals

The following list of books and guides dealing with African mammals covers national and even more extensive areas. These are general accounts which frequently provide keys or other guides to identification.

General

Best, A. A. and Raw, W. G. (1973) (eds.) *Rowland Ward's Records of Big Game. 15th edn.* (*Africa*). Rowland Ward's Publications, London.
Dorst, J. and Dandelot, P. (1970) *A Field Guide to the Larger Mammals of Africa.* Collins, London.
Meester, J. and Setzer, H. W. (1971–77) (eds.) *The Mammals of Africa: An Identification Manual.* Smithsonian Institution, Washington.

Central Africa

Malbrand, R. (1952) *Faune du Centre Africain Français* (*Mammiferes et Oiseaux*). Lechevalier, Paris.
Schouteden, H. (1948) Faune du Congo Belge et de Ruanda–Urundi. I – Mammifères. *Ann. Mus. Congo Belge, Tervuren Ser. 8°, Zool.,* **1**, 1–331.

East Africa

Astley Maberly, C. T. (1962) *Animals of East Africa.* Timmins, Cape Town.
Bere, R. M. (1962) *The Wild Mammals of Uganda and Neighbouring Regions of East Africa.* Longman, London.
Delany, M. J. (1975) *The Rodents of Uganda.* British Museum (Nat. Hist.), London.
Kingdon, J. (1971–79) *East African Mammals,* 3 vols. Academic Press, London.

Ethiopia, Somalia and Sudan

Brocklehurst, H. C. (1931) *Game Animals of the Sudan.* Gurney and Jackson, London.
Drake-Brockman, R. E. (1910) *The Mammals of Somaliland.* Hurst and Blackett, London.
Funaioli, U. (1957) *Fauna e Caccia in Somalia.* Government Printer, Mogadiscio.
Funaioli, U. (1970) *Guida Breve dei Mammiferi della Somalia.* Instituto Agronomico per l'Oltremare Biblioteca Agraria Tropicale, Florence.
Largen, M. J., Kock, D. and Yalden, D. W. (1974) Catalogue of the mammals of Ethiopia. I. Chiroptera. *Monitore zool. Ital.* (N.S.). Suppl. **5**, 221–98.
Setzer, H. W. (1965) Mammals of the Anglo-Egyptian Sudan. *Proc. U.S. Nat. Mus.,* **106**, 447–587.
Von Rosen, B. (1953) *Game Animals of Ethiopia.* Swedish-Ethiopian Company, Addis Ababa.
Yalden, D. W., Largen, M. J. and Kock, D. (1976) Catalogue of the mammals of Ethiopia. 2. Insectivora and Rodentia. *Monitore zool. Ital.* (N.S.), Suppl. **8**, 1–118.
Yalden, D. W., Largen, M. J. and Kock, D. (1977) Catalogue of the mammals of Ethiopia. 3. Primates. *Monitore zool. Ital.* (N.S.), Suppl. **9**, 1–52.

Malawi, Rhodesia and Zambia

Ansell, W. F. H. (1960) *Mammals of Northern Rhodesia*. Government Printer, Lusaka.
Astley Maberly, C. T. (1959) *Animals of Rhodesia*. Timmins, Cape Town.
Smithers, R. H. N. (1966) *The Mammals of Rhodesia, Zambia and Malawi*. Collins, London.

Southern Africa

Astley Maberly, C. T. (1963) *The Game Animals of Southern Africa*. Nelson, Cape Town.
Hill, J. E. and Carter, T. D. (1941) The Mammals of Angola, Africa. *Bull. Amer. Mus. Nat. Hist.*, **78**, 1–211.
Roberts, A. (1951) *The Mammals of South Africa*. Trustees of 'The Mammals of South Africa' Book Fund, Johannesburg.
Shortridge, G. C. (1934) *The Mammals of South-west Africa*, 2 vols. Heinemann, London.
Smithers, R. H. N. (1971) *The Mammals of Botswana*. Nat. Mus. Rhodesia, Salisbury.
Smithers, R. H. N. and Lobão Tello, J. L. P. (1976) Check list and atlas of the mammals of Moçambiquè. *Mem. Nat. Mus. Rhodesia*. **8**, 1–184.

West Africa

Allen, G. M. and Coolidge, H. J. (1930). Mammals of Liberia, pp. 569–622. In Strong, R. P. (ed.) *The African Republic of Liberia and the Belgian Congo*. Harvard University Press, Cambridge.
Baudenon, P. (1952) Notes sur les Bovides du Togo. *Mammalia*. **16**, 49–61, 109–21.
Bigourdan, J. and Prunier, R. (1937) *Les Mammifères Sauvages de l'Ouest Africain et leur Milieu*. Lechevalier, Paris.
Booth, A. H. (1960) *Small Mammals of West Africa*. Longman, London.
Bourgoin, P. (1955) *Les Principaux Animaux de Chasse de l'Afrique Noire Continentale Française*. La Toison d'Or, Paris.
Dekeyser, P. L. (1955) *Les Mammifères de l'Afrique Noire Française*. I.F.A.N., Dakar.
Gromier, E. (1936) *La Faune de Guinée*. Payot, Paris.
Gromier, E. (1937) *La Vie des Animaux Sauvages de Cameroun*. Payot, Paris.
Happold, D. C. D. (1973) *Large Mammals of West Africa*. Longman, London.
Jeannin, A. (1936) *Les Mammifères Sauvages du Cameroun*. Lechevalier, Paris.
Malbrant, R. and Maclatchy, A. (1949) *Faune de l'Equateur Française. II. Mammifères*. Lechevalier, Paris.
Raynaud, J. and Georgy, G. (1969) *Nature et Chasse au Dahomey*. Cotonou.
Rosevear, D. R. (1965) *The Bats of West Africa*. British Museum (Nat. Hist.), London.
Rosevear, D. R. (1967) *The Rodents of West Africa*. British Museum (Nat. Hist.), London.
Rosevear, D. R. (1974) *The Carnivores of West Africa*. British Museum (Nat. Hist.), London.
Roure, G. (1962) *Animaux Sauvages de Côte d'Ivoire et du Versant Atlantique de l'Afrique Intertropicale*. Imprimerie Nationale, Côte d'Ivoire.
Roure, G. (1966) *Animaux Sauvages du Togo et de l'Afrique Occidentale*. Ministère de l'Economie Rurale, Lomé.

Checklists

The following are lists of mammals known to occur within the country, area or region specified. They frequently include information on the distribution of each species listed but seldom provide information on their ecology and biology.

Allen, G. M. (1939) A Checklist of African Mammals. *Bull. Mus. comp. Zool. Harv.*, **83**, 1–763.
Booth, A. H. (1956) Some Gold Coast mammals not included in Cansdale's provisional checklist. *J. W. Afr. Sci. Assn.*, **2**, 137–8.
Cabrera, A. (1929) Catalogo descriptivo de los Mamiferos de la Guinea Española. *Mems R. Soc. esp. Hist. Nat.*, **16**, 1–121.
Cansdale, G. (1948) *Provisional Checklist of Gold Coast Mammals*. Government Printer, Accra.
Ellerman, J. R., Morrison-Scott, T. C. S. and Hayman, R. W. (1953) *Southern African Mammals 1758–1951*. British Museum (Nat. Hist.), London.
Frechkop, S. (1938) Exploration du Parc National Albert: Mammifères. Institut des Parcs Nationaux du Congo Belge, **10**, 1–103.
Frechkop, S. (1954) Exploration du Parc National de l'Upemba: Mammifères. Institut des Parcs Nationaux du Congo Belge, **14**, 1–83.

Glover, P. E. (1962) *A List of Mammals from the Mau-Mara area of Masailand.* Kenya National Parks, Nairobi.

Kuhn, H–J. (1965) A provisional checklist of the mammals of Liberia. *Senckenberg. biol.,* **46**, 233–44.

Rosevear, D. R. (1953) *Checklist and Atlas of Nigerian Mammals.* Government Printer, Lagos.

Sweeney, R. C. H. (1959) *A Preliminary Annotated Checklist of the Mammals of Nyasaland.* Nyasaland Society, Blantyre.

Swynnerton, G. H. and Hayman, R. W. (1950) A checklist of the land mammals of the Tanganyika Territory and the Zanzibar Protectorate. *J. E. Afr. nat. Hist. Soc.,* **20**, 272–392.

Periodicals

The following journals, periodicals and occasional publications are useful sources of information on the ecology of African mammals (those marked with an asterisk are exclusively African):

Acta Tropica; *Africana; *African Wildlife; *Annales Musée Royal de l'Afrique Centrale; Zoologiques; *Annals of the Transvaal Museum; *Arnoldia; Behaviour; *Biologica Gabonica; *Black Lechwe; *Bulletin de Institut Français d'Afrique Noire; Bulletin of the British Museum (Nat. Hist): Zoology; *East African Agriculture and Forestry Journal; *East African Wildlife Journal (now *African Journal of Ecology*); *Folia Primatologia; International Union for the Conservation of Nature Publications; Journal of Animal Ecology; Journal of Applied Ecology; *Journal of the East African Natural History Society; Journal of Mammalogy; Journal of Primatology; *Journal of the South African Wildlife Management Association; Journal of Wildlife Management; Journal of Zoology; *Koedoe; La Terre et la Vie; *Madoqua; Mammalia; Oryz; *Publications of the Institut des Parcs Nationaux Belgique; *Puku; *Revue de Zoologie Africaines; Zeitschrift für Säugetierkunde; Zeitschrift für Tierpsychologie; *Zoologica Africana.*

Index